READER'S DIGEST

HOW TO
PAY LESS
FOR JUST ABOUT
ANYTHING

HOW TO
PAY

PUBLISHED BY THE READER'S DIGEST ASSOCIATION LIMITED
LONDON • NEW YORK • SYDNEY • MONTREAL

CONTENTS

THE 6 'PAY LESS' PRINCIPLES

If you want to enjoy the best things in life without paying more for them than you need to, then it makes sense to learn how to spot – and secure – a bargain on everything you buy. **HOW TO PAY LESS FOR JUST ABOUT ANYTHING** is a modern shopper's bible, full of insider information and thousands of ideas, tips and resources to help you make wise decisions and get a better price, whether you are buying from a large store or a market stall, or paying for professional advice or a tradesman's services.

1 DEVELOP THE 'PAY LESS' ATTITUDE

Approach every purchase with the belief that you can do better than the asking price, and you're half way to doing just that. Train yourself to look for the money-saving angles in every situation, no matter how large or small the potential savings may be. Assume that other people are getting a bargain, so why shouldn't you? And remember that most goods and services have a healthy profit margin so there is usually plenty of room for manoeuvre.

2 FIND THE CHEAPEST PRICE

Do your research. There are now so many businesses vying for your custom with discounts and special offers that you can almost always find something cheaper if you know where to look. Check out our Resources boxes for recommended suppliers and information sources and, if you can, get onto the Internet to track down those good deals. It's a user-friendly virtual marketplace that really has brought bargain-hunting into the 21st century.

3 TAKE YOUR TIME

Don't be forced into a situation where you have to make a rushed purchase. You'll get the best deals if you book tickets in advance, or wait until that bathroom suite goes on sale, or keep a constant eye on camera prices so you can pounce when they drop. Give yourself time to shop around, weigh up your options and buy when the moment is right.

4 ASK THE RIGHT QUESTIONS

Learn the magic phrase that may get you a bargain: 'Is that the best you can do?' In other words, ask the seller to be resourceful on your behalf. You may find that you qualify for a discount, simply by paying cash. Or that a cruise will cost less if you go in May. That your insurance premiums will be lower if you meet certain criteria. Or that the coat you covet is going on sale next week. Most people really do want to help you – especially if you are friendly and smile.

5 USE YOUR BARGAINING POWER

Be prepared to haggle. Ask yourself how much the seller wants your business. Is he overstocked? Is he desperate to make his quota or his commission? Are you his only customer? Assume he wants to do a deal – you're probably right! Offer to buy more if he'll give you a discount. See if you can take a reduced service and pay less. Spot a flaw in the item and suggest a lower price. Find a rival offer and ask him to match it. On the other hand, bargaining also means being willing to walk away.

6 THINK CREATIVELY

If the price is still not right, don't give up. Be flexible. See if you can get a workman to lower his charges by offering to do part of the job yourself. Go in with friends to get a discount on bulk buys for everything from theatre tickets to vintage wine. Do a neighbour's gardening in exchange for free baby-sitting. That way, everybody wins – and everyone gets something for less.

HOW TO USE THE INTERNET TO

You've got to be a very dedicated shopper to compare prices at dozens of shops, but if you let a computer mouse do the work, you'll get results in a few minutes. Even if you don't own a PC, you can use an Internet café to hunt out the best bargains. And if you need help with computer skills, ring your local authority to find low-cost or free computer courses.

Most companies have websites, where you can get information on goods, services and prices, and can order online as well. If more information is all you require, you may be able to ask questions via email or get a contact telephone number to speak to someone.

We've selected the AA website to show you how to navigate round a typical site.

HOW WEBSITES WORK

When you visit a website, the first page will usually have a list of sections – much like departments in a large store. In the case of the AA's website, the line across the top covers AA Services, Motoring and so on. Each of these is a link to an individual section. The idea is that you can go straight to a particular section quickly.

JUMPING FROM PAGE TO PAGE

The rest of the page is worth checking, too, because you may also see the exact subject you're interested in – in this example, car breakdown cover is mentioned directly because it's a key subject. Move the mouse pointer to the underlined 'Breakdown cover' text and it changes to a hand. This shows that the text is a link – you can click on it to jump to a page with more information on this subject.

GETTING MORE INFORMATION

As you delve further into a website, you will find that there's often a lot more information that you typically find in a shop or a printed catalogue. Most companies try to provide as much information as possible to help you decide to buy. This page shows the prices and a summary of their Breakdown Cover, but there are also links to more detailed information, including the all-important Terms and Conditions so you can check the small print before signing up.

EMAIL FOR CORRESPONDENCE

If you decide to buy online, most online shops will ask for your email address as part of the payment process – it's used for sending order confirmations, delivery notes and other correspondence. So, if you don't have an email address and want to shop via an Internet café (good value at just £1–3 a half hour), you'll need to set one up in advance.

Some services are set up specifically to help out in this situation: if you join a web-based email service, such as **www.yahoo.co.uk**, you get an email address of your own, and you can use it to send and receive email messages from any PC – a friend's, a PC at work, or an Internet café's PCs. Most such services are free.

PAY LESS FOR EVERYTHING

READING THE WHOLE PAGE

On some web pages, the information takes up more than a single screen. If this is the case, a bar appears on the right side of the page, indicating that there's more of the page to see. To see the next screenful, press the [Page Down] key on the computer's keyboard.

DECIDING TO BUY

If, after browsing through the site, you find a service or product that you want to buy, look for a purchasing link or button. In this example, you click on the price for the type of service you want and then click on the Select button. Just follow the questions and options presented to you – the site is designed to be easy to use because the company wants your custom. You can always quit and come back later if you get confused.

ORDERING AND PAYING

This opens up a page where you can type in your address (for delivery) and payment details. Don't worry that you will make an expensive purchase by accidentally clicking the wrong button – you will be asked several times to confirm your command before your purchase goes through, just like on an Automatic Cash Machine. Almost all online shops offer credit card as a payment option, and it's a good idea to use this (see below, 'Is ordering online safe?')

HOW TO PAY

Q Do I have to pay for delivery?

A Some websites may offer free delivery for larger orders. In other cases, the savings you make almost always make up for the delivery cost.

Q Is ordering online safe?

A Online ordering is much like mail order: you are covered by distance-selling legislation, and if you pay by credit card, you are protected from losing your money if the goods or services you buy are defective.

Q How do I ask a question about my order?

A Look for a link to a 'Frequently Asked Questions' (or 'FAQ') page – this may address your query. If not, look for a Contact Us or Help page – it may contain a telephone contact number, or an address for sending questions by email.

Q What sort of receipt do I get?

A At the end of the purchase process, there will usually be a confirmation page with an order reference – print it out and keep it. The online shop may also send you an electronic receipt by email and a printed receipt with the goods you've ordered.

Eat healthily and well while sticking to a budget by assessing your culinary needs before you hit the supermarket. Learn when and where to shop, at home and abroad, and how to equip your kitchen without paying a fortune.

Food and drink

SHOPPING SENSE

Before you go food shopping, write down what you need. Searching for inspiration not only wastes time but you'll also end up buying too much. And never shop on an empty stomach. Munch on a banana or cereal bar on your way to the store – it will take the edge off your appetite, and you're more likely to save money by buying only what you need.

STICK TO YOUR LIST

Making a shopping list and sticking to it are two different things. Research shows that the average shopper buys one unlisted item from every supermarket aisle every time he or she goes shopping. If the store has ten aisles, that adds up to at least ten items, at about £1 each, every week of the year. That's an extra £520 you could have kept in your pocket.

TOP TIPS SHOPPING-LIST SECRETS

■ **Make a note** Keep a notebook and pen in your kitchen. As soon as you deplete your stock of a storecupboard item or are getting close to using up a necessity such as tea or milk, add it to the list. If you have a preference for a particular brand or store, note that down too.

■ **News items** When you see local newspaper ads with special prices on foods you buy regularly, circle the dates and clip them to your list, or make a note directly on your list for that store, noting the sale item and sale dates. That way, you won't buy something only to discover later that a similar item was on sale for much less.

■ **Group your list** Organise your shopping list in the same way as the store is laid out to prevent wandering – and possible impulse buying (see page 21). The more you wander up and down the aisles to pick up the next thing on your list, the more you'll be tempted by extra items. This simple organisational trick could save you 15% on shopping bills.

CASE STUDY

FAMILY MEALS PLANNED AROUND THE SPECIAL OFFERS

Diane Harding, with a family of four young boys and an athletic husband, plans her weekly shop around on-sale items she sees advertised in flyers and the local press. Once she would pick up just a few sale buys, which she would then make for that evening's meal. But now she's found a way to save even more. If minced beef is on sale, she'll buy enough for three meals: chilli con carne one night, beefburgers another night, shepherd's pie the third. If yoghurt is on sale, she'll buy enough for breakfast and dessert all week long, to mix with fruit or honey. By planning her meals around sale items and paying special attention to deals on meat and fresh produce – which account for half of her purchases – Diane can save 30% on her weekly food bill.

Stock up on store-cupboard items

SMART MOVES

These common staples and ingredients have a long shelf life. Buy them whenever you see them on sale, and be sure of getting the best price.

- Baking powder
- Breadcrumbs
- Caster sugar
- Cocoa
- Coffee
- Cornflour
- Couscous
- Flour
- Herbs (dried)
- Honey
- Ketchup
- Mustard
- Olive oil
- Pasta (dried)
- Pepper
- Pet food
- Rice
- Salt
- Soy sauce
- Spices
- Stock cubes
- Sugar
- Sunflower oil
- Tabasco sauce
- Tea
- Tinned fruit
- Tinned soup
- Tinned tuna
- Tinned vegetables
- Tomato purée
- Vegetable oil
- Wine vinegar
- Worcestershire sauce

■ **Weekly visit** Don't visit any store more than once a week. Generally, aim for a once-a-month big shop at a discount warehouse such as Makro or Costco (see page 24), or place a large online order (see page 25) to stock up on storecupboard items. You'll probably need to visit your regular supermarket about once a week for things that you buy in smaller amounts and every two or three days for perishable items such as milk, fresh fruit and vegetables. But remember, the more you shop, the more you will buy.

THE CHEAPEST TIME TO SHOP

You may be able to save money on some of the items on your shopping list if you shop late in the day, when retailers, and particularly market stall-holders, are likely to discount perishable items they want to shift. This can mean anything from half-price tomatoes to chilled soups, pasta sauces or yoghurts nearing their sell-by date.

DISCOUNT DELI

Check the deli counter for ends or offcuts of cold meats and cheeses and get a discount of 50% or more. The high turnover of such items ensures that the end bits won't be stale or past their best, just psychologically less appealing than a slice from a new joint or a wedge of uncut cheese. If you buy more discounted meat or cheese than you need at the time, you can freeeze the surplus.

ANALYSE YOUR PURCHASES

Most people are shocked by their food bills – and would be even more dismayed to see where the money really goes. You may find that more than 20% goes on non-essentials.

Record impulse buys Every time you pick up an item that's not on your shopping list, note it down in a different coloured pen. If you add more than half a dozen items, you are in danger of losing control of your spending.

Use a zapper to avoid checkout surprises If your supermarket has a bar code reader that you can use, check your total as you shop. Reconsider any impulse buys.

Add up all your receipts Each time you buy food – including sweets for the children, a sandwich for lunch or a bag of apples on your way home from work – keep the receipt. Save them all together and total them at the end of the week to see how much you are really spending on food and drink. Do this for a couple of weeks and then sit down and decide whether you can do without some of the items.

Separate miscellaneous from food items When you return home from a major shopping trip, categorise what you have bought. Tick off essential non-food items such as toothpaste, kitchen and cleaning supplies, clothing, stationery and pet food – that alone could account for a third of your bill.

Cutting down your food bill Take a look at your remaining food bill and use coloured markers so you can see what you have spent in different areas. Pick out snacks, biscuits and appetisers. Then highlight fizzy drinks, bottled water, alcohol, tea and coffee, followed by extravagant items such as desserts and expensive convenience meals. Highlight storecupboard items, which are a form of investment in your larder. What you should be left with is the fresh, healthy food you and your family will eat at mealtimes during the week. You can now work out what you can do without. This exercise could save you 20% on your food bill.

SAVE ON LAST-MINUTE BUYS

If you've forgotten something on your shopping list, consider whether you can wait until your next supermarket shop before picking it up at your local convenience store. You will usually pay for the privilege. Even some supermarket mini-shops have higher prices than their larger equivalents. Here's how the prices for the same items compare.

	CONVENIENCE STORE	SUPERMARKET MINI-SHOP	SUPERMARKET MAIN STORE
1 PINT MILK	£0.40	£0.38	£0.30
SMALL LOAF	£0.89	£0.55	£0.44
250g BUTTER	£1.29	£1.08	£0.82
TIN OF CAT FOOD	£0.55	£0.55	£0.47
100g CHOCOLATE	£0.45	£0.42	£0.39

Prices correct July 2004

BEST BUYS ON EVERYDAY FOODS

Make a list of basic foods you use regularly, and buy them in quantities suited to your needs. For example, if your family eats a lot of bread, it's worth stocking up when prices are low and freezing the excess for later.

SAVE ON FRUIT AND VEG

Buy fruit and vegetables from an outlet or greengrocer where you can select and weigh your own. You'll be able to buy the exact quantity you need and check that the produce won't be bruised or damaged more easily than if it's in a sealed pack. Loose fruit and vegetables also keep for longer than those wrapped in plastic and are often less expensive.

FROM THE MARKET STALL

If possible, avoid shopping for fruit and vegetables at the supermarket. Producers select individual, unblemished items of a similar size to look more attractive in the package, and this costs more. Smaller greengrocers and market stalls receive a lower-grade produce, which is just as good but less visually perfect. It will be cheaper, but you should select your individual items with care. Avoid market stalls where traders put items into a brown paper bag from a box at the back.

CHEAP FOR CHUTNEY

Discounted fruit needs picking over carefully. It may be cheap because it's fully ripe and needs clearing to make room on the shelf for a new delivery. This is fine if you'll be eating the fruit on the same day or plan on making

Get more per kilo

If you're planning to eat raw fruit, buy the smallest pieces as you'll get more per kilo. But, if cooking, buy larger (and fewer) pieces to avoid waste when they're peeled and prepared for the pot.

SMART MOVES

FRESH, FROZEN, TINNED OR READY-PREPARED?

Fresh is not necessarily the most expensive but you will pay a premium for vegetables that are both fresh and peeled, chopped or otherwise ready-prepared. Remember, though, that when you prepare vegetables such as peas yourself, you'll reduce the overall weight. Frozen vegetables are often good value, particularly when out of season.

VEGETABLES	FRESH	FROZEN	TINNED	READY-PREPARED
Green beans	£2.89/kg	£1.69/kg	£1.42/kg	£2.96/kg
Mushrooms	£4.39/kg	£1.60/kg	£3.10/kg	£2.40/kg
Cauliflower	£1.09 each	£1.26/kg	–	£3.49/kg
Peas	£2.00/kg	£1.29/kg	£1.24/kg	£7.11/kg
Carrots	£0.55/kg	£1.09/kg	£0.90/kg	£1.77/kg
Sweetcorn	£0.49 a cob	£1.15/kg	£1.20/kg	£1.90/kg

Prices correct July–August 2004

preserves and chutneys. If it has ripened too far or is likely to go to waste, it is probably not worth buying, even at a reduced rate.

REDUCED BUT NOT ROTTEN

Check reduced-priced vegetables carefully as well. Green vegetables such as beans and broccoli should look bright and fresh, root vegetables such as carrots or potatoes should be firm, and lettuces and leaf vegetables should be crisp.

SALAD SENSE

Pre-packed bags of prewashed salad can be 50%–70% more expensive than mixing ingredients and making your own salads. A 200g bag at around £1.49 costs the same as two romaine (cos) lettuces, three medium-sized iceberg lettuces or three curly lettuces – each enough for several salads.

WHAT'S IN SEASON?

Although fresh fruit and vegetables are less seasonal these days as crops are flown in from far and wide, many items are still much cheaper at their British seasonal times.

FRUIT AND VEGETABLES	PRICE IN SEASON	PRICE OUT OF SEASON
SPRING		
1kg RHUBARB	£3.50	£4.98
1kg ASPARAGUS	£5.60	£7.69
1kg BABY CARROTS	£0.90	£1.58
SUMMER		
1kg RUNNER BEANS	£2.35	£5.96
1kg STRAWBERRIES	£2.95	£6.23
AUTUMN		
1kg PLUMS	£3.50	£4.15
1 CAULIFLOWER	£0.79	£1.09
1kg COURGETTES	£1.00	£1.19
WINTER		
1kg BRUSSELS SPROUTS	£1.20	£3.64
1 CABBAGE	£0.55	£0.69
1kg LEEKS	£1.40	£1.79

PICK YOUR OWN

■ Picking your own will save you money – fruit and vegetables can be 30%–50% cheaper than shop-bought. To find local farms where you can pick your own, click on the 'Find a farm' link at **www.farmshopping.com** or ring 0845 2302150 ✉.

■ Although it's no longer possible to pick wild flowers, these rules don't apply to hedgerow fruits, such as blackberries and elderberries, nor to vegetables such as wild garlic and samphire grass.

■ British woods and forests are full of edible mushrooms that few people bother to pick. The Collins Gem *Mushrooms* (£4.99) is a handy guide to help you indentify mushrooms and toadstools, but if you are in any doubt as to whether a mushroom is safe to eat or not, leave it well alone.

■ Even the smallest flat should have space to grow herbs on a sunny windowsill, saving you pounds on the expensive pre-packed herbs sold in supermarkets. Basil, coriander, chives and parsley are easy to grow, and a packet of seeds costing just 59p will yield a constant crop for cutting that would have cost you £50 or more in the shops.

TALKING TURKEY

Many people only think of cooking turkey at Christmas, but it is an economical choice all year round – a 4.5kg bird will feed about a dozen people. You don't have to buy a whole bird, since turkey is available in supermarkets and at butchers as oven-ready joints, breasts, cubes, steaks and mince and is good value for family meals and barbecues.

THE TENDER TOUCH

Flank steak, stewing beef and other less-expensive cuts of meat are 10%–30% cheaper than choicer cuts, but they need longer cooking to make them tender. Plan in advance if you are going to use them; an Irish stew needs to cook for 2 hours, for example, though marinating for as little as 20 minutes will help to tenderise and add flavour too.

FALSE ECONOMY?

Cheaper minced beef may not necessarily be higher in fat than prime minced steak (the fat content of both will probably be less than 10%) but it's likely to have been made from a cheaper cut, such as shin or skirt. The meat will also have been hung for a shorter period so will need longer cooking to make it tender. Economy mince is fine for slow-cooked chilli con carne or a bolognese if you add plenty of herbs, wine and tomato purée for extra flavour. But buy prime mince for quick-cook homemade burgers.

CHICKEN PIECES

You can save on chicken pieces if you buy a whole chicken and cut it up yourself – all it takes is a good knife and a systematic approach. Whole chickens range from between £3 to £6 for a 2kg bird, compared to about £2.75 for 1kg of chicken thighs or £11.50 for 1kg of boneless, skinless breasts. Use the bones and any leftovers in stocks and soups. Roasted chicken wings make excellent party nibbles.

SMART MOVES

Add your own extras and save 40%

Many brands instantly bump up the price of a basic product by adding other ingredients such as sugar, seasonings and sauces, which you can easily mix in yourself, should you want to.

■ Avoid sweetened cereals – frosted cornflakes can cost almost 40% more than the unsweetened variety.

■ Salads with added dressing or croutons can be over 30% more expensive than salads that have no dressing or other additions.

DIET RIGHT: ARE READY-MADE DIET MEALS WORTH IT?

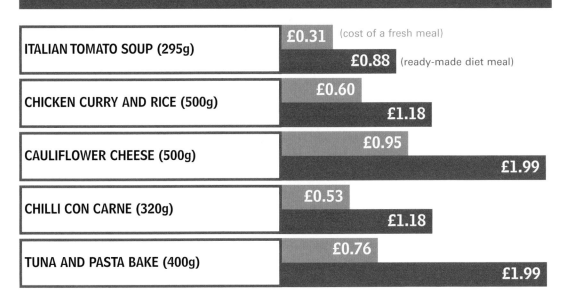

ITALIAN TOMATO SOUP (295g) — £0.31 (cost of a fresh meal) / £0.88 (ready-made diet meal)

CHICKEN CURRY AND RICE (500g) — £0.60 / £1.18

CAULIFLOWER CHEESE (500g) — £0.95 / £1.99

CHILLI CON CARNE (320g) — £0.53 / £1.18

TUNA AND PASTA BAKE (400g) — £0.76 / £1.99

SOMETHING FISHY

Although expensive, fish is an economical buy as it has little waste. Fresh fish should have plump flesh and bright eyes.
Avoid pre-skinned fillets The price of 1kg of skinned cod is £11.49 compared to £8.99 for unskinned. To remove the skin, grasp the tail firmly and hold a knife vertically while running it the length of the fish.
Pricing your prawns Unpeeled prawns cost around £3.99 for 225g; for the same price, you would get only 160g of peeled prawns. As peeling prawns is time-consuming, for convenience buy a smaller portion of peeled prawns than you need for a recipe and add cheaper chopped crab sticks to make up the weight.
Buy whole and bag up A whole 2kg–2.3kg salmon on special offer might cost £6.58 a kilo. If you cut it into fillets and freeze the surplus in individual bags, you will save nearly 40% over pre-cut fillets, which cost £10.50 a kilo.

TOP TIPS SPOTTING A BARGAIN

■ **Package appeal** One brand of jam might look appealing in its rustic jar, but check the weight on the label before you buy. The jar may contain only 400g of jam but cost the same as the plainer jar on the lower shelf weighing 500g.
■ **Staple diet** Fill spare freezer space with kitchen staples such as milk, cheese and bread on special offer. (See Can You Freeze It? on page 19.)
■ **Slice by slice** If you buy a lot of cold cuts such as salami and garlic sausage, invest in a meat slicer and buy them in a piece to slice at home. Unsliced, the meat will stay fresher for longer and you'll save around 15% on flat-packed slices.
■ **Get grating** Bags of pre-grated cheese cost around 30% more than a block of cheese. Look for reduced-price offcuts of cheese and grate your own. Freeze or keep in the fridge in self-seal plastic bags and make up mixes of different cheeses such as red Leicester, Cheddar, Edam and Gouda to add colour and variety to sauces and gratin dishes.

SAVE ON ETHNIC INGREDIENTS

If you cook a lot of curries, stir-fries or other Far Eastern dishes and have an ethnic store nearby, buy your staples such as rice, noodles, spices and sauces there. Basmati rice is expensive in an ordinary supermarket, where a 500g box of a popular brand is likely to cost around £1.50 compared to £4 for a 5kg bag from an Indian grocery store. You can make similar savings in Chinese or Asian stores on stir-fry sauces, chilli sauces and pastes, soy sauce and noodles.

BULK BUY FOR BARGAINS

USE YOUR LOAF
If you live alone, a loaf of bread frequently turns mouldy before you have a chance to eat it all. For fresh bread daily and no waste, buy a whole loaf and freeze it. The slices can be toasted from frozen or you can defrost them quickly in a microwave if you fancy a sandwich.

Take advantage of the seasonal glut of fresh produce and meat by buying it in bulk. Pay the lowest prices for as much of your favourite fruit and vegetables as you can store or freeze, and then give your taste buds a treat by eating fresh-from-the-freezer summer raspberries in January.

SEASONAL PRODUCE FOR STORAGE

Long-lasting vegetables and fruit can be bought in bulk from pick-your-own centres or farm shops at a fraction of the price per kilo in supermarkets.

Fruit and veg to keep A sack of potatoes or onions can be stored through the winter. You can also store garlic, apples, pumpkins, marrows and root vegetables such as carrots. Green vegetables can't be stored but freeze well. Tomatoes can be made into soups and sauces, then frozen.

How to store You need space in a cool garage or shed to ensure the produce doesn't go bad before you use it up. Root vegetables should be stored in crates, separated by sand or sieved soil. If you are short of suitable space, ask nearby friends or family if you can share with them.

YOUR FREEZER WILL PAY FOR ITSELF

Costing from £100, a large chest or upright freezer can be a money-saving asset, as the reductions on bulk-bought meat, jointed and ready-to-freeze, are significant. And you can cook double portions of meals, one for now and one for later, store seasonal fruit and vegetables and take advantage of supermarket discounts on perishable staples. Freeze food in single, double or family-size portions to suit your lifestyle.

TOP TIPS FREEZER FACTS AND FALLACIES

Don't waste frozen food by not caring for it properly. But there is no need to throw away what you can safely keep.

■ **Prevent freezer burn** Food will stay in better condition if you wrap it before you freeze it, excluding as much air as possible. This is particularly important when freezing meat which, if 'burnt' by ice, will become dry and tasteless.

■ **Use up quickly** Strong flavours such as spices, chillies and salt become more pronounced when frozen, and the fibres of meat, fish and poultry begin to break down. So smoked bacon and salted butter both have a shorter freezer life than unsmoked bacon and unsalted butter.

■ **Don't throw it away** A common myth is that food kept frozen beyond its recommended time is unsafe to eat. If properly frozen, food will never go 'bad' in a freezer, but over time its texture and taste will deteriorate. Use over-date food immediately on thawing and cook it thoroughly.

■ **When you must throw it out** Cooked dishes that thaw during power cuts and breakdowns but still feel cold should be transferred to the refrigerator and used as quickly as possible. Fresh food or cooked dishes that have thawed and no longer feel cold must be discarded.

■ **Refreeze safely** Bread, plain cakes and raw pastry can safely be refrozen, even if they have thawed, but will quickly become stale on rethawing. Fruit should be cooked before being refrozen, and will then be useful for making purées, coulis or jam.

FOR CHEAP YEAR-ROUND PRODUCE

Freeze fruit and vegetables as soon after harvest as possible.

Freezing fruit Rinse fruit (except soft fruit); leave stoned fruit whole, or stone and chop. Skin or peel peaches, apricots, mangoes and nectarines and freeze them in a light syrup with lemon juice added to prevent them from discolouring in the freezer. Spread currants, blackberries, raspberries and gooseberries out on trays, open freeze until solid and then pack into freezer bags and seal.

Freezing vegetables Peel and chop vegetables as required, and blanch for 2–3 minutes in a basket immersed in a pan of boiling, unsalted water to preserve their colour, flavour and nutritional value. Once blanched, plunge the vegetables into iced water, then drain, dry, cool and pack for the freezer immediately. Blanching times vary according to the vegetables being frozen but, as a general rule, the younger and more tender the variety, the less time it needs.

CAN YOU FREEZE IT?

It is not always clear what will and will not freeze successfully and safely, as these lists of similar items demonstrate. When in doubt, freeze only items that have been cooked. Although freezing halts almost all spoilage, bacteria in meat, and some enzymes that can cause further deterioration in fruit and vegetables (for example, potatoes, when frozen raw), are only destroyed by cooking at high temperatures.

FREEZES WELL	DON'T FREEZE
RASPBERRIES	WHOLE MELONS, BANANAS
SKIMMED, SEMI-SKIMMED MILK AND DOUBLE CREAM	FULL-FAT MILK AND COTTAGE CHEESE
EGGS (lightly stirred or separated)	EGGS (in their shell)
TOMATOES (for soups and sauces)	TOMATOES (for salad)
SPINACH	LETTUCE
POTATOES (fully cooked, or blanched in hot oil as chips)	UNCOOKED POTATOES
FRESH MEAT, POULTRY, FISH AND SHELLFISH	PREVIOUSLY FROZEN UNCOOKED MEAT, POULTRY, FISH & SHELLFISH (but once cooked they can be refrozen)
CREAMY DESSERTS (soufflés, mousses and cheesecakes set with gelatine)	FRUIT JELLIES, FRESH EGG CUSTARD

SUPERMARKET SAVERS

For many people, the most convenient way to shop is to buy their groceries, fresh produce and household goods under one supermarket roof. If your store is open 24 hours, try shopping when the aisles are clear.

WATCH POINTS TRICKS OF THE TRADE

Once you walk through their doors, supermarkets want you to spend, spend, spend, so be aware of the tricks they employ to part you from your hard-earned cash.

■ **Getting the runaround** The chiller cabinets containing basics, such as milk, juices and butter, are invariably at the back of the store, forcing you to walk past magazines, confectionery and countless other distractions to pick up a pint of milk. If you only need a couple of items, go to a store where you are familiar with the layout and leave with what you came in for.

■ **On the edge** Essential foodstuffs are usually displayed around the perimeter with the more costly ready-meals and prepacked items on the centre aisles. The more you shop in the outer aisles, the more you'll save.

■ **The eyes have it** Supermarkets have a trick of placing higher-priced goods at eye level. Look up, or down, to spot the regular-price items on the top or bottom shelf.

■ **All change** Just when you've mastered the layout of your local store, everything is rearranged. Avoid being tempted by unfamiliar displays and ask a member of staff to tell you where you can now find the items you're looking for.

■ **Wits' end** If you think the items displayed at the end of aisles are being sold at a reduction, think again. The eye-catching banners and signs are often masking excess stock selling at regular prices.

BUY MORE FOR LESS?

They are commonplace now, but it is still worth taking advantage of some supermarket best buys.
■ Buy-one-get-one-free
■ A larger quantity for the same price
■ Trial sizes at low prices
■ Jumbo or multipacks – but make sure you are buying something you know you'll use or will be able to finish by the 'best before' date.

BUT BEWARE

■ Avoid the three-for-the-price-of-two offers unless you really need three of the item – if you want one of something, don't let the supermarket tempt you to double your bill.
■ Make sure two-for-the-price-of-one deals aren't just a ploy for getting rid of old or unwanted stock.

CHECK THE UNIT PRICE

When comparing price tags, look for the lettering saying 'price per 100ml' or 'price per kilo'. This is useful for fresh produce or any item where pack sizes vary. Larger packs are often, but not always, better value than smaller ones, so check the unit price to make sure. Here are some prices we found in one shop on one day.

	EXPENSIVE OPTION	BETTER OPTION
Dried pasta shapes	500g size @ 68p per kilo	5kg size @ 54p per kilo
Mature cheddar	sliced @ £6.71 per kilo	whole, unpackaged @ £5.89 per kilo
Vine tomatoes	packaged @ £2.25 per kilo	loose @ £1.99 per kilo
Baking potatoes	loose @ £1.19 per kilo	prepacked @ 87p per kilo
Sweet potatoes	packaged @ £1.88 per kilo	loose @ £1.62 per kilo
Coke	12 x 330ml cans @ 11p per 100ml	2-litre bottle @ 6p per 100ml

BEAT THE SUPERMARKET PLANNERS AT THEIR OWN GAME

Supermarkets are laid out the way they are for one very specific reason – to make you part with your money. They are carefully designed by experts who use every marketing trick in the book to slow you down, tempt you with impulse buys and inspire you with delicious-looking and smelling food – we've all been enticed by the bakery smells pumped to the front of the store or the gleaming, colourful piles of peaches and red peppers. Next time you shop, see how many tricks you can spot, and don't play their game.

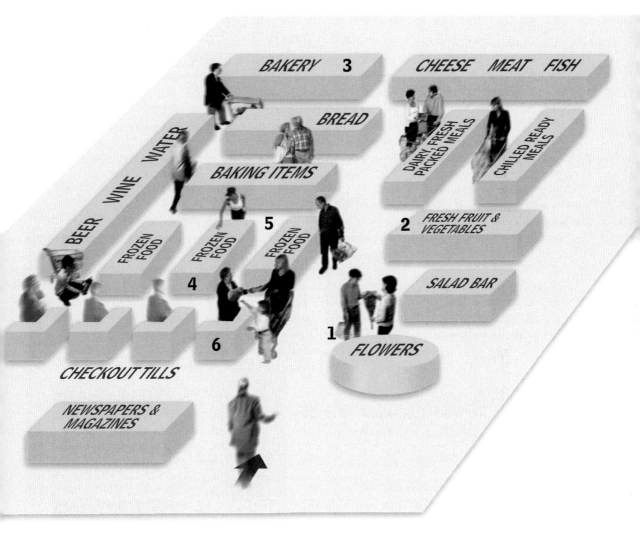

1 Flowers, fresh fruit and the salad bar entice you in and immediately gratify your senses. Wait to the end to see if you really need them.
2 Make smart decisions between prepacked and loose in the fruit and veg section. Don't be tempted by the salad dressing and dips, as often the most expensive are placed beside comparatively inexpensive produce.
3 If you have only come in for a loaf of bread, don't pick up a basket – you may become waylaid and end up filling it.

4 The chock-a-block end-of-aisle displays are made to look like a bargain dump bin, but don't be fooled – they may be full-price items.
5 Frozen food cabinets are positioned to block your path on the way to the checkout. Ready meals whet your appetite and are a convenience, but they're expensive.
6 Waiting in a queue can be boring, so don't even look at the checkout till items – they are impulse buys you don't need, and they usually have a high mark-up.

OWN LABELS ADD VALUE

Own-label goods are rarely prominently displayed – they may be stacked on the top or bottom shelves. The packs may look less interesting, but remember that dried and canned goods don't need fancy packaging.

Tasty copycats Own-label ranges are unlikely to be made by the market brand leader but by reputable companies that are often household names (even if the supermarkets are reluctant to reveal their source).

Significant savings Percentage savings on own label against the market leader are considerable, typically: 6 x 330ml cans of cola (50% less), pasta (40% less) and self-raising flour (50% less), (see table, right).

CUT OUT THE COUPONS

Flick through the supermarket's own magazine before you start shopping to judge whether you'll use the money-off coupons or offers inside. The coupons will be in the same place in the magazine each month. If you buy the products featured you could make substantial savings, in addition to recouping the price of the magazine.

Reap the rewards If there is a special offer on any food on your list, check for a coupon that will give you even more savings. Combining special offers with coupons will reward you the most.

Cross competition In order to entice you away from your regular supermarket, some stores will take their competitors' coupons. So even if you are shopping at Tesco, you may be able to use Sainsburys' vouchers.

BE A LOYAL CUSTOMER

Most supermarkets offer customers loyalty cards with which you earn points every time you shop. You won't save a fortune collecting the points – usually for every £1 you spend you earn one point and when your tally reaches 500 you're given a voucher worth £2.50 – but if you shop in the store anyway, why not?

Double up Look out for offers of bonus points on items you regularly use, but don't get carried away buying things you don't need.

Go further Vouchers can be used to reduce future shopping bills at the store but many cards also allow you to convert points into Air Miles (see *Good-value travel*, page 181).

> ## DISCOUNT DEALS
>
> Supermarkets usually have at least one basket or shelf of discounted stock somewhere in the store. Cans with torn lables, ends of lines, or packets or boxes with minor dents will all be heavily marked down – by as much as 60% or more – and are worth investigating. Buy cans without labels only if you're feeling adventurous. Never buy badly dented cans from any outlets as their seal may be damaged and the contents could be spoiled and highly dangerous.

SAVE MORE THAN 50% WITH SUPERMARKET OWN BRANDS

This table shows how much you can save by choosing a supermarket's own brand instead of nationally advertised brands. The savings vary but are always worth making. You could have saved £8.15 on this sample shopping list alone.

ITEM	SIZE	NAME BRAND PRICE	OWN BRAND PRICE	SAVED	SAVING
Low-fat spread	500g	£1.87	£1.17	£0.70	37%
Aluminium foil	300mm	£1.79	£0.72	£1.07	60%
Baked beans	4 x 420g cans	£1.48	£0.78	£0.70	47%
Breakfast tea	80 bags	£1.45	£0.31	£1.14	79%
Butter	500g	£1.64	£1.54	£0.10	6%
Cat food	12 x 100g	£2.72	£2.18	£0.54	20%
Cornflakes	500g	£1.24	£0.84	£0.40	32%
Fish fingers	300g	£1.34	£1.14	£0.20	15%
Ground pepper	40g	£1.55	£1.24	£0.31	20%
Herb tea	40 bags	£1.59	£1.39	£0.20	13%
Instant coffee	100g	£1.63	£1.11	£0.52	32%
Olive oil	500ml	£2.39	£1.41	£0.98	41%
Lemonade	2 litres	£0.86	£0.44	£0.42	49%
Paper towels	100 sheets	£1.14	£0.82	£0.32	28%
Washing-up liquid	500ml	£1.19	£0.64	£0.55	46%

SELL-BY DATES

Health and safety laws govern sell-by dates and responsible retailers abide by strict procedures for clearing stock, but just how much importance should consumers attach to these dates? Fresh food, such as fish and meat bought loose by weight, has no sell-by date stamped on its wrapping so it is left to the customer's common sense to store it properly and use it up quickly. Loose fruit and vegetables have no sell-by date, but even before you purchase it's easy to spot yellowing leaves, mould, shoots or shrivelled skin, indicating the produce is past its best.

Shelf life To bag a bargain, head straight for the supermarket bin containing a selection of items just about to pass their sell-by dates. Take advantage of these offers if you know you can use the items quickly. Sugar, salt and dried pulses will keep for a long period, as will canned food.

When small is best Olive oil and vegetable oils keep well after the bottle has been opened, but walnut and other nut oils become rancid within two to three months. This is why nut oils are sold in small bottles. Dried fruit also stores well (should it become over-desiccated it can be revived by an overnight soak in a little brandy, tea or water) but nuts need to be used up, particularly pine kernels, which quickly lose their flavour.

SHOPPERS' CHOICE

Cash-and-carry outlets and discount warehouses are a popular way to shop in the US and are increasingly popular over here. Check out how they can save you money.

JOIN THE CLUB

Cash-and-carry outlets sell primarily to a business clientele and the stock is purchased with them in mind. Members of certain professions can also shop there if they have authorisation, as can local community groups such as PTAs (Parent/Teacher Associations) and playgroups.

Makro UK To shop at Makro, businesses need to supply documents such as a copy of their VAT registration, copies of invoices over £50 and personal identification of the proposed cardholder before a trade card is issued.

Costco Wholesale This is a member-only cash-and-carry, offering trade membership for companies at an annual fee of £20 plus VAT, which includes a spouse card. Membership is also available to individuals over the age of 18 who currently work in or are retired from a variety of professions, including finance, local government, education, police, civil service, health service and the legal profession. The annual fee is £25 and, again, proof of identity is required such as employee ID card, payslip or certificate of professional qualification, plus a bank statement or current utility bill.

Buying in bulk Cash-and-carry stores are mainly designed for large-scale purchases. Tomato ketchup will be sold in a pack of two of the largest size bottles and fizzy drinks in packs of six 2-litre bottles. The savings are significant, but you have to be able to store goods for use over several weeks, and the ranges are limited and not in constant supply. Cash-and-carry outlets stock some regular items, but you may find that you visit for a specific type of food and it isn't in stock. If you can afford to buy in bulk, the meat, fish and delicatessen food is of high quality.

Club together Ask a neighbour who is a member of a cash-and-carry to consider buying in bulk for a group of local friends, who could then all take advantage of discounts of up to 30% on many everyday items.

TOP TIPS GET ONLINE

If you buy bulky items, such as bottled water, pet food, potatoes, soft drinks, baked beans, kitchen rolls or jumbo bags of snacks, it's worth thinking about shopping online.

■ **Compare prices** Browse retailers' websites to compare prices and services and then shop when it suits you. Most large online websites are geared to people's routines and will deliver at a time when you can be there to receive the goods.

■ **Avoid temptation** If you shop online, you're less likely to be tempted to impulse buy. Although many retailers charge a delivery fee, you'll almost certainly still save money when the cost is compared to visiting a supermarket.

■ **It pays to stay loyal** Once you've signed up, stores will be keen to keep you loyal. Watch out for special online prices, mail shots offering discounts and free delivery.

GOOD VALUE FARMERS' MARKETS

Our European neighbours shop regularly at their local town or village market and we're beginning to follow their lead. Farmers' markets are springing up all over the country and are good for seasonal fruit and vegetables. Produce should be cheaper and fresher than the local supermarket where it may have had to travel long distances to reach the shelves. Artisan goods, such as cheeses, bacon, honey, sausages or game, from small local suppliers tend to be expensive due to their superior quality and flavour and the labour-intensive way they have been produced. Farm shops are another excellent place to look for seasonal fruit and vegetables, as well as eggs and meat. Prices are highly competitive, especially if you buy items in bulk, such as a sack of potatoes or a whole lamb portioned and packed for the freezer.

WHERE TO SHOP ONLINE

Although most sites offer delivery over a wide area, enter your postcode before ordering to check you're covered, especially if you live in a remote area. To make sure you are getting the best value for money, use the price comparison website at **www.trollydolly.co.uk** – just select the type of goods you are interested in and a list of supermarkets and current prices appears.

www.tesco.com ✉ There is a service charge of between £3.99 and £5.99 which includes the cost of a personal shopper to select goods from shelves. There are two to three-hour delivery slots at the customer's preferred time.

www.asda.com ✉ The delivery area is limited at present and the delivery slots are agreed with individual customers, although they cannot be guaranteed. There is a £4.25 flat charge for all orders.

www.waitrose.com ✉ WaitroseDeliver operates in selected areas of the country, where you can order online, then have your shopping delivered, or collect from your nearest store.

www.ocado.com ✉ A company working in partnership with Waitrose, Ocado offers the same goods as those in Waitrose stores. There are one-hour delivery slots, offers of £10 off when £60 is spent, and free delivery over £75.

www.iceland.co.uk ✉ This site offers free delivery for orders over £40.

www.sainsburystoyou.com ✉ There is a £5 delivery charge on all orders, regardless of size and distance. Delivery seven days a week in two-hour windows.

www.marksandspencer.com ✉ Limited to cases of wine, fruit baskets and household goods. Delivery charges start at £3.50 with smaller parcels being sent by Royal Mail.

RESOURCES

CLUB, DISCOUNT, CASH–AND–CARRY AND FARMERS' MARKETS

■ Check out Makro **www.makro.co.uk** 020 8965 6655 ✉ and Costco Wholesale **www.costco.com** 0118 920 7105 ✉.

■ For a complete list of Farmers' Markets, see **www.farmersmarkets.net** 0845 230 2150 ✉.

■ For Freedom Food labelled farm produce from selected farms, try **www.farmgatedirect.com** 0870 754 0014 ✉.

■ For a directory of farm shops, speciality food retailers, farmers' markets and village stores in your area, log on to **www. localfoodweb.co.uk** ✉.

CASE STUDY

STRAWBERRY FAIR

When Liz Saunders was planning a summer lunch for her 50th birthday party, she wanted to provide strawberries for dessert for her 70 guests. First she weighed a single portion, then multiplied it to work out that she needed 8 kilos (17lb) for the party.

As a member of Costco, she made this her first stop. The packs of strawberries there contained eight large, identical fruits. There was no weight on the pack, so she didn't know how many to buy and suspected that these perfect specimens would not be especially tasty. Next she checked her local Sainsbury's, where strawberries were on special offer at £1.79 a punnet. The small print indicated this to be £3.92 a kilo but she could not be sure that the offer would be available on the day of the party. At the local farm shop, where there were also pick-your-own fields, the price was £2.95 a kilo, and

it was possible to order exactly what she wanted. This was much nearer to her home than Costco and cheaper than Sainsbury's. Being farm-fresh, the produce was delicious and she was also supporting a local supplier.

MEALS ON A BUDGET

Cheap meals can be both delicious and nutritious. You just need to know what's value for money and how to make the most of everything to hand.

DIY ALTERNATIVES

Buying everyday ingredients in larger quantities and preparing your own dishes at home is always less expensive than pre-packaged smaller portions. Mix and match your favourite ingredients for foods you eat regularly – and save up to 50% on the cost of ready-made items.

Salad dressings Make up a basic vinaigrette with three parts olive oil to one part wine vinegar, then add your own flavours, such as mustard, honey, sun-dried tomato paste, pesto, balsamic vinegar, light soy sauce or chopped herbs. Cut the cost by replacing half the olive oil with a cheaper oil such as sunflower.

Muesli Buy large bags of oats and wheat flakes from health food shops and add a selection of nuts and dried fruits.

Couscous Avoid packs with added flavourings, which can cost up to six times more than plain couscous. Buy your couscous unflavoured and add your own extras.

Tinned tuna A 400g can of plain tuna in oil or brine will save you around 50% on the cost of a smaller tin with added flavourings. Buy the larger tin and use in weekday family bakes and healthy main-meal salads.

TOP TIPS SPREAD THE COST

Make expensive meat and fish go further by mixing them with cheaper ingredients.

■ **Full of beans** Try replacing half the quantity of minced beef in a shepherd's pie with canned borlotti, black-eye or haricot beans.

■ **Veggie-value** Increase the quantity of vegetables and cut back on the chicken or prawns in a stir-fry, or make a vegetable-only version.

■ **Sensible substitution** Tofu is high in protein but only about half the price of good-quality braising steak. It absorbs the flavours of the food it is cooked with, so make a hearty casserole using half cubed beef and half cubed tofu.

■ **Curry flavour** Replace half the lamb in your favourite curry recipe with diced vegetables such as cauliflower, carrots and sweet or ordinary potatoes.

■ **Satisfying soups** Inexpensive green and brown lentils keep their shape when cooked. Simmer them in a well-flavoured stock, with chunks of gammon and baby onions.

LESSONS IN LEFTOVERS

Think of all the bread you casually throw away as throwing money in the bin. You wouldn't dream of doing that, so learn to transform leftovers into tasty bites and snacks.

Melba toast Remove the crusts, toast lightly under the grill on each side and then cut each slice in half horizontally. Return to the grill and toast until the slices curl. Cool, store in an air-tight container and serve with pâtés.

Rescue a disaster

Most people have experienced a bad cooking moment and probably thrown the results out in disgust. Being budget-wise means knowing what to do in a culinary emergency.

■ Heavy-handed with the salt when boiling vegetables or making soup or a casserole? Add a couple of peeled, raw potatoes or drain off half the liquid and replace with fresh water or stock.

■ Is your curry making your eyes water? Stir in some natural yoghurt to cool it down and serve as soon as it's ready. Longer cooking encourages spicy flavours to develop.

Breadcrumbs Make breadcrumbs using a food processor. Freeze in plastic bags, or spread out and leave until dry and crisp, turning over occasionally. Once dry, store the crumbs in a screw-top jar. The remnants at the bottom of your biscuit barrel are another good source of tasty crumbs. Crush to an even crumble with a wooden spoon and use as a biscuit base for desserts.

Croutons Cut a slice of toast into small squares and serve with soup or on salads.

Desserts Make a bread-and-butter pudding, summer pudding or an apple charlotte.

Bread bites Cut into squares, or slices if French bread, toast and spread with pesto, sun-dried tomato paste or simply drizzle with olive oil. Top with slices of mozzarella, goat's cheese, olives, cherry tomato halves, anchovies or other ingredients and serve as a snack.

GREAT-VALUE INGREDIENTS

Fortunately, the least expensive ingredients often turn out to be the most healthy, a bonus when it comes to making nutritious family meals (see recipes on page 28).

Tinned fish Sardines, mackerel and pilchards make tasty patés, and tuna is a favourite stand-by for casseroles; all can cost less than 50p a tin. The slightly more expensive salmon and mussels still make an economical treat.

Pulses At under 45p a tin, lentils, peas and beans are an inexpensive mainstay for vegetarian dishes. Dried pulses work out even cheaper, but the long cooking that some of them require adds to their cost.

Turkey cuts Because it is so low in fat, turkey is becoming more popular. The meat-to-bone ratio is quite high, so the price of fresh turkey compares favourably with chicken.

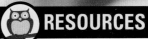

RESOURCES

RECIPE OF THE DAY

■ Find inspiration for your cooking by checking the recipes for budget meals on these websites: **www.sainsburytoyou.co.uk** 0845 301 2020 ✉ **www.bbc.co.uk/food/recipes www.recipes4us.co.uk**

■ Vegetarians can find a selection of recipes on The Vegetarian Society's website: **www.vegsoc.org/ cordonvert/recipes** 0161 925 2000 ✉. There are also economical vegetarian recipes on **www.frugal.org.uk**

TUNA FISH CAKES

COST FOR EACH PERSON: 50P
SERVES 4

450g (1lb) mashed potato
400g (14oz) canned tuna in brine, drained
2 tablespoons tomato ketchup
6 spring onions, finely chopped
1 teaspoon dried mixed herbs
1 egg, beaten
salt and pepper
85g (3oz) dry breadcrumbs
oil for frying or grilling

1 In a bowl, mix together the potato, tuna, ketchup, onions, herbs and beaten egg. Season and divide the mixture into eight equal portions. Shape each portion into round flat cakes and coat with the breadcrumbs.
2 Chill for 30 minutes to firm up the cakes and then shallow fry for 10 minutes until golden on both sides.
3 Alternatively, brush the cakes with a little oil and grill. Serve with a green vegetable or salad.

POTATO AND SAUSAGE FRITTATA

COST FOR EACH PERSON: 40P
SERVES 4

500g (1lb) potatoes, peeled and cut into small chunks
4 large sausages
2 tablespoons oil
6 large eggs
salt and pepper

1 Cook the potatoes until just tender and then drain.
2 While the potatoes are cooking, grill the sausages until cooked. Cut into bite-size pieces.
3 Heat the oil in a large frying pan and fry the potatoes until lightly browned. Add the sausages and stir well to mix with the potatoes.
4 Beat the eggs, season and pour into the pan. Cook until the eggs set on the bottom, then put under a hot grill to set the top.

FEED A FAMILY FOR UNDER £4

VEGGIE BEAN SOUP

COST FOR EACH PERSON: 45P
SERVES 6

2 tablespoons oil
2 leeks, thinly sliced
200g (7oz) carrots, finely chopped
250g (9oz) swede, peeled and cubed
600ml (1 pint) tomato juice
600ml (1 pint) vegetable stock
230g (8oz) can chopped tomatoes
400g (14oz) can kidney beans, drained
400g (14oz) cannellini beans, drained
salt and pepper

1 Heat the oil in a large pan. Add the leeks, carrots and swede, cover the pan and cook over a low heat for 10 minutes, stirring occasionally.
2 Add the tomato juice, stock and tomatoes and bring to a simmer. Cover the pan and cook for 20 minutes or until the vegetables are tender.
3 Add the beans, season and simmer for a further 10 minutes. Serve with warm crusty bread.

CHEESE, BACON AND BEAN PIE

COST FOR EACH PERSON: £1
SERVES 4

700g (1½lb) potatoes, peeled
  and cut into small chunks
1 tablespoon oil
350g (12oz) gammon steaks,
  cut into bite-sized pieces
1 leek, thinly sliced
100g (4oz) mushrooms,
  quartered
2 x 415g (14½oz) cans baked
  beans in tomato sauce
2 tablespoons warm milk
salt and pepper
75g (2¾oz) grated Edam
  cheese

1 Cook the potatoes in a pan of boiling water until tender.
2 Meanwhile heat the oil in a frying pan and fry the cut gammon for 5 minutes. Drain any excess liquid from the pan, add the leek and mushrooms and fry for a further 5 minutes. Stir in the baked beans and spoon into an ovenproof dish.
3 Drain and mash the potatoes with the milk, seasoning and cheese. Spoon the potato mixture over the gammon mix and spread out in an even layer.
4 Preheat the oven to 190°C/375°F/gas mark 5 and bake the pie for 30 minutes until golden brown. Serve with peas or sweetcorn.

MASALA VEGETABLES

COST FOR EACH PERSON: 70p
SERVES 4

2 tablespoons oil
1 large onion, peeled and chopped
3 carrots, chopped
450g (1lb) pumpkin or squash, peeled and cut
  into chunks
1 red pepper, deseeded and chopped
2 courgettes, cut into chunks
2 tablespoons curry paste
400g (14oz) canned chopped tomatoes
  with chilli
300ml (½ pint) vegetable stock
2 teaspoons cornflour
150g (5½oz) natural yoghurt

1 Heat the oil in a large pan. Add the onion and carrots and fry for 5 minutes. Add the squash, red pepper and courgettes and fry for a further 5 minutes, stirring occasionally.
2 Stir in the curry paste, tomatoes and stock, bring to a simmer, cover and cook for 15 minutes or until the vegetables are just tender.
3 Mix the cornflour with the yoghurt and stir into the pan. Simmer over a low heat for 5 minutes. Serve with rice.

GOURMET GOODIES

If you enjoy the good things in life but want to avoid paying top prices, it's worth finding suppliers who give substantial discounts, and timing your shopping for seasonal savings.

LUXURY CHOCOLATES AT SWEET PRICES

By keeping an eye on specialist chocolate retailers and shopping at the right places, you can bag a bargain. In particular, look out for sales offers just after Christmas, Easter and Valentine's Day.

Discounts online On the web, the Chocolate Trading Company **www.chocolatetradingco.com**  and Hotel Chocolat **www.hotelchocolat.com**  both offer discounted and sale items for stock that they want to clear quickly, which can be reduced by nearly 40%.

For true connoisseurs Mail-order chocolate clubs can also be worth joining if you are a dedicated chocolate lover who already spends a lot on your favourite indulgence. Hotel Chocolat's Chocolate Tasting Club offers a selection for £15.95 (each month or when you choose). Or for a lifetime membership fee of £70, the highly regarded Chocolate Society **www.chocolate.co.uk** or 01423 322 230  offers members a 5% discount off their mail-order shopping items, together with access to exclusive promotions and a large hamper full of chocolate goodies.

LOWER THE COST OF QUALITY COFFEE

Your local supermarket offers reasonable-quality coffee for around £2 for 225g (8oz), but for an unusual or higher-grade product, try a specialist supplier and get together with coffee-loving friends for bulk discounts.

Free delivery For an online supplier who offers quality products and free delivery on all orders, try Red Monkey Coffee **www.redmonkeycoffee.com** or 0870 207 4831 .

Wholesale discounts Although you can make savings at most coffee suppliers through mail-order or the web, Discount Coffee **www.discountcoffee.co.uk** or 0845 225 5000  offers exceptional value. With a £5 delivery charge on orders under £50, and up to 60% off wholesale prices for large orders, such as cases of 50 sachets of ground coffee or 4kg–6kg (10lb–14lb) of beans, the emphasis is on bulk buys, but they also have special offers on smaller orders.

Limit storage time Although you will save by buying in bulk, it isn't sensible to buy more freshly roasted coffee than you will use in under a fortnight as it will lose its flavour.

GET VALUE ON GOURMET MEAT AND GAME

For top-quality meat and game it's hard to beat Scottish butcher Donald Russell **www.donaldrusselldirect.com** or 01467 622601 . Prices reflect the high standard but watch out for seasonal bargains and the Value Boxes for year-round deals (such as eight meals for two of diced steak for £29.90). Delivery is free on orders over £100. Find producers of organic and free-range meat on **www.alotoforganics.co.uk**  and **www.foodfirst.co.uk** .

RESOURCES

FOOD-LOVER'S PARADISE

■ The supermarkets with the most successful premium quality ranges are (in order) Waitrose, Marks & Spencer and Sainsbury's. Find one on a high street near you.

■ The special offers at Gourmet World, who have a range of high-quality, award-winning products, are worth checking. Take a look at **www.gourmet-world.com** or phone 020 8748 0125  – free postage for orders over £65.

■ If you buy online from Merchant Gourmet **www.merchantgourmet.com** , you'll get free delivery and a free gift for orders over £15.

Seasonal prices Wait to buy game until the shooting season is well under way to make big savings, as prices are higher at the beginning of the season. The season for grouse runs from August 12 to December 10; for duck from September 1 to January 31; for partridge from September 1 to February 1; and for pheasant from October 1 to February 1. In a good year you can save even more by waiting until the end of the season when there is a glut and by buying directly from a local game dealer – check the Directory of Produce on celebrity chef Rick Stein's website **www.rickstein.com** ✉. You will tend to pay less for a large (usually tougher) bird than a young one.

SAVINGS ON SUPERIOR SEAFOOD

Seafood enthusiasts can benefit from specialist online or mail-order suppliers who offer value on larger orders.

Long-distance savings Try a mail-order company such as The Fish Society **www.thefishsociety.co.uk** or 0800 279 3474 ✉, which supplies nearly 200 kinds of frozen fish and seafood online and through a mail-order catalogue. Their stock is of high quality and environmentally friendly, and their special deals offer good value. A supplier of similarly high quality is Martin's Seafresh **www.martins-seafresh.co.uk** or 0800 0272066 ✉. This Cornwall-based company offers freshly caught seafood and will post anywhere in the UK. Postage is £5 on orders over £25 and free on orders over £100, and regular customers are entitled to discounts.

Buy in season Even if you are buying fresh fish in smaller quantities from a local supplier, you can still make savings by avoiding buying just before or after the low season in spring, when prices are higher. Crab and lobster are more expensive from January to March and mussels from April to August, but the price for prawns should be stable all year round.

CHANNEL HOP FOR CUT-PRICE CHEESE

You can buy a wide variety of high-quality cheeses by mail-order from companies such as Huge Cheese Direct **www.hugecheesedirect.co.uk** or 01323 641950 ✉, but for the best value make the most of your trips abroad. Prices can be an amazing 75% lower in France. For more on bargains abroad, see page 34.

FAIR TRADE BARGAINS

Many Fair Trade foods are worth buying for their gourmet qualities alone, and their prices are reasonable too. Highly recommended are Divine chocolate bars from Oxfam, Green & Black's Organic Cocoa and Fair Trade mangoes, both available from Waitrose and other supermarkets, and Traidcraft organic Seville marmalade, available online at **www.traidcraftshop.co.uk** ✉.

GIFT HAMPERS

For special occasions or impressive gifts that don't cost the earth, you can't go wrong with a hamper from one of Britain's top suppliers. Prices for ready-made hampers can be well over £100 a person, but you can order good-quality, reasonably priced hampers from Freshampers (**www.freshampers.com** or 020 7376 3185 ✉). Hampers start at £16.95 a person (minimum order is for four people), plus delivery from £10. (Orders are restricted to within 100 miles of Winchester.) You can reuse the packaging and the plastic cutlery, which can also be recycled. To order a hamper nationwide, contact Deli Rosslyn (**www.delirosslyn.co.uk** or 020 7794 9210 ✉), whose picnic hampers start at £15 a person.

GOOD DEALS ON WINE AND SPIRITS

Wine sales have grown rapidly in the last twenty years, but few of us are connoisseurs, so how do we decide which bottle to select from the crowded shelves?

KNOWLEDGE IS BUYING POWER

Don't assume that a high price necessarily indicates high quality. Although this is often true, some wines command higher prices than others for historic reasons or because of trends. If you learn about wine, you will be in a better position to spot the best-value vintages. Consider taking a course or setting up a wine club with friends or colleagues. You can arrange regular tastings where everyone brings a bottle of a particular type of wine.

CHEAPEST ISN'T BEST VALUE

If supermarkets have a wine on special offer at a knockdown price, it's worth giving it a try. However, with UK tax at more than £1 a bottle regardless of the quality of the wine, plus the cost of making and shipping it and the bottle itself, a wine costing around £2.99 is likely to be significantly inferior to one at £5, where a higher proportion of the cost relates to the wine itself.

SUPERMARKET WINNERS

In a 2003 *Which?* survey, Tesco's non-vintage Premier Cru Champagne triumphed over a variety of other champagnes, both supermarket brands and non-branded varieties, some of which cost up to £5 a bottle more. So don't be disparaging about own label brands on any type of wine; due to their desire to appeal to more upmarket customers and to their huge buying clout, own brand is often cheapest – and best.

HALF-PRICE BIN ENDS

These are odd bottles left over from a particular vintage or producer that the off-licence wants to shift. There are usually fine wines that can be picked up at bargain prices.

COMPARE PRICES OF WINE, BEER AND SPIRITS

Supermarket prices are generally better than those in off-licences, but keep an eye out for special promotions and bargains. Warehouse prices are the most competitive, and by choosing carefully you can save at least 20% on every bottle of wine you buy.

	OFF-LICENCE	SUPERMARKET	WAREHOUSE*
PENFOLDS SEMILLON CHARDONNAY 75cl	£5.69	£5.49	£5.22
CAMPO VIEJO RESERVE (RIOJA) 75cl	£8.29	£7.99	£5.69
YOUNGS BITTER 500ml	£1.25	£1.58	£0.75
BOMBAY SAPPHIRE GIN 70cl	£14.99	£18.74	£14.49
DOW'S LATE BOTTLED VINTAGE PORT 75cl	£9.99	£6.98	£6.63

* Warehouse wine prices are for bottles bought by the case, not individually.

UK prices correct September 2004

WAREHOUSE DEALS

Wine warehouses, such as Majestic, offer some great deals. They sell by the case of 12 bottles, although these do not all have to be the same type of wine. Check **www.majestic.co.uk** ✉ to find the location of their stores or order online.

LET'S PARTY

Investigate good deals, such as 'wine of the month' or '11 bottles for the price of 12' at supermarkets.
Sale or return To calculate how much wine to buy, bear in mind that a normal 75cl bottle will give six glasses of still wine and eight to ten glasses of champagne or sparkling wine. Arrange to return unopened bottles to your supplier.
Free glasses Wine shops normally lend glasses and offer a delivery service free of charge if you buy wine from them.

DRINK NOW NOT LATER

Most table wines sold in supermarkets and off-licences are designed to be drunk within one to two years rather than laid down. Store wines stoppered with corks on their sides or the corks will dry out, let in air and spoil the wine.

INVESTING FOR THE FUTURE

If you are lucky enough to get your hands on wines suitable for laying down, you can look forward to a treat later.
Conditions apply To ensure your wine is drinkable, let alone improved by laying down, you must have a suitable cellar or well-insulated area – an unsuitable environment will ruin it. Be prepared to store bottles for decades.
Which wines? Suitable wines include top-quality claret and vintage champagne or port – usually obtainable from a specialist auction house by the case, rather than from the local supermarket. For an up-to-date list of specific wines to lay down, see *The Guardian's* Superplonk column (also available on their website **www.guardian.co.uk**).

AVOID WASTING LEFTOVER WINE

Pour leftover wine into a smaller bottle and seal with a tight-fitting cork. Or use a pump that removes the air from a half-finished bottle so the wine returns to its unopened state.

LET IT BREATHE

You can improve an inexpensive bottle of red wine by opening it two or three hours before drinking.

RESOURCES

BUYING ONLINE
www.laithwaites.com
0870 444 8282 ✉
www.worldwines.co.uk ✉
www.virginwines.com
0870 164 9593 ✉
www.uk.chateauonline.com ✉

WINE CLUBS
www.wineontheweb.co.uk/ wineclubs ✉
www.decanter.com/learning/ wine_clubs.php ✉

WINE COURSES
■ For ten weekly two-hour evening sessions in Aberdeen, Birmingham, Edinburgh, Manchester and London (London £195, elsewhere £185) visit **www.wine-education-service.co.uk** ✉.
■ For courses from the Wine & Spirit Education Trust, call 020 7236 3551 or try **www.wset.co.uk** ✉.
■ For a home-study course costing £100, visit **www.thewinetutor.co.uk** ✉.

ONLINE GUIDES
■ For wines, log on to **www.ukwinesguide.co.uk**
■ For everything you need to know about Scotch whisky, visit **www.scotchwhisky.net** ✉.

BEST BUYS ABROAD

Discovering new foods and tastes is one of the highlights of travelling overseas. If you find local produce, or even authentic cooking equipment, that you particularly like, buy some to bring home. You can almost guarantee the price will be less than that of the same items for sale in the UK.

WHERE TO SHOP AND WHAT TO BUY

Follow locals to the food shops, off-licences and market stalls they patronise and so avoid buying obviously overpriced items aimed at tourists.

France Visit French markets for a tempting choice of cheese, honey and olive oil from the producer. Jars of mustard, cooking chocolate and strings of garlic are also good buys. Look out, too, for local produce, such as walnut oil from the Charente region. Stock up on table wine, local aperitifs and digestifs, and sweet muscat fortified wines.

Belgium Bring back chocolate – the quality is high and prices can be 60% lower than at home.

Italy Save money on food such as salami, Parmesan, Parma ham, panforte, sun-dried tomatoes, single-estate olive oils, aged balsamic vinegar, dried porcini mushrooms and perhaps a pasta maker. Take home wine, aperitifs, such as Campari and Limoncello, and even an espresso coffee maker.

Spain Pick up saffron, a paella pan, Pata Negra dried ham, dulce pimenton (smoked paprika), turron (nougat), olives, manchego cheese, sugared almonds and sherry at a fraction of the price in supermarkets in Britain.

Asia Ordinary Chinese or Indian teas will taste fresher than anything bought back home. Stock up on unusual whole and ground spices from local markets and bottled condiments that can be difficult or expensive to obtain in Britain, such as fish sauce, chilli paste and oyster sauce. You can find decorative and inexpensive china and wooden serving bowls and kitchen utensils, such as wooden steamers and strainers.

Middle East and North Africa Buy whole and ground spices from local markets, herbal, floral and fruit teas, honey, olives, Turkish delight, whole nuts in honey, dried fruits, and tagine dishes and Greek or Turkish coffee pots.

BUY YOUR DRINK ABROAD

Take advantage of trips abroad to stock up your wine cellar and buy cheaper spirits and fortified wines. If you don't have time for a vineyard visit, a trip to the local supermarket can yield bargains.

Direct from the vineyard If you're spending several days in a region, visit different vineyards and sample local wines in restaurants, noting what you like. On the last day, go back to your favourites to stock up. Make sure you can keep the temperature down on the way home – heat spoils wine.

From the supermarket Local wines will be the best buys, so try a variety during your stay, including aperitifs and digestifs. Avoid the cheapest as something quite palatable in the sun will seem to have lost its appeal when drunk back in Britain. Go for a mid-range wine abroad and you will have

RESOURCES

FOREIGN FIELDS

■ Find more information on the type of food you are allowed to bring back to Britain from abroad on the Food Standards Agency's website at **www.food.gov.uk** ✉.

■ For general advice, information on ferries and price guides on food bargains abroad (mainly France) try **www.day-tripper.net** ✉.

■ To arrange a vineyard visit, contact Arblaster & Clarke at their website **www.winetours.co.uk** or phone 01730 893344 ✉.

BRING IT HOME FOR LESS

Be sure to get the best value in the countries you are visiting by knowing what food and drink to bring home. The chart below shows some examples of good buys in commonly visited destinations – see what you can find! The prices in the purple-shaded bars are the sterling equivalent of what you would pay for the goods abroad and the red-coloured bars give the price of similar goods in Britain.

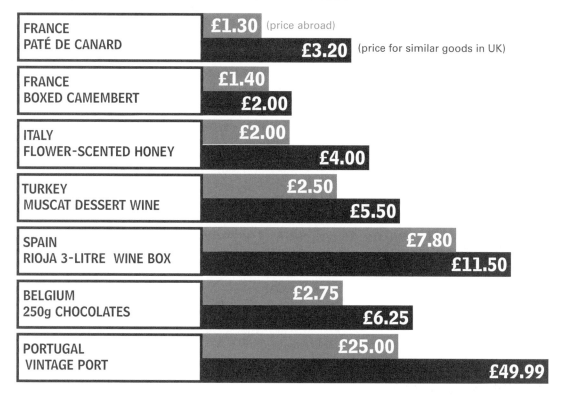

	Price abroad	Price for similar goods in UK
FRANCE — PATÉ DE CANARD	£1.30 (price abroad)	£3.20 (price for similar goods in UK)
FRANCE — BOXED CAMEMBERT	£1.40	£2.00
ITALY — FLOWER-SCENTED HONEY	£2.00	£4.00
TURKEY — MUSCAT DESSERT WINE	£2.50	£5.50
SPAIN — RIOJA 3-LITRE WINE BOX	£7.80	£11.50
BELGIUM — 250g CHOCOLATES	£2.75	£6.25
PORTUGAL — VINTAGE PORT	£25.00	£49.99

brought home a bargain. In France, for example, a bottle of good Cru Bourgeois wine should cost around £2.

Spirit savings European supermarkets sell spirits at comparatively lower prices in 1 litre bottles rather than the 70cl size customary in Britain. You could buy 1 litre of whiskey for £13.99 or 70cl for £11.99 – buy the larger size and save nearly 15%.

KNOW YOUR IMPORT RESTRICTIONS

Don't go to the trouble of shopping, packing and carrying only to find you have bought too much, or the wrong things.

Alcohol limits Travellers within the EU can bring back, duty free, up to 90 litres of wine and 10 litres of spirits, provided the alcohol is not for resale. See the Customs and Excise website at **www.hmce.gov.uk** ✉ for up-to-date information on imports from EU and non-EU countries or phone the National Advice Service on 0845 010 9000.

Other restrictions Always check what you can take out and bring in. Recent epidemics in Britain have resulted in restrictions on the importation of meat and milk products from many parts of the world. You can bring back any food on sale in an EU country, but nothing of animal origin from non-EU countries. India, curiously, forbids air passengers to carry ground almonds.

KITCHEN SENSE

A well-equipped kitchen needn't break the bank. Simply decide exactly what equipment you need and then invest well, buying the best quality you can afford.

TOP TIPS BUY VALUE-FOR-MONEY PANS

A set of three or four top-quality saucepans plus a robust frying pan will save you money in the long run, as cheap pans wear out quickly and need replacing.

■ **Hob matters** The type of pan you need depends on your hob – be particularly careful to select the right pans if you have an induction hob as these require pans to have a magnetic core, so only cast iron and enamel-coated steel pans are suitable. See the Cookware Guide at **www. gourmetcook.co.uk** ✉ for the correct pan for your hob.

■ **Choose the right pans** Copper pans are highly regarded as the best conductors of heat, but they are expensive and require a lot of maintenance. Stainless steel pans are cheaper and easier to care for. The steel should have a chrome/nickel content of at least 18/10. Brands to look out for are Stellar (around £100 for a 5-piece set including a frying pan) and Fissler (£350 for a 5-piece set), (**www.kingsofhagley.co.uk** 01562 885 236 ✉). Aluminium pans are flimsier but less susceptible to wear and tear if coated. Hard anodised pans are made from treated aluminium, but because the material is often coated, the surface is easily damaged. Cast iron is heavy, but is suited to long, slow cooking on an Aga-type range. Enamel-coated steel is also heavy, but more versatile than cast iron.

■ **Sets are better value** You can save up to 50% by buying entire sets rather than individual components. Check out the twice-yearly sales in department stores when top manufacturers sell boxed sets at knockdown prices.

CUTTING THE COST OF KNIVES

A set of good kitchen knives is a once-in-a-lifetime investment, and they are not cheap. To minimise the cost, know how to judge quality and shop around for a bargain.

Reliable makes A good-quality knife will be made in one piece, with the metal going right the way down the handle, which should be securely fixed. Brands that are noted for their quality include Sabatier (around £25 for a carving knife), Henckels and Global (both from £40 for a carving knife), (**www.cooks-knives.co.uk** 01877 33 99 00 ✉). However, Kitchen Devil knives were commended by *Which?* as the 'best value for money buy'; their carving knife is £18.95, available from hardware and kitchenware stores.

Mail order with caution You can find good mail-order deals, but make sure you can test the feel of the knife in your hand and send it back if it's not right. Culinaire on 01293 550 563 or **www.kitchenknivesdirect.co.uk** ✉ offers good deals on quality makes, including free postage and packing. It is worth spending money on a recommended brand as the knives will serve you well and may never need replacing.

ECONOMICAL STARTER PACKS

For people equipping their first kitchen, starter packs can be a good way to provide the basic tools and, like most bulk buys, can be good value for money. Just don't expect them to last for ever – they will eventually need to be replaced. But by then their owners should have learned how to care for their kitchenware and can buy more expensive, higher-quality products. You can buy a small set, including kitchen knives and other utensils, from around £15 from Littlewoods Index 0845 0752233 **www.index.co.uk** ✉ or an entire 44-piece kitchen starter set with pans, knives and other utensils for £22.49 from Kays at 0870 33 33 725 **www.kayslifestyle.co.uk** ✉. Students can often buy kitchen starter packs through their university Accommodation Office.

SAVING WHILE COOKING

Saving fuel doesn't just make financial sense, it also helps the environment by conserving precious energy. Make full use of your oven by cooking several dishes at the same time and maximise hob heat by placing steamers over pans.

OIL RESOURCES

Leave vegetable oil that has been used for deep-frying to cool completely before straining it through a coffee filter or fine sieve and pouring it back into a bottle for recycled oil. If it was previously used at a high enough temperature, it won't have picked up food flavours and so can be used again. Oil used for frying fish should be kept separate.

PUT A LID ON IT

Speed up cooking time by covering pans and casseroles with a tight-fitting lid. To make a loose lid tighter, put a sheet of foil under it.

JUST A CUPPA

When making tea, boil only the water you need instead of filling the electric kettle. According to the Energy Saving Trust, if we all did this we'd save enough electricity to power almost all our street lights.

A COLD START

If a roast or casserole needs to cook for more than an hour, start it in a cold oven and cook for the prescribed time. Reserve preheating for baking only.

SAUCEPAN SAVVY

Ensure the base of your pan covers the electric or gas ring so heat cannot escape up the sides of the pan.

ON THE BOIL

The cheapest and fastest way to bring water to the boil for cooking in a saucepan is to use your electric kettle.

DOUBLE UP

Steam fast-cooking vegetables in a basket over a pan in which you are boiling slower-cooking ones, such as potatoes, to save turning on a second ring.

PILE ON THE PRESSURE

Pressure cookers reduce cooking time by almost two-thirds. They are better than microwaves for tenderising tough cuts of meat and for cooking large quantities.

SLASH OVEN COSTS

Heating in the oven costs the same whether you're cooking two portions or ten. Maximise oven heat by cooking several dishes at the same time, especially cheaper cuts of meat that require long, slow cooking. Remove large joints and whole chickens or turkeys from the fridge an hour or so before cooking so they come to room temperature. If the centre of the meat is very cold, the joint will take longer to cook.

Looking good

The idea that you need plenty of money to look good is an outdated concept. There are even advantages to a small budget: limitations stretch the imagination and force you to think hard about how much you really want everything you buy.

MAKING THE MOST OF YOUR WARDROBE

Success with today's fashion relies more on individual style than a big bank balance. And style isn't about rushing out to buy a new season's look. A different approach to what you already own can be just as effective as a shopping spree – and more satisfying.

MAKE REALISTIC CHOICES

Common sense should be your first guideline. Before buying anything new, think about your lifestyle and select only items you'll wear often enough to justify their purchase. Make sure any additions will complement what you already own, choosing fabrics and styles that are easy to wear and maintain for maximum versatility.

Avoid dry cleaning As a rule, try not to choose fabrics that need dry cleaning. This is especially true of garments that will need frequent cleaning – you'll pay upwards of £2 each time they get dirty.

Linen lasts Linen is more resistant to deterioration when exposed to sunlight and high temperatures than cotton, but buy a linen blend if you like your clothes crease-free.

Buy denim for value Denim is one of the most comfortable and cheapest materials. It gives you lots of wear for your money – and grows in style with age.

Hard-working luxury Silk may be luxurious but it is also very durable and hard-wearing. It keeps you cool in summer and, because it is breathable and light, keeps you warm in winter – particularly if layered with other clothing.

Artificial fabrics have their place Fabrics such as viscose are hard-wearing and can be rolled for ease of packing without creasing. Recently developed materials like Tencel® have many of the advantages of natural materials, such as comfort, drape and strength, but with added ease of care and durability.

TOP TIPS BUILDING BLOCKS TO STYLE

A good clearout lets you start to create the building blocks to looking good. Look at your wardrobe as a whole. To maximise the number of outfits you can put together, focus on items that relate to each other.

■ **Simplicity pays** The most versatile clothes are simple – well-cut trousers or skirts and plain shirts and T-shirts.

■ **For all seasons** Try to choose fabrics that will take you through different seasons. Soft and crisp cottons, lightweight wool, soft knits, silk and fabrics with a hint of stretch will all work well across the seasons.

■ **Sartorial style** Traditionally, men have tended to have a smaller wardrobe and to buy clothes with a longer-term approach. This can be a helpful model for women too. A good tailored suit is a perfect example – it may cost a little more initially but it will last for ages and you can ring the changes by wearing it with different jackets, skirts and trousers and adding accessories to dress it up.

keep it simple

A NEW START
To revamp your wardrobe, pare it down to the clothes you actually want. This way, you'll avoid buying items that coordinate with clothes you no longer wear. Begin by separating clothes into three piles: dustbin; charity shop; pieces you want to keep.
Be ruthless and get rid of anything you haven't worn for the last two years. Don't keep something in the hope that you will lose weight or that it will come back into fashion.

WHEN TO SPLASH OUT

Spend a little more on the essential ingredients of a basic wardrobe – they will repay you in more ways than one.

Good-quality shirt Go for a simple, well-cut design in cotton or silk. It works well in the day with jeans or a casual skirt; at night with a slinky skirt or trousers; and as a summer jacket over a vest or camisole.

Quality mainstays When buying tailored winter outfits, be prepared to pay more for good-quality items, particularly with jackets and tailored trousers. Check they are lined and well-finished as well. You'll be rewarded with a better fit and clothes that stay looking good for longer.

The best accessories Your shoes, bags, scarves and belts should work with most of your wardrobe. Buy quality accessories in the sales to add style to more basic outfits.

BUY CHILDREN'S CLOTHES AND AVOID VAT

Petite shoppers (up to 5ft 4in and up to size 10) can benefit from the zero VAT rate on children's clothes. These days, children's ranges are imaginative enough to appeal to most adults. Children's shoe sizes generally go up to a size 5 or 6 (38 or 39), and clothes intended for 14–15 year olds may fit small adults.

DON'T SKIMP ON LINGERIE

When it comes to planning a wardrobe, underwear is too often overlooked. Ill-fitting lingerie can ruin the final effect of an expensive outfit. But you don't have to spend a fortune on designer lines.

Free fitting Before buying a bra, check out the styles available and take advantage of the professional measuring service offered by many department stores. It's free of charge and you don't have to make a purchase. Find a brand and style that suits you, then check online sources and catalogues for the same item at a cheaper price. For a list of websites offering a range of low-priced lingerie, log on to **www.price-paradise.com** and type lingerie in the web search box.

Slinky or sensible Marks & Spencer, Knickerbox and H&M offer a wide range of underwear sets in styles ranging from sexy to practical at £15–£40. For a real bargain, try Primark where you can get a set of bright lacy underwear for less than £10.

DESIGNER OUTFIT

LOW COST ALTERNATIVE

£120 £15

£45 £8

£350 £130

£200 £20

£150 £30

£225 £35

TOTAL £1,090

TOTAL £238

DESIGNERWEAR ON THE CHEAP

Knowing where to go for your designer suit can mean savings of up to £240 (new) or £379 (nearly new) on a Jaeger ladieswear wool suit (September 2004).

DESIGNER SHOP	**£439**
DESIGNER OUTLET	**£199**
SECONDHAND	**£60**

BESPOKE SUITS AT HALF THE PRICE

If you would like a bespoke suit but don't want to pay Savile Row prices, try using a visiting tailor from the Far East before paying expensive prices at home. Tailors from Hong Kong – such as Raja Fashions – frequently hold fittings in hotels across Britain. They email your design and measurements back to Hong Kong, and the suit is made and sent to you within four weeks. It can cost as little as £140, but check the details in advance – linings, for example, may not automatically be included in the price. For information on visiting tailors, see page 57.

Fabric choices Although pure wool is normally the recommended choice for a quality suit, a wool/synthetic blend is a good substitute and costs about 20% less.

HIRE OR BUY FORMAL WEAR EX-RENTAL

If you are put off wearing a formal suit by the cost, consider hiring one or even buying an ex-rental outfit.

For example, at Hire Society (**www.hire-society.com**) a traditional black dinner suit costs £195 to buy new, £39.95 to hire for 48 hours or £90 to buy ex-rental.

BUY MENSWEAR – SAVE UP TO 50%

Men's clothing tends to be less expensive and is often better quality than women's. If your style is casual, try the men's rails for a bargain but check the fit. Basic shirts, T-shirts and sportswear can be as much as 50% cheaper when bought in the menswear department.

DESIGNER OUTFIT — LOW COST ALTERNATIVE

TOTAL £1,065 — TOTAL £280

ASK YOURSELF

BEFORE YOU BUY

When you're making a purchase make sure you get value for money by asking these 'three by three' questions:
- What three things can I wear it with?
- What three places can I wear it to?
- What three ways can I accessorise it?

HIRE A HAT

If you need a ladies' hat for a formal occasion, don't waste money buying one. Try a hire company such as Get Ahead Hats – find a branch at **www.getaheadhats.co.uk** ✉ – a week's hire starts from £20.

BAGS OF STYLE

Look out for old leather handbags from charity shops or the family attic. Vintage handbags saved by your mother or aunt have a timeless appeal, and a secondhand Chanel bag would be a real style find. Camera cases and satchels also make unusual but stylish accessories. Clean up old bags with saddle soap, then use shoe polish and buff well. For a quick shine, rub with hand cream and wipe off with a tissue.

BEST FOOT FORWARD

■ If you are need shoes to match a dress for a special occasion, buy plain satin pumps and have them dyed instead of spending time and money searching for the right colour.
■ Strappy summer sandals bought in the end-of-season sales can double for evening wear.
■ Sew beads or sequins on plain canvas shoes for fun casual wear.

PRICE WATCH

For good deals on men's watches, cufflinks, wallets, belts, hats, gloves and scarves, plus clothing and gadgets, try **www.menkind.co.uk** 01372 365021 ✉.

ACCESSORISE FOR ADDED VALUE

Accessories add variety to your wardrobe, transforming clothes from ultra casual to dressed up, or taking a simple outfit from day to evening. A few well-chosen items can make a simple, inexpensive outfit look like a designer creation.

QUICK FIXES FOR SECONDHAND JEWELLERY

■ Repair gold or silver-plated jewellery with a fine paint brush and gold or silver spray paint. Spray a little paint onto a piece of cardboard, dip in the brush and touch up the chips.
■ To unknot a chain, lay it on a piece of wax paper. Put a drop or two of baby oil directly onto the knot. Use two needles to gently untangle the knot then blot the oil with tissues.
■ If the post on a pierced earring has broken, use a nail file to smooth off any residual glue from the back, then mount a new post with permanent glue.
■ If the pin on the back of a brooch is broken don't throw it away – put it on a chain to make a necklace, sew it to a jacket or repair it with permanent glue.

WINNING WAYS WITH SCARVES

A scarf is one of the most versatile accessories in your wardrobe.
■ Use a large woollen one as a winter shawl or poncho instead of a coat.
■ Twist a wide cotton scarf into a bikini top for the beach, or use a big scarf as a sarong.
■ Wear a narrow scarf or a necktie as a belt with jeans or casual trousers.
■ Use a small scarf to tie up long hair into a pony tail.

BUTTONS AND BOWS

The buttons and other trims used on designer or vintage clothes are sometimes worth more than the garment itself. Look for damaged secondhand designer outfits going for a song in charity shops, snip off the buttons and use them to give a touch of class to a plain jacket or sweater.

MONEY OFF DESIGNER SHADES

If you hanker after a pair of designer sunglasses and you don't need prescription lenses, you can usually save 15% on a stylish pair for men or women through designer websites and outlets (see pages 45 and 48), or save 17.5% by buying them VAT-free at an airport shop (see page 57). For the best protection, look for a sticker that specifies 100% UV blockage.

SOS (SAVE ON SHOE LEATHER)

Men's shoes are expensive, but you can find bargains without pounding the pavement by visiting the following websites:
■ Get 40% off Timberland shoes (for men and women) plus free delivery at **www.shoe-shop.com** 08700 117 227 ✉.
■ Invest in a pair of bespoke handmade shoes that last for 10 years for as little as £178. Go to Tower Bridge Shoes at **www. tailored-for-you.com** 01225 791 863 ✉.

A GIRL'S BEST FRIEND

If you are looking for jewellery in precious stones or metals, visit a wholesaler in London's Hatton Garden for the best prices. Get the names and numbers from the British Jeweller's Association, **www.bja.org.uk** 0121 237 1110 ✉.

BAUBLES AND BEADS

Jewellery doesn't need to be pricey. You can find colourful beads in craft shops such as Creative Beadcraft **www.creativebeadcraft.co.uk** 020 7629 9964 for under £1 a pack and make your own.

BARGAINS BY POST AND ONLINE

Shopping online is growing in popularity, although many shoppers still like to receive a catalogue to browse at their leisure and to pay by post or phone.

MAIL ORDER FOR 20% SAVINGS AND MORE

Mail-order shopping offers all the choice of the high street, often with more competitive prices and no hassles.

Stress-free shopping Browse a catalogue or a website, then order by phone or online so you cut out the hassle of shopping and can try on clothes in the peace and privacy of your own home.

Price advantage Prices are often lower than those in the shops because you can order direct from suppliers or from discount specialists.

Unisex shopping Many catalogues including Freemans, Kays, Choice for You, La Redoute, Lands End and Next offer extensive ranges for both men and women.

Free p&p Some companies offer free postage and packing under certain conditions. For example, Freemans and Kays offer free delivery and returns, and La Redoute often offers free postage. (See Resources, right for contact information.)

WATCH POINTS MAIL-ORDER PITFALLS

Although it can be convenient and economical, the main problem with mail order is that you have to rely on a catalogue (print or online) to judge an item's suitability. This can result in having to pay to return unwanted items.

■ **Try for size** Sizes aren't always standard so if you're new to a company, you may have to try a few garments before finding the right size. To counteract this, use a company that offers a free or heavily discounted first order – if you have to return anything, at least you won't lose out.

RESOURCES

CATALOGUES
For convenience you can't beat catalogue shopping. Compare prices to get the best deal.
■ At **www.catalink.net**, you can sign up free to receive paper catalogues by post or view catalogues online.
■ **http://buy.uk.shop.com/** has links to catalogue, online discount and clearance websites. Alternatively, order a free catalogue through the company's own website (see Resources, page 45) or call them direct:
Freemans 0870 606 6099
Kays and **Choice for You** 0870 333 3725
La Redoute 0870 050 0455
Next 0845 600 7000
Lands End 0800 376 7974
M&M Sports Ltd 01568 616161
Fashion World 0870 160 6100
Elvi 01527 506306

■ **Check the cost of returns** If you have to return or exchange an item, you may have to pay postage and packing – check terms and conditions before ordering as some companies offer free returns or don't charge if you return an item within a set number of days.

MADE FOR MEN

Many men hate shopping – even when it comes to buying clothes for themselves. Mail-order catalogues and online suppliers offer the perfect solution.

Casual chic Cheap and cheerful casuals can be ordered through companies such as Lands End, which has a free catalogue and website.

Going upmarket For the man who prefers a designer label, it's also possible to buy all the leading brands online at a fraction of high-street prices. Try web stores such as Brown Bag Clothing and Designer Discount (see Resources, below). The latter's product line includes designer accessories such as sunglasses and fragrances for both men and women.

> **COMPARE PRICES ONLINE**
> To make sure you are getting a bargain, use a price comparison website such as
> **www.kelkoo.co.uk**
> **www.dealtime.co.uk**
> **www.pricerunner.co.uk**

RESOURCES

HOT WEBSITES FOR MEN AND WOMEN

■ **www.kayslifestyle.co.uk** Fashion brands at affordable prices with 10% off your first order, free delivery, free returns and 14 days approval for online purchases on everything from clothing to perfumes and accessories. Brands include Levi's, Calvin Klein, Nike, French Connection, Peter Werth.

■ **www.choiceforyou.co.uk** A sister company to Kays but 10%–15% cheaper as there is no commission on catalogue sales. Catalogue prices are discounted by 20% for online purchases, and there is also an additional 10% off for first-time buyers.

■ **www.freemans.com** Substantial savings on clothes, footwear and sportswear.

■ **www.next.co.uk** Inspirational ideas from the Next Directory online.

■ **www.redoute.co.uk** A stylish collection of clothes with affordable prices.

■ **www.landsend.co.uk** Smart, comfortable casual clothes including petite and plus ranges for women and a tall range for men.

■ **www.debenhams.com** The popular high-street department store online with a wide range of men's and women's clothing from own brands to designer labels.

■ **www.bbclothing.co.uk** Only available online, Brown Bag Clothing offers you some of the best discounted prices on designer labels for both men and women including Aquascutum, Armani, Burberry, Dolce & Gabbana, Hugo Boss, Lacoste, Moschino, Paul Smith, Prada, Versace.

■ **www.yoox.com** Sizeable reductions can be found on last season's designer collections, from coats and suits to bags and shoes.

■ **www.asos.com** Fashion as worn by celebrities at low prices.

■ **www.kitbag.co.uk** Money-saving deals on top brands such as Nike, Adidas, Reebok and Umbro.

■ **www.mandmsports.com** End of ranges from big names such as Adidas, ranging from a third to a half off usual high-street prices.

JUST FOR WOMEN

■ **www.topshop.co.uk** The latest copies from the catwalks can be found here at reasonable prices.

■ **www.fashionworld.co.uk** Affordable fashion in sizes 12–32 with a free return policy.

FOR SIZE 16 AND OVER, CHECK OUT:

■ Elvi at **www.elvi.co.uk**
■ Dorothy Perkins at **www.dorothyperkins.co.uk**
■ Evans at **www.evans.ltd.uk**

JUST FOR MEN

■ **www.designerdiscount.co.uk** Up to 75% off designerwear
■ **www.eSuit.com** Suits at discount prices
■ **www.ebay.com** Buy and sell clothing and accessories.

PLAN YOUR SALES FOR GREATEST SAVINGS

Organise your sales shopping to make the most of the bargains at certain times of year. Some items are particularly cheap according to the season, such as end-of-summer ranges in July and end-of-winter ranges in January.

SALES SHOPPING – SAVE OVER 40%

Coats and outerwear A good time to buy a winter coat is in the January or February sales as department stores often do good reductions before spring fashions arrive. 'Classic' items – particularly in black – are not always put in the sales, but if you're flexible about the style and colour you want, you may get a great bargain.

Summer savings If you can wait to buy summer clothes until July or August, you will benefit from reductions of up to 40% on the prices at the start of the season. This also applies to the season's swimwear, which will be on sale at reduced prices by mid-summer.

January sales All items of clothing are slashed in price in the post-Christmas sales so that retailers can make room for the new season's stock. Remember that the sales often start before the New Year. Check in advance to see if an item you have been coveting will be on reduced in the sales.

50% OFF IN THE HIGH STREET

Items in high-street stores like Gap (find a local branch at **www.gap.com**) and New Look (01305 765000), whose selling point is their cheap, up-to-the-minute fashions, are expected to have a fast turnover. If they remain unsold for more than two months, they are relegated to the sale rail where you can grab them for as little as half their full price.

DISCOUNT OUTLET SALES – SAVE 80%

Big savings can be made in the sales merely by visiting your local high street, but for the real bargains try factory shops at sales time. Here, prices can be as much as 80% less than the nonsale high-street price.

HEAVILY DISCOUNTED HAUTE COUTURE

If your taste runs to the glamorous and expensive but your wallet doesn't, the designer sales may be for you. If you live in London, you're in luck because almost all of them are held in the capital – if you live elsewhere, it may be worth the cost of travelling to London for the day to pick up bargains at up to 90% less than the normal retail price. But be warned – if you are over a size 12, you may not find much of interest. Supermodel-sized shoppers (6–8) may pick up a real bargain. Be prepared to wait in long queues, to forgo the luxury of a dressing room and to jostle with the crowds for the best deals. In most cases, you may need to add your name to a mailing list at the shop or fill in a form online, through the relevant website, to be notified about future sales.

GETTING FURTHER DISCOUNTS

If you find an item of clothing you like that has a button or two missing or a loose thread, you may be able to get it at a further discount. Remember that you may be asked to waive your statutory rights if you buy a garment in the full knowledge that it has a fault.

BUY A CLASSIC FOR 70% LESS

Sale discounts at designer shops can vary from 25% to an enormous 70%. But, although they're quality-brand goods, the choice may be limited so don't be tempted to buy something ultra-trendy if it isn't exactly what you're looking for. Use this kind of shopping to boost wardrobe basics with good-quality names and special items that will give a touch of designer style to the rest of your clothes.

SALES ARE ONLINE TOO

When hunting for seasonal bargains, don't forget that the online retailers also hold sales at the same times as those on the high street. Here, too, items that have not sold during the season are heavily discounted – by as much as 50%, for example, at La Redoute. For more tips on buying over the Internet, see page 44.

 RESOURCES

RECOMMENDED DESIGNER SALES

■ **Designer Showroom Sale** (Central London, 020 7850 5075) End-of-season and sample sales four times a year for women. Find Marina Rinaldi, MaxMara and Passport.

■ **Oakville** (Central London, 020 7580 3686) Shop for Fendi and Ungaro at this fashion showroom where you'll find women's casual and dressy clothing at well below high-street prices.

■ **Wahl Fashions** (Central London, 020 7499 4000) Designer clothing for women from Plein Sud, C'est Duo and Beppe Bondi. Sales twice yearly – usually April and October. Often 50% less than retail price.

■ **The Designer Warehouse Sales** (North London, 020 7837 3322, or go to **www.dwslondon.co.uk** ✉) Entrance fee £2. More award-winning designer labels under one roof than any other outlet in the UK. Held over three days, 12 times a year, a major London sale for women and men. Buy Alberta Ferretti, Vivienne Westwood and Mandarina Duck at 60% less than retail. Local designers are also featured. Smaller items may be £10 or less.

■ **London Fashion Weekend** (West London, 0871 222 2314 or see their website at **www.londonfashionweek.co.uk** ✉) Entrance is £8.50 but you can find big reductions on women's and men's designer clothing and accessories. Most London

designers are here, from Jasper Conran to Philip Treacy – and many of the smaller labels.

■ **Designer Sale UK** (East London, 01273 470 880 or **www.designersales.co.uk** ✉) Substantial discounts here for women and men. Recent bargains include a leather jacket from RB for £30 reduced from £170, and Duffer of St George shirts for £26 reduced from £85. Cheaper items such as T-shirts go for £10.

■ **Della Finch Designer Sales** (South London, 020 7233 6385) Budget shoppers – women and men – will love this year-round designer heaven. You might even find something on the £5 rack. Labels include Armani, Moschino and Versace.

BUY HALF-PRICE AT FACTORY OUTLETS

For a bargain from both high-street and designer names, try visiting a shopping centre where discount outlets are gathered together in one place.

TOP TIPS SHOPPING WITHOUT DROPPING

Get the best value from your shopping trips by careful planning. Check purchases thoroughly and ask about the returns policy before buying apparent bargains on impulse.

■ **Big-name stores** To save on travelling, look for outlets that are anchored by well-known names such as Gap and have at least three stores you're interested in.

■ **Check first** Always telephone factory and outlet villages first to ensure they are still trading.

■ **Flawless** Check for flaws that may have caused their rejection. Sometimes garments are manufactured specifically for factory outlets and the quality isn't as good.

■ **Avoid impulse buys** Be clear about what you want. Don't be seduced by the low price if an item is out-of-date.

 **RESOURCES**

FACTORY OUTLETS IN LONDON

■ **James & Alden** (Edgware Road NW2, 020 8830 8008) The best place for bags, belts (from £3.50) and wallets (from £6).

■ **The Burberry Factory Outlet** (Chatham Place E9, 020 8985 3344) Sells top-quality clothing, shoes, jewellery and accessories. Men's shirts from £10, sports tops (slight seconds) for £11.95.

■ **Clark's Factory Shops** (Rye Lane, Peckham SE15, 020 7732 2530 and Powis Street, Woolwich SE18, 020 8854 3163) Sells footwear end-of-line styles or half-price slight seconds.

■ **French Connection/Nicole Farhi Outlet Shop** (Hancock Road E13, 020 7399 7125) Discounts on last season's stock, samples and seconds for women and men.

FACTORY OUTLETS OUTSIDE LONDON

For a list of factory outlets see www.shoppingvillages.com

■ **Alexon sale shops** (Shrewsbury, 01743 236319; Tamworth, 01827 310041; High Wycombe, 01494 464214; Luton, 01582 483422)

■ **Aquascutum factory shops** (Hornsea, 01964 536759)

■ **Bicester Village Oxon** (01869 323 200 and at www.bicestervillage.com) Savings of up to 60% on the previous season's branded goods for women and men.

■ **Clarks Village** (Street, Somerset, 01458 840 064 and at www.clarksvillage. co.uk) Up to 60% off famous brands for women and men.

■ **The Galleria Outlet Centre** (Hatfield, www.galleriacentre. com) Stores offer up to 50% discounts on this season's surplus or end-of-lines.

■ **Laura Ashley discount shops** (Colne, 01282 860166; Hornsea, 01964 536503; Street in Somerset, 01458 840405)

■ **McArthur Glen** (020 7535 2350, 020 7535 2449 and at www.mcarthurglen.com) Designer outlets in seven UK locations – Livingston, York, Mansfield, Cheshire-Oaks, Bridgend, Swindon and Ashford. The outlets offer up to 50% discounts on a host of top brands and designer labels.

■ **Mulberrry factory shop** (Somerset, 01749 340583) Find the latest designs on sale, many of which have substantial discounts.

■ **Paul Costello factory shop** (Ellesmere Port, 0151 357 1681)

■ **Peak Village Outlet** (Rowley, Derbyshire, 01629 735326 at www.peakvillage. co.uk) Stores offer up to 70% off a full range of fashions, shoes and accessories. Open every day except Christmas Day.

BARGAINS AT CHAINS AND SUPERMARKETS

A growing number of discount chains offer great bargains on brand-name clothing. And various supermarkets have added their own fashion ranges to the goods they stock at some very competitive prices.

DISCOUNT CHAINS OFFER UP TO 60% OFF

Chains of stores that offer hugely discounted clothing for all the family have spread nationwide. If you have web access, you can use their websites to find a store near you.

Matalan (01695 552400 and at **www.matalan.co.uk**) Matalan is a large chain of discount stores offering low prices on a range of fashion. Join at your local branch – lifetime membership costs only £1. As well as saving you up to 50% off high-street prices, they'll send you regular updates on new collections and special offers.

TK Maxx (**www.tkmaxx.com**) TK Maxx offers famous-label womenswear and menswear up to 60% less than recommended retail prices. You'll find big savings on a variety of genuine designer wear – from wardrobe basics such as jeans and shirts, to cashmere sweaters – if you're prepared to hunt through rails of clothes.

Primark (**www.primark.co.uk**) A low-cost chain, rather than a discount store, Primark stores offer items at up to half the price of even the cheaper high-street shops. They sell low-cost everyday clothing, with a good selection for children.

PICK UP A BARGAIN WITH THE FAMILY

Many supermarket chains now have their own clothing ranges – including designer labels such as Jeff and Co (Jeff Banks) at Sainsbury's and Fred + Florence at Tesco. Both George at Asda and Woolworths offer very competitive rates, especially on schoolwear.

 **RESOURCES**

BARGAINS GALORE
Dedicated bargain hunters will find a great source of information and comprehensive lists of secondhand and factory shops and other value outlets in *The Good Deal Directory*, available by phoning 01367 860016 or by visiting their website at **www.gooddealdirectory. co.uk** ✉.

SUPERMARKET BEST BUYS

The top bargains at the supermarket are everyday classic items such as white shirts and sportswear – you can save as much as 90% over department store prices.

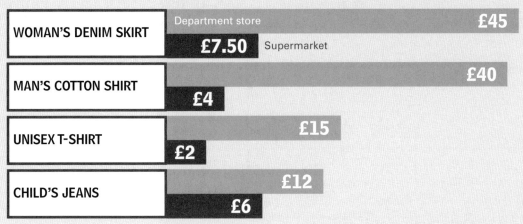

	Department store	Supermarket
WOMAN'S DENIM SKIRT	£45	£7.50
MAN'S COTTON SHIRT	£40	£4
UNISEX T-SHIRT	£15	£2
CHILD'S JEANS	£12	£6

Prices Oct 2004

BUY SECONDHAND FOR FIRST-RATE DEALS

If you are prepared to rummage through old clothes in vintage shops and markets, special bargains may await you. You could find nearly new designer dresses for as little as 10% of their original price.

FINDING MARKET BARGAINS

It is quite acceptable to haggle for a better discount when buying from street markets. First find out the seller's asking price to determine how low a price you can reasonably offer.

BEST MARKETS FOR SECONDHAND BARGAINS	
MARKET	**WHAT TO BUY**
Camden Lock, London NW1 Tube: Camden Town, Chalk Farm Monday–Sunday 10am–6pm	Designer clothes Also good for new and secondhand clothes and jewellery. Avoid the crowds at weekends.
Petticoat Lane, London E1 Tube: Aldgate, Aldgate E., Liverpool St. Sundays 9am–2pm	Mainly new but some secondhand street fashion and footwear, bags and leather goods.
Portobello Road, London W11 Tube: Ladbroke Grove, Notting Hill Fridays and Saturdays 8am–3pm	Clothes, footwear and jewellery. Best bargains at Ladbroke Grove end. Best secondhand clothes are on streets alongside the Westway and under the canopy at the junction with Portobello Road.
Spitalfields, London E1 Tube: Liverpool Street Sundays 11am–3pm	Designer and vintage clothing.
Affleck's Palace 52 Church Street, Manchester Sundays 9am–2.30pm	A large indoor market selling 'alternative' fashion and vintage clothing, with lots of retro styles and new designers.
The Barras 4–6 Stevenson Street, Glasgow Saturday and Sunday 10am–5pm	Clothing (new and secondhand), fake designerwear (be careful!), accessories and more.
Quayside Market, **Quayside, Newcastle** Sundays 9am–2.30pm	Secondhand clothes, amongst many other items (it's one of the largest Sunday markets in England), new clothing and accessories.
Rag Market (St Martin's Market) **Edgbaston Street, Birmingham** Tuesdays, Fridays, Saturdays 9am–5pm	Vintage (some designer) clothes, accessories, fabrics and makeup.
St Nicholas Market **Corn Street, Bristol** Monday–Saturday 9.30am–5pm	Clothing (new and vintage), jewellery, fabric and beads.

DRESS AGENCIES FOR DESIGNER DISCOUNTS

Dress agencies are the places to find secondhand designer clothes, bags, shoes and other accessories at savings of up to 75% and more. They are also an excellent way of recouping cash on garments you no longer wear. Agencies usually offer between a third and a half of the original price to sellers, and some allow you to reclaim or donate to charity clothes that are unsold after a couple of months. Most agencies won't consider clothes that are more than two years old, and the smarter ones accept only big names.

TOP TIPS FINDING CHARITY SHOP BARGAINS

Local charity shops can be an excellent source of bargains, but be prepared to set aside some time to look. And if you want designer goods, pick your area carefully.

■ **Ready to rummage?** Many charity shops including Oxfam, Scope and Age Concern are updating their image to make it easier to find designer bargains. But for real finds, you may still have to hunt through less-desirable items.

■ **Exclusive neighbourhoods** Naturally, the best bargains are more likely to be found in affluent areas. Pick the right shop and you may find a Nicole Farhi outfit for £25. Shops in West and Central London tend to yield high-quality goods but can also command higher prices – the smarter parts of other cities and suburbs may offer better value. Shops in the commuter belts and wealthier areas such as parts of Cheshire and the Home Counties can also be a good bet.

RESOURCES

LONDON DRESS AGENCIES

■ **Bang Bang** (Goodge Street W1, 020 7631 4191) Offers a good selection of younger styles, from cheap street fashion to designer labels.

■ **L'Homme Designer Exchange** (Blandford Street, near Baker Street W1) Get men's designer wear here. Trousers and shirts from £15, and suits from £90.

■ **The Loft** (Monmouth Street, near Covent Garden and Leicester Square WC2, 020 7240 3807) This shop offers items from contemporary designers for a third or so of their original price and a well-stocked £5 rail.

■ **Wellingtons** (Wellington Place, St John's Wood NW8, 020 7483 0688) Find a wide range of clothes and accessories for women, such as leather and suede jackets from £20; lots of Dolce & Gabbana; high-street labels and a bargain rail for under £20.

■ **The Anerley Frock Exchange** (Anerley Road SE20, 020 8778 2030) Large shop stocking women's clothes from Next and Gap to Versace.

DRESS AGENCIES OUTSIDE LONDON

■ **Elite Dress Agency** (35 King Street West, Manchester, 0161 832 3670) The largest dress agency in Europe, this shop offers clothes for all the family. Labels include Gucci, Versace and Paul Smith and high-street brands.

■ **Seconds Out** (High Street, Cookham, Berkshire, 01628 850371) Designers stocked include Gucci, Prada, Versace and Louis Vuitton at up to 75% reductions. Also offers a range of accessories including hats.

■ **The Uppingham Dress Agency** (2–6 Orange Street, Uppingham, Rutland, 01572 823276) A big shop selling over 4000 items from designers and high-street shops.

■ **Designer Exchange** (3 Royal Exchange Court, Off 17 Royal Exchange Square, Glasgow, Scotland, 0141 221 6898) Offers Chanel, Armani and Moschino and the high-street stalwarts. Past bargains include a Hermes scarf for £45 and a Moschino dress for £85.

■ **Best-value shops** Cancer Research and Oxfam are at the more expensive end of the charity clothing market. Prices at other nationwide charity shops and those run by smaller local organisations tend to be cheaper. But this does not mean that you won't still find bargains at the larger shops.

■ **Re-fashioned chic** Traid (Textile and Recycling for Aid and International Development) shops in London and Brighton are also worth a visit. Traid is 'the hippest charity chain in the UK' according to GQ magazine, and its staff have a reputation for paying more attention to the selection and organisation of their secondhand and customised clothing than most other shops in the sector. Traid's re-fashioned and customised garments and accessories, such as shirts, sportswear and bags, are now fashion must-haves.

■ **Children's couture** Look out for real finds in children's clothing, including designer names. These are often little-worn and a fraction of the original price.

WATCH POINTS USED CLOTHES

When shopping for secondhand goods, don't get carried away by the bargains. Be realistic about the item's suitability and the repairs and improvements you can make.

■ **Stain removal** If the garment is stained, assess whether you or a good dry cleaner would be able to deal with it.

■ **Costly repairs?** Try to judge whether you would be able to repair any damage yourself or whether you could pay someone else to do it and still save. Problems that are easily tackled include moving buttons and shortening the length. More tricky problems that are better left to the experts are alterations around the shoulder area and where the material is difficult to work with, such as leather or velvet.

■ **Avoid a fashion faux pas** When considering a vintage item, make sure it is in keeping with your personal style. And to avoid spending on something you will be unable to wear, keep current trends, colours and shapes in mind.

 **RESOURCES**

CHARITY SHOPS NATIONWIDE

Check out charity shops in your area.

■ Cancer Research UK **www.cancerresearchuk.org** 020 7009 8820

■ British Heart Foundation **www.bhf.org.uk** 08450 70 80 70

■ Oxfam **www.oxfam.org** 01865 311 311

■ Sue Ryder **www.sueryder care.org** 020 7400 0440

■ Traid **www.traid.org.uk** 020 8733 2580

LONDON CHARITY SHOPS

■ **Cancer Research UK** (Hill Street, Richmond, 020 8940 4581) Great for modern, stylish clothes at moderate prices.

■ **Crusaid** (Churton Street SW1, 020 7233 8736) The first place to go for quality high-street names as well as designer labels.

■ **Fara** (Fulham Road SW6, 020 7371 0141) Find designer cast-offs and handmade shirts for under £10.

■ **Oxfam** (Goodge Street W1, 020 7636 7311) There are many designer labels among the selection upstairs.

■ **Salvation Army Charity Shop** (Upper Street N1, 020 7359 9865) One of the best charity shops in London.

■ **Traid** (61 Westbourne Grove W2, HO telephone in Wembley 020 8733 2580) Find good-quality secondhand goods and inspired customised clothes and accessories. Traid currently has seven branches in London and one in Brighton.

VINTAGE VALUE

Although vintage clothes shops tend not to be as cheap as charity shops, you can still find good secondhand bargains in them. Many are stocked from the charity shops so will already have creamed off the pick of the garments. If you're short of time, it can be worth starting at one of the better-quality shops to find real retro chic.

NETWORKING – EVERYONE WINS

It's always satisfying to get a new item for your wardrobe or accessory drawer for nothing, or next to nothing. Organise like-minded friends and acquaintances to meet regularly to sell your unwanted items. Set a few basic rules, such as all clothes, accessories and jewellery must be of good quality and in excellent condition. Then, get selling to each other at knockdown prices. Guide prices could be:

■ Under £10 for big items such as coats, weather-proof/activity gear and shoes.
■ Under £5 for trousers, skirts and handbags.
■ £2 for tops and sweaters.
■ £1 for small accessories such as costume and other non-gold/silver jewellery, scarves and belts.

SWAP SHOPS FOR FUN AND GREAT VALUE

Swap shops are even more fun than network parties, but you need to work out what constitutes a fair swap. The best way is to put items into different categories and swap like for like – not just similar items but ones that are of approximate value. For example, if you had an expensive piece of jewellery that you don't wear any more you could swap it for top-quality, well-cut trousers; or you could trade an upmarket jacket for a skirt and top.

RESOURCES

SECONDHAND SHOPS

■ **Oxfam Original**, (London, 020 7437 7338 ✉) Sells pre-sorted designer and the better high-street brands as well as clothes from film and TV production companies.

■ **Revisions** (Brighton, 01273 207728 ✉) Lots of bargain-priced designer wear, such as Gucci shirts for £50.

■ **Armstrongs**, (Edinburgh, 0131 220 5557 ✉) Large, long-established shop selling fashions from the Victorian era, through to the present.

■ **Stitch Up** (London, 020 7482 4404) This shop specialises in secondhand cashmere as well as beaded cardigans and bags and new items from small independent designers.

ESSENTIAL READING

Bargain Hunters' London by Andrew Kershman £6.99, ISBN 0952291428

LOOK AFTER SWEATERS

Don't spend money on little shavers for sweaters. Gently remove bobbles with a cheap disposable razor.

TIE RESCUE

If you get a water spot on a silk tie, let the spot dry and then rub the spotted area vigorously with a hidden part of the tie. Small spots can be removed with soda water.

THE RIGHT HANGERS

Hang silk clothing on plastic or padded hangers. Wooden ones may cause snagging. Don't ever use thin metal dry cleaner's hangers – for any of your clothes.

MAKING CLOTHES LAST LONGER

Whether you live in jeans and T-shirts, jumble-sale finds or tailored separates, there is no excuse for looking scruffy. Treat everything in your wardrobe as if it cost five times the price.

SUEDE SHOES

■ To get rid of scuff marks, gently rub with very fine sandpaper.
■ Steam clean suede shoes by holding them over a pan of boiling water. Once the nap is raised, stroke the suede with a soft brush in one direction. Let the shoes dry before wearing them.

SPONGING SUEDE

Restore the nap on a suede garment by rubbing a dry sponge over it after each wearing.

GET THE MOST FROM YOUR LINGERIE

Ideally, all fine lingerie should be hand washed. If you don't have the time for this, enclose it in a bag to prevent it from getting tangled in the washer, and use the delicates setting. Do not use a dryer as this will damage the garments – if possible, dry lingerie naturally, away from direct sunlight.

SWIMWEAR CARE

To give your swimwear a longer life, rinse in cold water after each use to remove salt or chlorine, which weakens the stretchy fabric. Then hand or machine wash on a gentle cycle. Do not twist or wring out or hang to dry in direct sunlight.

EASY ON THE STARCH

Most manufacturers recommend that you don't use starch on clothes as it damages the fibres. If you have your clothes cleaned, ask for a light starch only. And if you apply your own starch, use a dry iron and make sure you clean it after use as starch build-up can stain clothes.

STAIN REMOVAL

Treat new stains by dampening a soft cloth with soda water and sandwiching the stained area between two layers of the cloth. This lessens staining, but wash or dry clean the garment as soon as possible.

PRESSING MATTERS

Dry cleaning is actually bad for clothes, as well as for your bank balance. If clothes are creased, not dirty, have them pressed instead. This is much less likely to weaken fabrics and will help to prolong the life of good-quality garments. To do your own pressing at home, use a damp cloth and a hot iron and keep the iron moving constantly. Or, to remove creases from most fabrics, hang the garment in the bathroom for 5–10 minutes, just after you've had a hot shower. The heat and steam will make the creases drop out without subjecting the fabric to chemicals.

SPILT WINE

Red wine spills needn't mean waving goodbye to a garment. Act quickly and either saturate the stain with white wine, or pour on plenty of salt followed by soda water. This should wash out the worst of the mark. Blot, and launder immediately.

PERFECT FINISH

If a silk garment has lost its finish and looks crumpled, try a little steam heat. Hang it in a steamy bathroom or lay a damp cloth over it and gently pass the iron over it.

SHOP ABROAD FOR BIG SAVINGS

Both the Internet and budget airlines have made purchasing goods from abroad increasingly popular. Get best value for money by knowing which countries offer the real bargains.

WHERE TO FIND THE BARGAINS

Paris is renowned as the fashion Mecca, but try looking for bargains farther afield, such as in Hong Kong, or in lesser-known shopping areas, such as Florence.

Hong Kong Fashion prices can be less than half those in New York, and diamonds are half the British price. For cheap clothes, try Stanley Market – a half hour's bus ride away from town, to the south side of the island. More discounted clothing and footwear is for sale in central Hong Kong at The Lanes (Li Yuen Streets, East and West).

United States In New York hunt for bargains in the Garment District in lower Manhattan. Try Century 21 for discounted designer clothes from the big names such as Prada and Gucci. Filene's Basement and TJ Maxx are also worth a visit. If you are prepared to travel out of town, you can shop at Woodbury Common – a huge outlet mall full of bargains from top-name designers – about an hour from Manhattan. Other centres, such as Orlando in Florida, also offer great deals on clothing. Remember American sizes are more or less two sizes bigger than British ones so if you are women's size 12 you will normally take an American size 8.

Athens Leather goods are particularly good value in Athens. Visit the sales in Athens in August and February for the best bargains. Try Ermou Street, off Syntagma Square, Eolou Street and Agiou Marou for clothing bargains and Kolonáki for designer clothes and accessories.

LUXURY GOODS AT WORLDWIDE DESTINATIONS

HONG KONG	£66
DUBLIN	£199
DUBAI	£200
SYDNEY	£295
NEW YORK	£430
PRAGUE	£450
ATHENS	£475
PARIS	£750
MILAN	£800

COMPARATIVE PRICES
Leather jackets of the same quality vary by as much as 1200% in price depending on where you buy them. Figures from Expedia.co.uk survey Nov 2003.

Italy The country is especially good for shoes and other leather goods. Remember that shops close for siesta from 2pm until evening so time your shopping accordingly. If you're in Florence, try The Mall, which offers designer bargains at up to 60% off.

Paris Visit during the January or July sales for bargains at the big department stores such as Galerie La Fayette and the big-name designers such as Louis Vuitton.

CHRISTMAS SHOPPING ABROAD

A weekend shopping package in New York costs from around £370 a person (based on two sharing), including flights and a three-star hotel (room only). Combine this with an exceptionally strong exchange rate, and you could discover that a sight-seeing holiday with treats like eating out and entertainment alongside your bargain-hunting will still be cheaper than buying the same goods in Britain.

BEWARE OF IMPORT DUTIES

If you are importing goods from non-EU countries such as Hong Kong or America you may have to pay import duties (payable on any purchase over £145), VAT and a handling charge, adding around 20% to the purchase price. But there is no duty or VAT on books, no VAT on children's clothes and no duty on computers. For up-to-date information and advice, check the Import & Export section of the government's Customs and Excise website (see right).

HIDDEN COSTS OF INTERNET BARGAINS

Duties and VAT apply to goods bought over the Internet, as well as those you bring back yourself. When calculating the price of items ordered from abroad, remember to add in the cost of postage and packing which, for bulky or heavy items, can be quite considerable, plus the import duty which may be applicable from some countries. Always make sure that you are ordering from a reputable company with a secure website. If you are not sure, don't order.

WATCH POINTS VAT-FREE SHOPPING

Shopping for fashion items at the airport can be a good idea if you are short of time, but be aware that with a bit of hunting you can probably find a better bargain at home.

Do a price comparison Decide what you want before your trip abroad and get some idea of prices locally. Note that the airport VAT-free price is based on the full high-street price, so you may get a better price at home in the sales.

Reserve your goods At the airport you can use the Personal Shopper Service to find your goods. Go for value, like Prada sunglasses at 17.5% less than high-street prices.

Leave bargains behind If you are travelling in the EU don't take your goods with you on holiday – use the free Shopping Collection Service to leave your purchases at the airport, to be picked up on your return (see below).

Avoid taxes If you take your VAT-free bargains with you while travelling outside the EU, and then bring them back with you to the UK, you may end up having to pay tax on them. Collect them on your return and save the tax.

RESOURCES

SHOPPING ABROAD
■ Before importing goods, check the Customs and Excise website at **www.hmce.gov.uk** ✉.
■ You may also want to view advice from the DTI on buying goods in Europe and over the Internet at **www.consumer.gov.uk** ✉.
■ For information on airport duty-free shops in the UK, visit **www.baa.com/shopping** ✉.

VISITING TAILORS
■ Raja Fashions (see Bespoke Suits on page 41) on 00852 2366 7624. For full details, see their website **www.raja-fashions.com** ✉.
■ Ash Samtani Clothing Ltd on 00852 2367 4285 or visit the website at **www.samtani.com** ✉.

HEAD-TO-TOE BEAUTY

An effective daily skincare regime can be yours for literally pennies. Check out DIY alternatives to expensive creams and treatments or find a supplier who offers real value.

LOW-COST TREATMENT FOR BLEMISHES

Rather than paying for special shop-bought treatments, which range in price from £3 to over £20, use a variety of tried-and-tested remedies for blemishes that cost just a few pennies. These often use products that you will already have at home.

Witch hazel or calamine lotion Dab on the cleansed, affected area before bedtime. Both treatments work just as well as more costly products.

Honey treatment Dab a little honey onto a blemish and cover it with a plaster. Honey kills the bacteria and aids the healing process.

Lemon juice healer Blemishes heal quickly if you dab them with a little lemon juice.

Potato cleanser To clear blackheads, rub your face with a slice of raw potato after cleansing.

TOP TIPS BEAUTY ON A BUDGET

By using inexpensive but effective products and household ingredients, you can avoid paying inflated prices for more slickly packaged beauty remedies.

■ **Star buy** A top London model agent happily admits to using E45 cream from the local chemist as her night-time moisturiser. At £3.75 for a 125g tub, it's one-tenth the price of more upmarket creams, and it works just as well.

■ **Soft as silk** Baby oil – at £1.92 for 300ml – can be just as effective as expensive cosmetics at removing make-up and softening skin. Olive oil is another great moisturiser at £1.20 for 100ml. You can also use it to bathe chapped hands, brittle nails and torn cuticles.

■ **All-purpose moisturiser** Vaseline jelly is great for slicking eyebrows and dabbing on dry skin under the eyes. For a plumper pout, mix it with sugar and massage it

into your lips. Coat rough hands in Vaseline then put on gloves; doing this for a few nights makes a big difference. The handbag-size pot for around £1.25 is still one of the best beauty products on the market.

■ **Pennywise toner** Remove every last trace of cleanser with witch hazel. Keep a £1.99 200ml bottle in the fridge for a cheap, quick pick-me-up.

■ **Anti-ageing therapy** Instead of laser treatment and expensive creams, dab vinegar on age spots daily until they fade, or rub them with the inside of banana skins.

SWITCH SUPPLIER – SAVE OVER 60%

By buying your favourite beauty products from a cheaper shop you can make worthwhile savings without having to switch brands.

Lower prices High-street discount stores like Superdrug and supermarkets such as Asda and Tesco give good deals on fragrances with savings of up to 70% on department store prices as well as good deals on many other own-brand and name-brand beauty products. Shop after Christmas for particularly good buys.

Web bargains Suppliers such as **www.buycosmetics.com** can yield savings of over 60% on top brand skincare.

Holiday savings If you holiday or take occasional shopping trips to France, you can pick up skincare, perfume and cosmetics for 20%–40% less than in Britain (look out for French brands like Chanel and Clarins).

TOP TIPS SAVE £20 ON A PEDICURE

Instead of heading for the local beauty salon where it can cost over £30, try a home pedicure for under £10. Your feet, as well as your bank balance, will appreciate it.

■ Using a massage brush or roller, massage the soles of your feet from the toes to the heels and then the instep.

■ Give your feet a footbath, then rub off hard skin with a pumice and push back the cuticles with an orange stick.

■ Finally, refresh your feet with a tincture such as lavender, thyme or sage.

LOWER THE COST OF MEN'S GROOMING

Men's grooming is big business, but you don't need to make a production of it or go overboard on designer products to look and feel your best.

Choose with care As with women's beauty products, you can reduce your spending by buying a cheaper brand that still does the job and choosing a more economical supplier. A mid-range brand of aftershave balm from a high-street retailer is a mere £3.79 – a good buy compared with a similar designer-branded product costing £30 or more from department stores. Good-value mail-order companies who offer a men's range, such as Yves Rocher (**www.yves-rocher.co.uk** or 0870 608 7575), may also be worth trying for products you use every day.

Save on aftershave balm To save on a favourite designer balm, use a neutrally scented low-cost balm from the supermarket as a base and add a little of the expensive balm, which will fragrance the entire bottle.

RESOURCES

ESSENTIAL OILS
■ Neal's Yard Remedies
www.nealsyardremedies.com
0161 831 7875 ✉
■ Essentially Oils
www.essentiallyoils.com
01608 659544 ✉
■ Check out these useful websites for beauty information and tips:
www.makingcosmetics.com
www.ivillage.co.uk/beauty
for women
www.ebay.co.uk for beauty items and great deals on beauty brands
www.bargainnavigator.com
for budget beauty
www.catwalk-queen.net
for great beauty tips
www.tips.tipking.com for tips on beauty and hair

SITES OF SPECIAL INTEREST TO MEN
■ Keenly priced shaving and skincare products are available at
www.shave.com ✉.
■ Find special offers and grooming tips at www.come-shopping.co.uk ✉.
■ For grooming products and advice go to www.menessentials.com ✉.

FRUIT FACIAL
COST 40P PER FACIAL

1 tablespoon mashed strawberries
1 tablespoon of organic natural yoghurt

1 Mix the strawberries with the yogurt.
2 Apply the mixture to your face and neck, cover with a warm cloth and leave it for a few minutes.
3 Rinse with cold water.
4 This is not suitable if you are prone to allergies.

FIRMING MASK
COST 29P PER MASK

2 carrots
1 tablespoon of potato flour
1 egg yolk

1 Finely grate the carrots, add the potato flour and egg yolk and stir thoroughly.
2 Wash your face and neck and immediately apply the paste.
3 Leave for 20 minutes.
4 Wash off with warm water and rinse with cold.

PAMPERING FOR PENNIES

Use inexpensive storecupboard ingredients for natural, old-fashioned homemade beauty preparations that contain no harmful additives, smell delicious and are always fresh with every use.

MASK FOR OILY SKIN
COST 19P PER MASK

Juice of half an orange
8 tablespoons of flour

1 Squeeze the juice into a bowl and stir in enough flour to make a thick paste.
2 After cleansing, apply the mask with a soft brush and leave it on for 20 minutes.
3 Wash off with warm water.

IVY MASSAGE OIL
COST £3.85 FOR A 2-3 MONTH SUPPLY

1 handful of fresh ivy leaves
100ml of wheatgerm oil
1 drop of rosemary oil

1 Put the ivy leaves in a jar and add the wheatgerm oil.
2 Seal and leave for two weeks in a warm place.
3 Strain through a fine sieve, add the rosemary oil, then pour the massage oil into a bottle and seal.
4 Massage into areas of cellulite using circular movements.
5 See warning below.

EXFOLIATING BODY SCRUB
COST 18P PER TREATMENT

2 tablespoons of double or whipping cream
1 tablespoon of salt

1 Put the cream and salt in a bowl and beat to a smooth paste.
2 In the shower or bath, gently rub the paste over your body using circular movements.
3 Shower or sponge off the body scrub afterwards.

MOISTURISING MASK
COST £1.30 FOR 3-4 MASKS

1 tablespoon of lanolin
1 tablespoon of petroleum jelly
3 drops of chamomile oil
3 drops of geranium oil

1 Combine the lanolin and petroleum jelly in a bowl, add the oils and stir in until thick and creamy.
2 Transfer to a small pot with a lid and store in a cool place for future use.

DEEP CLEANSER
COST 20P PER APPLICATION

1 Stroke on milk of magnesia with cotton wool balls, avoiding the eye area.
2 Leave for 10 minutes.
3 Gently remove with warm flannel and apply a moisturiser.

DRY HAIR SHAMPOO
COST 49P PER TREATMENT

1 egg white
2 egg yolks
1 teaspoon of honey
1 tablespoon of olive oil
Juice of 1 lemon

1 Whisk the egg white and fold in the yolks.
2 Stir the honey, olive oil and lemon juice.
3 Massage the shampoo into the scalp and thoroughly coat the hair.
4 Leave for a few minutes and rinse the hair, using plenty of water until all the shampoo has gone.

WARNING
Do NOT use rosemary essential oil if you are pregnant, have high blood pressure or suffer from epilepsy. Always consult a qualified aromatherapist if in doubt.

PATCH TEST
Essential oils are highly concentrated and can irritate the skin, so always take care, especially with a new oil. Dilute one drop in one teaspoon of carrier oil and test on your skin. Except for lavender and tea tree oils, pure essential oils should not be used on the skin.

BE CREATIVE WITH MAKE-UP

Don't spend money unnecessarily on expensive make-up. Often, a cheaper substitute will do just as good a job, or you can invest in a good-quality multi-purpose product. Keep costs down by knowing how to make your make-up last.

BUY MULTI-PURPOSE AND SAVE

It is in the cosmetics manufacturers' interests to sell you a separate product for each make-up stage. But it makes economic sense to use cosmetics with a double or treble life.

An eye pencil pays its way A soft light-brown eye pencil costing around £14 can be used for outlining lips, defining brows, shaping round the eye socket and putting a soft line under the lower lid. If you buy a separate lip pencil, brow pencil, eye shadow and eye pencil, the total could be £50.

Cost-cutting colour A blusher can act as eye shadow and be used for cheeks and lips. Or you can pay around £11 for a quality lipgloss that can also be a blusher and brow highlighter (total cost for separate products is around £30).

Dual-use bases Buy a foundation or moisturiser that also acts as a sun block. A good-quality foundation with UV protection costs from £10–£30.

Budget compacts Look out for a combination foundation and powder compact for little more than the price of a powder alone.

GOOD-VALUE SUBSTITUTES

You can make further savings by buying some products from non-cosmetic counters.

Low-cost powder Baby powder at around £1 for 500g costs less than translucent powder; apply finely with a large make-up brush.

All-round sheen Vaseline is a multi-purpose bargain at around £1.40 for 100g. It conditions lips, adds a subtle glow to cheek bones and defines eyelashes.

RESOURCES

FRUGAL BEAUTY
■ To order leading brand beauty products online at a discount, try www.slapiton.tv www.eskaye.co.uk or www.saveonmakeup.co.uk (free UK delivery and no minimum spend).
■ For recipes and ingredients on making your own cosmetics, check out the website www.makingcosmetics.com

FACING THE FACTS ON MAKE-UP

For essentials such as foundation, blusher, mascara and lipstick, check out supermarket brands such as Tesco and Asda. The price difference between these and the name brands from the top cosmetics houses is significant.

BRAND	LIPSTICK	FOUNDATION	BLUSHER	MASCARA	TOTAL
Designer name	£14.50	£20.00	£20.00	£16.00	£70.50
Mid-range	£8.00	£12.50	£8.50	£9.00	£38.00
Low-cost	£3.99	£5.99	£2.99	£4.49	£17.46
Supermarket	£4.50	£5.60	£3.50	£4.30	£17.90

AVOID WASTING MAKE-UP

Don't waste money by throwing away expensive cosmetics before you've used them up. Use every ounce of the product to make your budget stretch.

Lipstick first aid If a lipstick breaks in half, salvage it by softening the ends over a flame, joining them together and leaving them to set in the fridge.

Use a brush A lip brush is invaluable for rescuing the last of a lipstick and for creating a clean, professional outline. They vary in price from £1-£4.

Revive old pencils Dried-up eye and lip pencils can be softened overnight by putting them point down in a jar containing an inch of baby oil.

Nail varnish When nail varnish is past its best, dip the wand end into a jar of very hot water for five minutes.

Rescue crumbly powder Cakes of powder blush or eye shadow that start to crumble can be ground into loose powder and decanted into small jars.

TOP TIPS LONGER-LASTING MAKE-UP

A little know-how helps you to save money and time by avoiding having to constantly reapply makeup.

■ **Everlasting eyeshadow** Before putting on eye shadow, apply a light coat of cream foundation, blending with your little finger. The powdery shadow will bind to the foundation and stay in place longer than if applied directly.

■ **Longer lived lipstick** Your lipstick will last longer if you pat face powder over your lips, apply the lipstick, blot and powder again and reapply a final layer of lipstick.

■ **Nail varnish tricks** Make your nail varnish last longer by keeping it in the fridge. Bring it back to room temperature before applying to nails.

 **RESOURCES**

HOME SHOPPING
Some companies specialise in a shop-at-home service. They all offer good-value hair and beauty products delivered to your door by a trained beauty consultant. Prices tend to be lower than those in the shops, and you can browse their range at your leisure.

■ **Avon** Contact them for a brochure on 0845 601 4040 or at **www.avon.uk.com** ✉.

■ **Body Shop** Call 08459 050607 for details or visit the website at **www.uk.thebodyshop.co.uk** ✉.

■ **Virgin Vie** To receive a catalogue, call 0845 300 80 22 or go to **www.virgincosmetics.com** ✉.

REDUCE THE COST OF HAIRDRESSING

Don't be persuaded to get a haircut from an indifferent hairdresser, however cheap. The key to good-looking hair is a good cut, but you don't have to pay inflated salon prices.

CUT THE COST OF SALON VISITS

To reduce the cost of good hairdressing, keep salon treatments to a minimum, watch out for recommended freelances or offer to be a model for a hairdressing salon or school.

Minimise costs If your only alternative is a visit to an expensive salon, get the cut and skip the blowdry.

Hire a freelance If you hear of a good freelance hairdresser, who will cut your hair at home for a fair price, book an appointment immediately.

Become a model Check out special deals at hairdressing schools or trainee nights at established salons that are looking for models. The cut costs nothing, while the colour and perm are around £15 each. These deals are often advertised in the local press. The ads will state the requirements for a cut – in most cases you must be over 18 – and appointments are restricted to certain times. Often the stated booking fee is around £5, but the ad doubles as a voucher so showing it means that the booking is actually free. It is best to phone well in advance, book and turn up early. Make sure that you allow plenty of time as a trainee will take a lot longer than an experienced hairdresser.

TOP TIPS BUYING SHAMPOO

A recent report by *Which?* untangled some myths about shampoos. It tested a range of shampoos from the cheapest to the most expensive.

■ **Buy the best-value product** All shampoos tested cleaned hair efficiently but the cheapest shampoos did a better job than the more expensive salon products. The survey concluded that much of what we pay for is packaging, advertising and sophisticated fragrances.

■ **Supermarkets for savings** It established that it is cheaper to buy shampoos in the high street than in the salon, but even then not all outlets are equal, with supermarkets giving the best value. In the *Which?* test, Asda and Tesco charged the least for shampoos (all brands) and Boots charged the most.

■ **Salon products** If you are after specialist products that aren't available in supermarkets, try **www.salonlines.co.uk** ✉ and take advantage of the reductions.

MODEL DEALS AT THE SALONS

SALON	SERVICES	COST
L'Oreal Technical Centre, Hammersmith Road, W6 020 8762 4292.	Basic cut Colour or perm Call for a consultation appointment.	Free £13
Trevor Sorbie, Floral Street, WC2 020 7395 2907	Cuts and colouring. Supervised students style your hair. Appointments are booked depending on the student's availability.	Free
City College Manchester (**www.ccm.ac.uk**) 0161 957 1500	Cuts Colour Two campuses with hair and beauty schools	£4 about £9
Toni and Guy academies Branches throughout the UK. See **www.toniandguy.co.uk** or phone 020 7921 9100	Cuts Colouring or highlights	from £5 £20
Vidal Sassoon Branches throughout the UK offer substantial reductions on trainee haircuts. See **www.vidalsassoon.co.uk** or phone 020 7318 5205	High-fashion, cutting-edge looks, only for models aged 15–35. Subject to availability and you must book in advance.	Contact your local branch
Rita Rusk International 498 Gt Western Rd, Glasgow See **www.ritarusk.co.uk** or phone 0141 357 3333	Cuts Tints Highlights	£10 £15-£18 £20

AVOID HIGH PRICES

Even if you are attached to your professional hair-care brand, try to avoid buying hair products in salons as you will normally pay the full price. Many brands that were formerly available only in salons are now on the shelves in the high street. Try supermarkets, chemists and online retailers for better prices. For 300ml of a well-known 'professional' shampoo, the price can vary from £8.95 in a salon to £7.01 from an online retailer (see page 64).

DYE IT YOURSELF – SAVE OVER 90%

If your hair is in reasonably good condition and you fancy a colour change, consider doing it yourself, or with the help of a friend at home. The difference in price is striking – you can pay over £60 in a salon for highlights to long hair, but products such as L'Oreal's Couleur Experte allow you to achieve a similar effect at home for under £10.

INVEST IN CLIPPERS

For men or boys who like short, cropped hair, invest in clippers at around £20. With a haircut costing over £10, the clippers will repay the investment in two cuts.

RESOURCES

DIY HAIR?
Visit a website that gives you step-by-step guides to creating different hairstyles at **www.ukhairdressers.com** ✉.

Healthy living

Investing in your long-term health need not be an expensive option. Instead, take a balanced approach to diet and exercise, and stay up-to-date with what conventional and alternative medicine have to offer. You'll reap the benefits.

HEALTHY LIFESTYLE ON A BUDGET

Diets, fitness regimes, health plans – the complexities and potential expense of a healthy lifestyle can seem daunting. But the essentials for health are simple: a good, balanced diet and regular exercise of a type you enjoy and will continue to pursue. Both are a lot less financially draining than following health fads or paying for expensive treatments.

EIGHT ECONOMY WAYS TO GOOD HEALTH

Before you embark on a new health and fitness regime, keep in mind a few important points:

Healthy food can be cheaper Look at your diet and decide on the changes you want to make. A diet beneficial to your health can also be good for your bank balance – fresh fruit, vegetables, pasta and pulses are all much cheaper than convenience foods, which tend to be high in unhealthy salt, fat, sugars and starches.

Buy fresh This is a rule worth learning to live by. The longer your food has been stored, the less nutritional value it has and the worse it tastes.

Healthy ingredients Consider natural alternatives to shop-bought remedies and add vegetables and pulses to meals to make them healthier.

Drink more The average adult needs to drink 2 litres (3½ pints) of liquid a day. This can be made up of water, soft drinks, tea and coffee, but doctors recommend a maximum of three or four cups of tea or coffee a day.

Use the freezer If you buy and cook your own fresh food, you don't have to give up the convenience of an instant meal altogether. Make soups and stews in batches and freeze for occasions when you don't have the time to cook a full meal.

Think before joining a gym Never join a gym without considering the alternatives. Gyms aren't for everyone and they are expensive – consider walking, swimming, gentle stretching or cycling instead.

Set realistic goals Be sensible and tailor your fitness regime to your lifestyle. Aim for five 30-minute exercise sessions a week – if necessary, some of these can take a form that will fit into your ordinary activities, for example vigorous housework or a brisk walk to the shops. And you don't need to do the whole 30 minutes at once – you can vary your routine on some days by doing three 10-minute sessions.

Don't be a fitness fashion victim Avoid the temptation to think health and fitness is a goal that has to come with a hefty price tag (you don't need a £90 pair of trainers to find out if jogging is for you). But if looking fashionable is an urge you can't resist, then check out companies like M and M Sports (**www.mandmsports.com** ✉), who offer a range of top-name clothing and goods at between a third and a half of high-street prices.

RESOURCES

GENERAL HEALTH
www.healthyliving.gov.uk
✉ is a website offering good advice on exercise, eating healthily and other tips including nutritious and cost-cutting recipes. It also offers charts and calculators to help you to assess your current level of fitness.

YOU ARE WHAT YOU EAT

A healthy diet helps to keep you well and reduces the risk of serious illnesses such as cancer and heart disease. The good news is that there are lots of ways of introducing beneficial foods into your diet without making big, unpalatable changes, and at minimal cost.

HEALTHY DIET, HEALTHY WALLET

Although choosing the healthier alternative can save you money, a few foods that offer the best nutritional value can be expensive, but you need only use them sparingly.

Go easy on meat Make meat go further by cooking it in casseroles or stir-fries bulked out with cheaper ingredients such as beans, pulses or seasonal vegetables.

Cheap, healthy ingredients Basing meals on starchy foods such as rice, pasta and bread is not only good for a balanced diet but offers excellent value for money.

FIVE A DAY FOR LESS

Doctors agree that we should all eat five portions of fruit and vegetables each day. Here are the best-value ways of ensuring those five portions are a part of your daily diet.

Canned and frozen count too Your daily intake can include fresh, frozen, chilled, dried and canned foods; the health properties of some (like tomatoes) are even better in a canned form, as well as often being cheaper. Save more by buying the supermarket's own brand – it's just as nutritious.

FISH AND MEAT vs VEGETARIAN ALTERNATIVES

Although you may not want to become fully vegetarian, consider dropping fish or meat from your diet for at least one day a week. A 2004 study for National Vegetarian Week revealed that vegetarians visit hospital 22% less often than their meat-eating friends. Reducing your meat intake can be healthier and mean big savings on your food bill.

PRODUCT	DESCRIPTION/USES	PRICE PER PERSON
BEEF	Fillet steak	£4.00
CHICKEN	Whole roasting chicken	£2.00
TOFU	Soya bean curd. Rich in protein, calcium and vitamins. Useful in stir-fries.	£2.00
FISH	Cod fillets	£1.50
QUORN	Mycoprotein (derived from mushrooms). Low in fat, readily absorbs flavour, so useful in casseroles.	£1.00
NUTS	As homemade or pre-prepared tinned nutloaf. Can be roasted, grilled or fried.	£0.50
BEANS	Dried, tinned or fresh. For use in stews and casseroles.	£0.15

BEST-VALUE SUPERFOODS

Certain 'superfoods' provide excellent health benefits as well as offering great value. Include them in your diet regularly for maximum protection against disease.

FOOD	BENEFITS	PRICE
Broccoli	Full of goodness whether fresh or frozen. A good source of vitamin C, folate, iron, potassium and cancer-fighting compounds, it is useful in stir-fries and as a basis for homemade soup.	£1.17 per kilo
Citrus and other tree fruit	Juice or eat whole for fibre and Vitamin C. The antioxidants in some citrus fruits (including pink grapefruits and blood oranges) contain lycopene, which can help to reduce the risk of breast and prostate cancers.	Oranges from 15p–30p each
Soya/tofu	May help to reduce the risk of breast and colon cancer. Although soya milk can be an acquired taste, it is easy to introduce tofu occasionally as a cheap alternative to red meat and chicken.	Tofu from £1.39 for 250g
Spinach	Rich in antioxidants that help to protect against cancer; folate, essential for a healthy nervous system and proper brain function; and lutein, which is good for eye health. Steam lightly or eat small leaves raw in salads.	85p per kilo (frozen)
Tomatoes	Like citrus fruit, tomatoes contain lycopene and antioxidants that protect the immune system. Lycopene occurs in higher quantities in canned rather than fresh tomatoes.	£1.00 per kilo

Just juice One – but only one – of your portions of fresh fruit can be taken in the form of juice.

KEEP THE GOODNESS IN
Don't squander your money by making the effort to buy fresh fruit and vegetables and then carelessly destroying their nutritional benefits.

Fresh is best Eat fresh fruit and veg as soon as possible rather than storing – or use frozen.

Minimal cooking Don't cook vegetables for too long as you will overcook them. Cover to keep in steam.

Don't dilute vitamins Boil vegetables in as little water as possible without boiling them dry, then use the water as a nutritious stock for making soup.

Clever storage Cover and chill cut fruit and veg and don't soak or vitamins and minerals can dissolve away.

GROW YOUR OWN
Even if you don't have a vegetable plot, you can make savings by growing fruit and vegetables in your garden.

Be selective Don't grow vegetables you can buy cheaply in the shops; go for those that are sold at a premium, take up little space, yet are simple to grow. French beans, mangetout, sugar snap peas and cut-and-come again (or 'loose leaf') salad, such as 'Salad Bowl', will net you the biggest savings, especially if you grow them from seed.

Pot-sized plot If you have a courtyard or very small garden, you can still grow some fruit and vegetables in pots. In a 23cm–25cm (9in–10in) pot you can grow one aubergine, pepper or tomato plant; four climbing French or runner bean plants; 32 carrots; or three strawberry plants.

Save on herbs Grow the herbs you use most frequently in a window box, pot or a garden bed by the kitchen door so you can harvest them as and when they are needed. Many have nutritional and therapeutic benefits (see pages 75–77).

GET YOUR ESSENTIAL FATS FOR LESS

The omega-3 essential fatty acids are beneficial fats that can reduce the risk of a heart attack or stroke. You can increase the amount in your diet at minimal extra cost.

Swap meat for fish Replace at least one meat meal a week with oily fish. You don't have to go for expensive fish such as tuna or salmon; mackerel, sardines or herring are just as good, and canned sardines have the bonus of being high in calcium too, as the bones are edible.

Vegetarian option Top up your omega-3 oils by scattering a handful of pumpkin seeds on a salad or eating a few walnuts. Or eat 1–2 tablespoons of ground flax seeds a day: buy the seeds and mill or grind them yourself rather than taking expensive flax oil or ground flax seed supplements.

WATER ON TAP

Aim to drink up to 2 litres of water a day to ensure good circulation and digestion and to prevent dehydration and the fatigue and mental fuzziness that usually accompany it.

Tap water is just as good According to the Drinking Water Inspectorate, there are no health benefits from drinking bottled water. By drinking tap water instead of bottled you could save 50p–70p per person a day.

TOP TIPS BEST BUYS

To make sure you don't end up paying more for your healthier diet, you may have to make a few modifications to the way you shop.

■ **Bargains at the wholefood cooperative** Although supermarkets often offer value for money, wholefood cooperatives (see Resources, left) can be cheaper for healthy alternatives. We found cashew nuts at half the price bought in 1kg packs from a wholefood cooperative compared to the price in the supermarket where the biggest pack is 250g. The same applies to many herbs and spices.

■ **Buy dried not canned** Pulses such as kidney beans, chickpeas and lentils work out about 50% cheaper if you buy them dried rather than canned. But you do need to remember to soak them before cooking.

■ **Buy fruit not fizz** A can of a fizzy drink may contain up to 8 teaspoons of sugar, which encourages weight gain and is bad for your teeth. For a healthy alternative that contains valuable vitamins, mix 500ml of unsweetened fruit juice (orange or apple), with 500ml of water, chill and serve. It will cost just a quarter of the price of a canned fizzy drink.

RESOURCES

HEALTHY EATING

■ Use the website **www.foodstandards.gov.uk** ✉ to check out official Food Standards Agency advice on food, its supply and preparation.

■ For a list of wholefood cooperatives, farm shops and organic outlets near you, contact Big Barn Ltd 01234 871005 **www.bigbarn.co.uk** ✉.

GO ORGANIC THE COST-CONSCIOUS WAY

The organic food industry has grown significantly in recent years, with sales of organic goods now topping £1 billion a year and four out of five families buying some organic produce. Although organic food is still generally more expensive, by buying selectively you can keep costs down.

CHECK OUT THE CHEAPEST SOURCES

The big supermarkets supply over 80% of the organic food we buy but their prices vary considerably. A *Which?* survey in 2004 found that the price of a basket of 13 organic foods, including chicken, beef, milk, vegetables and general groceries, varied by more than £12 between six major high-street supermarkets. To ensure you get the best prices, look on the different supermarket websites or phone to check current prices before shopping.

Specialist shops Although buying from producers in smaller quantities than the supermarkets, small independent organic shops are not necessarily more expensive. Keep checking them for value buys.

Buy direct from the supplier Some larger organic farms have their own shops or farm gate sales, or attend farmers' markets (see page 69). Others sell by mail order. To find organic producers in your area, or those who supply a particular product mail order, visit the Soil Association website **www.soilassociation.org** ✉ and select the Organic Directory link. Save by comparing producers' prices online before making an order: prices for organic rump steak, for example, can vary by £5 per kg or more.

SELECTIVE BUYING

Going completely organic could increase your food bill by 40%–50%. But you can make your budget go further by buying just those foods that are most commonly subjected to, or contain, high levels of pesticides. They are:

- apples
- bananas
- green beans
- milk
- peaches
- strawberries
- oats
- peppers
- rice

COMPARE BOX SCHEMES

Run by an organic farm or delivery company, a box scheme puts together boxes of seasonal organic vegetables or fruit, or a mixture of both, for a fixed price and delivers it to your door. Some schemes list what will be included each week on their website and allow you to indicate what you don't like. Often eggs and other products can be requested too.

Avoid paying extra Prices start from £6, but a box for a family of four is more typically £15–£20. Box schemes are listed in the Soil Association Organic Directory (see Resources, right). Look for a company that delivers free in your area to get better value for money. Some schemes charge £5 or £6 delivery unless you order boxes over a certain price, which may be more than you need.

RESOURCES

GOING ORGANIC

■ For information on organic food and farming, including producers, farm shops and box schemes, contact the Soil Association on 0117 314 5000 or 0131 666 2474 (Scotland) or visit **www.soilassociation.org** ✉.

■ **www.alotoforganics.co.uk** is an organic search engine with links to a wide range of organic sites.

■ *The Organic Directory 2004–2005*, published by the Soil Association with Green Books, price £6.95, is a guide to organic products and services, from shops and box schemes to restaurants and holiday accommodation in Britain.

FITNESS FOR ALL

ASK YOURSELF

BEFORE YOU JOIN A GYM

■ What do you want from your fitness routine? Is a gym the best way to obtain it?

■ How close is the gym to your home or work? It should be easy and cheap to get there.

■ Have you looked at the alternatives? Compare a local authority gym (about £40 a month) with private facilities.

■ How long are you committing to? Joining for a whole year could be an unwise financial decision.

■ Check what is included. Is this a place that guarantees to update your fitness programme every 12 weeks or is subsequent contact with an instructor unlikely?

Despite increasing awareness of the health benefits of keeping fit, industry statistics show that the average person who joins a gym attends for just 12 weeks before reducing, or stopping, their visits. Private gym membership can cost over £800 a year – with some fitness clubs insisting on annual membership – so think carefully before signing up.

TOP TIPS JOINING A GYM

Having decided that a fitness gym or health club is for you, consider a few points before joining.

■ **Check out the venues** See what is available, decide how much to spend, then try at least three suitable gyms, preferably within 10–15 minutes of work or home. Book a viewing appointment, avoiding 5pm–7pm on weekdays.

■ **Don't be hasty** Never sign up after just one visit. Make a second visit at a busy time and question other members about the facilities. Ask staff how many members there are and the square footage of the gym. The ideal ratio of space to members is between 10:1 and 15:1.

■ **Haggle for a bargain** Don't be afraid to negotiate. It is a fiercely competitive market, so when you've decided on the gym you want to join, talk to the membership manager to see if you can get a better deal.

■ **Avoid the rush** Avoid the post-Christmas and pre-summer rush to sign up. Plenty of people will have the same idea and you will not get the best deals.

■ **Pick a promotion and save** Look out for special promotions. During quiet periods, you are sure to find trial memberships for a set number of weeks at a reduced price.

■ **Membership options** Consider reduced-rate, off-peak packages. These give restricted admission (before 5pm, or

ANNUAL FITNESS COSTS – THE COMPARISONS

Even a modestly priced local authority gym could cost you around £400 a year. So what are the alternatives?

A regular swim is good all-round exercise, excellent value for money and can burn up 500–700 kcals/hour; a pair of trainers will get you on the road for a regular run, burning 600–1000 kcals/hour; or you could invest in walking shoes and explore the countryside (130–240 kcals/hour).

PRIVATE HEALTH CLUB	£850
YOGA CLASS (twice a week)	£450
LOCAL AUTHORITY FITNESS GYM	£400
SWIMMING (assuming two visits a week)	£290
RUNNING	£50
COUNTRY WALKING	£50
EXERCISE VIDEO/DVD	£20

8am–4pm excluding weekends, for example) but are ideal if you are at home during the day and could save you up to 60% on the cost of full membership.

■ **Get a group discount** Gather a group of friends or work colleagues and get a corporate membership – most health clubs offer them for groups of 10 or more and there are sizeable discounts to be had.

■ **Pay as you go** Many local authority gyms have a pay-by-session option. This will work out more expensive if you are a regular user, but if you know your number of visits per month varies – you may find it more difficult to go in school holidays, for example – then this could be your best choice.

■ **Get value for money** Ask what you have to pay for and what is complimentary. Reputable clubs should give you a free day pass to try out the facilities. Be wary of enticing 'only if you sign today' deals and annual membership tie-ins.

INEXPENSIVE FITNESS ALTERNATIVES

If you aren't a gym person but still want to keep fit, there are many low-cost alternatives.

Walking is free Get off the bus or train one stop earlier and walk. If you work in an office, use your lunch hour to take a turn round the block or visit the nearest park. If you enjoy the countryside, make walking your weekend hobby. A brisk walk uses around 240–300 kcals an hour and is better for your cardiovascular (heart and lung) health than a stroll.

Step up to fitness Use the stairs instead of the lift or escalator and you'll burn up to 1,000 kcals an hour.

Try a taster Look out for introductory or taster sessions to fitness classes. Don't commit to a 26-week yoga or Pilates class before trying it. See if there are any centres offering a free or reduced-price opportunity to have a go first.

Good team work Team up with a group of friends and hire a village or community hall. You can get somewhere for a couple of hours that will cost about £20 and – if there are enough of you – you could even find a freelance instructor or personal trainer to take the class. Splitting the cost 10 ways will make it an affordable option.

Free recuperation If you have had a long illness or are recuperating from surgery, talk to your GP. Many surgeries now have arrangements with fitness centres where they can prescribe a set number of free sessions.

On your bike Buy a bike and start cycling – it is one of the best cardiovascular exercises and burns around 400–600 kcals an hour. Look out for secondhand bicycles advertised in your local paper, or buy from a local cycle auction – sometimes organised by schools or the police – or an online auction (see Resources, above).

HOME WORK-OUTS

If it's difficult to get to the gym or an exercise class or you'd rather exercise in the privacy of your home, there are various options. The key to successful home exercising is to be realistic about what you are likely to enjoy and so will continue to do. Otherwise any outlay, however small, will be a waste of money.

Use a video Invest in an exercise video/DVD and devise your own programme. Before deciding what to buy, look on www.reviewcentre.com to compare users' ratings and reviews of different videos – a frank 'this was definitely not for beginners' could save you a £15 mistake. The site also tells you what to expect to pay. It's also worth checking www.amazon.co.uk ✉ for new and secondhand prices.

Simple props work Invest in a few inexpensive pieces of equipment. A skipping rope (£6–£10) will give you a great cardiovascular workout, or get a fitball (£9.50–£14.00 from www.physique.co.uk ✉) – a superb piece of equipment recommended by fitness professionals to develop muscles in the trunk. Dumbells are around £10, or you can improvise with two same-size cans of baked beans (or whatever else you have in your storecupboard).

TOP TIPS EXERCISE MACHINES

The two most popular exercise machines bought for home use are the exercise bike and cross (or elliptical) trainer. Although these require more space and outlay than the equipment above, you can get bargains if you know where to look, and they'll cost much less than annual gym fees.

■ **Discounts on line** Look at www.exercisezone.co.uk ✉, www.powerhouse-fitness.co.uk ✉ and www.totallyfitness.co.uk ✉ for returned or refurbished items, ex-demonstration models and manager's specials. You can save 50%–75% of the cost of a new bike or cross trainer. Visit www.argos-sports.co.uk ✉ for cheap deals and a 14-day money-back guarantee; call 0845 430 2080 for expert advice.

■ **Don't go for the cheapest** It's better to buy a discounted or secondhand machine (look in your local paper or on ebay.co.uk ✉) than a cheaper new one that isn't as solid or has fewer programmes. Not only will you get a better machine for the price, but you'll also be able to resell it – should you want to – without losing much money.

■ **Must-have features** If you are to keep using your machine it has to give you an interesting workout. Look for one with a variety of programmes that vary the resistance level. Also go for a machine with a heart monitor.

BEST-VALUE SPORTSWEAR

You don't need to have the latest in fitness clothing in order to exercise. An old T-shirt and shorts or tracksuit bottoms are perfectly adequate to start with.

Brand names for less If you do decide you need specilised clothing, buy at factory outlet shops or on discount days at department stores such as Debenhams. But you're likely to find the best discounts on the Internet; sites such as lxdirect.com ✉ and www.mandmsports.com ✉ allow you to search by brand and give discounts of as much as 70%.

HOMEMADE REMEDIES

The average medicine cabinet probably costs about £30 to stock every three or four months. So save money by remembering that many foods, herbs and spices can be used as inexpensive medicines for a variety of ailments.

ACHING FEET

Add 3 tablespoons plain mustard to a bowl of warm water and stir until dissolved. Soak your feet for at least 15 minutes or until the water has cooled completely.

COLDS

Drink echinacea tea, a natural antibiotic that also strengthens the immune system. Or make a hot drink with the juice of half a lemon and a teaspoon of honey in a glass of hot water. The lemon is rich in vitamin C and the honey has antiseptic properties. (Do not give honey to children under 2 years old.) Garlic fights infection so use it in your diet to build resistance to colds and flu. It also helps combat coronary heart disease by cutting the levels of fatty deposits in the blood.

BAD BREATH (HALITOSIS)

Chew fresh parsley or mint leaves, or make your own herbal mouthwash. Boil 2 cups of water in a small pan, remove from the heat and add fresh parsley, and 2 teaspoons each of whole cloves, ground cinnamon and peppermint extract. Leave the mixture to infuse for an hour then strain into a jar. Seal and keep in the fridge for up to two weeks, using after meals to freshen the breath.

ACNE

Nasturtiums are a natural antibiotic. Make a tea from a handful of chopped leaves and boiling water and drink three times a day. Use as a face wash when cooled.

HANGOVERS

Honey – taken with vitamin C, plenty of water and a little caffeine – helps the body eliminate alcohol and overcome the effects of drinking too much.

COUGHS

To make a cough syrup, combine 3 tablespoons lemon juice and 1 cup honey with ¼ cup warm water. Take 1 or 2 tablespoons every three hours. Do not give to children under 2 years.

PMT

To ease pre-menstrual tension, two weeks before your period increase your intake of fruit, vegetables and low-fat dairy items and reduce caffeine and alcohol; eat at least every three hours and exercise regularly.

HEADACHES

For a nervous headache, drink a weak infusion of rosemary or basil. Infuse 1 teaspoon fresh rosemary leaves in a pint of boiling water for 5–10 minutes, then add lemon and honey to taste. For basil, infuse 1 teaspoon fresh chopped leaves in a cup of hot water. Drink once or twice a day. For a tension headache, place a hot compress (a heating pad, hot water bottle or hot towel) on the neck to relax the muscles.

EAR WAX

Flush out ear wax with a 50/50 mixture of hydrogen peroxide and warm water. Repeat twice a day until the wax softens and washes out.

INDIGESTION

To counter the discomfort of indigestion, drink a cup of mint or fennel tea, which you can buy as herbal tea bags. To make your own fresh mint tea, put 2 teaspoons chopped fresh mint leaves in a cup of boiling water and leave for 5–10 minutes to infuse. Strain, then sip slowly after meals. Alternatively, put 1 teaspoon sodium bicarbonate in a glass of water, stir to dissolve, then drink. The alkaline solution neutralises the acid in your stomach.

HEARTBURN

Bananas have a natural antacid effect, so if you suffer from heartburn – caused by excessive acid refluxing into the oesophagus from the stomach – eat a banana.
If you are pregnant and suffer from heartburn at night, eat an apple before bed.

INSOMNIA

Drink a cup of chamomile tea in the evening, or a sweetened milk drink. The sugars in the drink help the brain cells to absorb more tryptophan (in the milk protein) from the bloodstream. The brain converts tryptophan to a soothing chemical called serotonin.

MIGRAINE

Eat a couple of fresh feverfew leaves in a sandwich each day to reduce – and in some cases even prevent – migraine attacks. Do not eat the leaves directly as they can cause mouth ulcers. CAUTION: Pregnant women should not eat feverfew.

INSECT BITES

Relieve the itching and pain of all bites and stings by applying ice to the area. Treat bee stings by flicking out the sting horizontally (to avoid squeezing in more venom from the sac), then apply a paste of bicarbonate of soda and water. Treat wasp sings with vinegar. CAUTION: Allergic reactions to insect bites can be severe. If in doubt, get medical assistance immediately.

ARTHRITIS

Fill self-sealing food bags with ice and hold them against the affected joints for 15–20 minutes. Repeat several times a day until the swelling goes and the pain is relieved.
Alternatively, rub in a little plain mustard.

MOTION SICKNESS

Peel some fresh root ginger and chew before and during travel. Or chew candied ginger. Ginger is more effective in preventing travel sickness than some over-the-counter remedies and does not cause drowsiness.

CONSTIPATION

For a natural laxative, soak five prunes in orange juice or water overnight. Eat the prunes and drink the soaking liquid before breakfast. Or combine 2 cups tomato or vegetable juice with 1 cup sauerkraut juice and 1–2 cups carrot juice. Drink 1 cup at a time, refrigerating the rest.

SORE THROAT

Ease a sore throat with one of these homemade gargles.
■ Dissolve 1 teaspoon table salt in a cup of warm water.
■ Infuse 1 teaspoon dried sage or 2 teaspoons chopped fresh sage in a cup of boiling water. Cool before use.
■ Combine 2 tablespoons plain mustard and 1 tablespoon each of lemon juice, salt and honey with 1½ cups boiling water. Allow to cool.

OSTEOPOROSIS

For an inexpensive supplement, take sodium-free antacid tablets – they are just as effective as traditional calcium supplements but less expensive.

SUNBURN

Wrap ice cubes in a towel and apply to the sunburn to reduce soreness and swelling. To make a cooling solution, put 4 tea bags, 2 cups fresh mint leaves and 4 cups water in a saucepan. Simmer for 5 minutes, strain and cool. Apply with a face cloth.

NASAL CONGESTION

Garlic and onions are natural alternatives to over-the-counter decongestants. Eat as many as you can, either raw in salads or in cooked dishes. Inhaling steam is also a good remedy. Pour boiling water into a bowl and cover your head and the bowl with a towel. For extra benefit, add 6 drops of eucalyptus oil. Drink elderflower tea, which eases catarrh and relieves sinus problems.

TOOTHACHE

Soak a sterile cotton ball or piece of gauze with oil of cloves and apply to the area. If the ache has just started, a hot drink may help; for on-going pain, suck an ice cube for relief.

SAVE ON SUPPLEMENTS

With a few exceptions, a healthy diet should remove the need for vitamin and mineral supplements. But if you need to take supplements on a regular basis, you can still do something to reduce the cost.

DO YOU NEED THEM?

The sale of vitamins and minerals represents a multi-million pound industry. Those most likely to benefit are:

Pregnant women If you are trying to conceive or are already pregnant, a supplement of 400 micrograms of folic acid is recommended up to the 12th week of pregnancy. Vitamin A supplements should not be taken (and foods high in vitamin A, such as liver, should be avoided) to prevent damage to the baby's development.

Children Young children aged between 6 months and 5 years may need vitamin A and D supplements if they don't like dietary sources such as liver, fish, leafy green vegetables or red or orange fruit and vegetables, or if they have minimal exposure to sunlight.

Menopausal women Women who are going through the menopause or are post-menopausal may need calcium and Vitamin D supplements to help prevent osteoporosis. To get good value for money, buy calcium citrate, which is more expensive but is absorbed well by the body, instead of calcium carbonate, which is cheaper but not easily absorbed and which can lead to kidney stones. Vitamin E is also useful.

Those on restricted diets If you are a vegetarian or are following a restricted diet for medical reasons, you may need supplements such as vitamin B12, vitamin D, calcium, iron and zinc.

DISCOUNTS IN THE HIGH STREET

Look for promotions run by leading high-street retailers such as Superdrug and Boots, or health food chains such as Holland & Barrett. Three-for-two deals are often the cheapest way of buying supplements, and you can make considerable savings by buying in bulk. Be careful to check the best-before-dates and calculate how many you'll use within this period of time.

Supermarket savers Most supermarkets now stock a wide range of own-brand and branded supplements and often run discounts or buy-one-get-one-free offers.

ONLINE BARGAINS

Check Internet sites such as **www.hollandandbarrett.com** 0870 606 6606 ✉, whose own-label products usually offer some savings; **www.zipvit.com** 0800 028 2875 ✉, which has permanently reduced prices and challenges the shopper to find cheaper vitamins elsewhere; and **www.biovea.co.uk** 0800 917 4831 ✉, which offers free postage and packing on orders over £29.

Price comparisons You can also use a site such as **www.bestshopsearch.co.uk** ✉ to find advice, comparisons and information on where to go for the best buys. Select the

ASK YOURSELF

DO I HAVE A DEFICIENCY?

■ Do you have muscle spasms, cramps or aches?
■ Are you suffering from fatigue, apathy, poor concentration or depression?
■ Are you anaemic?
■ Do you have bone pain or osteoporosis?
■ Is your skin dry or scaly, or does it heal slowly?
If the answer is yes to any of these, it could be that you have a vitamin or mineral deficiency. Consult your GP, who may recommend supplements.

NATURAL SUPPLEMENTS VS CONVENTIONAL TREATMENTS

There are a number of vitamins, minerals and natural remedies that are proven to help with certain conditions. They also tend to work out cheaper than the equivalent conventional pharmaceutical products that provide the same benefits.

SUPPLEMENT	GOOD FOR	COST	PHARMACEUTICAL PRODUCT
Acidophilus	Settling the stomach when travelling abroad or when taking a course of antibiotics	£13.44/60 caps 45p a day	£2.99/5 sachets £2.40 a day (*Resolve*)
Aloe vera	Healthier hair, skin and nails	£5.94/60 caps 10p a day	£8.50 for 30 tabs 28p a day (*Perfectil*)
Cod liver oil	Healthier joints	£18.50/500 caps 4p–11p a day	£14.99/30 tabs 50p a day (*Seven Seas Jointcare*)
Evening primrose oil	Pre-menstrual tension	£9.95/240 caps 4p–8p a day	£2.79/20 tabs £1.11 a day (*Feminax*)
Ginseng	Helping the body resist all types of stress	£16.50/300 caps 6p–11p a day	£5.95/75 tabs 48p a day (*Stressless*)
Lavender oil	Relieving stress and insomnia	£4.50/10ml (dose 2–3 drops a day)	£4.15/16 tabs 26p a day (*Nytol One-a-Night*)

Health & Beauty category on the Home page, then Vitamins to display the vitamin categories.

SAVE ON A YEAR'S SUPPLY

If you need a particular supplement, look into discounts for buying a year's supply at once. At **www.purelyhealthdirect. co.uk** 0800 089 8900 ✉, you will find special prices for a year's supply. For example, a year's supply of their own brand of cod liver oil with vitamins A and D costs £6.50, a 15% saving over a similar supplement from another competitive online supplier and almost 50% cheaper than the equivalent (full-price) product in a high-street chemist.

VITAMINS AND MINERALS ON TRIAL

If in doubt, and after consultation with your GP, buy a small amount of a supplement that might be helpful. Don't go for multi-buys or a yearly supply until you have monitored your response. Keeping a diary of your diet and physical and emotional well-being can be a useful indicator of their effectiveness.

 **RESOURCES**

TAKING SUPPLEMENTS

■ To check the safe upper limits for supplements, visit **www.food.gov.uk/science/ ouradvisors/vitandmin/12028** and download the report by the Expert Group.

■ For a good all-round reference, try *Reader's Digest Guide to Vitamins, Minerals and Supplements*, £14.95, ISBN 0276 429303.

ALTERNATIVE THERAPIES FOR LESS

RESOURCES

NATURAL HEALING

■ The British Complementary Medicine Association represents more than 20,000 practitioners in Britain. Phone 0845 345 5977 or visit **www.bcma.co.uk** 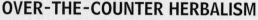 to find a practitioner in your area.

■ To find a medical herbalist, contact the National Institute of Medical Herbalists on 01392 426022 or visit **www.nimh.org.uk** 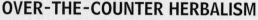.

■ For background on natural therapies, consult *Nature's Medicines*, Reader's Digest, £26.99, ISBN 0276 42793 or *Curing Everyday Ailments the Natural Way*, Reader's Digest, £26.99, ISBN 0276 42719.

Complementary and alternative treatments are now widely used and in some cases are available on the NHS. But there are also ways of enjoying the benefits of those that are not without breaking the bank.

ACUPUNCTURE FOR FREE

Long regarded as a mystical Chinese practice, acupuncture won the approval of the British Medical Association in 2000 and is now the fastest-growing complementary therapy used within the NHS. So before looking for a private acupuncturist, who typically costs £30–£40 a session, visit your GP: more than 2,000 GPs and hospital doctors are trained in acupuncture techniques and many physiotherapy departments in NHS hospitals now offer acupuncture.

ALEXANDER TECHNIQUE

If you have breathing disorders, joint or muscular problems associated with poor posture, difficulties with movement or coordination, you may have considered the Alexander Technique. A one-to-one session can cost £20–£30 an hour (with a series of sessions being needed), but you can sign up for group workshops and classes for much less. A single day class can cost just £14, and a series of four morning classes £25, for example. Go to the Society of Teachers of the Alexander Technique website **www.stat.org.uk** 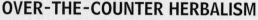 or phone 0845 230 7828 for details.

AROMATHERAPY OILS FOR 40% LESS

While you may not want the outlay of going to an aromatherapist, you can benefit from using aromatherapy oils at home (but take advice if pregnant, as some oils can be harmful in pregnancy). Many essential oils are thought to enhance mood – lavender and neroli aid relaxation, while bergamot and grapefruit are energising, for example. Others can help certain conditions. Though these oils can be expensive, the Internet provides some bargains – **www.essentialoilsdirect.co.uk** sells 10ml of lavender oil for £2.60, compared to the £4.50 you'd pay in a high-street chemist. Compare prices including 'p&p' carefully.

OVER-THE-COUNTER HERBALISM

A consultation with a medical herbalist costs £20–£50 a session and may help certain chronic complaints (see Resources, left). But for minor imbalances you can save by treating yourself – you'll find remedies in chemists, health food shops and on the Internet. Find a range of remedies, herbs and tinctures at **www.thinknatural.com** 0845 601 1948 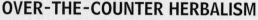 or go to **www.nealsyard remedies.com**

020 7627 1949 ✉.

HOMEOPATHY

The Society of Homeopaths has a list of qualified practitioners who are registered with them on **www.homeopathy-soh.com** 0845 450661 ✉. A consultation costs £40–£80, although there are often reductions for families and jobseekers. But check out these cheaper options:

Homeopathy on the NHS Some GPs take a course in homeopathy and practise as GP homeopaths (with the initials MFHom). Check with your local NHS Trust to see whether there is a GP homeopath in your area.

Homeopathic hospitals There are National Health Service homeopathic hospitals in Bristol, Glasgow, Liverpool, London and Tunbridge Wells. A GP homeopath can refer you to a consultant in these hospitals.

Homeopathy at home Many symptoms can be treated at home. Homeopathic remedies are widely available in high-street chemists and health food shops. Weleda have a guide to remedies on their website **www.weleda.co.uk** or you can obtain a free *Home Guide to Natural Medicine* by phoning Weleda on 0115 944 8200 ✉.

MASSAGE ON A BUDGET

There is nothing quite as relaxing as a massage, but the average session costs around £30 an hour. However, those in the know can pay a lot less.

Free treatment Massage – like many other complementary therapies – has seen a surge in popularity, with professional training courses, schools and courses at local adult education establishments cropping up all over the place. They often need 'subjects' on which students can practise, so find one locally and offer your services.

Make money from massage Consider training yourself – you will learn a skill to practise on family and friends and could even make a profit from it.

MEDITATION

We all know that when we are stressed we are more likely to succumb to illness, and recent research suggests that meditation can boost the immune system and reduce blood pressure, heart and breathing rates and muscle tension.

Joining a class Check in your local library, health food shop or adult education centre for meditation classes, which are inexpensive. Or join a yoga class, which incorporates an element of meditation at the end of the session.

Going it alone Meditate at home and it will cost you nothing except time. Set aside 20 minutes a day when you won't be disturbed and can sit comfortably and quietly. Concentrate on your breathing, or a certain word or phrase, or focus on the flame of a candle placed in front of you.

REFLEXOLOGY

An hour's session with a reflexologist costs £25–£35, but someone who is still training may be happy to practise for free. Approach an Association of Reflexologists' (AoR) accredited college (listed on the AoR website

RESOURCES

AROMATHERAPY AND MASSAGE

■ Contact the International Federation of Professional Aromatherapists for a list of schools and practitioners on 01455 637 987 **www.ifparoma.org** ✉.

■ To buy good-value aromatherapy oils, try websites that sell direct to the public such as **www.youraromatherapy. co.uk** ✉ and **www.essentialoilsdirect.co. uk** ✉.

■ For information on training in massage, **www.massagetherapy.co.uk** ✉ lists professional associations and governing organisations.

A BETTER DEAL ON MEDICINES

Whether you go to the doctor and come away with a prescription or treat yourself with an over-the-counter preparation, there are savings to be made.

GET THE BEST FROM YOUR PRESCRIPTION

Although no expense should be spared when it comes to your health, you can avoid spending money unnecessarily. Just because you have a prescription, this doesn't mean you will get the cheapest remedy.

Consult the expert Prescription medicines can be more expensive, so the first thing you should do is to seek advice from the pharmacist – sometimes it is cheaper to purchase the same drug over the counter rather than paying the prescription charge.

Prepay and save If you have a long-term illness or condition, consider buying a prepayment certificate. These act like a season ticket and cost £91.80 a year (2004 price) or £33.40 for four months. They are worth having if you need more than 14 items a year or five items in a four-month period. To buy a prepayment certificate, get form FP95 from post offices, pharmacists, Benefits Agency offices and Primary Care Agencies. Or download it from **www.dh.gov.uk/assetRoot/04/05/02/72/04050272.pdf** or call 0845 850 0030 to order one with a credit card.

Prescriptions may be cheaper If you have to purchase medication over a period, it can be cheaper to get a single prescription from the doctor that covers the whole time, instead of buying a pack of the medication each week. For example, hayfever tablets for two months cost £6.40 as a single prescription from the doctor, whereas even unbranded antihistamines can cost around £10 from the chemist for sufficient tablets for the same period.

GET FREE PROFESSIONAL ADVICE

NHS Direct is a free, 24-hour-a-day health advice service so, if you are concerned about an ailment that doesn't need immediate attention, make it your first port of call out of surgery hours and at weekends or on public holidays. Trained medical practitioners can be reached on 0845 4647, or use the website at **www.nhsdirect.nhs.uk** to search for information and advice on treatment.

SAVE BY BUYING GENERIC DRUGS

We are all familiar with the brand names of popular drugs, such as Panadol, Nurofen, Imodium and Clarityn. When a drug is developed, the manufacturer takes out a patent for exclusive rights to produce and sell it for a set period of time, normally 20 years. This is designed to help companies recoup their research and development costs. When that period elapses, other companies can produce their own versions. These are usually sold under the name of the active ingredient and are known as generic drugs. Sold in bulk by

---

keep it simple

SIMPLE SOLUTIONS FOR COLDS AND FLU

When you are suffering from a cold or flu avoid overspending on medication in an effort to get well.

■ Simple paracetamol will relieve fever and pain and costs around 15% of the price of flavoured sachets marketed for treating colds and flu.

■ Avoid spending on multiple products. To avoid an overdose, never combine paracetamol with other combination flu or cold remedies that contain paracetamol.

■ Drink plenty of water or fruit juice to prevent dehydration.

■ Use steam inhalation with menthol or eucalyptus added to clear the nose.

 **RESOURCES**

HEALTHCARE ✉
Find information on health issues on the following websites: **www.dh.gov.uk** gives information on prepayment certificates; **www.nhsdirect.nhs.uk** and **www.netdoctor.co.uk** give free health and medical advice.

major chemists and supermarkets, generic drugs can bring big savings for the canny consumer.

BUY MEDICINES FOR UP TO 80% LESS

You can save a considerable amount of money by buying generic medicines, which are just as effective as their branded equivalent. For example, hay fever sufferers could save £4 a week over the course of the pollen season. Branded medicines such as Zirtek, Benadryl, Clarityn and Piriteze all cost between £3.99 and £4.99 for a supply of seven tablets (a week's worth). Generic equivalents available in chemists, supermarkets and some discount stores cost from as little as 99p for the same length of treatment.

Name dropping To be able to ask for and recognise generic equivalents of common branded medicines, it helps to familiarise yourself with their names. See right for the names of generic drugs sold for common complaints and the chart below for potential cost savings.

TOP TIPS **FINDING THE RIGHT DRUGS**

To make sure you buy the products you want, you may need to ask for help and check the labelling.

■ **Ask a pharmacist** You will often find generic drugs readily displayed in supermarkets, but they will probably not be on display in the chemist's. You may need to tell the pharmacist specifically that you want the generic (or cheapest) version.

■ **Compare ingredients** If you're unsure of what you are considering buying, check that the name and amount of the active ingredients are the same in both the generic and the branded packet.

■ **Ignore the packaging** Don't let the often understated packaging of generic drugs put you off buying them. Supermarkets and major chemists aim to produce them as cheaply as possible, and this doesn't affect the effectiveness of the drug. All drugs are tested by the Medicines and Healthcare products Regulatory Agency and have a PL (licence) number on the box.

GET TO KNOW GENERIC NAMES

These are the non-brand names for medicines that you can buy over the counter to ease everyday ailments.

Allergies Loratadine, chlorphenamine, ranitidine (antihistamines)
Antiseptic Potassium permanganate solution, sodium chloride (salt)
Colds Benzocaine (spray, for sore throats), pseudoephedrine, xylometazoline (for nasal congestion), codeine linctus (for coughs)
Heartburn Aluminium hydroxide (antacid)
Muscular pain Ketoprofen (gel)
Oral hygiene, ulcers Chlorhexidine

A BITTER PILL TO SWALLOW?				
CONDITION	**GENERIC**		**BRANDED**	
HEADACHE	16 x paracetamol	£0.23	16 x Panadol	£1.85
MUSCLE PAIN	24 x ibuprofen	£1.25	24 x Nurofen	£3.29
HAY FEVER	30 x cetirizine	£4.99	30 x Zirtek	£14.95
DIARRHOEA	12 x loperamide	£2.20	12 x Imodium	£5.35
THRUSH	1 x fluconazole	£9.00	1 x Diflucan	£12.50
TOTAL	**£17.67**		**£37.94**	

LOWER-COST DENTAL CARE

If you are lucky enough to be one of the 44% of adults who are registered with an NHS dentist, then you hold the key to low-cost care. A shortage of dentists – especially those accepting new NHS patients – means that many of us will have to fund private treatment.

FINDING AN NHS DENTIST

Although it can be tricky to find an NHS dentist, for routine treatments it is worth it for the savings you will make (see chart, right).

Contact NHS Direct Ring NHS Direct on 0845 4647 or search their website **www.nhs.uk/england/dentists** for details of local practices offering NHS dental care.

Waiting lists Try phoning around local dentists, and if any practice is keeping a waiting list put your name down.

Dental Access Centres In some areas, people who aren't registered with an NHS dentist can get treatment at a Dental Access Centre. Contact your local NHS Trust for details.

Try your PCT Alternatively, contact your local Primary Care Trust (PCT) in England, local health authority in Wales, health board in Scotland or health and social services board in Northern Ireland. You should find them in the telephone directory under 'Health authorities and services'.

Keep your dentist If you are registered with an NHS dentist, be loyal and go regularly. Many will take you off their list if you do not attend for a stated length of time (typically 12–18 months).

COSMETIC DENTISTRY FOR LESS

Most practitioners offer a discount for early payment. None are shy about advertising their prices – a search on the Internet will reveal scores of practitioners – so compare costs carefully. If you want your teeth to be whitened, ask whether a home whitening service is available. This costs about half as much as the price of surgery-based procedures, although it is not quite as effective. Always check the dentist is experienced in cosmetic dentistry. Has he or she taken advanced courses in current techniques? Can you see before and after pictures and testimonial letters of clients who have had similar treatment? Does the dentist have imaging or presentation devices to help demonstrate how the procedure is done and what results might be expected?

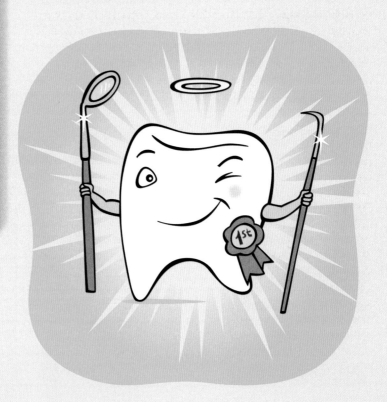

DENTAL CHARGES FOR COMMON TREATMENTS

Private treatment charges can vary widely, so it is worth obtaining several quotes, particularly for more complicated procedures such as crowns and implants.

TREATMENT	NHS	PRIVATE
BASIC EXAMINATION	£5.48	£25–£45
SCALE AND POLISH	£8.64	£25–£30
SMALL FILLING	£5.84	£28–£50
SMALL X-RAY	£2.72	£8–£10
ROOT FILLING	£58.72	£145–£300
CROWN (GOLD)	£75.64	£250–£450
IMPLANT	NA (not available)	£1,500–£3,000

Figures from British Dental Health Foundation, 8 September, 2003.

FREE NHS DENTISTRY

If you are eligible for free treatment, use your entitlement. If not, check the price of treatment before proceeding.

When is treatment free? Children, students, the elderly, pregnant and new mothers, and people on low incomes have a statutory right to free NHS dental care.

What do you pay? Everyone else must pay 80% of the cost of fillings, dentures and extractions, up to a maximum of £372 for a course of treatment (2004 figure).

BEST-VALUE PRIVATE DENTAL TREATMENT

If you have to go private, there are two schemes commonly used to help fund treatment.

Capitation and maintenance schemes These schemes involve the payment of a set monthly amount that is determined after your current level of dental health has been assessed. The scheme should then cover the costs of basic treatment. Be careful going this route as the service is often tied to your dentist, who will in turn be tied to one of the main schemes available. This may present a problem if you move to another part of the country: you may need to be assessed again by your new dentist and start a scheme anew.

Full cover plans The other option is full cover (or cash and full medical plans) which, for a monthly premium, cover you for a stipulated amount of treatment during the course of a year, and some will also offer cover for work following an accident. Make sure you check the level of cover as well as terms, conditions and any exclusions. Under these schemes, dental cover is sometimes an add-on to full private medical insurance.

 **RESOURCES**

PROVIDERS OF DENTAL PLANS

For capitation and maintenance schemes:
www.denplan.co.uk
0800 401402 ✉
www.practiceplan.co.uk
01681 677954 ✉
For full cover plans:
www.clinicare.co.uk
01462 688111 ✉
www.hsa.co.uk
08702 425454 ✉
www.bupa.co.uk
0800 001010 ✉.

ECONOMY EYE CARE

The market for spectacles and contact lenses is a fiercely competitive one, with local opticians, high-street stores, mail-order companies and Internet suppliers all vying for custom. Use this to your advantage to find the best deal.

GETTING AN EYE TEST

Having your eyes tested every two years will identify eye diseases before they affect your sight and can pick up health problems such as high blood pressure, diabetes and brain tumours. Optometrists charge between £17 and £30 for an eye test, so shop around.

Free checks Check whether you are entitled to free NHS eye tests (see box, left). If so, ask your optometrist for a NHS Sight Test form before you have the eye test.

Company perk If you work on a VDU your employer is legally required to provide an eye test and to contribute towards the cost of spectacles needed for VDU use.

Scot free If you live in Scotland, you will benefit from new legislation in the 2004–2005 legislative programme that grants free eye tests for everyone.

LOW-COST GLASSES AND CONTACT LENSES

If you need glasses or contact lenses you are not obliged to buy them from the optician where you had your eye test. Take your prescription and buy more cheaply elsewhere.

Savings on the Internet Online suppliers sell products at substantially lower prices than most high-street shops. You can find reading glasses for as little as £2 on the Internet instead of £35 plus (depending on frames) on the high street.

Major discounts Some larger high-street stores will match Internet prices, so phone to check before ordering online. Many also give interest-free loans and free discount cards, such as the 20/20 card, which gives 25% off designer frames, 20% off spectacle lenses and 10% off contact lenses.

Free trials Look out for promotions run by major contact lens manufacturers offering free contact lenses as a means of introducing potential customers to new products such as daily disposables, coloured contact lenses or bifocals.

French bargains Combine a day trip or holiday with a visit to a French optician and save up to 20% on glasses and 50% on disposable contact lenses. Check prices at home before you travel to ensure you get a bargain.

WATCH POINTS BUYING ON THE INTERNET

Make sure your Internet savings don't cost you dear.

■ **Compare like with like** Manufacturers make a range of different quality products at different prices. Check your Internet bargain isn't a cheaper alternative before buying.

■ **Check overall costs** Just because lenses are cheap doesn't mean you'll get the best overall deal. Compare the price of cleansing materials and postage and packing.

■ **Follow-ups** Internet purchases don't include the normal follow-up service you get from an optician, such as adjustments to frames or a contact lens check.

GET THE BEST-VALUE MEDICAL HELP

If you have an acute or life-threatening illness, you can usually depend on prompt treatment from the National Health Service. But many debilitating conditions have long waiting lists. So how do you get the treatment you need when you need it without paying to go private?

TOP TIPS GETTING THE BEST FROM THE NHS

If you don't have private health insurance and you want to avoid paying to beat the queues, you need to know the system so you can get the best from it.

■ **Check the waiting list** The government has targets for the maximum time a patient should have to wait for treatment under the NHS. Find out what the target is for your condition and how long you are likely to wait for local treatment.

■ **Ask for another referral** If the waiting time is longer than the government target, ask your doctor to refer you to a different hospital or area with a shorter waiting list. He may need to check that the local health authority will fund the treatment at another hospital.

■ **Contact the hospital of your choice** The Patients' Association Helpline (see Resources, right) may be able to help you identify a good hospital; your GP should be able to help or point you in the right direction, and it is also worth talking to your local Primary Care Trust (PCT) as well as their counterparts in surrounding boroughs or counties.

■ **European partnership** In some cases your local PCT may have identified a need for certain types of elective surgery that can't be met by its own hospitals and set up an agreement with a European provider. Check with your NHS Trust to see whether any such schemes are active.

■ **NHS private treatment** If you have a scheduled operation that is cancelled and the hospital is unable to offer you another date within a specified time, you may be able to be treated in a private hospital paid for by the NHS.

NHS TREATMENT ABROAD

If all else fails, you could take advantage of a European Court ruling that patients are entitled to seek treatment in other member states of the European Union if there is an excessive waiting list for NHS treatment. But this does not mean you can go abroad, have your operation and then send the bill to the NHS.

Conditions apply Treatment abroad is only possible when a local health authority has money in its budget but does not have the capacity in its hospitals. You are far more likely to be referred to a private hospital than get sent abroad.

Getting authorisation You'll need the support of your consultant and an E112 certificate authorising payment to the overseas hospital by your local health authority. This is provided by your local PCT, which has to get Department of Health approval. The process can take 6 weeks.

RESOURCES

LEGAL HELP
The Patients' Association represents the interests of NHS and private patients and looks after their legal entitlements. For advice, contact their helpline on 0845 608 4455 or visit **www.patients-association.com** ✉.

CASE STUDY

FRENCH LEAVE
Jack Simms, 73, had been waiting for a hip replacement for nearly a year.

'My daughter wanted me to go private, but without health insurance it was going to cost over £7,000 and there's no way I could afford that. Then when I moved to live near her we found that her local NHS Trust had an arrangement with a hospital in Lille and I got priority treatment. I was in hospital for two weeks to make sure everything was OK before I came home, and travelled back through the Channel Tunnel by ambulance. All my expenses were paid by the NHS Trust. But Jenny had to pay for her trip when she came to visit me.'

PRIVATE TREATMENT ABROAD – SAVE OVER 50%

If you are considering paying for private treatment, it pays to look abroad. Many European hospitals charge considerably less than private facilities in the UK. The chart below shows the comparative costs of four common elective operations. Prices include accommodation, food, surgery and post-operative care in hospital, but not travel costs.

OPERATION	UK COST (PRIVATE)	COST IN FRANCE	COST IN GERMANY
CATARACT	£2,000	£1,000	£890
HIP REPLACEMENT	£7,600	£4,000	£4,950
KNEE REPLACEMENT	£8,500	£3,000	£6,300
PROSTATECTOMY	£3,600	£2,700	£2,200

Know your rights Although the NHS is under a legal obligation to pay for treatment in European Union hospitals, it doesn't do so gladly. The main criterion in the decision to issue an E112 certificate is whether there has been any 'undue delay' in the provision of treatment. This may be taken to mean anything from four months to a year, depending on how painful or debilitating the condition is.
Locating a hospital You'll need to identify the overseas hospital and the consultant who will oversee the surgery. This is best done by your NHS consultant, although an application to any European Union teaching or university hospital should give successful results.

TOP TIPS PRIVATE MEDICAL INSURANCE

Private Medical Insurance (PMI) usually means you get medical treatment when you need it, but policies can cost as much as £3,000 a year. There are ways to make savings on PMI premiums – these will limit your choices and the type of service you receive but they might be worth it to secure a level of cover that suits both your needs and your wallet.
■ **Decide how much to pay** Decide in advance what you can afford. With PMI, you get what you pay for so it is important to make the right decisions at the outset.
■ **Flexible patients save** Insurers will usually give you a choice of three bands (typically A, B and C) ranging from a bed in the most expensive private hospitals through to medium-priced private hospitals and most provincial teaching hospitals. If you're flexible, you will be able to make good savings on the premiums.
■ **Large excess, lower premiums** Selecting a larger voluntary excess is another way of keeping the costs down, and you will be given the choice of paying the first part of any claim (anything from £100 to £1,500 or £2,000). There are different types of excess clauses – some are annual and others span the life of the policy, so check carefully.
■ **Budget policies** 'Budget'-type polices specify a limit to the number of days in hospital or the range and extent of treatments for which you are covered.

RESOURCES

ARRANGING PRIVATE TREATMENT
To find out more about private treatment options in Britain and abroad, look at **www.privatehealth.co.uk** ✉. Some independent companies have set up their own partnerships with hospitals in Europe and farther afield to provide a service for people looking for treatment abroad. Medical Treatment Choices Ltd 0191 251 9593 or at **www.treatmentchoices. co.uk** ✉ is one such company.

■ **Direct debit for 5% savings** Pay by direct debit. Most insurers will reduce your annual bill, typically by 5%.

■ **Join a group scheme** Group cover is cheaper. Some employers run schemes for staff and their immediate family, while certain professional institutions, trade unions and other bodies will also offer group schemes or pass on a discount to their members. This is a benefit worth having.

■ **Check the exclusions** Check that you understand the list of exclusions, which can be lengthy. You are unlikely to be covered for pre-existing conditions.

■ **Don't pay for travel** Make sure the policy you choose enables you to be treated at hospitals within easy reach of your home.

■ **Join online** Insurers have got wise to the operational savings they can make by encouraging customers to register and then manage their cover on line. Savings can be significant. One such provider is **www.xshealth.co.uk** ✉.

■ **Seek professional advice** As always, if you are thinking of committing to a big montly outlay it is worth talking to an independent financial adviser before you make a decision.

LOW-COST HOSPITAL CASH PLANS

Hospital cash plans are a less expensive alternative to PMI, designed to help with medical expenses rather than paying them in full. Cash payouts are small (they may pay £10–£90 for each day you are in hospital) but are useful if you are on a tight budget. Cash plans can also help towards optical and dentistry expenses, or visits to the chiropodist.

RESOURCES

HEALTH INSURANCE
For details of private medical insurance plans and cash plans, contact:
Western Provident Association on 01823 625230 or **www.wpa.org.uk** ✉
HSA on 08702 425454 or **www.hsa.co.uk** ✉.
For information on hospital cash plans, contact:
PHA on 0870 7700 942 or **www.cashplan.net** ✉
HealthSure on 0800 854 721 or **www.healthsure.co.uk** ✉.

COMPARING PRIVATE MEDICAL INSURANCE

Monthly premiums vary considerably, depending on the excess and the treatments excluded. The last two schemes are for hospital cash plans, shown for comparison, but these are very different policies and do not offer the same level of cover as PMI.

PROVIDER	EXCLUSIONS	BENEFITS	COST/MONTH
	Psychiatric care, specialist treatments, diagnostic tests	Nursing at home, private ambulance, NHS cash, minor surgery	**£18.49** (£500 excess)
	Minor surgery	Nursing at home, private ambulance, NHS cash	**£46.89** (£500 excess)
	Physiotherapy	Nursing at home, private ambulance, NHS cash	**£51.70** (£500 excess)
	Pays a yearly max of £42 dental care, £38 optical care, 80% of yearly max of £135 physio, £100 homeopathy, £90 hospital consultations, plus other benefits.		**£6.00** (no excess but maximum per year benefits)
	Pays 70% of yearly max of £100 dental care, 50% of yearly max of £100 optical care, outpatient surgery to £192, in-patient care to £2,912 and other benefits.		**£9.25** (no excess but maximum per year benefits)

Prices from Moneysupermarket.com, July 2004.

All figures are based on a single, non-smoking male, aged 45.

Practical parenting

According to recent research, raising a child from birth to age 21 can set you back as much as £300,000. And that's just for one child. There are some costs, such as childcare, that you may not be able to cut, but in areas such as baby equipment, clothing, food and outings you can make significant savings.

NEW BABY ON A BUDGET

The moment you find you are going to have a baby, you'll be deluged with information on what you can't possibly live without. Beware of such guidance; there are only a few things you really need, and many of these can be sourced at a discount.

BEG, BORROW OR BUY?

To avoid making expensive mistakes, don't rush into buying things for your baby.

Ask for advice Once you have had your 'anomaly' scan – about half-way through your pregnancy – start talking to friends and relatives with babies about what they have found most useful and what was a waste of money. Write a list of what you think you'll need at the outset and don't be tempted to stray from it.

Secondhand is good enough Save on large items such as prams, carry-cots and cots by borrowing them from friends whose children have outgrown them, or by buying them secondhand through the classified section of your local paper, from ads on supermarket noticeboards or on eBay (**www.ebay.co.uk** ✉). Also try a National Childbirth Trust (NCT) nearly-new sale – look at the news section on **www.nctpregnancyandbabycare.com** for your nearest sale or contact the NCT on 0870 770 3236 ✉.

SLEEPING SOLUTIONS

Dispense with the cost of buying a crib or Moses basket, which your baby will outgrow in a few weeks, by putting your newborn in a full-size cot. This is safe, as long as you position your baby with his feet at the end of the cot and his head half-way down (which stops him from burrowing under the sheets and overheating). Before buying secondhand, read the Smart Moves box on page 92.

SAVE ON BABYWEAR

You will be confronted with an enormous array of gorgeous babywear, but choose what's practical and good value – and accept offers of used baby clothes from friends.

The bare essentials For the first two or three weeks your baby will spend much of the time asleep, so vests and sleepsuits are the most practical. They are comfortable, easy to wash and don't need ironing. Buy a few sleepsuits and vests in the 'newborn' size and some more in size '0–3 months' before your baby is born. Look for good-quality fabric as they need to withstand frequent washing, but don't pay a fortune. Supermarkets or low-cost high-street stores such as Woolworths and H&M are usually the best value for multipacks, or buy in the sales.

keep it simple

BASIC EQUIPMENT

Basic baby needs are:

- A place to sleep
- Clothes to wear
- Something to drink
- Something to be transported in
- Nappies

FREE OFFERS

After your first trip to hospital for an ultrasound scan, you will begin to receive promotional literature and samples of goodies for you and the baby. Once you're confident about the health of your baby, sign up for anything that promises money-off vouchers and free samples. If you want to avoid being inundated by all and sundry, tick the 'don't pass on my details' box that all these leaflets must carry by law.

The low-down on cots

Buying a secondhand cot could save you more than £100.

You will need to check that:

■ the cot hasn't been painted by the owner. The paint may have been lead-based, and as lead is toxic, it's not worth taking the risk.

■ the teething rail is in a reasonable condition; these can be replaced, but make sure you can get the correct part before buying such a cot.

■ none of the screws and bolts are missing.

■ the slats aren't damaged and are no more than 6cm (2in) apart.

■ the catches on the drop-side are very secure, and the base fits properly. Whether you buy a new or secondhand cot, it is essential to purchase a new mattress. Research by the Foundation for the Study of Infant Deaths (FSID) has found that instances of cot death are increased with the use of a secondhand mattress, especially if the mattress comes from another home.

TOP TIPS BEST-BUY BABY CLOTHES

Many people enjoy giving baby clothes as presents, but they usually buy the small sizes which won't fit for long. Take advantage of this by not buying too many before your baby is born, then buy wisely to get the best value for money.

■ **Get the most wear** Always choose one size ahead of your baby's actual age. Sizes can be on the small side and babies grow quickly. Most 6-month-old babies can wear clothes size 9–12 months, 1-year-olds wear size 2 and so on.

■ **Stock up** When sales shopping, get clothes for the coming months. If your child is 9 months old in January, buy clothes for 18–24 months in anticipation of the following winter. In 'expensive' baby shops, head for the sale rails – there's nearly always one in Baby Gap, and bargains of up to 50% off – sometimes more – can be had.

■ **Designer modes** Be selective when buying up-market babywear. There's little point in paying top price for vests, plain tops or tights, for example – just mix in cheaper labels with some branded goods and you'll give the impression of full designer wear but pay a fraction of the cost.

■ **Good investments** If you are tempted by expensive clothing for your baby, consider whether it is good value for money. Trousers and practical dresses may be worn enough to justify the outlay, but avoid paying top price for an outfit for special occasions – it might only get one airing. See if you can borrow a special occasion outfit instead.

■ **Nearly new** For some real bargains, go along to nearly-new sales and secondhand babywear shops. Babies grow very quickly and favourite clothes are often relegated to the 'too small pile' long before they're worn out. You can benefit from what other people have had to throw out; some items may still carry the original shop tag, indicating that they've never been worn.

■ **Web buys** Good deals can be had on **www.ebay.co.uk** ✉. Select 'Home, garden & family', then the baby and clothing categories. You'll find secondhand and brand new designer and high-street baby clothes being sold for next to nothing. Other websites selling scarcely worn baby clothes include **www.basics4baby.co.uk** 01423 871093 ✉ and **www.dappernippers.com** 07905 929922 ✉.

BE WISE: IMPROVISE

■ You can make your own crib using a laundry basket or even a dresser drawer. As long as babies have a firm mattress and suitable blankets, they really don't mind where they are.

■ If friends or other family members are due to give birth a couple of months before or after you, why not halve the cost of a crib by sharing one? But you will still need to buy separate mattresses.

FEEDING, BATHS AND NAPPIES

Whether you breastfeed or bottle-feed, or opt for terry nappies or disposables, you'll be faced with a whole gamut of equipment to make your life easier. But the old ways are often the simplest (and the cheapest), as our mothers and grandmothers will tell us.

BREAST IS BEST – AND CHEAPEST

If you can, breastfeed your baby. Breast milk is free, convenient and has health benefits for you and your baby.
The costs of breastfeeding Don't be lured into spending unnecessarily. As a minimum you'll need two nursing bras and breast pads (washable ones are more economical than disposables). Wear loose T-shirts or blouses, and only invest in a (secondhand) breast pump if you are returning to work or you want your partner to share feeding with you.
The costs of formula You may not want to breastfeed or maybe you can't. If so, you will need to use formula milk, the cost of which mounts up (an estimated £350–£420 a year). Ask your baby clinic for their prices, and remember that if you receive income support you may be able to buy formula at the clinic at a reduced rate. Otherwise, keep an eye out for multibuy savings in chemists and supermarkets and stock up when you can – your baby will need formula milk for most of the first year.

SAVE ON STERILISING

Even if you breastfeed, you'll need to sterilise any bottles you use and, in the first stages of weaning, ensure that spoons and bowls are scrupulously clean.
Low-tech equals low cost The cheapest option is cold water sterilisation. You can buy sterilising tablets cheaply at a chemist's; simply add them to water and submerge your bottles in it.
High-tech alternatives Both electric and microwave steam sterilisers are more expensive options that may be worth while if you are bottle feeding. If you feel the time-saving benefit they offer is worth the extra outlay, shop around for the best deal before your baby is born. Also, keep an eye out for promotional packs that include free extras such as bottles and teats.

TOP TIPS BABY FOOD BONUSES

Between four and six months, your baby will be ready to begin supplementing her milk feeds with other foods that are cheaper than conventional baby foods.
■ **Frozen purées** To save money on shop-bought jars, buy a few flexible ice-cube trays and make your own purées (see Smart Moves, page 94). Freeze the purée as you would ice-cubes, then defrost the exact quantity you need for each meal, eliminating waste.
■ **Refilled jars** Recycle any empty shop-bought jars of baby food by sterilising the jar and its lid and then filling it with

RESOURCES

WEANING WISDOM
For general advice on weaning and recipes to make for your baby, see:
■ **www.nctpregnancyand babycare.com**
0870 770 3236 ✉
■ **www.babycentre.co.uk**
■ **www.forparentsbyparents .com** 0113 2455680 ✉
■ *New Complete Baby and Toddler Meal Planner* by Annabel Karmel, Ebury Press, £12.99
ISBN 009190031X

ASK YOURSELF

DO I REALLY NEED A HIGH CHAIR?
A baby can be fed in a portable car seat set in its upright position or simply held in your lap. Once your baby is able to sit upright, you can buy an inexpensive three-in-one booster seat (about £15 at catalogue stores). This seat, which has a seat belt and removable tray, can be strapped onto a sturdy kitchen or dining-room chair. The tray has a high position and a lower position to accommodate the child's size as she grows. When the tray is no longer needed, it can be removed and the seat can be used as a booster seat at the table.

homemade food. These small jars are ideal for taking out and about with you.

■ **Uses for cow's milk** Reduce the cost of formula milk by introducing diluted cow's milk to your baby's diet from the age of six months. It can't replace formula, but it can be used on cereal and in cooking.

■ **Safe leftovers** When using jars, spoon only the required amount into a bowl so you can use the remainder later.

EXTENDING THE JUICE

Don't waste your money on baby juices. Buy plain juice concentrates (the least expensive, but be sure they are marked 100% juice with no added sugar) and reconstitute according to the package directions. When you are filling a bottle or sipping cup, fill the container about one-third to half full, then top it up with water. Your juice will last longer and your baby will consume less fruit sugar, which can contribute to early tooth decay.

BATHING YOUR BABY

Every baby store has a wide selection of goods and products devoted to cleaning your baby. What should you buy?

Baby bath alternatives When considering whether to buy a baby bath, bear in mind that your baby will only fit in it for a few weeks, and most health visitors recommend that you only bathe your baby twice a week during the first six weeks. So instead of paying out for a bath that will get little use, why not bathe your newborn in the kitchen sink? She'll be quite safe and you won't have to bend over so awkwardly. Clean the sink thoroughly and line it with an old towel to prevent your baby from slipping. Then pull on

Make your own baby food

It's easy to save money by making food for your baby.

Homemade purées These work out much cheaper than shop-bought jars. Start off by introducing one taste at a time: puréed carrot, potato, parsnip, turnip, apple, pear, mashed banana or avocado. Later you can mix purées to make new flavours – apple and mango, for example, or carrot and courgette. As they grow,

don't be afraid to make your own concoctions using flavours you know they like. Babies generally love sweet potato, so try mashing sweet potato, salmon and broccoli together to make a delicious and nutritious meal. Just blend it down, using milk or water to get the right consistency, then freeze in meal-size containers.

Baby rice and cereals These are expensive, but did you know that baby rice is simply ground rice? Use a coffee grinder or a super-

efficient blender, pour in the rice grains, grind away and store the powder in the freezer in a resealable plastic bag.

Family food As your baby grows and you feel more relaxed about what they eat, structure mealtimes to fit in with your own – if you eat a sandwich lunch and a proper dinner, do the same for your baby. That way, your baby can eat a little of the family food instead of you having to buy and prepare different meals at different times of the day.

SMART MOVES

a pair of cheap white cotton gloves so you have a good grip on your little one. If you'd prefer to bathe your baby on the floor, look in discount shops for a rectangular washing-up bowl – it will do just as well.

Potions and lotions Save on the expense of baby toiletries: general guidance is just to clean your baby with water, since it is thought that baby bath and talcum powder can contribute to skin complaints.

Bath toys Plastic bowls, cups and spoons from the kitchen provide endless entertainment in the bath and help your baby to learn; and plastic sieves or funnels of different sizes make interesting water toys. Not only are these playthings free, but they often have the edge on expensive bath toys that are funny to look at initially, but are soon ignored by your infant because they don't allow actual play.

TOP TIPS WHICH NAPPIES?

You will have to decide which side to take in the great nappy debate. You have three options: traditional, terry-towelling nappies with plastic pants and disposable liners; the new, shaped reusable nappies; or disposables.

■ **Terry-towelling nappies** These are usually considered the cheapest, since after you have made the initial outlay for nappies, pins and pants, you can use them until your toddler is potty trained. But there is still the cost of disposable liners and washing and drying the nappies to be considered. If you go down this route, look out for nearly-new nappies that have been abandoned in favour of disposables. Because drying terries can be difficult,

keep it simple

BE PENNYWISE AT BATH TIME
■ Forget forking out for antislip mats or baby seats for the bath – one of the best ways of ensuring that your baby is safe in the bath is to get in too. You can join in the bathtime play and relax a little yourself.

■ You probably have the perfect substitute for costly baby talcum powder sitting in a kitchen cupboard: cornflour. It works just as well as baby powder to keep your baby dry, and it won't irritate her lungs if it gets breathed in – a big plus.

BABY CLUBS

Many supermarkets – including Sainsbury's and Tesco – operate baby clubs or 0–5 clubs. Join up and you'll receive newsletters or magazines with details of baby products, special offers in store and money-off vouchers.

RESOURCES

NAPPY LAUNDERING
■ Consult the National Association of Nappy Services (NANS) at www.changeanappy.co.uk/ 0121 693 4949 ✉, and the NCT (see page 91), to find out about laundering services in your area.
■ Your local authority may provide a nappy laundering service that is cheaper than comparable private laundering services.

especially in winter, and tumbledryers are expensive to buy and run, invest in an old-style drier that pulls up to the kitchen ceiling.

■ **Shaped reusable nappies** These are three times as expensive as terries to buy and also need cleaning. Find out if your local council offers a financial incentive for reusables; some give a rebate for not adding more nappies to a landfill site.

■ **Disposable nappies** These are the most popular option, and the most expensive. You can save as much as 4p a nappy by buying own-brand nappies, but if they don't fit as well or are not as absorbent, they'll be a false economy. Reduce the cost of branded nappies by signing up with the manufacturers so you benefit from money-off vouchers. And look out for multibuy offers in supermarkets, chemists and online.

■ **Nappy service** A laundering service for reusable nappies will collect your dirty nappies and drop off clean ones every week. But this can cost around £35 a month (a staggering £1,050 over two and a half years).

WIPE OUT EXTRA COSTS

You do not need to buy wipes for your baby. Instead, you can make them yourself.

Disposable wipes Cut a roll of strong paper towels in half crosswise. Put a half roll in a plastic container with a tight lid. Combine 1½ cups of water with 1 tablespoon of liquid baby bath soap. Pour the mixture over the towels to saturate them and cover the container. When you need a wipe, tear off a sheet from the roll.

Washable wipes If you use terry-towelling nappies, save more money by using washable wipes as well. Buy a bundle of flannels at a discount store or price club, such as Makro or Costco, and keep them in the bathroom near your baby's changing area. When it's time to change your baby, dampen a clean flannel in the sink and use that to wipe your baby's bottom. (If the baby has a really dirty nappy, dampen one flannel and rub a little soap over it, then dampen a second to rinse.) Toss the dirty flannels in your nappy bucket to wash and sterilise with the nappies.

NAPPY OPTIONS: COSTS OVER 2½ YEARS*

TERRY TOWELLING	Start-up £60 Liners £54 Detergent £75 Electricity £27 Washing machine depreciation £24.90	**£240.90**
SHAPED NAPPIES	Start-up £158 Liners £54 Detergent £75 Electricity £27 Washing machine depreciation £24.90	**£338.90**
DISPOSABLES	Size 1 nappies at 28 for £3.50; size 2 at 46 for £4.99 Size 3 at 38 for £4.99 and size 4 at 34 for £4.50 All own brand	**£700**

*This is the average time of a child in nappies. Costs calculated on the basis of six nappies per day.

BABY TRANSPORT

The choice of car seats, prams, pushchairs and sophisticated travel systems that combine all three is extensive. Don't be tempted to buy more than you need – with careful planning you can keep the costs down.

CHOOSING CAR SEATS

Buying a car seat is a necessity. Many hospitals won't allow you to take your baby from the maternity ward without one.

Seats that fit It is essential that a seat fits your car securely. The best way to ensure this is to go to one of the RoSPA (Royal Society for the Prevention of Accidents) centres – contact the Road Safety Department at your local council or visit **www.rospa.com** or phone 0121 248 2000 ✉ for details of your nearest centre – and find out which seats fit your car. Once you know, look at the many websites that sell baby goods to check out the cost – you can save up to 30% on high-street prices. Go to the RoSPA website **www.childcarseats.org.uk/links/manufacturers.htm** for a list of manufacturers' websites, which give recommended prices; and **www.childcarseats.org.uk/links/retailers.htm** (also a RoSPA site) for links to retailers' websites and their prices.

Stick with the basics To ensure you don't pay over the odds, try not to be seduced by gimmicks or glamorous fabrics. These won't make any difference to your baby and will get covered in the usual baby gloop of milk and biscuits just the same, negating your extra outlay.

WATCH POINTS CAR SEAT SAFETY

If you are offered a used car seat that fits your car, be very cautious. Your baby's safety is the top priority even if it costs a few pounds more.

■ **Take care with used seats** The protection offered by child car seats is reduced if it has already been in an accident or been thrown around the loft or garage. Consider a previously used seat only if you can be sure of its history – if it comes from a friend or relative, for example. Do not buy from the small ads or a secondhand shop.

■ **Follow instructions** Make sure the manufacturer's instructions are with the seat, so you can be sure you are fitting it securely.

■ **Check standards** The seat must meet the United Nations standard Regulation 44.03. It should have an 'E' mark.

■ **Look for ISOFIX points** The most secure car seats have ISOFIX (International Standards Organisation FIX) fitting points. Find out if your car takes an ISOFIX car seat, and if so, buy a car seat of this type.

PRAMS AND BUGGIES

The most economical choices for a newborn are either to buy a traditional pram secondhand and then go on to a buggy later, or to buy a two-in-one pushchair with a seat that adjusts from flat to upright, accommodating your child until he is happy to walk everywhere.

ASK YOURSELF

ARE BABY SLINGS WORTH IT?
These are great for carrying your newborn, and invaluable if you also have a young toddler, as they avoid the need for a double buggy. But as your baby gains weight, too much strain will be put on your back and you will have to stop using it once the baby weighs about 9kg (20lb). If you have a friend with a baby sling – especially one with head and neck support – ask if you can borrow it. Unless she is already pregnant, you can be sure you'll have finished with it before she needs it back.

CHANGING BAGS FOR HALF PRICE
When you are buying your first pram, you'll be enticed by the matching changing bag. These can be overpriced and are often quite impractical. Instead, look in sports shops or school outfitters for a roomy and comfortable backpack or bag that will accommodate all your paraphernalia (make sure you include a waterproof mat). You should end up with something at around half the price of a purpose-made changing bag.

PRAMS vs BUGGIES

When choosing a pram or pushchair consider your lifestyle. If you walk long distances (to the shops or friends), a traditional pram or three-in-one pushchair with carrycot might be the best option.
If you rely on public transport or travel by car look for a two-in-one that folds easily to go on the bus or put in the boot. Umbrella buggies (or strollers) are not suitable for newborns.

Think it through A pram will be cost-effective only if you have given some thought to what you really need. One with big wheels, for example, may look great but if it fills every inch of the boot, you'll end up buying a smaller one as well.

What to look for Make sure you know what's included in the price. Some prams come with raincovers and parasol, while with others you will have to buy these as extras.

Lightweight buggies Also known as strollers, these are suitable for babies from three or six months, depending on the model. If you will be using it occasionally, buy a sturdy, cheap model. If the buggy is for everyday use, be prepared to pay a bit more but shop around for the best deal.

Double buggies These are often a necessary evil but rarely receive much use, so it's always advisable to buy secondhand – but make sure that you find one with swivel wheels.

Resale value There is a thriving market in secondhand prams and pushchairs (look at the ads in your local paper and on www.ebay.co.uk ✉). If you make a wrong choice you can sell it on, whether it's a new pushchair or a traditional secondhand pram. Don't hang on to them – styles change and as they get older their value will drop.

BEST-BUY CAR SEATS

Car seats are described by stage or group when you buy them in the shops. Consider your options, bearing in mind your plans for future children. Buying group 0+1 and 2/3 combination will keep your child safe from birth to 11 for £200. Group 0+ and 1/2/3 combination will keep your child safe from birth to 11 for £155.

STAGE	GROUP	TYPE OF SEAT	WEIGHT	APPROXIMATE AGE	AVG PRICE*
1	0 0+	Rear-facing Rear-facing	birth to 10kg (22lb) birth to 13kg (29lb)	birth to 6–9 months birth to 15 months	£65
2	1	Front-facing	9kg–18kg (20lb–40lb)	9 months to 4 years	£110
1 and 2	0+1 combination	Rear and front-facing	birth to 18kg (40lb)	birth to 4 years	£120
3	2	Front-facing booster seat	15kg–25kg (33lb–55lb)	4–6 years	**
4	3	Front-facing booster seat	22kg–35kg (48lb–76lb)	6–11 years	£25
2, 3 and 4	1/2/3 combination	Front-facing booster seat	9kg–35kg (20lb–76lb)	9 months to 11 years	£90
3 and 4	2/3 combination	Front-facing booster seat	15kg–35kg (33lb–76lb)	4–11 years	£80

Information July 2004

* Prices given are average for the group. It is likely that car seats within the group will be found for both a lower and higher cost. ** Individual pricing not available (normally catered for in a combination of seats).

SAFETY AT ANY PRICE

Safety is something you don't want to take any chances on, but you don't need expensive equipment. Many people get by without stair gates and cupboard locks, but the success of this depends on your child. It's better to be safe than sorry.

WATCH POINTS HAZARDS AT HOME

The best method is to deal with situations as they arise, while keeping an eye on the obvious dangers. For example:

■ **Get a fireguard** If you have an open fire (real or gas), you will need a fireguard as soon as your child becomes mobile. Look out for secondhand guards, ask friends who have an older child and check out catalogue and DIY stores as they will often be cheaper than baby stores.

■ **Put away dangerous substances** Ensure that cleaning materials and medicines are kept well out of reach.

■ **Use safety devices** If your child is into everything, or you want to take every precaution, look out for special packs in DIY stores that include plug covers, cupboard locks and door stops. These starter packs work out much cheaper than buying individual packs of safety devices.

SAFETY CHECKS

Whether it's new or secondhand, before you buy equipment for your baby, you want to be sure it has not been recalled. The Royal Society for the Prevention of Accidents website **www.rospa.com** ✉ lists products that have been recalled by the manufacturers for safety reasons. (Select 'Product Safety' from the main menu, then The Trading Standards Institute product recall list or phone 0121 248 2000 for more information ✉.) The products listed include cribs, baby furniture, clothes, childproofing items, baby foods and formulas, over-the-counter medicines, car seats and buggies.

RESOURCES

SAFETY ADVICE

Although we all try hard to prevent injuries, each year more than 1 million children seek hospital treatment in Britain after an accident in the home.

■ The Child Accident Prevention Trust website at **www.capt.org.uk** or 020 7608 3828 ✉ has factsheets on aspects of child safety you can view online, and publications that can be ordered.

■ The government Home Safety site **www.dti.gov. uk/homesafetynetwork** has information on common accidents in the home and how to prevent them, including burns, chemicals, choking, bikes, garden safety and falls.

CUT THE COST OF CHILDCARE

For most working parents, the major outlay for the first five years is childcare. While it's essential to find a form of care that suits you and your child, cost is also a key factor. There are different ways of paying less, depending on your income and whether or not you work full time.

EXAMINING THE OPTIONS

If you have relatives who live nearby and are willing to look after your baby, you will make substantial savings on childcare and be confident that your child is with someone who loves them.

Sharing childcare If you have a job-share or work part time, you may be able to join forces with another part-time worker and take it in turns to look after each other's children. Check your legal position with your local Children's Information Service; if you look after someone else's child for more than two hours a day for payment you have to register as a childminder. Even if you don't need to register, you may have to increase your insurance.

Workplace nursery If your employer provides the site and is actively involved in the running of the nursery, you pay no tax on the benefit provided and have the reassurance and convenience of having your child nearby. Your employer gets full tax relief on the costs of running the nursery or play scheme, as well as happier employees. If you don't have a workplace nursery, ask if your employer will set one up.

Day nurseries These cost £80–£200 a week, but once your child is three years old you'll be eligible for a nursery education grant, which allows your child up to two and a half hours free nursery education five days a week. To claim, fill in an Early Years Education Parent Form, available from the nursery.

Childminders vs nannies Depending on where you live, childminding rates range between £2–£4 an hour for each child. Childminders can work out cheaper than a nanny if you only have one child. Nannies cost between £200 and £400 a week (£200–£250 to live in), but you'll need to pay your nanny's tax and national insurance contributions on top. A nanny is only really cost-effective if you have more than one child, or if you can arrange a nanny share with another family. Check with your local National Childbirth Trust group to see if they run a nanny share register.

CLAIMING BACK CHILDCARE COSTS

If you use registered childcare (a childminder or nursery, not usually a relative or nanny unless they are registered) you may be entitled to help with the cost through the Working Tax Credit (up to a maximum of £135 a week for one child and £200 for two or more children). To find out if you qualify, get the leaflet WTC1 'Child Tax Credit and Working Tax Credit: An Introduction' from the Post Office, or phone the Tax Credits helpline: 0845 9000 404.

RESOURCES

WHAT'S AVAILABLE

■ For details of childcare options in your area, visit **www.childcarelink.gov.uk** ✉ or phone the Children's Information Service on 0845 602 1125. The CIS will also have details of local places that are registered to provide free nursery education.

■ The National Childminding Association can give advice and information on childminders. The NCMA helpline is 0800 169 4486; their website is **www.ncma.org.uk** ✉.

■ For general Information on childcare and benefits, visit the Working Families website **www.working families.org.uk** ✉ or phone 020 7253 7243.

■ For information on the Working Tax Credit, visit **www.inlandrevenue.gov.uk** (0845 300 3900) ✉, the Department for Work and Pensions **www.dwp.gov.uk** (020 7712 2171) ✉, the Citizens Advice Bureau website **www.adviceguide. org.uk/em** ✉ or your nearest branch. See *Tax and benefits*, page 312.

HOLIDAY CHILDCARE

Once children have reached school age, full-time child care is no longer a priority for working parents. But there's still the problem of how to keep your children occupied once the holidays come around.

ORGANISED HOLIDAY ACTIVITIES

Summer and Easter camps are a boon to working parents, giving them peace of mind that their youngsters are being well supervised and learning new skills. Privately run day camps are expensive, charging from £135 to almost £200 a week, but there are plenty of other organisations that provide excellent supervised activities for much less.

Local authority schemes Holiday play schemes, organised by local councils, are run by qualified playworkers and offer daily fun for the kids from 8.30am to 6pm. They cost from £35-£90 a week, depending on the type of activity.

Camps and courses Don't book your summer holiday until you've found out what camps are on offer for any organisations your child belongs to, such as Guides, Scouts and Woodcraft Folk. Army, sea and air cadets organise residential skills-based courses costing under £100 a week.

YMCA holiday playschemes The YMCA (**www.ymca. org.uk** ✉) organises Easter and summer activities for children aged 5–14, offering sports, art and crafts and day trips. Week-long camps start at around £100 and may include transport, and there are discounts for booking early.

Sports-based activities Local sports or leisure centres are likely to have a full programme of holiday activities, ranging from free half-day sessions to football weeks costing around £35. For water sports fans, the Thames Young Mariners organise kayaking and canoeing days from only £12.50 (020 8940 5550 ✉). The King's Sports Camps (**www.kingssports camps.com** or 0870 345 0781 ✉) – run by registered national charity, The King's Trust – offer one-week courses costing £85–£90, and single or unemployed parents or those on income support may be eligible for an assisted place.

Arts and crafts Local museums and art galleries often put on free holiday activities. Check your local theatre, too, as some run drama classes for as little as £12 a day or £50 a week. Most churches also run holiday clubs for children.

ARRANGING CHEAPER CHILDCARE

Even if your children go to organised activities for part of the holidays, they need to be taken there. And there will be times when they are at home and need supervision.

Share the care Enlist the help of relatives and friends to drop off and pick up your children at their activities, or look after them at home. If possible, split your leave with your partner, so that you can each spend time separately with the children. Or arrange to share the services of a nanny or au pair with friends in the same position as you are.

Cheaper nannies Trainee nannies may welcome the chance to practise their skills with a family for a lower rate than a qualified nanny. Try advertising on a college notice board.

SPREAD THE HOLIDAY COSTS

During term-time, put a little money away into a short-term savings account for the children's holiday activities. In this way, not only will you spread the load of the inevitable extra expense but you will earn some interest on your money too.

keep it simple

PICK A PROJECT

Save money on activities outside the home by getting your children started on an inexpensive project to last them over the holiday, such as mega Lego building, putting together a large scrapbook or planting and tending a garden. This makes it easier for other people to cover for you as the children have a specific interest to occupy them.

Select seconds

Buy secondhand when you can – there are nearly-new bargains in many shops and sales.
■ **Coats and jackets** Usually well made, and last a while.
■ **Dressy dresses** Often good enough for resale once they are outgrown. This applies particularly to those for younger children.
■ **Never say no to hand-me-downs** Even if these items have seen better days, there are times when you need clothes for rough wear. Family and friends with older children will know you appreciate anything they can pass on.
■ **Teenage styles** Bygone styles sometimes appeal to teenagers. Visit car boot sales and flea markets together – you may make great finds.

SMART MOVES

GOOD-VALUE CLOTHES

Before long, fashions and branding will become important to your child. But there are plenty of ways to keep him happy, while looking after your wallet.

TOP TIPS EASY WAYS TO PAY LESS

■ **Storecard benefits** Sign up for storecards from the big department and chain stores, such as Debenhams, Bhs and Monsoon. You could gain 'points' to redeem against future purchases, advance notice of sales, or money-off vouchers and discounts. But avoid the high interest charges by always paying off your bill in full every month.

■ **Sales online** Many online catalogues start their sales ahead of reductions offered by post, and the same goes for the online outlet of some high-street stores. Register your email address to get advance notice of sales and any special offers.

■ **Get in the club** Look out for bargains in 'club' stores, such as Matalan and Costco, where you will find many items of clothing at rock-bottom prices.

■ **Discounted designers** Department stores such as Debenhams and discount stores like TK Maxx offer good-value ranges by top designers. If your child must have branded tops and trousers, look for them here, or try shopping sites such as **www.lxdirect.com** to get discounts.

■ **Branded sportswear** You can make savings on clothes and trainers at a factory outlet shop or on the Internet (try **www.sportzwear.com** and **www.sport-e.com**).

■ **School uniform** Most schools nominate a preferred outfitter, but don't accept that you must buy every item there. Look for high-cost items such as blazers at school sales. Blazers are often bought and not worn, and a secondhand one can look as good as new. Buy school shirts in multipacks at high-street stores and supermarkets. Grey, black or navy skirts and trousers in a non-specific style, can also be bought from high-street stores.

CASE STUDY

DRESSING FOR LESS
Anna's 9-year-old son Harry had outgrown his wardrobe. Faced with the expense of reclothing him, she started to shop around. First stop was the online auction site eBay, where she picked up a pair of trousers, long-sleeved top, T-shirt and unworn swim shorts – all designer-branded – for £26.60. She found four T-shirts for £2.50 each at Tesco and a hooded top, a parka jacket and a non-branded long-sleeved top, totalling £27, at the budget store Peacocks. Warehouse store Matalan and catalogue company Marshall Ward provided pyjamas, a T-shirt and shorts set, socks and pants and jeans for a total of £37.99, giving a total of £101.59. Similar clothes in high street shops would have cost twice as much.

A SEWING MACHINE CAN SAVE YOU MONEY

Because sewing machines have little resale value, you can usually pick up a used one cheaply. Consider a reconditioned model from a sewing machine shop. You should be able to get a good brand for £100–£125. Check out newspaper ads and car boot sales, but bear in mind machines bought this way will probably need an overhaul at a cost of around £60.

STYLISH REVAMPS

Bring old clothes right up to date by:
- Cutting off cotton trousers below the knee to make them cropped.
- Turning a summer dress into a skirt and a crop top.
- Cutting the arms to three-quarter length on a top or cardigan and adding a ribbon trim.

LONGER SKIRTS AND DRESSES

If you sew, you could buy a remnant of fabric that matches or contrasts with the dress fabric and stitch an additional panel to the hem.

Use simple sewing skills to give your children's clothes a new lease of life. Simple makeovers can help you to stretch your clothes budget but do consult with your children as they get older or your idea of stylish may be their idea of embarrassing.

NEW CLOTHES FOR NOTHING

PARTY CLOTHES MAKEOVERS

Unless there is a grand occasion such as a family wedding, your daughter won't need a proper party frock. Simply jazz up an inexpensive plain jersey or cotton dress, or a skirt or cropped trousers and a matching T-shirt, with some sparkly sequins. Glue more sequins to a pair of canvas sandals and she'll have a designer outfit.

LENGTHEN SLEEVES AND TROUSERS

- If the sleeves on a shirt or sweater get too short at the cuff while the body still fits well, transform the shirt into a short-sleeved version of the original (or in the case of a sweater, into a sleeveless vest). To add length to girls' trousers, buy a selection of braid, ribbon or trimmings and sew several strips of different ones to the hem on each leg.

CONCEAL STAINS AND SMALL TEARS

Cover them with a shop-bought motif such as a skateboard or a butterfly. You don't have to sew them on – use iron-on bonding fabric to hold them in place.

NO-FUSS FOOD

As with clothing, children become pickier and more brand-aware as they grow older. But a few tactical moves should make the shopping bill easier to swallow.

SHOPPING STRATEGIES FOR LOWER BILLS

Shop by yourself Taking the children around a supermarket, as well as being a logistical nightmare, will inevitably add to the bill items you wouldn't have bought if you were alone. So leave the children at home if you can – 24-hour supermarkets make this possible for many families.

Online shopping If the prospect of a late-night supermarket run is too much to contemplate, shop online. You'll follow your list far more closely and you should more than save the delivery charge, especially if you make use of the many money-off vouchers sent out by supermarkets in their bid to win new online customers.

Fill the freezer Stock up your freezer once a month at a good-value freezer store. The same items are often cheaper than at the supermarket, and you'll cut the weekly trip down to just fresh items.

Support your local market Make a saving on fresh fruit and vegetables by buying at a local market. Eggs may be less than half the supermarket price too.

BUY IN BULK, SERVE IN SMALL PORTIONS

Food producers love to offer small sizes of a product to entice parents – and children – with miniature portions. Don't be fooled by cute packaging – you're paying over the odds. For example, a small bag of crisps typically costs 39p, while a 24-pack bag of the same kind is on sale for £2.99 – 12.5p a bag. Always buy the largest packet of

FEEDING THEM WHEN YOU'RE OUT

The best way to save money on food when you're out is to take a packed lunch. But when you're struggling with kids, buggies and bags, you might not want to add flasks and sandwiches to the load. On a fine day when you can eat outside, go to a bakery or supermarket for filled rolls and a greengrocer for some fruit. You'll fill your children up with healthy food and should make a reasonable saving compared to eating in a fast-food restaurant.

Bake in bulk

raisins, crackers, biscuits and so on, but then transfer the contents to small plastic containers or bags that can be brought out when needed.

FOOD SIZE MATTERS TOO

There are ways to feed your children morsels that match their size and still hold down food costs. Blocks of cheese are less expensive than cheese sold in slices, but your children will enjoy the cheese more if you cut it into sticks or cubes. Baby carrots – less expensive when bought in big bags – look friendlier than big carrots. Alternatively, you could cut larger carrots into sticks yourself. For no-cost fun, cut sandwich bread with cookie cutters or roll narrow strips of bread spread with a filling into pinwheels.

JUST LIKE GRANDMA USED TO MAKE

While you may not always have the time to make meals from scratch, doing so will save money, and it's healthier too. Make it easier on yourself by thinking ahead.

Cook twice as much Whenever possible, make double the quantities and freeze half for future use. You can do this with pasta sauces, stews, savoury mince for shepherd's pie or lasagne, and stewed fruit for pie fillings or crumbles.

Bake in bulk Take a tip out of your grandmother's book and have a baking day. Biscuits, fairy cakes, muffins and sponges are all quick and easy to bake, and cost a fraction of shop prices. If you combine your baking day with cooking a roast lunch you'll use your oven to the full and save on electricity too. Involve the children in order to develop good food habits.

keep it simple

SAVE 50% ON JUICE CARTONS
Individual juice cartons may be handy, but they are expensive and create a lot of waste. Instead, use a reusable plastic bottle (sports bottles work well) and fill that with the juice of your choice. If you make it up from a frozen concentrate and dilute it with water you'll reduce costs even further. For a special treat, use half juice and half sparkling water.

FEEDING CHILDREN: PROCESSED COMPARED WITH FRESH

BOX OF BRAND-NAME SQUASH	£0.26
BRAND-NAME SQUASH, DILUTED AT HOME	£0.08
SNACK BOX WITH HAM AND CHEESE	£1.24
TWO BREAD ROLLS WITH HAM AND CHEESE	£0.40
READY-MADE SAUSAGES AND MASH	£1.64
HOME-COOKED SAUSAGES AND MASH	£0.63
READY-MADE RICE PUDDING	£0.42
HOME-MADE RICE PUDDING	£0.14
READY-MADE SHEPHERD'S PIE	£1.61
HOME-COOKED SHEPHERD'S PIE	£0.55

Prices are for each serving, and an average taken from three leading supermarkets in June 2004. Products used for both ready meals and fresh food are average for those available – neither premium nor value.

'MUST HAVE' TOYS AND FURNITURE

Babies and toddlers don't need fancy toys – most of all they need things that are age-appropriate and interesting. As your child grows there'll be ever more demands on your purse – for more toys, fancy kids' furniture and some way to accommodate their growing number of belongings.

TOP TIPS **THRIFTY TOYS**

■ **Simple ideas for babies** Don't buy soft toys, because your baby will be given lots and they provide little stimulation for very young children. It is better to buy the small, but perennially popular, items such as stacking cups, balls that rattle and wooden blocks. A baby gym is useful, and you can look for this in nearly-new sales and on eBay (**www.ebay.co.uk**).

■ **Sharing in the fun** Swap toys with friends to give your child maximum variety without spending a fortune. Alternatively, join a toy library, where you can borrow toys for nothing (or a nominal fee). For details of local toy libraries, ask at your local library or Citizens Advice Bureau, check your local council website or the National Association of Toy and Leisure Libraries' website **www.natll.org.uk** (020 7255 4600) ✉.

■ **Secondhand buys** Visit car boot sales and local school fêtes and Christmas bazaars. There is always a toy stall, and you'll find games, puzzles and toys, often in pristine condition. Trikes and bikes are quickly outgrown and can be picked up secondhand for a fraction of their original cost. Look out for bike auctions at local schools, where your child can try them before you bid.

TOYS FOR FREE

Making toys for your baby needn't take the skill and ingenuity of a *Blue Peter* presenter.
■ Make a shaker by half-filling an empty water bottle with dried lentils or rice. Ensure the lid is screwed on tightly.
■ Cover a cereal box with plain paper and then stick on pictures of animals, flowers or family photographs and cover with sticky plastic. Babies love looking at the pictures and will turn the box over and over.
■ Make a ball from scraps of different-textured material stitched together and stuffed with old tights. For extra interest, include a bell inside the ball.

Pay less for educational toys and books

The cost of toys and books can mount up. But there are a number of ways to reduce the expense of these valuable learning tools.

SMART MOVES

Toy libraries Toys designed to develop your child's imagination and reasoning powers are at the core of most toy libraries (see above for more information).

NCT sales The National Childbirth Trust holds annual nearly-new sales of toys and books in towns all over Britain. (To get more details on times and locations, see page 91.)

School fairs and sales Stalls run by parents often include toys that have been outgrown by their original owner, and are generally clean, well looked-after and in excellent condition.

Discount bookshops Chains such as County Bookshops have hefty reductions on the retail prices of children's books. Remainder book stores may also have many bargains.

Libraries Don't forget to borrow books from the local library – they are also a great source of videos, DVDs and CDs.

High-street stores Monitor stores for sales and spot discounts. This applies not just to the Early Learning Centre, but to more general retailers as well, such as Woolworths.

Museums Museum shops include many great toys and books – and reduce prices from time to time just like any other store.

FURNITURE

Today you can kit out your child's room with fabulous child-size furniture. While it may be worth buying a small table and chairs (which you can find secondhand), remember that by the time he starts school he'll already be growing out of them. To get value for money, it's much better to buy full-size furniture your child will grow into.

Bedding and curtains You can soften the feel of full-size furniture by choosing child-style fabrics for bedding and curtains, and decorating the walls with a fun border. All of these can be changed at a later date at little extra cost.

DOUBLE-DUTY BEDS

When it's time to buy a big bed for your child, consider one with a mattress set on a frame that has drawers underneath the bed. If space is limited or you have children sharing a room, this is a real space saver, providing storage and a sleep space in one. Alternatively, there are storage boxes on wheels that can be kept under beds without drawers.

Onwards and upwards For older children and teens, consider a loft bed with a storage or a study area below. You'll find a wide variety of prices and styles available in Ikea, DIY superstores and many furniture stores. Prices including bed, wardrobe and desk start at about £200.

TOP TIPS CREATING PRIVATE SPACES

If you have two children sharing a room, you probably face demands for more privacy than your house allows. Here are some low-cost suggestions for room dividers that give children some space of their own.

■ **Cheap bookcases** Place a free-standing bookcase, ranging from waist height to ceiling height, between the two beds. Or look for open metal bookcases (available at office liquidation stores), and bolt one side to the wall to prevent it tipping over. Your children will have more privacy and somewhere to store their belongings.

■ **Folding screens** Make simple wooden frames or use lightweight interior doors, and join them with hinges. Cover with fabric, or turn them into free-standing bulletin boards and let each child decorate their side of the screen.

■ **Curtain between the beds** Save money on a curtain by dyeing an old sheet, or use a 1960s-style curtain of beads.

keep it simple

CUSHION COMFORT
Instead of spending money on child-size chairs that are soon outgrown, try some penny-wise cushion ideas:

■ Buy a large foam cushion form and make a simple cover for it. Floor cushions allow a child freedom to cuddle up wherever they wish, and they are safe and easy for children to move.

■ Create a pile of old decorative pillows – if you don't have any, pick them up at car boot sales or in charity shops and have them dry-cleaned. Let your child make his or her own little nest for reading or listening to music.

OUT AND ABOUT

While toddlers and young children are easily entertained with water, a sandpit and swings in the park, older children demand more. Take advantage of low-cost entertainment for your children and make your money go further.

OUTDOOR FUN
Contact your local tourist office or consult the website of your local council for details of local places that offer the timeless attractions of tree-climbing, duck-feeding or an adventure playground for free. Most heathlands and parks are free to access. You will also find information on cycle routes, walks, events and free activities such as sports and drama sessions – often specially run by local authorities for children in the school holidays.

Join the National Trust Consider joining the National Trust ✉ or English Heritage ✉ – whichever has properties closest to you. The grounds provide exciting settings for outdoor play and you can look around interesting houses and castles as well. Some National Trust properties have tracker packs to help children explore. Find listings of family days and children's summer activities in the children's section of the website: **www.nationaltrust.org.uk/trusty/ index_static.htm** ✉. It's worth looking online for savings – a sizeable discount can sometimes be had if you pay by direct debit.

CULTURE VULTURES
Children's workshops There are children's workshops covering many different arts and crafts activities, from jewellery-making and mask-making to T-shirt decoration, and many more besides. Some workshop venues have individual websites, and others can be found by going to your local council website and selecting the children's events link. Local libraries and museums should also have useful information.

Theatre and dance Some theatres run special children's workshops. The Tricycle (**www.tricycle.co.uk**) do kite-making for 3-to-7-year-olds, story-telling for 9-to-13s, and drama workshops for older children. Their week's drama school is just £45 for 14-to-19-year-olds. The modern approach is catered for in the 2-day animation workshop at £20. Children may particularly enjoy open-air theatre such as Regent's Park or Edinburgh Castle.

Check out museums Entrance fees to museums are generally reasonable, especially family tickets and group bookings. Many museums are free – including some of the biggest, such as the Science Museum ✉ and the National History Museum ✉ in London, and the National Railway Museum ✉ in York. The larger museums and those with interactive exhibits and activities provide a whole day's entertainment. Some sports clubs have museums at their stadiums such as Manchester United or Lords, or for a football fan with no allegiences try the National Football Museum in Preston (**www.nationalfootballmuseum.com** ✉).

RESOURCES

NEWSLETTERS AND INFORMATION COVERING CHILDREN'S INTERESTS AND ACTIVITIES
■ The National Trust **www.nationaltrust.org.uk/** 0870 458 4000 ✉.
■ English Heritage **www.english-heritage. org.uk**/0870 333 1182 ✉.
■ For details of local events, visit your library or find out information from your local council website. Alternatively, visit **www.bbc.co.uk/events/ index.shtml** ✉ and search by region. Or check out **www.familiesonline.co.uk** ✉
■ To find museums of interest near you, visit **www.museums.co.uk** ✉ where you can search by location or museum type.
■ For information on loyalty card deals, visit **www.tesco.com/clubcard** or **www.nectar.com** ✉ (Sainsbury's).

EXTREME ADVENTURES

Day trips to theme parks are a treat for the children although they are known for being pricey. But there are ways around this.

Pay in advance Make savings by buying tickets in advance and booking online. Legoland (**www.lego.com/legoland** ✉) offers a 10% discount on tickets booked online, or phone 08705 04 04 04 for more information. The Alton Towers website (**www.altontowers.com**) sells family tickets, which could save you up to £14 (phone 08705 20 40 60 ✉).

Use loyalty points Supermarkets, such as Sainsbury's and Tesco have schemes whereby you can exchange loyalty points for tickets to theme parks for as little as £5.50.

FAMILY FARE REDUCTIONS

Buy a family railcard By paying just £20 a year, you can save 30% on most adult rail fares and 60% on child fares. There is also a railcard available to 16-to-25-year-olds, again priced at £20, and entitling the bearer to 30% off rail fares. These cards pay for themselves within a few trips, depending on the length of the journey.

Reduced fares Even if you don't have a railcard, anyone under the age of 16 is entitled to reduced railway fares (14 and 15-year-olds must carry a photocard as proof of age).

Travelcards An off-peak (after 9.30am) one-day family travelcard from London Transport for zones 1–6 will take one or two adults and up to four children all over London by tube, train or bus. It costs £3.60 for each adult and 80p for each child. There are no time restrictions on weekend travelcards and children travel for free. For more information, see **www.visitlondon.com/travel** ✉. There are comparable travel offers in many other parts of Britain. In Manchester you can buy a one-day Wayfarer group ticket that will give two adults and two children unlimited travel by bus, train or tram, with no time restrictions, throughout much of the northwest for £14. Visit **www.gmpte.com** ✉.

Plan ahead By using other travel websites such as **www.thetrainline.com** ✉ you can make substantial savings, as long as you specify your travel dates, avoid peak travel times and book at least a week in advance.

keep it simple

WHEN TO LEAVE THE CAR AT HOME

If you're taking the children out for the day, check at your local rail or coach station for family deals to places of interest and major attractions such as theme parks. These deals often include money-off vouchers or even the full price of admission. An all-in-one ticket for Leeds Castle in Kent, covering rail travel from London to the nearest station, coach to the castle and admission, costs £17.70 – a saving of £8 on what you would have to pay otherwise.

Family affairs

It is vitally important that your family is financially protected from unexpected events, and you are secure in old age. Find out about ways of reducing insurance and other costs, and entitlements that can help you.

LIFE AND HEALTH INSURANCE

If you have a family, or anybody who would suffer financially if you died, it is essential to take out life insurance. Yet many people leave their loved ones dangerously exposed – more than three million families have no financial protection against the death of the breadwinner. And death isn't the only threat to your family's financial security. Serious illness, either to the main earner or whoever is looking after the children, can be a major financial blow. You are three times more likely to suffer a serious illness such as heart disease or cancer before the age of 65 than die, so you should consider protecting yourself accordingly.

LIFE COVER OPTIONS

The good news is that life insurance is that rare thing, a product that has been getting steadily cheaper. So if you haven't got a policy, signing up could cost less than you think. And if you already have cover, you could save money by replacing it with a cheaper plan.

Term insurance The simplest, cheapest and most popular form of life cover is known as term insurance, taken out by more than nine out of ten people. You are charged premiums for a set term, typically 20–25 years, and your dependants receive a tax-free payout if you die within that period. There is no cash-in value at any stage, which means if you outlive the plan you'll get nothing back. But you are free to cancel your plan any time, simply by stopping your monthly premium.

Whole-of-life cover Life insurance that lasts for as long as you do, paying a tax-free lump sum whenever you die, is less common and more expensive. Premiums for this type of cover have fallen around 30% during the last five years, largely due to rising life expectancy and greater competition between insurance companies. If you took out a policy some time ago you could save money by ditching this in favour of a new, more competitive one.

TOP TIPS GET THE POLICY YOU NEED

Make sure you aren't paying for more insurance than you require by getting the right sort of policy at the right price.

■ **Check for options** It's worth looking for the lowest rate, either online, by telephone or using a specialist insurance broker. Don't just accept a plan that your bank or existing insurance company are offering, as you may well get a better deal elsewhere.

■ **Keep it simple** Life insurance is a simple product, and provided you buy from a reputable company offering a competitive deal, you can hardly go wrong.

■ **Pick a policy** If you are covering your mortgage, consider a 'decreasing' term policy, where the amount of insurance and therefore your monthly premium falls steadily as your outstanding mortgage is paid off. Other alternatives are 'level' term, where your monthly premiums and insured

---

MOTHERS AT HOME NEED LIFE AND HEALTH INSURANCE TOO

One in three mothers have no life or health insurance cover. They assume that because they aren't earning, they don't need to be insured. But it's worth considering how the father would look after the children if something happened to the mother. Mothers are worth £30,000 a year in unpaid housework and informal childcare. Most men couldn't afford to pay that from their salaries, and unless they have insurance, they could be forced to give up work.

PAYING LESS FOR TERM ASSURANCE

In 1999, 30-year-old Martin Hay took out £100,000 life cover over a 25-year term for £191 a year. At the time, this was the least expensive life insurance policy he could find. Fortunately Martin was not a smoker, or identical life cover would have cost him £268 a year. Five years later, in 2004, Martin found that there were now even cheaper term assurance policies available. He could pay less by switching to a new policy lasting for the remaining 20 years of his original contract. Martin could now buy cover for as little as £109 a year, saving £82 a year. (A smoker would pay around £200, saving around £70.) If Martin had been older, he would have made even greater savings by switching policies, though the annual premium would have been higher because of his greater age. Martin took out the new plan before ending his old policy, so as not to risk being temporarily without life cover.

amount remained fixed for the term of the policy, and 'increasing' term, where both premiums and insured amount increase every year.

■ **The cheapest option** Another insurance option is Family Income Benefit. If you die, this pays out a tax-free annual income to your family for the remaining term of the policy. This is cheaper than most term insurance policies, because if you die, say, with five years to go on your policy, it only has to pay out the remaining five years' worth of income, rather than the full lump sum.

■ **Avoid inheritance tax** Write the policy into trust (see page 115). This will ensure your tax-free payout falls outside your estate for inheritance tax purposes. Most insurance companies will provide the relevant trust forms.

HEALTH INSURANCE OPTIONS

The two most popular health insurance policy options are critical illness cover (CIC) and income protection. In an ideal world you would take out both, but most people choose one or the other.

Be sure of a payout

CRITICAL ILLNESS COVER

This form of health insurance pays out a tax-free lump sum if you are diagnosed with a serious illness such as cancer, heart disease or a stroke. Some policies cover up to 40 illnesses (check how many yours offers – and which ones), and you'll still receive the cash if you recover quickly.

Combine life and CIC Many people take CIC to cover their mortgage, and you can save money by taking a combined life and CIC policy over a set term. This will only pay out once, either if you suffer a serious illness or in the event of your death. As with ordinary life insurance, take several quotes in order to find a deal with the cheapest premiums, and write your policy into trust to avoid inheritance tax if you should die (see page 115).

INCOME PROTECTION

Sometimes known as permanent health insurance, income protection pays a tax-free monthly income if you fall ill and are unable to continue working. Unlike CIC, it pays if you are off work due to stress or back trouble, two of the most common causes of workplace absence.

Long-term benefits The income will continue until you recover or, if you don't, until you reach retirement age. This means if you fall seriously ill the policy could pay out for many years, although this makes income protection more expensive than CIC.

TOP TIPS REDUCING INCOME PROTECTION PREMIUMS

■ **Extend the deferral period** You can opt to receive benefits 4, 8, 13, 26 or 52 weeks after you stop working, living on your savings in the interim. This cuts your premiums, but still gives you protection from long-term sickness absence.

■ **Save on sickness benefits** Check how much the state and your employer will pay if you fall sick, as this could reduce the amount you need to fund yourself.

■ **Don't overinsure** Because the payout is free of tax, you only need to cover half or two-thirds of your salary. Work out how much you need to live on each month.

■ **Be sure of a payout** Income protection policies will pay out if: you are prevented from doing your own job; you are prevented from doing your own job and any other job to which you are suited by training and experience; or you are prevented from doing any job at all. The first definition is the one to opt for when choosing your policy. Although it will cost you slightly more, you are assured a payout.

MORTGAGE PAYMENT PROTECTION INSURANCE (MPPI)

Sometimes called accident, sickness and unemployment (ASU) cover, MPPI covers your monthly mortgage repayment for a limited period, so you don't lose your home following illness or redundancy. Payouts are tax-free. One in three homeowners now take out MPPI when they set up a new mortgage.

Cover costs Cover ranges from between £3.50 and £6 for each £100 of mortgage repayment you protect, so if your mortgage bill is £500 a month, you can pay between £17.50 and £30 to protect it.

Limited cover MPPI only typically covers you for 12 or 24 months. If you are ill or unemployed for longer than that, the money could dry up. Income protection covers you for much longer, although it doesn't protect against unemployment.

One or the other A good MPPI policy should allow you to buy accident and sickness cover without unemployment cover – or the other way around.

ASK YOURSELF

WHAT MPPI COVER DO I NEED, IF ANY?

To find out whether you need MPPI with accident and sickness cover, or unemployment cover, or both, ask yourself the following questions:

■ **If I'm made redundant, will I struggle to find a new job?** If there are plenty of opportunities in your field, you can probably do without the unemployment element.

■ **Am I eligible for MPPI unemployment cover?** You can't claim unemployment cover if you are self-employed, take voluntary redundancy, resign from your job, take early retirement in lieu of redundancy or work in temporary employment.

■ **What other insurance do I have?** If you have income protection, or access to a good sick pay scheme, you may only need unemployment cover, or no cover at all.

■ **Is my mortgage lender offering me a good deal?** If you are offered a policy where you pay more than £5 for each £100, you will probably find a better deal with another MPPI provider.

■ **When can I claim?** Some policies won't pay for the first 30 or 60 days of unemployment or illness, by which time you may have recovered or found a new job. Others allow immediate claims. Read the small print carefully.

WILLS AND INHERITANCE TAX

Dying intestate – that is, without leaving a will – means you lose your chance to divide your estate to make it more effective in avoiding inheritance tax (IHT).

TOP TIPS **SAVE ON WRITING A WILL**

You can produce your will in a number of ways, varying in complexity and cost. Make sure you choose the method that is most suited to your circumstances and budget. But be warned: self-penned testaments spark the majority of court cases.

■ **Do-it-yourself: £0** If you feel able to master the complexities of will writing, you can get a couple of books from the library and draw up your own. Following the essential wording for the beginning and end, you might be able to find your way through the subject well enough to write out your instructions. But you will need to make sure that it is properly witnessed and your executor knows where it is kept. This may not be the best solution if your family situation is complicated.

■ **Use a template: £10** Wills that have been preprinted, with blanks for the essential information you need to insert, are available for as little as £10 from leading stationers. First of all, you will need to calculate the worth of your 'net estate', which is the amount remaining in your name after funeral expenses and any outstanding debts have been deducted. Write down the full names of everyone you wish to benefit and how much they should receive, and make a gift of any residue – otherwise it could go to the Crown, or the wrong relative. While this is undoubtedly the cheapest means of drawing up a will, it is probably not the best if your affairs are at all complex.

■ **Online savings: £30** If you know what you want to achieve but aren't confident about drawing up your own will, look online for solicitors who will take your instructions over the Internet. This way, they will be checked over by an expert but you minimise your use of an expensive lawyer's time. As long as your instructions are clear and straightforward, getting your affairs in order could cost as little as £30.

■ **High-street solicitors: £100** If in any doubt, go to a solicitor, who will charge from £100 for a relatively straightforward single person's will, or around £150 for a couple. Take comfort from knowing that this outlay now could save your family thousands of pounds after your death. If you don't have a solicitor, contact the Law Society for recommendations. You can keep the time – and therefore cost – to a minimum by having a clear objective of what you want. Filling out a will template before visiting the solicitor will often help to clarify your thinking, even if the solicitor draws up the final version.

■ **Try your bank** Your bank almost certainly provides a will writing service. Contact your branch for details.

RESOURCES

WILLS AND INHERITANCE TAX

■ You can find a low-cost expert online. The Will Site, for example, can prepare a single will from £59, checked by a solicitor. Find it at **www.thewillsite.co.uk** ✉.

■ For information on making a will, contact The Society of Will Writers on 01522 687 888 **www.willwriters.com** ✉.

■ To view the Inland Revenue's information on inheritance tax, go to the website **www.inland revenue.gov.uk** ✉ and search for 'inheritance tax'.

INHERITANCE TAX PLANNING

Inheritance tax (IHT) is paid by your estate on your death if the value of your assets exceeds the nil-rate threshold of £263,000 (at the 2004–2005 rate). Anything above this threshold is taxed at 40%, unless it is left to your spouse or charity in which case no tax whatsoever is payable. The tax should be paid within six months, and your friends and family cannot benefit from your estate until the duty has been cleared.

Not just for the rich Many people regard IHT as a problem for the seriously wealthy, but millions of homeowners are likely to be caught in the net, because the value of their properties counts as part of their estate. With house prices rising much faster than annual increases in the IHT threshold, more and more people will face an IHT bill. But with a little planning and a simple procedure you can slash the tax you pay.

DISCRETIONARY WILL TRUSTS

Setting up a discretionary will trust now could save your loved ones tens of thousands of pounds in future tax bills.

Planning ahead Make a provision in your will for assets up to the current £263,000 IHT threshold to go into a discretionary trust, with the remainder going to the surviving spouse, and there will be no tax bill on either transaction. This effectively gives your estate a combined nil-rate band of £526,000, by using both you and your spouse's nil-rate band. Without the will trust, the nil-rate band of the first partner who dies is effectively lost. When the surviving spouse eventually dies, their assets, and those of the trust, will pass to children or other beneficiaries. Tax is only paid on any amount held by the second spouse that exceeds the IHT threshold at the time – the £263,000 previously transferred to the trust is free of tax.

> **keep it simple**
>
> **SAVE £100S ON LAWYERS' FEES**
> If you think that all your worldly goods will go to your spouse whether you have a will or not, think again.
> Brothers, sisters and even parents may make a claim which, if taken up, could cause your estate to be eaten up by costly lawyers' fees.

CASE STUDY

GAINING A GREATER INHERITANCE

John and Nancy Williams owned a house together valued at £400,000 and had other savings worth £50,000, giving total assets of £450,000. A few years ago, they drafted their wills to include discretionary trusts. John died in August 2004, and £263,000 (equivalent to the nil-rate band in the tax year ending 2005) of his estate passed to the discretionary trust. The remaining £187,000 went to Nancy. There was no inheritance tax (IHT) due at this stage. Nancy can now use assets held in the discretionary trust, effectively borrowing from the trust and giving IOUs that will be repaid upon her death. If, when Nancy dies, the value of her £187,000 is below the IHT threshold at the time, their estate won't have paid a single penny in tax. (Without the discretionary trust, Nancy would have inherited all £450,000 worth of assets on John's death.) On Nancy's death, everything she owns above the IHT threshold at that point will be taxed at 40%. The amount of tax paid will depend on how much her estate was worth and the IHT threshold at the time. For example, if she were to die in the same financial year as John, with assets still worth £450,000 and the IHT threshold at £263,000, the Inland Revenue would charge tax at 40% on £187,000. This would hand a massive £74,800 to the taxman – money that could have been saved for their children with a little more forward planning.

PENSIONERS' BENEFITS AND ENTITLEMENTS

Almost every pensioner is entitled to benefits. A number may apply to you, to boost your income or offset the costs of care at home or in a residential or nursing home.

TOP TIPS **COMMONLY MISSED BENEFITS**

Don't be one of the huge number of pensioners who are missing out on benefits – Age Concern estimates that £1 billion in pensioner benefits remain unclaimed each year. Make sure you keep up-to-date with the benefits systems. Even if you have savings or a large house, you should still check out your entitlements.

■ **Pension Credit** Experts estimate that nearly half of all pensioners are entitled to the tax-free Pension Credit. Introduced in October 2003, Pension Credit has two parts. The first part is a Guarantee Credit that gives a minimum income guarantee if you are aged 60 or over – it tops up income to £105.45 a week for a single person and £160.95 for a couple. The second part is a means-tested Savings Credit that provides extra money to many people aged 65. You may be eligible for the Guarantee Credit or the Savings Credit, or both. Contact your local Pension Service for help in filling out your claim on freephone 0800 99 1234, or see **www.thepensionservice.gov.uk/pensioncredit** ✉.

■ **Housing Benefit** Although this is means-tested, people over 60 may still be able to claim – even if they have some savings – and get help paying their rent.

■ **Attendance Allowance** One of the few benefits for the elderly available irrespective of income or savings, the Attendance Allowance is available to people aged 65 and over who need help with everyday tasks such as washing and dressing. The Benefits Agency decide whether you are eligible or not; get specialist advice from Age Concern or a similar agency on exactly how to fill out the form so as to present your case in the best way. The allowances in 2004 are £39.35 a week for help day or night, and £58.80 for help both day and night.

keep it simple

HOW TO APPLY FOR BENEFITS
Pick up information leaflets at your post office, social security office or local authority.

For help with your entitlements, contact your local social security office (in the phone book under Benefits Agency or Social Security) or the Department for Work and Pensions (DWP). Visit the DWP website at **www.dwp.org.uk** ✉ for information and to download relevant application forms.

CASE STUDY

INFORMED ADVICE NETTED £15.51 A WEEK
Valerie Roberts reaped the benefits of accepting help from a Pension Service officer in filling out her claim. A single woman living on her own, she was already receiving the Guarantee Credit part of the Pension Credit, which topped up her weekly income to £105.45. When she turned 65 in 2004, she became eligible to apply for the Savings Credit element of the Pension Credit, but was not sure whether she would gain anything by doing so, because the calculations seemed so complicated. An Age Concern fact-sheet advised her: 'You are likely to be entitled to Savings Credit if as a single person your income is less than around £144 a week and if as a couple your joint income is less than £211.50 a week.' Encouraged by this, she decided to claim with the help of the Pension Service and was delighted to discover that she would receive an additional £15.51 each week.

WATCH POINTS **HELP FOR YOUR HOME**

In addition to the usual benefits, pensioners can also get help with costs relating to maintaining their home.

■ **Heating and insulation** If you are 60 or over, your household is eligible to receive a tax-free Winter Fuel Payment. In 2004, this was £200 if you were the only eligible person in your household, £100 if there were others also eligible, and £200 for those receiving Pension Credit.

■ **Maintenance and repairs** Local housing authorities can provide assistance in repairing and improving housing, in the form of grants, loans, materials and labour. Contact your local authority or nearest Citizens Advice Bureau to see a copy of the local authority's Housing Renewal Policy.

FINANCIAL HELP WITH HEALTH CARE

Although some concessions – such as dental treatment – are means-tested, there are entitlements available which are automatic. Those aged 60 and over are entitled to free prescriptions and eye tests regardless of any savings they may have, although the cost of glasses is not subsidised.

TAKE ADVANTAGE OF TRAVEL ENTITLEMENTS

If you know your entitlements, you can benefit from the special rates offered to pensioners for many products and services on different types of transport.

Save 50%–100% on public transport People over the age of 60 can get a concessionary or free bus pass, which entitles the bearer to a discount of at least 50% on all bus travel within their local authority area. For information about free and concessionary bus passes contact your local authority or the nearest branch of the Citizens Advice Bureau.

Save up to 30% on train fares The Senior Railcard costs just £20 a year and provides fare reductions to anyone aged 60 or over. This saves a third off most rail fares in Great Britain, Northern Ireland and Eire. For details see **www.senior-railcard.co.uk** or phone the National Rail Enquiry Service on 08547 484950 ✉. Senior railcard users can also buy a Rail Plus Senior Card for £12 which gives savings of up to 25% on cross-border rail travel in Europe (phone 08705 848 848 or visit **www.raileurope.co.uk** ✉).

Save up to 50% on coach fares Half-price coach fares are available to anyone aged 60 or over on National Express coaches (**www.nationalexpress.com** or 08705 808080 ✉). Use Yellow Pages to check with smaller local participating coach companies. (See *Good-value travel,* page 182.)

CHEAPER TV VIEWING

Watch TV for free If you are aged 75 or over you are eligible for a free television licence for your household. You just need to apply for it. See **www.tv-l.co.uk** or call 0870 241 6468 ✉ for further details.

Concessionary licence The Accommodation for Residential Care (ARC) concessionary TV licence, costing just £5, is for those who are aged 60 plus and living in sheltered accommodation or a care home. Residents aged 75 or over are entitled to a free television licence. The full TV licence fee is paid for a television in a communal area.

RESOURCES

GREY POWER

■ Britain's two largest organisations working with and for older people are Age Concern **www.ageconcern.org.uk** 0800 009966 ✉ and Help the Aged **www.helptheaged.org.uk** 0800 800 6565 ✉. Both produce fact sheets on a wide range of subjects, including benefits, entitlements and care in old age. The Age Concern website in particular has links to many other organisations of potential interest to older people.

■ The Saga Group **www.saga.co.uk** 0800 414 525 ✉ aims to provide high-quality, value-for-money services for people aged 50 plus. These include holidays **www.sagaholidays.co.uk** or 0800 056 6088, a magazine (01303 771525 or 01303 771526) and insurance and financial products.

■ There are many websites specialising in education and leisure for the over 50s. Try: **www.laterlife.com** **www.seniority.co.uk** and **www.hellsgeriactrics.co.uk**

CUT THE COST OF CARE IN OLD AGE

Plan for the future and consider your options, so that if you or a relative needs to go into care, you can make an informed choice and know how to get the best deals.

TOP TIPS THE BEST DEALS ON CARE HOMES

There are essentially two categories of homes – local authority homes, and independent care homes (either private homes, or voluntary homes often catering for particular professions or religions). Get a copy of The Nursing Homes Directory (**www.ucarewecare.com** or ring 07092 035131 ✉), or the A-Z Care Homes Guide (**www.carehome.co.uk** or ring 01488 684 321 ✉), a national guide to care homes with 18,000 listings. For local authority homes, contact your local council.

■ **Get subsidised care if you can** The amount you pay for a place in a local authority care home is means-tested and subsidised where appropriate. The same holds true for independent homes if they accept residents on local authority funding. As the average weekly cost to stay in a care home is £329 (over £17,000 per year) having part or all of your fee paid makes a big difference to your finances.

■ **Try for a reduction at an independent home** If you are not receiving local authority funding, but your independent care home of choice takes local authority subsidised residents, find out what your local authority pays for a place; it may well be less than what a self-funding individual pays, and you may be able to use this information to negotiate a price reduction.

FUNDING CARE

Your local authority will examine your finances to determine whether you will have to pay towards care.

Property included For 2004–2005, if you have capital or savings over £20,000 (including the value of your home unless it's still occupied by your partner or a dependent relative) you will be expected to meet the full costs of care.

Council loans If you don't have a partner or dependent relative living-in, and must sell your home, and your capital and savings other than your home amount to less than £20,000, you can claim the right to have your local authority pay your fees for the first 12 weeks of care. After that time, if your house is still unsold, the local authority will lend you the amount of your fees, but you will have to repay them once you receive the proceeds of the sale.

TRANSFERRING ASSETS

Be careful if you are considering transferring assets to someone else in anticipation of your move into a care home (see left). There are now strict rules about 'deliberate deprivation of capital' and you could end up costing yourself and your family a great deal more than you were attempting to save.

Separate your assets

If you are living with a partner and one of you needs to move into a care home, the local authority will divide your income to calculate your contribution to care home fees.

■ As long as one of you lives in your home, its value won't be taken into account, so make sure your local authority is aware of the remaining resident.

■ Only 50% of any private pension should be taken into account.

■ Your savings will be divided equally. It's best to split your assets before the local authority becomes involved, and to make sure that any care-home costs are paid from the accounts of the person in the home.

SMART MOVES

LONG-TERM CARE INSURANCE

With care home fees escalating rapidly, it's a good idea to consider care fee payment plans that will pay your fees. There are two types of plan, both regulated by the Financial Services Authority: prefunded long-term care insurance (LTCI), which you buy in anticipation of future need, and an immediate care annuity, which is suitable if you have to move into a home and don't have any other provision. **What's in it for you?** The main benefit of these schemes is peace of mind that the care home fees will be paid for the rest of your life, and not just until your capital runs out. In addition, you hopefully still have some assets remaining after buying the annuity, which can cover any other expenses, or can be left to benefit your family.

HELP WITH THE COST OF CARERS

There is a benefit called Carer's Allowance that is available to those who look after someone else in an informal way – they might be a relative, a friend or a neighbour. To get it, the carer has to spend at least 35 hours a week giving personal care.

Find out if you qualify The carer has to be at least 16 years old, and the person being cared for has to be receiving an Attendance Allowance or a disability allowance. The Carer's Allowance is basically £44.35 a week (2004 rates), but it can vary depending on any other benefits the carer receives. It is not generally available to those who earn more than £79 a week (in 2004), though the carer's savings are not taken into account. Contact your local Benefits Agency, or claim online at **www.dwp.gov.uk** ✉ for details.

RESOURCES

HELP WITH CARE

■ Age Concern and Help the Aged have useful fact sheets (see *Resources*, page 117).
■ The Nursing Home Fees Agency **www.nhfa.co.uk** ✉ also has guidance on benefits and entitlements to help fund the cost of care.
■ Find out which are the best care homes by contacting the Commission for Social Care Inspection, which registers and inspects care homes. See **www.csci.org.uk** 0845 015 0120 ✉ for the address of your nearest office.
■ Care Choices at **www.carechoices.co.uk** ✉ has listings of care homes nationwide.

GETTING THE BEST CARE

These are the main types of care available for the elderly, both at home and in a residential facility. How much you pay for each level of care is affected by a number of personal circumstances and other relevant factors:

■ Your income, savings and capital (which may include the value of your home) are all taken into account when local authority social services calculate how much they expect you to pay towards your care.

■ Local authorities vary in their interpretation of relevant regulations and guidelines, and so differ in how much they will contribute, and their charges.

■ In addition, England and Wales, Scotland and Northern Ireland all differ in what they ask you to pay towards the cost of your care.

■ All the costs shown below may be reduced after means-testing.

TYPE OF CARE	SERVICE PROVIDED	COST
Home help	Household tasks and general care	£7–£15 an hour
At-home nursing	Nursing and personal care	£15–£20 an hour
Residential homes	Room, board and personal care	£300–£600+ a week
Nursing homes	Room, board and personal care	£400–£600+ a week

Animal matters

No one would claim that keeping a pet is primarily a question of cost. But why spend more than you have to when there are so many money-saving ways of obtaining and caring for a much-loved member of the family?

AFFORDABLE ANIMALS

Don't pay more than you need, but take care that an inexpensive pet does not bring long-term expenses.

RESCUED PETS ARE A DOUBLE BLESSING

Offering a caring home to an unwanted animal is a satisfying experience, and it can save you money too.

Benefits Animals offered through charities have normally been vet-checked, vaccinated, neutered and sometimes even microchipped. Some charities expect adoptive owners to pay towards these costs – the cost of adopting a vaccinated, microchipped, vet-checked, wormed, neutered dog from the RSPCA (Royal Society for the Prevention of Cruelty to Animals) is £85–£100. You will also receive free expert advice on the animal's care.

Potential problems Although many animals rehomed in this way make excellent pets, some come with ingrained behavioural problems. Be prepared to spend some time on retraining if necessary.

FRIENDS MAY NOT CHARGE AT ALL

If an acquaintance has an animal that has given birth, this can be an inexpensive way of acquiring a new pet.

Benefits You will usually be charged a fraction of the going price – if anything – though you should offer the cost of a similar animal (see Resources overleaf). This option lets you visit the animal many times before buying so you get to know your pet before making a commitment.

Potential problems Get a written guarantee if you pay a near-market price. If the animal is ill, or turns out to have congenital problems, it may be embarrassing to make a complaint, and having a guarantee document makes the situation clearer if you need to seek legal redress later.

FREE ADVICE BEFORE BUYING

If you have queries on types of pet, breeds or general care, take advantage of free resources.

Pet shops A good pet shop – though not a cheap option – can give you valuable guidance on buying a first pet, and you can get your money's worth if you ask for plenty of free advice, including after your pet is at home.

Rescue centres Organisations such as the RSPCA ✉, Cats Protection ✉, and Dogs Trust ✉ offer free advice to potential pet owners to help to prevent problems they may not have foreseen.

RESCUED PEDIGREE ANIMALS

If you want to adopt a rescued animal but have set your heart on a particular breed, it is quicker to contact a breed-specific rescue than to wait for your chosen animal to turn up at your local general rescue centre. Websites such as The Dog Rescue Pages at **www.dogpages.org.uk** ✉ list specialist canine rescues. For cats, try The Cat Rescue Resource on CatChat at **www.catchat.org** ✉, which has a similar list for cats.

keep it simple

COSTLY ERRORS

■ Don't buy an animal you don't have time to look after properly. Paying someone else to exercise and care for your pet can be costly – dogs need up to five hours a day to exercise, feed, groom and train.

■ Check bloodlines and avoid animals with a family history of ailments. Many pedigree dogs have inbred health problems, such as labradors with dodgy hips, cocker spaniels with autoimmune disease, bulldogs with breathing difficulties and dachshunds with bad backs. These breeds can have hefty long-term vet bills.

■ Don't buy an unhealthy animal. A dog or cat should have a glossy coat, bright eyes, clean teeth and an alert manner. A rabbit or other small mammal should have a rounded shape, a bird should be alert and fish should swim easily and have no lumps or fungal growths.

SPECIALIST BREEDERS

If you are after a particular breed of animal, or if you want to breed or show your pet, buying directly from a specialist breeder is probably the best option. Use a resource such as **www.breederdirectory.co.uk** ✉ to select a dog breed and locate a suitable breeder. Alternatively, you can contact the Kennel Club (0870 606 6750 or use their website **www.the-kennel-club.org.uk** ✉) to find registered breeders.
Benefits The price you pay will not have the percentage that is added by a pet shop, and you will have details of the background of the animal you are buying.
Potential problems There should be none if you make sure that the breeder sells animals registered with the accepted authority for the breed (the Kennel Club for dogs or the Governing Council of the Cat Fancy for cats) and that the animals are vaccinated and healthy. Ask if tests have been carried out for genetic disease, or whether there is a history of skin or joint problems, and try to see the parents as they should give you a clue to the animal's eventual size and temperament.

PEDIGREE PETS FOR LESS

A pedigree animal can be expensive, but there are savings to be made if you ask the right questions.
Not for show If you don't intend to show your animal, ask for a 'pet' standard rather than a 'show' standard. There may be a slight 'defect' in colour or posture that is unacceptable in a show animal but won't make the slightest difference in a family pet. You could get a pet standard Burmese cat, for example, for £100 rather than £200.
Golden oldies Animals that are too old to breed are also considerably cheaper but no less lovable. Opt for one in good health and with plenty of energy.
Don't follow the herd Popularity in breeds and colours changes from year to year, but this is purely subjective. If you opt for a less popular breed you could get yourself a fine animal and a real bargain.

SHARE A PET

If you can't afford the time or money for an expensive pet, you can still enjoy their companionship.
Horses and ponies These are beyond the reach of most households, but a particularly keen youngster could try volunteering at a local stable. Your child will learn about horses, get to feed and groom them and possibly be able to ride occasionally for free.
Volunteer pet care Local animal rescue centres, as well as many community schemes to help senior citizens, need people to walk animals and take care of pets' routine needs. By volunteering to help, you will gain much of the day-to-day pleasure of a pet for free.
Dog walking for the blind Sign up with your local charity for this worthwhile way to spend time with an intelligent, well-bred, well-trained dog.
Petsitting for the holidays Advertise locally or contact pet-owners' clubs to offer your services. Most owners would be glad to share their pet with you.

RESOURCES

CHECK PRICES AND AVAILABILITY

■ Get to know the market for cats and dogs by visiting the various shows and competitions. Crufts is the biggest dog show in the UK and is held annually in March at Birmingham's NEC. Discover Dogs, held at Earls Court in November, is another good event. For a list of smaller charity events, visit **www.dogpages.org.uk** ✉. For cats, call 01278 42757 or visit **www.ourcats.co.uk** ✉ for a complete listing of shows in all areas of the country, including the Supreme Cat Show, held at the Birmingham NEC in November.

■ To see what other people have paid for pets, from dogs and cats to exotic birds and fish, visit comparison websites such as **www.dooyou.co.uk** ✉ or **www.ciao.co.uk** ✉.

■ For more help with choosing a pet, see the RSPCA website **www.rspca.org.uk** (0870 3335 888) ✉ or the PDSA website **www.pdsa.org.uk** (0800 917 2509) ✉ or buy one of the RSPCA *Care for Your Pet* booklets, available at £3.99.

MEALS ON A BUDGET

Pet food outlets and discount Internet sites are a cheaper source of tinned and dry food than your local supermarket or pet shop. But there are other sources of cheap – and even free – pet food you should consider.

BUYING IN BULK
Check out the online shop at **www.petplanet.co.uk** (0845 345 0723) ✉, which offers special deals on all types of pet food, while **www.petsathome.com** (0161 486 6688) ✉ advertises its latest offers, though you will need to visit a store to buy. If you buy in sufficient bulk, you will often avoid delivery charges, so if you don't have room for storage, share with a friend.

CHEAP CUTS FROM THE BUTCHER
High-quality protein is essential to a healthy diet for cats and dogs and meat is a great source. Unlike humans, pets don't object to offcuts and the cheaper, less meaty cuts that cost very little, such as pigs' trotters and oxtail.
Raw or cooked Any fresh meat fit for human consumption can be fed raw, but any other meat must be well-cooked.
Cheap meat Meats such as offal and chicken wings are nutritious and cheap.
Bones for health Raw bones are great for teeth and a good source of calcium. Don't give cooked bones – especially chicken bones – to dogs (see right).

FREE VITAMINS FROM WEEDS
Garden weeds can be nutritious for rabbits, guinea pigs and small rodents. Wash them well before feeding to your pet.

BEWARE FALSE ECONOMY
Foods you should never give to your pet, no matter how cheap:
Dogs Cooked bones may splinter and cause injury or choking. Raw chicken bones, or chocolate in quantities, can kill.
Cats Vegetarian diets can't supply adequate nutrition. Milk can cause gastro-intestinal problems.
Rabbits Large quantities of dandelion can act as a laxative.
Birds Chocolate and avocado can kill parrot-like species such as budgies. A seed-only diet can also shorten your bird's life.

HOW COSTS OF PET FOOD COMPARE

A 1999 *Sunday Times* survey found that feeding your dog human-grade food from a supermarket, while not providing a complete diet, could actually work out cheaper than a conventional diet that was specifically manufactured for dogs. A *Which?* survey found that mid-range and even cheap complete diets for pets were just as nutritious as the most expensive ranges of pet food, at a saving of up to 75%.

| | Foods eaten by humans | Specially manufactured pet food |

DOG — CHICKEN WINGS, RICE & VEG / TINNED FOOD WITH MIXER
CAT — FRESH LIVER / DRY CAT FOOD
RABBIT — VEGETABLES / DRY RABBIT MIX

£1.00 per kilo   £2.00 per kilo

Delicious homemade treats

DIY DOG CHEWS

Don't buy your dog expensive rawhide chews – give him or her a carrot full of healthy vitamins.

Pennywise As a medium dog chew costs around 80p and a carrot costs only 6p, even if you have to replace the carrot frequently, this is a major saving.

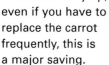

BUDGET CAT TREATS

Instead of buying cat treats, make your own for a fraction of the price. Mix the following ingredients, and place ¼ teaspoon dollops onto a greased baking tray.

- 185g tin of mackerel or tuna in oil
- 1 cup of wholemeal breadcrumbs
- 1 beaten egg
- ½ tsp brewers' yeast

Bake at 180°C/250°F/gas mark 4 for eight minutes. The treats can be kept for three weeks in the fridge or even longer if frozen.

Pennywise Cat treats cost around 80p for a 50g bag, whereas the recipe above gives you four times as much for less outlay. Fish provides valuable proteins, and the brewers' yeast contains fatty acids and B-complex vitamins for a glossy coat, healthy nervous system and fewer fleas.

NATURAL RABBIT TREATS

Although you can buy treats for rabbits, they're often not beneficial. Try the following instead – they're cheaper, and better for your pet too.

- Herbs, such as oregano, mint, parsley and thyme.
- Alfalfa (in moderation).

Pennywise Rabbit treats cost around £1.70 for a 120g bag, so growing your own treats is much cheaper.

BUDGIE RECIPE

Give your budgie a snack that will provide hours of chewing fun plus valuable vitamins by offering produce from your garden.

- Fresh eucalyptus or fruit tree twigs or branches.
- The heads of seeding grasses.

Pennywise You'll save the cost of manufactured budgie treats.

FEED FISH CHEAPLY

Save money on fish food by supplying your own.

- Fish love live foods and their condition improves noticeably when fed on them. Buying these from pet shops is expensive, so catch your own mosquito larvae, water fleas and daphnia from nearby ponds and water butts.

Pennywise Live foods cost around 50p a bag, whereas home-caught food is free.

Plants to include are chickweed, clover, coltsfoot, comfrey, cow parsley, groundsel, goosegrass, mallow, meadowsweet, plantains, sow thistle, vetches and yarrow.

TOP TIPS AVOIDING WASTE

You can get a great deal on the pet food you buy only to find it goes to waste because you don't serve it properly. Here are some canny ways of making food go further.

- **Cats eat more of lower-grade food** Cats tend to regulate their intake of vital nutrients. Feeding a cheaper, less-nutritious brand of cat food is not necessarily a cost saver – the cat has to eat more to derive the same benefit. Cat food should contain around 26% protein, in the form of meat, chicken or fish (vegetable protein isn't as useful).
- **Dogs are greedy feeders** Find out the best weight for your dog (your vet can advise you). Feed your pet a regime that suits that weight to avoid wasting food.
- **Rabbits pick and choose** If you give a rabbit a commercial rabbit mix consisting of grains, seeds and cereals, your pet will pick out the parts it likes and leave the rest. For less waste, feed your rabbit a good-quality pellet – which combines all these ingredients – instead.
- **Fish are usually overfed** Fish kept in tanks are usually overfed, which causes polluted water. Skip feeding your fish for at least one day a week for healthier fish.

PAMPER YOUR PETS

It's natural to want to buy your pet the finer things in life, from a luxury cage to a basket full of entertaining toys. Don't bother to feel guilty though – if you know where to look, you needn't break the bank providing for your pet in style.

DESIGNER LABELS AT DISCOUNT PRICES

It's true – Ralph Lauren has gone to the dogs, along with a few other top designers. If you hanker after a Burberry dog blanket or a Louis Vuitton collar and lead, factory outlet stores (check the Directory ✉ under designer names) are the best place to indulge your tastes. You can also snap up bargains at eBay (**www.ebay.co.uk** ✉). Check websites to see if your favourite designer does a range for pets. Z2 Clothing (**www.z2clothing.com** ✉) and other designer clothes sites often offer items for dogs, such as Burberry collar and lead sets in their accessories section.

DES RES FOR POSH PETS

If you have any carpentry skills and your pet needs a wooden hutch or cage, you can easily make your own or adapt a secondhand cupboard. If you sew, make inexpensive luxuries such as catnip mice or a dog blanket from luxurious fabric remnants such as brocade or velvet, or copy ideas on the cheap from upmarket glossy magazines.

RECYCLE YOUR OWN BELONGINGS

Dogs love to chew on cotton towels, knotted socks, cotton rope and old stuffed toys – but check these for safety before handing them over (see below). Cats enjoy chasing ping-pong balls or plastic golf trainer balls. Dogs and cats don't need a vast array of toys – let them play with a couple at a time and change them round every few weeks.

USE UP HOUSEHOLD WASTE

You can give rodents the cardboard middles from toilet and kitchen towel rolls to gnaw and use as tunnels.

---

keep it simple

CHEAPER BEDDING

For bedding for your rabbit or other small mammal, buy a straw bale from a farmer or wood shavings and sawdust from a carpenter. This is half the price of buying the same thing in small packs in the pet shop. If you own a paper shredder, use shredded paper for your pet's bedding. As long as you are shredding good quality, non-toxic paper, your pet will be happy.

JUST ONE CAREFUL OWNER

Local newspapers, classified ad magazines such as *Loot*, and websites such as eBay can be great sources of good-value secondhand cages and equipment, so if you can afford to wait, keep an eye on these sources until the right deal comes along. Just make sure you carefully disinfect anything that has been used by another animal.

WATCH POINTS DANGEROUS TOYS

When recycling household items for pets, take the following precautions:

■ **Cut off dangerous bits** Remove buttons and zips from clothing used as bedding, as well as eyes and any small plastic parts that could be swallowed from old soft toys.

■ **Check any wood** Ensure wood has not been treated with a toxic varnish or paint – if necessary, sand down to remove the surface, then re-treat.

LOWER VET BILLS

Of course, you should never stint on veterinary care when it is needed. But it's only wise to shop around for a reliable vet with reasonable charges, and to learn when a trip to the vet isn't necessary after all.

CATCH PROBLEMS EARLY

Make a habit of checking your pet's physical condition every day. If it is a tame animal, feel it all over for any lumps or bruising, and keep an eye on anything that seems unusual.

PICK A VET BEFORE YOU NEED ONE

A *Which?* survey in 2000 found that routine vet care for a healthy cat could vary by as much as £650 over the animal's lifetime, depending on the vet consulted and the area you live in, and concluded that some vets charge almost three times as much as others for routine procedures. So it pays to find a vet you can afford before you need one in a hurry.

Compare costs As there is no national structure for vets' fees, find out the costs of common treatments, such as vaccination, dental care and neutering, from several local vets. Ensure the vet you choose offers good value.

Get a quote Even if you already have a vet, get more than one quotation for any expensive treatment even if you feel it's best to go with your regular practitioner.

SHOP AROUND FOR MEDICINES

You can ask your vet for a prescription and take it along to a high-street pharmacy where it may be filled more cheaply. Most chemists stock products commonly prescribed for

ASK YOURSELF

SHOULD I TAKE MY PET TO THE VET?

Here are a few signs that indicate a prompt visit to the vet is in order:
- The animal is lethargic.
- It is shivering when asleep or has its eyes shut most of the time.
- Your pet is having trouble breathing.
- The animal won't eat.
- It has a severe wound, can't walk, is crying or sensitive to touch.

An ounce of prevention is worth £££ of cure

Get regular checkups Nip problems in the bud with a yearly checkup, costing £15–£30 for a cat or dog.

Think ahead Get to know what health problems your breed is prone to and be on the lookout for them. It is thought that there are 400 hereditary diseases in dogs alone. The Kennel Club publishes a list of breeds and conditions for which DNA tests are available at www.doggenetichealth.org ✉. The tests cost £30–£40 each.

It pays to vaccinate Protect your cat or dog from expensive, even fatal, diseases by getting the vaccinations recommended by the British Veterinary Association. Start in the first weeks of life and follow up with annual boosters.

Monitor weight Stand above your dog or cat and feel its waist. A healthy animal has an indentation behind its ribs. If you can't feel the ribs, chances are your pet is overweight. Ask your vet how much it should weigh, give it more

exercise and don't overfeed.

Keep fur clean to avoid disease Rabbits, for example, are prone to fly strike caused by flies laying their eggs in soiled fur.

Check teeth Tartar, plaque or gum disease can lead to trouble and eventual tooth loss. You can brush the teeth of a cat or dog with a human toothbrush and pet (not human) toothpaste to prevent problems and avoid expensive descaling.

Diet watch Dry food (as opposed to semi-moist) can lessen digestive problems, maintain healthy teeth and prevent obesity.

SMART MOVES

keep it simple

NURSE KNOWS BEST
For minor procedures, such as clipping claws, see a veterinary nurse rather than the vet. This should save you the cost of a full veterinary consultation, which is unnecessary for simple or routine treatments.

RESOURCES

CHECK OUT THE CHAINS
Though it's comforting to have a vet just down the road, regional chains such as Pet Vaccination Clinics (01564 823825 ✉) based in the Midlands specialise in cut-price vaccinations (complete puppy course £21), neutering (£15–£55) and microchipping (£15). Independent vet's fees can be double or more.
■ For free or subsidised pet care, contact one of these veterinary chains or charitable organisations:
RSPCA low-cost neutering vouchers and subsidised vet treatment **www.rspca. org.uk** ✉.
PDSA low-cost neutering vouchers and subsidised vet treatment **www.pdsa. org.uk** ✉.
Blue Cross free means-tested veterinary care **www.bluecross.org.uk** ✉.
Cats Protection half-price neutering vouchers and subsidised vet care **www.cats.org.uk** ✉.

veterinary treatment and will order others for you. According to the Competition Commission, British vets add up to 68% to the price when dispensing medicines.

FREE OR ASSISTED VETERINARY CARE
If you can't afford veterinary care, you may be able to take your pet to an animal charity treatment centre such as those run by the PDSA (People's Dispensary for Sick Animals), RSPCA or Blue Cross for free or assisted treatment.
Are you eligible? You must normally live in the centre's catchment area and be receiving either Housing Benefit or Council Tax Benefit. The number of pets treated may be restricted and some procedures excluded.
Special offers from private practices If you live outside a charity's catchment area, your pet may still be treated if you register with a private practice offering an assisted treatment service, such as the PDSA's PetAid scheme; or you may apply for a grant from the PDSA Special Request Scheme. Telephone 0800 917 2509 ✉ for more details.
Watch for free offers Announcements of free treatment will be on your local council's website, or you can phone for information. The local council's Animal Welfare service may offer free microchipping, vaccinations or neutering. Free or reduced-cost neutering is available from Cats Protection, the RSPCA and many small, independent rescue groups.

THE RIGHT INSURANCE

Some say it is better to save the money you might have spent on insurance premiums and pay your own vet's bills. Only you can weigh up the pros and cons of insuring your pet and decide which, if any, policy is best for you.

MODERN TREATMENTS AND BIGGER BILLS

Medical advances mean that it's now possible to extend a pet's life in ways that were once undreamt of. Today, a dog with a heart condition can be fitted with a £3,000 pacemaker, while a dog with arthritis can have a £2,000 hip replacement. And that is not all: one insurer reported a claim of £36,000 made by the owner of a dog who caused a road accident. Insurance might meet the expense of medical treatment or injury to a third party, but a lifetime's insurance cover can also mount up to several thousand pounds.

WATCH POINTS INSURANCE PITFALLS

A *Which?* survey found that it costs from £50 to £500 a year to insure a dog and £30 to £200 for a cat. Most pet insurance will cover vets' bills for illness and injury, third-party or accidental damage, replacing a deceased pet and disposing of its body, and advertising and paying a reward for a lost pet. Some bargain policies have restrictions such as on cover or payout, or a large excess. Others may vary the fees depending on your locality and the breed of animal insured. Insurance companies will not pay for routine treatments such as vaccinations or neutering.

■ **Maximum claim limit** Check that the maximum claim for one incident falls within a reasonable limit for your pet. For example, a dog that is involved in a traffic accident can cost thousands of pounds to restore to health. When a four-year-old labrador was hit by a car, his owner paid £800 for X-rays and surgery to treat the dog's injuries. Had the dog been insured, this would almost certainly have been fully covered, as the maximum claim limit for most pet insurance policies is generally between £1,500 and £6,000.

■ **Restrictions on cover or payout** Some policies restrict the length of time you can claim for the cost of treating a long-term condition, or put a ceiling on how much money you can claim for treating the condition. This could mean that if your pet is insured and then becomes chronically ill, you may eventually find yourself paying the treatment costs, even though your pet is insured. Avoid this by making sure you choose an insurance policy that will pay out for an indefinite period of time for an ongoing medical condition.

■ **Age limit** Many older pets are uninsurable unless they have been covered by the same insurer from an early age. If an older pet is taken on by an insurance company, the owner will have to pay much heftier premiums than would be paid for a younger animal of the same kind. In addition, you may have to pay a percentage of the total cost of each claim.

■ **Excess payment** Check the amount of the excess and whether it's payable for each claim. Excess fees for veterinary treatment are usually around £50 for each claim

keep it simple

THE BEST POLICY
■ Insure pets from an early age.
■ Insure more than one animal with the same company.
■ Choose a policy with relevant discounts – for senior citizens for example.
■ Make sure the company has the General Insurance Standards Council (GISC) stamp.

BETTER DEALS FOR CITY DWELLERS
If you live in an urban area, choose an insurer that does not price its policies according to where you live. Because vet bills tend to be more expensive in the city, if you choose an insurer that varies fees according to location, you will pay a higher premium for urban living.

for a single condition in one year. The excess for third party liability is generally higher – normally £75–£100 for a dog.

■ **Increase in premiums and limited claims** Many policies automatically increase your premium once you have made a claim. In addition, there may be a limit to the number of claims you can make each year. Make sure you know before you sign on the dotted line.

■ **Exclusions** All policies exclude expenses arising from medical conditions that existed before the policy was taken out. For example, the owner of a cat with diabetes took out a pet insurance policy, but as the diabetes was classed as a pre-existing condition, the owner still had to bear costs of £42 a month for treating the diabetes. Had she insured her pet before the condition developed, the insurers would have paid for the diabetes treatments, although they may have increased the insurance premium.

■ **Switching to another insurer** Because a new policy will exclude all pre-existing conditions, changing to a different insurance company means that the new insurer will not cover the cost of treatment for any conditions for which the old insurer was paying.

RESOURCES

COMPARE INSURANCE RATES

■ Get links to insurance companies offering competitive quotes on **www.find.co.uk** ✉.

■ Compare insurance rates on **www. moneysupermarket.com** ✉.

CHOOSING THE BEST-VALUE PET POLICY

These policy terms are based on a pedigree labrador retriever in the Home Counties, aged 3–4 years. Pedigree animals carry a higher premium as they can have more problems; policies for a pedigree cat or a young mongrel in a city would be different.

Policy Example/ Annual Premium	Maximum annual Vet fees/ Excess each claim	3rd Party Liability/ Excess each claim	Death benefit	Holiday cancelled	Reward if lost	Most suitable for
A £62.50	£1,500/£49	£10m/£75	£350	No	£100	Owners who don't take expensive holidays
B £92.50	£1,500/£49 + 35%	£1m/£75	£350	No	£100	Older dogs (8 years plus)
C £105.24	£2,000/£49	£1.5m/£75	£750	£1,000	£600	Pedigrees/valuable dogs
D £119.04	£3,000/£40	£1m/£200	£300	£300	£300	More than three pets (10% discount)
E £129.91	£3,500/£50-£80 +15% of fee over £500	£2m/£250	£500	£500	£500	Dogs likely to need expensive vet treatment
F £202	£5,000/£35	£2m/£75	£1,000	£1,500	£1,000	Dogs likely to need expensive vet treatment
G £204.11	£6,000/£60	£2m/£250	£1,000	£2,500	£1,000	Valuable dogs; cover for life

Rates as of August 2004

CAREFREE HOLIDAYS

Your holiday will be anything but relaxing if you have to worry about your pets while you're away, or pay nearly the cost of your own holiday on their sojourn at the local kennel. Luckily, there are answers both at home and abroad.

TAKING PETS ABROAD

Although taking cats and dogs to Europe is easier than it was pre-2000, it is still an expensive business. Travelling with your pet by car is the most convenient and cheapest option. But you will have to pay for microchipping, vaccination, a blood test, and a PETS (Pet Travel Scheme) certificate before setting off, and tick and tapeworm treatment before you return – normally totalling around £200. (Most of this expense will have to be repeated each year you travel, except for the microchipping.) But this may be a cost-effective option for longer stays abroad, especially if you take trips regularly.

Countries in the PETS scheme European countries to which you can safely take your pet under PETS rules include Austria, Belgium, Denmark, Finland, France, Germany, Greece, Iceland, Italy, Luxembourg, the Netherlands, Norway, Portugal, Spain, Sweden and Switzerland. Non-European countries include Australia, New Zealand, USA and Canada. For an up-to-date list, see the Pet Travel Scheme on the DEFRA (Department of Environment Food and Rural Affairs) website at **www.defra.gov.co** ✉.

PETS WELCOME HERE

If you are taking a holiday in the UK, it often makes sense to take your pet with you. Use an online resource such as **www.k9directory.com** ✉ or a book such as *Pets Welcome!*

by Anne Cuthbertson, 2003, ISBN 1850553491, or the AA publication *Pet Friendly Places to Stay*, ISBN 0749537795, to find suitable accommodation for you and your pet.

BETTER BOARDING

Boarding may be the best option for dogs who need daily exercise, and for pedigree animals where having a vet on call is a service worth paying for. Prices are £6–£10 a day for a dog (depending on its size) and about £5.50 for a cat. You may be able to ask for a reduction in rates if you book more than three months in advance, if you are a frequent customer or if you are boarding more than one animal.

Get recommendations If possible, use a boarding service recommended by friends or seek the advice of your vet who should know of reputable local ones.

Contact the council Your local council can give you the names and rates of boarding kennels in your area. There are no national or even local guidelines on charges, but the Competition Commission is more critical of inflated kennel charges than any other pet-care cost, so be aware that some kennel charges are way out of line.

See for yourself Always visit a boarding kennels before deciding that this is where you want to leave your pet.

 **RESOURCES**

REGISTERED PETSITTERS

If you have to use a petsitter, be sure of a reliable, value-for-money service by checking that they are registered with the National Association of Registered Petsitters. In addition, always ask for and check references.

■ You can find more information about petsitting services on the web at sites such as **www.dogsit.com** ✉ and **www.ukpetsitter.com** ✉.

■ Some housesitting agencies also offer petsitters who will look after your pet in your home, making sure it is fed and exercised.

TOP TIPS CHEAPER PETSITTING

Petsitting prices ranges from being totally free to costing more than boarding. The main advantage is that your pet can stay in familiar surroundings.

■ **Book visits from a qualified veterinary nurse** Getting a professionally qualified pet carer to come to your house is affordable but not cheap at £8–£10 a visit. Your best bet for finding such a person is to contact your local vet.

■ **Get live-in petsitting for free** You'd be surprised how many animal lovers would relish the chance to stay in a nice house or area in exchange for looking after your pet. If you have to pay for this service, on the other hand, it could cost you £30–£40 a day, plus travel expenses. If this is your choice, make sure you use someone who is registered and worth the fee you are paying.

■ **Go halves with a neighbour** If you find that neighbours are going away at the same time, you may be able to share their care arrangements.

■ **Swap petsitting for babysitting** It may be easier to ask a neighbour to petsit if you can offer something they would value equally in return – babysitting, for example, lawn mowing or ironing.

■ **Form a petsitting club** Team up with pet owners in your vicinity and work out a petsitting rota. Local pet clubs should be able to put you in touch with like-minded individuals.

■ **Ask a friend** Pet-loving friends who have none of their own may be willing to come and stay with your animals.

You can make your parties memorable affairs and still watch the budget – a little careful planning will leave you with more to spend on the things that really matter.

Special occasions

GETTING IN THE MOOD

Setting the scene is one of the most important aspects of planning a party, as the right decorations and lighting will put guests in a festive mood. With imagination and canny shopping, you can transform your home for very little.

BARGAIN DECORATIONS

Look at your social diary and plan ahead – having a stock of cheaply sourced party goodies and decorations will spare you from expensive last-minute shopping.

Gift and craft shops Prices at gift and knick-knack shops can be more reasonable than at specialist party shops. Scour card shops for balloons, banners and celebration confetti. Craft and fabric stores often have all sorts of party décor. Watch out for sales and cheaply priced oddment bins.

Chains and supermarkets Discount superstores such as TK Maxx and Matalan, DIY stores and supermarkets all stock many items that can be transformed into decorations, as well as partyware such as paper plates, cups, party-bag gifts and prizes. Supermarkets offer discounted items after an event such as Halloween, Christmas and New Year; buy them and save them to use next year.

TOP TIPS ATMOSPHERIC LIGHTING

Appropriate lighting is crucial in creating a welcoming ambience. Use party lights and a good selection of taper-style and column candles to help give a party atmosphere with a minimum of expense.

■ **Change colour** Swop plain light bulbs for coloured ones for about £1 each. Warm colours give a flattering soft glow to a room, while cool colours can help conjure up a mood for themed occasions such as a Halloween party.

■ **Reusable party lights** Start snapping up strings of indoor/outdoor Christmas lights during post-festive sales. These tiny lights, costing from under £6 for 50, add instant enchantment to any party scene, indoors or out. You can reuse them and they can be left unattended, unlike candles.

■ **Grab bargains** Tealights can cost as little as £5–£6 for 100, and larger candles are not expensive when bought in bulk. IKEA's plain white candles are £3 for a pack of 50. Leading candle-maker Price's Candles (**www.prices-candles.co.uk** 01234 264500 ✉) has lots of factory outlets and a retail outlet in Battersea, south London.

■ **Make the most of singles** If you have leftover single candles in a variety of shades, place them in a matching pair of candelabras on the dining room table or mantelpiece for a colourful display. Buy candelabras cheaply from a street market or in secondhand and charity shops.

■ **Cooler candles** To save even more money on candles, store them in a sealed box in the fridge and light them when cold. They will burn more slowly.

■ **Bargain garden lights** If you are throwing an evening party, place tealights in old jars and use wire to hang them in trees or along a fence. Or set them in paper bags half-filled with sand and position around a patio.

RESOURCES

PARTY PLANNING
■ For free online invitations, visit **www.globalflight.net** ✉.
■ For good-value bouquets from £9.99 online, try **www.bunches.co.uk** ✉ or phone 01623 750343.
■ Buy cheap candles online from **www.just-candles.net** ✉.
■ For cheap party lights, try **www.christmastimeuk.com** or phone 01427 667270 ✉.

COMPARE THE COST OF ROSES

If your heart is set on roses, here's what you could pay for a dozen. The more expensive roses are arranged with foliage and tied with attractively presented cellophane and ribbons, so choose cheap bunches and make your own floral arrangements.

MARKET	£5.50
TESCO	£13.99 FOR 15
WWW.BUNCHES.CO.UK	£26.99
INTERFLORA	£43.25
WWW.0800-BLOSSOMS.CO.UK	£45.95

All prices 2004 and, except for the market, include delivery

FRUGAL FLOWERS

Flowers always add style to a party, but can be expensive. Committed money savers grow their own flowers for cutting, or ask a green-fingered friend who is coming to the party to donate some. Even if you have to buy shop-bought flowers, you can still keep down costs.

Bunches in season Only buy flowers in season, as the more exotic the bloom, the higher its cost. Buy flowers in bunches of the same variety as flower arrangements tend to cost more and will limit your options.

Choose your supplier Supermarkets are a source of cheap flowers, especially when the blooms are near their sell-by date. Avoid buying flowers at petrol stations where prices can be extortionate and the flowers may not last.

Save at street markets Street markets always have flower stalls and their blooms are reasonably priced and cheaper at the end of the day when the flowers need to be sold.

Bulk buys at flower markets Search your local directory for flower markets in your area. You will have to buy in bulk, but the savings are definitely worth it (see *Homes and gardens*, page 215).

FLORAL FILLERS

Use greenery – preferably from your own garden – to make floral displays go further. Herbs such as rosemary or lavender last well and give arrangements a wonderful scent.

Artful artifice Combine paper, silk or ceramic artificial flowers with fresh greenery. They can be used year after year.

Fruit and nuts When making a table centrepiece or wreath for a door, use fresh fruit, vegetables and nuts for an inexpensive arrangement.

Bowers of green For a stunning effect, lop off branches from shrubs or trees such as bay or fir, wash off any insects and place them on bare walls or on a buffet table. Remember, though, that you are not permitted to take greenery from public places.

GILDING THE LILY

Flowers are lovely on their own but you can make them look more special, or even tie them in to your party theme, by adding a few finishing touches.

■ Cut or buy seasonal foliage to fill up the vases. Or use good artificial foliage – no one will be able to tell the difference.

■ Add stems of gypsophila or carnations, which are inexpensive and complement roses. Mixed displays always look more opulent.

■ Add some seasonal decorations: ribbons, ears of corn, small glass ornaments, paper or wooden shapes glued to the end of lengths of wire. Your party theme will suggest other options.

■ Finish your bouquets with a wrap of coloured cellophane or tulle.

THEMED PARTIES

Building your party menu and decorations around a theme or specific event will help you to make a big splash for less money. Why? Because the choices of food and décor will be clearer, allowing you to tailor the party for effect rather than expense.

70S FLASHBACK

Dress in hot pants, flares and psychedelic clothing. Dance to Gloria Gaynor, the Bee Gees and the Village People. Lava lamps and disco balls make great decorations. A perfect meal is a cheese fondue, and then get your guests to play charades and guess the '70s personality. This retro-style party theme can be adapted to suit any era and any music, and so is ideal for someone with a milestone birthday.

MONOPOLY PARTY

Meet up with friends at a café or bar in the morning and divide into teams. Each team is given tasks to perform at various Monopoly-style sites and must prove they have been there. Community chest and Chance cards are dares to be done at designated times. Meet back at home in the early evening. Give prizes to the winners, then prepare easy, hearty food such as baked potatoes with a selection of fillings.

STAR TURN

Rent a karaoke machine, or buy a 'Karaoke Classics' CD for £5 and let your friends do their best Elvis Presley or Cher impersonations. Just warn your neighbours first, or invite them. Serve a punch of fizzy wine and fruit juice, with finger food such as chicken wings.

ETHNIC POTLUCK

Ask each guest to choose a different country and bring an appropriate dish. As the host, you provide beverages, tableware and linens. Play CDs of appropriate music and ask a travel agency or the tourist board for posters or brochures to use in decorating.

MEXICAN NIGHT

Create a Latin fiesta by decorating your venue with strings of lights, cacti, colourful balloons and streamers in red, green and yellow. Dance to sounds of the mambo, samba and tango. Serve tortilla chips with salsa, wraps filled with chilli, re-fried beans, sour cream, guacamole, cheese and lettuce, and ask your guests to bring bottled beers.

CATERING ON A BUDGET

Whether you are planning simple nibbles for a few friends or a formally catered event on a large scale, there are plenty of ways to save on the costs of the party food without skimping on style.

TOP TIPS MAKE FOOD GO FURTHER

Choose and serve food in the right way and you can provide a sumptuous spread while sticking to your budget.

■ **Save with spreads and dips** Make expensive ingredients such as smoked salmon go further by combining them with dressings, cream cheese and vegetables in dips and spreads. Serve spreads with crackers and breads, or use them as fillings for puff pastry shells and wraps.

■ **Two for the show** Even at a formal sit-down meal you can drop a course and serve two rather than three. This suits many people's appetites, and as long as the serving is leisurely your guests will still enjoy time at the table. Either serve a main course and dessert with a good selection of bread to start, or starter and main course only with chocolates and coffee to finish.

■ **Avoid too many choices** Most people will have one or two slices of meat, but if they are offered fish as well they may choose both – and then eat only half of each. Serve the main dish on a plate – whether the fish or the meat – to prompt guests to choose one or the other.

■ **Serve on a platter** For a sit-down dinner, serving side dishes family-style on a platter in the middle of a table – rather than as restaurant-style individual portions – makes them go about 20% further.

A FORMAL AFFAIR

Many people like to make celebrations such as significant birthdays, wedding anniversaries and christenings formal affairs with a slap-up sit-down meal or lavish buffet. If you want to have a special party, getting caterers in could be the solution, and it could be less expensive than you think.

Choosing a caterer Shop around for different packages until you find one that suits you, as prices vary considerably – some simply bring the food, while others will also supply linen, crockery, a marquee, waiters and more.

Draw up a budget To avoid a larger bill than you were planning for, set a budget and stick to it. Don't be persuaded to have any extras, or a more 'sophisticated' menu, unless they are within your price range. Unnecessary frills could add up to 25% to your overall costs. Agree what is included and get a written quote.

Work with your chef If you are dealing with a large firm, find out if they have flexible deals – ask if altering the set menu will cost more, or whether it can save you money. If your caterer is a one-woman band, see what cost-cutting suggestions she can make or whether you can save by helping her prepare some of the food.

Delivered to your door Party delivery services bring finger foods or ready-heated party meals to your door at a fraction

---

CALCULATING QUANTITIES

Get your quantities right and you will avoid wasting food or appearing stingy.

■ If you are serving buffet food alone, allow 8–12 pieces for each person.

■ 450g (1lb) of pasta serves 4–6 people at a sit-down meal or 8–12 at a buffet.

■ For a mixed buffet, allow 110g–170g (4oz–6oz) of meat, fish or cheese for each person.

■ A sit-down meal should contain 140g–170g (5oz–6oz) of meat or fish for each person and three vegetable dishes.

A MOUTH-WATERING MENU YOU CAN AFFORD

The two impressive menus below are for a self-catered formal summer dinner party for 10 people, but Menu B is half the price of Menu A because it is based around seasonal and other inexpensive ingredients and cuts out unnecessary extras.

MENU A

Scallops served in chicory cups with a creamy wine and ginger sauce

Roast duck with foie gras stuffing served with kumquat and brandy sauce

Shredded sprout and cabbage sauté

Roast pumpkin and sweet potato

Individual chocolate truffle tortes served with a foaming Cointreau sauce and candied cape gooseberries

Irish coffee and luxury Belgian chocolates

cost for each person: £18.00

MENU B

Steamed asparagus bundles served with shrimps in lettuce cups with a tangy lime hollandaise sauce

Tender chicken breast fillets filled with goats' cheese, tomato, spinach, courgette, peppers and walnuts, rolled and baked and served with watercress sauce

Green vegetable medley – runner beans, garden peas and spring onions, stir-fried in a balsamic dressing

Potatoes Normandy

Individual summer puddings served with a foamy lemon syllabub sauce

Fresh coffee served with homemade mocha truffles

cost for each person: £9.00

of the price of getting caterers in. A luxury two-course dinner for 15–20 people might cost around £10 a head whereas bringing caterers to cook at your venue would cost over £20 a head.

Cut costs by helping out See if you can reduce your bill by doing some of the chores, such as picking up the drinks, yourself. Using your own linen, glasses, china and cutlery could save more if you don't mind doing the washing up.

Hiring tables and chairs Look in the Yellow Pages under Catering Equipment Hire for local companies and compare their price lists. If you have access to a van, save on delivery charges by picking up and returning the equipment.

Coordinated approach Save on hiring damask tablecloths by draping white linen sheets over the tables so they come almost to the ground. Then lay your own smaller coloured cloths on top or make some from fabric remnants. Add good-quality paper napkins in a matching colour.

Save 50% on waiting staff For formal occasions where waiting staff are required, ask your friends or neighbours if their teenage sons and daughters might be willing to work for some extra cash.

DEALS YOU CAN DRINK TO

STOCK UP ON HOLIDAY

If you are planning a large party, make dramatic savings by visiting the wine and beer warehouses in France on your way home from holiday. These are usually situated in convenient stop-off points near ferry or shuttle terminals and are open seven days a week throughout most of the year. Typical bargains include bottles of vintage wine for under £1 and a wide selection of discounted champagnes, so it could even be worth making a special trip. (See *Eating and drinking*, pages 32–34.)

Alcohol can be an important part of a social event, but do not feel obliged to offer a full bar or any spirits. Beer and wine are usually sufficient, or stick to one spirit in keeping with your guests' tastes or a seasonal theme, such as a fruit rum punch in summer or eggnog with brandy in winter.

TOP TIPS FINDING A BARGAIN

The cost-conscious party-giver should make it a rule never to pay full price for wines. Take advantage of discounts given for buying in bulk. Watch out for retailers that offer other services that help you cater for guests – for example, free glass loan and a sale-or-return policy.

■ **Wine warehouses** Wine warehouses are large stores, either dotted around Britain or on the Internet, that offer substantial discounts on a wide selection of alcohol. Recent deals include 50% off cases of wine, 20% off champagne and knockdown prices on bottles of Pimms, whisky and gin. Some sell wine or beer by the case only and offer additional party services such as free glass loan, chiller bins and ice. They usually have a sale-or-return facility, which is useful as it can be difficult to judge how much alcohol you will need at a party – this way, you only pay for what you drink.

■ **Cheap wine online** Search the net for good deals on wine when planning your party (see Resources, left). Many companies offer wine, cocktail mixes and champagne at enticing prices. For example, **www.virginwines.com** offer an impressive range of fizz. You can either mix your own case of 12 bottles or pick up a special case deal. If you try one of the wines they have recommended and don't like it, they will refund the cost of the bottle.

ALCOHOL-THEMED PARTIES

Planning a party around a particular beverage is an easy and low-cost party idea as friends can bring a favourite tipple.

Wine and dine Ask guests to bring a bottle to a dinner party – specify that it should go with a particular course or dish – then make sure you drink their donated wine with the appropriate food. Wine and cheese parties are also popular.

Bring on the brew With the explosion of microbreweries, there is now an exciting variety of beers. Host a beer-tasting party and invite your friends to bring a six-pack of their favourite stout, pale ale, amber ale or bitter. Mexican, Indian and Chinese food are all enhanced by beer, so appetisers from these cuisines make a good accompaniment.

DISCOUNTED READY-MIXED DRINKS

There are plenty of ready-mixed drinks to choose from in supermarkets and off-licences, as well as cash-and-carry stores where they can cost under £1 a bottle. They have a shorter shelf life than wines and spirits, so when stores overstock, you can buy at half price or on a buy-one-get-one-free basis. Check that you will use them by the use-by date.

RESOURCES

ONLINE DRINK SUPPLIERS

■ Try the following websites ✉ to compare prices:
www.dealtime.co.uk
www.discountwines.com
www.luk-wine.co.uk
www.majestic.co.uk
www.oddbins.com
www.tesco.com/winestore
www.virginwines.com

■ For cheap glass hire – 50 wine glasses at £6.30 for three days or £10.50 for a week – try HSS (branches nationwide) at www.hss.com or phone 0845 728 2828 ✉.

NON-ALCOHOLIC FRUIT FIZZ
MAKES 10 SERVINGS

■ In a large saucepan, combine 25g (1oz) each frozen raspberries and strawberries, 1.3 litres (2¼ pints) water, 350g (12oz) sugar, 10 whole cloves, ½ teaspoon ground cardamom, six strips orange zest and 1 split vanilla pod.
■ Bring to a boil over a medium-high heat; reduce the heat and simmer, uncovered, stirring occasionally, for 10 minutes.
■ Strain through a fine sieve and discard the solids. Cool to room temperature, and then stir in 450ml (16fl oz) orange juice and chill.
■ Just before serving, stir in 450ml (16fl oz) chilled sparkling water.
■ Serve over ice and garnish as desired.

ANNIVERSARY FRUIT PUNCH
MAKES 8 SERVINGS

■ Drain the liquid from a 215g (7½oz) can of apricot halves, reserving half the juice.
■ Mix the juice with a bottle of sweet white wine, 450ml (16fl oz) orange juice, 200ml (7fl oz) pineapple juice and 1 tbsp lime juice.
■ Dice half of the canned apricots.
■ Fill one-third of a large jug with crushed ice. Pour the wine mixture into the jug and top with the diced apricots.
■ Garnish with sprigs of mint.

CLASSIC SANGRIA
MAKES 12 SERVINGS

■ In a large pitcher, mix 1.7 litres (3 pints) fruity red wine such as burgundy, 225–450ml (8–16fl oz) brandy, Cointreau, cassis, or other fruit-flavoured liqueur, and 6–8 tbps lemon juice.
■ Stir, and add 225ml (8fl oz) of sugar syrup.
■ Add orange and lemon slices, pitted cherries or pineapple rings. Chill well.
For white sangria, use dry white wine such as Chablis, Grand Marnier or other orange-flavoured liqueur, and lemon or lime-flavoured tonic.

HOMEMADE PARTY DRINKS

Making your own refreshing drinks costs much less than ready-mixed drinks or even wine and beer. Served in a pretty jug or punch bowl, they add a festive spirit to any party.

SUMMER WINE CUP
MAKES 24 SERVINGS

■ In a large punch bowl, mix 4 bottles of dry white wine with 1 bottle of dry sherry.
■ Add 225ml (8fl oz) of sugar syrup and stir.
■ Top up with 1.5 litres (2¾ pints) lemonade and add ice cubes.
■ Garnish with sprigs of mint, sliced apple and a few strawberries.

BASIC SUGAR SYRUP
(FOR SANGRIA AND SUMMER WINE CUP)

■ Combine 450g (1lb) sugar and 600ml (1 pint) water in a heavy-bottomed saucepan. Cook over a moderate heat, stirring often, until the mixture comes to the boil and the sugar dissolves.
■ Remove the pan from the heat, cover and leave for 10 minutes to dissolve any remaining crystals, and let stand to cool.
■ Pour into a jar or bottle with a tightly fitting lid. Makes 600ml–700ml (1–1¼ pints).
■ Make up to two days before use and store in the fridge.

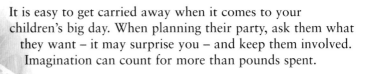

CHILDREN'S PARTIES FOR A SONG

It is easy to get carried away when it comes to your children's big day. When planning their party, ask them what they want – it may surprise you – and keep them involved. Imagination can count for more than pounds spent.

LOW-COST INVITATIONS

Children love to make their own birthday fliers. If they have access to a computer, they can design and print off as many invitations as they need. Older children can email them to save on paper and postage. Or you could photocopy or print a photo of your child onto card and write a message by hand on the back.

TOP TIPS PARTY ENTERTAINMENT

Hiring a magician, juggler or face painter can be expensive, ranging from £70 for 40 minutes to £140 for two hours. Party games that you organise yourself can be just as much fun for younger children and cost next to nothing.

■ **Classic games** Old favourites, such as Musical Bumps, Musical Chairs, Blind Man's Buff and Charades, don't require any special equipment and are perennially popular.

■ **Dressing up** Children love dressing up, so put a selection of colourful clothes, hats and shoes into a large box and let them create their own costumes, with a prize for the best.

■ **Treasure hunt** Write clues on slips of paper and send the children off to hunt for treasure – such as small sacks of chocolate coins – in your house or garden. Older children might prefer a supervised scavenger hunt in a local park.

CASE STUDY

HAVING A GREAT TIME OUT OF DOORS

Helen Pearce was determined to disguise the fact that the birthday party she organised for her 7-year-old daughter Katy wasn't going to be as lavish as some of her friends'. Luckily, Katy was born in May so it was a pretty good bet that the weather would be fair, and a Sports Day party – where the children would be perfectly happy to make their own entertainment – seemed the ideal option. Helen and her husband, Michael, turned their lawned garden into a professional-looking venue by painting white lines on it for a mini-running track and other athletic events, which really impressed Katy's classmates. Now that the stage was set, Helen planned a simple picnic and let the children make their own ice-cream creations (with supervision!) for dessert. When choosing items for the party bags, Helen thought like a child. She found inexpensive toys, such as 99p cars for the boys and 55p bracelets for the girls. She also included a balloon (99p for 8), a home-baked biscuit and a small packet of sweets (bought at 75% off the usual price in a post-Easter sale). The party was such a success that Katy's 9-year-old brother Scott wants to do the same. Though his birthday is in October, Helen is planning an outdoor barbeque and lots of athletic events to keep the children warm.

PARTY OUTINGS FOR LESS

When children get too old to have in-house parties, amusement parks, adventure playgrounds and swimming pools are popular venues.

Home catering Party outings will be much cheaper if you can take your own food, cake and party bags.

Get the numbers right Find out if there is a minimum number of guests you have to invite. Many places, such as Madame Tussauds, London (020 7935 6861 ✉), London Zoo (0870 400 3000 ✉) and Thorpe Park (0870 444 44 66 ✉), have group discounts.

Minimise the price You can usually save £1–£2 a head by booking in advance rather than paying on the day. Some venues, such as Legoland (**www.legoland.co.uk** 08705 04 04 04 ✉), offer a 10% discount if you book over the Internet. And bowling alleys, for instance, often charge less during the slower summer months.

Free and low-cost outings Visit free museums or events, such as The British Cartoon Centre (020 7278 7172 ✉) or the Changing of the Guard in London, and low-cost venues such as art galleries and small open farms. Try Forestry Commission parks for a picnic or barbeque, or go to the seaside by train. Many children never travel by train so this will be a double treat (see *Practical parenting*, page 108).

RESOURCES

CHILDREN'S PARTIES

■ For ideas and a directory of suppliers, visit **www.kidspartysurvival guide.com** ✉.

■ These books give plenty of ideas for children's party games: *Practical Parenting Party Games* £5.99, ISBN 0600606945, and *Collins Gem Family and Party Games* £4.99, ISBN 0007122705.

■ Look at **www.cadbury. co.uk** ✉ for recipe ideas for chocolate party cakes and biscuits.

COMPARING PARTY BUDGETS (FOR 10 CHILDREN)

TYPE OF PARTY	VENUE	FOOD	CAKE	PARTY BAG	PRIZES	ENTER-TAINMENT	TOTAL
At home with homemade food, games	£0	£20	£2	£15	£10	£0	£47
Swimming pool, homemade cake	£65	£20	£2	£15	£0	£0	£102
Soft play centre, bought cake	£95	incl.	£10	£15	£0	£0	£120
Cartoon theme in hired hall, bought cake	£60	£50	£15	£35	£15	£0	£175
Hired venue, entertainer, homemade food	£60	£20	£2	£15	£5	£100	£202
Hired venue, face painter, bouncy castle, bought cake	£60	£20	£10	£15	£5	£150	£260
Legoland off-peak*, picnic, bought cake	£227.70	£20	£10	£15	£0	£0	£272.70

Prices August 2004

*£15 for each guest based on a minimum of 15 paying guests booking in advance.

GLAD TIDINGS AT CHRISTMAS

Although it does not feel right to be miserly during the festive season, you don't have to spend lots of money to have fun. Get the whole family involved in the preparations and approach Christmas as a family activity – you will enrich your time together as well as saving money and adding a personal touch to your decorations and cards.

SPEND LESS ON DECORATIONS

If you are willing to be adventurous and shop away from the high street, you can save a small fortune on decorations – leaving you more to splash out on presents.

Car boot and garage sales You can pick up a bargain just before or just after Christmas. Look for unused tablecloths, candleholders, strings of lights, ornaments, boxed presents and artificial trees. Scour sales advertised in local papers throughout the year, especially from September.

Fabric and craft shops Watch for sales, usually just before and after Christmas, as well as end-of-line or old-stock bins. You should be able to pick up glitter glue, fabric remnants (a piece of red cloth to cover a small side table, a piece of velvet to embellish a cushion, or a holly print fabric to wrap up a present), shiny ribbon, foam stamps and shaped scissors. You may also find decorations at 50%–70% off the full price.

DECORATE LATE – SAVE OVER 50%

Start a family tradition of buying and decorating a tree on Christmas Eve and you will be surprised at the bargain-basement price you can get. Visit your local street market on the weekend immediately before Christmas and the traders will be practically giving away the trees.

Make your own decorations

Be creative and get back in tune with the spirit of Christmas.

Recycle old decorations Pile inexpensive glass ball ornaments into a bowl or basket to decorate a windowsill or shelf.

SMART MOVES

Cut out paper snowflakes Fold a square piece of white paper in half, then in half again. Now fold the square into a triangle. Cut out shapes along the outer edges of the triangle. Open up the paper and you have a snowflake. Tape to windows or hang as ornaments.

Make Christmas oranges Using double-sided tape, stick a strip of festive ribbon around the circumference of an orange. Repeat the other way, so you have a ribbon running vertically and horizontally all round. Push whole dried cloves into the outer skin of the orange and place in a bowl, or hang up using a looped ribbon.

Fill a bowl Use bright red and green apples, golden oranges and satsumas bought cheaply from a street market. Tuck in sprigs of holly and small conifer boughs. Include Brazil nuts, walnuts and hazelnuts, which can be nibbled throughout Christmas.

Use tree trimmings Cut off the lower branches from your Christmas tree before setting it in a holder and use them to make a wreath or a swag for the mantelpiece.

Go for natural beauty If you have a cotoneaster or holly bush in your garden, cut branches to make inviting natural decorations. Add a bow and fairy lights strung through the branches. Or pick up nuts, bare twigs and fir cones on a walk through the woods. Leave them plain or spray paint gold, silver or white. Arrange the nuts and cones in bowls, or tuck them along the mantelpiece or on shelves and windowsills.

COMPARE THE COST OF CHRISTMAS TREES

TREE TYPE	SIZE IN METRES (FEET)			
	1.2–1.4M (4–4½FT)	1.5–1.7M (5–5½FT)	1.8–2M (6–6½FT)	2.1–2.4M (7–8FT)
ARTIFICIAL TREES				
Braemar pine	–	£65	£49.99	£145
Glendale spruce	£39.99	–	£69.99	£110
Fibre optic	£21.99	£49	£49.99	–
White spruce	£49.99	–	£77	£120
Blue springfield with cones	–	£69.99	£94.99	£124.99
REAL TREES				
Norway spruce	£20	£23	£25	£37
Nordman fir	£25.99	£32.50	£39.99	£49.99
Fraser fir	–	£29.99	£36.50	£41.50
Scots pine	–	–	£30	–

Information **www.birstal.co.uk** and *Gardening Which?* July 2004

BARGAIN CHRISTMAS TREES

For many people, a home at Christmas needs a tree, but an expensive natural tree is not the only choice available.

Tree farms for value If you want a fresh tree, your best bet is a tree farm (see Resources, right). The prices are good, and the tree is fresh and so will last longer and look better. Selecting and chopping your tree can be fun for all the family. Many tree farms offer hot chocolate or mulled wine to warm you up while you chop and shop.

Choose a cheaper variety Nordman firs have excellent needle retention (some don't drop their needles at all), but they will set you back 30% more than an ordinary Norway spruce. Limit needle drop on a spruce by slicing off the top when you bring it indoors and watering the tree well – a 1.8m (6ft) tree drinks 600ml (1 pint) of water a day.

Artificial trees The most economical approach is to invest in an artificial tree. Though the better-looking trees cost more, this is a one-time investment that should pay for itself within a few years. You can buy the trees plain, with lights or completely decorated, depending on your budget. They go up in minutes, will serve you well for years and are cheap if you buy them during post-Christmas sales.

Mini-trees If you live in a flat, or if putting up a full-sized tree is more trouble than it is worth, consider a miniature tree, either artificial or real. At Christmas, prices rise according to height, so small trees can be a bargain.

Deep-rooted trees The most expensive but environmentally friendly option is to buy a container-grown, rooted tree from a nursery and plant it in the garden after Christmas. If you have the space, you can do this every year, enhancing your property and preserving memories of Christmas for a generation or more.

RESOURCES

CHRISTMAS TREES THROUGH THE NET

■ Try these websites for Christmas trees:
www.birstall.co.uk
www.money.msn.co.uk
www.xmastreesdirect.co.uk
www.christmastreeland. co.uk ✉.

■ The British Christmas Tree Growers' Association offers a list of growers who sell quality trees on 0131 644 110, or visit their website **www.christmastree.org. uk** ✉.

Fun and inexpensive gift baskets

Gift baskets full of lots of little treats are often more pleasing than a single present costing double the amount. Try to tailor-make them to the recipient for an even more delighted response.

Young baby Fill an inexpensive basket with practical items the parents will appreciate, such as sleepwear, vests, bottles, bibs, nappies, a snuggly, booties or socks – plus a rattle and a cuddly toy.

Young children Line a basket with a bright T-shirt, then add a packet of coloured pencils, a box of crayons, safety scissors, stickers, comics, a small car or doll and packets of favourite sweets.

Older children Line the basket with a T-shirt printed with a favourite band's logo. Add some suitable toys or games, and a computer-printed 'certificate' offering to take the child to a local 'splash slides' pool, to the cinema to see a latest release or on a shopping trip.

Older relatives Line a basket with velvet, then fill it with accessories for his or her favourite hobby, such as golf tees, balls and a shoe brush; a trowel, packets of seeds and a mini watering can; or a book on world travel, sun lotion and brochures for cruises.

Almost anyone Put decorative fabric covers over the lids of small jars of homemade jam, lemon curd or chutney, or a selection of luxury foodstuffs, and secure with a ribbon. Tuck into a basket lined with gingham and straw.

Recycling is free When Christmas is over, recycle your tree by taking it to the Christmas tree skip at your local garden centre. The trees are shredded and recycled as mulch.

SEASON'S GREETINGS

The cost of sending greeting cards can soar to over £1 a card, but you can share seasonal cheer for much less.

Shop after Christmas Cards are reduced by up to 70% in January, so shop for next year's cards then and tuck them away until you need them.

Create cards for free Some of the cards you receive are just too beautiful to throw away. Using last year's cards, cut off designs and motifs, and glue them onto card blanks either as a central feature or a pattern. Embellish the cards with glitter or embossed lettering. Or make gift tags by cutting the central motifs from cards, punching a hole at one edge and tying on a ribbon. Cards can also be made cheaply from note cards with suitable illustrations – why pay extra for a printed Christmas salutation?

Transform old cards for decorations For attractive paper garlands, cut the front of old cards into strips and make interlocking chains to hang on a tree, edge a mantelpiece or brighten a staircase. For unique napkin rings, cut 5cm (2in) strips from the cards, form them into a circle and glue or staple the ends together.

The last post Posting your cards on time allows you to send them second class instead of first. This is especially cost-effective for cards going overseas.

Email greetings Bypass the Post Office altogether and create cards on your computer to send by email. The website **www.egreetings.com** offers ready-designed cards you can send free to family and friends at home and abroad at just the click of a button.

PURCHASING POWER

Smart Christmas shopping means buying presents you think a person will like when you spot them, and when the price is right. Look for gifts throughout the year. Holiday trips, craft and country fairs, gift shops at museums and botanical gardens, auctions and flea markets are all excellent sources of one-of-a-kind presents. Earmark a drawer or the back of a cupboard as a designated gift store. Then, when Christmas – or birthdays and other special occasions – approach, you can reach in and produce the ideal present for anyone on your list.

MAKING MEMORIES

For a unique Christmas present – as well as for a milestone birthday, wedding anniversary, graduation or retirement – make a scrapbook or collage. Use photographs, decorative papers and other memorabilia. Ask friends, family members and colleagues to contribute a written memory of an event or conversation shared with the recipient to include in the present. Or make a personalised calendar featuring 12 photographs that show a special moment in the person's life. The recipient can then enjoy your gift all year long.

PERSONALISED GIFT WRAP

With wrapping paper costing £1 a sheet or more, decorating your own gift wrap is a rewarding project, as well as a creative way to add a personal touch to a present. Using thin brown parcel paper or another type of paper with the equivalent thickness, paint with acrylic paint and sponge, potato print, stencil, fingerpaint or draw designs to create one-of-a-kind wrapping paper. Fabric also makes an excellent wrap, especially for awkward shapes, and can be bought very cheaply (£1 a metre for sheer fabric or tulle, £2 a metre for cotton) in fabric warehouse sales, end of lines or on street markets. Tie with satin ribbons.

SAVE ON SEASONAL PLANTS

Don't wait until the last moment to buy poinsettias or forced bulbs, when they will cost double and have suffered from sitting too long in heated shops. Buy them early and keep in a cool spot until you need them.

Garden centres DIY stores with garden centres, such as B&Q and Homebase, tend to offer good deals on Christmas flowers and bulbs.

Web bargains Scour the Internet for a new breed of florist who offer inexpensive bouquets for same or next-day delivery – for example, bouquets from **www.bunches.co.uk** ✉ start at £9.99 (first-class delivery), while at **www.crocus.co.uk** ✉ they're priced from £24.95 (courier delivery).

WEDDINGS FOR THE (PRICE) WISE

There is a current trend for elaborate, costly weddings, often paid for by the bride and groom themselves rather than the bride's parents. But you don't have to splash out on a lavish ceremony and reception – some of the most memorable weddings are simple, elegant and affordable affairs.

SPENDING TO SAVE

A little initial outlay can save a lot of unnecessary expense – planning and prudence are worth it.

Coordinated discounts A wedding coordinator costs from £500 but could save you big money by negotiating discounts from preferred suppliers. Find one in the Yellow Pages, in wedding magazines and at wedding fairs, or log on to the website **www.weddingguide.co.uk** ✉.

Peace of mind Wedding insurance costs £50–£100. It covers mishaps such as a damaged dress, the theft of presents, double bookings and cancellations due to illness.

Bank on it A dedicated bank account for all wedding funds will stop you from eroding your funds with unofficial spending. And just in case, set aside 5% extra for any unforeseen expenses.

Facts on file A wedding file in which you keep a running total of all wedding-related expenditure will help avoid any nasty surprises.

MOVE THE DATE AND SAVE UP TO 50%

Instead of getting married on a Saturday in June, which is popular and so costs more, choose another month and day – January, February, March and November are quieter times for suppliers. With less competition for the resources you want, you can get a much better rate. Your honeymoon will cost less, too, if you go out of season – Venice, the Seychelles or even Cornwall are more romantic without the crowds.

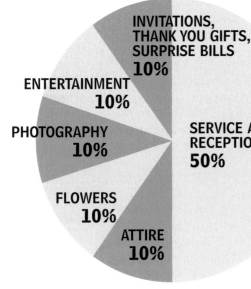

INVITATIONS, THANK YOU GIFTS, SURPRISE BILLS **10%**

ENTERTAINMENT **10%**

PHOTOGRAPHY **10%**

FLOWERS **10%**

ATTIRE **10%**

SERVICE AND RECEPTION **50%**

CONTROLLING YOUR BUDGET

Professional wedding organisers advise that the best way to control your budget is to decide how you are dividing it up. These are the proportions they recommend.

GETTING VALUE FROM YOUR RECEPTION

While the cost of the wedding itself is predictable – £67.50 to get married at a Registry Office, and a sliding scale of charges at a church, ranging from £275 to £575 depending on the kind of church, the number of clergy and whether you have bells and a choir – the reception is where you can be creative. Depending on the venue and arrangements, you can choose to spend – as well as save – a little or a lot.

LOCATION	WHAT YOU CAN EXPECT	POSSIBLE SAVINGS	TYPICAL COST*
Outdoor beauty spot	A romantic beach or country setting would be ideal for a memorable party. Apply to the local council for the cost of hiring the location.	Plan an old-fashioned picnic to keep costs to a minimum. Take hampers full of cold food, plus a gazebo, rugs and a few small tables and chairs.	£50 plus picnic
Church hall	Hire of a church hall costs around £15–£25 an hour at weekends. You may need to hire tables, chairs, linen and crockery and pay for flowers and decorations.	There is often access to a kitchen with crockery and glasses, so you can do your own catering as well as your own decorations and flowers.	£250 plus catering
At home	An economical solution if you have a large house. You may have to hire caterers, a marquee, chairs and tables.	For a small party, save on caterers by having a barbeque in the garden, with casual seating.	£700– £2,000 plus catering
Restaurant	For a medium-sized affair, hire a private room. The cost of the meal can be fixed.	For a smaller reception, a large table in the main dining area is a cost-effective solution, although you will lose privacy.	£100+ but the meal may be expensive
Caribbean resort	A wedding package, added to the cost of a week in Antigua, includes bouquet, sparkling wine, cake, decorations and registrar.	Tour companies may provide wedding packages free if your guests book rooms. You can expect your guests to pay their own costs, except reception.	£2,000 plus catering
Botanical garden	Lush landscapes all year, perfect for photos. Many are equipped for functions, such as London's Kew Gardens and Bristol's Wildwalk.	Smaller gardens or the orangery of a country house offer an attractive backdrop at a lower price. Member discounts may apply.	£1,800 plus catering
Country club or hotel	Usually includes catering and decorations, so you pay for convenience. If you hire the whole hotel, you'll pay more for exclusivity.	Save by limiting numbers. Choose a Friday or Sunday, which are cheaper than Saturday. Get a discount for overnight guests.	£2,500 including minimal catering

*before any savings

TOP TIPS A SWELL PARTY

Even with limited resources, which effectively rules out a formal sit-down dinner, you can treat your friends and family to a stylish and elegant reception.

■ **Buffets may be better** A sit-down meal requires one server for every three to four tables, and you pay for every one. A buffet requires servers only at the serving tables.

■ **Alternative meal times** A morning wedding lends itself to a champagne brunch or a light lunch. An early afternoon ceremony could be followed by high tea with lavish sandwiches and strawberries and cream. A late afternoon service is perfect for a cocktail party with finger foods.

■ **Healthy desserts** Because you will be serving cake, do not feel you must offer other desserts. A platter of fresh fruit is an attractive and refreshing finish to any meal. If you want to dress up fruit such as strawberries or raspberries, offer whipped cream on the side.

■ **Discount catering** Look in the Yellow Pages under Schools and Colleges – Further Education to find a catering college and ask them for a quote for waiting staff and food.

BUDGET FOR BEVERAGES

Wine, beer, and a good selection of non-alcoholic beverages, plus champagne or sparkling wine for the toasts, is a less pricey and more satisfying approach than an open bar.

Bring your own The markup on alcoholic drinks is steep, so to save money buy your own rather than getting it from the caterer. But for a reception in licensed premises, such as a hotel or country club, check the corkage charge – it can range from £5 to over £30 for each bottle of champagne.

Toasting the bride Champagne or another sparkling wine really makes the toasts special, but not everyone wants to drink it throughout the reception. Save the bubbly for the toasts, and you can then invest in a better-quality wine.

Best of the bubbly If champagne rather than sparkling wine is your drink of choice, shop around for the best deal. During an end-of-summer wine offer, one supermarket offered Pol Aimé champagne in cases of six for under £58 (under £10 a bottle).

Alternative drinks For an afternoon reception, Pimms or a fruit punch may be cheaper and more appropriate than champagne. A winter wedding could lend itself to mulled wine or spiced cider; the heat of summer calls for jugs of white sangria.

GOOD DEALS ON CHAMPAGNE

CHAMPAGNE TYPE	COST/BOTTLE (12-BOTTLE CASE)
Brut Reserve	£12.80
Brut Rosé	£16.50
Louis Dornier Brut	£16.99
Vintage	£22.00
Laurent Perrier Brut	£23.99

Source: Prices from Majestic Wines, August 2004

CASE STUDY

HIGH STYLE ON A LOW BUDGET

When Julia and Richard Millbank were planning their summer wedding, they looked at where they could make savings without losing out on style. For invitations, they bought A5 parchment card and 50 envelopes for £40 and asked Richard's father if he would write them in his neat italic handwriting, saving at least 50% on printed cards. Julia looked in bridal boutiques for a dress but her favourite cost £1,500, so she asked a local dressmaker to alter her grandmother's gown for £100. Richard decided to buy an ex-hire morning suit for £160, which would come in useful for future formal occasions and eventually pay for itself in hire fees saved. The couple opted for an outdoor buffet reception in Julia's aunt's large garden. They decorated trestle tables with sumptuous brocade curtains bought at an auction for £50, adding pots of orchids at £5 each from a flower market. As the evening drew in, mini-lanterns (£14.95 for 10) strung through the trees gave a magical light.

Non-alcoholic options Offer plenty of non-alcoholic drinks too. Sparkling water, lemonade, fruit juices, or punch are all appropriate and will save you money.

LET THEM EAT CAKE

These days, you are not limited to the traditional fruit cake. You may want to try a more modern and less extravagant option, such as a lighter sponge.

Traditional fruit cake This is the most expensive cake to buy or make, but it can be cut into modest squares to make it go further. Choose a small fruit wedding cake for you and your partner to cut, and keep a second, simpler iced cake ready to be served out of sight.

Keep it square When you are working out portions, take into account that a square cake will provide more portions than a round cake of the same size.

Finish it yourself As fully iced cakes from a commercial bakery can easily cost £200 or more, ask the baker for a less elaborate 'occasion cake' – the same fruitcake and icing, but much cheaper. Then ask a relative or friend to personalise it as your wedding gift. Marks and Spencer sell plain luxury iced cakes ready to decorate and build into tiers – a 27.5cm (11in) fruit cake providing 60 portions costs around £45.

Individual fairy cakes A delightful alternative to make or buy, little fairy cakes are becoming popular with modern brides and will add a light-hearted touch to any reception. They can be personalised with guests' names or decorated to suit your colour scheme, and displayed in a tower or on tiered stands.

Keep it simple Intricate decorations take time, and time costs money. Instead of sugar flowers, pop some of your bouquet flowers in a tiny vase and use that as a topper for your cake.

THE DRESS OF YOUR DREAMS

Looking – and feeling – like a million dollars is, fortunately, not determined by the amount you spend on your dress.

Something old Visit antique shops and charity shops, as many brides wear their dresses once and then give them away. Also try the local papers and the eBay website.

Something new Try wedding warehouse sales – bridal dresses are from £149 and bridesmaid's dresses from £24. If you want a traditional designer gown, a less expensive route is to rent it. Check the Yellow Pages or the ads at the back of wedding magazines for hire shops.

Sew simple You may be able to make a simple style yourself, or have it made up from a pattern. Ask a friend or relative to help as their present to you.

Family heirlooms If it is still in good condition, the gown worn by a relative can work well. Pay a good dressmaker to alter the gown to fit you perfectly for around £120. Look in the Yellow Pages or ask your local dry cleaners if they have an alteration service.

Low-cost options An elegant ivory suit, a knee-length antique lace gown, or a dress in your favourite style can all be suitable wedding attire. Or choose a wedding dress that could easily be adapted for other occasions in the future, as this will save money in the long run.

Designer dresses at 25% off Oxfam have seven shops (Birmingham, Chippenham, Coventry, Leicester, Heswall, Southampton and Eastbourne), with their own bridal departments. They sell both new (a £700 designer dress for £150) and secondhand wedding dresses; and they can even find something special for your guests from pageboys to mother of the bride. Look at **www.oxfam.org.uk** ✉.

Off the peg Keep an eye on your favourite dress shop as you might find an evening dress suitable for your bridesmaids. One bride bought stylish, plain silk shifts from Wallis at £69.99 each for her two bridesmaids in their early twenties. They loved them and wore them to parties later.

A SPECIAL INVITATION

Instead of choosing traditional engraved invitations, look at the options at your favourite stationers. If these are still too expensive, consider the homemade approach.

Printing versus engraving Good printing looks handsome and costs about half as much as engraving. Paper quality affects cost too – a pretty, lightweight paper can be 70% cheaper than heavy card.

Your own fair hand A hand-written invitation that really reflects who you are, is much more intimate and evocative than a printed one, and costs little except time. If you cannot hand-write your invitations, ask a friend who is good at calligraphy. You can buy exquisite stationery and even good-value do-it-yourself invitation kits.

Special effects To dress up plain invitations, add wax seals, embossed stamps, foil or ribbon. Sprinkle a little confetti or potpourri inside the envelope before you seal it.

Hi-tech invites Design and print your invitations on a computer – you can download graphics from the web and use a fancy font. You could also scan in images of the venue.

CUTTING A DASH

■ Hiring a morning suit costs from £50, although the average cost of a wedding outfit is £197, according to a *You & Your Wedding* magazine survey. Look out for offers, such as free hire for the groom if six or more members of the party hire from the same company.

■ Consider buying rather than hiring. At most rental outfitters, you can buy a secondhand morning suit for only two or three times the single hire fee, which means it will pay for itself after just a few more formal occasions.

■ Don't be stifled by tradition or feel pressurised to wear a frock coat and top hat. If you already have a smart suit or dinner suit, wear this and spend the money saved on a new shirt, tie or waistcoat.

BUDGET BLOOMS

Flowers are beautiful in their own right and don't need to be extravagant to look elegant.

The bouquet Use only flowers in season and either arrange them yourself or ask a friend or relative to help. You could even use a kit, available from florists, to make a silk flower bouquet.

Decorations for the ceremony and reception Buy pot plants, which cost less than cut flowers and will not wither and die. Tie ribbons around the pots and let guests take them home.

TOP TIPS FINAL FLOURISHES

You can give your wedding an individual, stylish touch without breaking the bank by using local amateur talent rather than paying for professionals.

■ **Classic cars** Hiring a Rolls-Royce limo to get the bride to the ceremony is a time-honoured but expensive tradition that could set you back over £500. Ask through your local vintage car club to see if a proud owner would like to show off his prized horseless carriage for the day.

■ **Making music** Check with local music schools or universities to hire a good cellist, organist or soprano for the ceremony. Or play a CD of birdsong or other music that has a special meaning for you as background music. For the reception, check colleges for student dance bands and vocalists who might meet your needs and be less expensive than professional musicians.

■ **Photography deal** Ask the photographer if he will just deliver the negatives and proofs. You will make big savings if you print the photos and create a wedding album yourself.

■ **Candid camera** Hire a professional photographer just for the formal line-ups, and ask a friend to shoot informal photos at the reception. If you use a digital camera, you can email photos to your guests.

■ **Hidden cameras** For informal moments you'll treasure, put a disposable camera on each table. Online suppliers offer cameras from £1.25, or from £2.99 with flash.

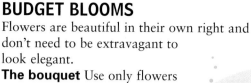 **RESOURCES**

WEDDING ADVICE AND INFORMATION ON THE INTERNET

■ Visit eBay for wedding supplies at **www.eBay.co.uk**

■ For information about wedding planning, try **www.confetti.co.uk** or **www.webwedding.co.uk**

■ To record the event, try **www. disposablecamerashop.co.uk**

■ For bouquets and flower arrangements, visit **www.weddingflowers freeservers.com**

■ To compare prices of drinks for a wedding party, visit **ww.champagne-cellar.co.uk**, and **www.virginwines.com**

Leisure and hobbies

Make your money go further so you can enjoy more of the good things in life – whether it's trips to the theatre, dining out with friends, pursuing hobbies or expanding your horizons.

DINING OUT ON A BUDGET

Although eating out is a luxury, you can treat yourself without breaking the bank. Take advantage of special deals and plan in advance, so you have time to find the right offer.

CASH IN ON OFFERS

Keep an eye out for special offers that will make your meal a real steal – such as two for the price of one.

Newspaper deals Watch both local and national newspapers such as *The Times* and *The Daily Telegraph* for special offers and coupons, especially early in the year when business is slow. You will generally have to choose from a set menu, and drinks are often extra, but you could find yourself enjoying a two-course meal at a good restaurant for just £10 a head.

Watch the web Regularly check websites such as www.lastminute.com ✉ and www.toptable.co.uk ✉. These sites offer special deals throughout the year; for example, lastminute's set meals for two in many major cities range from £9.50 (two-course) to £15 (three-course). Lastminute also has an 'Eat out for under £15' page. Toptable has a similar page of low-price deals and a 'Special offers' link, giving users exclusive deals such as free wine or free dessert when you use their services to make a booking for your meal. www.5pm.co.uk has many offers such as £5 for two courses. You will need to register with them, which is free, in order to book a table.

AVOID HIGH WINE PRICES

One of the major expenses when eating out is the wine, so you can make a substantial saving by bringing your own bottle to establishments that allow this.

The unlicensed option Although unlicensed (or Bring Your Own) restaurants, where you can drink your own wine with your meal, are more common in America and Australia, there is a growing trend for them in Britain. To find a BYO restaurant near you, look at the Bring Your Own Bottle Directory website www.wine-pages.com/byoblist.shtml ✉.

Beware of the corkage charge Most BYO restaurants levy a 'corkage charge' – a charge decided by the management for serving wine brought by customers – on BYO wine. It is normally charged by the bottle and can be anything from a few pounds upwards, so check before you dine to avoid paying more than you bargained for, and instead of taking two bottles take one large one.

Budget eating Most BYO restaurants are small and inexpensive, so they won't stretch the budget when it comes to paying for the food.

TIMING IS EVERYTHING

Save up to half the cost of a meal by visiting a restaurant for lunch instead of dinner. The average cost of a meal at a well-known restaurant is £30, but their two-course lunchtime

---

keep it simple

STILL WATER FROM THE TAP
When you order still water with your meal, order a glass or carafe of tap water, rather than bottled water. For a very slight taste difference, you will save the cost of the bottled water, which is not only expensive to begin with, but also carries a high mark-up in most restaurants.

 **RESOURCES**

RESTAURANT DEALS
To help you plan your value-for-money meal in London, look at:
■ *Time Out London Cheap Eats Guide*, £6.99
■ www.lastminute.com ✉, www.toptable.co.uk ✉ and www.5pm.co.uk ✉. All offer special-value meals nationwide.

RESOURCES

MOTORWAY ALTERNATIVES

To avoid paying high prices for eating out while travelling on the motorway, research your stops before you set out. Plan a short detour into a small town, and phone the local tourist office for places to park and good-value food.

■ **www.5minutesaway.co.uk** ✉ lists restaurants, pubs and other facilities within five minutes' drive of motorway service stations.

■ Good Guides publish both *Good Pub Guide* at £14.99 (ISBN 91899303) and *Great Food Pubs* at £5.99 (ISBN 91885167). Or text 'goodpub' to 85130 from your mobile phone to get details of the nearest pub on their list. The cost is 50p plus call cost.

■ *AA Britain's Best Afternoon Tea* at £9.99 (ISBN 0749839771) is published by the AA and the Tea Council.

menu is just £15 a head. Or dine in the evening during the week, when cut-price set menus may be on offer, instead of at a weekend when prices are often higher.

BE A PIONEER DINER

One way of paying less for a gourmet meal is to visit new restaurants soon after they have opened – prices are naturally lower before a new venue develops its reputation. This can be a bit of a gamble, but if you watch the reviews in the dining sections of the local and national papers and at sites such as Dine Online (**www.dine-online.co.uk** or **www.restaurant-guide.com**), you can get some idea of what to expect and a price guide.

TAKE THE SET MENU

To reduce the bill, it's worth giving the restaurant's set menu a try instead of choosing your own dishes. Set menus are designed to allow the restaurant to charge a little less for meals and still give you a delicious culinary experience. Restaurants that only offer a set menu are even better value as they have far lower overheads.

AVOID THE TIPPING TRAP

Don't automatically tip at restaurants; first make sure that service isn't already included in your bill and don't be embarrassed to ask if it's not clear. It often is, especially if you are a group of more than six people. Give tips to reward good service: 10% is the usual amount or 15% if the service has been exceptional.

MOTORWAY MADNESS

Avoid motorway service stations where refreshment prices can be double what non-motorway equivalents charge (£3 for a sandwich and £1.80 for coffee). Spend a few extra minutes to drive to somewhere cheaper. Pubs and cafés in nearby towns will have better food at a lower price (see Resources, left). Find them by reading guide books such as *The Rough Guide to Britain*, available in libraries, and making a note of eating places they recommend.

Bring-and-dine clubs

SMART MOVES

If eating out is beyond your means, or you don't want to travel far to find fine dining, get together with like-minded people to save on costs and still create a real sense of occasion. Organise a bring-and-dine club with a group of friends or neighbours. Arrange to meet regularly – perhaps once a month – at someone's home and each bring a different element of a three-course meal: one of you can organise a starter, someone else the main course and a third person the dessert. Other people can take charge of the table decorations and wine. You all get to try new foods and wines in different settings and the costs are split between all the participants, allowing big savings. Even a lavish meal in a carefully arranged setting will cost much less than the normal restaurant equivalent.

For example, a sirloin steak at a Harvester restaurant costs £11, while a similar home-cooked meal bought from the supermarket can cost as little as £4-£5.

BARGAIN-BASEMENT EATING

If your budget is really tight but you still want to enjoy the luxury of eating out, there are other ways to experience very cheap or even free meals.

The proverbial free lunch Look out for luncheon vouchers, which may be offered to you by your employer or on training courses and seminars, when trains or flights are delayed, as part of a tourist package or as compensation for bad service. You can use them towards the cost of a meal at over 33,000 outlets in Britain, including restaurants, cafés sandwich bars, fast food outlets and most big supermarkets. You can even pick up luncheon vouchers free for agreeing to complete surveys for some research companies; for example, PineCone Research **www2.pineconeresearch.co.uk** offers a £4 voucher when you complete a survey for them.

Vouchers for discounted dining If you don't object to participating in surveys, keep an eye on websites such as **www.Vouch4me.com**, which offers a selection of two-for-one dining vouchers at various restaurants. Other websites, such as **www.wishvalue.co.uk**, offer a selection of discount vouchers for cheap eating out if you register with the company holding the promotion.

RESOURCES

LUNCHEON VOUCHERS
For information on luncheon vouchers, contact **Accor Services** 0845 3304433 **www.luncheonvouchers. co.uk** ✉.

PRE-THEATRE DINING

To get value for money while enjoying an indulgent evening out, consider a dinner and show package, available from **www.lastminute.com** ✉. We found a package including top-price seats for a West End musical (usual price £45) and dinner at a nearby restaurant (average cost a head £40) costing just £40 a person, making a saving of £45.
Or, in summer, take an up-market picnic and eat it in a nearby park or on the riverbank.

THE WINE LIST: GETTING VALUE FOR MONEY

Each restaurant has its own pricing policy, with mark-ups typically ranging from 200% or 300% upwards. The mark-up covers the expertise of the buyer, so get value from your spending by trying a wine you don't know, then checking it out at a wine store.

TYPE OF WINE	RESTAURANT PRICE	RETAIL PRICE (TYPICALLY)	MARK-UP
House wine	£12	£3-£4	300%-400%
Mid-range	£30	£10	300%
Superior	£100+	£30-£50	200%-300%

TIPS
■ Don't order by the glass: if two or more of you are drinking a few glasses of wine it can work out 20% cheaper to order by the bottle.
■ Unless you spot a wine you know, opt for one from the same region as the restaurant's cuisine: these should have been chosen with more discernment.
■ Discuss the choice with the sommelier or waiter. Ask for their recommendation within your price bracket.
■ If in doubt, pay a few pounds more for wine, then skip the coffee.

LOW-COST ENTERTAINMENT

Evenings out at the theatre, trips to the cinema and days out with the family visiting places of interest need not be occasional treats. Find out about cut-price ticket deals so you can make your money go further.

TOP TIPS CUT-PRICE THEATRE TICKETS

If an evening at the theatre appeals but the price of a ticket puts you off, use the cut-price offers and special deals that are available to those in the know.

■ **Preview deals** Book for previews before the show has been reviewed – these first few performances are normally offered at a reduced rate and sometimes even half price.

■ **Off-peak shows** Look in national and local newspapers for adverts offering discounts on major shows at quiet times of the year. By quoting a reference number from the paper when booking through the box office, you can benefit from as much as a 50% reduction or a two-for-one offer.

■ **On-the-day reductions** Buy tickets for West End theatres half price on the day of performance at the official booths in Leicester Square (Monday to Saturday 10am–7pm; Sunday noon–3pm) and Canary Wharf DLR station (Monday to Saturday 11.30am–6pm). At Leicester Square, queues start forming from 9am in summer and a little later in winter, so get there early. Visit **www.officiallondontheatre.co.uk** ✉ and select 'TKTS Ticket' for a guide of what will be on sale.

■ **Lend a hand** Volunteer for a scheme such as Shape Arts **www.shapearts.org.uk** 020 7619 6160 ✉ to be an escort-driver and accompany an elderly or disabled person to the theatre – you'll have expenses paid and watch the show free.

■ **Just the ticket** London Transport offers season ticket holders cheap tickets to many London events. Visit **www.thetube.com** and click on the 'Going Out' link, or enquire at a London Transport booking office.

■ **Save up to 70%** At some theatres, standby tickets are offered an hour before a show starts to the over 60s, unemployed, students or theatre union members with valid ID – although there is the chance you might not get in.

CASE STUDY

THEATRE WONDERLAND
Retired teacher Sonia March lives in north London and the theatre and musicals have always been the love of her life. Now she has time to indulge herself, but with a limited income she makes sure she gets value for money. One week she went with a friend to a preview of *Singin' in the Rain* at Sadler's Wells on Tuesday, each paying just £8 by booking well in advance. On Wednesday they got tickets for a matinée performance of *Les Misérables* at less than half price through the Leicester Square ticket booth. Then to round off the week, they took advantage of the £10 Travelex Season at the National Theatre and saw *Measure for Measure*, enjoying a free jazz concert in the foyer beforehand. All in all, Sonia paid a total of £43.00, making a saving of around £45.00 on normal prices.

JOIN A MAILING LIST

If you're a keen theatre-goer, it's worth getting on the mailing list of your favourite venues. If possible, book direct rather than through an agency, who add a hefty fee.

Direct from the theatre The National Theatre ✉, Royal Shakespeare Company ✉ and many other theatres nationwide charge around £10 a year to send you performance schedules. You get priority booking and discounted ticket offers (such as evenings where all seats are £10), including premières. For an online listing of UK theatres, see **www.theatresonline.com** ✉. Visit your library or information centre for local theatre details.

Web mailing lists Ticketmaster, **www.latestevents.com** ✉ and SeeTickets **www.seetickets.com** ✉ all make special offers of their free services available to subscribers.

Join a newspaper club Newspapers including *The Times*, *The Sunday Times*, London's *Evening Standard*, the *Daily Telegraph* and the *Sunday Telegraph* all run theatre clubs. For little outlay, you can take advantage of the special offers regularly published in the papers. Phone the box office number given in the paper for your discounted tickets.

LITERARY EVENINGS

Look out for special events at nearby bookshops. Many now host literary evenings or poetry events which are free or charge a nominal fee that may include a glass of wine. You could hear your favourite authors read their latest work or discover some exciting new writers.

TOP TIPS MUSIC FOR A SONG

To find cheap tickets for the opera, contact the venue to find out whether they are offering any special deals. The easiest way to do this is to browse their website or phone their enquiry line before booking.

■ **For opera lovers** The Royal Opera House ✉, The English National Opera ✉, The Welsh National Opera ✉, and Scottish Opera ✉ offer limited numbers of reduced-cost tickets to encourage opera-goers. When Opera North ✉ perform at Leeds Grand Theatre groups of 10 or more can get a 20% discount plus a free seat for the organiser. Phone Opera North for information on this and other offers.

■ **LSO** The London Symphony Orchestra (020 7588 1116 ✉) offers up to 20% discount for booking multiple events. It also gives regular free lunchtime recitals at St Lukes, Old Street, London ✉, in addition to free public rehearsals.

■ **Outdoor culture** Many local groups put on free or inexpensive events during the summer when audiences can be seated outdoors. Churches, pubs and parks are the usual venues. These types of entertainment are normally advertised on church notice boards and in local papers.

■ **Visit a music school** Many music schools, such as London's Royal Academy of Music ✉, allow observers to listen in on rehearsals for students, as well as giving free entrance to public recitals undertaken as part of their degree. These are often of an exceptionally high standard and give a fascinating insight into music education. Look in the Yellow Pages to find music schools in your area.

SUPPORT YOUR LOCAL PLAYERS

Save on the cost of attending a big show by supporting the smaller fringe groups, pub theatres and good local societies. Amateur dramatic and opera societies often give outstanding performances for a fraction of the price of the professional ones. Your local paper and library notice boards will have announcements about performances. Internet users can go to **www.amdram.co.uk** to get information about amateur theatre productions across Britain.

 **RESOURCES**

OPERA AND CONCERT TICKETS
Look at the following websites to find a discounted deal for a night at the opera:
■ Click on the Classical and Opera link on **www.lastminute.com** ✉.
■ Check the Performing Arts section for opera listings and offers on **www.ticketmaster.co.uk** ✉.
■ For listing of opera and concerts nationwide, including minor venues, go to **www.concert-diary.com** ✉. Contact the venues direct for tickets.

CHEAP CINEMA TICKETS

Whether you are a dedicated film buff or an occasional cinema-goer, there are ways you can see a film for far less than the full price.

'Early bird' deals For films starting before noon, tickets can cost between half to a third less than the standard price.

Cheap days Check with your local cinema to see if they have discount days. Many cinemas offer cheaper tickets if you go before 6pm, or on Monday to Thursday. Fridays and weekends are almost always more expensive.

Become a member Cinema chains such as UCI ✉ and Odeon ✉ encourage visitors to their cinemas and websites to register with them and receive offers such as food vouchers and trailer CDs. Many also offer free membership to Kids' Club, Odeon Movie Mob or similar groups. Once you join, you can take a child to the cinema during weekends and school holidays for a cost of £1–£2 for a child, and at UCI an accompanying adult gets in free. Students also often qualify for discounts.

DISCOUNTED EXCURSIONS

Many organisations and schemes offer discounts to members, so if you already belong to any of them, take advantage of your entitlement. If not, you may find it worthwhile joining.

Two for the road The AA has two-for-one offers to members, such as entrance fees to Kew Gardens and English Heritage sites. They also offer ticket deals to attractions such as Legoland, where a child gets in free with an accompanying adult. For membership details, contact the AA on 0870 600 0371, or visit **www.theaa.com** ✉.

Supermarket days out Large supermarket chains, such as Tesco and Sainsbury's, reward customer loyalty through their points schemes. Points can be exchanged for tickets to all kinds of attractions and museums, saving you up to 75% of the normal price (see *Practical parenting*, page 108).

Banks offer discounts Many high-street banks offer current accounts whose monthly fee entitles holders to discounts on days out and other types of entertainment. The Royal Bank of Scotland's Royalties current account, which costs £5 a month, gives holders discounts on days out and dining. If you hold this type of account with a high-street bank, take full advantage of these offers.

Savings for frequent visitors The National Art Collections Fund offers its members unlimited free access to more than 200 museums, galleries and historic houses across Britain that normally charge for admission. The Art Fund card also grants free or discounted entry to major exhibitions. Single membership costs £23–£35, depending on age; family membership is £52 and includes any children under 18 living at the same address. For details call 0870 848 2003 or visit **www.artfund.org** ✉.

Print your own coupons A number of websites offer discounts for family days out, such as two-for-one deals. The website **www.daysoutuk.com** ✉ has 62 attractions to choose from. To benefit from offers, you need to print your own coupons and take them along to your chosen venue.

RESOURCES

CUT-PRICE CINEMA
To find good deals at cinemas try the following:
- The *Independent* **www.independent.co.uk** ✉ – sign up for the Arts Card for free tickets to film previews.
- Odeon cinemas **www.odeon.co.uk** ✉
- Orange film offer **www.orange.co.uk entertainment/film/cma/ overview.html** ✉
- UCI Cinemas **www.uci.co.uk** ✉
- UGC cinemas **www.ugccinemas.co.uk** ✉
- Vue cinemas **www.myvue.com** ✉

keep it simple

BFI MEMBERSHIP
If you join the National Film Theatre section of the BFI (British Film Institute ✉) you get one free ticket a year, £1 off tickets for yourself and up to three guests and money off tickets to cultural events across London. Annual membership is £24 (2004); go to **www.bfi.org. uk/showing/nft/about/join. html** or phone 020 7815 1374 for how to join.

The group solution

Save 20%–50% on ticket prices by forming a group of eight or more people.

■ Contact the venue to check their policy on group booking: the number of people needed to qualify as a group and the discount applied varies.

■ To assemble enough people, try placing an advert on the notice board of your local club, school or church organisation.

■ The larger the group, the lower the prices should be. If you don't feel the discount is large enough, don't be afraid to haggle.

FREE EXTRAS

■ Extra concessionary rates are normally given to certain groups – children up to 16 and pensioners – for midweek matinées.

■ If your group contacts a venue in advance, you may get more free extras. For example, Clyne Gardens and the Botanical Gardens in Swansea will provide either a guided tour or give an informative talk to members of your group if you arrange this with the gardens before the visit.

COACH TOURS

■ If you can't find a large enough group to qualify for big discounts, try joining a coach tour. Check your local paper or information centre for offers.

■ Transport costs, parking charges and show tickets are included in the price.

■ The whole package often costs less than the price of a ticket alone.

FREE TO THE PUBLIC

Many museums, galleries and tourist attractions in major cities do not charge entrance fees and often merit several visits.

Public museums Most public museums are now free and offer both adults and children an educational as well as entertaining day out.

Free art Entry is free to the permanent collection of most regional art galleries as well as famous London art museums such as the National Gallery and Tate Modern.

Visit the House of Commons British residents can participate in free guided tours, which are available on some weekdays by contacting their MP. Phone the House of Commons information service on 020 7219 4272 (**www.parliament.uk** ✉) if you don't know who your MP is and they can find contact details for you. To round off the day, you could visit Westminster Abbey, which is free for evensong. For details of other free attractions in the capital, visit **www.londontourist.org/free.html** ✉.

Local government websites Websites run by your local authority (which will end in **.gov.uk**) often list free attractions and events in your area, as well as other cheap days out.

Free walks As walking is not only free but a convenient way to see the sights, work out an itinerary that includes some spectacular scenery or historical landmarks. Maps are often free at local transport centres.

DAYS OUT AT A DISCOUNT

If you are in the know, you can save pounds on days out to popular attractions such as gardens, zoos and theme parks. Visiting in low season, using special-offer coupons or seeking out smaller venues can all cut ticket prices dramatically.

VISITING GARDENS

Check magazines such as *BBC Gardeners' World* for occasional money-off vouchers for gardens around Britain.
RHS members free Members of the Royal Horticultural Society ✉ get free entry to the Society's gardens and other privately run gardens, as well as reductions on tickets to major horticultural events such as the Chelsea Flower Show ✉. Membership costs £40 a year.
Private views For a list of allotments and private gardens open to the public for charity, contact the National Gardens Scheme or look in *The Yellow Book* (see Resources, left), published annually by the National Gardens Scheme ✉.

HERITAGE SITES FOR ALL

If you enjoy visiting Britain's wealth of heritage sites on a regular basis, join organisations that give you free entry.
National Trust sites The National Trust ✉ has more than 300 properties and gardens in its care. Yearly membership including free entry and parking costs £36 for an adult. For membership details, call 0870 458 4000 or visit **www. nationaltrust.org.uk** ✉ (see *Practical parenting*, page 108).
A sense of history English Heritage maintains over 400 historic sites. For £34 a year, you get free entry to castles, monuments and fine homes. Call 0870 333 1182 or visit **english-heritage.org.uk** ✉ for details.

TOP TIPS A DAY AT THE ZOO

As with many other days out, visiting the zoo needn't be an expensive experience as long as you are aware of the pitfalls.
■ **Avoid high season** Some zoos offer lower admission at low season. Woburn Safari Park ✉ offers winter tickets at less than half the price of high season, and the London Aquarium ✉ offers off-peak entry for around £1 less.

■ **More is cheaper** Many zoos offer reductions to groups (normally 15 or more people or, for London ✉ and Whipsnade ✉ zoos, 20 or more).

■ **Try smaller attractions** Lesser known wildlife parks and animal experiences such as butterfly farms are cheaper than bigger zoos. Use the Internet or local tourist office to find these smaller sites.

CHEAP THRILLS

Although theme parks are not cheap, you can save by buying tickets in advance.

Coupons and loyalty points Keep an eye on newspapers for special offer coupons and also on your supermarket's loyalty points scheme. Both Sainsbury's and Tesco's schemes allow you to buy tickets to many theme parks with your points, reducing the cost by up to 75%.

Website bargains Check on eBay **www.ebay.co.uk** ✉ for cut-price tickets for many major attractions; sometimes they are available at a third of the normal price. You can also save up to 10% by booking on the theme park website.

SAVE ON THEME PARK TICKETS

The chart below shows how much a family of four can save by buying a family ticket instead of individual tickets, and visiting off-peak. If you are likely to visit more than three times a year (or four times for Thorpe Park), it pays to get an annual pass.

PARK	CONTACT DETAILS	INDIVIDUAL	FAMILY	ANNUAL
ALTON TOWERS	Alton, Staffordshire 08705 204060 www.altontowers.com	£97 peak £74 off-peak	£82 peak £68 off-peak	£195
CHESSINGTON	World of Adventures, Surrey 0870 444 7777 www.chessington.com	£56 no off-peak	£56 no off-peak	none
LEGOLAND	Windsor, Berkshire 08705 040404 www.legoland.co.uk	£86 peak £80 off-peak	none	£200
THORPE PARK	Chertsey, Surrey 0870 444 4466 www.thorpepark.com	£97 peak £65 off-peak	£75 peak £50 off-peak	£240

Information July 2004.

Prices given for individual and family tickets, and annual family passes, are costed for a family of four with two children under 12.

CUT THE COST OF HOBBIES

Hobbies needn't cost a fortune. Even if you are collecting or need specialist equipment or materials, you can indulge in your chosen pastime without paying over the odds by buying secondhand and taking advantage of special deals.

ANTIQUES AND COLLECTABLES

The price-conscious collector can save money by knowing where to shop and using free resources.

Secondhand bargains When starting up a collection, don't head for big auctions. Instead, browse the classified ads in your local paper, or visit car boot sales and house contents auctions. Look in the Yellow Pages for local salesrooms.

Free expertise Gain free insider know-how from web pages such as **www.atg-online.com/Default.asp** ✉. By logging on, you can join **www.antiquestradegazette.com** ✉, which gives guide prices and other trade information.

STAMP-COLLECTING BARGAINS

Most stamp-collecting begins as an inexpensive hobby, using stamps found on envelopes. Keep costs under control as you expand your collection.

Contact an office Besides asking friends and relatives for used stamps, particularly those with contacts abroad, ask anyone who sorts the mail in an office – large, international companies are ideal.

Collect together There are groups that can help you collect stamps economically: The Great Britain Philatelic Society **www.gbps.org.uk** ✉, The National Philatelic Society **www.ukphilately.org.uk/nps** ✉, Stamp & Coin Mart **www.stampmart.co.uk** ✉ and Linns Stamp News International stamp magazine website **www.linns.com** ✉.

Find bargains in magazines Buy a philatelic magazine, such as the *GB Journal*, the magazine of the Great Britain Philatelic Society, which also organises postal auctions; *Stamp Lover*, the magazine of the NPS; or *Stamp & Coin Mart*. All carry ads for swaps wanted.

KEEP GARDENING COSTS DOWN

Let your garden grow without incurring large costs by finding ways of getting discounts on supplies and equipment.

Cheap supplies Let nature provide what you need for your hobby. Collect seeds one year to grow the next, take cuttings and swap them with other gardeners you know and save your vegetable waste to make compost. Gardening on the cheap takes time, but if you have time to spare, you can create a successful garden for very little outlay.

Group discounts By joining your local horticultural society, you can take advantage of discounts on garden chemicals and supplies. Membership charges tend to be very low and are more than recouped in savings. Phone your council and ask if they have a list of local societies, check in your

Read more for less

If you love reading, keep the costs of your hobby down by not paying the full price for books.
Secondhand books For a wide range of books try secondhand bookshops. Many have their own websites and an online catalogue, such as Barter Books, **www.barterbooks.co.uk** 01665 604880 ✉.

Discount books For new books and secondhand titles, search the big online suppliers, such as Abebooks **www.abebooks.co.uk** ✉, Amazon **www.amazon.co.uk** ✉ and BOL **www.uk.bol.com** ✉. You may make a saving of more than 50%. Amazon may offer a book either new or secondhand – for a best deal take secondhand.
Book clubs If you are a regular reader, it may be

worth joining a book club. The Book People **www.thebookpeople.co.uk** 0870 607 7740 ✉ offer discounted books online or from their catalogue.
Book groups If you have friends who also like to read, form a reading group and assemble a private library. All members have access to a wider range of reading material than their own individual collections.

library for information or ask other gardeners living nearby.
Rent an allotment If you want more space for growing your own vegetables, rent an allotment. Apply to your local council (parks, recreation and leisure department) who will advise on locations and availability. The cost of a plot varies depending on size and facilities provided, but the average nationwide is £25–£30 a year for a 250m² plot. A 50% concession is available if you have a state pension or receive benefits. For general advice contact National Society of Allotment and Leisure Gardeners **www.nsalg.demon.co.uk** 01536 266576 ✉.

SEWING AND KNITTING ON A BUDGET

With a bit of searching, needlework enthusiasts can find bargains that will save them the cost of several new patterns.
Bargain fabrics Search in secondhand clothes shops and charity shops for unusual textiles for cushions and throws. Markets and discount fabric outlets are another inexpensive source. Keep a note of how much fabric you need for your favourite patterns so you can buy the right amount when you chance on a bargain such as pure wool for £2 a metre.
Patterns for pennies Look in charity shops and car boot sales for secondhand stitching books and dress patterns. Many embroidery and knitting patterns, for items such as Aran sweaters, don't date. Search **www.ebay.co.uk** ✉ for patterns as cheap as 99p, many of them vintage.
Stitching showcases Visit needlecraft shows, advertised in stitching and craft magazines, where you find a lot of suppliers with special promotions.

ECONOMICAL ART AND CRAFT SUPPLIES

If your hobby requires craft-related material, get together with like-minded people to benefit from group discounts.
High-street bargains High-street arts and crafts suppliers often offer discounts to art society members and students. Find details in your local library or on your council website.
Online bulk buys Online suppliers such as Craft Depot **www.craftdepot.co.uk** ✉ offer craft-related materials at discounted prices, particularly if you buy in quantity.

RESOURCES

NEEDLEWORK FOR NEXT TO NOTHING

For free patterns and cut-price fabrics look at:
■ **www.woolworks.org** ✉ offers free knitting patterns.
■ **www.cross-stitch-club. co.uk** ✉ has free cross-stitch patterns.
■ For designer fabrics at up to 50% discount contact Discount Fabrics & Wallpaper on 08705 239955 or visit **www.homeinteriors.co.uk** ✉.
■ For silks, satins and sequinned fabrics, contact Online Fabrics on **www.online-fabrics.co.uk** 024 7668 7776 ✉.

MAKING MUSIC

The cost of musical instruments can be enough to deter some would-be players, but you needn't allow financial considerations to put paid to your dreams.

CHECK THE CLASSIFIEDS

Many good deals can be found in the classified ads. Almost-new instruments should be at least 25% cheaper. Look at www.prepal.com ✉, for current secondhand market prices.

STRINGS FOR BUDDING PLAYERS

A stringed instrument for a child, such as a violin, is better rented than bought because a child will quickly outgrow quarter or half-size versions. When your child is big enough to handle a full-size instrument, purchase a good-quality secondhand one. Take expert advice from a tutor or knowledgeable friend to ensure you make the right purchase.

WHEN TO HIRE

If you are taking private lessons, consider hiring your equipment until you are sure you have made the right choice. Many music shops offer hire schemes for used and new instruments: you can offset the hire fees paid against the purchase of the instrument should you wish to buy it.

BE WARY WITH PIANOS

Repairing a badly treated upright piano can cost as much as £3,000, so take expert advice before buying secondhand.

SCHOOLS' PURCHASING POWER

Child-sized woodwind and brass instruments tend to be better value new than stringed instruments, so you are safer buying these, although the same problems of a child outgrowing them quickly apply. Ask your local authority schools' music centre if they have any secondhand instruments for sale, or whether there is a local authority-assisted purchase scheme.

SPECIALIST SOURCES

For good deals on musical instruments, try:
Dawkes Music 01628 630 800
www.dawkes.co.uk ✉
John Packer Ltd 01823 282386
Signet Music www.signetmusic.com ✉
Music Attacks www.musicattacks.com ✉
London's Denmark Street WC2 has many music shops – look at www.tinpanalley.co.uk ✉.

ADDED EXTRAS

Always ask if the carrying case is included in any price quoted. Often it isn't. Be prepared to haggle with the retailer. Ask if he'll throw in some extras for free – wood polish, reed, extra strings, tube cleaners, straps or even a music lesson.

GREAT-VALUE OUTDOOR PURSUITS

Many hobbies, such as birdwatching, cycling and rambling, require little additional outlay once you have bought the basic equipment. Although some of this may be expensive, you can still keep costs down if you know how.

WATCH PENNIES ON BIRDWATCHING

Before investing in a pair of binoculars or telescope, contact the RSPB (The Royal Society for the Protection of Birds). They organise events where you can try them in the field and give advice on choosing equipment to match your budget.

Magazine ads The RSPB's magazine *Birds* and most photographers' magazines carry adverts for new and second-hand equipment. Many of the listed specialist suppliers will part-exchange your old items.

Try a dealer Specialist high-street dealers such as Jessops (0116 232 6000 ✉) or Kay Optical (0208 648 8822 ✉) can be good for new and secondhand binoculars. A basic pair costs £50–£150 new, and a better-quality pair £350 – though the same pair would be only £50 secondhand. You may find binoculars in your local paper for as little as £15.

SAVE ON FISHING

By avoiding the peak season and finding cheap sources of equipment and bait, you can enjoy fishing on a budget.

Buy secondhand Both eBay and your local paper can be a fruitful source of cheap, almost-new items, sold by people who have quickly upgraded their fishing equipment.

Mail order Bait can be expensive when ordered in small quantities from your local tackle shop, but the mail-order companies that advertise in publications such as *Angler's Mail* and *Angling Times* often offer a better deal, especially if you buy in bulk. Team up with fishing friends or join your local fishing club to save money on bait. For listings of fishing clubs in Britain, look at **www.go-fishing.co.uk** ✉.

keep it simple

HIRE, DON'T BUY
If you want to avoid the cost of buying all your equipment, or aren't sure whether you'll continue with a new-found hobby (such as camping or skiing), consider hiring it, at least until you are sure you want to continue. Beans of Bicester offer ski wear and camping equipment for hire by the day as well as equipment for sale. Contact Beans of Bicester 01869 246451 **www.beansonline.co.uk** ✉.

FISH FOR A DISCOUNT AT THE POST OFFICE
If you are a pensioner or registered disabled, take advantage of the discounted fishing licences available only at Post Offices.

Go low-season to cheaper waters Buy off-season day tickets for lower prices – game (fly) fishing waters often charge less at non-peak times (that is, before 31 May). Although fly fishing is generally more expensive than coarse fishing (both for equipment and for tickets), game fishing in man-made lakes is generally cheaper than river fishing.

Fishing on the net The Environment Agency's website **www.environment-agency.gov.uk** ✉ is good for special offers on fishing. A recent promotion was for people who may not normally fish – juniors, over 50s and women – to take up fishing in the West Country. New anglers were offered a day's fishing, an instructor, equipment and any fish caught, with no need to buy a rod licence – all for £5.

SPORTS EQUIPMENT AT A DISCOUNT

Buy secondhand if you can. The difference in price between a barely used and a full-price item from your local sports shop can be as much as 70%.

High-street shopping High-street shops such as Argos Sports (**www.argossports.co.uk**) often carry cheap sports and fitness equipment, particularly in their sales.

Internet bargains For expensive specialist items, search online for sites that offer discounts, such as Jags Online **www.jags-online.co.uk** ✉ or Exercise Zone **www.exercisezone.co.uk** ✉. You can save more than 50% on clearance and sale items.

WALKING AND CAMPING

Specialist camping dealers are not always the cheapest for basic equipment. Check other sources to bag a better deal.

High-street bargains Find cheap camping equipment – for example, tents, airbeds, cooking equipment and mats – in high-street shops such as Argos, Nettos or Halfords.

Discount shops The Outdoor Megastore **www.outdoormegastore.co.uk** ✉ is an online clearance warehouse for many top-name brands of outdoor clothing and equipment. The online shop World of Camping **www.worldofcamping.co.uk** ✉ have good sales discounts.

Make do and mend Walking boots should not be bought secondhand; boots that have been 'worn in' to fit someone else's feet will never be comfortable. If your old boots are worn out, have them repaired by a company like Feet First (**www.feetfirst.resoles.co.uk** 0114 258 9529), who specialise in resoling outdoor footwear. A resole repair costs £30–£35, whereas a new pair of boots costs around £50–£100.

Used maps and guides Book sites such as Amazon have many secondhand maps and guide books on all parts of Great Britain. For a list of those currently available, see the Explore Britain website **www.xplorebritain.com** ✉.

Cut-price tents Attend camping exhibitions (such as the Caravan and Outdoor Leisure Show ✉ at Earl's Court, London, in November, or one of the smaller camping events held throughout the summer), where you can try out equipment and pick up a good deal at reduced prices if you buy there and then. If you're looking for a tent, wait until the end of the show – you may make substantial savings by buying one of the tents set up for the exhibition.

GOLF EQUIPMENT AT A DISCOUNT

Brand new golfing equipment is expensive – a 16-piece starter set costs around £130 at Argos. Secondhand shops, websites and your local golf club can help soften the blow.

Sourcing secondhand Many general secondhand shops carry golfing equipment discarded by their original owner. Online auction sites such as eBay can also be a source of bargains, as are local papers and boot sales. It is also worth asking friends who are keen golfers and are upgrading clubs if they are thinking about selling their old set.

Go to the specialists Specialist online shops such as Online Golf www.onlinegolf.co.uk ✉ also have special offers and clearance bargains on discontinued lines.

Shop abroad Take advantage of business trips and holidays to stock up on golfing equipment – in September 2002, the *Sunday Telegraph* reported that Orlando, Florida, had golfing equipment priced at least 35% lower (and equipment for other sports 20%–30% lower) than in Britain. Research comparative prices on the web or at specialist golf shops in the UK before you go.

BETTER-VALUE BICYCLES

Buying a bicycle secondhand can be good value but if you don't know much about them, take along a friend who does.

Go private Buy secondhand from a private seller (through a newspaper or bike magazine ad). It's generally cheaper than buying from a retailer who stocks used models.

Bike auctions These can be excellent places to pick up bargains. Local schools and the police often run them. Look at local ads, or ask at your local police station for details.

Buying new For good advice, look for shops that are Association of Cycle Traders (ACT ✉) members and have staff that are CyTech accredited. The best times of year for bargains are autumn, when shops make room for new stock, and January and February when there are sales.

Cheap and cheerful Buying a low-cost basic model for about £150 rather than opting for a lower range of specialist bike which could be as much as £400–£500, can be a sensible option if you're not sure how much you'll use it. Once you have a couple of years of cycling experience you'll know better how you want to spend your money.

keep it simple

MUNICIPAL VS CLUB
Many local councils run golf courses and charge around £10 for 18 holes. Private clubs charge a minimum of £30 a round, and you have to be a member or be playing with one. Rules and etiquette on municipal courses also tend to be more relaxed, so they are good places for beginners or youngsters to start.

SAVING ON SPORTS

If you enjoy spectator sports, you can get great discounts for big matches, or make savings by watching good amateur teams instead. And if you prefer to participate, you can save money on even the more expensive sports.

TAKING PART AT LOCAL LEVEL
If you enjoy participating in a sport, join a local club or team. Membership at local level isn't expensive and you will have access to the club's equipment and coaching. At a rowing club in Avon, prospective members get two free lessons before joining at £17 a month. Contact Sport England ✉ to access a wide variety of local clubs, from aikido to wrestling. Or visit your local government office's website or your library for more information.

SPECTATOR SAVINGS
Save on the price of a ticket to a sports event by organising a group of friends, or an outing from your sports society, school or work. TicketMaster offers discounts of 50% or more to organisers of groups, and other ticket sellers offer similar discounts. If you go as part of a group you can expect to save 10%–20%.

Take a cheap seat Buy one of the cheaper higher seats in a stadium, where you will have all the excitement of the game and still get a good view of the action if you take binoculars.

MEMBERSHIPS AND SEASON TICKETS
If you are a fan of a particular sport or team, or have friends with whom you can share the costs, a year's membership or a season ticket could be a worthwhile investment.

Do you need a season ticket? For truly dedicated football fans, being a season ticket holder saves you money if you intend to watch most of the games and assures you of a seat at the really big matches. For example, a premier league club currently charges around £15–£35 a match and £450–£1,060 a season ticket. If, as a season ticket holder, you attend every home game of a premier league club, you can generally save around £50 for the season.

Alternative packages Some football clubs, such as Fulham FC, sell other packages for those who don't want to fork out for a season ticket. The 10 Match Deal allows the supporter to attend ten home league matches of their choice. Each match is graded according to the standard of the opposition; matches against top premiership clubs are in categories A or A Plus. The 10 Match Deal includes entrance to two of these games, and eight to any other matches. The package costs £260 (concessions are available) and can save up to £48. See **www.fulhamfc.com** ✉.

Going local Joining a local or county-level cricket club can bring big savings if you are likely to watch a lot of matches. For example, a year's club membership of Lancashire County Cricket Club costs £145 (with large discounts for pensioners, students and children), for which you get free access to home matches. Contact England and Wales Cricket Board ✉.

AVOID THE FINALS
Avoid the most popular events, such as finals, and instead attend one of the earlier events in the sporting calendar. For example, in 2004, first-round Wimbledon tennis tickets for Centre Court booked in advance (through a ballot) were £30, whereas tickets to the finals were £75. If you want to go to Wimbledon for the experience or just to watch tennis, rather than to see the champions, then there are cheaper ways still. If you are not averse to an early start and a long queue, you can buy your ticket on the day and pay as little as £6 for a ticket to Court No 1. Or you could purchase a resold ticket after 5pm for just £3. See **www.wimbledon.org** ✉.

 **RESOURCES**

SPORTS CLUBS AND EVENTS
■ Sport England
08458 508 508
www.sportengland.org ✉
■ The Sports Council for Wales 029 2030 0500
www.sports-council-wales.co.uk ✉
■ ScottishSport, online only, includes hill walking and snow sports
www.scottishsport.co.uk ✉.
■ **www.ukathletics.net** ✉ lists local athletics clubs and sells tickets to many athletics events.

Membership perks If rugby union is your sport, you may find it worthwhile joining a rugby union football club. You will receive a preferential discount on tickets, as well as discounts on all rugby paraphernalia. Find your local club listed in the telephone directory. For match and ticketing details, visit the national club websites **www.rfu.com** ✉, **www.wru.co.uk** ✉ and **www.scottishrugby.org** ✉.

SAVING ON SWIMMING
Whether you fancy the occasional quick dip or are keen to start a keep fit regime, swimming is an inexpensive hobby. Most public swimming pools charge £2–£3 for use of the pool, although swimming lessons cost more. You can often save money by purchasing blocks of swim sessions in advance, which can be used at your convenience.

RUNNING REDUCTIONS
Running is free if you simply don a pair of trainers and run around your local park. But for little extra cost you could join a running club and benefit from discounts as well as the social aspects and the competition. Most running clubs cost around £20 to join, with concessions for the young and old, and include entrance fees to races, the use of an affiliated sports centre and discounts at local sports shops. Find a club near you at **www.running-world.net/clubs-uk.html** ✉.

HORSERIDING AT A DISCOUNT
Although riding lessons are quite expensive, costing around £45 an hour for a private lesson in west London and £25 an hour in the country, there are ways of avoiding a big outlay.
Student membership If you are a student, join the university or college riding club for cheaper riding deals.
Offer your services If you are an experienced rider, contact local livery stables and private horse-owners. Many people don't have the time to exercise their own animal and would welcome an experienced, trustworthy rider.
Fair exchange Some local stables will even give free lessons in exchange for regular help from a volunteer.
Pay by the month Some riding schools will give you a reduced rate if you pay by the month for weekly lessons, so it is always worth asking.

DIVING FOR LESS
If you want to learn to dive, taking a course in Britain may not be the cheapest option.
Dive on holiday If you book a diving course while you are on holiday, you can save up to 75% of the cost of a course in Britain – which normally costs up to £400 for a basic five-day course. Avoid school holidays to bag a bargain, but look out for PADI-certified centres (Professional Association of Diving Instructors ✉) worldwide to ensure expert tuition.
Dive in the UK For value for money, search dive magazines and websites for discounted courses. For example, the Dive-In Centre at Whittlesey in Cambridgeshire has special offers such as a Discover Scuba Diving evening for £15. Use a resource such as the UK Dive Guide **ww.ukdiveguide.co.uk** ✉ to find a diving school near you.

How's that?
Tickets for the last day of a Test Match are not sold far in advance, in case play has ended. But if the match does run into the fifth day, then the tickets are cheap – or even free. Tickets at Edgbaston for days 1-3 are £30–£40, for the Sunday £20–£30, but for the fifth day could be as low as £3 depending on the stage the game is at. Or, if you have bought a Sunday ticket and the game runs over, you can attend the Monday game free.
■ Tickets for the new 20/20 day-night matches are £10 for an adult and £5 for a concession.
■ Watching cricket at a local match is free. In country areas just take a deck chair and some refreshments, although many clubs, even village ones, have a bar.

SMART MOVES

A NEW SKILL FOR LESS

Whether you want to learn a new skill simply for your own satisfaction or to add an impressive extra to your CV, there is often a way to avoid paying full price for the privilege.

BACK TO SCHOOL

Education authorities, clubs and societies offer adult learning opportunities at many local schools and colleges. Check when you book whether you qualify for reduced fees – which can be as little as £5 a term – or even a free place.

Jobless freebies If you are unemployed and the subject of the course is work-related, you may be eligible for free training and assistance with associated costs, including travel, equipment, books and childcare. To find out more, contact your local JobCentre about New Deal and Work-Based Learning for Adults.

Low-wage discounts If you are not unemployed but are receiving a means-tested benefit such as Working Tax Credit, or are on a low income, you may be eligible for heavily discounted fees – contact your chosen college to find out.

Free courses The government-sponsored initiative LearnDirect offers free online taster courses in many subjects and full courses in IT, business management, languages and essential life skills. It encourages participation in learning for everyone by providing local LearnDirect centres where you can access the courses with the help of trained staff. Find out more about courses, fees and centres from your local Adult Learning Centre or visit **www.learndirect.co.uk** ✉.

Over-50s courses If you are over 50, you may find your local college runs special over-50s courses with a social element built in. If you are over 60, you'll also benefit from reduced fees for these tailor-made courses.

TRY A MODULE

Many colleges offer modular courses for those unsure of whether they want to commit to long-term study. You can enrol and pay for only a short module, which you can use towards a qualification if you decide to take this route later. This could be a cost saver if you are not sure whether a particular course would suit you.

KEEP STUDY COSTS DOWN

Benefit from student castoffs by buying educational books from secondhand bookshops. Many bookshops specialise in course books so you shouldn't have far to look, particularly if you live near a university or college. Discounts of over 50% on new prices are common. Or post a message on the college notice board saying what you need and offering to buy.

SEARCH THE WEB

As Internet access is now widely available, save money by taking advantage of inexpensive learning resources available on the web. Use a search engine, such as **www.google.com**, to find out about your chosen subject.

COMMUNITY LEARNING CENTRES

If you are seeking low-cost classes, find out the location of your nearest Community Learning Centre. These centres are highly subsidised and are able to offer extremely good value. Some courses, in computing and languages for example, are given for free.

Learn from your peers Use a search engine such as Google or Alta Vista to find a forum, email list or bulletin board to join, and receive the benefit of other students' learning experience in your chosen subject. Your college may also have a forum or email list you can join.

Online courses Many websites offer free online courses, such as the BBC's short language courses for holiday-makers in European languages. Visit **www.bbc.co.uk/languages** and **www.bbc.co.uk/learning** for other courses. Free courses in IT, business development and personal development are at **www.freeskills.com** ✉, and **www.learndirect.co.uk** ✉ offers similar courses for a fee.

Global learning The recruitment agency Manpower offers its employees free access to over 1,100 web-based courses. A few of their courses from their Global Learning Centre are available to anyone at **www.manpower.co.uk/jobseekers /main_global_learning_centre.asp/** ✉.

International courses Because courses are online, you are not limited to those based in Britain. For example, you can enrol for up to three courses at the Virtual University (**www.vu.org**), based in America, for $15 each term.

Distance learning colleges If a course at your local college is too expensive, find out whether a college specialising in distance learning offers the same course. Prices are often considerably cheaper and the courses even more flexible than the part-time or evening courses offered at local colleges and universities. Find databases of courses on **www.distance-learning.co.uk** ✉.

TAKE ADVANTAGE OF EVENING CLASSES

Prospectuses are usually available at your local library or distributed via the local paper before the start of term, but you can contact the course provider at any time for advice.

Artistic value Evening classes that require potentially expensive equipment and materials, such as pottery and art, are often particularly good value. Schools are able to take advantage of educational discounts that are not available to the general public and you benefit from the discounted rates.

Special deals for starters Some classes offer first-timers' deals, such as the first two classes for the price of one.

Term discounts Some organisations give a discount for paying for the whole term's classes in advance, which is worth considering if you know you'll like the course.

OLD-FASHIONED PURSUITS

Take a step back in time to discover some old skills and you will find yourself a rewarding hobby.

Flower power Many flower clubs exist in towns or villages where you can buy flower-arranging equipment cheaply and be treated to demonstrations. Find out more about your local club from NAFAS (National Association of Flower Arrangement) on 020 7247 5567 **www.nafas.org.uk** ✉.

Ring those bells Most people in England live within a short drive of a church with a ringing band. There is rarely any fee to join and you will be taught to ring. If you are asked to ring for a wedding, you get paid. Contact the Central Council of Church Bell Ringers on **www.cccbr.org.uk** ✉.

RESOURCES

FINDING A COURSE
To find out about courses in your area and fees:
■ Contact your local colleges or visit **www.lifelonglearning.co.uk** 0800 101 900 ✉ or **www.learndirect.co.uk** ✉.
■ For information on short courses visit **www.hotcourses.com** ✉.
■ Adult learners can find out about the courses available to them and funding from **www.waytolearn.co.uk** ✉.
■ For free basic IT, business and personal-development courses see **www.freeskills.com** ✉.
■ Full-time, part-time or summer courses in London are covered by Floodlight; either buy the magazine guides at bookshops or visit **www.floodlight.co.uk** ✉.

Good-value travel

Spending more on a holiday doesn't always mean having a better time, especially if you constantly have to check your wallet. Armed with this suitcase of tips, you can make the most of your hard-earned cash and get more from your holiday experience.

FUN-FILLED HOLIDAYS ON A BUDGET

As many as 40 million Britons take a holiday every year. The average family of two adults and two children plans to spend £1,150 on a long summer holiday, but ends up spending £1,500. That leaves plenty of scope for savings.

IS ALL-INCLUSIVE WORTH WHILE?

The advantage of all-inclusive deals is that you can budget for the whole trip. They are ideal for families with teenagers who have big appetites, want to graze all day, and are after non-stop action, but might not be such good value if you just want to read on the beach.

Caribbean catch All-inclusive packages to the Caribbean represent good value for money if you want to take part in a lot of water activities. But check the small print as deals often exclude motorised water sports.

Cost of living That two-week holiday in Brazil might seem like a real bargain because it includes all meals, but once you realise that a large, delicious meal for two can be had for less than £2, it may not appear to be such a good buy. The Caribbean is a different matter, though, as the cost of eating out is actually higher than in Britain.

Free drinks Check whether alcohol is included, and whether that means often undrinkable local brands. Some deals, surprisingly, exclude mineral water, which can bump up the cost of your drinks bill considerably if you have children or are in a hot country.

TOP TIPS ACTIVE HOLIDAYS

If you are seeking an active break or want to take in the sights, then package holidays catering for specific interests are often both fulfilling and good value.

■ **Coach travel** If you are keen to take in the scenery of your chosen destination then a coach tour offers cost-effective travel. A ten-day trip to the Austrian Tyrol costs from £309 a person at **www.consorttravel.com** ✉. The price includes coach travel, accommodation at a 3-star hotel on a half-board basis, excursions and entertainment.

■ **Walking holidays** For a seven-day holiday walking in Spain and France, including half board accommodation, maps and transport of luggage, see **www.worldwalks.com** ✉. Their prices are from £320 a person. You can book through **www.expedia.co.uk** for cheap flights from Britain.

■ **Seeing the world** Attractive deals can be found at **www.travelsphere.co.uk** for escorted holidays worldwide. A seven-day tour of Beijing and Xian including flights, meals, accommodation and excursions costs from only £699.

■ **Family deals** Specialising in holidays in Scotland **www.familyholidays.biz** ✉ is an ideal site to search for families with young children who like activities. A golf package for two adults and two children including seven nights accommodation, four family golf lessons, 9-hole golf round, seven-day course pass and car rental costs £1,600.

Group holidays and shared accommodation

Real savings can be made by organising holidays that lend themselves to sharing accommodation.

Skiing holidays Chalets are perfect for groups, small or large, although it is obviously cheaper if you use all the available space. A self-catering apartment for six in Chamonix, France, cost £88 a person for a week. A half-board catered chalet in Chamonix for ten cost £304 a person for a week in 2004. See **www.chaletfinder.co.uk** 01453 766 094 ✉.

SMART MOVES

Villas in the sun Prices for villas vary hugely, but of course if a villa accommodates more people, the cheaper the price per person will be. In September 2004 **www.villastogo.com** were advertising a villa for 10–12 in the Algarve for £755 a week (£64 each); a similar villa for 2–6 was £570, (£95 each). If you want to save money – and ensure the children have playmates – look at villas that accommodate two families.

Gites in France Similar economies can be made on larger properties in France. Rural properties are cheaper than those near a beach, so consider a gite inland with a pool.

FREE SIGHTSEEING SPECIALS

When you travel to a city, visit the tourist office to find out about any free tours the city sponsors. Before you set off, check out a directory of tourist offices around the world by going to **www.tourist-offices.org.uk** or telephoning 0870 241 9084 ✉.

Walking tours Many towns and cities have inexpensive walking tours with excellent guides that charge far less than big tour operators do. Guided walks around London cost as little as £5.50 each, paid on arrival. For more information see **london.walks.com** or phone 020 7624 3978 ✉.

History hounds If you are interested in architecture or history, the tourist office can direct you to the relevant local societies. They may be sponsoring tours or educational programmes and you can further your education in a way that you enjoy for little or no cost.

Civic amenities Don't forget that city parks, museums, universities and libraries often have free or discounted tours on specific days or at special times. With careful research and planning, you may be able to coordinate dates and find several tours for free.

THE NORTH/SOUTH DIVIDE

With cheap flights available to many destinations in Europe, the main cost of your holiday is living expenses.

Better value According to a 2004 *Which?* survey, Malta, Turkey and the Czech Republic offer the best overall value for hotels, eating, car hire and items such as bottled water. Spain, Portugal and Greece came a close second.

Cheap living If you are self-catering, it is worth taking into consideration how your destination rates on local expenses. Check out the table below for grocery costs.

VISA MARK-UP

Margins in the travel industry are so tight that agents have to do what they can to make their money. One area with big mark-ups is visas. One traveller paid his tour operator £35 for a visa for Egypt, yet when he arrived at the airport in Luxor he realised it would have been a simple case of paying £15 on arrival, and in fact the queue was longer for those who had prepaid the premium.

VALUE FOR MONEY AT YOUR DESTINATION

CZECH REPUBLIC	£12
TURKEY	£13
GREECE & GERMANY	£16
HUNGARY, ITALY, POLAND & SPAIN	£17
BELGIUM & CROATIA	£18
MALTA, PORTUGAL & BRITAIN	£19
AUSTRIA, CYPRUS, FRANCE, IRELAND & THE NETHERLANDS	£20
SWITZERLAND	£23
DENMARK	£26
NORWAY	£27

The table compares the cost of a 200ml bottle of Nivea sun cream, a can of Coca-cola, a 1.5 litre bottle of Evian water, a large tube of Pringles, a 24-exposure Kodak film, and ten postcards and stamps in 10 European countries.

WATCH POINTS RIP-OFFS ON LOCAL TOURS

■ **Reps on commission** When your holiday reps bully you into that welcome meeting, bear in mind that they make significant commissions on every trip they sell to you.

■ **Shopping sprees** If you do go on a trip with your tour operator, the chances are it will be in a coach full of tourists from home. You may also get taken to shops for souvenirs where your rep will get a percentage of everything you buy.

■ **Go local for half the price** Tour operators can charge two or three times the price of a tour with a local company. On a trip to Egypt, you could get a tour of nearby temples in an air-conditioned, chauffeur-driven car with a guide for less than half the price of a trip with your tour operator. Ask for contacts at your hotel, or look out for information centres. If you have a clearer idea of your movements once you reach your destination, you could use an Internet café to search for local information.

■ **Comfort zone** Despite the cost advantages, there may be a language problem with a local, so if something goes wrong, it may be easier to deal with your tour operator. And, of course, take care and make sure the local guide is legitimate and authorised to conduct a tour.

Holidays that pay their way

THE NATIONAL TRUST
Visit **www.nationaltrust.org.uk** or call 0870 609 5380 ✉ to find out about NT working holidays – anything from painting a lighthouse to herding goats – which cost from £60 a week.

They include hostel-style accommodation and all food in one of 100 attractive locations in Britain. Participants also receive the bonus of one year's free entry to National Trust properties around the country, worth £36 (see *Practical parenting*, page 108, and *Leisure and hobbies*, page 160).

WORKING ABROAD
If you want to go farther afield, you could try grape picking in France or protecting a nature reserve in Nicaragua.

■ To find out more about paid and unpaid work in the UK and abroad, check **www.anyworkanywhere.com** ✉.

■ A directory of opportunities for volunteer environmental work in 150 countries, including Canada, Costa Rica, Peru, Brazil, Ireland and Russia is at **www.workingabroad.com** ✉.

There is an allowance based on the local cost of living for some of these destinations, but it is only payable if you have two years' relevant experience in the line of work that you are planning to undertake. Most volunteer programmes provide you with room and board, the amount of which depends on the country.

■ For a rewarding long working holiday in destinations such as Australia, New Zealand, South Africa, the USA and Central America, visit **www.worktravelcompany. co.uk** ✉.

SMART MOVES

BE YOUR OWN TRAVEL AGENT

More than a fifth of British travellers now use the Internet to book their getaway, and the savings can be substantial. But travel agent or Internet, make sure you know exactly what you're getting for the price.

ONLINE REVOLUTION

The Internet is an invaluable tool for the independent traveller, allowing you to take control of your plans and search out a bargain.

Save 70% online Some promotions are only available online and fares are often reduced because companies can cut out the cost of a salesperson. The Internet also gives access to companies around the world without the cost of international telephone calls.

Cheap hotels A website that claims to have the cheapest hotel rates on the Internet is **www.cheeptravel.co.uk** ✉. This site has secured discounts of up to 75% on some hotel rates in top destinations. There are also links to other sites such as **www.totalstay.com** ✉ which offers up to 70% off.

Flights and car hire Many sites enable you to book flights and car hire (see Resources, left). Travel sites suggest that you book car rental as far in advance as possible and consider renting for a full week to get special package rates (see page 183). There are also Internet sites where you can buy insurance (see page 194) and book airport parking (and save up to 20%, see page 181).

AGENT OR INTERNET?

It's a good idea to visit a travel agent and check their website as well. They don't always have the same offers and information and there are advantages to each. Talking over your needs with a real person can get you advice you didn't know you needed, while the Internet gives you control over your own research.

DIY versus package Agents (including those online) have access to packages that aren't available to individuals, so you won't necessarily save money by arranging your holiday yourself. But in 2003 the American investment bank Goldman Sachs found that in 80% of cases it was 26% cheaper to book accommodation and flights yourself rather than buying a package through a British tour operator. On a holiday for £1,200 you could make a saving of £312.

TOP TIPS MAKE THE MOST OF THE WEB

■ **Check the market** Look at five reputable websites before making a booking.
■ **Be one step ahead of your agent** Check out a travel agent's website first, even if you end up calling them anyway. Search facilities are far more sophisticated than they were just a few years ago, but pricing structures in the travel industry are complicated and you may need the help of an agent to get things straight.

■ **Website savvy** To make your research faster and easier, bookmark your favourite sites for bargain travel, hotels and cars on your computer. Comparison shopping will be much quicker and simpler every time you use the computer to make reservations. You will need access to a printer to print out a hard copy of your reservations.

■ **See come-ons coming** Sites often advertise an unbelievably good price that turns out to be unavailable.

■ **Watch out for booking charges** Hidden charges, such as taxes, may only be added on at the time of booking. Check totals carefully.

GET INVOLVED

If you want to do more than save money, and would like to foster international friendships, there are various ways.

Join the club Women Welcome Women (01494 465441 or **www.womenwelcomewomen.org.uk** ✉) is a unique organisation. Offering cross-cultural experiences and mind-opening insights into different lifestyles, WWW has 3,500 members from 70 countries around the world. Members must be female, aged 16–80, and either request to be hosted or undertake to host another member for a period to be agreed. There is no membership fee, but a donation of £25 is suggested.

Town twinning Contact your local council to find out if your town is twinned with towns in Europe or farther afield. If so, get involved in the twinning association and take advantage of the exchange visits that are often organised between families.

GET THE BEST FROM YOUR AGENT

If you don't have the time and energy for making your own travel arrangements, then use a travel agent.

Look for unbiased advice An agent you know and trust can be an indispensable source of information and good fares. Discuss all your requirements with the agent and make sure they understand what is important to you. But be aware that your agent could have an agenda other than getting you the best prices, as many airline companies offer bonuses to the travel agencies that sell the most tickets.

Read 'the guide's guide' Before you commit yourself, ask to see the 'insider's guide' to your destination. Under the counter, every agent has a copy of a valuable reference book called the *Gazetteer*, which carries detailed independent information (from climate to accommodation) about every possible holiday destination.

WATCH POINTS AGENCY CHECKS

■ **Hidden extras** Read the small print of brochures and travel agreements to make sure you don't miss added extras. Watch for additional charges, such as taxes.

■ **Be safe rather than sorry** Bear in mind that even if a smaller agent offers a cheaper price, they may pose a financial risk. Seek out the ABTA (Association of British Travel Agents) or ATOL (Air Travel Organisers' Licensing) symbols. That way, you'll have financial protection if the tour operator goes bust.

RESOURCES

FREE ACCOMMODATION
If you are keen to travel but don't want to fork out for accommodation, then organise a holiday exchange with someone who lives at your chosen destination.

■ **Stay4free** (**www.stay4free.com** ✉) is an organisation founded by world travellers for everyone from businessmen to backpackers. Without charging a fee, the site puts you in touch with people offering free accommodation.

■ If you don't mind the idea of another family living in your house while you are on holiday, consider a house swap. You can find a suitable exchange partner through well-established agencies (see page 185).

Look for unbiased advice

CUT-PRICE FLIGHTS

With intense competition among airlines on many routes and reduced-price tickets available from both airlines and travel companies online, you can often pick up a real bargain. Do your research thoroughly before booking and consider all the available options.

FLIGHTS ON THE INTERNET

In the last year, one third of British travellers have used the Internet to buy an air ticket. But with sites such as **www.trailfinders.com** ✉, **www.travelbag.co.uk** ✉ and **www.bridgetheworld.com** ✉, the number of options online can be overwhelming. That's where **skyscanner.net** ✉ – a dedicated flight search engine – comes in. It compares budget air travel in Europe, with an easy-to-use search engine looking at both budget and scheduled flights. Skyscanner doesn't take bookings, but it gives links to the relevant airline.

No frills versus comfort On a day in June 2004 we searched the Internet for a price on a flight from London to Malaga and it came up with 20 flights, including a best price of £52.99 (£41.99 plus tax) on easyJet. A British Airways flight, with a fare of £84 (£55 plus £29 surcharges), offered more comfort and free food, which is often not available on the cheaper airlines.

TELEPHONE MANNERS

If you decide to call the phone reservation numbers given on travel or airline websites to buy a flight instead of booking online, learn these tricks to make the most of your phone time:

Do your homework first Check newspapers or online sources to get a sense of the best fares and which airlines are offering specials. You can use this information to spur the agent into topping the deals you've already found.

Call early or late If you catch a ticket agent at a time when they're having fewer phone calls, you're more likely to get their full attention and their help in finding the best fares. What if BA is offering a great deal, but you prefer Virgin? Ask the Virgin agent if they can match the rival offer.

Last but not least Use every ounce of charm you have. We've found that a good strategy is to get the agent on your side by being a relaxed, humourous customer.

CONSOLIDATORS AND CHARTERS

If you're planning a trip to a popular holiday destination, it always pays to check the following options:

Consolidators A consolidator buys up blocks of air tickets and then sells them at a large discount. You will see advertisements for consolidators in the travel section of most large Sunday newspapers. This can yield excellent prices on tickets to major overseas destinations, including the Caribbean, Australia and New Zealand, and Asia. But you'll find a number of restrictions on the tickets, so you must be willing to be flexible to maximise savings this way.

CASE STUDY

GOING TO THE SOURCE
Rebecca Compton wanted to fly from Heathrow to Bangkok. After she checked the availability of flights and the price of tickets with several of the travel sites, she went directly to the airline's website. Rebecca compared the lowest fare from her search with the airline site and managed to make a saving of £30. It doesn't always work that way, but it's worth trying. Airline website addresses are almost always **www.airlinename. com** (for example, **www.ba.com**).

Charter flights These can be purchased as 'air only' or in combination with tour packages that offer discounts on hotels. They almost always fly non-stop to highly popular holiday destinations and, as with consolidators, there will be fewer options on seating and availability. Use a knowledgeable travel agent to protect yourself from scams and last-minute cancellations.

TIMING IS EVERYTHING

In many travel guides, the virtues of making reservations early to save money are extolled over and over again. They are right. You'll usually get a better price if you make reservations several weeks in advance, and you're more likely to get the flights and seats you want.

Wait and gamble But booking early isn't always best. Most airlines don't offer a supersaver fare until close to the departure date. Do you wait, hoping the airlines drop their fares, or take the safe route and buy tickets well in advance? It depends on the nature of your trip and the strength of your nerves.

The smart approach Keep an eye on normal low fares to destinations you're interested in so you get to know the range of prices. Then, if you really need to travel at a certain time, on a specific date, start checking fares about six weeks before your trip. When you see one that you know is reasonable and meets your needs, go ahead and book it.

Save 85% as a courier

SMART MOVES

Working trip If you really want to save money on air fares, consider travelling as a courier. This is an increasingly popular way of cheap travel and, depending on your destination and the time of year you travel, you can save 30%–85% of the regular ticket price.

What's involved You'll need to travel alone, dress smartly and travel light (carry-on bags only in some cases). You'll be travelling with a package (frequently documents) on behalf of a courier company to deliver to a legitimate company.

Signing up For reliable information on becoming a courier, contact the International Association of Air Travel Couriers on 01291 625656 or visit their website www.aircourier.co.uk ✉. You can join the association by filling in an application online and then check for flights on the website.

The deal You buy the ticket and receive instructions for meeting the courier company's representative on departure and arrival. The ticket is usually a return ticket which allows you to remain at your destination for 14 days (90 days or longer on flights to the Far East and South America).

Maximise savings The more flexible you can be, the more you can save. You'll get the best bargain on airfares closest to the package delivery date.

GIVE UP YOUR SEAT AND SAVE £150

If you have a very flexible schedule and are prepared to take a gamble, try to get a ticket on a popular flight – one that tends to be overbooked. If there are too many passengers, the airline will ask for volunteers to give up their seat in exchange for a £100–£150 travel voucher. If the later flight keeps you at the airport overnight, the airline will sometimes throw in free accommodation too.

Making the upgrade

It's hard to get an upgrade on a flight, but there are still some tricks that may work.

Frequent flyer points These are the best way to get an upgrade.

Use your charm Be polite, non-demanding and even humorous to the person at check-in.

Cause to celebrate Bring proof of a birthday, anniversary or honeymoon – and make it known.

Dress well Clean and neat is essential.

Popular airline You're more certain of success if the airline is likely to be oversold in economy.

Quiet days Monday to Thursday is usually the best time.

Single seat You have a better chance if you are travelling on your own.

Be flexible If you wait until the last minute, you may get a further discount, but you'll often have to be flexible about things such as non-stop flights, dates, times and seats.

High-street bargains You can usually secure a cheaper flight from the larger high-street travel agents than by contacting the airlines direct, especially on long-haul trips.

BE CONTRARY

Do the opposite of what everyone else is doing. Not only will you escape the crowds and higher accommodation prices, but you are more likely to get a better deal.

Fly off-peak It is usually cheaper to depart on a Tuesday, Wednesday or Thursday and stay over one Saturday night. Flying late at night or early in the morning may also save you some cash, although the price reductions are often negligible and the inconvenience considerable.

Off-season success Wherever possible, travel outside the main holiday periods. If you are travelling to Sydney, Australia, for example, you can fly in May for under £600, whereas it may cost you as much as £1,200 in December.

WATCH POINTS HIDDEN COSTS

■ **Taxes** Many airlines do not include the price of taxes and other charges until the flight is actually booked. This is, on average, £30 on return economy flights to Europe and up to £70 farther afield, according to *Which?* The Advertising Standards Authority rules that print adverts have to include all non-optional charges, but this does not apply to websites.

■ **No refunds** If you cancel a trip, taxes and charges should be refunded. But many airlines, including easyJet, do not make refunds after 24 hours of booking, and only issue credit in exceptional circumstances.

■ **Inconvenient airports** No-frills airlines often fly to airports in an out-of-the-way city. For example, Ryanair fly to Gerona. To get to Barcelona from there, it is a €15 euro return coach trip taking an hour each way when your one-way flight may have only cost the equivalent of €20 euros.

■ **No public transport** If you decide to save money by flying very early or late, bear in mind that public transport may not be running, so that the money you save on the flight may be spent on a taxi to the airport.

■ **No meals** Budget airlines often cut costs by not providing in-flight meals. Avoid buying food in-flight, which is sold at a hefty mark-up, by bringing your own.

■ **Long stopovers** If money takes precedence over time, it may be worth having a stopover. You could save £50 on a long-distance flight to India if you are willing to spend six hours in an airport in the Middle East.

TOP TIPS MAKE THE MOST OF AIR MILES

There are thought to be around 117 million travellers globally with frequent-flyer accounts, but many of us don't make the most of them, with 8 trillion unused air miles at the last count. Airlines generally award one air mile for every mile flown on a full-price flight, and some airlines even give a reduced allocation on discounted flights. If you are a frequent flyer, these miles will soon accumulate.

■ **Choose your route** Only use air miles for expensive routes, certainly not one covered by a budget European airline. That said, you would need to buy £230,000 worth of shopping to qualify for a holiday in Australia, according to a *Holiday Which?* report in 2004.

■ **Partners make prizes** Check out the list of partners for each programme. Gone are the days when you just got air miles for flying. Supermarkets, hotels, car hire and other services often offer frequent-flyer miles that you can use to acquire free airline tickets more quickly. Check for partnerships between airlines; many allow miles to be used towards the purchase of tickets on other carriers.

■ **Play the field** Look at other airlines involved in air miles schemes. Many people mistakenly think that they can only use frequent-flyer air miles for the airline that issued them. Don't presume this airline is the best one to save with.

■ **Stay on top** Remember to ask about extra miles and always keep your boarding card to prove your entitlement if the air miles are not credited. Book as far ahead as possible as there is often limited availability.

PARKING PLUSES

Unless you have efficient public transport or someone willing to get you to and from the airport, you will probably end up leaving your car in a car park. Remember to book ahead or, if you have an early start, take a room in a nearby hotel that includes holiday parking.

Long-term bonuses Most airports have adequate long-term parking provision, and frequent shuttle buses run between parking lots and the departure gates. But the cheapest option is an independent satellite parking lot near the airport. They charge about 50% less than long-term airport parking costs, offer a shuttle bus service and are usually fenced in as well as guarded.

Parking plans on the net We checked three websites and found the following for a week in September 2004. The site **www.parkandsave.co.uk** 0870 733 0542 ✉ claims to offer discounted cheap rates for all major airports, with space at Heathrow car parks for the week in question costing £76. But if you stay in one of its suggested hotels for one night the inclusive price starts at £96. This compares with the full BAA (British Airports Authority) car parking charge of £112; but by booking a day ahead this charge also drops to £76. Call 0800 844844 or visit **www.baa.com** ✉. The site **www.parkaph.co.uk** ✉ has prices between £57 and £84, according to the provider. The helpful site **www.airport-parking-shop.co.uk** ✉ searched five parking companies and gave transport time from each to the terminal, along with the frequency of transfers. The lowest price for our dates was £57.

Short-term losses The closer the car park is to the airport, the higher the parking fees tend to be. Never leave your car in short-term parking for more than an hour or two. Many airports have a free period if you are just picking someone up. Stansted has a free parking area in the short-term lot for 15 minutes but if you go over your free time it costs £2.60 for up to 1 hour and £4.70 for 2 hours.

RESOURCES

FACTS FOR FREQUENT FLYERS

■ **handbag.com/travel/ advicefortravellers/ff** gives general information about frequent flyer schemes.

■ **www.globalflight.net** has more in-depth information. For an annual fee of £90, this site provides independent analysis of 120 airlines' frequent flyer schemes, so that you can plan your trip to get the best deal.

BY LAND AND BY SEA

With the plummeting cost of air fares, travelling overland or by ferry can easily be more expensive than a flight. Although pricing structures are generally complex, the trick is – as with flying – to book ahead as far as possible as cheaper tickets are sold on a first-come, first-served basis.

COACHING SESSIONS

Taking the coach is one of the cheapest ways to travel long distances both in Britain and farther afield.

Go to the 'funfare' National Express offers 'funfares', but only on its website, **www.nationalexpress.com** ✉. Fares are between £1 and £7 each way for travel between London and 20 cities, with no additional charges. As 'funfares' are only loaded into the system a month in advance, the opportunities are usually limited to late or early departures or arrivals.

Golden-age benefits Most people know about discounts for students, but over-60s can automatically travel half-price on most National Express services without a discount card.

DON'T GO OFF THE RAILS

The fare structures of the different rail companies can be confusing. First Great Western, for example, has six different main standard fares: Apex, SuperAdvance, SuperSaver, Advance, Saver and Open (see chart below). Call National Rail Enquiries or see their website **www.nationalrail.co.uk** ✉ for rail tickets and information on all companies.

RESOURCES

TRAIN TRAVEL

- If you are not sure which company you need, a good site that covers them all is **www.qjump.co.uk** or call their help desk on 0870 0007 245 ✉.
- **www.infotransport.co.uk** ✉ has a full timetable for all companies as well as listings of rail websites, including Eurostar.

PLAN AHEAD AND SAVE ALMOST 500%

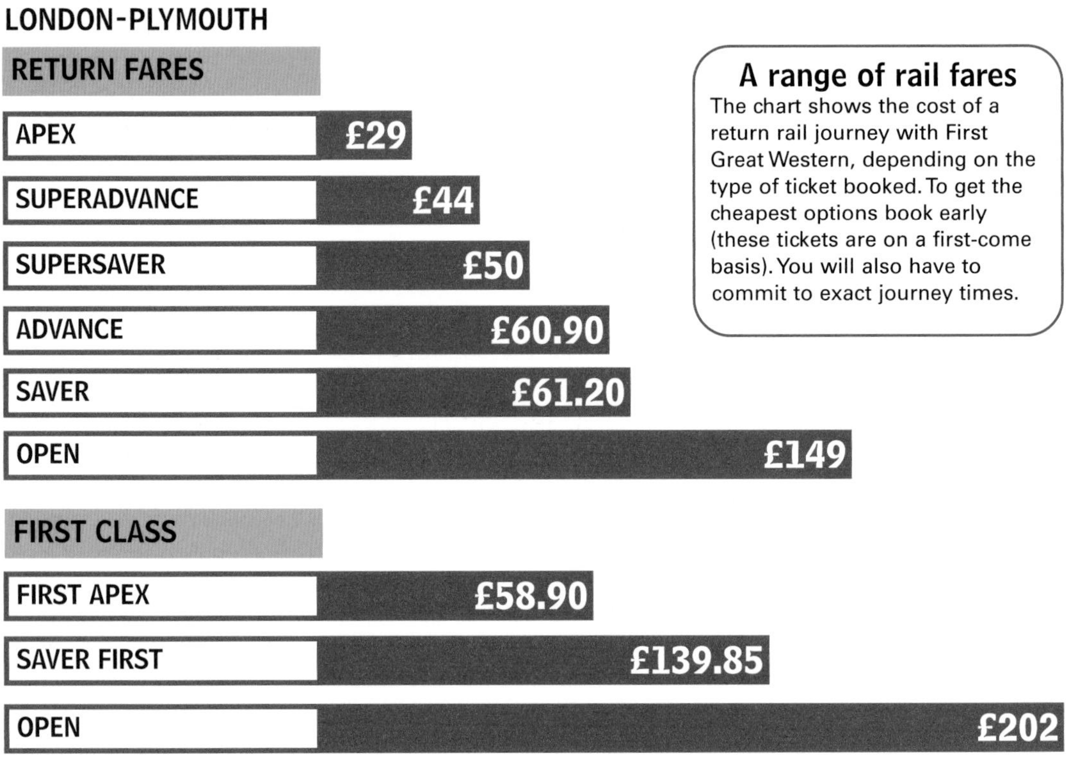

LONDON-PLYMOUTH
RETURN FARES
APEX £29
SUPERADVANCE £44
SUPERSAVER £50
ADVANCE £60.90
SAVER £61.20
OPEN £149
FIRST CLASS
FIRST APEX £58.90
SAVER FIRST £139.85
OPEN £202

A range of rail fares

The chart shows the cost of a return rail journey with First Great Western, depending on the type of ticket booked. To get the cheapest options book early (these tickets are on a first-come basis). You will also have to commit to exact journey times.

Family discounts Most passengers are unaware of the GroupSave option. In the case of First Great Western, on selected journeys groups of three adults travelling together can get a 34% discount, groups of four adults can get a 50% discount and up to four children can travel with either group for just £1 each.

FAIRER FERRIES

A transformation as dramatic as the low-cost airlines revolution is taking place with cross-channel ferries. In summer 2004, a new ferry service was launched that eradicated complex price structures and restrictions.

Call direct Trying to find the cheapest fare by Internet has, until now, been a complicated process, whether you use an independent site or the website of the ferry company. Our research showed it is usually better to call the company direct, even given the small online discount offered. The exception is Speedferries, the new company based on the Ryanair model (**www.speedferries.com** or 01304 20 3000 ✉), which operates a cars-only service between Dover and Boulogne. It has highly competitive fares, an easy-to-use website and a £10 discount for booking online.

Stay for more than a day Day returns to France by ferry usually cost as little as £40, but if you want to go for longer a single can work out at £100. There is nothing to stop you travelling on two day returns. Although companies do claim that their conditions prohibit this and they can charge you the difference, in practice it is unlikely to happen.

Special offers Companies are eager for custom and some offer as much as 40% discount for bookings made well in advance. On the other hand, be flexible and stay on the lookout for last-minute offers. Go mid-week – Saturdays are the most expensive. For the cheapest option, take an overnight ferry.

CLEVER CAR HIRE

Free upgrades It's worth taking a chance by booking the cheapest car going, which is usually also the smallest. Because these cars are limited in number, the rental agency will sometimes offer you an upgrade. If they initiate the upgrade, make sure you don't pay more for it, especially if you reserved ahead with a credit card.

Get extra insurance? In Britain, many car rental offices will try to sell you insurance but it's almost always a waste of money. Check with your own car insurance agent or your credit card company. You'll probably find the coverage offered by the rental company is simply duplicating the cover you are already paying for. But when hiring overseas make sure you are fully insured – in this instance the rental company's insurance will probably be the best and most convenient deal.

Fill her up? In the past, the car you rented would always have a full tank and it would save you money to return the car full of petrol, preferably from a cheap petrol station. Now you'll often be getting a car with only a half tank and it makes no sense to put in more fuel than necessary. Ask for details before you rent, then follow the cheapest option.

ASK YOURSELF

DO I NEED TO PICK UP MY RENTAL CAR AT THE AIRPORT?
If you arrive late in the day and are staying in the city near the airport, consider taking the shuttle to the city centre and renting the next day. This will save you a day's hire cost and the trouble of finding your way in an unfamiliar city when you're tired after a flight.

CAR HIRE WATCH POINTS

■ Ask when you book if it's cheaper to pay in local currency at your destination, or in sterling at the time of booking.

■ In America you will need supplemental liability insurance (SLI), typically to $2 million, and collision damage waiver (CDW). You can buy SLI much cheaper from **www.worldwideinsure.com** before you travel, and your credit card may cover CDW.

■ Always check that the rental is for unlimited mileage, or you risk an additional bill when you return the car.

■ Local taxes may apply; check when you book.

■ An extra driver, a different drop-off location and a driver under 25 may cost more. Make sure you know what you really need and compare deals offered by different companies.

ROOM FOR RENT

For some people, a luxury hotel is the only place to stay. But many others know that the money saved on a hotel room leaves more for food, sightseeing, shopping and other enjoyable activities.

DISCOUNT BOOKINGS

Decide how much time you will spend in your room, then book accordingly. If you're staying in a resort, the quality of the room matters more than if you're touring several cities.

Discount booking sites The directory website **www.ukhotels-net.com** ✉ lists hotel rooms in Britain, many of them discounted. Late booking is effective: two days before the summer bank holiday, 2004, this site offered a room at the 5-star Grosvenor House Hotel, London, at £69 a person, nearly 50% off the normal rate. Other sites worth checking are **www.roomstobook.co.uk** ✉ (B&B and hotels in the UK) and **www.cheaphotelsworldwide.co.uk** ✉, which claims to give up to 70% discount.

Budget chains Hotel chains such as Travel Inn (**www.travelinn.co.uk** ✉) and the international chain Ibis (**www.ibishotel.com** ✉) offer good-quality accommodation at reasonable prices. You are guaranteed a clean, en-suite room with amenities such as a television, kettle and hair dryer. Their independent counterparts are likely to be more expensive. For example, a double room at a Travel Inn or an Ibis hotel in Edinburgh costs, on average, £60 a night. A double room in an independent hotel of the same standard would cost around £80.

TOP TIPS SAVE ON ACCOMMODATION

■ **Save 50% at weekends** Most hotels cater mainly for business travellers and have tempting deals for the weekend. Time your big-city escapes and go half price.

■ **Ring late at night and save 10%** Reserve a room when the person at the reservation desk will have time to talk to you. A friendly chat may lead to a better deal.

■ **Ask for a lower room rate and save 10%** Simply asking 'Is that the best you can do?' can lower the price.

■ **Ring from the lobby and save 25%** If you arrive without a reservation at a big hotel, don't go to the front desk. Ring from the lobby instead – the desk clerk won't know you're already in the hotel and may feel he has to offer you a better deal to get you to make a booking. With smaller hotels, ring from outside on your mobile.

■ **Get the corporate rate for 15% less** If you find yourself staying at a hotel more than once, even if you're not on business, ask if the hotel has special rates for frequent guests or corporate travellers.

■ **Pay with a credit card and save up to 15%** If you're travelling abroad, wholesale exchange rates give companies better deals than individuals. By paying your hotel bill with a credit card you should find you're quids in when you get your statement.

RECEPTION

LHR

NYC

Venice

Ring from the lobby and save 25%

NOT JUST FOR YOUTH

If you want a comfortable room and delicious food in an excellent location from just £10 or £12, depending on location, contact The Youth Hostel Association of England and Wales (**www.yha.org.uk** or 0870 770 8868 ✉). It's open to all, including senior citizens, families and couples.

Cost-conscious membership The 2004 membership fee for adults was £14 a year and family membership £28, but group only £14. Members also get membership of the International Youth Hostel Federation (HI), which offers more than 4,500 places to stay in 60 countries worldwide.

Reward yourself Freenites & More is a reward scheme run by HI. By staying in hostels in participating countries, you collect points that you can use for free nights when you travel to hostels around the world (see **www.freenites.com**).

Royal living for pauper prices Many youth hostels are in characterful buildings or locations. At Carbisdale Castle in Scotland, a bed in a shared room is just £13 a night.

APARTMENTS AND VILLAS

Instead of staying in a hotel, look at renting a house or apartment; there are many available in major cities as well as at beach and rural locations.

Trawl the net The Internet is the best resource for finding personal rentals. With Daltons holidays **www.daltons holidays.com** ✉ you can rent a three-bedroom villa for six people off season in the Algarve for £295 a week – just £50 a person. City apartments are also good value. Reasonably-priced, attractive holiday apartments in Prague can be found at **www.apartments.cz** ✉. A two-bedroom apartment for four people in the centre of town costs just over £100 a night. This works out at roughly £25 a person, which is far cheaper than staying in a hotel of the same standard.

STAY ON CAMPUS FOR HALF PRICE

Many universities and colleges rent rooms during the holidays when few students are around. The bathroom may be down the corridor, but the savings will more than make up for that. The rooms are clean, though they lack glamour. Kings College in London (**www.kcl.ac.uk** 020 7848 1700 ✉) has rooms in four central locations, including London Bridge and leafy, bohemian Hampstead; 2004 prices for individual rooms in London Bridge are £29.50 and £26 in Hampstead, including breakfast.

House swap

Fair exchange There is a form of accommodation available around the world that is completely free – the house swap. The idea began in America around 50 years ago, and now there are more than 30 agencies globally. All potential exchangers must register with an agency for an annual fee, and they then have access to the details of exchange partners worldwide. Boats, caravans and other types of accommodation are included too.

Selling points When you write up the listing for your entry, be sure to include all the amenities that would make your home particularly appealing: access to public transport; historic sites or cities nearby; parks, mountains, lakes, rivers or areas of natural beauty; theatres, museums, shopping; sporting venues or amusement parks. If you have regular access to a health club, swimming pool, tennis courts, golf club, beach or special parking, include this information in your listing.

Check the contract The home exchange networks have standard contracts available. It should include a guarantee that swappers will pay replacement value for any damage.

Established agency The world's major exchange company **www.homelink.org.uk** 01962 886882 ✉ covers 50 countries with over 200 offices. It is UK-based and has been operating for 50 years. Even before you become a member (£95 annually) you can look at their directory of properties with photographs.

SMART MOVES

FRUGAL FAMILY FUN

Entertaining the children and having fun on holiday needn't have a hefty price tag. Don't discount some of the more time-honoured traditions of getting away from it all that will keep children amused, as well as other, gentler pursuits that senior citizens may prefer.

PACK UP YOUR TENT

Depending on the weather (although the children will love it rain or shine), one of the best family holidays is also the cheapest: camping. If you already own equipment, the major outlay is food and petrol.

Low-cost rentals If you don't own any equipment, try to hire or borrow some from friends for the first outing or two, to see if you enjoy the camping experience; or start out on a site where everything is provided. For a family of four, this can cost 60% less than buying your own tent if you only use it for one year.

Pick and choose Campsites range from remote settings to privately owned grounds that have a full range of facilities including shops, entertainment rooms and swimming pools. Fees vary considerably too. At some municipal sites you can pitch a tent for as little as £3 a night, while private grounds can charge up to £15 or £20. The Camping and Caravanning Club at **www.campingandcaravanningclub.co.uk** or 024 7669 4995 ✉ publish *Your Big Sites Book* annually for members with 3,500 sites listed. Annual membership costs £29 (2004 price) plus a £5 joining fee.

Thrifty campers Keep costs down by bringing your own food and storing it in a cool box – or even a mini fridge with a car adapter if you have one. You can also save money by organising your own entertainment and keeping excursions to a minimum.

RESOURCES

CAMPSITES

■ For child-friendly camping holidays in Britain and Europe, consider the following:
www.canvasholidays.co.uk
01383 629 000 ✉
www.eurocamp.co.uk
0870 9019 410 ✉
online.haven-holidays.co.uk
0870 242 5678 ✉
www.uk.haveneurope.com
0870 242 7777 ✉

■ For a list of campsites across Britain, try www.camping.uk-directory.com ✉. Its search engine allows you to find facilities such as electric hook-ups.

RESPONSIBLE TOURISM

If you are concerned about the impact your family holiday has on the environment as well as the cost to your pocket, consider the following.

Responsible Travel Marketing carefully screened holidays in the UK and abroad, **www.responsibletravel. com** ✉ has links to the tour companies, lodges and hotels who take your booking. Under the budget travel section you can stay in a highland lodge for £10 a night, or

a B&B in Snowdonia for £19 a night (2004 prices). A self-catering cottage for four on the Lycia coast in Turkey will cost just £200–£250 a week, excluding flights.

Responsible rambling If you have older children who enjoy walking, Ramblers Holidays on 01707 331133 or **www.ramblersholidays.co.uk** ✉ offer walking holidays worldwide for all budgets. They try to use local resources and facilities, and put profits back into the community.

Package tour operators Major companies such as Thomas Cook ✉, Cosmos ✉, Virgin ✉ and First Choice ✉ often advertise free child places, but you'll need to book early as they are limited. These companies are all members of the Federation of Tour Operators ✉, who agreed in 2004 to report on their commitment to sustainable development.

EXPLORE BRITAIN

You need not travel overseas to find an interesting diversity in landscape and culture.

Walking is free Go walking in the Welsh hills or visit the remote craggy islands in the west of Scotland. For example, holidays from Hillscape at **www.wales-walking.co.uk** ✉ start at £222 a person per week, including bed and breakfast, a packed lunch, tea and evening meal.

Stay on a farm Young children love the experience of a working farm. For inexpensive B&B and self-catering farm accommodation, contact Farm Stay UK on 024 7669 6909 or visit **www.farmstayuk.co.uk** ✉. In 2004, a Cumbrian cottage for eight cost from as little as £130 a week.

Family adventures Visit **www.family-travel.co.uk** ✉ and pay a small access fee for plenty of well-researched, up-to-date information.

CHILD-CENTRED RESORTS

If roughing it doesn't appeal and you want a stress-free holiday for the whole family, shop around for a resort that is set up for children. Many companies offer a range of children's programmes with child-friendly play areas, clubs and even baby-sitting services.

Cost versus convenience These resorts often have a high price tag, but if you shop hard and think off-season, you'll find a programme to suit your family at a price you can afford. Although the price can seem daunting, the cost is all-inclusive and good deals can be found. The travel company Mark Warner (0870 770 4227 or **www.markwarner.co.uk** ✉) offers a free child's place on all two-adult family bookings made before the end of January.

TRUST THE TRUST

The National Trust (**www.nationaltrust.org.uk** 0870 458 4000 ✉) has over 200 historical buildings and gardens in England and Wales. The National Trust for Scotland (**www.nts.org.uk** 0131 243 9300 ✉) has 100 properties.

Tailor-made tours If you are not a member and want to visit several sites while you are visiting an area, consider buying a touring pass that grants admission over a period of seven days (£16 in England; £17 in Scotland). See *Practical parenting*, page 108, and *Leisure and hobbies*, page 160.

CONSIDER A CRUISE

Sailing off into the sunset sounds romantic until you start pricing those luxury cruises. Although they may seem expensive at first, just about everything is included. So the real savings can be made on land, with wise buying before you embark.

SURFING FOR SALES

Using your computer to check out specials can save you big money, even if you end up having to use a travel agent or booking directly through the cruise company.

Get an overview Surfing several sites can give you a good feeling for the cost of a cruise and how to save a few hundred pounds.

Dream deals The site **www.cruisecontrolcruises.co.uk** (0870 909 7540 ✉) promises that if you find one of its cruises at a cheaper price within 24 hours it will match that price. It also features late deals and special attractions – for example, a Caribbean cruise for nine days for £1029. A 14-night Mediterranean island cruise was available for £899 through **www.cruisedirect.co.uk** (0871 226 0964 ✉) while **www.cruisedeals.co.uk** (0800 107 2323 ✉) showed a trip taking in Sardinia, Italy, France and Spain for £549 all-inclusive. Regular 2004 prices for the same holidays from the cruise lines could have cost twice as much.

CONSOLIDATED SAVINGS

Consolidators are the middlemen between the cruise lines and the consumer. Each cruise line will usually provide a consolidator with a number of cabins for each cruise. The consolidators' deals can be as much as £400–£500 cheaper than those offered by travel agents, and include bonuses such as an upgraded cabin or £50–£100 onboard credit.

Scour the newspapers You can find advertisements in the travel section of most major newspapers under either 'consolidators' or 'discounters'. There are several websites now in operation, too, such as **www.cruiseplanners.co.uk** (0870 528 0000 ✉), **www.bestatholidays.co.uk** (0870 709 3007 ✉) and the website for the Association of Special Fares Agents **www.asfa.net** ✉, which is the platform for discount travel specialists and consolidators.

CRUISE CONTROL

A travel agent that specialises in cruises can save you money. They buy up space on certain cruises in bulk at a hefty discount and are therefore able to offer you a better bargain.

Assess the agencies Check with more than one agency that specialises in cruises. Try the ones listed under Dream deals above or, alternatively, **www.cruisepeople.co.uk** (0800 526 313 ✉) or **www.voyanacruise.com** (020 8515 4890 ✉). Some agencies will push one cruise line more than another to get a bonus for extra sales. So to get what you want, find an agent that is willing to review all your options. The Passenger Shipping Association ✉ runs a retail

SAVE £100 ON DISCOUNTED AIR FARES

Most cruise packages include just about everything but the air fare. Many lines will offer you a discounted fare with an airline partner, but don't automatically buy into this. Use all the tricks for cut-price flights (see page 178) to find the best price to fly to your port of departure. You may save yourself £100 or more. Or you may find that the air fare the cruise line offers is indeed the best. One advantage of booking a flight with a cruise line partner is that if the flight is delayed or cancelled, the line will honour your booking and get you to the ship another way.

agents' accreditation scheme for high-street travel agents who are experts on cruise holidays. To find an accredited agent in your locality, visit **www.discover-cruises.co.uk** and select the 'cruise information centres' link or phone 020 7436 2449.

Be either early or last-minute Cruise lines give a big discount to those who pay well ahead, netting you a saving of up to 45% on the brochure price. (For P&O you needed to book by August 31, 2004, for cruises from the March 2005–March 2006 brochure.) The same goes if you wait until the last minute and book close to the sailing date, when the cruise line may have cabins it needs to fill. We found a last-minute deal on **www.lastminute.co.uk** ✉ for a cruise to Iberia on one of P&O's most popular liners for £435 – 65% less than the regular price.

TOP TIPS ON-BOARD ECONOMIES

Here are a few before-you-embark tips to keep extra costs from spoiling your cruise experience.

■ **Tips, trips and tipples** Food and entertainment are included but tips are not – and they can add up to over £30 a week for each person. Many shore excursions are extra, bumping up the cost by another £50. So are drinks other than coffee and tea. Check what is included carefully.

■ **Go your own way** Don't limit yourself to the planned excursions from the ship. Contact the tourist bureaux of the ports you'll be visiting beforehand and see what they can offer you. Doing your own land tour can be more fun, better tailored to your interests, and a lot cheaper. Just be sure to get back on time so the ship doesn't leave without you.

■ **Room without a view** Inside cabins are just as spacious as outside ones and generally cost about 60% less. The only thing you'll miss is the view from your room, but if you plan to be out and about most of the cruise, this shouldn't be a problem. Spend the money you'll save on the cabin on treats

RESOURCES

DIRECT LINES
After checking the bargain travel sites, it might save you money to check each cruise line directly. Even if the sites don't book travel, you can get a better idea of the ships and the amenities they offer before you buy.
Royal Caribbean
www.royalcaribbean.com
0800 398 9819 ✉
P&O
www.pocruises.com
0845 355 5333 ✉
Fred Olsen
www.fredolsencruises.com
01473 742424 ✉
Cunard
www.cunard.co.uk
0845 071 0300 ✉
Norwegian Cruise Line
www.uk.ncl.com ✉

Freighters – low costs on the high seas

SMART MOVES

Alternative cruise If you are adventurous, look into taking a cruise by freighter. On average these cost £65 a day for each person, plus any dues and taxes. Voyages normally take 40–120 days, although segmented trips are available so it is possible to take a 14-day cruise.

Select company Freighters generally carry no more than 12 passengers, but they don't usually allow children under 13 or seniors over a certain age.

Level of comfort There are fewer amenities than a luxury cruise ship but you may find a small pool, a library, a lounge and deck chairs. Life on board is more casual; there are no formal dinners, casinos or organised activities.

Varied routes Freighters have an itinerary, but they are subject to change depending on the cargo. The trips are generally longer and they visit more unusual

ports of call than a normal cruise ship.

British departures Travelling on a freighter costs half as much as on a regular cruise ship. The fee covers everything onboard except alcohol. If you want to look into freighter cruises that start from British ports, contact:
Andrew Weir Shipping
020 7265 0808
www.aws.co.uk ✉ or
The Cruise People Ltd
020 7723 2450
http://members.aol.com/CruiseAZ /freighters.htm ✉.

SPENDING POWER

While many holidaymakers spend months poring over travel brochures, many do not even give a second thought to how they will pay their way once they've reached their destination. Buying foreign currency can be an expensive business, but you can minimise costs by avoiding the pitfalls.

CURRENCY CREDITS

Check the newspaper or Internet (see Resources, right) for the current exchange rate – it should vary little between banks. But check out the various options available for commission-free currency.

Post-office pluses You might not associate the Post Office with foreign currency, but it is keen to promote its banking facilities, including no commission or handling fees.

Travel agents Check your local travel agents. Some of the larger ones, such as Thomas Cook and First Choice, offer commission-free currency and travellers cheques.

Free for all You don't have to be a customer of a particular financial institution to enjoy the benefits of its promotions. Lloyds TSB offers commission-free foreign currency to both customers and non-customers (summer 2004).

TOP TIPS GET THE BEST RATES

■ **Get some local currency before you go** That way, if there is no ATM (Automated Telling – or 'cash' – Machine) on arrival, you won't have to go to a cambio or other exchange booth, or to an exchange office at the airport, which will give a poorer exchange rate. Airport booths also charge 3% commission instead of the banks' 1% or 2% – that is £6 against £2 or £4 on £200.

■ **Shop around for the best deal** To compare charges made by banks and other travel money providers, go to **www.moneyfacts.co.uk** and select the Surveys link.

■ **Check the offer** If you are offered an exchange with no commission, check the rate isn't really poor. If the deal includes commission-free buy-back of any surplus when you return, keep all receipts.

■ **Use a bank rather than a hotel ATM** To avoid hidden charges while abroad, find an ATM at a bank which has an alliance with your bank. Check with your bank or building society to find out about their global alliances before you travel. If you have a debit card with the Cirrus or Maestro logos, you should be able to use it internationally in ATMs. Whether or not you will be charged a transaction fee depends on your bank or building society – their website should provide this information. To find the Cirrus/Maestro ATMs in the region you are visiting, go to **www.mastercard.com/cobrand/maestro/atm** ✉.

■ **Take traveller's cheques as well as cash** Most insurance policies only cover up to £250 in cash lost or stolen, whereas traveller's cheques will be replaced by the provider within 24 hours. Clydesdale Bank, Lloyds TSB and Tesco, among others, don't charge commission or handling charges for traveller's cheques.

ASK YOURSELF

AM I GETTING THE BEST RATES?

■ Always check current exchange rates in a newspaper or on the Internet before buying foreign currency.

■ Look for a provider offering commission-free currency at a competitive exchange rate; a commission-free deal can be poor value if the rate is unfavourable.

USING YOUR PLASTIC CAN BE DRASTIC

A report published in January 2004 by Nationwide Building Society says that we lose £350 million each year on foreign currency fees or commission by using a credit card. It might be the most convenient method of paying, but it's also the most expensive.

Credit card charges Many credit cards charge an extra 2.75% on overseas transactions, bumping up the cost of your overseas trip. If you spend £1,000 on plastic while overseas, you face an extra £27.50 in charges.

Whacked for cash Withdrawing cash on your credit card – from a bank or ATM – is even more costly, as you can pay withdrawal fees of up to 2% on top of the foreign usage charge. Take out £1,000 worth of cash and you could pay total charges of up to 4.75%, costing £47.50. You also pay interest from day one on cash advances, which could add another 1.5% a month to your credit card bill.

Rare exceptions Nationwide Building Society's Classic card has a cash withdrawal fee of just 1.25% and no foreign usage loading. London Victoria's SAGA has no ATM fees if used at a VISA cashpoint abroad (1.5% from January 2005) and only a 1% loading outside the European Union.

CHECK BANK CHARGES

It's not only credit cards that attract extra charges; many banks and building societies also charge customers extra fees for using their debit cards to withdraw cash while overseas. Using a Barclays or alliance member cash machine will incur a handling fee of 2.75% of the amount you withdraw. Using a NatWest debit or cash card will incur a 2.65% fee.

Zero rates Nationwide charges no commission on foreign transactions and no fees for use of its debit card abroad.

SAVING ON HOLIDAY ESSENTIALS

Even before we leave the country, we each spend on average £430 in preparation for our holidays. But it is simple to reduce the cost of basic holiday expenditure on items such as sun cream and film.

Special offers Stock up on sun protection in October when prices are cheaper, but bear in mind that the effectiveness of sun cream diminishes after a year. Alternatively, look out for buy-one-get-one-free promotions in Boots or other major chemists at the beginning of the season.

Supermarket sweep Special offers aside, you're better off buying sun cream from the supermarket. A *Holiday Which?* report concluded that buying travel products at the large supermarkets is far cheaper than at the big-name high-street chemists. One brand of sun cream was 65% cheaper.

At the airport If you've forgotten the sun cream and decide to stock up at the airport, you'll find that products are cheaper in the chemist after passport control, as they are tax-free – although this still costs more than at the supermarket. Consider how costly your destination is before opting to buy holiday essentials abroad. Prices for holiday consumables in eastern and southern European countries are generally the cheapest, whereas the cost of sun cream in Portugal is the highest.

RESOURCES

CHANGING RATES

There are many websites with a currency converter. So, you have no excuse not to be up to date with the latest rates.

www.bankrate.com
www.currencies.co.uk
www.currencies4less.com
www.money.msn.co.uk

If you don't want to use the Internet, check your daily newspaper or pop into the high-street bank and check there.

CONFIDENCE TRICKS

Scams, thefts and rip-offs often take place in urban areas in less-developed countries. Most happen in the first day or so (you may think you blend in but you probably don't), and the majority are opportunist. This means you can avoid them.

■ Be wary of anyone who approaches you, particularly around popular tourist sites.

■ Always agree a price for taxis (if there is no meter) and tour guides in advance.

■ Watch out for porters who take you to unofficial taxis which overcharge you. Don't use unlicensed cabs in any city.

■ Take care of your bags and money especially in crowded areas and when you are distracted, for example when trying to find your way around on a strange metro. Take your time and zip up bags and pockets.

keep it simple

SAVE ON THE 100% MINI-BAR MARK-UP
In a hotel, the quickest way to blow your budget is by using the mini-bar. Visit the local shops and stock up on bottled water, beers and juices, and a few snacks too. Keep these in your room and you'll save exorbitant charges on similar items. And you should always eat breakfast if it's included in your room rate.

MOBILE RATES
Before you travel, find out your network provider's rates for making and receiving calls abroad. Orange (**www.orange.co.uk** 0500 802080 ✉) offers their clients this information free. Text 'FROM' followed by the country you are visiting to 159, and you will receive a text detailing the costs of using your Orange phone in that country.
However, your network provider's partner networks in the country you are travelling to may not charge the same rates. As mobile phones connect automatically with the strongest signal, you may end up paying the fee from any of these foreign networks. Although you can't dictate which network you connect with, check the different rates with your network provider before you travel to save yourself a shock.

Film and camera supplies Take advantage of offers where you receive a free film with photo processing and two-for-one offers in supermarkets and chemists. Without these special offers, supermarkets are the cheapest source for films and disposable cameras; print film can be up to 50% more expensive at leading high-street chemists. Generally speaking, it is cheaper still to buy film when you are abroad, and especially if you are visiting Denmark.

DON'T WASTE YOUR TIPS

What to tip for and how much varies greatly from country to country. Ask locally so you neither insult your waiter nor tip unnecessarily. As a rough guide, the following would be expected after a meal in a mid-range restaurant.
Australia and New Zealand Tipping is still relatively new here. In Australia 10%–15% is usual in restaurants in the bigger cities. In New Zealand tip 5%–10% only if you receive special treatment.
France, Germany and Italy Service of 10%–15% is added to meals, but 5%–10% extra is normal for good service.
Greece 15% is added to bills but it is the custom to leave a little extra or round up the bill.
Japan Tipping is not expected; if a tip is given for outstanding service, enclose it in a small envelope sold exclusively for this purpose.
Scandinavia Service charges and tips are included in restaurant bills; leaving an additional gratuity is unnecessary.
South America A 10% service charge is added to your bill, but because wages are so low an extra 10% or more is expected by everyone from waiters to car rental agents.
Spain Service is included in the price of meals and drinks but additional tipping is commonplace – usually 5%–10%.
United States A tip of 15%–20% is virtually essential. You will tend to find a high level of service in America and you risk insulting people if you don't show your appreciation.

DINNERS FOR PEANUTS

A memorable meal can be a highlight of any holiday. But avoid situations that will leave a nasty taste in your mouth.
Don't act the tourist Always be wary of special tourist menus. They might be cheap, but dishes are often mass-produced and made with inferior ingredients.
When in Rome... Pick the restaurant that is full of local office or manual workers and have the dish of the day or set menu, which will be the best value. Avoid à la carte eating as this is most costly.
Eat early Many countries lunch at noon, and the specials are the first things to run out. Lunch is usually better value for money than dinner, especially in France where lunch is the main meal of the day.
Check the price In some countries, you are asked to select food from a hot or cold cabinet. Don't do this unless the prices are clearly displayed. If in doubt, ask to see a menu or have the price written down.
All-inclusive? Check whether taxes and service are included in the bill. It is easier to ask about local practices at your hotel beforehand than to wait until the bill comes.

TOP TIPS CHEAPER MOBILE CALLS

Think again before using your mobile phone to stay in touch with home. If people call you, you pay for the additional cost of the call and you will be charged a high fee to access voicemail, even in a country as close as Ireland. In many countries you can buy a phone card to use in a public phone box, so you can keep track on your spending. But if you must use your mobile, here are some money-saving tips:

■ **Don't use prepay** Prepay users generally pay more than monthly users, so look at changing your contract if you travel overseas a lot.

■ **Understand the charges** Most networks have a bewildering system of charges. A survey in 2001 by the communications watchdog, Oftel, found only a quarter of users knew the charges for receiving calls and only half knew how to reduce their bills. Some have a minimum unit of one minute, so you pay for all fractions of minutes.

■ **Get the cheapest plan** Compare the costs of different networks. Some, such as O2, T-mobile and Vodafone, offer monthly international call plans.

■ **Get texting** To send a message is around half the cost of a one-minute call.

■ **Precautionary measures** Make a note of your serial number and phone number so that, if the phone is lost or stolen, you won't be charged for any calls you haven't made.

CUTTING ONLINE COSTS

■ Most people know that phone calls from hotels can be high, but Internet costs in hotels and resorts are normally inflated as well.

■ Ask at reception for the nearest Internet café, or check online before you go: www.cybercafes.com ✉ is a database of cyber cafés worldwide. The café rates are normally cheap, and you know exactly what you are spending at the time, not two weeks later when you eventually get your hotel bill.

■ Many public libraries in Britain and overseas have free Internet access.

CUT THE COST OF CALLING HOME

There are big differences in the cost of calling Britain from abroad, depending on whether you use a mobile, the hotel phone, a landline or a public payphone. This table shows typical costs per minute. Conversions are from local currency in September 2004. When phoning from the US, check the provider, as charges vary greatly.

	ORANGE MOBILE	INTERNATIONAL HOTEL	LANDLINE	PAY PHONE
FRANCE (Paris)	70p Pay monthly £1.20 Pay as you go	£1.17 for first 15 mins then 22p up to 32 minutes	15p 8p between 17.00 and 0800	30p*
GERMANY (Berlin)	70p Pay monthly £1.20 Pay as you go	£1.36	8p	41p
INDIA (New Delhi)	£1.30 Pay monthly £1.40 Pay as you go	£2.91 + 8% tax	9p	9p
AUSTRALIA (Melbourne)	70p Pay monthly £1.30 Pay as you go	£5.05	8p –18p	**
USA (New York)	£1.10 Pay monthly £1.30 Pay as you go	same as landline	6p –£1.12	1p – 7p*

* Using a prepaid phone card   ** Rates vary widely; not available for publication

BUY ONLY THE INSURANCE YOU NEED

We waste more than £250 million a year on overpriced insurance, according to Nationwide. While more and more of us will spend time researching the best holiday deal, we don't do the same when it comes to travel insurance.

SAVE ON YOUR TRAVEL AGENT'S DEAL

Many travel agents now insist that you have cover if you travel with them, so this is no longer an optional expense. But buying insurance from a travel agency can cost three times what it should and there are lots of easy options for arranging your own.

TOP TIPS KEEP PREMIUMS DOWN

■ **Free insurance** Some credit cards and banks offer free travel insurance, but check the small print beforehand as the benefits may not be as good as they sound. If you do have to claim on your credit card, it won't affect your claims history.

■ **Home insurance** Your baggage and more expensive personal items, such as cameras and jewellery, may already be covered on your home insurance policy. Check before taking out extra cover.

■ **Multi-trip policies** An annual multi-trip policy means that you can be covered for short trips in the UK as well as longer holidays abroad. A European policy for a single adult costs as little as £28 at **www.travel-insurance-web.com** ✉ and **www.simpletravelinsurance.co.uk** ✉. You only have to take three breaks in Britain or Europe and you will be ahead – three single trip policies would cost at least £57.

■ **Combined policies** Look out for combined couple or family policies. These can save you 20% or more on the cost of individual policies, especially if you're buying Multi-trip cover. Travel-Insurance-Web.com ✉ and Simple ✉ both have an annual family European policy for £42.

■ **Buy online** Save up to 30% of the cost of the policy by buying online rather than over the phone.

MAKE SURE YOU CAN CLAIM

Always check the small print of your policy and take a copy with you so you can inform your insurer immediately of any claim you need to make.

Reporting a crime It is vital to make sure you meet the criteria for reporting a crime. Most companies stipulate that the police must be notified within 24 hours of any incident and will expect an official report for your claim to be validated. If you are unfortunate enough to be the victim of a crime, you may be too distressed to think clearly, so make sure you are prepared in advance for this eventuality.

Free EU health coverage Although form E111 only covers basic medical problems such as a broken leg, it could save you a great deal in an emergency. You are entitled to this medical cover and it's free, so get a form from the Post Office, fill it in and have it certified before you go.

RESOURCES

GOVERNMENT GUIDELINES

Insurance companies should be members of the Financial Ombudsman Service or General Insurance Standards Council. Check on the Foreign Office website **www.fco.gov.uk/travel** or call 0870 606 0290 ✉ for more details of what should be covered in policies and details of companies.

PENSIONERS CAN SAVE POUNDS

Insurance premiums can double at the age of 65, particularly with annual policies. Age Concern and Help the Aged have no upper age limit on annual policies. Some of the best deals for those aged 65 to 69 can be found on line at **www.netcoverdirect.com** ✉ or with Marks & Spencer Money at **www6.marksandspencer.com** 0800 068 3918 ✉.

COMPARE POLICIES AND SAVE

Don't just compare the cost of the policies, consider details of the relative cover. Look for a policy that provides for medical treatment of at least £1 million in Europe and £2 million farther afield, and £1 million personal liability. You'll need extra cover if skiing or doing extreme sports.

■ Check for any exclusions.
■ Check that the company is a member of the Financial Ombudsman Service or General Insurance Standards Council.
■ Check that you are covered for winter or extreme sports; many policies exclude them unless you pay extra.

Multi-trip for one adult (12 months worldwide)

INSURER	COST*	MEDICAL EXPENSES	BAGGAGE	VALUABLES	CANCEL-LATION	EXCESS
SIMPLE	£42/£59.85	£10 million	£1,500	£250	£3,000	£50–£250
DIRECT TRAVEL	£51/£74	£10 million	£1,500	£200–£300	£3,000–£4,000	£40–£100
TRAVEL PLAN DIRECT	£52.50/£73	£5 million	£1,750	£200	£5,000	£40
GO TRAVEL INSURANCE	£55.65/£59.50	£5 million	£1,500	£250	£3,000	£50–£250
LLOYDS INSURANCE	£67.48/£74.97	£5 million	£1,500	£300	£5,000	£15–£70
LEADING EDGE	£73/£98.55	£5 million	£1,500	£200	£1,500	£50–£100

Single trip for one adult (7 days worldwide)

INSURER	COST*	MEDICAL EXPENSES	BAGGAGE	VALUABLES	CANCEL-LATION	EXCESS
TRAVEL PLAN DIRECT	£19/£35.80	£5 million	£1,750	£200	£5,000	£15–£70
DIRECT TRAVEL	£23/£50	£10 million	£1,500–£2,000	£200–£300	£3,000–£6,000	£35–£100
SIMPLE	£23.15/£52.70	£10 million	£1,500	£250	£3,000	£50–£250
PRIMARY DIRECT	£24.40/£55.45	£10 million	£1,500	£250	£3,000	£50
GO TRAVEL INSURANCE	£25.20/£50.41	£5 million	£1,500	£250	£3,000	£50–£250
LEADING EDGE	£27/£37	£5 million	£1,250	£200	£1,000	£50–£100

*Costs show normal rate followed by rate including winter sports
On multi-trip policies, maximum trip length is 31 days

August 2004

Homes and gardens

Creating a comfortable, efficiently run home need not be an expensive business. Find out where to buy bargain furniture and appliances on a shoestring, and how to keep your home and garden fresh and welcoming.

FURNITURE BARGAINS

When you are buying furniture, don't just go to your nearest department store and buy something there and then. If you know where, when and how to shop, you can save money on good-quality furniture that will give you years of use.

TOP TIPS PLACES TO BUY A BARGAIN

There are plenty of outlets where you can save money on buying furniture, whether new or secondhand.

■ **Department and furniture store sales** The key to getting the best bargains in the sales is to get there early. For publicity purposes, some department stores sell a limited number of high-priced products at rock-bottom prices – for example, a £1,500 sofa for £200 – but this might mean queuing all night or longer.

■ **Seasonal savings** These days, sales are not just restricted to winter and summer since stores have clearance bargains throughout the year – try Homebase (0845 077 8888 ✉) and MFI (08702 400417 ✉) for seasonal savings of up to 50%.

■ **Buy online** Online stores are cheaper than showrooms because their overheads are far lower. Always ask a retailer if they have a website, as prices might be less than in the store.

■ **Bid at auctions** These can be the source of great bargains resulting from house clearances. Look at the catalogue, inspect items you're interested in and register with the auction house. Set a budget and keep to it when you're bidding. Remember there's usually a premium of 15% plus VAT to pay on top of the purchase price.

■ **Online auctions** Bidding online gives you access to literally millions of products at knock-down prices. You are free to browse but will need to register before buying. Compare the price of the item you want to buy with its retail price so that you know how much of a bargain you're getting. Pay by credit card for added security.

■ **First-time buys** Some mail-order and online retailers give generous discounts on first orders to attract new customers. For example, Littlewoods (0845 707 8810 ✉) and The Cotswold Company (0870 241 0973 ✉) give up to 20% off initial purchases, and Next (0845 600 7000 ✉) takes 15% off early orders from their latest catalogue by new and existing customers.

■ **Buy ex-showhome** Consider buying furniture previously used on display in a showhome (see Resources, right). Prices depend on an item's condition, but you'll usually pay between a quarter and a half of the retail price.

■ **Check ex-display items** Department and furniture stores often sell ex-display pieces at half price or less, so it's always worth asking if there are any on sale. Examine pieces carefully, as you might be able to get further reductions if they are damaged. You can then carry out repairs at home.

■ **Factory shops** These sell surplus stock cheaply, including cancelled orders, returns, last season's stock and ends of ranges. Contact a manufacturer or store to see if they have a factory outlet, but be prepared to travel because most

RESOURCES

WEBSITES FOR FURNITURE BARGAINS

■ View everything in the good-value, twice-yearly Argos catalogue at **www.argos.co.uk** ✉.

■ Find beds and mattresses at knockdown prices at **www.bedsdirect.com** ✉.

■ Check the biggest online auction house at **www.ebay.co.uk** ✉.

■ Another easy-to-navigate auction site is **www.ebid.co.uk** ✉.

■ Find a huge range of discounted furniture at **www.furniture123.co.uk** ✉.

■ A website that includes brand names such as Jaybe and Limelight is **www.furniture busters.com** ✉.

EX-SHOWHOME STOCK

Stock previously used in showhomes, but still in good condition, can be found at the following:

■ The Showhome Warehouse on 0870 333 1556 or see online at **www.showhome warehouse.co.uk** ✉.

■ Trading Interiors on 020 8397 4730 or see the website **www.roomservice group.com** ✉.

companies only have the one. Larger items are discounted the most, so if you are after a sofa, bed or dining table, a long journey may well be worth your while. For half-price top-quality upholstery, try Habitat's Clearance Department in Wythenshawe, Lancashire (0161 902 0441 ✉) – delivery charges start from £25 – or Wesley-Barrell in Witney, Oxfordshire (01993 893100 ✉) – where delivery is included in the price.

■ **Office furniture suppliers** Many outlets sell secondhand desks, chairs and other workplace items bought as a job lot in the hope of a quick turnover. Perhaps a small filing cabinet could be painted and turned into a bedside table, or a metal locker converted into a wardrobe for a child's room.

■ **Junk and charity shops** Visit shops in affluent areas that are likely to have better-quality furniture. Best buys are items such as large wardrobes or tables that won't fit the average room, or pieces in unpopular colours. Stripping and revarnishing or repainting a useful item could be a good-value option.

■ **Investigate skips** Not for the faint-hearted, but a rummage through a skip can pay dividends in terms of furniture finds. Look in wealthier neighbourhoods where the residents are more likely to throw out better pieces.

■ **Newspaper ads** There are bargains to be had but it pays to do some research. Check what the item costs new and examine it for damage, as you are unlikely to have any recourse if it breaks or won't fit in your room. Include the cost of cleaning in your calculations.

■ **Haggle for a lower price** Ask retailers for a discount if you pay cash or buy several items together. They are most likely to agree to this if you're buying items they're keen to shift, such as discontinued lines or end-of-season stock.

WATCH POINTS BUYING FURNITURE

■ **Practicalities** Measure your doors and hall before buying a large piece of furniture. It won't be a bargain if you have to remove windows to get it in. If you are likely to move house, sofas with removable arms are a good investment – without arms they will go round any corner.

■ **Hidden extras** Check whether or not delivery is included in the price. Some companies dispatch free but others – particularly stores – charge as much as £50 for large items. If delivery is included in the price, it is worth asking if they will knock something off if you pick it up yourself.

■ **Unwanted goods** Find out if you can return online and mail-order buys without incurring a delivery charge.

INVEST IN THE RIGHT BED

A bed needs to be comfortable and supportive to give you a good night's sleep. You should go for the best you can afford as, with a little care, it should last at least ten years.

Buy just the mattress Even if your mattress needs replacing, your bed base might still be in good condition so you'll save the expense of a whole new bed. If you don't need a new bed, spend more on the mattress for longer life.

Longer-lasting sprung mattresses The more springs a mattress has, the firmer and longer-lasting it will be.

FLATPACKED – NIGHTMARE OR DREAM?

Flatpacked pieces are cheaper than ready-assembled – and easier to get home. But make sure you get value for money by checking the quality and avoiding problems with assembly. Follow these tips to ensure that your furniture lasts as long as possible:

■ Examine the made-up samples in-store for potential problems such as flimsy drawers.

■ Read the instructions carefully before you start and check you have all the pieces.

■ Make sure that there is a contact for replacement parts.

■ Paint or varnish untreated wood or MDF after assembly to give a smooth surface that is easy to clean.

Pocket-sprung mattresses – where the springs are housed inside individual pockets – are better quality and will last longer than those with open or continuous coil springs.

Don't buy a secondhand mattress However cheap a secondhand mattress is, it will be a false economy as it will have moulded to the shape of the previous owner and won't support you properly. But there's no need to throw out an older, good-quality mattress that has become soft – slip a thin sheet of plywood (around £34 for a double-sized piece from a timber yard or DIY store) underneath for extra support and it will last for another couple of years.

Incorporate storage Divans often have storage drawers underneath, which is often a cheaper option than buying a separate chest of drawers.

VERSATILE SOFABEDS

A sofabed rather than a spare bed is a good compromise if space is tight. Consider how often it is likely to be used.

Buy cheaper for occasional use Less expensive models, from around £250, have a metal mesh base and thin foam mattress and are fine for occasional use. For regular use spend around £500 on a bed with a slatted base and sprung mattress which is more comfortable and will last longer.

A SOFA TO MEET YOUR NEEDS

Although an expensive sofa will give you years of service (see chart below), you may prefer to opt for a cheaper model so you can buy a new one as fashions move on or your circumstances change.

Smaller means cheaper When considering sofa size, think about how many people are going to sit on it. If it will rarely be more than two, why pay more for a three seater?

Choose loose covers If you're worried about the sofa showing the dirt, go for loose covers with built-in fabric protection. Machine-washable covers are cheaper to clean than those that are dry-clean only.

keep it simple

GET VALUE FROM YOUR MATTRESS

To prolong the life of your mattress and get better value from it, turn it over and then around lengthways every couple of months. Stick a piece of masking tape on the mattress with the date it was last turned, in order to keep track of when the mattress needs turning again.

ARE YOU GETTING VALUE FOR MONEY?

You can pay anything from £200 to over £1,000 for a sofa, so it's important to ensure you are getting value for money. Always ask how the sofa is constructed, because these are the parts you can't see, and go for the best your budget allows. Better-quality, more expensive sofas are built to last and often carry a ten-year guarantee. Bearing this in mind, a £1,000 sofa might not cost much more per year than a £200 one in the long run.

COST OVER TIME	SOFA CONSTRUCTION
£200 SOFA = c.£55 PER YEAR	**£200–£350**: Softwood frame with elasticated webbing and foam padding; foam-filled cushions. Lasts about 5 years.
£500 SOFA = c.£80 PER YEAR	**£500–£800**: Hardwood frame with fibre padding and zigzag springs; feather and fibre or foam cushions. Lasts about 8 years.
£1,000 SOFA = c.£50 PER YEAR	**Over £800**: Hardwood frame with glued, screwed and dowelled joints; coil-sprung seats; horsehair or Dacron padding; feather/down or feather/fibre cushions. Lasts about 20 years.

REVAMP WICKERWORK

You can often pick up wicker pieces for next to nothing, and they look just as good in a bedroom as on the patio or in a conservatory. You'll pay less if the seats are saggy – to tighten them, turn the chairs upside down, wet the underside with a damp sponge and leave for 24 hours to dry and shrink. Give the wickerwork a new-look colour change by spraying with acrylic paint.

FIRM UP A SAGGY SOFA

Make an old sofa more comfy by fitting a piece of plywood beneath cushions for under £10. Or replace foam in cushions – pay about £30 for foam cut to fit four cushions.

CREATE A HEADBOARD FOR A BED

Give a plain divan bed an instant headboard with a length of fabric, a throw or a lightweight rug hung from wooden dowelling or a broom handle fixed to the wall behind the bed.

REPLACE WARDROBE PANELS

If wardrobe door panels are marked or broken, take them out and use a staple gun (a good investment at around £20) to staple lengths of gathered fabric in their place.

PREVENT TABLE LEGS FROM WOBBLING

Tables usually wobble because one leg is shorter than the others. Lengthen the leg by cutting a piece of cork to the right size and gluing it on with wood adhesive. This is a lot easier than shortening the other legs.

SCRATCHES ON WOOD

Rub small scratches with half a walnut kernel to restore the colour. Repair deeper scratches by rubbing with a wax crayon of the same colour until the crack is filled. Then cover a small piece of wood with a soft rag and rub across the filled scratch to remove surface wax. Buff with a soft cloth and the scratch should be almost invisible. Make white rings fade by rubbing them with toothpaste.

EASY COVER-UPS

Reupholstering a sofa is expensive – expect to pay at least £200. The easiest and least expensive way to disguise worn-out seating is to drape an attractive bedspread, throw or blanket over it. If you need to buy fabric, the cheapest option is cotton calico which can then be dyed to match your decor. This costs about £1.85 a metre from department stores such as John Lewis. For a more fitted look, use a staple gun to fix fabric to the underside of the sofa to stop it slipping off.

STRENGTHEN FLIMSY SHELVES

Screw battens under the back edges of shelves for extra support to prevent bowing.

TURN PACKAGING INTO FURNITURE

Throw an attractive piece of fabric over a sturdy cardboard box or a plastic or wooden crate for an instant, no-cost coffee table.

DEALING WITH STICKING DRAWERS

If drawers are not sliding in and out smoothly, rub the runners with a candle, a bar of soap or petroleum jelly. If they still stick, rub gently with fine-grade glasspaper or an emery board and re-apply the wax or soap.

STRENGTHEN A CHEST OF DRAWERS

Take out flimsy hardboard drawer bases and back panels, and substitute chipboard to make them more solid. A large sheet costs about £5 from Wickes – half the price of plywood. Alternatively, use wood recycled from old furniture.

INSTANT UPGRADES

With a little imagination and a coat of paint, some different fabric or a change of accessories, you can give your latest furniture bargain a fresh, more stylish look for just a few pounds. Make budget buys look better and last longer, and restore furniture bought secondhand.

USE UP LEFTOVER PAINTS

If you have any leftover paints and are decorating a child's bedroom, try painting each drawer in a chest-of-drawers a different shade, or paint wardrobe doors a contrasting colour to the frame.

TRANSFORM WOOD WITH PAINT

The finish will be far more professional if you sand first or remove old paint with paint-stripper. Streamlined tables and chairs are much easier to strip than ones with fussy mouldings. Ornate chairs may require professional stripping (from around £25), so bear this in mind when buying. Coordinate mismatched wooden kitchen and dining chairs by painting them all the same colour.

NEW HANDLES FOR OLD

Replace plastic knobs or handles on furniture with smart metal or chrome ones, from as little as £2 each.

FIND HOME ACCESSORIES FOR LESS

Soft furnishings, tableware and other accessories help create a stylish, individual home. There are plenty of outlets where you can find these items heavily discounted, so you'll never have to pay full price for anything again.

TOP TIPS WHERE TO BUY

■ **Factory shops** Look out for seconds, last season's designs, ends of lines and surplus stock, at reductions of at least 30% (see Resources, right).

■ **Warehouse sales** Some suppliers of furnishing fabrics hold clearance sales twice a year, including Designers Guild (**www.designersguild.com** 020 7893 7400 ✉) and Osborne and Little (**www.osborneandlittle.com** 020 7352 1456 ✉). Put your name on their mailing lists.

■ **Factory shopping villages** Prices might not be as low as in individual factory shops, but the advantage of shopping at one of these centres is that there are lots of stores under one roof, stocking fashions as well as homewares. Traditional sale times – January and June – are the best times to shop. Two of the biggest are Bicester Village in Oxfordshire, and Cheshire Oaks Designer Outlet at Ellesmere Port on the Wirral. For more centres, see **www.shoppingvillages.com** ✉.

■ **Permanent discount stores** TK Maxx and Matalan are the two big names here and each has a wide selection of brand new bedding, towels, curtains, cushions and crockery at great prices. TK Maxx stocks brand names, whereas Matalan sells own-brand goods.

■ **Across the Channel** Popular French-made homeware is worth checking out if you are planning a holiday or day-trip to France. Provençal fabrics and Le Creuset pans are just two potential bargains (both 30% cheaper than in Britain).

BUYING BARGAIN FABRICS

■ Check fabric carefully for quality when you buy at a discount. If you are buying seconds, look out for loose threads, crooked edges and other flaws. Make sure colours of separate items such as towels are a good match.

■ Many sofas and chairs come with an indication of how much fabric is needed for loose covers. If this information isn't provided, take measurements with you so you don't buy too much or too little.

■ If you particularly like a fabric and think you might find various uses for it, buy more of it than you need – you are unlikely to find it again.

CASE STUDY

NEW HOME, GREAT SAVINGS

When newlyweds Sarah and Dan Bell were furnishing their flat, they really made their budget stretch. At the Homebase sale they netted a sleek leather sofa for just £500 – half the original price. They also got curtain material at 75% off from a nearby fabric warehouse – buying extra to make a cloth to cover a dated but sturdy dining table discovered for only £30 in a junk shop. Crockery came from a Denby Factory Shop, where plates, bowls and mugs were 25% cheaper. For all their bedding and other household linen, they saved 15% by putting in their first order with a mail-order company. The money they saved soon added up to fund an exotic holiday.

RESOURCES

FOR LISTS OF SUPPLIERS
■ **www.gooddealdirectory.co.uk** ✉ has details of factory shops and warehouses with home accessories at discount prices; see also **www.homesources.co.uk** ✉.

FABRICS
■ **Christy Mill Shop** in Hyde, Cheshire, is the factory shop for Christy towels **www.christy-towels.com** 0161 368 1961 ✉.
■ **Knickerbean** has four outlets in southern England for low-priced quality fabrics **www.knickerbean.com** 0845 130 5900 ✉.
■ **Laura Ashley** has a factory shop in Hornsea, East Yorkshire **www.lauraashley.com** 0871 9835 999 ✉.
■ **Sanderson** sells fabric and bed linen at up to 70% off **www.sanderson-online.co.uk** 07895 830044 ✉.
■ Suppliers of secondhand curtains, **The Curtain Exchange** has branches all over England **www.thecurtainexchange.net** 020 7731 8316 ✉; see also Curtains Encore in Dorset **www.curtainsencore.co.uk** 01258 455 221 ✉.

QUALITY TABLEWARE
■ **Dartington Crystal** has stores nationwide selling discounted glassware **www.dartington.co.uk** 01805 626241 ✉.
■ **Denby** has ten factory shops plus special offers sold online **www.denbypottery.co.uk** 01773 740899 ✉.
■ **Spode** has a factory shop for bone china in Stoke-on-Trent **www.spode.co.uk** 01782 744011 ✉.

■ **Fabric discount shops** These outlets can afford to charge lower prices as they are selling direct to the public with no middleman involved. Fabrics are often manufactured at the same mills as leading brands, but at a fraction of the price (see Resources, above).

■ **Supermarkets** Buy food and furnishings together in the big chains, which now have an impressive range of homewares, bedding and cushions. Asda and Morrisons in particular have very competitive prices, with double duvet sets at just £6.97 in Asda, and faux suede cushions at £6 a pair in Morrisons in summer 2004.

■ **Secondhand curtain shops** There is a big market in secondhand curtains, with the stock often sourced from showhomes or customers who have simply changed their minds. Prices are a third to a half of what you would pay brand new (see Resources, above).

CHOOSING CHEAP CHINA AND GLASS
Almost perfect Items marked as seconds often have imperfections that are almost invisible. But still examine pieces carefully for chips and cracks before you buy.
Buy in bulk Boxed sets of china or glassware usually cost less than buying individual pieces.
Check on replacements If you are buying a matching set, check whether it is being discontinued. If so, you may still be able to get replacements through a china-matching service, though these can be expensive. Check out **www.lostpottery.co.uk** (0870 732 4462 ✉) or **www.tablewhere.co.uk** (020 8361 6111 ✉).

PAY LESS FOR CUSHIONS
■ Make your own cushion covers from recycled materials such as embroidered tablecloths, silk scarves and remnants from charity shops.
■ Restuff cushions that have gone flat, using feathers from a pillow.

BEST-BUY KITCHEN APPLIANCES

When you are shopping for domestic appliances, check all the consumer information you can find, either online or at a library. Look for efficiency ratings and repair records, and research what features are available. Make a list of the features you really need and look only at appliances that meet these requirements.

TOP TIPS WHERE TO BUY APPLIANCES

■ **Department stores** Check these out at sale times for the best bargains. Many stores such as Debenhams ✉ have preview days for account customers, and it may be worth opening an account as you will get a further discount on your first purchase. John Lewis ✉ is known for its keen pricing policy and excellent after-sales service – all major appliances have a free two-year warranty.

■ **Electrical superstores** Dixons ✉ and Comet ✉ are two of the best, and you will find even better bargains on their websites, both on own-brand and name-brand models.

■ **Independent stores** Small doesn't necessarily mean more expensive, as prices need to be competitive to keep customers. Buyers and Sellers in Ladbroke Grove, London (0845 085 5585 ✉) is one of the largest and best independent outlets and offers a nationwide delivery service.

■ **Buying online** Without the overheads of running a store, online retailers can afford to cut costs on large and small appliances. We found a Russell Hobbs metal kettle from an online source at 25% cheaper than from a high-street store.

■ **Old stock** Many manufacturers update their products annually, so you will find last year's models going cheap. Always ask in-store if you can't see any on display, as retailers are often only too pleased to shift them.

■ **Ex-display** White goods and smaller appliances which have been on display are often substantially reduced. Haggling may get you an even better deal.

■ **Secondhand** Only buy reconditioned appliances from a reputable retailer. Contact the manufacturer to find out where they are sold. Never buy electrical items from a newspaper small ad, as they could be dangerous.

ARE TOP BRAND NAMES VALUE FOR MONEY?

You pay a lot more for leading, top-end brand names than for own-label or lower-end products. So are they worth the extra expense?

Unnecessary extras The extras you get for a greater outlay may be largely cosmetic – more streamlined, contemporary looks – or the choice of more features. If you are happy with a standard appearance and are not likely to use a wide range of extra features, cheaper models should prove adequate.

Money-saving technology It is worth bearing in mind that more expensive brands are often the leaders in incorporating cutting-edge technology into their appliances, which could save you money in the long run. For example, a faster spin

---

What's worth paying for and what's not

Before you buy a fridge or fridge freezer, think about which features will save you money in the long term – and which ones are not worth paying for.

WORTH IT

■ **Frost-free function** With this function, you won't have to worry about defrosting your freezer.

■ **Auto-defrost** Regulates the temperature to prevent frost building up and so keeps the freezer working more efficiently.

■ **Easy-clean shelves** These just require a wipe with a damp cloth, so you won't need to buy expensive cleaning products.

NOT WORTH IT

■ **Chilled water dispenser** Get into the habit of keeping empty bottles filled with tap water in the fridge.

■ **Ice dispenser** Keep ice cubes in a freezer bag so they are always on hand.

■ **Egg and bottle racks** These take up too much room; better to organise the space yourself.

IT PAYS TO SHOP AROUND

APPLIANCE	RRP	CHAIN STORE PRICE	INTERNET PRICE
Fridge (larder)	£310	£260	£220
Fridge freezer	£430	£360	£330
Dishwasher	£300	£250	£215
Cooker (gas)	£950	£730	£670
Cooker (electric)	£640	£490	£450
Washing machine	£380	£350	£280
Tumble dryer	£285	£250	£205
Washer dryer	£530	£500	£400

You can make big savings by shopping around for kitchen appliances. In the chart to the left, you can see how you can save up to 30% on the RRP (Recommended Retail Price) of typical top-end brand names by buying at an electrical chain store or Internet shop.

Delivery charges not included. Information July 2004

speed in a washing machine will leave clothes drier. If you use a tumble dryer, which is expensive to run, these clothes will dry off quicker and so reduce your electricity bill.
Greater reliability One thing worth paying more for is greater reliability. In a 2004 *Which?* survey, Miele and Bosch dishwashing and laundry products were found to be far more reliable than less expensive brands, including Hoover and Hotpoint. A more reliable product will last longer and save on repair bills, so would be a better buy over the long term.

ARE EXTENDED WARRANTIES WORTH IT?

Decline an extended warranty when buying your appliance. Some retailers charge up to half the cost price for a five-year warranty which is very likely to go unused.
Pay for repairs You will be better off paying for repairs as and when needed – and remember that most appliances come with at least one year's warranty, or more if you buy from John Lewis or pay with certain credit cards.
Multi-appliance warranty If you do want the security of a warranty, a multi-appliance one covering several products is better value – for example, British Gas ✉ offers breakdown cover on up to three appliances for £10.50 a month.

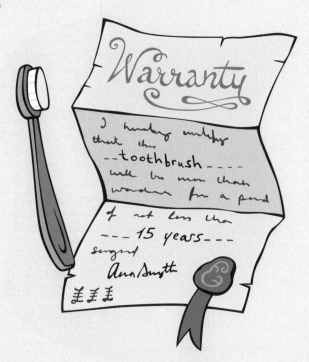

TOP TIPS BUYING APPLIANCES FOR LESS

■ **Opt for freestanding appliances** These are cheaper than built-in or integrated appliances and you will be able to take them with you if you move.

■ **Smaller size, not price** Most appliances are a standard 60cm (24in) wide, but many ranges have slimline models designed to fit into tight spaces. A smaller size doesn't mean a lower price – they cost as much as full-sized models.

■ **Go for white** A white finish often costs less than chrome or stainless steel, and is easier to keep clean.

■ **Choose two-in-one** Appliances with combined functions, such as a washer dryer or fridge freezer, cost less than buying each separately.

TOP TIPS FRIDGES AND FREEZERS

The choice of cooling products has never been greater nor has the range of prices. You can pay from about £150 for a basic larder fridge up into the thousands for an all-singing, all-dancing American-style fridge freezer. So how can you find the right type of fridge and freezer for your needs without breaking the bank?

■ **Think vertical** A vertical fridge freezer costs less than two separate appliances placed side by side and will make full use of space in a confined area.

■ **How much capacity do you need?** A fridge freezer with a total capacity of about 277 litres (9.8cu ft) is adequate for most families, so there is no point in buying extra space that you won't use.

■ **Freezer on top** Models with the freezer at the top usually cost less than those with the fridge at the top, but are less convenient as you have to bend down to open the fridge.

■ **Economical chest freezer** If you buy frozen food in bulk or freeze your own garden produce, think about investing in a separate chest freezer with a lidded top, which can be stored in the garage. With prices starting from around £100, these cost less and are cheaper to run than upright models.

■ **Buy to suit how you eat** Look at how the fridge and freezer areas are split and buy a model that reflects how you shop. If you eat mostly frozen foods, you will need a larger freezer and smaller fridge, whereas if you are a fan of fresh produce, go for a larger fridge area.

FREEZER CARE

If you look after your freezer, it will not only last longer but also cost less to run.

Keep the freezer full Freezers are more efficient when full, so fill in the gaps with tightly packed newspaper.

Defrost the freezer If your freezer is not frost-free, defrost it once the frost is 6mm (¼ in) thick. The thicker the frost, the harder the freezer has to work and the less efficient it will be. Never scrape the frost away with metal utensils, as you could damage the surface.

DISHWASHER DECISIONS

Unlike most other kitchen appliances, a dishwasher is not regarded as a necessity. But there are benefits in investing in one and they save time standing at the kitchen sink.

DELIVERY AND INSTALLATION

■ Check delivery charges and ask whether the appliance can be installed on delivery. Can the old one be taken away at the same time, and is there a cost for this?

■ By law, gas appliances must be installed by a registered CORGI engineer.

■ You will need to contact your local authority regarding disposal of a fridge, but this is normally free.

ENERGY EFFICIENT

Fridges, dishwashers and washing machines are graded according to their energy efficiency. Buy appliances with an A rating for lower running costs. An A-grade fridge freezer can cost up to £46 cheaper a year to run than a similar, older, G-grade model.

What is the best size? Consider how many place settings you need room for. Most standard-sized models take 12 settings – around 76 pieces of crockery and 64 items of cutlery. If you have a large family, a model that takes 14 settings might be more suitable, so you don't have to run the machine so often.

Hygiene and economy Dishwashers are more hygienic and economical than washing by hand. They use half the amount of water and less than 10p of electricity per wash. The best machines have an AAA grade for cleaning, energy efficiency and drying performance.

Keeping the noise down If your kitchen is close to your living area, you will need to check the noise level on cheaper models – more expensive machines have better insulation.

Check the features Choose a machine with programmes and features that suit you, so that you don't pay out for ones you don't use.

keep it simple

COOKER CARE
Keep hobs clean, as food won't be cooked efficiently if the area of contact with the pan is reduced by a coating of dirt. Wipe off spills while the hob and oven are still warm to save on elbow grease and detergent.

WATCH POINTS CUT THE COST OF RUNNING A DISHWASHER

Make savings on energy bills by using the most economical cycles to suit your purposes. Operate the dishwasher only when full for maximum energy savings.

■ **Quick wash** Use this cycle for lightly soiled dishes and when there's no time to wait for a full cycle.

■ **Economy wash** Suitable for plates that aren't too dirty, this cycle uses less water and electricity.

■ **Don't use half load** This is a false economy. Running the dishwasher when half full only saves about 25% on energy, so wait until you have a full load.

■ **Timer delay** This function lets you set the machine to come on at a time to suit you. This is an excellent cost saver if your electricity charges are lower at night.

■ **Don't stint on detergent** Make sure you put detergent in every wash and top up rinse aid and salt as required. Omitting these is a false economy as the machine won't wash properly without them.

■ **Clean the filter** Keep your machine clean by scraping food off plates and removing deposits from the filter after each wash, or debris may coat the next load.

CLEVER COOKER CHOICES

You probably use the cooker more frequently than any other kitchen appliance, but it's quite possible to find a good-quality model that suits your needs at a reasonable price.

Freestanding is cheaper As with other appliances, a standard freestanding cooker costs less than a built-in oven and hob. Modern cookers fit in so neatly that you don't sacrifice good looks if you choose this option. Range-type cookers are increasingly popular, but cost upwards of £500.

Gas versus electric Most hobs and ovens run on electricity or gas, or are dual fuel,

SMART MOVES

consisting of a gas hob with an electric oven. Electric cookers are cheaper to buy than gas, but gas cookers are more energy-efficient to run. Halogen and induction hobs are also available, but at a price – expect to pay at least £500 for them.

Fan-assisted ovens It is worth paying a little more for a fan-assisted oven as it cooks more quickly and distributes heat more evenly to prevent food from drying out.

WHAT TO LOOK FOR WHEN BUYING A WASHING MACHINE

A washing machine is a must for most households because doing your own laundry costs far less than you would pay in a launderette.

Don't be tempted by fancy features Most laundry loads require one of just three programmes: low temperature with a short spin; colourfast/delicates wash with a short spin; hot wash for cottons with a long spin.

Economy features But do look out for options such as half-wash and economy-wash programmes that help you use your machine efficiently.

Check the grading Washing machines are graded from A to E for wash performance, energy efficiency and spin efficiency, with AAA rated models the most efficient.

Drum capacity Choose a model with a larger drum capacity if you have to deal with big loads of washing on a regular basis. This is also useful for washing bulky items such as duvets which you would otherwise have to take to the launderette or dry cleaners.

TEMPTED BY A TUMBLE DRYER?

Tumble dryers are expensive to run, but are often a necessity in busy households, especially during winter months.

Vented or condenser dryer? Vented dryers, which release the hot air outside, are cheaper than condenser dryers but need to be positioned near a window or exterior wall. Condenser dryers can be positioned anywhere and give better results overall.

Consider a washer dryer This combines the features of both appliances and costs less than buying them separately. It doesn't require venting and is a practical option if you are short on space. However, it means you can't wash and dry at the same time. The drying function is also slower and less efficient than in a separate tumble dryer, and if one part goes wrong, it affects the whole machine.

TOP TIPS DOING YOUR LAUNDRY FOR LESS

Set yourself some rules to save water, electricity and money.

■ **Wash full loads** It is more economical to wash a full load so, if necessary, add tablecloths, dishcloths or seldom-washed items to fill the machine. Alternatively, use the half-load economy button if your machine has one.

■ **Use cold water rinses** Rinsing with cold water uses less energy than using warm water.

■ **Don't overdo the detergent** Even very dirty clothes won't wash any better with more detergent and it may leave a film on fabrics.

INVEST IN THE RIGHT VACUUM CLEANER

Buying a good-quality vacuum cleaner can save hours of cleaning time and add years to floors and furnishings by removing dirt and grit. Vacuum cleaner prices start at around £50, but it's probably worth spending more to get the performance you want. Go for as much motor power as possible – up to 1,600 watts or so.

Traditional bagged models These are cheaper than the bagless cyclone type, though you will need to buy replacement bags, which can cost about £1 each. See **www.vacuumbagsonline.co.uk** 07870 697 728 ✉.

Reuse bags three or four times When using an upright hoover with a bag, simply clip off the top, empty out the dirt, fold the top edge over and staple it closed.

Empty the bag frequently Even a half-full bag can sap up to 40% of a vacuum cleaner's suction power.

Save wear and tear on your cleaner Pick up hard objects such as coins and paper clips before you vacuum.

MICROWAVE MAGIC

Microwaves can cook a meal in just a few minutes and so are much cheaper to run than conventional ovens. A standard microwave oven that cooks, defrosts and reheats food costs from about £30, while one with a grill costs from around £65. A combination microwave with a convection hot air oven costs from around £100 but is still very economical to run.

How will you use it? If the microwave is just for reheating and defrosting, it's not worth paying for extra features.

PURCHASING SMALL APPLIANCES

Be selective when buying small appliances. The only essential ones are a kettle, a toaster and an iron.

Check out kettles Plastic kettles cost less than metal ones. Go for one with a fast boiling time – the fastest boils in around two minutes. A kettle with a concealed element is more resistant to limescale, or put a few glass marbles in the bottom to help prevent limescale from accumulating. Expect to pay a minimum of £15.

Today's toasters Toasters range from basic models to ones packed with features, so think what you'll use it for. Prolong a toaster's life by emptying the crumb tray regularly, and using wooden tongs rather than a knife to remove trapped slices (with the toaster unplugged, of course). A basic four-slice toaster can cost as little as £9.

Select a steam iron Irons range from a traditional dry model to a high-powered steam generator. Opt for one with a steam/spray feature, which can cost as little as £5 and will make stiff fabrics easier to iron, so won't need to be switched on for as long.

RESOURCES

CHECK OUT WEBSITES
■ These are some of the best websites for cheap kitchen appliances:
www.appliance-direct.co.uk 01332 547580 ✉
www.appliance-world.co.uk 0870 757 2424 ✉
www.comet.co.uk 08705 425425 ✉
www.cheap-washing-machines.co.uk ✉
www.dixons.co.uk 0845 850 0545 ✉
See also the Home and Garden section within **www.amazon.co.uk** ✉.
■ For spares and ex-display plus new try **www.ukappliances.co.uk** 0870 760 6600 ✉:
www.unbeatable.co.uk 01293 543 555 ✉
www.vacuumcleanersdirect. co.uk 0870 609 3001 ✉
Bid for bargain, returned and ex-display items from Comet at **www. clearance-comet.co.uk** ✉.

CUT THE COST OF CLEANING

Furnishings, flooring and household fittings will last longer if they are cleaned on a regular basis. There's no need to spend much money on proprietary cleaning products, as you can make many of your own for a fraction of the price.

TOP TIPS PAY LESS FOR CLEANING PRODUCTS

You can slash the cost of cleaning products by using the cheap, readily available substances listed below, some of which you will no doubt have around the house already. Each has multiple uses and is effective on a wide range of different surfaces.

■ **Ammonia** Use household ammonia in solution with water on windows, glass surfaces, mirrors, ceramic tiles and cooker hobs. Caution: avoid inhaling fumes, and contact with skin or clothing. Cost: £1.65p for 500ml.

■ **Bicarbonate of soda** This mild alkaline powder will clean china, stainless steel, fridges and freezers, ovens and plastic furniture. It can be sprinkled on a damp cloth or applied as a paste mixed with water for light scouring; or use as a solution in water when soaking china, for instance, or washing surfaces. Cost: 50p for 200g.

■ **Borax** Domestic or laundry borax softens water and breaks down grease. It's good for cleaning enamel surfaces, ceramic tiles, windows and mirrors, and for dissolving grease in sinks and drains. It will also clear tannin stains in teapots. Use it dry, as a paste with water and vinegar, or in a solution with water. Caution: wear gloves if you have sensitive skin. Cost: £2.00 for 750g.

■ **Lemon juice** Applied neat or added to water, the acidity of lemon juice clears tarnish on brass and copper, removes limescale, rust and stains on marble and plastic worktops, and is effective against unpleasant smells (see page 214). Cost: 65p for 200ml.

ASK YOURSELF

IS IT WORTH BUYING A SUPERMARKET'S OWN-BRAND CLEANERS?

The answer is yes, but the saving is not always very great. Often the difference in price between a famous-name cleaner and the supermarket's own-brand equivalent is 20p–30p. But it's always worth checking the difference. We spotted an own-brand cream cleaner (54p for 500ml) that was under half the price of the market leader (£1.14), and an all-purpose kitchen cleaner that was £1.61 for 500ml but just 98p for the supermarket's own label – over a third less.

Recipes for success

Raid your kitchen cupboards for bicarbonate of soda and lemon juice, and solve cleaning problems for a fraction of the price of branded products.

SMART MOVES

DRY CARPET SHAMPOO

Sprinkle bicarbonate of soda generously over the carpet, leave for 15 minutes, then vacuum thoroughly.

Cost 50p; cost of branded carpet cleaner: £2 plus.

OVEN CLEANER

Mix bicarbonate of soda with a little water to make a thick paste and spread over baked-on grease. Leave overnight, rub with a plastic scrubber and rinse.

Cost 50p; cost of branded oven cleaner: £3.

MILDEW REMOVER

Mimimise mould and remove mildew from a shower curtain by applying a paste of bicarbonate of soda and lemon juice. Soak, then rinse in warm water.

Cost 50p; cost of branded mildew remover: £2.

TAP DESCALER

Rub chrome taps with half a lemon to remove scale and scrub inside them with a toothbrush dipped in vinegar.

Cost 50p; cost of branded limescale remover: £2.50.

■ **Washing soda** Use to soften water and break down grease, in a hot-water solution. It will clean cooker hoods, extractor fans, hard flooring and drains. It will also clear green corrosion on brass and copper. Caution: wear gloves. Cost: 75p for 1kg.

■ **White spirit** A turpentine substitute, white spirit is used neat to clean gilt picture frames and remove wax polish build-up. It can also clear rust spots from acrylic sinks. Caution: it is highly flammable. Cost: £1 for 750ml.

■ **White vinegar** Used neat in a solution with water or as a paste with borax and water, vinegar cleans windows, glass surfaces, ceramic tiles and wooden furniture. It can help to remove hard-water deposits from taps, toilet bowls and sinks, and works as a descaler for kettles. (See also Smart moves, page 213.) Cost: 1.20p for 1 litre.

SAVE BY USING COMMON HOUSEHOLD ITEMS

Proprietary cleaners and stain removers will set you back pounds, but sometimes the solution is much closer to home, and costs just a few pennies.

Bread Rub dirty marks on wallpaper gently with a piece of fresh white bread. This also works with Venetian blinds.

Paper Clean grease spots on wallpaper by blotting with a clean paper towel, brown paper or blotting paper and then pressing a warm (not hot) iron over it.

Salt Use salt to absorb red wine spilt on carpet or fabric. Apply immediately after the accident, then brush or rinse away later. Cost of a carpet cleaning spray: £2 for 500ml.

Talcum powder Pour talc over a grease stain on cloth, leave overnight, brush the talc off and wash the cloth as normal. Cost of a stain remover spray that does the same job: £2 for 100ml.

Baby oil Make stainless steel appliances gleam by gently rubbing them with cotton wool dipped in a little baby oil.

Toothpaste Clean dirty grouting between wall tiles by rubbing with toothpaste, or try a mild bleach solution.

Denture cleaning tablets Use as a kettle descaler. Fill the kettle with cold water, add a couple of denture cleaning tablets, leave overnight, then rinse thoroughly. Cost of a branded kettle descaler: £1.20.

WATCH POINTS LOOK AFTER FLOORS

If you take good care of floors and floor coverings, they will reward you with years of service. Protect them from damage, clean regularly and deal with stains promptly.

■ **Use a doormat** The easiest way to keep floor-cleaning costs down is by preventing dirt from entering your home in the first place. Look in IKEA stores ✉ or the £1 shops found in many towns for inexpensive, heavy-duty mats to place outside every exterior door. Put thinner ones just inside the doors to prevent dirt being trodden into carpets and wearing down the fibres.

■ **Clean carpets once a year** Hire a carpet cleaner from a hire shop such as HSS ✉ or get quotes from local cleaning firms. Expect to pay at least £25 a room but look out for special 'whole house' deals. Ask about a discount if you move all the furniture out of the room beforehand, as this

keep it simple

BRIGHTEN LIGHT BULBS
Restore the effectiveness of your light bulbs by dusting them with a dry cloth when switched off. A dust-free bulb shines up to 50% brighter than one that is dirty.

CLEVER WAYS WITH CLEANING EQUIPMENT

■ **Wipe windows with newspaper** Rub newly washed windows with crumpled newspaper as the ink will make the glass shine. Cost of a chamois leather: £5.

■ **Cleaning cloths** Cut up old terry nappies, towels, T-shirts, sheets and dishcloths. Cost of a pack of ten branded cloths: £1.

■ **Make a polisher for a wooden floor** Tie a duster round a soft broom and use this to apply polish. Cost of replacement head for a floor polisher: £3.

will save the cleaners' time and mean they can fit in more jobs that day. For help in finding local carpet cleaning companies, contact the National Carpet Cleaners Association (**www.ncca.co.uk** 0116 271 9550 ✉).

■ **Disguise marks** Rub small scratches on wooden floors with fine steel wool, then mix a little brown shoe polish with floor wax and rub in well. Remove scuff marks on vinyl by rubbing with a clean pencil eraser.

■ **No-cost disguise for a worn area** Disguise a small worn patch on a carpet by filling in with a felt-tip pen in the same colour. Test on an inconspicuous corner first to check for a good colour match.

■ **Attack stains immediately** Soak up spills with a paper towel as soon as they occur, then squirt the stain with soda water, and blot and repeat. Never rub the stain. If the spill discolours your carpet, apply a half-and-half solution of white vinegar and water, then dab and blot with clean rags repeatedly until the mark disappears. Cost of a branded carpet stain remover spray: £2.

SAVE ON CARE FOR CURTAINS AND BLINDS

Clean curtains and blinds at least once a year to prevent dirt build-up shortening their life.

Buy machine-washable curtains Wash curtains yourself to save on expensive dry cleaning bills, which can be as much as £50 for a pair of curtains. If the curtains are too large or heavy for your machine, wash them carefully in the bath and hang to drip dry on a washing line.

New rings for old Boil dirty metal curtain rings in a solution of two parts water to one part vinegar and rub dry with a clean, old towel to make them come up like new.

Cleaning roller blinds A roller blind cleaner bought in a shop costs £3 for 500ml. Instead, unroll washable roller blinds and sponge with a solution of water and washing-up liquid. Or dry-clean blinds by laying on towelling and rubbing with flour. Clean Venetian blinds in a mild soapy solution too.

TOP TIPS A GLEAMING BATHROOM

There's no need to pay out for proprietary bathroom cleaners. Use washing up liquid (cost: 70p for 500ml) and a little white vinegar instead.

■ **Bathtime basics** If you clean a shower or bath immediately after use, when steam has loosened any dirt, you should only need to wipe over surfaces with a damp cloth plus a small amount of washing-up liquid, or white vinegar for stubborn marks. Wipe soapy film off tiles with a

Ten ways with white vinegar

Vinegar is cheap, at £1.20 a litre, long-lasting and has myriad uses.

Kettle cleaner Fill with equal parts vinegar and water, boil, allow to cool and leave overnight.

Window washer Add a few drops of vinegar to water in a plant mister. Cost of a branded window cleaner: £2.

All-round bathroom saviour See below for cleaning baths, tiles, taps, screens and shower heads.

Plaster perker Mix one part vinegar to three parts water to clean water-stained plaster on walls and ceilings.

Iron restorer Fill a steam iron with a 50:50 solution of vinegar and water. Run the iron on the steam setting until dry and repeat with clear water.

Rust buster Soak rusty screws or nails in vinegar for several days until the rust dissolves, then scrub with an old toothbrush and rinse.

Mould preventor Wipe kitchen cupboards and the bread bin with a cloth soaked in vinegar. Cost of a branded mould remover: £2.

Fabric softener White vinegar makes a great substitute and doesn't affect allergy sufferers as it contains no chemicals.

Vacuum flask reviver Clean a flask by filling with a half water/half vinegar solution, then rinse with clean water.

Hand freshener Rinse hands in vinegar to remove onion, garlic or fish odours.

SMART MOVES

mixture of one part vinegar to four parts water. Cost of a branded bathroom cleaner: £1.20 for 500ml.

■ **Cleaning a shower unit** Remove hard-water deposits on shower doors and screens by wiping with vinegar. Leave for 30 minutes, then rinse. Unscrew and soak a shower head in a bowl of warm vinegar to remove scale, using an old toothbrush to clear the holes. Cost of a branded limescale remover, liquid or spray: £3 for 500ml.

■ **Descaling taps** If there is a build-up of limescale on taps, scour with vinegar, then cover with a plastic bag. Leave for a couple of hours, then rinse.

TOP TIPS A SPARKLING KITCHEN SINK AND WORKTOPS

Many kitchen cleaning products can scratch porcelain and stainless steel sinks, so try one of these easy – and much cheaper – ideas instead.

■ **Cleaning porcelain sinks** To remove stains from a porcelain sink, soak paper towels with bleach and spread them over the bottom of the sink. Leave for 30 minutes, remove and rinse with cold water. Cost of a branded kitchen cleaner suitable for porcelain: £1.50 for 500ml.

■ **Keep stainless steel sinks clean** Remove water marks with white vinegar. Rub persistent marks with a paste of bicarbonate of soda mixed with water. Cost of a branded stainless steel sink cleaner: £2.50 for 250ml.

■ **Remove limescale** Get rid of limescale from around plug holes by rubbing with a piece of cut lemon. Cost of a branded limescale remover: £3 for 500ml.

■ **Hygienic worktops** To avoid the need for a major cleaning job, wipe worktops daily with hot, soapy water, rinse and wipe dry. Rub stains with a damp cloth and bicarbonate of soda. If the stain persists, wipe with a cloth moistened with a little bleach. Cost of a branded kitchen worktop cleaner: £1.50 for 500ml.

NATURAL PESTICIDES

Homemade remedies can work just as well as shop-bought pesticides, and are safer and kinder on your wallet.

INSTEAD OF:
Ant killer
Mothballs
Fly strips

USE:
Dried mint or ground cloves
Cedar chips or lavender bags
Lengths of brown paper soaked in boiled and cooled sugar water

MAKE YOUR OWN AIR FRESHENER

Fill a spray bottle with water and add ten drops of an essential oil – try rosemary, eucalyptus, pine, lavender or citrus.

CLEAR SMELLS WITH LEMON

Remove fishy or garlic smells from a wooden chopping board by rubbing the board with a cut lemon. And put citrus peel down an electric waste disposal unit to clear smells.

SIMPLE SOLUTION

Remove unwanted odours from inside the microwave by heating up a slice of lemon in a bowl of water or a bicarbonate of soda solution.

SCENT OF CLOVES

Simmer cloves in water for a delicious smell that is welcoming in winter.

FRAGRANT BATHS

Pop about eight drops of a relaxing essential oil such as neroli or sandalwood into your bath.

ADD THE SCENT OF BAKING BREAD

Warm brown sugar and cinnamon gently on the stove to fill your home with delicious baking smells. Take care that the mixture doesn't burn.

ABSORB ODOURS

Place a saucer of vinegar next to the cooker to absorb strong odours.

FRESHEN UP AS YOU VACUUM

When you do the vacuuming, put a couple of drops of essential oil into the dust bag and the scent will be dispersed around the house.

KEEP AIR FRESH AND SWEET

Kitchens and bathrooms can harbour unpleasant smells, but there are plenty of ways to get rid of them cheaply or for free. You can make your own air fresheners and room fragrances. Essential oils cost from about £3 a bottle from health food shops, but a little goes a long way and they last well.

LAVENDER SACHETS

If you grow your own lavender, snip the heads off the stalks, let them dry, then make your own sachets using scraps of muslin or thin cotton.

FREE THE FRIDGE OF SMELLS

Put a bowl filled with clean cat litter in a fridge that is going to be switched off for any length of time to absorb smells.

SWEET POMANDERS

Keep wardrobes smelling sweet with homemade pomanders. Stud oranges, lemons or limes with whole cloves, then hang from a piece of leftover ribbon.

FLOWERS AND PLANTS IN YOUR HOME

Add colour to your home with beautiful flowers. Knowing where and what to buy and how to look after them will ensure you get value for money.

SHOPPING FOR FLOWERS

The best bargain flowers are home grown, so plant them in your garden if you can.

Get reductions Supermarkets and street markets are a good source of well-priced flowers – buy at the end of the day when the flowers are often reduced.

Flower markets If you're buying for a special occasion or want exotic varieties, visit a flower market, where you'll find flower and plant stalls selling plants at wholesale prices – about half those charged in florists' shops. Prime examples include the Columbia Road Flower Market, in Shoreditch, London (open 8am to 2pm on Sundays only), and Manchester Flower Market, in Piccadilly Gardens in the city centre (open 11am to 5pm, Thursday, Friday and Saturday).

LONG-LASTING BLOOMS

Buy flowers that last a long time, such as chrysanthemums and carnations. Lilies are expensive but last for two weeks and have an intense fragrance that will fill the whole house. Ensure that you change the water every three days.

Longer-life flowers Cut flowers from the garden just before they are in full bloom. That way they will open indoors and you will need to replace them less frequently.

Delicate scents Sweet peas are easy to grow, have a long-lasting scent, and the more you cut, the more they flower. Freesias are also a good choice for a fragrant flower. Not all colours are strongly scented, so before you buy you may want to sort through and select the most fragrant.

Houseplants Move a pot plant around until you find a spot where the plant is happy. Don't be tempted to overwater if the plant looks unhealthy – it could just need a spot in stronger sunlight.

TOP TIPS FOR HEALTHY HOUSEPLANTS

Houseplants are a great investment as, if looked after properly, they can last for years. Help keep them healthy with these old-fashioned methods that cost nothing.

■ **Aerating the soil** Mix a few tea leaves or coffee grounds into the plant soil to aerate it.

■ **Tea-time** Give plants a boost by watering occasionally with leftover cold tea.

■ **Leftover water** Add cooled water used for boiling eggs as it is full of nutrients.

■ **String solution** Water small house plants while you are away by using a piece of string. Place one end in the soil and the other in a bucket of water positioned higher than the plant. The string will gradually draw the water from the bucket to the soil.

SMART MOVES

TRADITIONAL ALTERNATIVES TO FLOWER FOOD

■ Add a couple of aspirin tablets to the vase.

■ Pop a few drops of lemonade into the water.

■ Add a few drops of bleach to disinfect the water, but don't overdo it or you will kill the flowers.

■ Add a couple of coins – the dissolving minerals are believed to extend the life of flowers.

Ways to make cut flowers last longer

■ Buy from a reputable source, and ensure flowers are well wrapped for protection.

■ Choose flowers with firm petals or with buds that are coloured, which shows that they've absorbed enough food to develop fully.

■ Put them in lukewarm water – it has less oxygen, which prevents air bubbles in the stem blocking water uptake.

■ Clean vases thoroughly after use – bacteria kills flowers.

■ Snip stems at an angle to increase the area that can absorb water.

■ Strip off all leaves that would be below the waterline to help keep the water clean.

■ Use flower food as instructed. It contains flower-friendly sugars to feed the flowers and encourage buds to open as well as preservatives to prolong their life.

 **RESOURCES**

GARDEN DESIGN
The following may
help you to plan your
garden for less:
■ Software, such as the
*Punch Master Landscape
and Home Design*
price £12.99, or *Geoff
Hamilton's 3D Garden
Designer* price £16.99
■ Websites, such as the
Royal Horticultural
Society at **www.rhs.org.uk**
✉ and the BBC site at
**www.bbc.co.uk/gardening/
design** ✉.

CREATIVE GARDENING ON A BUDGET

Whether you are designing a new garden from scratch or improving what you already have, a lot of work is involved, though with careful planning this can cost surprisingly little. Shopping around and doing the hard graft yourself rather than paying others to do it will reap dividends, both in your garden and for your wallet.

DON'T FIGHT NATURE

Take time to find out about your soil and growing conditions and then select only those plants that will thrive there naturally. Local weeds and wildflowers should also provide clues as to the species of plants that are easy to grow in your garden.

Give plants what they need Identify ways to improve growing conditions to give plants, bulbs and seeds every chance in life.

Choose good stock Buy the best-quality plants you can afford to ensure maximum growth and value for money.

TOP TIPS PLANS FOR PENNIES

A professional garden designer may charge several hundred pounds for a detailed garden plan, plus more again for buying the plants and carrying out the work, but there are ways of keeping the cost of planning and planting out a garden well below this level.

■ **Design it yourself** Design your own landscaping and planting plan. There are dozens of books, CDs and websites (see Resources, left) that can help you come up with the right solution for your garden.

■ **Plant it yourself** If you have your garden professionally designed, then do the work yourself.

■ **Hire a student** Contact a local horticultural college to see whether you can hire a student to design your garden.

■ **A garden centre may help** Visit your local garden centre or nursery – staff are often very knowledgeable and may agree to draw up a plan for free or a modest fee on condition that you buy the plants from them.

■ **Visit a DIY store** It is worthwhile trying large DIY chains with garden sections. For instance, Homebase offers good-value tailor-made garden plans, and you will also get discount vouchers towards their extensive stock of plants, paving and equipment. A detailed plan, including information on plant varieties, arrangements, features, paths and patios, costs from £110 for a garden up to a 100m² (1,100sq ft) in size.

LANDSCAPING NEEDN'T COST THE EARTH

Paving stones, soil and gravel can be a major expense, so buy larger quantities for the biggest savings and look out for secondhand bargains.

Buy in bulk It is far more cost-effective to purchase materials in large quantities, and it is cheaper still to buy them when you can from a builders' merchant rather than your local garden centre or a DIY store such as B&Q. Gravel, for instance, costs just £1.39 for 25kg from the DIY chain store/builders' merchant Wickes, whereas a 5kg bag from B&Q costs £1.48.

Don't go it alone If you are planning to cover large areas of ground, ask neighbours if they plan to landscape their gardens and share the costs. That way you can buy larger quantities and share the cost of delivery.

Bargain paving You may be able to pick up paving stones secondhand. Keep an eye out for anyone renovating their garden, and see if they will sell off unwanted paving slabs cheap. You may even be lucky enough to find some in a skip.

FEATURES FOR THE COST-CONSCIOUS

Ponds, arbours and arches add interest to a garden, but can be expensive to buy and install. With a little know-how you can keep costs down by making your own.

Bargain barrel ponds Ideal for a small garden, a miniature pond made from a half barrel is portable so you can take it with you when you move. Although you can buy barrels at a garden centre for £25–£40, you may be able to strike a bargain if your local pub has any spares.

Arches for the thrifty Rather than paying £50 or more for an arch from a garden centre, save by making your own from flexible plastic plumber's pipe. Key with glasspaper, apply weatherproof paint and attach to wooden supports. Alternatively, reuse timber from a dismantled shed or fence.

BUYING PLANTS ON A BUDGET

Your options for obtaining plants vary from the most expensive garden centre to the humblest roadside stall, but in all cases, make sure you buy viable stock.

Do a deal with friends The cheapest option is to get into the habit of swapping cuttings with friends.

Savings on the road Roadside stalls, where an amateur gardener sells off surplus stock, can be great value.

Shop-bought bargains DIY chain stores are often cheap, as are large supermarkets – prices can be up to 40% less than at nurseries or garden centres, though the choice might be limited.

Reliability costs Garden centres and nurseries are the most expensive option, but the variety and quality of the plants will be high, so they are less likely to die and need replacing.

Look out for perennials Small perennial plants are good value for money, particularly ones that can be divided easily. Buy one perennial and divide it into two or three plants.

Bulbs for value The most economical bulbs are ones that multiply yearly in the same position. Daffodils and other varieties of narcissi, snowdrops and crocuses are good value.

Avoid cracked containers Don't buy a plant in a cracked container, even if it is reduced, as the roots may be damaged.

MAKE YOUR OWN COMPOST

Since compost from a garden centre can cost from £1 for a 28-litre bag, get into the habit of making your own compost – it is easy, environmentally friendly and virtually free. You can make a suitable container using a plastic bin with holes

HOW TO MAKE A GARDEN LOOK BIGGER

Create the illusion of size and space in your garden by fixing an old mirror to a wall or fence in a position that gives an attractive reflection, and training plants to conceal the mirror edges.

A LAWN FOR 75% LESS

It is far more economical to sow grass seeds than plant turf, though you will have to wait for the results. Turf for 40m² (432 sq ft) costs around £130 (including delivery), whereas seed for the same area costs £20. You will need a lawnmower if you don't have one already – look for bargain buys in summer sales, newspaper adverts and car boot sales.

drilled round the side. Alternatively, nail together pieces of recycled timber from a wooden palette and wrap with galvanised chicken wire. You can use a piece of old carpet as a lid. Almost any organic kitchen waste can be used for composting, especially vegetable peelings, as can clothes and furnishings made from natural fibres, cut into small pieces, and lawn mowings.

TOP TIPS **PROPAGATE AND SAVE**

Propagating your own plants will save you a great deal of money in the long term, and is immensely satisfying. The most common ways to do this are by growing plants from seed or taking cuttings.

■ **Savings from seeds** A single adult plant can cost as much as a packet of seeds that yields 30–50 plants, so buy seeds or collect them by scooping out from ripe fruit or vegetables, or tying a paper bag round plants and gently shaking. Store dry seeds in film canisters until you are ready to plant them indoors or out.

■ **Cheaper cuttings** Depending on the type of plant, you will need to take cuttings in spring or late summer. Make your own mini cloche by securing a plastic bag over the pot to retain moisture and warmth. Once it has been moved outside, place an upturned jar over the plant for protection against the elements, snails and slugs.

■ **Recycled containers** Rather than paying for plastic plant pots or seed trays, grow seeds and cuttings in plastic food containers or yoghurt pots, and use wooden lollipop sticks as markers.

■ **Keep bulbs for another year** Frost kills non-hardy bulbs, so dig them up once they have finished flowering and keep them in a frost-free garage or shed throughout the winter. Store them inside old tights, tying a knot between each bulb so they are not touching each other, to minimise the risk of disease.

Improve your soil for free

There are various ways to improve your soil's texture and fertility for next to nothing.

■ Improve drainage in clay soil by working it gently with a fork.

■ Add well-rotted manure. You shouldn't have to pay for this as many stables and farms are only too glad to have it taken off their hands. Make sure it is well-rotted or it will burn your plants. You may have to find somewhere to store manure while it rots down, such as an out-of-the-way corner at the bottom of the garden.

■ Perk soil up with homemade compost.

TOP TIPS CONVERTING CONTAINERS

Virtually anything can be used as a planter, so forget buying pots from the garden centre at a cost of £5–£50. A container should be able to hold enough potting compost for root growth, and have drainage holes to prevent plants becoming waterlogged. Pierce the bottom with a drill or bradawl to make holes before planting.

■ **Add style to plastic** Use leftover paint to add a bright splash of colour to cheap plastic pots, or stick pieces of broken tiles onto waterproof grout for a colourful mosaic finish. Stick shells onto a painted pot or window box for a striking three-dimensional effect.

■ **Antique pots for less** Fashionable antique terracotta pots from exclusive gardening stores are expensive. Create an aged effect on a new pot by painting it with yoghurt to encourage the growth of algae and moss.

■ **Re-use a sink** Old troughs and sinks can make splendid planters. A butler's or Belfast sink works best. Or try a child-size bath galvanised with rust-resistant zinc.

■ **Versatile tyres** Old tyres can be stacked for increased depth. Paint them to improve their appearance.

■ **Drainage included** A metal colander makes a wonderful hanging basket and has ready-made drainage holes. Add a liner if compost is in danger of falling out. Then attach three lengths of chain (from DIY shops) and hang from a bracket.

■ **Transform rubbish** Any of the following containers can look effective when filled with geraniums or other bright flowering plants: a catering-size oil can, ceramic potty or chamber pot, wheelbarrow, terracotta chimney pot, wellington boot or an old mop bucket.

GROW YOUR OWN HERBS

Grow herbs from seed in a pot and make savings on the cost of repeatedly buying them from the supermarket. Plant herbs such as basil, chives, parsley and sage together in a sunny spot, but grow rosemary on its own as it has a tendency to take over. Many varieties will thrive for years if they are regularly pruned.

SAVING WATER

Knowing how to water your garden efficiently and how to conserve water will cut costs, particularly if your water is metered (see Household finance, page 298).

Conserve and save Buy an inexpensive water butt or use a plastic bin or other watertight container to collect rainwater. You'll need to place it under a downpipe from the guttering so that the water is channelled into the container.

Re-use water Recycle used water from basins and bath water without much bubble bath.

Beware chemicals Don't use water from the dishwasher. Chemicals in the detergent may be harmful to your plants.

Treat thirsty lawns Spike a dry lawn with a fork to encourage water to penetrate the soil.

Mulch for moisture Old carpet and newspaper efficiently retain water – place around the plants and disguise with soil. Chipped bark, lawn mowings, animal manure and garden compost can also be used.

SPEND AT LEAST 25% LESS ON COMPOST

When planting up containers, reduce the amount of compost you will need by placing an upturned plastic pot in the base, or add pieces of polystyrene packaging to pad out the compost.

 **RESOURCES**

FOR THE THRIFTY GARDENER
Use the following resources to save money on your hobby:

■ The Henry Doubleday Research Association (HDRA) website contains tips on making your own compost. Find it at **www.hdra.org.uk** ✉.

■ *Which?* conducted a survey comparing many commonly available composts. You can find the results at **www.which.net/gardening which/shopping/compost.pdf**

■ Websites, such as Sisley at **www.sisley.co.uk** ✉ and GoneGardening at **www.gonegardening.com** 0845 1 300 100 ✉, offer discounts for bulk buys of compost and gravel.

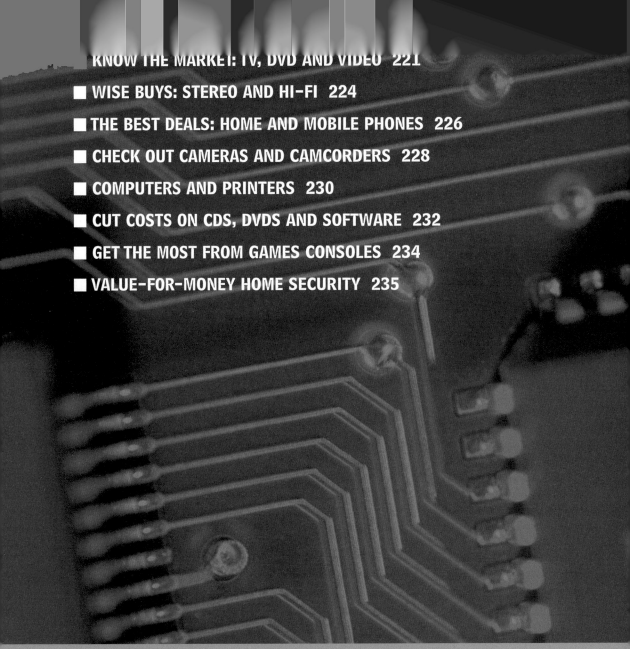

Electronic equipment

With competitive Internet prices and constantly evolving technology, a little homework can save you a lot of money.

KNOW THE MARKET: TV, DVD AND VIDEO

There's huge potential for saving money when you're choosing TV and home cinema electronics. The cash saved by smart buying on just a single item is often enough to justify an extra purchase, such as a surround sound setup or even a collection of DVD films.

CHOOSING THE RIGHT TYPE OF TV

Make an informed choice about which type of TV to buy so you purchase the model that suits your viewing habits.

Staying mainstream You get the best value for money by buying the most mainstream TV choice – a 28in widescreen tube-based TV. Competition between dealers is so fierce that £300 will get you a brand-name TV. If you choose to purchase a larger set, be prepared for the higher cost; there's a big hike in prices for a 32in screen – you'll pay as much as £200–£300 more.

Save money or space? Thin panel TVs look stylish and modern and take up a fraction of the space of normal tube-based TVs, but you pay dearly for the privilege, as the chart below shows. You will save around £700 by buying a normal 28in TV compared to a similar-sized LCD model.

False economies If you do decide to get a thin panel LCD TV, be wary of the lowest-cost models. Some 13in–15in models sell for as little as £300, but the corner-cutting compromises make these a false economy. They look great when viewed straight ahead and up close in a shop, but back home the screen will be too small and the viewing angle too narrow for comfortable viewing from your sofa and armchairs. Their ideal use is in a caravan or small bedsit.

Plasma problems The best of the large plasma screen TVs are impressive, but the technology is still in its infancy and this shows in the picture quality of the cheaper models. Some plasma TVs don't even include a TV tuner which can cost an extra £50–£200. Prices continue to fall, too – so wait for a few years and not only will you get far better picture quality but you'll also save £1,000 on today's prices.

TV PRICE COMPARISONS

For TVs with a screen size up to 32in, the choice is between tube-based and LCD TVs, with a big premium for LCD's slim lines.

For larger sizes, only projection TVs (most of which use tubes) and thin panel plasma TVs are available.

TYPE OF TV	PICTURE SIZE	PRICE RANGE	FUTURE PRICE FALLS
Tube-based TV	14in–32in	£50–£700	Minimal
LCD TV	13in–42in	£300–£3,500	Likely – up to 50%
Projection TV	42in–61in	£800–£2,000	Minimal
Plasma	32in–50in	£1,700–£7,000	Likely – up to 50%

222

WHERE TO GET THE BEST DEAL

The chart below shows the typical price range for a 28in TV at different types of dealers. But price apart, they each have advantages.

Check the terms and conditions of mail-order and online dealers for after-sales service and returns policies.

| LOCAL INDEPENDENT SPECIALIST
Knowledgeable staff and good after-sales service | £399–£420 |

| HIGH-STREET RETAILER
You can see what you are getting and benefit from special deals | £350–£380 |

| MAIL-ORDER/ONLINE SPECIALIST
The best choice and most competitive pricing | £299–£319 |

RESOURCES

DISCOUNTS ONLINE
The Internet is the best way to find good deals on a new mainstream TV as magazines tend to concentrate on the expert end of the market. For comparisons look at:
www.kelkoo.co.uk
www.uk.pricerunner.com
www.compareprices.co.uk

MAKE REAL SAVINGS

When you're shopping for a DVD player, ignore the free DVD movies used as an incentive on a particular model. It's rarely possible to find a set of films that you already plan to buy; instead, concentrate on finding what you want at the cheapest price.

SAVE ON YOUR SET

If you want to pay less for your next TV, or for other home cinema electronics, you will need to look further than your nearest high street or shopping centre.

Brand names on the cheap Use an online price comparison site to save a small fortune on the cost of a brand name TV (see Resources, left).

Impulse buying Supermarkets can use their buying power to sell TVs and DVD players at low prices – as little as £230 for a 28in widescreen TV, for example. They can be great deals, but you can rarely check the picture quality, so ask about the return policy before buying on impulse. The same applies to mail-order and online retailers.

Check picture quality If you're a home cinema enthusiast looking for an LCD or plasma TV, audition each model by using an action-packed DVD movie to test quality. In particular, look out for screen smearing, where the screen just can't keep up with the speed of the action.

Buying a used TV As TVs can last for years, there are some great used bargains as other people upgrade their sets. Look in your local newspaper's classified ads or online at **www.ebay.co.uk** ✉ or **www.loot.com** ✉. Used TVs have little or no warranty, so offset the risks by paying much less: never offer more than half the new price of a similar model.

Local deals A local shop can rarely match online prices on new goods, but they sometimes display Manager's Specials. There may also be discounts on unwanted returns or equipment with minor cosmetic flaws. Look for a 20% or higher discount, but avoid items with functional problems and make sure you get a full warranty.

VIDEO AND DVD OPTIONS

VHS video recorders are on their way out – they are being replaced by the latest digital technology with better features and better value. VHS will soon be obsolete, so don't spend money on a VHS recorder or pre-recorded movies.

DVD for movies Don't buy another VHS tape. For the cost of three movies – about £30 – you can buy an entry-level DVD player. You can run both a VHS and a DVD player on your TV as long as it has multipule SCART sockets; if not, buy an adapter for £10-£15 from an electrical store.

Region-free DVD The most valuable feature on any DVD player is a 'region-free' facility. This lets you play all DVDs, regardless of the region of the world that the disc was originally released in, giving you more freedom and access to lower prices when shopping for movie discs (see page 232).
Recorder options DVD recorders require you to buy blank recordable DVDs to record TV programmes. The alternative is a model that includes a hard disk that you can use in addition to blank discs. It costs a little more – from £300 – but adds flexibility to your data filing and can save you the cost of buying DVD discs, at about £2 each.

DIGITAL TV

There are hundreds of digital TV channels available in dozens of package deals and tariffs. Subscription fees can wipe out savings made on buying your TV, so choose carefully and read the small print.
No strings attached The cheapest way to try out digital TV is Freeview. You buy a set-top box for a one-off cost of £50–£90 and there's no installation or subscription fee to pay. The only additional cost may be a new rooftop aerial, which costs about £80 plus installation at £40–£50 – your retailer should be able to advise you if you need one. Freeview is the best option if you're just interested in getting the BBC's digital channels and 24-hour news. Talk to your TV dealer, visit **www.freeview.co.uk** or phone 08708 80 99 80 ✉ to see if it is available in your area.
Digital TV packages For a wider choice of channels, you need to sign up for a satellite or cable TV package. The equipment is free to rent, but you must subscribe to a channel package that can cost anywhere from £160 to £600+ each year. To get value for money, it's vital that you are as picky as possible about the channels you realistically think you will use (see the table below).
Contract flexibility When you sign up, check the terms and conditions in the subscription contract. See if downgrade options are included in the period you're signing up for. This is important as it lets you switch to a cheaper channel package if you find you're not watching premium channels.

CABLED OPTIONS

Not all areas are able to receive cable TV – it depends whether the cables have been laid. If they have, you are sure to know as you will be receiving offers for subscribing to their packages. If you are in any doubt, check on **www.ntl.com** ✉ or **www.telewest.co.uk** ✉.

CHOOSING THE RIGHT DIGITAL TV PACKAGE

The most heavily promoted **full packages** are those that include movies and sports. These typically cost £40–£50 a month and include many channels that you will rarely, if ever, watch. If you're unsure whether you'll take full advantage of the movies and sports channels, you might be better off signing up for a **basic package**. All digital TV companies make it easy to upgrade later, should you find you want to.

	MONTHLY			PER VIEWING
	BASIC PACKAGE	FULL PACKAGE	EXTRA CHANNEL	PAY-PER-VIEW MOVIE
SATELLITE	£13.50	£40	£5–£6	£3.75
CABLE	£19	£49.50	£5–£10	£3.50

WISE BUYS: STEREO AND HI-FI

Whether you want to eke hi-fi sound quality out of a music centre budget, or snap up the latest MP3 player for a song, spend a little time on research. You can make your hi-fi as easy on your wallet as it is on your ears.

PRICE CHECK

Get an instant survey of prices by going to an online price comparison site (**www.pricerunner.com** ✉ or **www.kelkoo.co.uk** ✉) and using the audio section to browse through hundreds of deals at dozens of dealers. There are across-the-board savings to be had, such as a top-branded mini-system (small-size amps and speakers) that costs £185 on the high street discounted to £155 at an online retailer.

STICK TO BASICS

Stereo manufacturers produce dozens of similar models, each with an added feature or slightly higher power output than the next. They want you to decide on more features than you really need. Don't get taken in; before you go shopping, make a list of your must-have features. Concentrate on these features alone and ignore the added extras, no matter how little each one adds to the cost.

DON'T BE A FASHION VICTIM

Electronics makers frequently change the styling of their stereos to make them look up-to-date without changing the specification. Use this to your advantage by hunting out last season's stereos – look for dealers who specialise in discontinued stock such as **www.richersounds.co.uk** as well as dealers on **www.ebay.co.uk** ✉. You'll still get a full year's guarantee and the same sound quality as current models, but you'll make significant savings. A personal CD player that cost £49.95 last year can be bought for as little as £19.95.

BUYING USED

Hi-fi and stereo equipment is usually very reliable, and it's a good used-buy because most depreciation happens in the first year. Steer clear of cheap stereo systems with damage or wear and tear, and look instead for vintage hi-fi separates. If you're buying from a private seller, test the equipment before buying – especially if there are moving parts, such as a turntable, which would be expensive to repair.

UNWANTED GIFTS

It's a fact of life that not all gifts are wanted. Where gifts can't be returned to the original shop, they are often sold through classified newspaper ads or online auctions (**www.ebay.co.uk** ✉ or **www.loot.com** ✉). Browse an auction site shortly after Christmas and you'll find plenty of nearly new MP3 players, portable CD players and other electronics gifts – at prices that are lower than those in the January sales.

TOO GOOD TO BE TRUE

Beware of auctions held at temporary locations, such as closed-down shops. The prices may be appealing, but the goods are often poor quality and you have little redress if things go wrong.

'Bait and switch' Watch out for shops that advertise amazingly low prices but have sold out of the special deal once you reach the store. It's a common sales technique to get you through the door. Don't buy something else; return home and do some more research.

SYSTEMS VERSUS SEPARATES

For the best sound quality, opt for a system of separates – £200 will buy a CD player, amplifier and speaker separates that will be leagues ahead of a £200 all-in-one stereo system.
Building a system Begin with a decent amplifier, leads and speakers. Make sure the amplifier has enough inputs to link up to as many separates as possible, such as a CD player, TV, DVD player, turntable and tuner. If you want your amp to support surround sound for your TV, look for an amp with 5.1 channel sound.

AN EYE ON THE FUTURE

The fastest-changing area in stereo is the MP3 and portable music player. You can use them with recordings made from CDs or with music downloads (see pages 232–233). To get the best prices, don't just go to electronics dealers but try online computer stores such as **www.pcworld.co.uk** (08702 420444 ✉) or **www.dixons.co.uk** (0845 850 0545 ✉).

WATCH POINTS EXTENDED WARRANTIES

Retailers offer tempting warranties that insure goods beyond the initial guarantee period, but they are rarely good value.
■ **The cost of cover** Extended warranties add 15%–20% to the cost of stereo equipment. Unlike big appliances, such as washing machines, most home stereos are reliable.
■ **Look at the big picture** If you have, say, £2,000 of home electronics, extended warranties might add another £350. The saving you make by not buying the warranties will let you replace almost any item should something go wrong after the first year's guarantee runs out.

UPGRADES CAN SAVE £100s

If your current stereo system works fine, but you want better sound quality, think about upgrading part of it. This is one of the biggest advantages of a separates system, but you can do the same for cheaper stereos, too. For example, buying a pair of hi-fi speakers for £100 will give a cheap stereo a new lease of life for a fraction of the cost of a completely new system.

CASE STUDY

HI-FI THAT PAYS FOR ITSELF

When Jim Miles wanted to upgrade his old stereo system, he opted for a completely different setup. 'I took one look at the glitzy stereos in the shops and saw that I would be paying for stuff I didn't want – like a tape deck and radio tuner. I'd pay over the odds to get better sound than from my old stereo. 'I mentioned this to a friend at work and he told me he bought old hi-fi separates from online auctions. I checked it out and was amazed to see that some hi-fi was becoming collectible, with buyers from all around the world. I took the plunge and built up a system of separates. I've now got great sound quality and I know that each day my vintage hi-fi actually goes up in value. You can't say that about a new stereo.'

THE BEST DEALS: HOME AND MOBILE PHONES

If phone bills are a constant drain on your finances and you feel you are paying over the odds, it's time to find better mobile and landline deals. Whether your friends and family live nearby or on the other side of the world, there are plenty of phone companies ready to do business with you.

SAVE £160+ ON YOUR MOBILE

Most new mobile phones are aimed primarily at teenagers and technophiles. If you don't want to take video clips, photos or check email and surf the Internet, opt for a basic phone. With Pay As You Go contracts, the difference between a basic phone and an all-singing, all-dancing model is around £180. With a monthly contract, you can save £160 on the initial price, depending on the subscription deal you opt for.

MOBILE MONEY-SAVINGS

Buying and using a mobile phone can be a costly business. Many phones are expensive and the call charges can mount up alarmingly. But there are ways to control these costs.

Assess your needs Before buying a new phone, try to draw up a list of your phone habits – it will help you to choose the right network and tariff. What will the volume and length of your calls be on weekdays and at weekends? Will you be calling landlines or other mobiles? Which networks do your friends and family use?

Pore over the tariff charts It is difficult to compare mobile networks by their adverts because they concentrate on free talk time, text messages and other incentives. As a result, they rarely cover the cheapest deals – which can be as little as £5 a month. Visit the websites of each company so you can see the full range of prices, or buy a copy of *What Cellphone* or see their website **www.what-cellphone.com** and study the network comparison charts.

Cashback deals Many contracts offer money back, usually on the condition that you stay with the network for a year. The money will come as a bill credit, not cash, but this is worth while if you are happy with your choice of network.

CASE STUDY

SWITCHING TO A BETTER TARIFF

Tony Bond was perfectly happy with his mobile phone until he realised how much he was spending on it unnecessarily.

'I'm not actually a big fan of mobile phones but they are necessary. When I started out on my own, I got one so that customers can always get in touch with me, then I don't lose out on new business. I started out on a £19 monthly tariff with 60 minutes of talk time a month; I thought two minutes a day was a likely figure. But I've hardly made any calls on it – just on a few rare occasions, so all those minutes have been wasted.

'When the contract was up, I found a £5 a month deal. There's no free talk time, but that suits me fine. I've used the £14 a month saving to upgrade from my dial-up Internet connection to Broadband.'

Switching made easy Mobile phone companies make it easy and rewarding to switch to their service, and once your initial contract term is complete, your current supplier has to oblige. With a little research, you are certain to find lower monthly fees, and/or a better phone for a modest one-off charge. Call your current supplier, too – see if it can offer an incentive for you to stay aboard.

EXPLORE ALL YOUR LANDLINE OPTIONS

Deregulation of the landline phone means that there are now money-saving UK and international services, and you don't have to switch from BT or change your phone number to take advantage (see *Household finance*, page 301).

Independent phone companies You can save up to 50% by signing up with one of these new services, such as Onetel and Planet-talk (see Resources, right). Many work with your BT or cable phone line to provide cut-price calls. Typically, you add a short code in front of the number you're calling which routes your call through the cheaper service.

Long distance for less Many independent phone companies buy up capacity in the global phone networks and offer discounted international calls. You can cut these charges at a stroke – for example, calls to America from 14p/minute at peak times to 2.5p/minute. Similar savings are available for other countries too. Try Tele2 and Alphatelecom (see Resources, right) for this service.

Telephone and cable TV Cable TV companies can provide a telephone connection over the TV cable. If you're thinking about signing up for digital TV too, the combination of digital TV and telephone by cable may work out cheaper than keeping a BT line and subscribing to satellite TV.

Can you switch? Beware of complications if you decide to switch away completely from your BT landline. You can keep your current phone number but you may not be able to transfer other services, such as ADSL Broadband.

TOP TIPS CUTTING CALL COSTS

The charge for each call you make may only be a few pence, but when totted up it can make for a nasty surprise on your monthly or quarterly bill. The good news is that you don't have to look hard to find cheap – or even free – options.

■ **Free weekend calls** If you like to chat for hours, wait until the weekend. Some services offer free weekend calls in addition to cut-price weekday calls.

■ **Free calls to friends** You can get free calls to family and friends by getting together and signing up for a service that encourages calling circles (**www.talktalk.co.uk** ✉).

■ **Directory enquiries** If you often use directory enquiries, find out which is the most economical provider: the cheapest are under half the cost of the most expensive (see *Household finance*, page 303). Visit **www.118tracker.com** ✉ for a price comparison. Many of the 118-based companies offer to connect you automatically to the number you have asked for. But beware: you will be charged at a much more expensive rate than if you dial the number yourself – it could be more than twice as expensive as a normally dialled number, so never take this option.

RESOURCES

PHONE COMPANY ROUNDUP ✉

Phone services, tariffs and call charges change constantly, so check with the phone companies from time to time.

www.118tracker.com
www.alphatelecom.com
www.bt.com
www.ntl.co.uk
www.o2.co.uk
www.onetel.co.uk
www.orange.co.uk
www.planet-talk.co.uk
www.talktalk.co.uk
www.tele2.co.uk
www.telewest.co.uk
www.three.co.uk
www.tiscali.co.uk/services/smarttalk/
www.t-mobile.co.uk
www.virginmobile.com
www.vodafone.co.uk

CHECK OUT CAMERAS AND CAMCORDERS

With the arrival of the digital age, there's an opportunity to save money in still and video photography. Don't let the initial cost of switching over to digital deter you – you will be rewarded with lower running costs and better results.

GETTING THE BEST PRICE

If you visit a high-street electronics shop, you'll see only a fraction of the full range of cameras and camcorders that are available. You'll get a wider choice and lower prices online. For instance, there are savings of £90 to be had on a typical mid-range digital camera over high-street prices of £229.

Instant research Use a price comparison website such as **www.kelkoo.co.uk** or **www.pricerunner.com** to get the full picture on prices for any camcorder or digital camera. A basic camcorder ranges from £250 to £350, for example.

Good used deals You can pay just £60 for a name-brand camera with a good specification by buying from an online auction. Used digital cameras can be bought cheaply and make an excellent second camera for the children to use.

Bad used deals Camcorders are much more risky to buy used as their moving parts can go wrong and are expensive to fix. If there's no remaining warranty, a cheap camcorder could end up being a waste of money.

ANALOGUE CHEAPIES VS DEARER DIGITALS

Think twice before buying an analogue (film-based) camera or camcorder (VHS-C, 8mm or Hi-8). Digital equivalents cost a little more to buy, but will cost less in the long run.

Film costs A digital camera saves on both film and processing costs. If you take many photos, the long-term saving will more than cover the cost of a more advanced digital camera. And you can discard the pictures you don't want before printing them either at home or at a processing centre, where they'll cost from 10p–20p a print, or at a high-street photo centre, where you connect your camera and select the images you want. But the cost varies at these centres from 29p to 49p depending on the number of prints.

ASK YOURSELF

DO I NEED TO GO DIGITAL?

■ If you are happy with your analogue compact but would like more control over your prints, consider buying a flatbed scanner instead of replacing your camera. Flatbed scanners can be bought for under £50 from computer stores or online and deliver images scanned from a 35mm print as good as those produced by a digital camera.

Accessorising on a budget

For digital camcorders, buy a handful of accessories to maximise the value you get from your purchase.

SMART MOVES

Extra tapes It makes sense to buy tapes in bulk. Not only is it cost-effective, but running out of tape at a special family event can be a potential disaster. Tapes bought singly cost around £5, but bought in multi-packs they can cost as little as £3.

Extra battery power Running out of power in the middle of filming is also frustrating. Go online to find an extra rechargeable battery pack (see Resources, right). A regular pack will be about £20, but it is better to opt for the high-capacity battery (around £40) if you are expecting to do longer filming sessions.

Get a tripod A tripod is a must-have for camcorders, and a budget model will only cost around £15 from a high-street shop.

GO DIGITAL AND SAVE ON FILM COSTS

One of the benefits of digital cameras is that you don't have to worry about the cost of developing film, which encourages you to make greater use of your camera. Once you have transferred the images to your PC you can select which images to print either at home or at a processing centre. This chart shows how your savings on film costs can mount up. On this basis, your digital camera could pay for itself in two years.

AVERAGE USAGE	ANNUAL PHOTOS	COST OF FILMS	COST OF DEVELOPING AND PRINTING	TOTAL ANNUAL COST FOR FILM DEVELOPING
Medium	200	£36	£32	£68
High	400	£72	£64	£136

Analogue tape costs As more digital tapes are sold, fewer analogue tapes will be made and their cost is likely to go up. Eventually they will become uneconomical to produce.

Difficult editing If you want to transfer photos or videos on to a PC for editing, it's more costly and difficult with analogue cameras and camcorders. Many DV (Digital Video) camcorders connect directly to a computer; analogue camcorders require a converter which costs £40–£75.

FOCUS ON FEATURES THAT MATTER

Don't be lured by sheer number of modes and menu options into buying an expensive model. Picture quality and convenience (light weight, long battery life) are what matter.

The right type of zoom Both camcorders and cameras tend to have two types of zoom: optical and digital. The optical figure is the one that contributes most to good picture quality. Don't base your decision on the digital zoom figure.

Exposure controls Check for options that automatically help you to compensate for tricky lighting conditions, such as shooting people against a bright sky or snowy backdrop.

Easy computer connection A DV Out or USB socket makes it easy to connect a digital camcorder or camera to a PC, with little or no extra outlay.

Ignore the gimmicks Don't pay extra for gimmicky features such as built-in special effects on a camcorder or movie modes on a digital camera.

CAMCORDER WARRANTY QUESTIONS

Digital cameras are very reliable and you're unlikely to need an extended warranty. But both analogue and digital camcorders have complicated mechanisms and many moving parts, and repairs out of warranty can be expensive.

Insurance policy The most likely risk to a camcorder is accidental damage while you're out and about. Your home contents insurance may already cover this at no extra cost – check your policy before buying extra cover.

Breakdown cover For other causes of failure, you can take out an extended warranty at the time of purchase. This costs around £80 for an extra two years after the initial 12-month warranty runs out.

 **RESOURCES**

COMPUTERS AND PRINTERS

Computers and printers are cheaper than ever before, and some decent bargains are on offer. You can also save on consumables and get a good deal on your Internet connection.

WHAT TO BUY

All the manufacturers use virtually the same internal components in their PCs. This means there is little difference in reliability or cost of parts between companies.

Buying mail order If you're buying a low-cost PC, you can save £50–£100 by buying from a mail-order computer maker instead of a branded model. If you're spending more – say for the fastest PC with components chosen for games performance – the saving could run to £200 on a £1,000 PC. Check out computer magazines such as *Computer Shopper* ✉ and *Computer Buyer* ✉ for current bargains.

Check the spec When shopping around, look closely at the specification (the components used in the PC). A single difference could account for a £100–£200 price difference.

Look out for returns You can make big savings on computers that have been returned to the manufacturer. They may not have been used, or even opened – for example, stock returned by bankrupt firms. Check manufacturers' websites (Dell, IBM, Compaq ✉, for example) for details.

Avoid used computers Older PCs will be slower and are usually poor value. Also, if the files on a PC's hard disk have been corrupted, it may never work properly.

PLAY THE WAITING GAME

Each new generation of PC comes with a slightly faster processing chip than the last, and prices are high when the new chips are first launched. But wait a few months and prices fall. For example, a 3GHz notebook that sold for £1,400 when first introduced cost just £1,000 after a year.

CHOOSE THE RIGHT INTERNET ACCESS

Whatever Internet access you have been using, it's worth checking to see if it's still the best choice. Broadband prices have dropped and some deals now cost as little as the cheaper flat-fee dial-up connections. If you've been using Broadband for more than a year, take advantage of the price drops and switch to a cheaper supplier.

TYPE	COST (TYPICAL)	SPEED (RELATIVE)	CONTRACT
Pay as you go	1p/minute	very slow	No contract required
Flat-fee dial-up	£8–£16/month	very slow	Monthly subscription only
150K Broadband	£16–£18/month	slow	12-month contract normally required
256K Broadband	£18–£20/month	moderate	12-month contract normally required
512K Broadband	£20–£28/month	fast	12-month contract normally required
1Mb Broadband	£30–£35/month	very fast	12-month contract normally required

Cut the cost of computer consumables

Today's computers use blank CDs, ink, toner and paper. The costs can mount up over a year, so shop around for the best deals.

SMART MOVES

Compatible ink and toner You don't have to stick to the manufacturer's own brand of ink or toner cartridge. If you have a popular model, check out the prices for compatible alternatives – you will find you can easily cut the cost by up to 40%.

Ink refills Try an ink refill kit the next time your cartridge runs out. Although fiddly to do, by refilling the ink reservoirs you can cut the cost to £5 or less.

Paper supplies Use copier grade paper for your draft print outs and save the inkjet and photo paper for your final prints only. Go direct to an office supplies company and buy in bulk to maximise the saving: buying five 50-sheet packs of premium photo paper brings the typical high-street price down from 46p to just 32p a sheet.

Blank CDs and DVDs (CD-Rs) If you don't use paper or blank discs quickly enough to make a bulk buy worth while for yourself, get together with family and friends to share the saving. You'll also share the delivery cost, helping everyone out.

Net prices A little surfing on the Internet will save you money on all manner of computer consumables. Try the following general stationery sites:
www.staples.co.uk ✉
www.theinkfactory.co.uk ✉
www.viking-direct.co.uk ✉

UNNECESSARY ADD-ONS

Bundle deals, which generally consist of a computer, printer, extra add-ons and stacks of software, are popular in computer shops. They look tempting at first, but often hide poor value.

Unwanted software The bundled software may be advertised as 'worth £500' but it is often outdated or unpopular. If the software isn't exactly what you're looking for, don't let it influence your decision.

Imperfect add-ons The extra hardware included can be a poor choice. For example, the printer may be slow or expensive to run due to high ink cartridge prices.

Choose your own bundle Any computer dealer can put together exactly the bundle of hardware and software you want. Give the same specification to two or three dealers and choose the one that gives you the best price.

THE PORTABLE PREMIUM

Notebook computers (or laptops) are ideal if you need to use your computer away from your desk or if you are short of space. But, comparing like for like, you'll save £300–£500 by buying a bulkier desktop computer.

STAY UP-TO-DATE

If you're ordering any computer hardware from a catalogue, never quote the price listed. Instead ask for the current price. Prices often change week by week, so tell dealers what you want and let them quote you their best price.

BEWARE WARRANTIES

Don't waste money on an extended warranty. While it may be worth while for a notebook, especially if you use it for work, a desktop PC is relatively cheap and easy to repair.

keep it simple

DIY CAN SAVE YOU £30–£50
PCs are very easy to upgrade – you can swap internal components to make your PC faster or to add more features. By doing it yourself, you'll save the £30–£50 labour fee that many computer dealers charge. Go to the Internet for help: a search on 'upgrade PC graphics card', for example, will turn up lots of advice and even step-by-step guides.

CUT COSTS ON CDS, DVDS AND SOFTWARE

keep it simple

SHOPPING INTERNATIONALLY

■ If you buy CDs or DVDs from outside the EU, it's tempting to put in a bigger order to offset shipping costs. But beware of going over the £18 Customs limit, or you will have to pay duty and VAT (approximately 22%) on top. There may also be a handling fee.

When you've saved a packet by buying your electronic gadgets at the best price, don't blow your savings by buying full-price CDs and computer software. Make your money go further by using your computer to shop online; half an hour's effective surfing will save money and shoe leather.

BUYING USED DISCS
As long as it plays perfectly, a used CD or DVD is a sensible buy; over time the savings can be enormous. In a typical music collection of 100 CDs, an average saving of £4 for each CD will buy a new TV and DVD player.

Shop locally Local and independent music shops may have a pre-owned section to browse.

Look online Online auctions have a far wider selection, with typical CD prices of around £5.

Watch out Before buying at a car-boot sale or temporary fair, check that the disc is legitimate, and not a pirated copy.

BUY SONGS INSTEAD OF CDS
If you don't like all the songs on an album, see if the songs you want are available from an online music service, such as **www.apple.com/itunes** rather than buying a CD. You can download individual songs from thousands of albums for 79p each, build up a music collection on your computer then transfer the songs to an MP3 player or create your own CDs. Although it's difficult to quantify the savings you'll make if you compare the cost of the downloaded tracks with the same number of tracks on purchased CDs, at least you'll have the satisfaction of knowing that you've only paid for those tracks you enjoy listening to.

REPLACING OLD WITH NEW
Are you sitting on a goldmine? If you have a collection of music or film in old formats – vinyl and VHS, respectively – they may be worth selling. To find out if any of your old records are valuable, use the Search feature on an auction site such as **www.ebay.co.uk** ✉ to see how much the same records fetch. Online auctions are perfect for getting the best price for items that are otherwise hard to sell and you can reinvest your newly earned cash in more CDs and DVDs.

REGIONAL VARIATIONS
Movie studios release DVDs with regional codes to restrict the sale of discs to a particular area – America or Europe, for example. If your DVD player is region-free, see page 223, you can watch discs bought anywhere in the world. This allows you to shop internationally, and by visiting American sites and buying from the American ebay website (**www.ebay.com** ✉), you can get DVDs cheaper than in Britain. Expect to pay around one-third less, but remember to factor in other costs (see Keep it simple, left).

🦉 RESOURCES

MUSIC DOWNLOAD SITES
Steer clear of websites that provide pirated music and buy music from legitimate websites such as:
www.apple.com/itunes
www.od2.com
www.napster.co.uk

TOP TIPS AUCTION BUYING

Buying online at an auction can be fun, but don't let the excitement get in the way of your better judgment.

■ **Check the seller's profile** To gauge the seller's reliability, check his feedback score. This shows the number of people who have left positive feedback about the way the seller has done business with them. You can read the feedback comments too.

■ **Bid late** By bidding as late as possible, you avoid revealing your interest to other bidders and help to keep the price down.

■ **Check originality** If the auction description doesn't make it clear that you're buying an original CD or DVD, ask the seller directly in an email sent via eBay. Don't pay £5 for a pirated disc worth 50p.

CD AND DVD CLUBS

Be wary of joining any CD or DVD club that offers a great discount to join but then requires you to buy a certain number of regular price discs during your membership. The lack of any discount on these discs always outweighs the initial saving you made when you signed up.

ACADEMIC DISCOUNTS ON SOFTWARE

Is there a student or teacher in the household? If so, you may be entitled to an academic discount. The savings can be considerable. The most popular office software suite costs around £300 to buy normally, but can be legally purchased for around £100 for students and teachers.

TRY BEFORE YOU BUY

Pay less for your computer software by buying only what you really need. There are two ways to try it before buying.

Shareware Because it has few marketing and packaging overheads, shareware (software that you can download on a trial basis) tends to be £10–£25 cheaper than the equivalent shop-bought software. Check user reviews and ratings to find out which programs are worth downloading; **www.downloads.com** ✉ and **www.shareware.com** ✉ are just two sites with thousands of reviews available.

Official demos Many software companies create downloadable demos and trial versions of their packaged software. These demos can be large and slow to download, but it's a great way to get more value from Broadband if you are connected.

FALLING GAMES PRICES

When a computer game is new, almost all shops sell it at very close to the manufacturer's list price – typically £30. Within a few months, discounts of £5–£10 become common, and within a year it may fall to half-price. After that, the most popular games are often repackaged into a 'classic game' budget line-up with a selling price of £8 or so.

RESOURCES

SUPERSTORE SAVINGS
By shopping for CDs and DVDs online, you'll often save £3 or more on high-street prices. Online shops also have the advantage of a searchable catalogue that makes it easy to find the most obscure discs. Good sites include:
www.101cd.com
www.amazon.co.uk
www.cd-wow.com
www.mvc.co.uk
www.loaded247.com
www.play.com
www.sendit.com

GET THE MOST FROM GAMES CONSOLES

A video games console can be expensive to buy and cost even more if you are constantly paying out for new games. By waiting for inevitable and substantial price cuts and finding alternative means of buying games, you can have fun at a fraction of the cost without falling prey to the marketing ploys of the manufacturers.

BE WARY OF THE LATEST CONSOLES

The best way to save money on video games consoles is never to buy the latest console when it's first launched. Manufacturers are careful to manage supply and demand to keep prices right up at list price. Consoles get to their natural prices – about 25% lower – after six months or so. After a year or two, they can fall to half their original price.

AVOID GETTING INTO FORMAT WARS

When a brand new type of games console is launched, there is always the possibility that it may not make the grade. If the new format proves unpopular, software companies stop making games for it. It's best to hold tight and deduce the longevity of the console before splashing out. Popular consoles such as Playstation 2 and Xbox will have a never-ending stream of new games and are a far better investment.

WHO NEEDS A DVD PLAYER?

Many new consoles work as DVD players, able to play back DVD movie discs as well as games. You could save £40 or more on the cost of buying a separate DVD player.

TOP TIPS BUYING GAMES

The cost of new video games is also high, and when they are just launched, you often have to pay close to the full list price – thanks to heavy promotion and pre-launch hype.

■ **Wait it out** If you can bear not to have the newest, must-have game you'll benefit from waiting a few months to decide on whether to purchase or not. Read the user reviews on the Internet (see Resources, left) or in your favourite games magazines to see which games have failed to live up to the hype, and save the expense of buying a dud.

■ **Buying used** CDs and DVDs are immune from viruses so are worth tracking down. Small local shops are best for pre-owned games – expect to pay half price or less. You can also look more widely by searching Amazon's used section (**www.amazon.co.uk**) and online auctions.

■ **Rent-a-game** Instead of buying games, join a video game rental service. You pay a monthly subscription (£10–£15) to rent the games by post. When you have mastered – or got bored with – the game you have rented, you post it back and choose another game to rent. This gives you the benefit of playing a wide selection of games and, if you're a games fanatic and rent two games a month, you'll pay as little as 25% of the cost of buying them when they're first released.

VALUE-FOR-MONEY HOME SECURITY

Installing an effective alarm system will not only give you peace of mind, it can also be the key to paying a smaller insurance premium. But you'll need to do your homework to ensure you make the right choice.

CHECK WITH YOUR INSURANCE COMPANY

To help decide which type of alarm or home security system to install, first call your insurer to find out how much of a reduction in premium you will get for the various types of system you're considering. You may also find they insist on the alarm being fitted by an approved National Security Inspectorate (NSI) installer.

CHOOSING THE RIGHT TYPE OF ALARM

A professionally installed alarm can cost £400–£1,000, depending on the size of your home.

Siren call The most basic alarm is a bells-only system: if the sensors detect an intruder the alarm sounds, but nothing else happens. You're relying on a neighbour or passer-by to report the alarm bell ringing, so it's a poor investment for rural or isolated homes, and even in a city it may be ignored.

Monitored response The alternative is the same setup of sensors and alarm box, but with an added monitoring system. The alarm is connected to a 24-hour call centre which calls your home – to catch any false alarms – before contacting the police. Monitoring can add an extra £5–£20 per month, but is essential for isolated homes.

FALSE ECONOMY

If you have good DIY skills, you may be tempted to buy an alarm kit from a DIY superstore and install it yourself. Although you can make substantial savings (a bells-only system costs £40–£250, depending on the number of sensors and the size of your home), you might be wasting your money. Before buying and installing a DIY kit, check with your local Crime Prevention Officer that the police will respond to the system – they have strict guidelines about which systems they will respond to. To check, log on to **www.met.police.uk/crimeprevention/alarms.htm** or phone 020 7230 1212 ✉.

MULTIPLE DISCOUNT

Save money on having a police-approved system installed by getting together with neighbours in your street and negotiating a discount with an NSI installer.

Home repairs and improvements

Doing repairs and maintenance yourself, tackling problems before they get expensive and making sensible improvements helps you to pay less to preserve the value of your home.

PAYING LESS IN AN EMERGENCY

Calling out a plumber or other tradesman in the middle of the night because of an emergency is extremely expensive. But there are ways of keeping costs down.

TOP TIPS PAY LESS TO PROFESSIONALS

Increase your chances of finding a reputable tradesman who will do a good job for a fair fee by adopting these strategies.

■ **Don't use the phone book** Unless you have a dire emergency, such as serious flooding or sparking electrics, never use the emergency plumbers or electricians in the phone book. They charge a prohibitive call-out fee – as much as £100 – plus high hourly rates thereafter.

■ **Call someone you know** Compile a list of local tradesmen whom you have used before and can trust, and keep it to hand so you can find it quickly in case of an emergency. Because you already have a working relationship, they are more likely to come quickly, and less likely to charge a high call-out fee.

■ **Check existing home insurance** Many home insurance policies include a 24-hour helpline with lists of reputable companies who will send someone in an emergency. Check to see if your policy includes this service.

EMERGENCY DIY

Avoid an emergency call-out fee by making your own repair, temporary or permanent. Plumbing problems are usually the ones that can't wait.

Fixing a leaking pipe If you can spot the leak and it is from a compression fitting – a heavy brass component – tighten the nuts with a spanner. A leak from a soldered fitting – a smaller copper joint – can be fixed using J&B Cold Weld or a similar two-part adhesive, with the pipes drained before you begin. If you are in any doubt about your repair, get it checked by a plumber later.

Drain rods for a blocked drain You can hire drain rods for £12 or buy a set for under £50. Find the manhole and remove the cover. If it's full of water, fit the corkscrew end onto the drain rods and push them into the gulley at the bottom, away from the house. Work the rods backwards and forwards, pulling them out from time to time so you can remove anything the corkscrew has picked up. If the manhole is empty, use the rods in the opposite direction.

Unblocking a sink With a sink plunger, force water down the waste pipe. If that doesn't work, look under the sink for a bowl or U-shaped trap , place a bucket beneath it, then unscrew and flush with water from the taps. Remove residue with an old toothbrush.

Unblocking a toilet Put on a latex glove and feel around the other side of the U-bend. You should be able to remove anything you find there. If you can't find anything, push the head of an old-fashioned cotton mop into the toilet bowl base and work up and down as you would a sink plunger.

ASK YOURSELF

IS EMERGENCY REPAIR INSURANCE WORTH IT?

Emergency repair insurance is generally worth the premium, typically £50 a year for emergency cover only and a lot less than a call-out charge. In an emergency, the insurance company will quickly send a tradesman to sort it out. Areas covered by policies include problems with central heating, gas, electricity and plumbing. Make sure you know what is covered, and what the insurance company defines as an emergency, so there are no unpleasant surprises.

MAKING A BROKEN WINDOW SAFE

If the glass is still in place or the hole is small, lay strips of duct tape along the cracks to hold it together. If a lot of glass has gone, you'll have to board up the window. Work from the outside if possible, and lay down newspaper to catch the splinters. Wearing gloves and safety glasses, pull out the loose glass, then remove the putty with a hammer and chisel to free the rest of the glass. Cut a piece of hardboard large enough to overlap the putty and secure with tacks or light nails. Seal the edges with duct tape.

CUT THE COST OF EXTERNAL REPAIRS

Water can be highly destructive to flat roofs, brickwork and even interior decoration if you do not maintain the exterior of your house. By catching small problems before they escalate into major emergencies, you'll avoid heavy bills.

KEEP A LID ON ROOF REPAIRS

Felt for a flat roof Repair flat roofs with torching-grade roofing felt, at £40 a roll. You'll need a blowtorch (costing about £50) and a gas bottle, but the repair will last indefinitely. Apply the felt when the roof is dry. Cut a patch 15cm (6in) larger all around than the affected area. Heat the shiny side of the felt until the bitumen melts, then position it. Tread down from the centre outwards to avoid bubbles.

Paint over a leak For an emergency repair to a flat roof that is leaking, paint the leaking areas with a bituminous roofing treatment such as Acryflex or Flexacryl from a DIY supplier (£40 for 5 litres). You can do this while the roof is wet, or even when it's raining. If the roof has deteriorated all over, buy a 50-litre tin and paint the whole roof. The same products also work on flashings.

Save on replacement tiles Keep an eye on builders' yards, skips and demolition sites, looking for cut-price or free replacement tiles or slates that match the colour of your roof. Then, when you need to make a roof repair, you won't be forced into an expensive rush purchase.

---

keep it simple

SAFETY FIRST
When working above ground level, make safety your top priority. Don't be tempted to save money by taking a chance with an old ladder. Hire or buy the platform or ladder that you need to do the job safely. Ladders can be hired from HSS Hire Shops **www.hss.com** 0845 728 28 28 ✉ at a cost of £28–£96 a week. If you have any doubts at all about working from a ladder or platform, call in a professional.

WHAT YOU SAVE BY DOING IT YOURSELF

CLEANING MASONRY WALLS		
HIRED POWERWASH	£35	
HIRED WORKMAN		£130 plus

REPAINTING A FLAT ROOF WITH WATERPROOFING SOLUTION		
REPAINTING YOURSELF	£80	
HIRED WORKMAN		£200 plus

REPOINTING BRICKWORK		
REPOINTING YOURSELF	£10	
HIRED WORKMAN		£25 per m²

APPLYING SEALANT TO MAKE GUTTERS AND PIPES WATERPROOF		
APPLYING YOURSELF	£5	
HIRED WORKMAN		£120

PROTECTING GUTTERING WITH CHICKEN WIRE		
APPLYING YOURSELF	£1	
HIRED WORKMAN		£120

Are you up-to-date with routine checks?

Regular checks cost nothing but can prevent expensive problems occurring.

SPRING

■ Remember to have the chimney swept. Call in a chimney sweep to clear blockages (for around £50) before they cause costly trouble.

■ Check masonry for cracks and fix any that appear by replacing damaged bricks.

■ Check pipes are straight, leak-free and unblocked. Straighten downpipes, clear leaves and flush with water.

■ Check gutters for cracks. Fix with roofing mastic – around £12 for 2.5 litres.

SUMMER

■ Ensure the drive is free of holes. Fill any that appear. A 25kg bag of pre-packed tarmac costs around £10.

■ Check flat roofs for wear. Paint Acryflex (about £15 for 5 litres) on cracks or tears.

■ Check window sills and fences for rot. Treat if necessary (see page 240).

AUTUMN

■ Check pipes and roofs for leaves, blockages and leaks. Remove leaves, flush out pipes and fix leaks.

■ Check insulation on pipes, especially in well-insulated roof spaces, which get cold.

WINTER

■ Check the lower chimney for soot. Clear out if needed.

■ If you go away in winter, remember to leave the heat on low to avoid burst pipes.

MAINTAIN SOUND GUTTERS

Within six months, the effects of rainwater overflowing from a blocked gutter can damage a wall, inside and out.

Install a leaf guard Keep leaves out of gutters by installing a leaf guard costing a few pounds from a DIY store, or make a leaf guard for pennies by bending a piece of chicken wire over the top of the gutter.

Fix cracks and holes Use waterproof exterior sealant to fill small cracks in gutters; fill bigger holes cheaply with self-adhesive flashing. Epoxy-based car body repair paste effectively fills small cracks in metal gutters and downpipes.

Plastic gutters cost less When replacing gutters, choose plastic ones that need no painting and are easier to maintain than metal ones. Use plenty of clips to prevent the gutter bending when full of rain. You may be able to buy a special connector to join the plastic to a metal gutter that is not being replaced. Seal the joint with roofing mastic.

CURING DAMP WALLS

A permanently damp wall costs money by reducing the effectiveness of your domestic heating, and causes condensation that eventually ruins the plasterwork.

Weatherproof walls Bricks in old walls often absorb water, even if the pointing is sound. Having checked that the problem isn't a defective damp course – call in an expert if you're unsure – paint the exterior with two coats of silicon waterproofer (about £6 a litre). Buy a 5-litre 'no name' tin from a builders' merchant as it's half the price of branded products, but make sure it's a type that allows condensation to escape. Fill any defects in the wall by applying a sand and cement exterior filler, dyed to match the bricks.

Prevent condensation Nine-tenths of interior damp is due to condensation. Improve the ventilation in affected rooms before you do anything else – this may be enough by itself. Turning up thermostatic radiator valves by 5°–10° may help too. If these measures don't work, buy a dehumidifier. These cost £150–£250 but are effective and much cheaper than wall insulation, which can cost thousands of pounds.

TROUBLE-FREE PATHS AND DRIVES

Paths and drives invariably get covered in weeds and can be damaged by harsh weather. Give them a low-cost facelift.

■ **Save on weedkiller** Use thin bleach (50p a litre) instead of weed and moss-killers (about £5 a litre) for paving. On a sunny day, brush the weeds with the bleach – it will kill shallow-rooted moss and other weeds but won't harm the plants with deeper roots.

■ **Refurbish paving** Cover cracked concrete drives and paths with gravel. Don't pay to remove the concrete – it will help keep the gravel in place and clear of soil.

■ Build a low retaining wall with a row of bricks to retain the gravel. Cut costs by 60% by buying gravel by the metre from a builders' yard instead of in bags.

REPAIRS AND REPLACEMENTS FOR WOODWORK

Wood is the traditional and best material for windows, doors and floors. It is a renewable resource, easily repaired and lasts for a long time if correctly maintained.

WELL-MAINTAINED WINDOWS AND DOORS

Cut costs on maintaining windows and doors by tackling problems yourself in good time.

Use car body filler A cheap way of repairing window sills that have rotted in a few areas is to chisel the rotten wood out, paint the sound bare wood with top-quality wood preservative to prevent more rot, then fill with car body filler. This is less expensive than wood filler – especially if you buy a large tin from a car parts wholesaler – and just as effective. Sand until smooth and paint as normal.

Save 50% plus on sash window repairs Rattling or draughty sash windows can often be repaired using standard beading and parting beads – around £1 a metre at any good timber yard. If you don't have the skill yourself, a good joiner should be able to overhaul one sash window a day – less if you are lucky, longer if the whole sill has to be replaced. Allow £150 a day for time and £30 a window for materials, as opposed to £300 plus for a made-to-measure sash window, including the cost to fit it.

 **RESOURCES**

USEFUL WEBSITES

■ Get DIY advice on maintaining and repairing woodwork on **www. eHow.com** ✉ and **www. experthomeadvice.com** ✉.
■ For suppliers of windows and doors, check out **www.homesources.co.uk** ✉.

WINDOWS

■ For reputable glaziers contact the Glass and Glazing Federation at **www.ggf.org.uk** 0870 042 4255 ✉.
■ DIY stores such as Wickes **www.wickes.co.uk** 0870 6089001 ✉ have low-price PVC-U windows, starting from £70.

■ Andersen Windows **www.blackmillwork.co.uk** 01283 511122 ✉ offers a particularly wide range of windows, plus doors.
■ Protech **www.thebb group.co.uk** 01325 310520 ✉ sells windows, conservatories and specialist glazing online.
■ The Original Box Sash Window Company **www.boxsash.com** 0800 783 4053 ✉ makes casement windows, as well as traditional sash windows.

DOORS

■ DirectDoors.com **www.directdoors.com** 0131 669 7310 ✉ sells exterior and interior doors.

■ Distinctive Doors **www.distinctivedoors.co.uk** 0114 232 3379 ✉ is a specialist supplier of domestic doors.
■ Doors Select **www.doorsselect.co.uk** 01625 262400 ✉ stocks interior doors and timber mouldings.
■ Kershaws Door Warehouse **www.door-warehouse.co.uk** 0845 126 0270 ✉ sells exterior and interior doors, including manufacturers' seconds.

DOOR FURNITURE

■ Handles Direct **www.handlesdirect.co.uk** 01422 358111 ✉ sells door fittings and handles for kitchen cabinets.

Replace putty the proper way If putty is loose or missing, scrape the old putty out with a chisel, down to the bare wood. Knead fresh putty until workable, then hold it in your palm while you press it in place with your thumb. Smooth the surface and shape it to match the other windows with a scraper or knife dipped in water so it doesn't stick to the putty. When it has hardened paint the new putty in the same way as wood.

Stop the rot If the bottom of a door or the sill has started to deteriorate, remove paint from the affected area and treat with two coats of wood-hardening resin, then fit a weather bar (£5 from a timber yard). This will divert rain from the door bottom. Paint with two coats of exterior paint.

Strengthen doors Close up loose joints in the corners of a panel door by knocking them together with a mallet, then running two or three one-inch wood screws through the side rails, about 3cm (1½in) in from the edge. Countersink the heads so that they disappear, fill and then coat with paint.

LOW-COST TIPS FOR TIMBER MOULDINGS

You can avoid hiring a carpenter to carry out repairs to internal woodwork by investing in the right equipment. And with a little knowledge, you can keep repairs to a minimum.

Pay less for the perfect fit The main problem when fitting new architraves around doors and windows is cutting the mitres. But if you invest in a chop or mitre saw (about £20 for a manual version or around £50 for a cheap electric one), there will be no need to call in a professional and your corners will be completely accurate and neat.

Rule out replacements When fitting new internal woodwork, always paint the back with wood primer as well as the front. This prevents the wood from splitting as it dries out, so you won't have to replace it again.

EXTERIOR TIMBER REPAIRS

■ Strengthen elderly wooden fences with ready-made metal plates shaped so you can nail horizontal arris rails back onto fence posts. Loose boards and gravel boards – hardwood timber planks fixed to the bottom of panels to stop damp causing the panel to rot – can be nailed back in place with galvanised clout nails, and rotten boards replaced with new from a timber yard. Two coats of coloured exterior wood preservative will protect a fence for 5 years.

■ Rotten fence posts can be saved by sinking a concrete stub into the soil, then bolting the post to the concrete stub. Or, if enough of the post remains, push it into a spiked metal socket.

TIMBER TROUBLES – PREVENTION vs CURE

PROBLEM	CURE	PREVENTION
Wet rot	Woodwork with extensive wet rot must be replaced – and costs can quickly escalate over the £1,000 mark.	Cure wet rot early yourself with rot killer, wood filler and a coat of paint for under £20 (see opposite).
Specialist woodworm treatment	If woodworm has spread, it can cost from £1,000 to eradicate it from a small house. Specialists have to drill holes in floorboards, joists and stairs to spray in chemical treatments.	If you do it yourself, treatment could cost under £50. Ask a timber preservation company for a free report on the problem areas – often included with a no obligation quote – then buy your own fluids.
Dry rot	Extensive dry rot can cost thousands of pounds to eradicate from a small house.	Maintain a waterproof roof, sound brickwork and good underfloor ventilation.

GOOD-VALUE FLOORS AND FLOOR COVERINGS

Avoid expensive mistakes by asking yourself a few questions before you buy. Will the flooring receive a lot of wear and tear? Is it important that it's waterproof? Does the floor covering need to muffle sound?

STUNNING SOLID WOOD FLOORS

Save on carpets by exposing wooden floors. With only a little money and effort, your boards can look beautiful.

Sand it yourself Instead of paying hundreds of pounds to have floorboards stripped professionally, hire a heavy-duty sander for around £70 a weekend or £100 a week (plus glasspaper at around £2 a sheet).

Save on stripping If you have fairly new floorboards, you may be able to get away with scrubbing them with hot water and detergent before applying a suitable finish.

Do the preparation If you do decide to hire a professional, save money by doing some preparation yourself. Replace any damaged floorboards with boards taken from an area that will be covered by a rug. Then carefully remove any protruding nails that may damage the sander.

CARPET LORE

With carpeting, you generally get what you pay for and high quality will last longer, so buy the best you can afford. Because floors set the tone for your décor, carpeting is an area in which long-term savings should outweigh up-front costs. And with carpet warehouses and department stores competing for business, it is worth visiting several outlets to find high-quality carpeting for a reasonable price.

Fitting a carpet Paying to get your carpet fitted professionally is worth it; it will almost certainly look better than if you do it yourself, unless you are laying foam-back carpet. When looking for the best deal, price the cost of the carpet and fitting together – a more expensive carpet coupled with an in-house fitting service may cost less than buying a cheaper carpet and sourcing the fitting from elsewhere.

Pros and cons of wool and synthetic Synthetic carpet costs less and should wear well, but wool keeps its looks longer. Consider opting for a wool-synthetic mix that looks good but is less expensive than all-wool.

Pay less for a bedroom carpet A carpet in a bedroom will be less heavily used than one in a living room or hall so you can go for a cheaper option.

COMPARE THE COST OF FLOORING

SOLID WOOD FLOOR	£50
WOOL TWIST PILE CARPET	£20–£40
UNTREATED SLATE	£25
WOOD-EFFECT LAMINATE	£20
SHEET VINYL	£15
VINYL TILES	£10
FOAM-BACK CARPET	£10

These are typical 2004 prices per m² for different types of flooring – though costs for each vary.

Never skimp on underlay Buying poor-quality underlay is a false economy. A good-quality underlay will extend the life of your carpet by 40% or more and can be reused when the time comes to replace the new carpet on top.

Cut down on waste Make sure your carpet retailer doesn't supply you with a large roll of carpet that may be more than you need once all the awkward corners have been trimmed off. A skilled carpet fitter should use off-cuts to fill in awkward gaps, so you can save by having a carpet properly measured and fitted, especially for areas such as stairs.

Look out for hidden costs Major carpet retailers sell carpet at a reasonable price but inflate the cost of grips and underlay. Ask whether underlay and grips are included, or whether your existing ones can be reused. Check whether you can buy them more cheaply from a DIY store.

WIPE-CLEAN FLOORING

Look out for sales at DIY and high-street stores. You can lay most types of laminate and vinyl flooring yourself.

Pay less for a wood floor Wood-effect laminate is the low-cost alternative to laying a solid wood floor. If the surface beneath is flat and in good condition, lay it yourself. Use a specially designed waterproof laminate, such as one with the Aqua Protect logo, in a bathroom or kitchen.

Cheapest for bathrooms Cut the cost of flooring in a bathroom or kitchen by opting for hard-wearing vinyl – the least expensive choice.

Cost-conscious choices for tiles If you want clay flooring, buy quarry tiles – they are half the price of terracotta, which cost about £25/m². For a real stone floor, which costs on average £60/m², untreated slate is often cheapest, but will stain – so use a suitable stain protector (around £20 a litre). Fake a stone floor with laminate tiles (around £25/m²) or top-quality vinyl that looks like stone (up to £45/m²) – and both are cheaper than stone to lay.

USE NATURAL-FIBRE FLOORING WISELY

Avoid having to replace natural flooring sooner than you anticipated by taking into account its intended use. Each type has its own strengths. Like carpet, natural flooring looks best when fitted professionally.

■ **For heavy traffic** Buy sisal or coir – the most hard-wearing options – for areas that receive a lot of use. Don't put natural flooring down where food or drink may be spilled, or in a bathroom, because damp could make it rot.

■ **For comfort underfoot** Soft, silky jute is a good choice for bedrooms, whereas coir, for instance, may be too prickly.

RESOURCES

FLOORING SUPPLIERS

■ Some leading suppliers of flooring are listed in www.homesources.co.uk ✉.
■ iFloor.co.uk www.ifloor.co.uk 0800 358 0103 ✉ sells a wide range of flooring online.

CARPETS

■ For where to buy a carpet near you, plus buying tips, visit www.carpetfoundation.com 01562 755568 ✉.
■ UK Carpets Direct

www.ukcarpetsdirect.com 0191 418 7396 ✉ is an online carpet superstore.
■ The Discounted Carpet Underlay Company www.discounted-carpet-underlay.co.uk 0845 644 0623 ✉ sells carpet underlay online at trade prices ✉.
■ RugsUK.com www.rugsuk.com 0808 108 9657 ✉ has many rugs at low prices online ✉.

OTHER FLOORINGS

■ 1926 Trading Company www.1926trading.co.uk 0800 587 2027 ✉ sells real

wood floors at discount.
■ The Tile Warehouse www.thetilewarehouse.com 0115 939 0209 ✉ has a vast selection of tiles at their Nottingham base.
■ World's End Tiles www.worldsendtiles.co.uk 020 7819 2110 ✉ runs a mail-order service.
■ Amtico www.amtico.com 0121 745 0800 ✉ specialises in tile-effect vinyl.
■ Slate World www.slateworld.com 020 8204 3444 ✉ has the biggest slate range in Britain.

SMART DECORATING CHOICES

Painting and decorating is an inexpensive way to give your home a makeover, turning dark spaces into light and airy ones. Here's how to pay less when renovating your existing decorating scheme.

PAINTING POINTERS

Bear in mind that painting a wall almost always costs less than covering it with wallpaper.

Don't skimp on preparation The secret of a successful result lies in the preparation. Make sure your walls are as smooth as possible before starting to cover them with paint, paper or tiles.

Buy match pots Avoid choosing the wrong paint colour by painting sample patches on all four walls of a room, or on large pieces of white paper (lining paper is ideal) which you then stick on the walls. Examine each colour under natural and artificial light to see if you still like it. Match pots cost between £1–£3 each.

Mix your own If you want a bright colour of paint, save money by buying cheap white emulsion and adding a strong-coloured emulsion – a match pot will often be enough –

DON'T PAY TO RE-PLASTER

■ Use thick lining paper to give walls a smooth surface, then coat with emulsion paint.

■ When a damp problem has been cured, get rid of stained patches without paying a plasterer. Smooth the plaster with glasspaper or an electric sander, use oil-based paint to seal the stain, leave to dry, then paint with oil-based eggshell.

■ If a leak makes internal plaster bubble, scrape out the damaged plaster and repair with ready-mixed plaster. Prime with emulsion diluted with up to 10% water, then paper or paint with emulsion.

 RESOURCES

DECORATING

■ Decorating Direct **www.decoratingdirect.co.uk** sells materials and tools online at trade prices with delivery free for orders over £50 ✉.

■ Homesources **www.homesources.co.uk** ✉ lists many suppliers of paints and wallpapers.

PAINT

■ Suppliers of a wide selection of paints:
Crown Paints **www.crownpaints.co.uk** 0870 240 1127 ✉
Dulux **www.dulux.co.uk** 01753 550555 ✉
B&Q **www.diy.com** 0800 444840 ✉
Focus Do It All **www.focusdoitall.co.uk** 0800 436436 ✉

Homebase **www.homebase.co.uk** 0845 077 8888 ✉

■ Cuprinol **www.cuprinol.co.uk** 01753 550555 ✉ to protect interior and exterior wood, walls and floors.

■ Hammerite **www.hammerite.com** 01661 830000 ✉ for interior and exterior paint.

WALLPAPER

■ Major suppliers of wallpapers:
Coloroll **www.coloroll. co.uk** ✉
Crown Wallcoverings, Anaglypta and Vymura **www.cwvgroup.com** 01254 222800 ✉
Harlequin **www.harlequin.uk.com** 08708 300032 ✉

■ The Wallpaper Shop **www.thewallpapershop.net** ✉

offers 25% and more off leading brand wallpapers, and sells online.

■ Wallpaper Orders UK **www.wallpaperorders.co.uk** ✉ is another discount online outlet.

TILES

■ The Tile Association **www.tiles.org.uk** 020 8663 0946 ✉ provides product and supplier information for wall and floor tiles.

■ Topps Tiles **www.toppstiles.co.uk** 0800 783 6262 ✉ is a low-price chain with branches throughout Britain.

■ Marlborough Tiles Factory Shop, Marlborough **www.marlboroughtiles.com** 01672 512422 ✉.

■ For details of Pilkington's Tiles factory shops visit **www.pilkingtons.com** 0161 727 1000 ✉.

until you get the desired shade. Make a note of exactly which colour you added, and how much, in case you need to make up more paint.

WALLPAPER ECONOMIES

Before you buy expensive wallpaper, check out the sales at your local decorating stores, and online shopping outlets that sell designer wallpaper at a discount all year round (see Resources, left).

Try before you buy Just like paint, look at wallpaper samples in the room you intend to decorate in both daylight and artificial light, and so be sure that you have made the right choice.

Buy less paper If you select an expensive wallpaper, use it as a focal point and hang it on one wall only.

Paint on paper Combine textured paper with paint for an economical yet stylish look. Textured wallpaper in white or cream is often cheaper than the coloured equivalents.

SAVE THE EXPENSE OF RETILING

Look out for cheap tiles in factory shops and discount warehouses. These outlets have overstock in perfect condition as well as seconds.

Paint over tiles Paint over old tiles for a new look at a fraction of the cost of re-tiling. Clean the tiles and remove all traces of dust, then apply a tile primer, followed by tile paint, both at about £10 for 750ml. Alternatively, paint an all-in-one tile paint directly onto the tiles, at a cost of about £15 for 750ml.

Refurbish existing tiling For under £10 you can give ageing tiling a fresh look by regrouting. Scrape out as much of the old grout as possible – you can buy a grout removal tool for around £2 or make your own from an old hacksaw blade. Regrout, using an ice lolly stick to smooth the grout between the tiles.

Replace cracked tiles Save retiling whole areas by just replacing any damaged tiles. Wearing safety glasses, drill a hole in the centre of a damaged tile and chisel it out along with old grout to give a flat surface, working from the centre. Then replace and regrout. If matching tiles aren't available, replace with tiles in contrasting colours.

Salvage not necessarily cheaper When replacing quarry tiles or trying to match old brickwork, try a salvage company such as the Coventry Demolition Company 0247 654 5051 ✉, who specialise in reclaiming reusable materials. But as the cost of reclaimed materials can be high, also try other sources such as council recycling centres and farm sales.

keep it simple

When decorating, keep waste to a minimum and look after your tools to avoid having to replace them often.
■ Use the smallest possible quantity of white spirit or brush cleaner.
■ Soak brushes in the same jar of white spirit overnight if you plan to use them again next day.
■ After you finish decorating, make sure you clean all traces of paint from brushes and rollers. Prevent damage to brushes during storage by securing paper around the ends.

DESCALE WASHING MACHINES AND DISHWASHERS

Lime scale shortens the life of your machine and causes breakdowns, so descale regularly. Remove furring from inside a washing machine by running it on empty with 600ml (1 pint) of white vinegar, followed by a rinse wash. For a dishwasher, add a cup of white vinegar and run the empty dishwasher on a rinse-and-hold cycle. Then add detergent and run through a cycle to clean the machine.

KEEP FILTERS CLEAR

Clean filters in the washing machine and tumble dryer on a regular basis. Similarly, remove food particles from the dishwasher filter once a week.

TIPS FOR TROUBLE-FREE KITCHENS

Save money on calling out the professionals by dealing with minor problems before they become costly repair jobs. Better still, avoid problems occurring in the first place by regular maintenance. It doesn't cost a penny to carry out a few basic housekeeping chores every week or so. These precautions will keep machines running smoothly and save on repairs.

CHECK FIRST

If your washing machine or any other major kitchen appliance starts to play up, run some checks before you resort to calling in the repair men.
- Is the machine properly plugged in?
- Are the sockets and fuses all OK?
- Check the electrical cord isn't damaged.
- Is there a filter that is clogged up?
- Check that the machine is level.
- Is there some other basic check you could carry out that just might save you an expensive call-out fee?

TOUCH UP PAINT SCRATCHES

A local appliance dealer can sell you touch-up paint. A scratch on a washing machine or fridge quickly creates rust, which spreads the damage. For minor blemishes, paint on a thin coat, allow it to dry and smooth it out with a fine rubbing compound used on car bodies. For deeper gashes and nicks, build up paint in layers, allowing each one to dry before adding the next.

OPEN WINDOWS WHILE YOU COOK

Ensure that you have good airflow through the kitchen. Wash extractor grilles regularly to prevent moisture build-up. If condensation is a problem, install an extractor hood over the cooker.

AVOID BLOCKED PIPES

Put a handful of washing soda and boiling water down the plughole regularly to prevent the U-bend from filling up with food waste. Keep tea leaves, rice and vegetable peelings out of sinks – use a bowl to catch them and prevent them clogging the plughole.

BALANCING ACT

Appliances work best when level, so use a spirit level to check from side to side and back to front. Screw legs or castors up or down as needed.

CHECK THE SEAL ON THE FRIDGE

Put a torch with a beam into the fridge, shut the door and switch off the kitchen lights. Any light leaking out of the fridge is a sign that the seal is damaged. Mend it cheaply with silicon sealant, or buy a replacement seal at an appliance store.

WHEN NOT TO DO IT YOURSELF

Don't attempt a DIY repair if the appliance is still under guarantee or extended warranty. Instead, get the maker or warranty provider to fix it.

A QUICK FIX FOR A WASHING MACHINE LEAK

If the hose on your washing machine springs a leak, fix it cheaply by replacing the faulty hose at your local DIY store.

GIVE YOUR FRIDGE ENOUGH SPACE

Make sure there is enough space between the fridge and the wall for adequate air flow. Keep the coil at the back of the fridge dusted. Check the fridge temperature setting and defrost timer from time to time and adjust as necessary.

DISHWASHER DODGES

■ To check that the spray arm of a dishwasher is working, make a note of its position before you start the machine and then again halfway through a cycle to see whether it has moved.
■ If the spray arm is clogged, you can clear it easily with a skewer or a stiff wire. Then rinse the arm well with water.
■ Fix jammed dish racks by loosening the rollers by hand or unscrewing and replacing them.

LOWER THE COST OF HOME IMPROVEMENTS

A well-chosen new kitchen or bathroom can transform your home and even add to its value. Look in the sales, visit discount warehouses and factory shops and consider ex-display models. Adding more space to your home will also increase its worth. You save more by getting a good deal on materials and managing the building process carefully.

SAVE ON BUYING A NEW KITCHEN

Get 50% off ex-display units As most ex-display kitchens are sold 'as seen', you won't be able to demand a refund if you find a fault, so check well before buying.

Free kitchen planning Many kitchen suppliers will plan your kitchen for you for nothing if you take along a set of detailed measurements, including dimensions of windows, doors and existing appliances.

Cut delivery costs If possible, transport the kitchen units home yourself.

Save on fitting costs Using the supplier's own fitters adds up to 50% to the cost of a new kitchen. There are two ways round this. One is to employ independent fitters you have found yourself. Or do a lot of the work yourself, including removing the old kitchen and assembling the units, and ask

---

SERVICE POINTS AND APPLIANCES

Keep existing service points to reduce electrical and plumbing costs when fitting a new kitchen.

Also cut out the cost of new appliances by using your existing ones. If you opt for new appliances, remember you are not obliged to buy those offered by the supplier with the kitchen. Sourcing from a discount store could save you anything from 10%–25%.

 **RESOURCES**

KITCHENS AND BATHROOMS

■ For advice on planning and buying a kitchen or bathroom, plus a guide to products, contact The Kitchen Bathroom Bedroom Specialists Association **www.ksa.co.uk** 01905 726066 ✉.

■ For suppliers of kitchens and bathrooms, see **www.homesources.co.uk** ✉.

■ For outlets that sell kitchens and bathrooms at discount prices, visit **www.gooddealdirectory.co.uk** ✉.

KITCHENS

■ Find discount stores and sales offers for kitchens at **www.kitchens.co.uk** ✉ plus details of many other kitchen suppliers and products.

■ You can shop online for cabinet doors at Just Doors **www.justdoors.co.uk** 0870 200 1010 ✉ and Doorsdirect **www.doorsdirect.co.uk** 01423 502040 ✉.

■ Also check out The Replacement Kitchen Door Co **www.replacementkitchendoor.co.uk** 01708 865386 ✉ and The Kitchen Doctor **www.thekitchendoctor.com** 0500 855555 ✉.

■ National Brands **www.national-brands.co.uk** 0151 260 8967 ✉ sell famous-name freestanding kitchen units at a discount from their Liverpool outlets.

■ Good-value kitchens are available from:
IKEA **www.ikea.co.uk** 0845 355 1144 ✉
Magnet **www.magnet.co.uk**

01325 744344 ✉.
MFI **www.mfi.co.uk** 08702 400417 ✉

BATHROOMS

■ Bathrooms.com **www.bathrooms.com** 01883 732470 ✉ is a comprehensive online directory of products and suppliers.

■ The Bathrooms Manufacturers Association **www.bathroom-association.org** 01782 747123 ✉ has an online directory of products and suppliers including free fact sheets.

■ The Bathroom Discount Centre **www.bathroomdiscount.co.uk** 020 7384 4222 ✉ has a warehouse in Fulham, London.

■ Bathroom Express **www.bathroomexpress.co.uk** ✉ is an online store with keenly priced bathrooms.

the kitchen fitters for a discount. Consider doing the basic installation too: major retailers such as B&Q will even advise on how to plumb in a new washing machine.

UPGRADING YOUR EXISTING KITCHEN

Pay a fraction of the cost of a new kitchen by adding new doors and work surfaces to carcasses already in place.

Revamp doors Buying new cabinet doors costs from £25 a door, while painting doors that are too good to replace costs just £10 for wood or melamine primer (750ml) plus £10 for 750ml of satinwood or melamine paint. Then fit new knobs or handles – knobs from Screwfix Direct (see Resources, page 253) are about £8 for five, for example.

Replace the worktop A new worktop is another way of making a big change for little outlay. Fitting a worktop is a job for a professional. The price of a new worktop for the average-sized kitchen plus fitting starts at around £300.

Retile the kitchen For around £100, you can retile a kitchen yourself. Alternatively, change the tile colour with tile paint (see page 245).

REVAMPING A BATHROOM

A new bathroom costing from £750 including installation, can be a good investment. By doing small jobs yourself you can maintain its condition for little cost.

Quick fix Patching up scratches on an enamel bath costs just a few pounds and saves on the expense of a new bath.

Upgrade your taps Elegant taps give an inexpensive bathroom suite a designer look, and cost from about £30 for two from a plumbers' merchant or discount store.

Buy a new suite A new bathroom suite is as little as £200 from a superstore like B&Q. The cheapest bathroom suites at these and similar suppliers are known as 'contract suites'.

Pay less for fitting The cost of bathroom installation is at least as much as the suite itself, so doubling the cost of the job. Some suppliers, such as B&Q and MFI, offer an installation service. But you may get a better price if you find your own plumber. Don't use heavily advertised bathroom fitting services – somebody has to pay for all those adverts.

MAKING AN OLD SHOWER GOOD AS NEW

If a shower is sluggish, don't just buy a new one. Mineral deposits from the water may be clogging the head. Unscrew the head and take it apart. Put all the pieces in a bowl of white vinegar and leave them to soak for a few hours. Use a brush to remove any stubborn sediment and rinse all the pieces well. Reassemble the shower head and screw it back into place. Fitting a new hose often helps as well.

ASK YOURSELF

CAN I GET A GRANT FOR REFITTING MY BATHROOM?

Check with your local council to see whether grants are available. They are generally only available for the elderly, those on benefit or with a disability, or if you live in a deprived area. See *Family affairs*, page 117.

HELP IN PLANNING AND COSTING HOME IMPROVEMENTS

■ If requested, the Federation of Master Builders **www.fmb.org.uk** 020 7242 7583 ✉ will send you a free copy of *The Essential Guide to Home Improvement*.

■ Local Authority Building Control **www.labc-services.co.uk** 020 7641 8737 ✉

■ National Home Improvement Council **www.nhic.org.uk** ✉

■ Royal Institute of British Architects **www.riba.org** 020 7580 5533 ✉

■ Royal Institute of Chartered Surveyors **www.rics.org.uk** 0870 333 1600 ✉

■ Royal Town Planning Institute **www.rtpi.org.uk** ✉

BUILDING AN EXTENSION

Free advice on the cost of extensions is available from the Royal Town Planning Institute and the National Home Improvement Council (see Resources, left) or online at **www.estimators-online.com** (0161 286 8601 ✉).

Get planning permission Skimping on proper checks can prove to be an expensive mistake in the long run. Although you may not need it, always check on planning permission. In addition, ensure that the planned extension complies with Building Regulations by checking with your local authority or the LABC (see Resources, left).

Do you need an architect? Many people assume that architects are only for grand projects and that they cost the earth. But architects' fees are only about 15% of the total building cost. For this, you get full professional back-up, plans that work, help in negotiating the cost of builders and materials and supervision of the building project, which in itself can save you thousands. Find a qualified architect through the Royal Institute of British Architects (see Resources, left).

Discount for DIY Adding an extension is of course a job for a professional builder. But you may be able to cut costs in the later stages by tackling the final decorating yourself.

CONVERTING A LOFT

The cavernous space in your loft could be converted into habitable rooms. Doing so might add up to 30% more usable floor area in a two-storey building, and nearly twice as much in a bungalow. A loft conversion costs less than a home extension of the same floor area, because the shell – the roof and floor – is already there.

Don't skimp on advice Check Building Regulations first by contacting the LABC (see Resources, left), and get a surveyor to find out if joists – which are often much weaker than on the first floor – need strengthening.

Make more space cheaply Adding a pull-down ladder to the loft opening and nailing a better floor in place is an economical way of getting more storage space. If you don't need a staircase and don't mind having a ladder, you don't need planning permission. You can add a floor and ladder to a loft for about £1,000.

Cut the price of stairs You can also save on the expense of having a staircase built – and save valuable space – by choosing a ready-made spiral staircase, if fire regulations permit. These start at just a few hundred pounds and look stylish too. Check the small ads in the newspapers for low-cost or secondhand stairs, or put in a wanted ad yourself.

Use an independent builder In general, it's cheaper to employ a builder than to go to a specialist loft conversion company that has fixed and promotional costs. But check that the builder you are considering has a good track record in successful loft conversions – ask for a reference and get the builder to obtain permission for you to see other jobs the firm has completed locally.

ADDING A CONSERVATORY

The cheapest way to give your home extra living space is to build a conservatory. It is normally classed as a home extension, which means you need to apply for planning permission, and you should check Building Regulations too.

Where to buy You can order a conservatory from a specialist supplier or you can buy the components and arrange for assembly yourself. The cost-conscious DIY chain stores such as B&Q (see Resources, page 253) sell conservatories and will install them once the site has been prepared. Buying end-of-line and end-of-season models can slash costs from standard prices, which start at about £2,000.

Low-cost framing PVC-u is the most economical choice for the framing system (aluminium, steel and timber being the other options) and requires less maintenance afterwards.

Install it yourself The bill for professional installation can be over £1,000. But you can save most of the cost of erecting a conservatory by doing it yourself and getting friends in to help, especially if you know someone who is in the building trade and has professional skills. Conservatories come with clear instructions and doing most of the work yourself should not prove difficult, as long as you have had some experience on smaller projects.

 **RESOURCES**

CONSERVATORIES
■ For suppliers of conservatories, visit **www.homesources.co.uk** ✉.
■ **www.conservatories.co.uk** ✉ is an extensive directory of suppliers and anything to do with conservatories.
■ **www.bestquote4 conservatories.co.uk** 0870 165 7280 ✉ lists lower-priced stock.
■ **www.conservatories online.co.uk** 0800 169 2200 ✉ offers information on materials, suppliers and special offers.

COSTS AND RETURNS ON HOME IMPROVEMENTS

Check with local estate agents to see what the potential added value of a planned home improvement might be before you go ahead.

Every street has a top price for the value of properties, and no improvement will take house prices beyond that level.

AREA	CONSIDERATIONS AND COSTS
NEW KITCHEN	Costs from around £1,000 to £10,000 plus installation costs of around 50%. A good kitchen may add 5% to the value of your home, or at least make it easier to sell.
NEW BATHROOM	Costs from a few hundred pounds to update with a basic suite to £3,000–£5,000 to convert a box room with new plumbing, but an extra bathroom could add 10%–15% to the value of your home.
CONSERVATORY	Costs from around £2,500 to £30,000 or more, but increases the light and space in your home as well as improving its saleability. Could add 10% when you sell, but don't overestimate this value – a £30,000 conservatory might recoup its costs in an idyllic rural setting but is unlikely to add that much in town.
BEDROOM EXTENSION	Costs from £12,000 upwards, and adding an en suite can cost another £3,000 or more. A properly built extra bedroom could add up to 15% to the value of the property, so it's worth it if you do a good job, especially if house prices are rising.
LOFT CONVERSION	Costs start at around £7,000 and rise to £30,000 or more, with further costs for an en suite – but a spacious converted loft could add up to 10% to the value of your property and give you attractive new living space. Take care not to make your property 'top heavy'.

BUYING MATERIALS, TOOLS AND FITTINGS

Do some research and compare prices before you buy materials and tools for building work. There are always bargains or discounts to be had if you take the trouble to check various sources.

TOP TIPS SAVE MONEY ON MATERIALS

■ **Shop at DIY chain stores and online** The chain stores and online outlets are often excellent value for money because of their bulk buying power. In addition, Internet shopping outlets don't have the overheads of retail stores. Which DIY chain store is cheapest varies from item to item. In general, prices are lower at Wickes but their range of products is not as great as that offered by some other DIY stores, such as B&Q.

■ **Save 50% at a builders' yard** Pay less for building materials such as bricks by visiting a builders' yard rather than a DIY retailer. Buying on the high street or at a DIY store can double or even treble costs. As a private buyer at a builders' yard, you won't be offered items as cheaply as a professional builder would be, but if you buy in bulk you should be able to negotiate a discount. Just try asking 'What is your best price?'

■ **Negotiate a further discount** If you are buying several items at the same time, you could negotiate further discounts. For example, buy sand and cement with bricks and ask for free delivery.

■ **Look out for money-off days** Some DIY stores hold 10% or 20% discount days for their regular customers and/or senior citizens.

■ **Buy at source and install it yourself** A glazier who comes to measure up and then returns with the correct pane of glass will charge a large call-out fee and for the work on top of that. But you can measure the window yourself, then simply ask him to cut a pane and sell you some putty at a total cost of just a few pounds.

■ **Architectural salvage yards** If you are fixing up an older property or like a period look, reclamation and salvage yards can be sources of inspiration. Look for low-cost materials or interior fittings such as baths, toilets, sinks and fireplaces. Keep your eyes open, too, for good timber, stained glass and ironwork, or root around for unusual door handles or brass knobs to give your low-cost schemes a sense of individuality (see Resources, right).

■ **Check demolition sites for bricks** These are a good source of free bricks with a weathered appearance that fits in better with existing older houses and garden walls. But take care – some Victorian brick simply crumbles, and some old bricks may be covered in mortar or they may not be frost-resistant.

LOWER PRICES: SUPERSTORES vs LOCAL BUYS

■ **Check the superstores** Out-of-town superstores don't have to pay high-street rents and so can pass savings on building materials, tools and fittings to customers. They also cut prices to the bone on popular items and offer loss leaders too. But you may do better on brushes, paint, door handles and other basic items at your neighbourhood hardware shop.

■ **Compare local prices** Check the Yellow Pages for local shops and phone rival stores to compare prices for the same item.

■ **Scour the small ads** You can often find cut-price new or nearly-new items. Some are offered free if you collect them. Local papers also print discount vouchers on certain items.

■ **Place your own ad** Find just what you want on a buyer-collects basis to drive down the price.

PAY LESS FOR TIMBER

When buying wood in quantity, go to a timber yard. Prices for bulk buys will be lower than a DIY store, and staff can advise you on the most appropriate wood for your needs.

Buy secondhand Reclaimed timber will cost less than new wood, though prices vary according to quality. But be aware that timber yards will refuse to cut secondhand timber because nails, screws and grit damage cutting tools, so you will probably have to cut it yourself.

Keep an eye on skips and building sites Valuable old timber is often junked, and for £10 a builder on the site may even deliver it to your front door.

Old hardwoods You might pick up a beautiful piece of teak or mahogany in an architectural salvage yard in the form of a door, panelling or fireplace surround.

Avoid timber troubles Look carefully for woodworm exit holes, warping and moisture staining before you buy.

Check the ends for quality Some secondhand wood is merely veneer-covered chipboard, and inside it resembles compacted sawdust.

BARGAIN HUNT

■ **Junk shops**
Look for old brass handles, hinges and doorknobs to complement home improvements.

■ **Car boot sales**
Save money on fittings and accessories. The best bargains go early, but it's worth a late afternoon visit to scoop up last-minute discounted items. You can pick up great bargains in affluent areas, where the quality is likely to be higher and the vendors may sell for less.

RESOURCES

PRODUCT INFORMATION
■ Call The Building Centre **www.buildingcentre.co.uk** 020 7692 4000 ✉; calls are charged at £1.50 a minute.

DIRECTORIES OF SUPPLIERS
■ Homesources **www.homesources.co.uk** ✉ lists suppliers of products related to DIY and the home.
■ The Good Deal Directory **www.gooddealdirectory.co.uk** ✉ lists discount outlets selling DIY-related products, fixtures and fittings.

DIY CHAIN STORES
■ Argos **www.argos.co.uk** 0870 600 8784 ✉ lets you reserve online, then pay and collect in-store.
■ B&Q **www.diy.com** ✉ has stores and provides an online shopping service.
■ DIYnot **diynot.com** has hundreds of information pages written by experts, as well as an online shop.
■ Focus Do It All **www.focusdoitall.co.uk**

0800 436436 ✉ also lets you shop online.
■ Homebase **www.homebase.co.uk** 0845 077 8888 ✉.

DIY ONLINE/MAIL ORDER
■ Screwfix Direct **www.screwfix.com** 0800 096 6226 ✉ offers online shopping and mail order on a massive range of items.

DIY TOOLS SOLD ONLINE
■ DIYtools.co.uk **www.diytools.co.uk** ✉
■ Draper Tools **www.draper.co.uk** 023 8026 6355 ✉
■ Toolbank **www.toolbank.co.uk** 0800 068 6238 ✉

BUILDERS' MERCHANTS
■ Build Center **www.build-center.co.uk** 0800 529 529 ✉ has branches throughout Britain, and you can shop online.
■ Buildbase **www.buildbase.co.uk**

0800 107 2255 ✉ also has many branches.

SALVAGE YARDS
■ The Architectural Salvage Index **www.handr.co.uk/ salvage_home.html** 01483 203221 ✉ is a database of items wanted and for sale, at £10 an entry.
■ Salvo **www.salvo.co.uk** 01890 820333 ✉ has lists of local salvage dealers.

PLUMBERS' MERCHANTS
■ Plumb Center **www.plumbcenter.co.uk** 08701 622 557 ✉ has branches throughout Britain.
■ Plumbworld **www.plumbworld.co.uk** ✉ is an online shopping outlet.

LIGHTING SOLD ONLINE
■ Lighting Direct **www.lighting-direct.co.uk** 01923 333000 ✉
■ Lightsaver.co.uk **www.lightsaver.co.uk** 0121 350 1999 ✉
■ The Lighting Superstore **www.thelightingsuperstore. co.uk** 01225 704442 ✉

ENERGY-SAVING HOME IMPROVEMENTS

If your utility bills are high, you may be able to lower them by making smart alterations to your home. Being energy efficient need not cost a lot of money – it's possible to make a big difference for very little outlay.

INSULATE FOR THE GREATEST SAVINGS

A sure-fire way to lower your heating bills is to improve the insulation in your property.

Insulate the loft Save heating costs by laying a glass fibre insulation blanket over the joists or filling the spaces between joists with loose-fill granules. Since up to 25% of your home's heat is lost through the roof, you should recoup the cost within a few years.

Check existing insulation Older houses often have only a thin layer of insulation. Ideally, it should be at least 20cm (8in) deep. If you top it up by 10–15cm (4–6in), you could save as much as £40 in a year.

Lag the pipes Lag hot water pipes with fibre bandage or flexible foam tube, which you can buy from a plumbers' merchant or DIY store. You could save more than just the cost of lost heat – proper insulation helps to stop pipes freezing and bursting in winter.

Insulate the hot water tank Put an 8cm (3in) thick insulating jacket around your hot water tank to reduce heat loss by up to 75%.

SIMPLE DRAUGHTPROOFING

You can lose up to 15% of the heat in your home through draughty doors and windows, and another 10% through the floors.

Keep draughts out A brush or PVC seal for external doors costs just a pound or two from your local DIY store. Draught-excluding tape can be used around offending doors or windows.

Seal up floor cracks Filling cracks between floorboards with newspaper or sealant reduces draughts. If you've just sanded your floor, save the sawdust from the sander to mix with PVC and fill small cracks for a seamless finish.

SEALING WINDOWS AGAINST THE COLD

The average house loses as much as 20% of its heat through the glass in windows; look at ways of reducing this wasteful heat loss – double glazing can cut this by as much as half.

Save £40–£60 a year with double glazing Although you won't recoup the cost with the amount you save on heating bills, the other benefits associated with double glazing can make the expenditure worthwhile. These benefits include the fact that all your old windows and frames are replaced with new ones, and the double glazing provides insulation against noise and smells and greater security against break-ins. For an average home, initial expenditure on double-glazed windows would be around £5,000, with a projected fuel saving of approximately £60 a year from the most energy-efficient option, low-E (low-emissivity) double glazing.

Save £30–£40 a year with secondary glazing
Generally less expensive than full double glazing, but also slightly less effective, secondary glazing covers existing windows with sealed panels. This type of glazing is worth considering if your windows are sound or you want to keep a period look to your home. The windows have sliding panels and are also available as hinged units, and so they can be opened and closed.

Save £30–£40 a year with low-cost options Have your windows professionally treated with low-E (low-emissivity) film, which costs about £40 a metre, including installation. A low-E coating usually lasts about five years. Cheaper still, install sheets of low-E film, plastic or vinyl over windows yourself (low-E film is tinted, so you may prefer to use one of the alternatives). Cheapest of all, fix insulating film over the windows with adhesive tape. Shrink the film with a hair dryer until it is free of wrinkles.

SMART MOVES

Don't pay for heat you don't need

■ Use your home heating system as efficiently as possible to maximise savings on energy (see *Household finance*, page 298).
■ If your heating is not already controlled by a timer and thermostat, have them installed. If you don't have a thermostat, check the temperature regularly and adjust the heating controls when your house gets warmer. This way, you avoid paying for heating when you don't need it.
■ Having your boiler checked annually can pay for itself, as a well-maintained boiler is less likely to develop costly problems, and saves gas by burning it efficiently.

HOW MUCH MONEY EACH YEAR CAN YOU SAVE ON ENERGY?

CONDENSING BOILER AND UPGRADED HEATING CONTROLS	£140
25cm (10in) LOFT INSULATION	£80–£100
CAVITY WALL INSULATION	£70–£100
DOUBLE GLAZING	UP TO £40
NEW ENERGY-EFFICIENT FRIDGE FREEZER	£35
TURNING DOWN THERMOSTAT BY 1°	£20
INSULATING JACKET ON HOT WATER TANK	£15
INSULATING HOT WATER PIPES	£5

ESTIMATED TOTAL £395

Figures based on information from Energy Saving Trust/2004

The average British household spends £610 a year on fuel, but may not be doing everything possible to keep bills to a minimum. This chart shows how fuel bills can be reduced substantially with energy-efficient measures, adding up to an approximate saving of £395–£455 on annual fuel bills for the average British home.

HARNESS SOLAR POWER

Save on fuel bills by making use of free solar energy. Whether you have solar panels or not, there are various ways in which you can use solar energy to heat your home.

Install solar panels The most popular way of utilising solar energy is to preheat cold mains water so that less gas, oil or electricity is needed to supply hot water. This is usually achieved by putting a solar panel measuring 3–4m² (3.6–4.8 sq yd) on the roof, facing roughly south. Although solar panels work best in sunny weather, they still function in cloudy conditions and could provide about half your hot water energy needs over the year. An installed system costs between £2,400 and £5,000. DIY kits cost about £1,500. Grants are available through Clear Skies (funded by the DTI) – check their website at **www.clear-skies.org** or ring 0870 243 0930 ✉.

Retain warmth in cold weather During winter, allow as much sun as possible into the house. On sunny days, open blinds and shutters, and tie back curtains. Trim evergreen trees and shrubs that shade the windows. As soon as the sun starts to go down, close the blinds or curtains to hold the heat inside.

Keep cool in summer For the summer, take the opposite approach. Plant deciduous trees to shade the house in hot weather, and install awnings over south-facing windows. Close your windows and curtains by mid-morning when the temperature begins to rise, or leave them closed if you'll be out all day. If temperatures cool down after sunset, open up the house to take advantage of any breezes.

TOP TIPS INSTALL BATHROOM FITTINGS THAT CUT HEATING AND WATER BILLS

Install new energy-efficient models when you come to replace bathroom fittings.

■ **Add a shower** Consider putting in a shower if you haven't already got one. A three-minute shower uses a quarter of the water of a bath. With a low-flow shower-head, you save even more.

■ **Reduce water flow** Fitting inexpensive low-flow shower heads and taps in your home is a simple fix you can do yourself and will reduce the amount of water you use by half, without decreasing the performance of the fittings. Follow the manufacturer's instructions – all you'll need is a wrench or pliers to do the job.

■ **Stop the shower while you soap** Check out shower heads with an off-on switch that lets you interrupt the water flow while you soap up, shave or shampoo and then resume the flow to rinse.

■ **Buy a low-flow loo** When you replace a toilet, get a new low-flow model (which is now required in all new construction). They use only 7.5 litres (1½ gal) each flush, compared with the 16 litres (3½ gal) the old type use.

---

keep it simple

HEATING
Central heating systems run less efficiently when they are full of trapped air. To save on heating costs, and prevent the radiators rusting internally, bleed them once a month to release air, using a square key available from DIY stores.

LIGHTEN UP

Invest in compact fluorescent bulbs. They fit in the same sockets but use only about a quarter of the energy. They also last ten times longer than their incandescent cousins – doubling your saving. Buy from a supermarket or online (for example at **www.tesco.com** ✉) or your local electricity supplier, and save on the initial cost as well.

PAY LESS FOR PROFESSIONAL HELP

Finding good workmen and dealing with them fairly and wisely prevents costs from spiralling out of control.

TOP TIPS GETTING THE BEST PRICE

Always compare prices before settling on a particular builder or workman, and check out other ways of saving money too.

■ **Ask for written quotes** Collect at least three different quotations (not estimates) for a job, and get them in writing. This gives you some comeback in case of problems. Make a careful list so you can ask each tradesman the same questions. Ask for an itemised quote, so you can compare like with like – 'making good', or replastering and clearing away rubble, should be clearly stated. Make sure the tradesman's full name and address is on the quote, so you can follow up with legal action in case of trouble.

■ **Combine jobs** You may get a better price if the builder who repoints the brickwork on your house also does some work on your garden wall, for example – and you will save on further call-out fees.

■ **Choose a one-man band** Using a VAT-registered builder will automatically add 17.5% to your bill. If you find a small sole trader who is not registered for VAT, you will save £87.50 on a £500 job.

■ **Do unskilled work yourself** Cut the price of a job by doing some of the preparation – lifting old floor coverings or removing old tiles, for example – before asking tradesmen for a quotation.

DON'T DIY

Beware of tackling jobs yourself if they:
■ require specialist knowledge about gas or electricity. By law, gas appliances must be installed by a Corgi-registered gas fitter (see Resources, page 258). And electrical appliances must be installed to Institute of Electrical Engineers (IEE) standards;
■ are dangerous – for example, working at height from an unsecured ladder;
■ are likely to land you with further problems you can't fix yourself, as when knocking down an interior wall that might be structural, for instance.

keep it simple

■ When looking for a builder or other tradesman, start by asking for personal recommendations from friends who consider they have had good work done at a reasonable price.
■ If it is at all possible, ask to see examples of past work by a builder or tradesman who you are interested in hiring.

CHECK OUT GUARANTEES

Look for value-added extras The man who installs your new alarm system could offer a year's free guarantee followed by a cut-price annual contract, saving you money on repeated call-outs. And you could get a discount on your home insurance for a properly installed and maintained security system, too.

Read the small print Some guarantees last for just a year and charge an excess after that – so having a 'guaranteed' damp-proof course, for instance, could mean that after one year you have to pay the same firm again if you want them to check their work. If the guarantee is not worth the paper it's written on, ask if there's a discount for doing without it.

HOW TO GET FREE HELP

Many specialists will survey a job for free. Their advice can save you money as, armed with the knowledge, you might then decide to tackle the job yourself.

Measuring up for carpet Retailers will measure up for carpet for free, though some may be wary of handing over the dimensions to you. To estimate the dimensions for yourself, simply divide the total cost of the carpet by its price per square metre. Use graph paper to roughly estimate the area and check their sums.

Timber specialists Specialist companies will assess timber troubles and give you a free estimate. For example, they will track down the source of any woodworm and assess how extensive the damage is. You can then ask the company to sell you the chemicals to do the job yourself much more cheaply – and compare prices in your local DIY store too.

WATCH POINTS GREAT RIP-OFFS

There are always unscrupulous workmen who are ready to exploit the average person's lack of specialist knowledge.

■ **Passing experts** Beware of the chap who knocks on

your door to say he has some tarmac left over from road works and will resurface your drive at a cut-price rate. Almost certainly he will do a poor job, and once he has the money you will never see him again.

■ **Eagle eyes** Your suspicions should be aroused by the man who says he has just noticed that one of your slates is loose or missing, but he will fix it for £50. Of course, he has no proper roof ladder or equipment and damages several other slates in the process – and the bill runs into hundreds. Take a long, hard look at the roof yourself, through a pair of binoculars, and only let a local roofer who is well known in your area touch it.

■ **Invisible fixes** Don't believe the workman who services your boiler and then explains that a vital part needs replacing at a cost of several hundred pounds. Decent workmen leave you the packaging, the receipt and the damaged part to show that they really have changed the part they say needed mending. If in doubt, stop the work and get some other free quotes.

■ **Mysterious damage** Watch out for a plumber who works in your loft and then spots discoloured water coming from your taps, or the chimney 'expert' who discovers smoke in the bedroom. Cowboy builders can create problems so that they get paid to fix them. If you suspect this is the case, stop the work and call the council's Trading Standards department right away.

CONTROLLING THE JOB

While your builder will manage the day-to-day running of the job, it is up to you to take control, plan for contingencies and avoid costly misunderstandings.

On schedule Agree a timetable of works and payments, and try to negotiate a rebate for every day the job is late.

Be assured Get proper insurance before you proceed with major work. For any job, check that your workman is properly insured in case he damages your property.

Don't pay too much up front The deposit should be no more than 25% of the total cost. Negotiate a 10% retention at the end to give you, say, two weeks to one month to assess whether the job has been properly done.

Check before you sign If the delivery man won't wait while you check items are in good order, amend the delivery note to say 'goods unseen' before you sign for them.

Record progress Keep a detailed log of the works, and take regular photographs of what has been done. Get receipts for every payment you make.

Job satisfaction Don't sign any satisfaction agreements until you are 100% satisfied. If you are not, ask for a discount or for the job to be completed properly. In case of problems, try to negotiate an amicable solution. If necessary, you can seek advice from your local Trading Standards Authority (see the Trading Standards Service website **www.consumercomplaints.org.uk** ✉ or your local Citizens Advice Bureau. As a last resort, you can take legal action cheaply and simply through the Small Claims Court. Costs start at £20 depending on the disputed amount, but you will probably need to hire a solicitor as well.

keep it simple

Communication is the key to a successful and cost-efficient building project.

■ Make sure you understand what is happening at all times. Don't let tradesmen's jargon confuse you – if you don't understand exactly what is meant, ask.

■ If you don't like something that has been done, say so at once – it will be easier and cheaper to change it immediately rather than later on.

■ To avoid the possibility of misunderstandings, write down any changes agreed mid-project.

■ If you start running over budget, let the builder know – he may be able to help by suggesting additional ways of saving money.

Buying and running a car

It's easy to take running a car for granted, but when you realise it's likely to be the second or third most expensive item in your weekly budget, it makes sense to get your priorities and your sums right.

BUYING A NEW CAR

A new car is a luxury, so be sure that a nearly-new one would not suit your needs just as well. But if you do decide to buy new, getting the right car and the right deal needn't be a hassle if you follow some basic consumer guidelines.

DO YOUR RESEARCH

Save money by doing some background research first. Read car reviews and check prices in magazines such as *What Car?* and *Parker's Car Price Guide*. Surf the web for good deals and keep an eye on showroom prices.

Set a budget Include tax and insurance (see page 272) in your budget and stick to it. The biggest considerations are the age and model of the car you intend to buy.

Stay flexible List the features you want in your new car, such as engine size, number of doors, optional extras and fuel economy, and place them in order of importance. Finding several makes and models that fit your needs will give you more bargaining power – and help you to pay less.

Factor in depreciation You lose thousands of pounds as soon as you drive a new car off the forecourt. Some lose up to 20% of their value the moment you pick them up. But you can cut those losses by choosing models with lower depreciation – a top-of-the range luxury model could lose more than £8,000 immediately, while a mid-range family saloon could cost £1,000 in initial depreciation. If this is a major concern, consider a year-old car – almost as good as new but up to a third less in price.

Compare costs The purchase price may be low but the running costs high. Since the AA estimates that running an average car costs £3,600 a year – and that's without allowing for the purchase price – it pays to do your sums (see below).

RESOURCES

FIND THE BEST PRICES
Compare prices for new cars by checking the following sources:
RAC at **www.rac.co.uk**
08705 722 722 ✉
AA at **www.theAA.com**
0870 600 0371 ✉
www.autoebid.com ✉
www.jamjar.co.uk ✉
www.virgincars.com ✉
www.motorpoint.co.uk ✉
www.ebay.co.uk ✉
www.which.net ✉
What Car? magazine
www.whatcar.com ✉

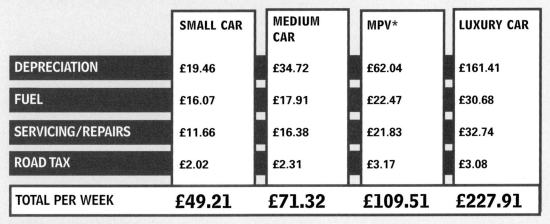

CONSIDER RUNNING COSTS

How much will your new car cost to run? Costs vary widely depending on the size and make of car you choose. If you travel 12,000 miles annually, these are the weekly costs, excluding any financing arrangements such as loans.

	SMALL CAR	MEDIUM CAR	MPV*	LUXURY CAR
DEPRECIATION	£19.46	£34.72	£62.04	£161.41
FUEL	£16.07	£17.91	£22.47	£30.68
SERVICING/REPAIRS	£11.66	£16.38	£21.83	£32.74
ROAD TAX	£2.02	£2.31	£3.17	£3.08
TOTAL PER WEEK	**£49.21**	**£71.32**	**£109.51**	**£227.91**

* Multi-passenger vehicle

Information July 2004

SCOUR THE MARKET

The difference in price between British and European-sourced cars has narrowed in recent years, but you can still gain by knowing where to get the best bargains (see below).

FRANCHISED DEALERS

Most new cars are sold by franchised dealers, who are tied to a particular manufacturer. Although increased competition and government pressure is helping to bring prices down, franchised dealers' prices are still high. Save time and money by test-driving a new car at your local dealer and then going for a cheaper deal elsewhere – or haggling (see page 264).

INDEPENDENT DEALERS

Although you'll only get absolutely new cars from franchised dealers, you may find 'pre-registered' new cars – with only delivery mileage – at independent dealerships. They are often cheaper than franchises and you can haggle to reduce prices.

BUY CHEAPER ON THE INTERNET

Online car supermarkets offer worthwhile discounts on new cars and you can bring the price down further by being flexible about the model or colour. Visit websites such as **www.autoebid.com** ✉, **www.jamjar.co.uk** ✉, **www.virgincars.com** ✉ or **www.motorpoint.co.uk** ✉ for discounts of up to 15%.

■ Travelling to another part of the country to pick up a cut-price car you have found on the Internet will cost you the journey but could save you thousands of pounds on the price of the car. Many dealers will deliver to your home for a relatively small charge.

SAVE MONEY BY BUYING ABROAD

You can benefit from lower European prices by importing a car, though the savings are not as large as they were before the rules governing car sales changed from 2000 onwards.

Contact a European dealer Save on importer's fees by going directly to a dealer in Europe. But you will be responsible for the costs involved in getting the car home, such as your travel expenses and other costs (see Watch Points, opposite). Savings made will also be reduced if you have to make long international calls to dealers abroad.

Use a specialist For peace of mind, use a company that specialises in importing vehicles from Europe and ask for a breakdown of the cost. Virgin Cars, for example, don't have any hidden extras, and all their cars have UK specifications. An agent typically charges between £300 and £1,000. For further details, visit **www.carimporting.co.uk** ✉.

Consider a high-spec import Buying a car that has been built for a country outside the EU, such as Japan or America, can be a way of getting a high-specification car at a good price. But check out manufacturing standards, warranty, servicing and the availability of spare parts, or it could cost you more in the long run. You will also need a Certificate of Conformity to make it legal for British roads. Such an import may be harder to sell, and could depreciate faster. For more information, see the AA and RAC websites.

WATCH POINTS BUYING ABROAD

Compare prices and make sure you know what you are getting, including any hidden costs.

■ **Check out European price surveys** Look at the European Commission's car price comparisons, available at **europa.eu.int/comm/competition/car_sector/price_diffs/**, as car prices vary within Europe. Holland and Belgium are generally cheapest.

■ **Hidden costs** Watch out for extra importing costs, such as transit plates, VAT and registration.

■ **Specifications and warranty** Make sure the car has the same warranty with the manufacturer and the same specifications as the UK model. Cars that do not have a valid Certificate of Conformity (see above) from the manufacturer will need to pass a Single Vehicle Approval (SVA) test before they can be driven legally.

CUTTING DEALER COSTS

Phone several dealers – don't just go to the nearest. But the chances are that you won't get the best possible deal until you're actually sitting in a showroom with the salesman.

Set your price Find the wholesale price of the car you want by using *Glass's Guide to Car Value* (the trade vehicle valuation guide) or see **www.glass.co.uk**, and read *What Car?*, *Parker's Car Price Guide* and other car magazines to find who is offering the best deal. Add a small profit for the dealer – say £300. Then ring round different dealers offering that price. Once one offer is made, make a note of it and phone other dealers to see if they can beat it. After you have negotiated the best price, visit this dealer to check that they have the exact car you want to buy.

RESOURCES

SOURCES OF HELP WHEN BUYING FROM ABROAD
Detailed information about importing a vehicle into the UK can be found on government websites:
■ VCA (Vehicle Certification Agency), under FAQ (Frequently Asked Questions) **www.vca.gov.uk** 0117 952 4235 ✉
■ The DVLA (Driver and Vehicle Licensing Agency) **www.dvla.gov.uk** 0870 240 0010 ✉
■ Further useful information in Watchdog Guides on **www.bbc.co.uk/ watchdog/guides_to/ importinganewcar** ✉
■ Many questions on car-buying abroad are also answered on **www.buy-abroad.com** 01692 400 999 ✉.

CHEAPER DEALS FROM EUROPE

Variations in European car prices are less than they were several years ago, and Britain no longer tops the 'most expensive' list, but good buys can still be found.

Here's how average British prices compare with those in Belgium and Holland. Prices (September 2004) are in Euros and exclusive of tax.

CAR MAKE AND MODEL	BRITAIN	BELGIUM	HOLLAND	CHEAPEST	SAVING
FIAT PANDA	€8,693	€7,554	€6,953	HOLLAND	€1,740
NISSAN MICRA	€10,096	€9,752	€9,252	HOLLAND	€844
FORD FOCUS	€14,998	€14,492	€13,146	HOLLAND	€1,852
VW PASSAT	€15,642	€17,072	€16,903	BRITAIN	€1,430
RENAULT ESPACE	€23,645	€23,185	€20,749	HOLLAND	€2,896

Plan your timing carefully A good time to buy is just as the new registration models arrive on March 1st and September 1st, because dealers will offer discounts on earlier models to make room for the new ones. Buying at quiet times – just before Christmas or in bad weather when the showroom is deserted – can result in big savings too.

Hitting the target Closing the deal on a Saturday afternoon at the end of the month can pay off, because selling one more car may help your salesperson hit their target – and make them more likely to give you a better deal. Choose the right time, and you could even get away with offering the cost price without an added profit for the dealer.

Ask for extras Use your bargaining powers to get what you want, such as a CD player, air conditioning, power steering, road tax or a better model. Try implying that you can always go to the dealer down the road for a better deal and that if they won't throw in the extra you want, the other dealer probably will.

Buy ex-display Pay less by buying an ex-display vehicle or loan vehicle. Make sure you get a new car warranty with it for better coverage.

Choose an older model Wait until a new model is just out. Unless you yearn for the latest model, opt for the slightly older one and save enough for a good holiday. But remember that older models will depreciate in value much more quickly than the latest one.

TOP TIPS LEARN TO HAGGLE

Dealers build in a generous profit margin because they know customers will haggle – and the better you are at it, the more you can save. Take a friend along to keep you from being drawn in to the sales patter.

■ **Don't be put under pressure** Don't wait until your current car is failing – being desperate will put you in a poor bargaining position.

■ **Be prepared** Have your research at your fingertips, with the latest models, prices and options.

■ **Have a starting point** When it comes to haggling, start at about 10%–15% off the list price.

■ **Be discreet** If you've fallen in love with a car, don't let it show. You'll save more by playing it cool and acting as if you're undecided between several models. And don't let friendly feelings for the sales staff cloud your judgment – you can be pleasant without letting them take advantage.

■ **Don't play the numbers game** A salesperson who asks, 'How much would you like to pay each month?' is using one of the oldest tricks in the book. Typical car loan interest rates are between 6%–8% over 1–10 years, depending on whether the loan is secured or not. Paying £200 a month is not economical if repayments stretch over years – aim for a loan of around three years' duration.

■ **Be willing to walk away** If you don't feel good about the deal or the dealer, your instincts could be right. And if the dealer asks why, say so – you could see a huge shift in attitude and a get better deal that way.

■ **Go over the details** Does the price cover delivery charges and number plates? Are the special features you want

KEEP YOUR OLD CAR OUT OF THE DEAL

You might get a good deal on your new car, and then be fleeced on the trade-in. Fix a price for the new car, then get the best price you can for your old one, possibly by selling it privately.

included? If you have agreed a good price, ask the dealer to waive these fees. If he won't, ask for free servicing or complementary extras.

■ **Read the warranty carefully** How long does it last, what does it exclude and what conditions are imposed for it to remain valid?

WATCH POINTS FINALISING THE DEAL

Unless you're certain that this is the car you want, don't put any money down until the deal is finalised. Doing so means you lose all your bargaining power.

■ **Don't lose your deposit** If you put down a non-refundable deposit and then there are problems, you could lose the money. Ask for a receipt so you have evidence for the Trading Standards office if this becomes necessary later.

■ **Check cancellation terms** Check that there is a clause in the contract that lets you cancel it if there is a hitch, such as a delay in delivery.

■ **Get the manager's signature on the contract** The sales staff may not have the authority to make any changes to the contract – you need the highest official signature possible.

■ **Test drive your new car** When you go to pick up your new car, check every detail and test drive it before finalising the contract. If there are any problems, draw them to the seller's attention and ensure any minor repairs are agreed in writing before proceeding.

■ **Know your rights** If serious faults appear after you have taken the car home, you are normally protected under current legislation. Stop using the car and complain to the seller in writing as soon as possible after purchase – you could be entitled to a full refund. See the Trading Standards website at **www.tradingstandards.gov.uk** ✉ or contact your local Trading Standards office for further advice.

CASE STUDY

SHOPPING ABROAD PAYS DIVIDENDS

Surrey teacher Lisa Brown saved a small fortune when she shopped for a new 5-door Volkswagen Polo. She checked car magazines and dealers' websites until she was confident she had found a bargain UK price of slightly under £10,000 for her chosen model. Then she scoured the Internet until she found an authorised dealer in Europe offering a UK-spec car for an 'on the road' price of £2,000 less (including the extras she wanted, such as her preferred colour 'misty lilac', an electric sunroof and a CD player). Her car would take up to six months to be ready, but at that price, Lisa was prepared to wait. To maximise her savings, she was prepared to travel to the showroom in Holland to collect it. She estimated the cost would be around £180, including the flight out, transport to and from the dealership, petrol and a ferry ticket for the return journey, but when she discovered the dealer could arrange delivery to her door for an additional fee of £200, she decided to go for this no-hassle option.

FINANCING YOUR CAR

Save money by finding the best finance – opting for the convenient deal offered by the car dealer usually means you'll be paying more than you need to.

CHOOSING THE RIGHT DEAL

Broadly speaking, there are four ways to finance the purchase of a car:

Cash The cheapest in the long run, but you may not get the best price from a dealer who prefers income from interest.

Loan You can borrow the entire amount from a bank or lender. Then you are in the same position as a cash buyer, but you will pay interest.

Dealer finance This is like a loan, but it involves a deposit and generally higher interest rates, which might make the dealer more likely to offer a better price on the car.

Leasing You pay a monthly amount to lease a car from a dealer. At the end of the lease period, you can either purchase the car or return it. Interest rates are usually the highest of all finance options. At the start of the agreement you will be quoted a 'final payment' (also known as a 'balloon payment' figure or GFV – guaranteed future value). This is the amount due if you decide to keep the car after your agreement has ended, and is based on an estimate of your annual mileage. What you pay is calculated by subtracting your deposit and the GFV from the car price and then adding interest.

ASSESS CAR FINANCING CHARGES

LOANS FROM BANKS, MOTOR ORGANISATIONS AND DEALERS

LENDER	LIST PRICE	DEPOSIT	CREDIT CHARGE	TOTAL PRICE	MONTHLY PAYMENTS	APR
Bank loan	£9,000	NA	£974	£9,974	£277	7%
Motor organisation loan	£9,000	NA	£952	£9,952	£276	6.1%
Dealer A finance	£9,000	£1,536	£1,524	£10,524	£139	10%
Dealer B finance	£9,000	£900	£1,491	£10,491	£261	11.9%

LEASING FROM DEALERS AND MOTORING ORGANISATIONS

LENDER	LIST PRICE	DEPOSIT	MILEAGE	GFV	MONTHLY PAYMENTS	COST OF FINANCE	APR	RENTAL + GFV
Dealer Lease	£8,995	£1,536	12,000	£3,169	£159	£1,434	10%	£10,429
Motor org lease	£8,645	£0	10,000	£3,277	£197	£1,724	8.9%	£10,369

The charts show financing arranged over 36 months on a Fiesta/Corsa type car.

Figures correct September 2004

'Dealer lease' example If you negotiate a price of £8,995 with the dealer from your estimated yearly mileage of, say, 12,000 the dealer calculates a GFV of £3,169. This is a 'wear and tear' calculation – the higher the mileage, the lower the GFV. As the finance is calculated by subtracting the GFV and any deposit from the agreed price, £8,995 minus £1,536 deposit and £3,169 GVF gives the amount of £4,290 to be borrowed. At an APR of 10%, this comes to £5,724 over 36 months. After 36 months, you can return the car to the dealer (having spent £7,260 in deposit and finance) or buy the car outright by paying the GFV to the dealer, in which case the total cost of the car will be £10,429.

TOP TIPS **PAYING FOR YOUR CAR**

If you borrow money to finance your car, check out websites such as **www.moneyfacts.co.uk** ✉ or magazines such as *Your Money* (from newsagents or phone 020 7404 3123) or *Moneyfacts* (0870 2250 100), for best rates.

■ **Check the details** Look at the APR (annual percentage rate) and the length of any loan, instead of just the monthly repayments. Ask for the total – most finance packages turn a £10,000 car into a £12,000 car by the end of the loan.

■ **Bank borrowing** Consider bank borrowing, especially if it offers a 0% interest introductory period. But check the APR once the introductory period ends. How easily can you then move the debt to another lender to take advantage of a second 0% interest period?

■ **Reduce your debt** Bring down your total repayments by putting down the largest possible deposit and going for the shortest possible loan.

■ **Pay cash if you can** As new cars depreciate immediately, borrowing money to buy one is bad debt. Paying cash is the best option, if at all possible.

keep it simple

BUY YOUR COMPANY CAR If you have a company car and you're about to lose it, perhaps because it is due for replacement or you are retiring, consider buying it outright. You know its history, and that it has been properly serviced, so it could be a bargain.

COMPARE THE COST OF CAR TAX

For cars registered before 1st March 2001, car tax is in two bands based on engine size – engines smaller than 1549cc cost £110 to tax, and engines larger than this are £165. Cars registered after 1st March 2001 are taxed according to their CO_2 emissions on a sliding scale from £65 to £160. The following chart shows 12 months' tax for petrol, diesel and alternative fuel cars. For biggest tax savings, choose a vehicle in bands AAA or AA.

EMISSION BAND	EXAMPLE	CO_2 EMISSIONS GM/KM	PETROL	DIESEL	ALTERNATIVE FUEL
AAA	Honda Insight	less than 100	£65	£75	£55
AA	Vauxhall Corsa	100–120	£75	£85	£65
A	VW Polo	121–150	£105	£115	£95
B	Audi A3	151–165	£125	£135	£115
C	Ford Focus LPG	166–185	£145	£155	£135
D	Nissan Almera	over 185	£160	£165	£155

BUYING A USED CAR

Buying nearly new is the simplest way to pay less for your car. Since many new models can lose up to half their value in the first two years, buying a two-year-old car gets you a half-price bargain that is still in good shape and unlikely to incur high repair bills.

BUYING FROM A DEALER

Buying from a dealer is expensive but gives you most comeback in case of problems. Non-franchised dealers are generally cheaper than the franchises and are more likely to be flexible on price. For extra security, buy from a dealer who is a member of the RMIF (Retail Motor Industry Federation). The conditions of membership require them to provide a good service, and you can go to their National Conciliation Service in the event of a dispute. Contact the RMIF at **www.rmif.co.uk** or 0845 758 5350 ✉.

Recommended dealers Ask your local garage and friends for personal recommendations.

Check out the warranty Is the warranty competitively priced, or can you negotiate?

Bargaining power Since dealers have a wide range of models in stock and tend to be in convenient locations, they give you plenty of bargaining power. If you don't like what you see, you can easily go elsewhere.

LOOK FOR AN AUCTION BARGAIN

Buying at auction can get you a real bargain. If you are lucky, you may find a six to twelve-month-old car at a saving of between 20% and 50% off the new car list price.

Have you got the knowledge? As you have just a short time to check the car over, you need to know what you're looking at – or take along someone who does.

Professional organisations For security, only buy from auctions that are members of the Society of Motor Auctions (contact the RMIF, see above for details).

CAR SUPERMARKETS AND THE INTERNET

Prices at car supermarkets are low because the stock tends to be imported or ex-fleet vehicles, and the companies source their vehicles in bulk. Whether you buy from a supermarket or through the Internet, have the vehicle thoroughly inspected and check both the spec and the warranty to ensure you buy a vehicle with a genuine UK specification. Remember to find out how much you will be charged for delivery – one major car supermarket charges £250.

Finding supermarkets Companies to try include Virgin (0845 274 1000 **www.virgincars.com** ✉) and Motorpoint (Derby, Burnley and Glasgow, 0870 125 4321 **www.motorpoint.co.uk** ✉), as well as the long-established Fords of Winsford (0845 456 3770 **www.fow.co.uk** ✉). For a list of British car supermarkets, visit **www.car-supermarkets.com** ✉.

Web purchases Buying a car from an online car dealer such as Jamjar (**www.jamjar.co.uk** ✉) can bring even bigger

DEALING WITH THE TRANSACTION

If making a private purchase, don't be tempted to hand over large bundles of cash. The best way to pay is by a banker's draft or building society cheque; if the vendor has any doubts he or she can call your bank and get it validated over the phone while you are there.

CASE STUDY

BEWARE OF OUTSTANDING FINANCE

When London motorist Marcus Stanley spotted a diesel estate with a For Sale sign in its window, he nearly fell for one of the oldest scams around. The vendor wanted £3,500, but offered a £1,000 discount. The delighted would-be buyer told his local mechanic, who was suspicious and told him to get an AA or RAC Data Check.

Mr Stanley refused at first, baulking at an extra £35 until he realised how much more a dodgy car could cost him. The AA found that the car was not stolen, but had £4,500 of finance still owing. The vendor may have been planning to pay the outstanding sum with the proceeds of the sale, but Mr Stanley couldn't take the chance that he would have to pay the outstanding amount. 'I didn't buy the car, and potentially saved myself the £4,500 liability for finance on top of the £2,500 I would have paid for the car,' he says now. 'I would strongly advise anyone who is looking to buy a used car privately to carry out a check. I've also learned to be a bit more cautious in general – not everyone is as honest as they look.'

savings than those to be made from ordinary car supermarkets. And on auction websites the feedback section gives you opinions on individual sellers – **www.ebay.com**, for example, lets you check the comments of other customers.

CHEAPER FROM A PRIVATE SELLER

Privately sold cars are cheaper than those bought from dealers. View the car at the vendor's home in daylight and in good weather so you can check it over thoroughly and get a feel for how well the car has been maintained.

■ **Try negotiating** You can save a tidy sum by negotiating – many vendors are willing to reduce the price for a sale.

■ **When to complain** Although buying privately can be the cheapest way, your legal rights are limited. Cars are sold as seen, so you have no comeback if it is faulty. But if the vendor has described the car wrongly – for example, by saying that it has had only one previous owner when you can prove that it has had more – then you can claim for compensation. But you may not get redress even if you win a legal battle, so check the vehicle thoroughly before buying.

GOOD-VALUE BUYS

You can save serious money over the long term by choosing a used company car, as it is likely to have been well maintained. You can find them at auctions, car supermarkets and some secondhand dealers who specialise in them. Ask to see the log book of the owner.

■ **Used executive cars with a full service history** The first owner of an executive car is often a company, which will have had it serviced regularly and borne the losses of the initial depreciation. The advantage is that you will get a good-quality, well-serviced car at a knock-down price.

■ **High-mileage cars** A car with high mileage could be a bargain, especially if your annual mileage is low. A company car that has been driven for thousands of motorway miles at high speed is usually in better mechanical condition than a smaller car that has spent years on stop-start city driving, which takes a heavy toll on the transmission and brakes.

keep it simple

CHECK OUT PRICES
Before you start negotiating, look at a current copy of *Glass's Guide* or visit **www.glass.co.uk** for a list of prices for new and used cars. Or check **www.whatcar.com** or **www.autoexpress.co.uk** and negotiate from the prices shown – never from the advertised price. Compare running costs, performance information, reliability and insurance levels for different makes and models in the Car Buyer's Guide at **www.theAA.com** or in *What Car?* magazine.

WATCH POINTS BUYER'S CHECKLIST

Check the car over thoroughly, either yourself if you are knowledgeable or using an expert mechanic or inspector from a motoring organisation for a small fee (see opposite).

■ **Test drive the car** Take the car for a long test drive, including hilly terrain, stop-start town driving and driving at speed. Listen carefully to the engine and use any problems to help you make a decision – or get it checked out, then negotiate a discount.

■ **Look at the service record** Are any parts due to be replaced? For example, a replacement cam belt costs a couple of hundred pounds, but if it fails you might have to buy an entire engine.

■ **Check the MOT certificates** All cars over three years old must have annual tests. Check that the recorded mileage rises steadily each year. If it doesn't, this could indicate that the car has been 'clocked' – the mileometer has been turned back to show a lower figure. If you are suspicious, ask a mechanic or inspector to look at whether the recorded mileage fits in with the condition of the car – or just walk away.

■ **Look at the mileometer** If the digits are misaligned, the mileage may have been tampered with.

■ **Examine the interior** Badly worn items such as seats and pedals can suggest high mileage more accurately than an odometer reading, especially if there is no service history.

■ **Cheap check for accidental damage** Run a magnet over the bodywork – as it is attracted only to metal, it will show up any dents that have been touched up with body filler.

■ **Look for signs of damage** Damp patches on the carpet could suggest a leak.

■ **Check the tread** A 2p coin should stay wedged in the tyre tread, unless the tyre is badly worn. Anything under 3mm of tread will need replacing.

■ **Ask about the warranty** Dealers may offer a limited warranty – for example, 30 days on a used car. Ask for a longer warranty as part of the deal, and check the terms carefully – most exclude 'wear and tear', and some limit the number of claims.

SAVE MONEY BY SPENDING MONEY

You can avoid expensive repair bills by having a used car checked out by an expert. The RAC, which examines 350,000 vehicles annually, says that 40% of vehicles examined had at least one potentially dangerous fault – and 80% had faults that would cost over £200 to fix. One in three had faults that would have made them illegal to drive on the roads and over half would have failed an MOT.

SAVINGS TO BE MADE ON BUYING SECONDHAND

Check out the new and used prices of six popular types of car ranging in size from modest to luxury. The used prices (dealer and private) are for a two-year-old car with average mileage (approx 10,000 a year) and in good condition.

CAR TYPE	NEW	DEALER	PRIVATE
SUPER MINI	£8,830	£5,430	£4,885
SMALL FAMILY	£11,030	£6,440	£6,160
LARGE FAMILY	£16,937	£8,170	£7,410
MPV	£19,750	£12,595	£11,935
EXECUTIVE	£37,426	£14,490	£13,355
LUXURY	£60,390	£34,875	£33,885

Prices from Parker's, September 2004

■ **Arrange an inspection** Both the AA and the RAC (see Resources, page 261), inspect cars for a fee starting at around £90, or you can get your local garage to check a car for around £50. For another £35, either the AA or the RAC can also check that the car has not been written off by insurers following an accident, and that it is not still subject to a hire-purchase agreement. Or opt for a complete package at around £180 from the AA or RAC, including all checks.

■ **Cheaper for members** Cut the cost of inspection by using your own motoring association – the AA and RAC offer substantial discounts to members.

SORTING OUT PROBLEMS

Take advantage of any problems with the car you want to buy by insisting on a better deal.

■ **Negotiate a discount** Take a written report from the AA or RAC back to the vendor to negotiate a discount. Private vendors will usually reduce the price rather than lose the sale. Most reputable dealers will simply carry out the work for free, saving you the cost of future repairs – and a good garage should then check that the work has been properly completed without charging you again.

■ **Ask for extras** 'If the dealer says he can't go any lower, then push for some extras – mud-flaps, or even a tank of fuel,' says the RAC. Other extras to negotiate include a CD player, a year's road tax or a better specification.

■ **Getting your money back** If you run into problems, act immediately. 'A newer vehicle should be in better condition than a 10-year-old secondhand car,' says the RAC. 'For example, a nearly new secondhand car purchased at premium market rates which, within a few days, develops a defect that would never usually appear on such a low-mileage vehicle, does not meet this standard. So you may be entitled to compensation, or your money back.' See Watch Points, page 265 for what to do if there are problems.

Getting a good deal on your old car

Whether you sell your car privately or trade it in, slick presentation increases the chance of a good price.

■ Put together a seller's pack. Showing that you have a full service history, especially with a franchised dealer, can make your car worth more – and so can showing that you've had tyres or engine parts replaced recently.

■ Check out your local scrap yard – find one in the Yellow Pages or use a parts-finding service such as Breakerlink on 08707 806655 or **www.breakerlink.com** to replace missing parts.

■ Hide paint chips and scratches with a touch-up stick from your local car-care store, polish the car and replace worn mats.

GET THE CHEAPEST INSURANCE

The canny approach to finding the right car insurance is to search for a policy that suits both your particular vehicle and your circumstances.

CHECK PREMIUMS BEFORE BUYING A CAR

Check insurance premiums before you splash out on a new car. The AA lists premiums for each type of car at **www.theaa.com** ✉. Some imported cars, for instance, can cost more to insure than British-made cars, simply because they tend to be more expensive to repair.

HOW INSURANCE COSTS ARE SET

The amount that you pay depends on several factors.
Insurance group The insurance group reflects the size, specification and cost of repairs of the vehicle. Factors include the car's performance, image, and maximum speed. The car's cost when new, the cost of parts, and the price and availability of its body shell are also taken into consideration. Each time you go up a group, your insurance costs grow by £30, so for a car in a higher group, you could pay an extra £200 annually over the most economical car.
Age and occupation of insured driver Someone in their twenties will pay more than someone in their fifties, and a publican will pay more than an accountant.
Postcode The postcode where the car will be kept has an effect on the premium. Some areas, such as inner cities, are more high-risk than others, and whether the car will be parked on the street or in a garage will also be relevant.
Driver's record The past record of the driver, including convictions and insurance claims made, will have an effect.

BUY THE APPROPRIATE INSURANCE POLICY

Choose insurance that suits you and your car. Third-party insurance is usually cheaper, but if you have a valuable car, a comprehensive policy will give you security.

■ Third-party insurance covers the cost of damage you may cause to someone else, their vehicle or property.

■ A third-party, fire and theft policy also pays out if your car catches fire or is stolen.

■ Fully comprehensive insurance will cover repairs to your vehicle, after an accident.

FINDING THE BEST-VALUE INSURANCE

Insurance premiums vary depending on the type of insurer and policy you choose. With the help of an Internet search site, we were able to locate comprehensive policies that were even cheaper than the third-party policies from the same broker.
The quotes shown below are yearly premiums for a family car belonging to a 45-year-old man, who lives in Birmingham, parks in a garage and has no convictions and no recent insurance claims. Prices are taken from **www.confused.com**, **www.insuresupermarket.com** and individual insurers, September 2004.

TYPE OF INSURER	3RD-PARTY, FIRE & THEFT	COMPREHENSIVE
Broker 1 (via Internet search site)	£252.64	£214.83
Broker 2 (via Internet search site)	£253.44	£232.54
Insurance Company (direct)	£370.07	£401.64
High-street broker	£221.26	£313.86

GETTING A COMPETITIVE QUOTE

Decide whether you would prefer to do your own research or let a broker do the work for you.

Ask around You can cut premiums by taking several quotes or using a broker to find the cheapest deal. Use a price comparison service such as **www.moneyfacts.co.uk** or the AA's broker service **www.theaa.com/services/ insuranceandfinance/gisc.html** 0870 606 0483.

Is a broker worth it? In shopping for insurance, it is worth considering the cost of your own time. There are many suppliers of insurance quotes and a host of brokers, both on the high street and the Internet. The variations you find between insurers may well be outweighed by the amount of time you spend searching. But if you choose to work with a broker, go for one who makes their money on commission from the insurer and does not also charge a fee to their customers.

TOP TIPS SAVING ON MOTOR INSURANCE

There are many ways in which you can bring down your premiums, depending on your age and circumstances and the type of motoring you do.

■ **Insure through your motoring organisation** The RAC, for example, gives members 12 months for the price of 11.

■ **Pay the cheapest way** Paying online by direct debit will give the biggest discount – Esure gives a 10% discount.

■ **Opt for a bigger voluntary excess** You'll have to pay more upfront in case of an accident, but you could save in the region of £50 on a £600 premium by increasing the excess from £100 to £350.

■ **Avoid making minor claims** If you claim for minor incidents, you'll simply push your premiums up.

■ **Save money on an old car** If your car is now worth only £1,000, there is no point in insuring it as though it were still worth £6,000. Tell your insurer when your car is ageing and pay less by insuring it for just third-party, fire and theft instead of with comprehensive cover.

■ **Invest in better security** Tell your insurer if you have an approved car alarm system – not only will it help protect your car, it will bring premiums down too.

■ **Garage your car** Your insurers will give a discount if your car is garaged at night.

■ **Tell your insurer if you move** Cars kept in inner city areas and those with high crime rates typically cost more to insure, but you can still make savings within a local area: in one Newcastle postcode, annual premiums range from £320 to over £700 depending on the exact address.

■ **Buy a safe make** If your car is a make with a good safety record, cut premiums by ensuring your insurers are aware of this. Check consumer reports – airbags, good side-impact protection systems and anti-lock brakes can all help to reduce premiums.

■ **Limit named drivers** Reduce insurance costs by limiting the number of named drivers on your policy. If just you and your partner are insured, costs will be low – add a teenage child, and they will typically soar. But insuring a child through the parents' policy is much cheaper than asking the

keep it simple

KEEP AN EYE ON YOUR PREMIUMS
Check your car insurance premiums yearly – rates change and you may find that last year's best buy has been undercut.

Cut 20%-30% off your insurance

Consider taking extra qualifications to cut insurance costs.

■ Insurers offer discounts of 20%-30% to younger people who take the Pass Plus driving test, designed by the DSA (Driving Standards Agency)
www.passplus.org.uk
0115 901 2500 ✉.

■ Both RAC (who own BSM **www.bsm.co.uk**) and the Institute of Advanced Motorists **www.iam.org.uk** 020 8996 9600 offer advanced driving tests. Experienced drivers could see their premiums fall if they let their insurers know they have passed.

SMART MOVES

young adult to take out their own insurance, and costs typically fall fast after the first year if there are no claims.

■ **Get a policy for mature drivers** Older people can cut costs by choosing a policy aimed at the over-50s, such as those offered by Saga (**www.saga.co.uk** 0800 015 4752 ✉). Savings can be in the region of £80 a year on a comprehensive policy.

■ **Check your annual mileage** Negotiate the best deal based on your annual mileage. If you do less than 10,000 miles a year, tell your insurer and you should pay substantially less. If you do more than 60,000, premiums are likely to rise sharply.

■ **Keep within the law** Premiums rise steeply once you have points on your licence, and insurance companies won't pay out if an accident results from your breaching the terms of your insurance – for example, if you drive while under the influence of drink or drugs. For a serious drink-drive accident, most insurers would pay third-party damage only and might then seek to reclaim the money from the driver through the civil courts.

■ **Drop coverage if abroad** Anyone who spends part of the year abroad – from young people on a gap year to a retired couple wintering in the sun – should tell their insurers. Dropping the coverage during the time the car is not in use could save a substantial amount.

■ **Opt for joint insurance** Save money by taking out joint insurance, especially if your occupation pushes up premiums (see page 275).

RESOURCES

CHECK THE FACTS
Compare online motor insurance quotes as well as reviews of the main providers on:
www.cheap-car-insurance.uk.net
www.ukcarinsurance directory.co.uk

HOW THE SCOTTS CUT THEIR INSURANCE PREMIUMS

James and Jill Scott got a shock when their new insurance quote landed on the doormat. The premiums had soared from £300 a year to £897 when they added their 21-year-old son Chris to the policy.

They queried the quote and were told that adding the inexperienced driver, who had three motoring convictions, made up about 75% of the increase. But they learned too that the premiums would drop after a year if Chris had no further accidents, saving £86. Buying Chris his own insurance policy would cost even more, but there were measures the Scotts could take to reduce their current bill. They kept the car garaged at night, saving £20, and chose a larger voluntary excess – £600 instead of £200, saving a further £11. Chris took a Pass Plus test to save 20% of the premium, and both parents became members of the Institute of Advanced Motorists, altogether saving £187. Insuring the car through their motoring organisation and reducing the annual mileage helped save around £40. By taking these measures, the Scotts managed to reduce their insurance premiums by £344.

SWEET DREAMS

WATCH POINTS JOB-RELATED INCREASES

If your insurance costs are much higher than those of the couple next door, even though you have no points on your licence, you could be paying more because of your occupation. The AA charges £573 to insure a female estate agent, GP or teacher driving a new Mini Cooper S 1.6 living in the DL10 postal district in North Yorkshire, but £603 for a restaurateur and £769 for a journalist with the same car in the same area. Why should this be the case? 'This is all based on risk,' says the AA, 'and particularly where alcohol is involved in some way. Publicans command a higher premium; so do club or restaurant managers as their cars are often left out at night while the premises are cleaned up and late-night revellers are about.'

■ **Cite your partner's occupation** Insurance costs for couples are normally lower than insuring the same two people separately.

■ **Park more securely** Leaving the car at home or parking it more securely at your workplace can bring down your insurance premiums – let your insurer know.

■ **Reveal the facts** Concealing vital truths about your occupation from your insurer in order to save on premiums could cost you money. If your car is stolen or broken into under circumstances that relate directly to your profession, you could find that your insurance (except for the third-party cover) is invalid.

■ **Business use** Even if you use your car only occasionally for business, make sure you opt for business use. It might not increase your premium at all, and you will be covered if you have an accident on one of those rare business trips.

keep it simple

SAVE MONEY WITH A PROFESSIONAL ORGANISATION

You may be able to bring down high, job-related car insurance premiums if you are a member of a professional organisation. Many professional associations have an insurance scheme offering discounts. For a small fee, the Transport and General Workers' Union offers an insurance top-up package for members who are professional drivers. This includes compensation for loss of licence due to injury and help with legal fees for traffic offences.

COST-CUTTING DRIVING AND MAINTENANCE

Save money on fuel and avoid large garage bills with these simple strategies and checks.

TOP TIPS MAXIMISE FUEL ECONOMY

Britain has the highest fuel prices in Europe, but you can cut your bill with cost-saving measures that are cheap – or even free.

■ **Think ahead** Rapid acceleration and braking are heavy on fuel – take your foot off the accelerator when you approach a red light, and then brake gently. Accelerate gradually too. Gentle driving in town can cut fuel costs and emissions by more than 10%.

■ **Select high gears** Drive in the highest gear you can.

■ **Don't leave the engine ticking over** You simply waste fuel by leaving the engine ticking over to warm it up.

■ **Turn off your engine** When it's safe, turn off your engine when you stop.

■ **Avoid short journeys** These run up the highest fuel bills and the most wear on your car, so walk to the corner shop.

■ **Cut your speed** Save on fuel by driving more slowly. For example, on motorways sticking to the 70mph speed limit instead of speeding at 85mph will save you up to 25% in fuel consumption.

■ **Close the windows** Open windows create air resistance.

■ **Remove the roof rack** An empty roof rack pushes up fuel consumption by around 11.5%, and a fully laden one by up to 30%.

■ **Reduce weight** Empty the boot and roof storage box. Extra weight means fewer miles to a litre.

■ **Don't use unnecessary accessories** Air conditioning can use up to 10% more fuel.

■ **Plan your route** High winds, bad weather and rough terrain can all reduce fuel efficiency.

LOOK FOR THE CHEAPEST PETROL

Petrol prices vary considerably and supermarkets are often cheapest. Check out the best local prices at **www.aapetrolbusters.com** ✉. Filling a large tank at the cheapest outlet could save you £5 a week.

Avoid premium grade If your car's engine isn't designed for premium grade fuel, paying for it is a waste of money. It will not produce more power or improve engine performance.

HAVE YOUR CAR SERVICED REGULARLY

Having your car serviced regularly keeps it in good running order, improves fuel efficiency and helps you to avoid large bills when an unchecked minor problem causes serious damage. For example, worn-out brake pads result in damage to the brake discs, which will then need replacing. For a small family car, new brake pads cost around £30 a set, as opposed to around £130 if you have to replace the discs as well.

MAKE THE CHANGE TO CLEANER FUEL

■ Think about converting your car to run on cleaner fuels, including natural gas or liquefied petroleum gas (LPG).

■ Petrol costs about twice as much as LPG, although LPG gives you around 20% fewer miles to a litre.

■ Making the change costs over £1,000, but PowerShift grants are available to convert your car.

■ New LPG cars cost a couple of thousand pounds more than petrol or diesel versions.

■ Consider changing to an electric car, particularly if you make mainly short journeys. Petrol/electric hybrids can travel around 60 miles on a gallon.

■ Find out about grants for energy efficient cars on **www.transportenergy. org.uk** 0845 602 1425 ✉. The Energy Saving Trust at **www.est.org.uk** 0845 727 7200 ✉ and Friends of the Earth at **www.foe.co.uk** 0808 800 1111 ✉ also have information on using cleaner fuels.

Stay local A small local garage will normally charge less for servicing than a franchised dealer, so ask for quotes before taking your car in. Check and compare the hourly labour charge, which will probably be the largest part of the bill. Having your car serviced by a franchised dealer is 35% more expensive than using an independent garage, according to a 2001 MFBI (Market Facts and Business Information) survey.

WATCH POINTS TOP GARAGE SCAMS

■ **Extra work discovered mid-job** When you take your car for its MOT, the garage may discover major work that needs doing before it will pass the test. You should shop around for the best price, but you can't – the car is already stripped down and the MOT certificate is about to run out. The answer is to use an independent MOT centre for a £40 test well before the certificate expires. Once you know what needs to be done, research the best quote for the work.

■ **Unquoted labour charges** A repair costs £340, but the bill comes with an extra £60 charge for stripping down the engine – two hours' labour at £30 an hour. You've been cheated – the bill should include stripping down the engine for the job, or the garage should tell you beforehand that there will be a separate charge. Explain why you feel the bill is unfair, and ask for a reduction. Say you will approach the local Trading Standards office if you aren't satisfied.

■ **Extra work done without agreement** The garage manager tells you that they found a major fault – so they fixed it and doubled your bill. A reputable garage would

Save money by checking your car yourself

Keep your car running well with these cheap – or free – checks:

Oil Check the oil every other time you fill up with petrol and top it up when it runs low. Change the oil regularly – every three months or 3,000 miles, whichever is sooner – using the recommended grade. Check the other fluids at the same time, including brake fluid and power steering fluid.

Windscreen wipers Check your wipers – smearing suggests that they are wearing out. Try cleaning them first, checking the edges and smoothing them down with fine-grade glasspaper if they are rough. Or buy new ones to slot into place. Fix a bent wiper by switching off the ignition to stop it mid-stroke, then grip it with two pairs of pliers to twist it gently until straight.

Tyre tread Examine the tread on tyres regularly. Uneven wear suggests that you should ask your garage to fix the tracking and wheel balance. At the same time, get them to switch tyres front and back to maximise their life.

Antifreeze Top up antifreeze in winter to reduce the risk of emergencies and expensive garage recovery.

Lights Avoid emergency replacements by checking all your lights weekly at dusk and replacing any blown bulbs.

Battery Check the battery regularly. If you need a new one, buy the longest-lasting one your car can take – it'll help prevent problems with the starting, charging and electrical systems and save money in the long run.

Tyre pressure Make sure your tyres are inflated as specified for the car to ensure fuel economy.

Leaks Puddles under your car can be caused by leaking brake fluid, oil or windscreen wiper fluid. To detect problems early, before any really expensive damage has been done, use a small clear or white plastic jug or bowl to catch the leaking fluid and examine it to pinpoint the problem.

SMART MOVES

have called you first. The solution? First, ask friends and neighbours which garage they recommend or, if you're new to the area, use a larger garage that is part of the Retail Motor Industry Federation scheme (ring 08457 58 53 50 ✉ to check). In case of trouble, you'll be able to ask the RMIF to arbitrate.

■ **Work not done** Your car has had its major service, but you're suspicious – did they really do the work? Check the oil – if it's black and dirty, they haven't changed it. Check coolant levels too – if they're low, they haven't done the job properly. Complain to the garage and the council's Trading Standards department (see Resources, page 270), and find a better garage.

CAR CLUBS FOR OCCASIONAL DRIVERS

If you need a car just occasionally – even for as little as an hour at a time – use a nonprofitmaking car club, such as Car Plus (**www.carclubs.org.uk** 0113 234 9299 ✉). Book a car through a central office using the phone or Internet, then pick it up from a designated parking space less than ten minutes' walk from your home or workplace.

■ **Save on car expenses** With a car club, you get access to a car without having to own it, so you save on servicing, maintenance and garaging costs.

■ **Reasonable rates** You pay £100 annual membership plus a £100 returnable deposit, and can hire a car for £2–£3 an hour plus 15p–20p mileage rate including fuel.

■ **Comparing costs** An occasional driver, who needs a car for, say, four weeks during the entire year for outings and holidays, may find it more economical to rent than to buy, particularly over the short term. Total annual costs (including tax, running costs, insurance and petrol) for a Ford Fiesta bought through a leasing deal would be around £3,350. And if the car was bought outright, the annual cost would obviously be much higher in the first year. But renting a car outside London for the same number of days would cost around £980. Even taxis for £20-worth of weekly shopping trips would only add £960 to the bill. Adding the cost of fuel still only brings the total to around £2,100. And you will save on parking costs and fines.

JOIN A CAR POOL

Being part of a car pool can enable you to share costs between several drivers. In some parts of Britain, such as Leeds, you can use special lanes for cars carrying more than one occupant.

■ **Cheaper insurance** The ABI (Association of British Insurers) say that if you are a driver in a car pool scheme, your normal motor insurance still applies – but if you are in any doubt, you should contact your insurance company. Some insurance companies even offer reductions for people in a car pool.

■ **Cheaper parking** Check with your employer or car park operator. They may offer better spaces, discounts or even free spaces for car pool drivers.

■ **Tax breaks** Ask your accountant what you can deduct for car pooling expenses.

---

keep it simple

SAVE ON PARKING COSTS

■ Cut car park costs by investing in a season ticket.

■ Park away from the high street – parking is cheaper or free out of town.

■ Park legally – parking fines of £40 or more can add up to a sizeable bill over the year. If you do get one, pay it promptly as many councils double the charge after a couple of weeks.

■ Save on parking charges – and fines – by using park-and-ride schemes, especially in congested cities.

DIY VALET SERVICE

Keeping your car looking clean and shiny needn't involve expensive trips to the car wash or valet service, or investment in special car-cleaning products. Soapy water, baking soda and vinegar are natural cleaning agents that do an effective job and cost next to nothing.

SAVE MONEY ON DE-ICING

If your windows and windscreen ice up overnight in winter, pour a jug of hot (but not boiling) water over them and switch the wipers on for a few seconds. Any ice that re-forms can then be cleared easily with a scraper, and you'll save on cans of de-icer.

HOMEMADE WINDOW CLEANER

Save money on ready-made window cleaning solutions by mixing warm water with a little white vinegar in a clean spray bottle.

REMOVING INSECTS

Squashed insects on the windscreen and bodywork can be removed simply with one or two cups of baking soda mixed with two cups of warm water in a clean spray bottle. Soak the insects for a couple of minutes, then rinse with a hose, using a sponge to remove the insects.

DEMIST YOUR WINDSCREEN

Buy an inexpensive blackboard rubber for under £1 and keep it under the front seat. It's handy for wiping the windscreen if it gets steamed up.

REMOVING OIL STAINS

Remove oil from the garage floor with white spirit and a layer of cat litter. Once the litter has absorbed the oil, sweep it up and use white spirit on remaining stains.

CLEANING CAR ASHTRAYS

To help eliminate the stale smell of cigarettes, place baking soda or clean cat litter in your car's ashtray.

WASH YOUR CAR YOURSELF

Save up to £5 a week at the car wash by doing the job yourself. Always wash a car in the shade, and when the engine is cool – a hot surface dries the water too fast, leaving unsightly spots.
Rinse the car with a hose to loosen dirt, then turn the tap off to save water. Use one bucket of soapy water – a little dishwasher detergent is fine – and one bucket of clean water. Use the hose again for the final rinse.

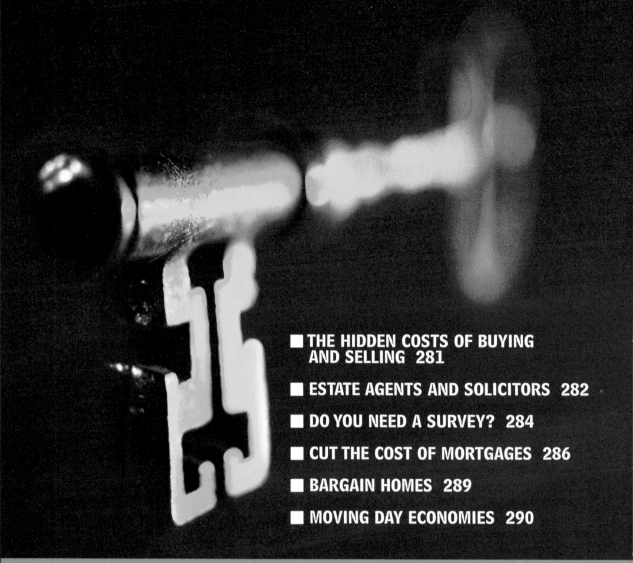

Buying and selling property

Buying a house is the biggest financial transaction
of most people's lives, but it needn't be daunting.
There are plenty of opportunities for saving money
on purchasing, professional fees, mortgages and
moving expenses.

THE HIDDEN COSTS OF BUYING AND SELLING

House buying and selling is an expensive business. Before you even consider the cost of your mortgage, there are fees, taxes and other charges that can run into thousands of pounds. And as house prices rise, costs rise too. The table below shows typical costs, but you can make savings.

TOP TIPS LEARN WHERE YOU CAN SAVE

Although some costs, such as stamp duty, are unavoidable, many other expenses involved in property transactions are variable. You can make considerable savings by good research and doing some of the work yourself.

Explore all options Estate agents' fees vary, so shop around – and even investigate selling your house yourself (see page 282).

No stamp duty Although you normally have to pay stamp duty on properties valued at above £60,000, houses in some disadvantaged areas are free of stamp duty up to a value of £150,000. See **www.inlandrevenue. gov.uk/so/pcode_search.htm** or phone 0845 603 3135 ✉ to find out whether your purchase qualifies.

Cut conveyancing costs Although solicitors' fees vary depending on the amount of work involved, they have recently become more competitive, so it's worth getting several quotes. If the sale is simple and you are good at research and form filling, you can cut costs substantially by doing your own conveyancing (see page 283).

Save on surveys If the property is in good repair, you may not need a full structural survey. Make initial checks yourself to see whether you need an in-depth survey (see page 284).

Cheaper moves Removal firms' charges vary, so be sure to get several quotes, both from your departure point and your destination, as you may find that one is considerably cheaper. You can also save on removal fees by doing some of the work yourself (see page 290).

STAMP ON COSTS

You can't avoid stamp duty, but you can avoid paying more than is necessary.

■ Look for a house priced under the closest stamp duty band limit (see below). A house priced at £250,001 attracts a 3% rate, whereas one priced at £250,000 involves 1% stamp duty.

■ If you are selling, set a price just below the cut-off point to increase its attractiveness to potential purchasers. But beware: don't try to evade stamp duty by cutting the house price and bumping up fixtures and fittings: the Inland Revenue take steps to prevent this.

■ For a free online stamp duty calculator, see the Inland Revenue website: **http://sdcalculator. inlandrevenue.gov.uk**

House value	Stamp duty rate
0-£60,000	0%
£60,001-£250,000	1%
£250,001-£500,000	3%
Over £500,000	4%

Information July 2004

HOW YOU CAN SAVE ON FEES AND TAXES

Estimated cost savings on a property priced at £260,000.

	TYPICAL	COULD REDUCE TO
ESTATE AGENT'S FEE	£6,500 @2.5%	£2,600 by negotiating a 1% fee
STAMP DUTY	£7,800	£2,500 or less by negotiating price below 3% threshold
SOLICITOR'S FEES	£1,500	£750 by going online to find a cheaper solicitor
SURVEYOR	£500	£200 by getting a report and valuation only
REMOVALS	£600	£400 by doing some of the work yourself
TOTAL	£19,150	£8,600 Pay less than half price

ESTATE AGENTS AND SOLICITORS

Professional help, although expensive, can save you worry and hassle when buying and selling your home. But you can save money by negotiating fees. You could cut costs even more by doing your own advertising or conveyancing.

SAVE £4,100 ONLINE

Cut out the estate agent and sign on with an Internet sales site (see Resources, right). Costs are likely to be between £20-£199 for options such as a For Sale board, an online advert and even a virtual tour. HouseWeb (**www.houseweb.co.uk** ✉) estimates that their average customer saves £4,100 by selling this way.

WATCH POINTS SNAGS WHEN SELLING

Be aware of the pitfalls when selling your house, otherwise your money-saving efforts may be counterproductive.
- **The right price** A problem with DIY selling is underpricing. To check that the price you set is reasonable, see **www.upmystreet.com** ✉.
- **Paper money** Newspaper ads give limited exposure, and you might pay £100 for just one week's insertions.
- **Contract length** Do not tie yourself to a long contract with an estate agent in case you want to change agencies.
- **Check the charges** You should be given written details of charges and when they are payable at the outset (see box below).
- **Advertising costs** Some estate agents make additional charges for advertising and For Sale boards.
- **Official bodies** There is a degree of reassurance if your agent is a member of the National Association of Estate Agents ✉, but only membership of the Ombudsman for Estate Agents ✉ scheme offers independent mediation, should you need it.

keep it simple

HOME INFORMATION PACKS: MONEY SAVERS?
- You may be able to attract buyers by paying for a home information pack (HIP). The government plan to make this obligatory in early 2007. They stipulate that the seller must pay for basic survey information – costing up to £500–£600.
- For free information on HIPs go to the website **www.rics.org/public/** ✉ or visit **www.channel4.com** and click on 'Mortgages and homebuying'.

Choose the right agency deal

Estate agents' charges vary from 1% to 4% depending on the deal. As increases in house prices have far outstripped rises in agency costs, you are justified in arguing for the lowest rate.

SMART MOVES

Sole agency This is normally the cheapest option. You make an agreement for a set period. The agent cannot claim commission if you sell privately but if you sell through another agent, both get commission.

Joint sole agency Two agents work for you on a sole agency contract. This is usually a little more expensive than a sole agency agreement.

Multiple agency A number of agents work for you and the one who gets a sale takes the commission. This is often the most successful, and expensive, option.

Sole selling rights The agent gets commission however the house is sold – even if you sell it to a friend or colleague. This is obviously unfair, so avoid it.

'Ready, willing and able purchaser' If the agent finds a purchaser able to buy, commission is payable, even if the sale does not go through. So again, avoid signing agreements that include this type of deal.

TOP TIPS UP YOUR PRICE BY £5,000

You are likely to achieve a quicker, more profitable sale by showing your home in its best light to potential buyers. A well-presented house could add thousands to the selling price.

■ **Declutter** Put into storage any items that make the place look crowded or untidy. The house may look spartan for a while, but a tidy, spacious appearance will attract buyers.

■ **Redecorate** Spruce up any areas that look worn – the cost of a lick of paint and a little elbow grease can add several thousand pounds to a sale. Finish any half-completed DIY jobs – a well-maintained house is always worth more.

■ **Clean and sweeten** Give the entire house a thorough clean, eliminating any pet odours, dust and grime.

■ **Tidy the garden** Do some outdoor housework – make sure the grass and hedges are trimmed and that the flowerbeds look attractive.

■ **Lighten up** Maximise the light in all the rooms by ensuring the windows are sparkling. It may even be worth redecorating in lighter shades to increase the impression of airy spaciousness.

■ **Give rooms a role** The function of each room should be obvious, so make sure a three-bedroom house has three proper bedrooms, for example. If necessary, add a bed to a former junk room or a table to a dining room.

■ **Create a good atmosphere** On the day prospective buyers come to view, add welcoming touches such as vases of fresh flowers, scented candles or a fire in the grate.

DO YOU NEED A SOLICITOR?

Solicitors' fees for conveyancing are one of the major costs in buying and selling property. In theory you can do it yourself. Plenty of help is available on the Internet and through books, and the standard legal forms cost only a few pounds.

DIY drawbacks Although conveyancing is largely a form-filling exercise, a mistake can be costly. Mortgage lenders may not deal with someone who is not legally qualified, or may impose higher charges. If it all goes wrong, you could end up paying a solicitor to sort out your mess.

Shop around If you don't have the courage for DIY, at least take advantage of the competitiveness of the conveyancing market. It is easy to get a range of quotes from the Internet (see Resources, right) or by phone from local firms. Current online quotes to sell a £200,000 house and buy a £250,000 house anywhere in England and Wales range between £620 and £1,100 (each excluding duties and searches of about £3,000). Look out for offers such as nil charges if the transaction does not go through and a guarantee of no extra charges. Note that you may pay around £100 more for leasehold transactions, depending on their complexity.

Go out of town If you live in a major city, get a quote from a solicitor in a more rural area as prices can be much lower.

Fix the price Some solicitors work on a time basis, others may quote a fixed price. Agree the terms at the outset so you know where you stand. If your bill is higher than expected, complain to the firm promptly. If you are not satisfied, contact the Law Society's Consumer Complaints Service ✉ (see Resources, right).

HELPFUL INFORMATION

■ The National Association of Estate Agents website **www.naea.co.uk** is the place to find a local estate agent.

■ The Office of Fair Trading guide, *Using an Estate Agent to Buy/Sell Your Home*, is available at **www.oft.gov.uk** ✉.

■ The *Which?* book, *Buy, Sell and Move House*, is available at **http://shop.which.net** or from bookshops.

■ The *Which?* website at **www.which.co.uk/moveit** ✉ has guides to DIY house-selling.

■ Either check the Ombudsman for Estate Agents website at **www.oea.co.uk** or phone 01722 333306 ✉.

■ You can sell online through sites such as **www.use-the-mouse.com** or **www.houseweb.com** ✉.

■ For advice, try **www.adviceguide.org.uk** ✉, the Citizens' Advice Bureau at **www.citizensadvice.org.uk** ✉ and **www.england. shelter.org.uk** ✉.

■ To find a solicitor, use the Law Society website at **www.lawsoc.org.uk** or phone 020 7242 1222 ✉.

■ Get conveyancing quotes from **www.property-conveyancing -online.co.uk** ✉, **www.britishlaw.net** ✉ and **www.easier2move.co.uk** ✉.

DO YOU NEED A SURVEY?

Fewer than 20% of buyers get a professional structural survey of the house they want to buy. Although this might not prove a problem for most buyers, for others the cost of a survey might have saved them the several thousand pounds they then had to spend on putting structural problems right.

SURVEYS FOR LESS

If you decide on a full survey, make sure you get your money's worth. Ask questions about what will be included, and have the surveyor comment on specific matters of interest, although bear in mind that extra work may add to the cost.

Discounted surveys Your lender's surveyor may accept your commission at a discount by doing the survey at the same time as the lender's valuation report.

Finding a surveyor To find a surveyor consult the Royal Institute of Chartered Surveyors on 0870 333 1600 ✉. Their website **www.rics.org** also has information on surveys.

WATCH POINTS IS A FULL SURVEY NEEDED?

If you are buying any of the following, get a full structural survey to avoid paying to fix problems after the sale. A good survey may mean you can negotiate on the sale price, or decide not to go ahead with a sale at all.

■ A property built before 1900 – it may have developed significant faults over the years.

■ A listed building.

■ A building of unusual construction – a timber-built or thatched house of any age warrants a full survey.

■ A house you plan to renovate or change.

■ A house that has been renovated or altered.

■ A place with obvious problems such as signs of damp, very old electrics or a damaged roof.

Different surveys and their costs

SMART MOVES

REPORT AND VALUATION
Gives a basic description only – the number of rooms and the type of construction. Also gives an estimated valuation.
Cost: Up to about £220.
Needed: Always.
Required by lender.

HOMEBUYERS' SURVEY
Looks at easily visible features – measurements of rooms, any obvious defects or repairs needed such as damp, rot or woodworm. Includes a valuation.
Cost: £400–£500.
Needed: Optional. Highlights obvious problems.

FULL STRUCTURAL SURVEY
Very detailed survey – may lift carpets, look in loft, test electrics and plumbing. Can answer specific questions, such as 'Could we knock down this wall?' No valuation.
Cost: From £500–£1,000+.
Needed: Optional. Shows underlying problems.

GET MONEY OFF THE ASKING PRICE

We're not suggesting that you do your own buildings' survey. But check the following to get an idea of the condition of the property. There are three strong reasons to do this:
■ It may indicate a full survey is needed.
■ You may discover things that will turn out to be costly or persuade you not to go ahead with the purchase.
■ You may find ammunition for getting the seller to drop the price, so don't be put off by problems. Cost the repairs carefully by calling in a specialist and estimating any inconvenience costs. Show your calculations to the vendor and lower your offer.

WHERE?	WHAT'S THE PROBLEM?	CALL A SURVEYOR
OUTSIDE		
WALLS AND ROOF	■ Is the brickwork in good repair? Cracks could indicate subsidence. ■ Crumbling mortar? The walls might need an expensive repointing job. ■ Is the roof in good order? Damaged slates could indicate leaks. ■ Are gutters and drains damaged or blocked? ■ Are the windows in good order – or will they need replacing? REDUCE YOUR OFFER BY £1,000–£10,000	✔ ✔ ✔
THE GARDEN	■ Who is responsible for the hedges and fences? (See the deeds.) ■ Are there fences? If not, you may have to pay for them. ■ Might those large trees close to the house cause subsidence? REDUCE YOUR OFFER BY £500–£1,000	✔
INSIDE		
DECOR	■ Is the decor dated, extreme, or very shabby? Don't dismiss the cost and disruption of redecorating the whole place. ■ Could that brand new redecorating be an attempt to hide defects? REDUCE YOUR OFFER BY £4,000–£5,000	
ELECTRICS AND PLUMBING	■ Can you trust old-style switches and obvious DIY wiring? Definitely not. ■ Ask to run the taps. Do they work? How long does it take for the hot water to come through? You may inherit problems. REDUCE YOUR OFFER BY £1,000–£4,000	✔ ✔
WALLS AND CEILINGS	■ Do those ceiling stains indicate leaks? If so there are probably plumbing or roof problems. ■ Are those cracks just settlement or something more sinister? ■ Is that musty smell damp? And is the wood panelling covering defects? REDUCE YOUR OFFER BY £2,000–£10,000	✔ ✔
RUNNING EXPENSES		
BILLS	■ Are fuel bills, council tax or insurance very expensive? Check the cost of running the house. REDUCE YOUR OFFER BY £500–£1,000	
GENERAL UPKEEP	■ How much will the beech hedge surrounding the large garden cost to cut each year? It could be over £300. ■ Do you realise a thatched roof will need replacing every 15–20 years – and could cost from £15,000–£20,000. ■ Are you prepared for the maintenance costs of that swimming pool? REDUCE YOUR OFFER BY £300–£20,000	✔
LOCAL KNOWLEDGE	■ Check on possible problems such as noise nuisance from traffic. Chat to the neighbours or check out the local council website. Visit **www.upmystreet.com** ✉ or another site for local information.	

CUT THE COST OF MORTGAGES

A mortgage is a means of borrowing money to finance a property purchase. As with any other loan, you have to pay interest to the lender until the loan is repaid. Mortgages are available from sources such as banks, building societies, Internet lenders and specialist mortgage companies.

FINDING THE BEST MORTGAGE

You can find out about available mortgages through specialist magazines or the Internet and approach the lender direct, or ask a broker to find you the right deal.

A better deal? Brokers should trawl the whole market for you and point out the pros and cons of different loans. They may also get cheaper deals than you could by going direct.

Avoid fees Some – including most big brokers – charge fees, amounting to as much as 1% of the mortgage, or £1,500 on a £150,000 mortgage. You can haggle over fees and maybe

---

Know your mortgages

REPAYMENT
You pay some capital and some interest with each monthly payment, until the whole loan is paid off at the end of the term (usually 25 years).
Good for: Steady and reliable repayment of the whole mortgage.

FLEXIBLE
Mortgages that allow for changing circumstances. You may be able to make overpayments or underpayments without penalty.
Good for: Borrowers whose financial status may change significantly.

TRACKER
The rate varies, but is fixed at a certain level above or below the Bank of England base rate.
Good for: Housebuyers who want to benefit from any drops in the base rate.

DISCOUNT
For a specified term, you pay interest at a discount on the lender's standard variable rate (SVR), after which you pay at the SVR. Redemption penalties may apply.
Good for: People who want to benefit from lower rates at the start.

FIXED
The interest rate is fixed for a period – usually five or ten years. Redemption penalties usually apply.
Good for: Buyers worried by rising rates who need security at the start.

INTEREST ONLY
Your monthly payment covers interest only, leaving the capital outstanding at the end of the loan. In order to pay off the capital at maturity, you take out a savings plan (ISA, pension or life policy) at the start of the term. This, in theory, should grow enough to

cover the capital. But endowment mortgages – a type of interest-only mortgage using a life policy – have been controversial in recent years as many policyholders have ended up with a shortfall at the end of the term.
Good for: Risk takers. Can be cheaper than a repayment and may even result in a lump sum at the end.

OFFSET ACCOUNT
Your current or savings account and your mortgage are combined in one account. When money (such as your salary) goes into your current or savings account, it reduces the overall debt, so you pay less interest. This can allow the mortgage to be paid off more quickly.
Good for: Buyers with healthy current or savings account who don't object to being tied to a particular bank.

PAY LESS ON YOUR MORTGAGE?

TYPE OF MORTGAGE	INTEREST RATE %	MONTHLY REPAYMENT	TOTAL PAYABLE OVER TERM
Offset Tracker (assumes £15,000 savings held)	Base rate + 0.8	£602.20	£180,883
3% discount over 2 years	3.24	£486.79	£194,029
Fixed 5 years	5.84	£721.24	£196,939
Standard variable rate	6.24	£659.05	£198,163

Figures show details for a £100,000 repayment mortgage over 25 years (Norwich & Peterborough Building Society, July 2004)

ASK YOURSELF

IS IT WORTH SWITCHING OFTEN TO GET THE BEST DEAL?
■ It may be. Keep your eye on prevailing market rates compared to what you are paying.

DO REDEMPTION PENALTIES APPLY?
■ Redemption penalties will probably mean it is not worth switching more often than every two or three years.

WILL I PROLONG MY MORTGAGE?
■ If you start a new 25-year mortgage each time you switch, you are postponing the day when you pay off your loan.

get a reduction, but it is far better to choose a broker who doesn't charge a fee.

Compare rates yourself You can see from the mortgage examples above that the lowest initial repayment rate does not necessarily result in the cheapest mortgage overall, and a dramatic difference in the interest rate at the outset may not make a big difference to the total cost. The offset tracker mortgage in the table is cheapest because interest is calculated daily and so can immediately reflect any drop in the interest rate. If the calculation is monthly, or even yearly, it will not reflect a lower interest rate for a long while, so you end up paying more. But, if interest rates rise, daily calculation will reflect these faster too.

WATCH POINTS BEWARE HIDDEN COSTS

Don't be seduced by lenders' advertising. Seemingly attractive deals may not necessarily suit your circumstances.

■ **Cash costs** A number of lenders now offer cashbacks – a percentage cash refund each year. These are appealing but you may have to pay an uncompetitive interest rate and face big redemption penalties that make the deal less attractive.

■ **Large mortgages** Some lenders add a charge, known as a mortgage indemnity guarantee (MIG), for large mortgages. Avoid deals that carry this extra expense.

■ **Insure cheaply** Lenders may try to persuade you to buy their house insurance. You are likely to get it cheaper if you shop around.

■ **Expensive moves** Beware of redemption penalties if you move your mortgage during the penalty period. These range from £150 to 3–6 months' repayments, or as much as 6% of the outstanding balance.

SAVE MONEY WITH 'SWITCH AND SAVE'

If you have had your mortgage for several years and are paying your lender's SVR (standard variable rate), you can save thousands of pounds by switching to a cheaper deal.

HAS YOUR DISCOUNT RUN OUT?

This simple question could slash thousands off your mortgage. Although your discounted mortgage may have been a good deal to start with, you can save by switching as soon as the discount period has ended. The table below shows that a borrower paying 6% could save £116.46 a month by moving to a two-year discounted 4% deal, which is a saving of £2,795 over the discount period.

Change lenders Your existing lender may make a better offer, but mortgage companies are typically keener to bring in new borrowers than to keep existing borrowers happy with low rates. You are more likely to get a worthwhile deal by switching to a new lender.

Avoid charges When you switch, you pay off the existing mortgage and take out a new one. This entails a number of charges, so find a lender who will pay them to entice customers who are just switching loans rather than moving.

WATCH POINTS SWITCHING COSTS

Before you rush into switching your mortgage, check to see whether you will really save.

■ **Short-lived savings** Most really cheap deals are for a short period, say two years. They may carry big penalties to make it harder for you to move again.

■ **Total charges** There will be a valuation charge (£220) and legal costs (£350), and there may also be a discharge fee from your existing lender (£100) and a booking fee on a fixed rate mortgage (£300). This all adds up to nearly £1,000, or 1% of a £100,000 mortgage – a percentage which will seriously reduce the benefit of a rate switch, although some deals will pay for all of these.

■ **Rates vs fees** The larger your mortgage, the less significant the fees will be in percentage terms. Someone with a big mortgage might save more by switching to a low rate and paying fees, while a smaller borrower could find it more cost-effective to go for an interest rate that is not as low but where one-off costs are paid by the lender.

■ **Find the alternatives** Shopping around is crucial. Even if you use a broker, ask them to look at several deals.

■ **The right deal** While you are going to the trouble and cost of switching, think whether a different type of mortgage would benefit you too – repayment rather than interest only perhaps, or offset rather than conventional.

RESOURCES

MORTGAGE COSTS

The Internet is a good starting point for finding information on mortgages, and many sites offer calculators to work out how much you can borrow and what your mortgage will cost.

■ Look at **www.lcplc.co.uk** (fee-free broker) ✉, **www.fool.co.uk** ✉ or **www.charcolonline.co.uk** ✉.

■ Financial data publisher MoneyFacts offers a daily update on top deals, available by fax on 090 60760701 (calls cost 75p a minute max).

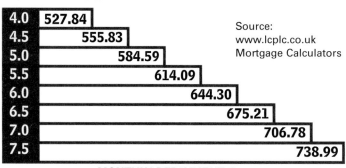

EFFECTS OF INTEREST RATE CHANGES

£100,000 repayment mortgage over 25 years

INTEREST RATE %

4.0	527.84
4.5	555.83
5.0	584.59
5.5	614.09
6.0	644.30
6.5	675.21
7.0	706.78
7.5	738.99

Source: www.lcplc.co.uk Mortgage Calculators

MONTHLY REPAYMENT £

BARGAIN HOMES

If you are not in a position to spend vast sums of money on becoming a home owner, or are simply looking for a good buy, then try your luck at an auction or go for a property that other buyers find unattractive.

TOP TIPS BUYING CHEAPER AT AUCTION

■ **Make a dry run** Attend an auction first as a practice outing to get a feel for how it works and pick up tips on how to do it. Learn the jargon: the reserve price is the minimum price the seller will accept, and the guide price is what the auctioneer thinks the house might fetch.

■ **Hold back on professional fees** Only pay the legal and surveying costs on a property on which you are reasonably sure of making a successful bid. If you are unsuccessful, the pre-sale costs of several hundred pounds will be wasted.

■ **Don't underestimate** Do not assume you will pay less than in a normal sale. There are many types of property for sale at auction, from well-presented houses and flats to barn conversions and even former churches – not just repossessed and dilapidated houses.

■ **Plan ahead** Start getting auction catalogues, issued three weeks before the sale. You can buy them from the auctioneers (the Royal Institute of Chartered Surveyors' ✉ website has a list, plus useful FAQs at **www.rics.org/ help/faq/auctions.html**). There are also subscription services with details of sales nationwide at **www.eigroup.co.uk** (0870 112 3040) ✉ and **www.property-auctions.net** (01772 621909) ✉.

■ **Have a mortgage offer in place** Don't miss out on a bargain by failing to apply for a mortgage first. You must have an offer in hand when you turn up at the sale.

■ **Get the right house** At the sale, double-check the lot number and catalogue number – otherwise you might buy the wrong house.

BUY ON A BUDGET

Joint purchase One option is to buy jointly with a friend. You will need to be 'tenants in common' rather than the 'joint tenants' arrangement which is more usual between couples. This makes things easier should one of you die. You will also need to have an arrangement which sets out how the property is owned and a legal agreement about what is to happen if one of you wants to sell.

Shorter leases You could look for a flat which has only a short lease outstanding. Most flats start with a 99-year lease, but mortgage lenders may lend on shorter leases, down to about 50 years. Once you have lived in the flat for two years you could get a 90-year replacement lease. Landlords are obliged to grant these on many properties. You will need to increase your mortgage in order to pay for the replacement lease – maybe another £15,000 on a flat which cost £120,000 at the outset. Use a solicitor who specialises in short-lease properties. Don't forget to renew the lease after two years, otherwise, you could find the place hard to sell.

---

keep it simple

MAKE AN OFFER
Houses can be sold privately before an auction sale – so if you are keen you could try making a pre-sale offer through the auctioneer. Or, if the lot fails to make its reserve and is not sold, try approaching the auctioneer after the sale with an offer.

ADVENTUROUS HOMEOWNING

Steer clear of the conventional approach and go for properties or situations that might not appeal to the average home buyer.

■ Try to anticipate current trends and buy in an area that is up-and-coming but not yet fashionable.

■ Learn to see the potential in apparently undesirable properties – smells can be banished, and a little DIY can solve many problems.

MOVING DAY ECONOMIES

Whether you use a professional mover or do it yourself, you can make big savings if you know the ropes.

CHOOSE A CHEAPER MOVER

When selecting a removal firm, get several quotes. Decide where you are prepared to economise.

Shop around A range of quotes on a fairly standard move can vary by around £200. You can get different quotes from Internet sites such as **www.reallymoving.com** ✉. If you live in a big city, consider hiring a company from an outlying area – it will sometimes be cheaper.

Agree a price Expect to pay several hundred pounds for a professional removal firm. The total will depend on the firm, how many possessions you have, how far you have to go and whether anything needs special handling. A typical bill is around £600; negotiate a lower price by agreeing to handle some special items yourself.

Move early in the week Removal firms are less busy then, and you may get a cheaper rate. Avoid Fridays, which are the busiest days for removals.

Book as early as you can Some firms charge more for bookings made at short notice.

Provide parking Make sure a parking space has been cleared as near your house as possible. Costs may rise if movers have to park at a distance.

Check professional associations If possible, choose a firm that is a member of the British Association of Removers (BAR). Ignore logos of other organisations shown on removers' advertising: some are not worth much, and the industry is not regulated.

HITCH A LIFT

The free online service **www.reallymoving.com** ✉ offers a mini-move. This lets you take advantage of the fact that many removal lorries are travelling around the country with spare capacity. If you don't have a huge number of items to move, you can use this service to find a removal firm that is already travelling to your destination and will offer a competitive price for including your move.

TOP TIPS PAY LESS FOR MOVERS

- **Declutter first** Don't pay to move things you don't want in the new house. Take them to charity shops or ask special furniture charities to pick them up. You could also make some money selling items at a car boot or garage sale.
- **Save £200 on packing up** If you're using a professional removals firm, you can save money by handling some or all of the packing yourself. Certain firms, such as Pickfords, offer a range of packing services, from delicate items only to everything in the house – the difference between services is around £200.
- **Save £70 on packaging** You can also save by buying your own packing materials. Some companies offer complete kits containing self-

SAVE £600 ON DELAYS

Ask the removal firm whether extra charges apply if there are delays on the day – some charge double in such circumstances.

SAVE £100 ON INSURANCE

Don't pay for special insurance from the remover if your contents are covered under your normal household policy. If not, consider moving small valuable items yourself, under existing insurance.

assembly boxes, bubble wrap and tape for £30–£70. Alternatively, you could use old newspapers for wrapping, and linen or towels for protecting valuables.

■ **Get free boxes** For no-cost packing boxes, visit your local supermarket. The vehicle hire firm, Practical Car & Van Rental, recommend Sainsbury's banana boxes, as they stack, have handles and are free.

■ **Move your own garden tools** In addition to transporting small valuables under your own insurance, consider moving the contents of your garden shed or garage yourself and storing them at your new address. Obviously this only makes sense if you are moving nearby and your seller has some space in the garage which he will agree to let you use. Make sure the storage area is secure, particularly if you are storing valuable items.

GO THE DIY ROUTE

With a little forethought, preparation and elbow grease, big savings can be made by shunning the professionals and moving all your possessions yourself. If you or a friend are happy driving a 35-cwt van, and you can rally the troops to help you lug your wardrobe downstairs, it is perfectly feasible. By using a cheap but reliable van rental service (preferably one that has been recommended), making as few trips as possible and travelling at off-peak times, you are sure to save a small fortune.

Van hire Costs will depend on the size of van and the length of time you want to keep it, so try to keep both to a minimum, but be realistic. Get a quote first, and check that this is actually the amount you will pay; petrol and other expenses may be added. You will need to show your driving licence so don't send it off to the DVLC to have the address changed before moving day.

Use the Internet Compare costs of van hire and find a competitive quote. Big-name companies in city centres will cost more than independent hire places outside the city. A well-known van hire company in Edinburgh charged £126 for two days, whereas an independent hire company outside the city quoted £55 for the same period.

RESOURCES

GET THE BEST PRICES

■ To find a range of quotes on moving, including mini-moves use **www.reallymoving. com** ✉.

■ The British Association of Removers lists removal firms at **www.removers.org.uk** or phone 020 8861 3331 ✉.

■ For a big removals firm with a range of packing services, try Pickfords at **www.pickfords.co.uk** ✉.

■ To hire a van suitable for removals, try Practical Car & Van Rental at **www.practical.co.uk** or phone 0121 772 8599 ✉.

■ Buy your own packing materials online at **www.bigbrownbox.co.uk** ✉, **www.theboxstore.co.uk** ✉, **www.removalboxes.org** ✉.

Savings on the day

Use common sense to make sure you don't lose out on moving day.

Have a moving party Get your friends to help with carrying boxes and any last-minute packing.

Take it away Remove everything that you are not contractually obliged to leave behind, within reason. Don't forget ornaments, pot plants, curtain rails and screw fittings. Make a last-minute check in lofts and cellars.

Switch off Don't end up paying for utilities that your buyers will end up using – notify all the relevant companies. The website **www.iammoving.com** ✉ makes this easier by automating the process. Take a final reading of all meters and turn everything off before you leave.

Switch on Changing utilities suppliers could get you a cheaper deal. Check **www.energylinx.co.uk** ✉.

Are you at the mercy of your household bills? It doesn't have to be like that. You can cut hefty slices out of what you pay for your fuel, telephone service, insurance and even water. Instead of being a passive consumer, you can take control.

Household finance

BALANCING THE BOOKS

Get a clear picture of your household finances by putting together a budget showing your income and expenditure (see overleaf). If you find you are overspending, the good news is that, by shopping around, you can save at least 10% on household expenses such as utilities and telephone bills without noticing any difference to your lifestyle.

IMPROVE CASH FLOW – SAVE £30 A MONTH

Every time you go overdrawn at the bank it can cost you as much as £9.50, plus the interest charges you incur – as much as 33.8% on an unauthorised overdraft. If three standing orders take your account unexpectedly overdrawn, bank charges of over £30 will be levied. Make a budget to see all your outgoings clearly, and time the payment of your bills to coincide with money coming in to your account.

SETTLE YOUR BILLS TO SUIT YOU

Notice when your utility bills – gas, electricity, phone, water – arrive and see if the timing suits you. Perhaps you've been receiving your quarterly telephone bills just when your bank

ALLOW FOR SAVINGS

When you are working out your budget, bear in mind that the recommended savings rate is 10% of your take-home pay. If you aren't achieving this, you may be ill-prepared for future expenses.

CASE STUDY

REGAINING CONTROL

Londoners Richard and Caroline Stanswick, 38 and 33, both worked in the banking industry. But their joint current account was regularly overdrawn by much more than they'd reckoned on. Before pay day, they would often be more than £1,000 in the red. 'We both knew we had to sort it out,' says Richard.

Looking at past bank statements, Caroline added up how much the couple had paid in overdraft fees and interest. It came to £156 in one year alone.

'It was such a waste!' she says. 'But it finally prompted us to work out what was going wrong.' The couple set everything out on paper – how much money they had coming in and how much they'd been spending based on their habits over the last six months.

'The whole thing made us aware of how we were throwing money away by failing to plan,' says Caroline.

At the same time, the couple switched their electricity and gas supply to a cheaper provider and plumped for a lower cost phone service. Within three months, they were managing to spend

well within their monthly income of £3,650, saving around £150 a year in overdraft interest, £180 in energy costs and an estimated £200 in phone charges.

balance is at its weakest. In this case, set up monthly direct debits. Having a regular amount coming out of your account just after you get paid will give you much more control over your expenditure and is the first step towards cutting back.

THE ADVANTAGES OF DIRECT DEBIT

When you pay by direct debit, you benefit from your supplier's money-off policy for this method of payment. You could get as much as £50 off if you buy both gas and electricity from the same supplier. If you don't already pay

SMART MOVES

Work out a monthly budget

Make your household budget in four easy steps. Being able to list all your debits and credits will make it much easier for you to analyse and control what you spend and when you are spending it.

1 TOTAL INCOME

Add up all the money that you can expect to receive during the month. Note when it goes into your account so that you can better plan when you make various payments.

- Regular pay cheques and bonuses, or pension payments
- Part-time or freelance income
- Interest
- Dividends
- Other income such as rent on properties, benefit payments or income from a trust

2 FIXED EXPENSES

Next, total all the regular payments you make during the month.

- Mortgage or rent
- Electricity, gas, water
- Home telephone
- Insurance: home, contents and car
- Insurance: life, medical, income protection
- Internet service, cable or satellite dish
- Mobile phone
- Pension, savings, investments
- Debt payments such as car loans or other hire purchase
- Commuting expenses
- Memberships and subscriptions

3 VARIABLE EXPENSES

Now add up all the payments you make that vary from month to month.

- Food, beverages, household products
- Car maintenance: petrol, oil, upkeep
- Home maintenance and improvement
- Furnishings, appliances
- Clothing
- Personal grooming
- Recreation: eating out, sports and cultural events, movies
- Holidays
- Gifts and contributions
- Health care not covered by insurance

4. THE MOMENT OF TRUTH

Subtract all your fixed and variable expenditure from your total monthly income. If you spot any problems, see where savings can be made or how cash flow can be improved. This chapter will show you how to cut at least **10%** from your electricity, gas, home telephone and insurance bills alone; look in the Index for hundreds of ways to make more savings every month.

Even if your budget is not tight, any excess cash floating around in your current account can be put to better use in a high-interest savings account.

So it pays to have firm control of your monthly finances, and a detailed budget is the only way to do that.

your utility bills by monthly direct debit, it is a good idea to switch for this reason. And, of course, your suppliers want you to agree to this pre-arranged payment as it makes business more predictable for them.

Regular income, regular payments If you have a regular monthly income, then having your bills paid each month – and at a predictable, year-round level – will help you to keep on top of your money matters and avoid overspending.

BENEFITS OF PAYING QUARTERLY

If you can easily handle the quarterly bills when they arrive, there is an advantage in staying with this method of payment.

Earn some interest By paying your bills quarterly, you can hang on to your money for slightly longer before handing it over to the utility companies. In this way you can take advantage of your bank or building society's interest rates.

Get tax-free interest Save by keeping the money set aside for your bills in a tax-free ISA (Individual Savings Account). If you usually spend £180 a quarter on electricity, but you kept this amount in a tax-free ISA, it could earn £8 a quarter in interest. This gives you an idea how much value there is in holding onto your money for as long as you can.

ESTIMATED BILLS

It's tempting, if you get an estimated gas or electricity bill, to call the freephone number and give your actual meter reading to the company. But you can be clever about this.

Free credit If the estimated reading is below your actual reading, isn't the company actually giving you free credit? As long as you can afford the higher bill that will come when they do read the meter, why not let it lie for a while? If they're charging you over £40 less than you really owe them, that means about £2 in interest for you over that quarter. And another £2 next quarter if they still don't come to read your meter. It may not be much, but it all adds up.

ARE YOU PAYING TOO MUCH?

You should still monitor your bills once a direct debit has been arranged to make sure that the amount you're paying isn't too high. If this is the case, you will have built up a credit, which most suppliers do not repay automatically. You will need to request a refund and adjust your direct debit accordingly. Some suppliers do refund the credit automatically, but only when it reaches around £150.

CHOOSING A FUEL SUPPLIER

In the late 1990s, the government broke the monopolies on the provision of electricity and gas. Before that, you didn't have any choice about who sold you either form of energy – it had to be the local provider. Now you can choose – and save up to £150 a year in the process.

SWITCHING SUPPLIERS

There are now around 70 licensed suppliers of gas and electricity in Britain. The fuel suppliers are in sharp competition with each other, leading to lower prices for the consumer. The pipes and cables running into your house may be owned by a separate company from the one supplying your energy, so you don't need any new pipework or wiring to switch providers.

Shop around The supplier you choose can be based at the other end of the country. For example, a couple in Kent could buy their electricity from ScottishPower if they happened to offer the cheapest deal.

Which company should you choose? Ask friends and neighbours which suppliers they use for gas and electricity. Find out if they made any savings when they switched and if they are satisfied with the service.

Check the Internet The Internet is the best place to get information about how much less you could be paying for your energy. There are several websites that give detailed price comparisons (see Resources, left), which will vary depending on your postcode and the amount of energy your household uses. Often these sites will switch you online, although you will have to sign paperwork at a later stage.

 **RESOURCES**

COMPARE PRICES
■ The following websites will help you to compare prices and switch energy suppliers:
www.uswitch.com
www.unravelit.com
www.ukpower.co.uk
www.switchandgive.com
www.theenergyshop.co.uk
■ Ofgem is the regulator for the gas and electricity industries.
Phone 020 7901 7000 or fax 020 7901 7066 or go to www.ofgem.gov.uk ✉.

CUT YOUR ELECTRICITY BILL

If a family spends £430 a year on electricity with their current tariff with Southern Electric, they could save the amounts shown below by changing their supplier.

SUPPLIER	SAVING
SCOTTISH POWER (Online Energy No Standing Charge plan)	£105.73
BASIC POWER (Standard plan)	£102.77
SCOTTISH POWER (Green plan)	£89.93
SWALEC (Standard plan)	£78.21
VIRGIN HOME ENERGY (Standard plan)	£62.23
POWERGEN (Age Concern plan)	£60.00
GREEN ENERGY UK (Green Energy 10 plan)	£54.91

Information: uswitch.com, 2004

CASE STUDY

AN OFFER THEY COULDN'T REFUSE

Sandy and Gill McBain had bought their electricity supply from Scottish Hydro-Electric for years. In Aberdeen, many of their friends did the same. But a year ago, when a work colleague of Sandy's mentioned he'd saved money by changing to another company, Sandy did some research into the matter.

'We found out that we could save £76 by hopping over to British Gas – paying £374 instead of the £450 we were shelling out at the time. If we'd been using gas too, we were told we would save another £134 a year. But Scottish Power had a better service rating, so we went with them instead.'

The savings still added up to around £70 a year. Then, a few weeks ago, the McBains were contacted by their old supplier. Did they want a special deal for returning customers? They'd have no standing charge

to pay and an even lower tariff than with ScottishPower. So they switched back and saved even more.

'Staying faithful to one company really doesn't pay,' says Sandy.

CHANGE YOUR PLAN

When you've done your research and got a good idea of how much less you could be paying, have a word with your current energy provider.

Same company, different plan Some companies have ten or more different plans and may be able to offer you a different plan from the one you're on that will match the savings you would make if you switched. So you can benefit from the savings without the bother of forms to sign and a different bill format to get used to.

Other benefits Some energy providers offer plans that include benefits such as no standing charge, or give Air Miles or other incentives.

ELECTRICITY FOR NIGHT OWLS

If you can organise your household to use power-hungry appliances such as washing machines and dishwashers at night by putting them on a timer, you could cut up to three-quarters off your electricity bill.

Change to a cheaper tariff Electricity companies in Britain offer cheap rate power for seven hours during the night – for this reason, these cheaper tariffs are called Economy 7. If you change to Economy 7, you pay around a quarter of the normal unit price for power used at night, depending on the supplier. Typically, the tariff applies between 1am and 8am. Even if you use only 20% of your electricity between those times, it is probably worth switching to Economy 7.

QUALITY OF SERVICE

Most of the websites give star ratings for the quality of service provided by the energy suppliers. It may be worth paying attention to this. But as long as you don't tie yourself into a long-term contract, you can easily switch to another supplier if you're dissatisfied. On the other hand, if you are prepared to sign up for a certain period, you may get an even better deal on the energy you buy.

DISHWASHER'S RINSE-AND-HOLD CYCLE

Use it only when dishes must be held overnight and odours may result. Use the lightest washing cycle for dishes that aren't very dirty. It uses less hot water and energy.

RUN ONLY FULL LOADS

Use your dishwasher and washing machine only if there is a full load. These appliances are some of the most energy-intensive in your home.

CHECK YOUR CISTERNS EVERY THREE MONTHS

Faulty ball or float valves in toilets and header tanks waste water.

SAVE WATER AND ENERGY

Conserving heat and light is where you can make some big savings – at least 15% on your yearly fuel bill, or £91.50 on an average bill of £610 for a family of four. If you have a water meter or switch to the metering system, you can save even more money every day.

DON'T DRAIN BATHWATER IN WINTER

Wait until it's cooled. You've paid to heat the water, so it might as well heat your house for as long as possible.

FIT A SAVE-A-FLUSH

This water-saving device saves 1 litre (2 pints) of water every time you flush. It costs about £1 and could save you 10% on your water bill.

USE A BUCKET OF WATER TO WASH YOUR CAR

Save water when cleaning your car by using a bucket of soapy water and a sponge rather than a hosepipe. Or use the hose briefly just to rinse off the soap.

USE A BOWL

When washing up or preparing vegetables in the sink, don't let the tap run.

FIX DRIPPING TAPS

A tap losing one drop of water a second will waste 15 litres (3 gallons) a day – at a cost of more than £40 a year.

TAKE A SHOWER

A quick shower uses 20% of the water a bath does, but watch out – power showers use about the same amount of hot water as a bath.

KEEP A JUG UNDER THE SINK

When you have to run water to get it hot, use a plastic jug to catch the water instead of letting it go down the drain. Use it for your houseplants or humidifier.

KEEP COOL WATER IN A COVERED JUG

Put the jug in the fridge so you don't have to run the tap for a long time to get a cold drink. Change the water every day.

USE THE OVERRIDE

Override your central-heating timer whenever you think the heating is unnecessary.

TURN DOWN YOUR THERMOSTAT

Just one degree lower cuts heating bills by 10p in the pound.

STANDBY COSTS MONEY

TVs, DVDs, sound systems and especially computers all use electricity on standby. Get in the habit of switching them off and save £10 a year.

TURN YOUR CENTRAL HEATING OFF HALF AN HOUR EARLY

The house will stay warm until you are in bed. In an average 3-bed semi you'll save £10-£12 a year.

USE A PLUG-IN LIGHT

If you have small children who like the light on at night, use this money-saving option.

BLOCK CHIMNEYS

If you're not using your fireplace, block the chimney with newspaper to prevent heat loss.

CLOSE YOUR FRIDGE DOOR QUICKLY

Stop cold air escaping. And never put hot food straight into the fridge.

SWITCH OFF ELECTRICAL ITEMS AT THE WALL

Many use some electricity if they're still connected, even when switched off. So don't use the microwave as a clock – a battery-powered clock uses less power and the batteries last over two years.

SWITCH OFF HEATING APPLIANCES

Switch off an iron a few minutes before you stop using it. Heating devices use more power than anything else.

REDUCE YOUR HOT WATER TEMPERATURE

Turn it down to 60°C (140°F) and save between £10 and £20 a year.

TURN OFF LIGHTS

Get your family into the habit of turning off electrical devices when they leave a room.

CLOSE YOUR CURTAINS

Stop heat escaping, especially if you don't have double-glazed windows.

THE BEST PRICES FOR OIL AND SOLID FUEL

The market for heating oil and solid fuels is smaller and less competitive than for gas and electricity, but there are still considerable savings to be made.

SAVING ON HEATING OIL

If you use oil to heat your home, you've always been able to shop around. But are you making the most of that freedom?

Phone around When your oil tank is getting low, don't just order your next supply from the company you used last time. Phone around to find the cheapest price – and save as much as £18 on a 1,250 litre (275 gallon) domestic tank.

Check money-off vouchers If your usual supplier has sent you a money-off voucher to keep your custom, factor this into your calculation, although it won't necessarily make their oil any cheaper for you than the most competitive price from your ring-around. By shopping around like this, you can easily save £15 on a £200 tank of oil.

Put in a big order Wait until your oil tank is low before ordering more fuel – you get a cheaper rate for orders over 1,000 litres (220 gallons). But don't let it run out altogether or you could face a £60 bill from a heating engineer for bleeding the air out of your boiler.

Club together with neighbours It's not usually feasible to have a very large domestic tank as they're expensive and tougher environmental regulations will apply – which spells even more cost for you. But you can club together with neighbours to order your oil together. If you can order 5,000 litres (1,100 gallons) at a time between, say, five households, you'll each save around 7% on the cost of your oil.

Start your own co-op If there is no one already running this type of co-op for ordering oil, take the initiative and start one yourself. If you get ten households on your list, you could be ordering 10,000 litres (2,200 gallons) at a time. And the more people you have on your list, the less it will matter if some don't need to join the order each time.

USE THE YELLOW PAGES FOR OIL AND COAL

Forget web-based research when you're shopping for heating oil and solid fuel. Your old friend, the Yellow Pages, is your best resource.

Heating oil Turn to the 'Oil Fuel Distributors' listing and circle the numbers of five suppliers. Tell them how much oil you want to buy, and how soon you need it, and ask for their best price. This will be a per-litre price. Then ask if there are any discounts available.

Coal Prices for coal vary more widely between suppliers than heating oil prices – even more reason to shop around. As with oil, the Yellow Pages are your best starting point for checking prices. Choose five local coal merchants and phone around for the best price. Do the same each time your bunker is nearly down to the base and you could save yourself around £20 on ½ tonne of house coal.

keep it simple

STOCK UP FOR WINTER
Coal and other solid fuels are cheaper in summer, so think ahead. By buying between June and September, you can typically pay £4 a tonne less than if you leave it until the autumn.

CHEAPER CHATTING

Competition in the telecoms market has become intense – and it's a money-saving boost for you. Where BT once stood alone, there are now hundreds of companies vying for your custom, which means more choice and a cheaper service.

CHANGE YOUR LINE SUPPLIER

There are only three major phone line providers – BT, NTL and Telewest. If a cable network exists where you live check their prices for installation, line rental and calls. While BT is now forced to let other companies operate its lines – so you can have a BT line but use another company for your calls – NTL or Telewest customers have to use their tariffs.

TV and Internet deals NTL and Telewest offer some competitive deals when you use them for multi-channel TV and the Internet. But they tend to be very expensive for calling mobiles. Check all the services you use most.

CHANGE YOUR CALL SERVICE PROVIDER

Changing your phone line supplier is not always feasible. There may not be a good alternative service where you live, or its deals could be tied in with a cable TV or Internet service that you're not interested in. Perhaps you just don't want to change your phone number. But there is another option that doesn't require the installation of new wires in your house. You simply arrange for all your calls to be routed through another phone company. The technical term for this is 'Carrier Pre Select' (CPS). When making local calls, you might have to dial the STD code as well. But apart from that, everything should be the same. You simply instruct the new company to take over your calls.

Work out savings in advance Every company has a different charging structure. Where some types of call may be cheaper, others are more expensive. If you frequently make calls to mobile phones, your bill will rocket unless your service provider offers a good deal on calls to mobiles. If you find that you're not satisfied with the new service, you can always switch back to BT, or to another company.

RESOURCES

MAJOR LINE PROVIDERS
BT
Dial 150 from a BT line or visit **www.bt.com** ✉.
NTL
For national sales enquiries phone 0800 183 0123 or visit **www.ntl.com** ✉.
Telewest
For enquiries phone 0800 953 0002 or visit **www.telewest.co.uk** ✉.
■ For best value telephone services, log onto **www.moneysavingexpert. com** or **www.uswitch.com**

SMART MOVES

Which package?

The various packages offered by different call providers can be confusing. But it's worth battling on through them to find the best one. Most of them tend to follow BT's discount packages:

Basic: No monthly fee, but high call costs.
Fixed call cost option: Reduced cost daytime calls; evening and weekend calls at a set price, e.g. BT Together Option 1 (£2 a month).
Inclusive evening and weekend calls: Reduced cost

daytime calls; local and national calls in the evening and at the weekend are inclusive, e.g. BT Together Option 2 (£8 a month).
Inclusive UK calls 24 hours a day: All calls to UK landlines are inclusive, e.g. BT Together Option 3 (£19 a month).

USE A CHEAPER 'OVERRIDE' SERVICE

You can sign up with various companies to use their service for some calls only. So if you have family living overseas, choose a company that gives a good rate for calls to that country. Just dial the four or five-digit prefix they give you and connect through their service. They'll bill you for those calls separately from BT.

USE CHEAPER 'NORMAL' NUMBERS

Many companies use 0845/0870/0871 numbers (see below), which can be expensive and are rarely included in any inclusive minutes offered with your phone provider's package. But companies often give normal geographical phone numbers on their literature for callers from abroad. Use these even when you're in the UK – as normal rate calls, they will be included in your inclusive minutes. Visit **www.saynoto0870.com** which lists normal number options for many non-geographical numbers.

WHEN IS LOCAL RATE NOT LOCAL RATE?

Most of us are familiar with 0800 numbers, these are free. But other non-geographical prefixes have varying charges. Do we know what we are paying for these – and which to avoid?
- **0800** Freephone, or no charge to the caller.
- **0845** Local rate, or up to 5p a minute.
- **0870/0871** National rate, or up to 10p a minute.
- **09** Premium rate, between 10p and £1.50 a minute, or a fixed single charge. Charges for these calls vary according to the operator you use to make the call, and the type of service.

CUT THE COST OF CALLING A MOBILE PHONE FROM A LANDLINE

This chart compares the costs of calls from landlines on different tarifs and from different providers, to a T-mobile phone, based on 10 minute daytime call.

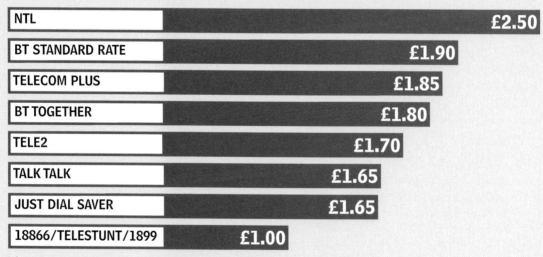

NTL	£2.50
BT STANDARD RATE	£1.90
TELECOM PLUS	£1.85
BT TOGETHER	£1.80
TELE2	£1.70
TALK TALK	£1.65
JUST DIAL SAVER	£1.65
18866/TELESTUNT/1899	£1.00

Information: www.moneysavingexpert.co.uk, 2004

CASE STUDY

DONNA MINIMIZES HER BILL

When Donna Ware moved away from home and got a flat of her own in Hartlepool, the phone was one of the main things she appreciated, as she could chat to her friends as long as she liked.

'Before, Mum or my brother Joe were always knocking on the door after ten minutes,' she says.

But never having had to deal with the phone bills before, she had no idea how much she was paying.

When the first quarterly bill came through, it was for £452. 'My jaw dropped! I could afford it, but I didn't want another one like it.' A friend at work told her to try some other phone companies. But she didn't like the idea of switching and she still had enough paperwork to deal with following the purchase of the flat.

She called BT and asked if there was anything she could do. They offered to put her on their BT Together Option 2 package. For a fee, she then had unmetered calls at

evenings and weekends. She made sure she only spoke to her friends in those 'free' times, and managed to cut her next bill to £151.

TOP TIPS CUT YOUR PHONE CHARGES

Think before you pick up the phone. Use all the benefits that your tariff offers and avoid making unnecessary and expensive calls which all mount up.

■ **Don't call mobiles from a landline** If you must do it, keep the call short or ask the person you are speaking to if they have a landline you could call. Mobile to mobile is often cheaper than landline to mobile.

■ **Look carefully at your bills** Notice which calls were expensive so you can be aware of the cost when you are making them next time.

■ **Use cheap rates** Find out the times of your call provider's cheap rates. BT's cheap rate begins at 6pm and ends at 8am. Wait until 6pm to make evening calls.

■ **No 09 calls** Never call 09 premium-rate numbers.

■ **No come-ons** Don't be tempted by scams that require you to call a number to find out if you have won a prize. You will usually end up with £10 on your phone bill.

■ **Answer your phone** If you let people leave messages and call them back, then you will have to pay for the call.

■ **Get a chatter's plan** If you want to talk to friends for ages, sign up with a package that lets you do this free.

■ **Stop before you start** Before you dial, ask yourself if you really need to make that call.

DIRECTORY ENQUIRIES

■ Since competition opened up in the market for directory enquiries services, 118 800 has consistently been one of the best value services, with a 29p connection charge and 9p per minute charged after that.

■ One-Tel customers have the advantage of a free directory enquiries service at 118 111.

■ If you are online, you can find the information you need without paying any extra. Go to **www.118500.co.uk www.ukphonebook.com** or **www.192.com**

■ Or try **www.yell.com** (Yellow Pages online) for free access to its listings.

GET WISE TO COUNCIL TAX

Every year, your local council sets the level of tax residents have to pay. But this doesn't mean there's nothing you can do about your bill. Check that you are paying the correct amount for both your home and your situation. If you aren't, you could save over £100 a year.

DISCOUNTS AVAILABLE

There are various discounts that you might be entitled to when paying your Council Tax, so don't miss out.
Home alone Are you the only adult occupant of your home? If so, you are entitled to a 25% discount on the full rate of council tax – the Reduction for Single Occupancy. Let the council know if your circumstances change – the discount can usually be backdated if necessary.
Other discounts You can claim a 50% discount if no one is living in the property; if all the people living in the property are disregarded for tax purposes; or, in some areas, if it is your second or holiday home.

IS YOUR PROPERTY CORRECTLY VALUED?

All homes are categorised by the Inland Revenue according to the market value they would have had on a certain date. This is only updated every 15 years or so, so work out if your property is currently in the correct band.
Ask your neighbours Check by asking neighbours with houses of similar value what band they are in. If your house is in a higher band, it may be worth querying the valuation. Call your local Inland Revenue Valuation Office for advice.
If your valuation is downgraded This could mean a windfall for you. The last round of valuations may have been more than ten years ago. You could then be eligible for ten years'-worth of rebates on your council tax. But beware – if you make a query, the valuation could be lifted into a higher band, and you could face a hefty retrospective council tax bill. So think carefully before trying this.

PAYING YOUR BILL COST-EFFECTIVELY

What is the most cost-effective way of paying your bill? Your council will usually give you two choices: monthly direct debit or the whole bill in one go.
Gain interest with direct debit It is rarely worth paying the bill all in one go. Council tax is a large amount of money – often around £1,000 or more. The tax-free interest you could earn on £1,000 is about £45 a year, so the longer it stays in your interest-bearing account, the more you will gain. If you pay by monthly direct debit you will generally be given two or more payment dates to choose from each month, and the money will slowly trickle out month by month throughout the year.

INSURING YOUR HOME AND POSSESSIONS

Insuring your home is vital to enable you to recover financially in the event of misfortune, which could otherwise cost you tens of thousands of pounds. Buildings insurance covers the structure and fittings of your home, while house contents insurance covers your possessions. Buildings insurance will be a stipulation of any mortgage agreement.

A GOOD DEAL ON BUILDINGS INSURANCE

Your current insurer might not be giving you the best deal, so ask for quotes from several other companies.

Consider remortgaging If your mortgage lender insists you use their insurance company for your buildings cover, think about changing to a lender who'll leave you free to choose your own insurer.

Charges for switching Some mortgage lenders charge you if you switch insurer, so take this into account when you work out the savings you'd be making with a new policy.

Ask your insurer for a better deal Before changing insurer, speak to your existing insurer and see if they will give you a better deal. Having a few lower quotes up your sleeve can be persuasive. If they cut your premiums by enough, you can save the paperwork of changing company.

Buy from the same company You might be able to save £50 or more a year by buying your contents and buildings insurance from the same company.

Increase your excess and save 20% Ask your insurer to recommend savings you can make. They might tell you that if you double your excess, they will take £50 a year off your premium, for example.

Claim-free years count Ask for lower premiums – if you have never made a claim, you could save as much as 30% on your yearly premiums.

WATCH POINTS PERILS OF UNDERINSURING

It's important to keep your insurer up to date with the rebuild cost of your home (see below). If disaster struck, it could badly damage your finances too.

■ **Keep up to date** With rebuild costs having risen steeply over the last few decades, there are many cases where houses are insured for only a third of the real cost of rebuilding them. To calculate the rebuild cost of your home you need to know its dimensions, which you then multiply by the current building cost for each square foot – this depends on where you live and the age of your house. As a guide, visit the website of the Association of British Insurers at **www.abi.org.uk** ✉, which works out this sum automatically.

■ **Don't be caught out** In 1990, North Wales was struck by floods. The damage to homes was devastating and many people were unable to afford the necessary repairs. After the disaster, it was found that 15% of properties had no buildings insurance, 40% had no contents insurance and 50% were underinsured.

ASK YOURSELF

DOES IT NEED INSURING?

It's easy to be scared into insuring everything but there's no point in paying premiums to insure items that are cheap to replace or unlikely to get damaged. And there might be cheaper ways of protecting your more expensive items.

■ **Covering antiques** Do you have items of antique furniture worth more than £2,000? Check the single item limit of any contents insurance policy. If a piece is worth more than that, ask each insurer you approach how much they would charge to insure it. It may be cheaper to find an insurer with a high single item limit.

■ **Frozen assets** If you have a large chest freezer, the value of the frozen food could be substantial, so choose a policy that covers it. A small freezer may contain only £25 worth of food at any time and not be worth insuring.

■ **Save £70** Accidental damage insurance can add £70 a year to a combined buildings and contents policy. If you have children or are keen on DIY, then you might benefit from this extra cover. Otherwise, consider saving the cost of these premiums.

FINE PRINT ON CONTENTS INSURANCE

Before you search for the best deal on insuring the contents of your home, have a good look around your house or flat. Work out, roughly, how much it would cost you to replace everything you own should it all be destroyed.

Value expensive items There are many different options in contents policies, and often a limit on what the insurer will pay out for single items. If you have an antique piece of furniture, it could easily exceed this. Jewellery, too, can be worth more than a claim would yield. Make sure these items are valued and listed with the policy, or you could lose out.

Check conditions of cover Check that you are abiding by the provisos of your insurance. For instance, it might be a condition of the cover that you have locks on your windows, and that keys are taken out of the inside of doors. If you don't comply with these conditions, the insurer can easily refuse to honour a claim.

Check out your coverage

- What is the policy excess?
- Does the sum insured cover jewellery?
- Is new-for-old cover standard when making a claim?
- What cover is there under accidental damage?
- Do you have to pay an extra premium for bicycles?
- Is the food in your freezer covered?
- What is covered if a burst pipe causes damage?
- Will your business equipment be covered?
- Are you covered while you are abroad?
- Will the policy pay out for third-party liability claims?
- Does the policy include a legal helpline? This can help save you upwards of £60 on the fees you would have to pay for specialist legal advice.

WHO GETS A LOWER RATE?

Some categories of people may qualify for lower household contents insurance rates as they are likely to be better risks than others.

Pensioners Saga (**www.saga.co.uk** 0800 015 4752 ✉) and Age Concern (**www.ace.org.uk** 0845 606 5075 ✉) are specialists in insurance for pensioners. But most insurers give lower rates the older you are, since they reckon pensioners' homes are almost always occupied and less vulnerable to burglaries.

People who've moved to a safer area All household insurance is postcode rated, so if you live in Devon or Cornwall, for example, you will get a better price for your cover than if you live in Bristol or another big city.

Responsible lifestyles Insurers may lower premiums for non-smokers, for example, as this may decrease the likelihood of fires. Ansvar (**www.ansvar.co.uk** 01323 737541) gives 3% discounts to non-smokers, non-drinkers and active churchgoers with its Home Connect insurance.

TOP TIPS **PREVENTION LOWERS PREMIUMS**

Take a few precautions and don't forget to tell your insurer you have done so.

■ Join your local Neighbourhood Watch scheme or start one in your area. Get a crime prevention officer to inspect your home and report on his findings.

■ Install a burglar alarm, window locks and five-lever deadlocks to final exit doors.

■ Get a fire extinguisher and a smoke alarm.

DON'T STAY LOYAL TO THE SAME INSURER

Each year, when your insurance comes up for renewal, do some research to see if you could be getting a better deal elsewhere.

Use Yellow Pages Pick five insurers from the Yellow Pages and phone them up in turn. When they give you a quote, ask them for a reference number and write it down. Otherwise, if you decide to buy that policy later, you could have to give them the same information all over again.

Try the internet Many insurance websites will give you an online quotation. Save yourself time by having all the information about your property and contents to hand.

Use a broker This is an easy way to search for the best quote from several insurers at the same time. But don't be lulled into thinking that a call to a broker means you don't have to go any further. The list of insurance companies that brokers use is far from comprehensive. The direct insurers won't be included, and they often offer the best value of all.

RESOURCES

USEFUL CONTACTS

The Association of British Insurers is the trade association for the UK's insurance industry, representing about 400 companies. Contact them for information at 020 7600 3333 or **www.abi.org.uk** ✉.

■ Log onto **www.find.co.uk** for a list of home insurance firms.

COMPARING QUOTES FOR BUILDINGS/CONTENTS INSURANCE

This table shows how you can pay differing amounts for insuring the same property, and that the key levels of cover vary.

It refers to a three-bedroom semi-detached house in rural Gloucestershire, built in the 1960s, with a rebuild cost of £150,000.

INSURER	ANNUAL PREMIUM	...WITH ACCIDENTAL DAMAGE	...WITH PERSONAL POSSESSIONS	NOTES
A	£223.65	£291.90	£315.00	£150,000 max. rebuild cost; £20,000 max. contents; £100 excess; £2,500 personal possessions
B	£254.78	£335.27	£385.15	£400,000 max. rebuild cost; £60,000 max. contents; £100 excess; £2,500 personal possessions
C	£205.07	£284.45	£339.26	£250,000 max. rebuild cost; £35,000 max. contents; £100 excess; £3,000 personal possessions

Information from individual insurers, 2004. Note: Other details and conditions of the policies vary.

Tax and state benefits

Although many taxes are unavoidable, you can avoid paying more than you should if you understand how they work.

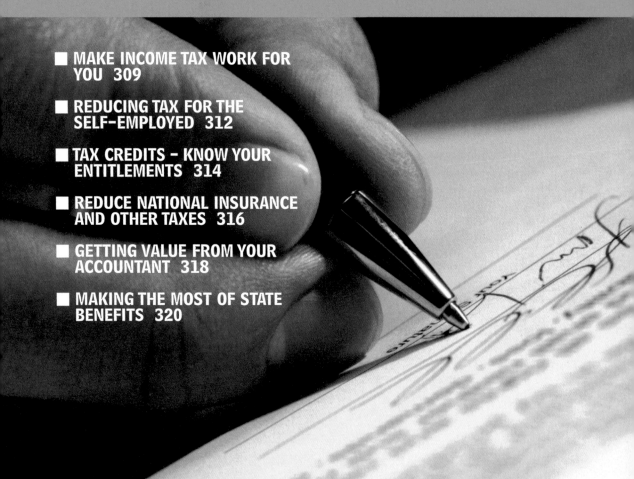

MAKE INCOME TAX WORK FOR YOU

Although everyone with an income above a set amount must pay income tax, you can save money by ensuring you are given the correct tax code and claiming all the allowances and credits to which you are entitled. To do this, you need to understand the basics of the taxation system.

HOW INCOME TAX WORKS

By law, we have to pay a proportion of the money we earn in income tax. Each person has a personal tax-free allowance – £4,745 in 2004/2005 – that they can earn before tax has to be paid. Above that level, three bands apply at different levels of income: 10%, 22% and 40%.

Employed or self-employed? If you are employed, tax is deducted from your salary, along with National Insurance contributions. If you are self-employed, you must declare what you have earned in each tax year by the end of the following January, and pay the tax you owe.

Self-assessment The Inland Revenue runs the self-assessment system. You fill in a multi-page tax form and submit it. Self-assessment is for people with more complex tax affairs including the self-employed, business partners, company directors and higher-rate tax payers. Nine million people fall into the self-assessment system. This may save you money, so if you think you could be self-assessed, contact your local tax office (see Resources, page 310). The phone number can be found in your local phonebook or at **www.inlandrevenue.gov.uk/local/index.htm** ✉.

TOP TIPS SAVING TAX

According to one company that promotes independent financial advice, 9 out of 10 UK adults pay too much tax. Make sure you are not one of them.

■ **Check your tax code** If you're employed, the Inland Revenue gives you a tax code, which your employer uses to deduct tax from your pay. Check this code on your payslip or your Inland Revenue coding notice (see page 310 and Resources, right). Around 1 in 10 codes are incorrect because the tax office has been sent the wrong information.

■ **People over 65** Pensioners should always check they've been given their higher age allowances. The Inland Revenue doesn't always notice 65th birthdays, but being 65 at any time in a tax year qualifies you for a higher allowance. Check your code straight away, and query anything you don't understand with your local tax office.

■ **Understand banding** Make sure you understand the rules governing the top rate of tax you have to pay as this affects the savings schemes suitable for you. Although income on interest from your savings counts towards your banding, remember that tax is applied to your income only after allowances and credits that apply to you have been deducted. Also, if you are a higher-rate tax payer, you need to claim relief on personal or stakeholder pension contributions, or you will miss out.

GET OVER £4,000 TAX-FREE

If you're a homeowner with spare rooms, you may be able to rent them out tax-free. Under the government's 'rent-a-room' scheme, you can charge rent of up to £4,250 tax-free, within a given tax year. This only applies where the property is your main residence, and the lodger shares facilities with you.

 **RESOURCES**

CHECKING TAX RATES
To check current rates of income tax, and where the bands begin, see **www.inlandrevenue.gov.uk/rates/it.htm**

■ Make sure you're not paying too much tax. Check your payslip details on this website: **www.digita.com/taxcentral/home/employment/payslipcalculator**

CHECKING YOUR TAX CODE

Your code is a number followed by a letter. The number indicates the tax due on your income. The letter shows how it should be adjusted if the government makes tax changes.

Avoid emergency tax code You'll be put on an emergency tax code if the Inland Revenue doesn't have enough information about your previous job. Try to change this as soon as possible. The emergency code is based on the personal allowance for people under 65. Even if this is your correct allowance, you may pay too much tax for a while. This happens because the emergency code doesn't give you the benefit of any tax-free pay that may have built up before you started your new job. You can make sure you are on the correct code by checking your payslip details on the website listed in the Resources box on page 309. If you think there has been a mistake, contact your Inland Revenue office.

The costs of the wrong tax code If you carry on working with the wrong tax code, you could end up paying too much tax – which means lending the tax collector money which could be earning interest for you. Or you may not be paying enough tax – which could lead to more being deducted from your monthly pay cheque next year.

Look beyond the current year If you're on the wrong tax code, it is likely it was wrong last year too. Make sure that it's put right, and you could be in for a welcome tax rebate.

MORE THAN ONE JOB?

Perhaps you have two jobs or several part-time jobs. If so, ask your tax office to split your personal tax allowance between your employments. If you earn less in total than your personal allowance, you should not have to pay tax.

A POOL CAR MEANS NO TAX

If you use a car for work, try to make sure it is a pool car. There is no tax payable on this at all. To qualify, the car must be available to – and be used by – more than one

RESOURCES

WHERE IS YOUR LOCAL TAX OFFICE?
Correspondence from the Inland Revenue will display the address of your local tax office at the top. You will also find the phone number in your local phonebook, or go to **www.inlandrevenue. gov.uk/local/index.htm** ✉.

UNDERSTANDING TAX CODES

LETTER	MEANING
L	The basic personal allowance.
P	The full personal allowance for those aged 65–74.
V	The full personal allowance for those aged 65–74, plus the full married couples' allowance where the elder spouse was born before 6 April 1935, if you are liable at the basic rate of tax due to the size of your income.
Y	The full personal allowance for those aged 75 or over.
T	There are other items the IR needs to review in your tax code or you have asked them not to use any of the other tax code letters.
K	The total allowances in your code are less than the total deductions to be taken away from your allowances.

WKI or MI after any of these codes indicates you are on emergency, or week/month 1, tax code (see above).

TAX OFFICE SWALLOWS JULIA'S PAY RISE

After leaving her job, receptionist Julia Robbins took five months off to go to India. She came back in September and started in her new job.

'I was all travelled-out by then, and really looking forward to the new job. It was going to be great having that bit more money to live on,' she said. Her salary was set to go up to £16,000 from her previous £14,100. But at the end of the first month, she was disappointed to find that her net pay had hardly changed. It wasn't until January that one of her colleagues pointed out she might have been put on an emergency tax coding.

Julia went to the payroll department and asked them about it.

'They said they'd never even got my P45, even though I could have sworn I'd put it in the post to them months before I even started!' But the man in the department rectified the situation just in time for the next pay day, and Julia was delighted to find an extra £620. She had been reimbursed for overpayments.

The man in payroll explained that the emergency tax code hadn't taken account of the fact that Julia was only working for seven out of the twelve months of that tax year.

employee. Normally, it shouldn't be kept overnight at or near an employee's home. If the car is used privately, this must be incidental to business use.

TOP TIPS SAVINGS FOR MARRIED COUPLES

Although a married couple's allowance now only applies to older couples, money-conscious couples can still save on tax by splitting their assets in the most tax-efficient way.

■ **Divide your assets** One way for married couples to pay less tax is to make full use of their tax-free personal allowances. If, for example, one of you is a top-rate taxpayer and the other a basic rate or non-taxpayer, you can halve your tax liability by transferring income-yielding assets, such as building society deposits or shares, to the lower earner. Instead of paying 40% tax, as a couple you could be paying 20% or less. And as married couples do not pay capital gains tax when transferring assets between them, this is a good way to reduce your joint income tax bill.

■ **Halve joint assets** When completing a tax return, if you are married, make sure you only enter half of the income from assets held jointly.

■ **Older couples can benefit** Since April 2000, the married couple's allowance only applies to couples where one of the partners was 65 on or before 5th April 2000. But eligible couples who failed to claim still have 5 years and 10 months after the end of the relevant tax year to claim the allowance.

■ **Claim tax back** Once you have divided your assets, remember to claim back any tax that has already been paid on bank and building society accounts by completing and sending off form R85, available from the local branch of your bank or building society.

SAVE ON WORK-RELATED TRAVEL

A company car could be a perk worth having. Although a company car is taxable as a 'benefit in kind', the tax you pay could be less than the purchase and running costs you would incur if you owned your own car.

Obviously the more mileage you do, the more you will benefit.

But to reduce tax liability choose a fuel-efficient car (see Keep it simple, page 317).

And even if you don't have a company car, you can still save on work-related travel by claiming a mileage allowance from your employer, who should pay you a reasonable allowance (around 40p per mile for 2004/2005).

REDUCING TAX FOR THE SELF-EMPLOYED

It is a common assumption that there are huge tax advantages to being self-employed. But self-employed people have many expenses, such as transport costs and electricity bills, that don't apply to employees. Although these expenses are non-taxable, they can still add up to a hefty sum. To minimise tax bills, all business expenses should be claimed for and tax forms completed on time.

TOP TIPS TAX FOR THE SELF-EMPLOYED

If you work for yourself and are taxed under the rules for Schedule D Case I or Case II, make sure you claim all the allowable expenses you can. These expenses can be offset against tax, which reduces your taxable income.

■ **Claim for your home office** If you work from home, put in a claim for the proportion of the household bills that relate to your workspace, such as the cost of water, light, heat, power, property insurance, rent and security.

■ **Include all business meetings** Even if you are in business with your spouse, occasions where you discuss work – in a restaurant, say – are legitimate business expenses and the cost can be deducted from your tax bill.

■ **Don't forget admin costs** Claim for all your administrative costs such as phone bills and stationery.

■ **Add in reading material** You can claim for the cost of relevant trade and professional journals. A lot more of your reading may be for work purposes than you realise. If you take a daily paper to keep up with the business news, then this is also a deductible expense.

■ **Claim for travel** Put in a claim for travel and hotel accommodation costs related to your business.

■ **Loans for less** You can also include interest on bank and other loans that relate to your business.

■ **Mending matters** The cost of repairs and maintenance of business equipment are also legitimate expenses.

■ **Using the car for business** Include motoring expenses if your car is used for work, such as AA membership, petrol or diesel and parking charges. Include any driving you do to social occasions when the primary purpose is to meet work contacts or new customers.

■ **Record everything** You must keep accurate records of all your expenses if they are to be allowable for tax purposes.

MAKE USE OF YOUR FIRST YEAR ALLOWANCES

If you have a small or medium-sized firm and you buy capital items such as furniture or equipment, you can claim a first year tax-free allowance of 40% of its value. This is higher than the normal 25% capital allowance, a tax allowance that takes account of depreciation of business assets such as machinery and motor vehicles. To qualify, you have to have a turnover of less than £11.2 million, assets of less than £5.6 million, and fewer than 250 employees.

---

keep it simple

EXPENSES ARE TAX-FREE, NOT FREE!
Keep a frugal office, and only buy what you really need to run your business efficiently. Don't let the knowledge that you can write off these expenses against tax influence you to spend more freely than you would otherwise.
That new integrated phone/email/fax machine might look attractive, but does it really do any more than the equipment you already have?

Payments on account

If you're self-employed, you will usually have to make payments on account to the Inland Revenue – two payments during the year which, added together, reflect the amount of tax you were due to pay the year before. But if your income drops, complete and send off the Inland Revenue form SA303 to reduce those payments on account. Don't let your money sit in the Revenue's coffers when it could be in your account or earning interest in a deposit account.

SMART MOVES

A LEASE CAN MEAN LESS TAX

It may be worth leasing new equipment rather than buying it. You can normally claim only 25% of the cost of buying new equipment in the first year – it is classified as a capital allowance – whereas you can claim back 100% of the cost of a lease as a business expense.

WATCH POINTS PAYING YOUR TAX ON TIME

Don't join the million or so taxpayers who end up having to pay £100 fines for being late returning their self-assessment forms.

■ **Pay on time to avoid a fine** You must get your completed tax return to the tax office by the end of September following the tax year (the tax year ends on April 5th) if you want the Inland Revenue to calculate your tax, or by the end of January if you calculate it yourself. All money owed must be paid by the end of January. If you don't, you will pay a fine of £100 and be charged interest on the amount you owe the Revenue.

■ **Late payers risk paying more** If you leave your return till the end of January and you miscalculate your tax liability, you could have to pay a fine and interest for the amount you owe. In this case, it's safer to overestimate it but better still to have done your return by the end of September so it will be calculated for you.

■ **Avoid overpayment** Tax bills must be paid on time, and once you are established as self-employed for tax purposes you will be asked to make payments on account. This is usually two payments a year – one before the end of January and one before the end of July – which together equate roughly to the amount of tax payable for the previous tax year. If your income drops substantially, you can ask to have your payment on account reduced.

SAVING TOWARDS YOUR TAX BILL

Whether you pay less tax when you're self-employed or not, at least you are allowed to hang on to it for longer. Often, you don't have to pay the tax for months or even more than a year after the income has been generated. This gives you the opportunity to put that money to work in the meantime.

Save the right amount A good habit to get into is to put aside a certain percentage of all gross earned income to cover tax and National Insurance. Provided you are likely to fall into the basic rate tax bracket – earning £33,000 or less in one tax year – then putting aside a quarter of gross earned income should cover your subsequent tax bill. Once you have two years experience of how much tax you actually pay, you will be able to get a better idea of how much you need to put aside. It may be as little as a fifth.

Use a high-interest account The money you put aside for tax is best kept in an easily accessible savings account, paying as high a rate of interest as possible. The interest you can earn on your tax money is substantial. For example, if you earned £28,000 during the year and gradually put a quarter of this away in an account paying 4.5% in interest, you could earn around £315 in interest on the money before you have to pay it to the Inland Revenue.

Keep invoicing

Invoice clients as early as possible. Check when they normally pay invoices and submit your invoice so it will be ready to be paid at this date. Many companies pay as late as possible, but don't accept this without a fight. Make sure that the client has actually received the invoice, and then chase them up just before the due date, not after it.

RESOURCES

FOR THE SELF-EMPLOYED

■ The Inland Revenue has a special helpline for the newly self-employed on 0845 915 4515. It also has a line for the self-employed who have queries about NICs (National Insurance Contributions) on 0845 915 4655. The Self-Assessment helpline is on 0845 9000 444 and the Tax and Benefit Advice Line is on 0845 608 6000. Alternatively, you can write to your local tax office (see **www.inlandrevenue.gov.uk/local/index.htm** ✉). Always quote your UTR number (Unique Taxpayer Reference number).

■ The FSB (Federation of Small Businesses) has a website that includes advice about tax at **www.fsb.org.uk** ✉.

TAX CREDITS – KNOW YOUR ENTITLEMENTS

In April 2003, the government introduced two new tax credits, replacing the previous system. Under the tax credit system, the Inland Revenue actually hands out large amounts of cash to working families. But you won't receive this extra help automatically so it's important to understand whether you are eligible, how to claim if you are, and to get your claim in as soon as possible.

WHAT ARE TAX CREDITS?

Tax credits are intended to support families and make working worth while for them, especially when the high cost of childcare is enough to make having a job pretty pointless for many parents. There are two types of tax credit – Working Tax Credit and Child Tax Credit.

WORKING TAX CREDIT

Working Tax Credit supports working people on a low income by topping up earnings. There are extra amounts for working households in which someone has a disability. You can claim it if you're employed or self-employed, and it includes support for the cost of childcare.

Who qualifies? If you are on a low income, you might qualify for Working Tax Credit if you're working 16 or more hours a week and are 16 or over, and are responsible for a child; or if you're 16 or over and have a disability. You might also qualify if you're 25 or over and work for 30 hours a week or more, or if you're 50 or over, work 16 or more hours a week and return to work after you've spent time on certain state benefits.

Childcare costs Families who pay a registered or approved childminder, or use a registered nursery, and who have one child may receive up to 70% of childcare costs up to the value of £135 a week; those with two children or more may receive up to 70% of childcare costs up to £200.

WHO QUALIFIES FOR CHILD TAX CREDIT?

Child Tax Credit is paid to the main carer of the child/children and is not dependent on whether the carer works. To receive Child Tax Credit, you must be responsible

RESOURCES

TAX CREDITS
For more information about tax credits, see www.inlandrevenue.gov.uk/taxcredits or call 0845 300 3900 ✉.

HOW MUCH PER ANNUM COULD YOU GET IN TAX CREDITS?

ANNUAL FAMILY INCOME	ONE CHILD – NO CHILDCARE	ONE CHILD – £70 A WEEK CHILD-CARE COSTS	THREE CHILDREN – NO CHILDCARE	THREE CHILDREN – £100 A WEEK CHILDCARE
£5,000	£5,015	£7,565	£7,905	£11,545
£10,000	£3,810	£6,360	£6,700	£10,340
£25,000	£545	£810	£1,150	£4,790

Source: Inland Revenue, Autumn 2003

CASE STUDY

TAX CREDITS HELP MAISIE BACK TO WORK

Before Marcus and Maisie Straw had Jasmine, their oldest child, now eight, both of them used to work at the local branch of a bank.

'That's where we first met,' says Maisie. 'But I didn't go back after my first maternity leave. I wanted to be at home for Jasmine, and Jordan, when he came along three years ago.'

Marcus earns £14,000 a year, which is enough for the family to get by on. But when Maisie wanted to go back to work part time, she didn't know whether it would be worth it, since she'd have to pay £70 a week to a day care centre.

'Then one of the mothers at playgroup told me you can get tax credits to help with your childcare costs, so I phoned the number and applied then and there.'

Now Maisie earns £4,500 a year. The day care centre fees are £3,640 a year, but this is more than offset by the £5,195 the couple get in tax credits.

for at least one child who is 16 or younger, or 16–19 and in full-time education, or has left school, doesn't have a job yet and has registered with the Careers Service or Connexions Service **www.connexions.gov.uk** ✉ 080 800 13219. In the tax year 2004–2005, it is payable to couples whose combined annual income is £58,000 or less.

HOW TO CLAIM

You can claim tax credits in two ways: either phone the Inland Revenue on 0800 500 222 and ask for a claim pack or go to **www.taxcredits.inlandrevenue.gov.uk** ✉ and apply online. People who already receive tax credit should automatically receive a Renewal Pack from the Inland Revenue by July in the relevant year.

MAKING A LATE CLAIM

If you discover that you have been eligible for tax credits for some time, but haven't claimed them, or that you should have received more in tax credits, the Inland Revenue will backdate your claim for up to three months or the date you became eligible. You must make your claim by the 5th July. You can tell the Inland Revenue of your change of circumstances either by using their website or phoning their Tax Credits helpline (see Resources, left).

WATCH POINTS AVOID FINES FOR OVERPAYMENTS

Tell the Inland Revenue as soon as your circumstances change. If the changes cause you to be paid tax credits to which you are no longer entitled, you could be liable for a £300 fine, as well as having to repay all the money you owe, back to the time when the change in circumstances occurred. Here are some typical scenarios that would mean you could be receiving too much in tax credits:

■ There has been a change to your status as a single person or as part of a couple.

■ You have not made any childcare payments for more than four consecutive weeks.

■ There has been a reduction of more than £10 a week in the cost of your childcare for more than four weeks in a row.

GET THE BENEFIT

At some point during your working life, you may be offered a choice between a fringe benefit, such as a company car, or the equivalent in salary. Although you have to pay income tax on fringe benefits, you don't have to pay National Insurance contributions on them, so it can be worth taking the benefit rather than the salary to save on NICs.

REDUCE NATIONAL INSURANCE AND OTHER TAXES

Most people have to pay NICs (National Insurance contributions) when they work. The class and level of contributions changes throughout your working life, but what you pay counts towards certain benefits, including your state old-age pension when you retire.

WHICH CLASS OF NI DO YOU PAY?

Class 1 – paid by people who work as employed earners and their employers.

Class 1A and **1B** – paid by several categories of employers.

Class 2 – flat rate contribution paid by the self-employed.

Class 3 – voluntary contributions paid by people who want to protect their entitlement to the state pension, and who don't pay enough NI in another class.

Class 4 – profit-related contributions paid by self-employed people who also pay Class 2 contributions. These contributions don't count towards benefits.

HOW MUCH NI DO YOU HAVE TO PAY?

It depends on your earnings. There is an Earnings Threshold of £91 a week (check the current level), and an Upper Earnings Limit of £610. Between these levels, you pay Class 1 contributions at the rate of 11%. For earnings above the top limit, you pay 1%. For example, if you earned £615 a week, you would pay 0% on the first £91, 11% on £92–£610 and 1% on the remaining £5. To find out more about NI, ask the Inland Revenue for a leaflet, or get one at **www.inlandrevenue.gov.uk/leaflets/ca01.pdf** ✉.

DON'T PAY TWICE

If you have two jobs, National Insurance contributions will be deducted from both. But there is an annual maximum amount that you should pay in NICs, so you can apply for a refund if the combined deductions will exceed this. Or, if you know in advance that you will pay too much, you can apply for a refund by obtaining a deferment certificate by the start of the tax year.

DON'T LOSE OUT ON CAPITAL GAINS TAX

If any asset you have grows in value and you then sell it, the difference between the acquisition cost and the selling price – the capital gain – is taxable.

Annual exemption Everyone is entitled to an exemption of £8,200 (in 2004/2005). This is the amount of capital gains you can make before CGT (Capital Gains tax) applies.

Don't be afraid Many people fear that Capital Gains tax will seriously erode any revenue from a sale. But there are various types of relief available, and costs such as fees are allowable against the gain. A self-assessment tax return must be filed if you are in a capital gains situation.

WHICH CAPITAL GAINS TAX RATE APPLIES?

Take your taxable income plus any taxable gains (after relief and allowable costs) less £8,200 exemption to find the relevant range, then check the rate.	RANGE	RATE
	0-£2,020	10%
	£2,2021–£31,400	20%
	over £31,400	40%

Rates for 2004-2005

TOP TIPS PAY LESS CGT

Couples can avoid CGT by splitting assets sensibly. You can also offset losses against gains to reduce your liability and time any gains so that they are spread over several tax years.

■ **Divide to maximise exemptions** If you have assets that have built up a capital gain, transfer them between you and your spouse and use both annual exemptions.

■ **Lowest rate tax** The rate of CGT that is levied depends on the income tax band of the person concerned. So try to ensure that the spouse paying income tax at the lower rate is the one who ends up with the taxable gains.

■ **Think ahead** For example, if you have lost money on the stock market recently (there are few investors who have not), you can carry your losses forward to future tax years and offset them against any gains you might realise.

■ **Report losses** To offset losses against gains, you need to report any loss to the Inland Revenue within 5 years and 10 months of the date when the loss occurred. If you want to carry forward losses, you must notify the Inland Revenue of your intention within six years, but once you have done this, there is no time limit on when you have to use the losses that you have brought forward to offset gains.

■ **Timed gains** If you know you are going to make taxable gains, be clever with timing. If in 2004/2005 you will sell assets of more than £31,600 and make more than £8,200 in capital gains from it, split it into two transactions. Dispose of one portion within that tax year and the other in the next. This way, you'll use the exemptions for two tax years.

■ **Keep assets** If you make a capital gain on an asset that does go over your annual exemption, don't forget to claim taper relief. The basic idea is that your assets can grow in line with inflation tax-free, and only growth that goes above that is to be taxed. The longer you've held the asset, the less of the gain is taxable. For example, if you've held an asset for more than 10 years, then only 60% of any gain is taxable.

■ **ISA trick** Participants in employee share schemes who sell shares after exercising their options may have to pay CGT. To avoid this, they can use the 90-day period from the date they exercised the share option to transfer the shares into an ISA (see page 328), where they can then be sold tax-free.

INHERITANCE TAX (IHT)

Your estate doesn't pay this tax until after your death. There are plenty of ways you can keep it to a minimum for those you leave behind (see *Family affairs*, page 115).

---

keep it simple

DRIVE A GREENER COMPANY CAR If you are about to choose a new company car, select carefully to keep the tax you pay on it within the flat rate of 15%. Generally, you should buy a car with a smaller engine and one that is more fuel-efficient. It is the CO_2 emissions that can push up the tax level. See the Society of Motor Manufacturers' and Traders' website **www.smmt.co.uk** or call 020 7235 7000 ✉ to find out CO_2 emissions by car model.

 **RESOURCES**

DO YOU MAKE MONEY FROM PROPERTY? If you have a buy-to-let investment, or make money from buying and selling property, take a look at the Tax Café website's tax-saving tips for property investors **www.taxcafe.co.uk** or phone 01592 560018 ✉.

GETTING VALUE FROM YOUR ACCOUNTANT

Having the expertise of an accountant on your side can, in some circumstances, save you hundreds or even thousands of pounds in tax. On the other hand, you do have to pay for the service. Is it worth employing one? Unfortunately only an accountant can tell you this, but at least the initial consultation should be free.

DECIDE WHETHER YOU'LL SAVE

Try to find an accountant who is recommended by someone you trust. Arrange a meeting; find out if they will be able to save you money and how much their fees would be. It may be that you are already well aware of how to minimise your tax bill and the fees could not justify the convenience of having an accountant prepare your tax return for you.

HELP FOR DIY ACCOUNTANTS

If you decide that your affairs are sufficiently straightforward and that you have the necessary skills to do your own accounting, you can get help from the Internet by using software such as Intuit's TaxCalc (see Resources, left) and from the Inland Revenue itself.

LEARN FROM THE EXPERT

If you use an accountant to complete your tax return, be canny about it. Take a good look at how they have done it, and which expenses they have been able to claim for you. Use the accountant as your tutor – then consider saving yourself the fee next year by doing it yourself.

Drawing a salary from your small business

Tax rules on small businesses are in flux at the moment. But there may be ways an accountant can minimise your tax if you run one.

SMART MOVES

In the past people have been able to draw a minimal salary and pay themselves the rest of the company profits as a dividend. Many have cut their tax bill to less than 1% in this way. Things have changed, but consult an accountant to set your business up in the most tax-efficient way.

TOP TIPS MINIMISING ACCOUNTANCY COSTS

To keep your accountant's fees to a minimum, do a little research before hiring one. As there is no set scale of fees, fee scales vary considerably, so it pays to get at least three quotes for the services you require.

■ **Fixed rates often cheaper** Accountancy services may be charged for by the hour, with costs such as phone calls and letters being itemised separately. Some will charge a fixed annual fee, which can be paid monthly. If you can find a suitable firm who charges a fixed rate for particular services, such as completing an annual tax return for you, this is often a cost-effective option.

■ **Hire a junior and save** Charges may vary depending on the seniority of the accountant involved, so you may be able to save by having a more junior member of staff deal with your account, as long as you are happy to work this way.

■ **Beware of price hikes** Check that charges will not rise steeply after the first year – many reputable firms are willing to give you a guarantee that this won't happen.

■ **Shop out of town** As with many professionals, accountants in London and other major cities usually charge more than those in smaller towns, so it may be worth going to one from a different area or using an online service. A smaller firm may give you a more personal service too.

■ **Don't pay a rush fee** If you give your accountant plenty of time to do the work you require, you are likely to pay less than if you need work completed quickly.

■ **Be organised** Your accountant will charge more for records that require a lot of additional work. By keeping clear records yourself, and particularly if you use a software package recommended by your accountant, you can minimise the work that they have to do and reduce costs.

■ **Deduct fees** Remember that your accountant's fees are a business expense and can be used to reduce your tax bill.

BEFORE HIRING AN ACCOUNTANT

Use the initial consultation to ask these questions:
■ Are they qualified? Look for the words 'chartered' or 'certified'.
■ Who are their other clients? It's helpful if the accountant has experience with people in similar circumstances or other businesses the same size as yours, or in the same field.
■ How do they charge? Hourly fees are most common, but you may be able to arrange a fixed fee for a certain job such as a tax return.
■ Can you work with this person? Take a moment to consider whether this person has understood and responded to your requests. If you feel the communication is poor, try a different accountant.

DO YOU NEED AN ACCOUNTANT?

If your financial affairs are fairly simple, you can probably save the cost of hiring an accountant by doing the work yourself. On the other hand, if your affairs are complex – for example, if you are self-employed or want tax advice – the money a properly trained accountant can save you will usually repay the cost of hiring one.

LEVEL OF SERVICE	SUITABLE FOR	COST
DIY ACCOUNTANCY	Employed people with no complicating factors such as a requirement for tax advice.	Your time, plus any potential savings you miss due to lack of expertise.
BOOKKEEPING	Small businesses who require help with keeping track of their finances.	from £25 an hour
BASIC ACCOUNTING	Clients who wish to keep costs down, using a newly qualified accountant or using an Internet-based service.	from £65 an hour
FULL ACCOUNTING	Clients with complex affairs who want a full service that includes tax advice.	from £100 an hour

MAKING THE MOST OF STATE BENEFITS

Every year, hundreds of millions of pounds in benefits cash reportedly goes unclaimed. Through lack of knowledge, many people who are entitled to benefits don't even apply. Don't miss out. Find out what there is, and if you qualify for benefits, take them – they're yours!

KNOW WHAT YOU CAN CLAIM

Benefits are paid out either by the Social Security Agency, the Inland Revenue or regional councils. All depend on your circumstances, but some are paid regardless of income. Use the Resources (left) or contact your local Social Security office to find out which benefits apply to you.

- Attendance Allowance
- Bereavement Allowance
- Budgeting Loans
- Carer's Allowance
- Child Benefit
- Child Tax Credit
- Cold Weather Payments
- Community Care Grants
- Council Tax Benefit
- Crisis Loans
- Disability Benefits
- Funeral Payments
- Health Benefits
- Help – mortgage interest
- Help – prison visits
- Home Energy Efficiency Scheme
- Housing Benefit
- Incapacity Benefit
- Income Support
- Jobseekers Allowance
- Maternity Allowance
- One-off 70+ Payment
- Over 80 Pension
- Pension Credit
- Severe Disablement Allowance
- Social Fund
- Statutory Maternity Pay
- Sure Start Maternity Grants
- Widowed Parent's Allowance
- Winter Fuel Payment
- Working Tax Credit

DEALING WITH UNEMPLOYMENT

If you become unemployed, take action as quickly as you can. To minimise any loss of income, claim benefits as soon as possible and take your finances in hand.
Put in your claim Contact your local Social Security or Jobs and Benefits Office ✉ right away and claim any applicable benefits. If you have a mortgage or rent to pay, ask about help with mortgage interest or Housing Benefit. Check on the progress of your claim every few days.
Identify your priorities Make sure you can pay the most important bills – rent, council tax, electricity, gas and TV licence. If you can't pay your utility bills, your Benefits Office may be able to help. If there is anything else you can't pay, let the company concerned know as soon as possible. Then get advice from a Citizens Advice Bureau ✉, which can help work out a payment plan with any creditors.
Get a new job Once your finances are safe, start job hunting, making use of all the resources and advice available. Visit your Jobs and Benefits Office, and use the library to look in a variety of local area newspapers.

keep it simple

WORK AS A TEAM
If you find yourself facing a sudden drop in income it can feel like a catastrophe. But try to turn the situation around, and see it as a challenge. Get your family involved and solve the problem together. Hold a family meeting. Be upfront and honest with them, and ask for their suggestions. Even the youngest of children can have ideas about how to save money. And no one will resent the cuts if they can feel part of the team.

HELP FOR THE SICK OR DISABLED

If you find yourself unable to work due to sickness or disability, find out which benefits apply to your situation and claim as soon as you can. If you're too ill to make a claim yourself, get help from someone you trust or ask your doctor to contact Social Services for you.

Claiming Incapacity Benefit To get this Social Security benefit, you must have paid enough National Insurance Contributions at the right rate and at the right time, but if you're under 20, or under 25 if you were in education or training at least three months immediately before you were 20, then you might be able to get Incapacity Benefit even if you haven't paid enough NI. If you claim Incapacity Benefit, you might be able to get Income Support as well.

Accommodation costs For help with your rent or mortgage, ask the Benefits Office about how to apply for Housing Benefit or assistance with your mortgage interest.

Check your entitlements Check out the list opposite to make sure you've claimed all the benefits to which you're entitled. If your income is about to fall, you need to make sure the essentials are secure.

Help for the disabled Find out if you qualify for the 'disabled element' of the Working Tax Credit. This is for people who meet the conditions for Working Tax Credit and have an illness or disability that puts them at a disadvantage in getting a job. To find out more, visit the Inland Revenue website **www.inlandrevenue.gov.uk/taxcredits** or phone the helpline on 0845 300 3900 ✉. You may be able to claim Disability Living Allowance, which is a Social Security benefit for people under 65 who need a lot of help with personal care because of a physical or mental illness or disability. Or you may be able to claim it if you have a disability that means you need help getting around.

MATERNITY BENEFITS

When you're going to have a baby, your employer has certain obligations and there are benefits you can claim. If you're fortunate, your firm will have more generous maternity benefits than the legal minimum.

Statutory Maternity Pay This is for women who've been in the same job throughout their pregnancy, and whose earnings average £67 a week or more. It's paid for 26 weeks. Your employer pays it to you and then claims the money back from the Inland Revenue. You can get it even if you don't intend to go back to work after having the baby, and you don't have to pay it back. For the first six weeks you receive 90% of your previous pay, and after that you get the basic rate of around £100 a week.

Notify your employer You must tell your employer – in writing – at least 21 days before the start of maternity leave. Say that you are pregnant, the expected week of childbirth, and the date you intend to start maternity leave.

Maternity Allowance This benefit is for women who don't qualify for Statutory Maternity Pay, for example because they have changed jobs during pregnancy or are self-employed. It is worth around £102.80 a week at present, and lasts for 18 weeks. Ask your Benefits Agency ✉ for details.

Help with housing You might also be eligible for Council Tax Benefit and Housing Benefit (see below).

Get a Sure Start If you or your partner are getting Income Support, Jobseeker's Allowance or some types of Tax Credit, you qualify for a £500 Sure Start grant from the Social Fund to cover purchases for the baby. You don't have to pay it back, and it doesn't matter if you already have savings.

HELP WITH HOUSING

The two benefits given to those who need help with costs related to accommodation are paid by the local council rather than a central government agency. They are both means-tested and depend on your type of housing.

Council Tax Benefit (CTB) You might qualify for this benefit if you are on a low income, have little in savings or all of your council tax is paid for you. If you have more than £3,000 saved, or £6,000 if you're 60 or over, then this will reduce the benefit you get. If you have more than £16,000, then you usually won't get any benefit. You will get a CTB claim form with a Jobseekers Allowance or Income Support claim form. Or contact your local council and ask for a form.

Housing Benefit In some areas this is called Local Housing Allowance. You may be eligible if you pay rent to a private landlord and are on a very low income. As with CTB, if you have savings this will affect how much housing benefit you can get. And the amount you receive depends on a number of factors, such as whether other people live with you and whether the rent is reasonable for your accommodation.

BENEFITS FOR THE BEREAVED

From 2001, the old widow's benefits, which applied only to women, were replaced by bereavment benefits, which apply to both men and women. If your spouse dies, there are several benefits to which you may be entitled.

Help for younger spouses Regardless of age, you should be entitled to a one-off payment of £2,000. Bereavement Payment is based on your late spouse's NI contributions. You can get it if you're under 60, or if your spouse died before being entitled to a Retirement Pension.

Widowed Parent's Allowance If your spouse dies when you're bringing up children or if you are a widow expecting your late husband's baby, you can claim this allowance. Again, your late husband or wife has to have paid NI contributions. In 2004, the weekly rate was £79.60.

CLAIM PENSION CREDIT – GAIN OVER £100 A WEEK

Nearly half of all pensioners are entitled to Pension Credit (see table, right) but over two million of those eligible don't claim. There is no upper limit on your savings, but savings over £6,000 will start to count against what you receive, and if your income is over £144.23 a week if you're single or £211.50 for couples, you probably won't receive any Savings Credit. Still, it is worth checking your eligibility. Contact your local Pension Service ✉ or use the freephone number 0800 99 1234 for help with claiming. Have your NI number and details of your income and savings to hand.

COMMON BENEFITS YOU MAY QUALIFY FOR

BENEFIT	WHAT IS IT?	WHO CAN CLAIM?	WHAT YOU MAY RECEIVE (PER WEEK)
JOBSEEKERS ALLOWANCE	Benefit for the unemployed – divided into contribution-based and income-based benefits.	Unemployed or those working less than 16 hrs a week. They must be available for work at least 40 hrs a week.	For single people aged 25 and over, the benefit is worth around £55.65.
DISABILITY LIVING ALLOWANCE	Available for the disabled. It's split into two parts, mobility and care, which attract different rates.	Those under 65 who are disabled.	£39.35 for help day OR night; £58.80 for help day and night; £15.55 for part-time help.
COUNCIL TAX BENEFIT	A benefit that can pay some or all of your Council Tax.	Those on low incomes.	Some or even all of your Council Tax may be rebated.
MATERNITY ALLOWANCE	Benefit lasting 18 weeks, for women expecting a baby.	Women who don't qualify for Statutory Maternity Pay.	Approx £103.
PENSION CREDIT	Divided into two parts – Minimum Income Guarantee (MIG) and Savings Credit.	MIG is for the over 60s. Savings Credit is for the 65+ whose income exceeds the set level due to savings or pensions.	MIG for single people is £105.45; couples get £160.95. Savings Credit is up to £15.51 or £20.22 for couples.

For the over 45s If you're not bringing up children, you might be eligible for the weekly Bereavement Allowance. In 2004, the weekly maximum rate was £79.60. To get it, you have to be over 45 when your spouse died or when your Widowed Parent's Allowance ended. The rate varies depending on your age – from 30% at age 45 to 100% at 55 and over.

WHERE DO YOU MAKE CLAIMS?

Check the phone book for your local Social Security or Jobs and Benefits Office. See the Directory at the back of this book for further help in finding Goverment and local offices.

ASK YOURSELF

CAN I SAVE ON MY COUNCIL TAX?
You may be able to reduce your Council Tax banding if you can answer 'Yes' to any of the following questions:
- Do I live mainly in one room?
- Do I need space for a wheelchair?
- Am I receiving the guarantee part – the amount that everyone eligible is entitled to receive – of the Pension Credit, Housing Benefit or Council Tax Benefit?

Saving, borrowing and investing

There are a few fundamental financial truths that
don't change over time. If you master them and
stay on top of current trends, you can maximise
your assets and provide for a secure future.

SURER SAVING AND BETTER BANKING

Even if you only have a small amount of spare cash, there are ways of making savings grow into worthwhile amounts. And while you're at it, check out your banking habits – they're probably so familiar that you fail to notice the fees your bank takes from you to make its vast profits.

KEEP SOME CASH ON HAND

Keep enough money available so that you can pay regular bills and cope with unexpected expenses.

Rainy-day savings You never know when you might need cash at short notice, to repair the car or a leaking roof or to cover the cost of sickness and redundancy. It's vital to create a savings fund to protect yourself and your family.

Cover necessities Even cutting out all the little luxuries, the average person needs at least £700 a month to cover essential bills and debt repayments such as credit cards, loans and mortgages.

Emergency funds You should save at least three, ideally six, months' salary in a safe, instant-access savings account so you can get your hands on it in an emergency. This will also save you from having to raise expensive credit when you can least afford it.

GET THE BEST RATE FOR YOUR SAVINGS

Keep an eye on your cash. If your current account starts showing a healthy surplus, shift some of the money into a high-interest savings account to make it work for you.

Introductory bonus Many savings accounts offer an introductory bonus of around 0.5% for the first six months, but after this rate has ended you might get an ordinary return. Either choose an account with a good long-term rate, or switch after the introductory period is over.

Give notice Check out accounts with 30 or 60 days' notice of withdrawal. These often give a higher interest rate and they stop you from dipping into your emergency fund.

ISA allowance If you pay tax, use your annual cash ISA allowance to invest up to £3,000 a year in a special savings account and you won't pay any income tax on your interest. Rates can be good, as banks and building societies compete for new customers. Some of the best rates are offered by online banks and local building societies.

Fluctuating interest rates If you expect interest rates to rise, consider a tracker account that pledges to match any future increases for a set period. If you expect interest rates to fall, you could fix your interest rate for one, three or five years. But if rates rise, you could lose out. Don't tie up money in a fixed-rate account if you might need it later.

Minimum payments Some accounts insist you pay a minimum sum of between £50 and £2,000 into your account each month. Only open this type of account if you're sure you won't miss a payment, otherwise you won't get that attractive interest rate.

CASE STUDY

SAVE A HEALTHY £3,000 A YEAR

Until his girlfriend pointed out how much money he was frittering away, Alan Brown, 28, had nothing left at the end of each month to put aside for savings. By trimming back on crisps, chocolate, alcohol and cigarettes, Alan is now saving nearly £3,000 a year. With the average pint of lager now costing £2.29, one pint fewer a day saves Alan £836 a year. And by stopping his 20-a-day smoking habit, he is now a whopping £1,825 a year better off. Also gone are his daily 40p packet of crisps and 45p chocolate bar (saving him a further £310 a year). Now, as well as feeling healthier, Alan has healthy savings, too.

KEEP AN EYE ON YOUR INVESTMENTS

Once you've decided to invest some money, keep track of how it's performing and change to a better deal if necessary.

Compare ISA rates Check out www.moneyfacts.co.uk ✉ and www.moneysupermarket.com ✉ for savings and cash ISA comparison tables, or read the money section in your weekend newspaper. Switch if your rate doesn't match up.

No branches Telephone, postal and online accounts, especially Intelligent Finance (**www.if.com** 0845 609 4343 ✉) and Safeway Bank (**www.safeway.co.uk** 0800 995 995 ✉), offer more competitive rates, because they don't have the cost of a branch network.

Annual equivalent rate (AER) This rate puts accounts on a level playing field by showing the annual amount you receive, regardless of when you take the money. It also includes the impact of introductory bonuses.

MAKE THE MOST OF YOUR BANK ACCOUNT

Many people set up a current account with one of the four big high street banks – Barclays, HSBC, NatWest and Lloyds TSB – and never think of changing. The banks know this and don't work hard to keep your custom. They typically pay a miserable 0.1% interest on current accounts but hit you with heavy penalties if you go overdrawn.

Find a better deal The Consumers' Association website **www.switchwithwhich.co.uk** ✉ helps you find a better current account and demonstrates how easy it is to switch. Online banks Smile and First Direct perform strongly in the association's regular surveys.

Don't go overdrawn If you think you might need an overdraft, seek authorisation from your bank first. Banks may charge 15% interest on an authorised overdraft, but a hefty 30% if you don't tell them first. They also charge fees up to £25 a day (subject to a £75 monthly maximum), plus charges of between £10–£25 for any cancelled payments.

---

keep it simple

CLEAR DEBTS BEFORE SAVING

Instead of putting spare cash in a savings account, use it to pay off your mortgage. Many lenders offer flexible mortgages that allow you to make regular overpayments. You might be paying 6% on a lender's standard variable mortgage rate, whereas you will get little more than 4% on its best savings rate. It makes even more sense to pay off credit card and store card debt. Many credit cards charge more than 15% while store cards can charge up to 30%. No savings account on earth will come close to that.

Be flexible with offset mortgages

These flexible mortgages work as a current account, allowing you to pay extra money into your mortgage or borrow back that money whenever you wish. This works in your favour for two reasons. First, you receive the mortgage rate on your savings, which is always slightly higher than savings rates, and second, you don't pay any tax because you are saving rather than earning interest. Offset mortgages are available from a number of lenders, including Intelligent Finance and Woolwich Open Plan, as well as building societies such as Yorkshire, Coventry and Norwich & Peterborough.

THE BENEFITS OF OFFSET MORTGAGES

This type of mortage will benefit homeowners with:
■ High levels of savings.
■ Large sums of money in their credit account earning negligible interest.
■ High credit card or personal loan bills – you repay the debt at the much lower mortgage rate.
■ Higher-rate tax – a mortgage rate of 5.45% is equivalent to a return of 9.08% for this group.
■ Fluctuating incomes – reduce your account or borrow back, according to your earnings.
■ The desire to pay off their mortgage early – paying an extra £100 a month on a £70,000 mortgage will clear your mortgage eight years early, saving you thousands of pounds.

SMART MOVES

THE COST OF BANK CHARGES

Banks vary slightly in how they bill you for transactions such as money transfers and overdraft charges, and some costs are unavoidable. The examples shown below are typical, with little to choose between high street and online banks. Do complain to your bank if you have been hit with excessive charges without good reason.

TRANSACTIONS WHILE OVERDRAWN	£30 PER CHEQUE OR OTHER ITEM
SAME-DAY TRANSFER (CHAPS)	£20 PER TRANSFER TO ANOTHER UK BANK
EXPRESS CHEQUE SERVICE	£15 PER CHEQUE
STOPPED CHEQUE	£10 PER CHEQUE UNLESS LOST OR STOLEN
BANKER'S DRAFT	£10 PER STERLING DRAFT
UNAUTHORISED OVERDRAFT	£10 EACH DAY
COPY STATEMENT	£5 PER STATEMENT

Charges correct at July 2004

Beware surcharging ATMs Following a high-profile campaign, many banks and building societies waived the charges on drawing out money on cash cards. Now, some have sold their cash machines to private operators, who charge up to £1.75 every time you withdraw your money. Make sure your local ATM isn't stinging you. Alternatively, use free supermarket cashback schemes.

DON'T DRAW CASH ON YOUR CREDIT CARD

You face an extra charge if you draw cash on your credit card, ranging from 1.5% to 2% of the money you withdraw. Credit card companies also charge interest immediately, rather than waiting for the standard 56 days, as with shop purchases. Avoid this except in emergencies.

EARN CASH FROM YOUR CREDIT CARD

If you pay off your credit card balance every month, swap your current card for a cashback card, available from Abbey, Alliance & Leicester, Halifax, Royal Bank of Scotland and Smile. You get a typical rate of 0.5% back on every purchase. Put all your spending on your card – a big-ticket purchase such as a £2,000 holiday earns you a bonus of £10. Spending £1,000 a month this way would earn you about £60 a year, payable as a credit to your account or a yearly cheque – a bonus more attractive than Air Miles.

USE A WINDFALL WISELY

When you have a windfall – bonus, gift, cash for extra work – use the rule of thirds to determine how you'll use it.
One third for the past Use one third to pay off a debt.
One third for the present Take the second third to make a home or personal improvement you want.
One third for the future Put the final third into some sort of savings or investment.

CANCEL UNWANTED DIRECT DEBITS

More than three out of four people who cancel their gym membership or a magazine subscription pay for an extra two months by forgetting to tell their bank. Remember to cancel your direct debits or standing orders the moment you want to stop paying.

TAX-EFFICIENT SAVINGS

The taxman doesn't just want to take a bite of your income, he's also after your savings. But there's plenty you can do to keep his hands off your money, whether it's taking steps to safeguard your earnings or making sure that any money you invest pays the best possible returns.

PLAY THE PERFECT PARTNERS GAME

If your spouse or partner is in a lower tax band than you are, consider shifting your savings into their name as they will pay less tax on the interest.

Significant savings A top-rate taxpayer earning 4% a year on savings worth £15,000 would get interest worth £600 a year but lose £240 of that to the taxman. They could save that by shifting the money into the name of their non-taxpaying spouse. If their partner pays basic rate tax,

THE BEST TAX-EFFICIENT SAVINGS

SAVINGS VEHICLE	ANNUAL MAXIMUM	PURPOSE
Individual Savings Account (ISA)	Invest up to £7,000 a year in stocks and shares through a maxi ISA. Alternatively, invest up to £3,000 in the stocks and shares of a mini ISA, £3,000 in a mini cash ISA and £1,000 in life insurance. The investment limit in a maxi ISA falls to £5,000 from April 2006.	An ISA can be used for almost every investment purpose, from long-term stock market savings to a tax-free deposit account. All returns are free of most income tax and all capital gains tax.
Friendly Society bonds	Invest a maximum £25 a month or £270 a year in a tax-free bond run by mutual organisations called friendly societies.	Most commonly used by parents and grandparents investing for children in so-called 'baby bonds'. You have to maintain your monthly investment for a minimum of 10 years. Watch out for high charges, especially early on – with many bonds the entire first-year contributions could be swallowed up in charges. But, some now charge just 1% a year.
National Savings	You can invest up to £60,000 in tax-free savings certificates.	Savings certificates, Children's Bonus Bonds and Premium Bonds all pay tax-free interest or prizes. Backed by the government and so low risk.
Stakeholder pensions	Pension savings plan that allows you to invest up to £3,600 a year. Higher-rate taxpayers earn 40% tax relief. Basic-rate taxpayers and non-taxpayers earn 22%.	Must be used to buy an annuity before the age of 75. You can claim a 25% tax-free cash lump sum at this point. Thereafter, all returns are subject to income tax, depending on your tax bracket at the time.

HOW TAX ERODES YOUR RETURN

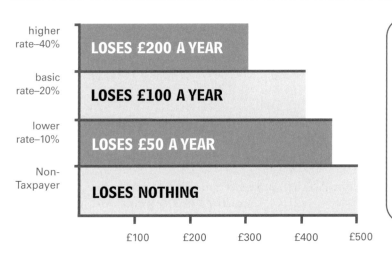

higher rate–40%	**LOSES £200 A YEAR**
basic rate–20%	**LOSES £100 A YEAR**
lower rate–10%	**LOSES £50 A YEAR**
Non-Taxpayer	**LOSES NOTHING**

£100   £200   £300   £400   £500

> This chart shows how much savers in different tax brackets receive in interest on £10,000 in a savings account that pays 5% a year. Though rates paid on savings interest are lower than income tax rates, only a non-taxpayer would reap the full £500 pounds interest earned, with the taxman not getting a penny. So other forms of saving may be a smarter option.

they can still make savings. In this case, shifting that £15,000 into their partner's name would reduce the tax bill from £240 to £120.

Word of warning Make sure your relationship is solid before transferring your life savings – you could lose everything if an untrustworthy partner were to run off with your fortune.

Reclamation Non-taxpayers should make sure they don't get taxed by mistake. Complete Inland Revenue form R85, available from your bank or building society, to reclaim tax automatically deducted from your savings. Why give it to the Inland Revenue when you don't have to?

USE YOUR ISA ALLOWANCE
Use your Individual Savings Account (ISA) allowance. You can save up to £7,000 a year from tax in a 'maxi' ISA, with a choice of investment components. Couples can shelter £14,000. A 'mini' ISA is also available, but the investment limit is £3,000 and the components are fixed.

Cash ISA The safest way to use your ISA allowance is to buy a cash ISA. You can save up to £3,000 a year. If you have savings sitting in a deposit account, transfer them into a cash ISA; interest is tax-free and rates can be more competitive. Shifting £3,000 of savings into a cash ISA paying 4.5% saves a higher-rate taxpayer £54 a year and a basic-rate taxpayer £27.

MAKE A SOUND INVESTMENT
Saving tax is important, but it's even more important to choose the investment that's right for your personal circumstances. As any financial adviser will tell you, never let the tax tail wag the investment dog.

FAMILY FINANCES

A well-planned saving strategy will help the whole family prepare for the future. Get more for your money by starting to invest while your children are small, and save even more by claiming all your tax breaks and entitlements.

SET UP A CHILD SAVINGS ACCOUNT

A good way of teaching your children about the value of money, and making sure they don't squander it when they get older, is to set up a savings account in their name.

Best interest rates Almost every bank or building society offers children's savings accounts, often giving away goodies such as stickers, cuddly toys and birthday cards. Don't be distracted by free gifts – go for the best interest rate. The delights of compound interest will hopefully prove more attractive than fluffy toys in the longer run.

STOCKS AND SHARES FOR THE LONG TERM

You might think the risky nature of the stock market makes it the wrong place to invest money for your children, but the reverse may be true. Stocks and shares are a risk in the short term, but over long periods such as 10 or 20 years they have dramatically outperformed other types of savings. If you start saving when your child is born, you are setting the money aside for at least 18 years – enough time to override short-term volatility.

Spread the risk You can choose the safer option by saving in a fund such as a unit trust or investment trust. Some investment fund managers promote funds targeted at parents and grandparents who wish to invest

---

MOST COMMON MISTAKES IN FAMILY FINANCE PLANNING

- Only one family member is involved in financial affairs.
- There is no budget for the family.
- There is insufficient cash available to handle emergencies or new opportunities.
- Employee benefits are poorly understood and mismanaged.
- Investments are not diversified.

CASE STUDY

SET UP FOR LIFE

Helen Kirby, 20, is delighted that her parents had the foresight to start saving on her behalf shortly after she was born. 'They didn't have much cash to spare but decided the best way to save was little and often. So they put £20 a month for me in a high-interest savings account – they didn't really notice the money leaving their account, but its value was gradually mounting in mine.' Over time they increased the monthly sum to £40, and now the savings account holds more than £10,000. This is proving a real boon now that Helen is studying at university. 'Most of my friends have already racked up large debts, but I've got this financial cushion to fall back on.'

Helen's parents always taught her the value of money and how to look after it wisely. 'They set up another account in my name when I was 12 for spare pocket or Christmas money. The account only holds a few hundred pounds, but the lesson it taught me about handling my cash was invaluable.' Helen isn't just relying on her parents – she has a part-time job working in a local coffee shop one afternoon a week and every Saturday. 'This brings in a bit of extra money and helps keep things ticking over. Some of my friends expect to graduate with five-figure debts, but I'm hoping to keep mine to just a few thousand pounds. Then I want to start saving for a deposit on my first flat.'

on behalf of children, but there is absolutely no reason why you should plump for these. What really counts is the underlying performance of the investment, and some children's investments have performed badly. Ignore marketing gimmicks – make your choice in exactly the same way as any other investment.

LOW-RISK NATIONAL SAVINGS

A Children's Bonus Bond from National Savings is a low-risk, tax-efficient savings account targeted at children. The headline interest rate is actually better than it seems, because all returns are free of tax, provided you hold the bond for five years. You can invest up to £1,000 in each bond issue.

SAVE WITH A CHILD TRUST FUND

In future, the government-backed Child Trust Fund (sadly, only benefiting children born after September 2002) may be a popular tax-efficient way to save for your children.

Lump sum The state will pay £250 (£500 for low-income families earning full Child Tax Credit) into a fund held in the child's name. There may be a further state payment when the child turns seven.

Feed the fund The aim is to encourage friends and families to top up the account (which cannot be cashed in until the child turns 18) to a maximum £1,200 a year. From April 2005, parents with eligible children will receive a voucher when claiming Child Benefit. They can use this to open an account with a range of different firms, including banks, building societies, friendly societies and investment fund managers. Shop around for the best rate.

How you gain The Child Trust Fund saves you money in two ways. First, you don't pay any income tax or capital gains tax on the returns. Second, charges are limited to an annual fee of 1.5%, lower than many rival investments.

AVOID TAX ON CHILD SAVINGS

Children have the same tax allowances as adults and so can earn £4,745 (from April 2004) in savings interest each year before paying tax. To prevent parents using their children as a tax dodge, the Inland Revenue will tax parents on any interest above £100 a year – £200 if the original investment came from both parents. But this doesn't apply to accounts opened by friends and other family members.

Set up a trust Parents who want to make bigger investments can protect themselves from tax using a 'bare trust', which states you are holding the assets in trust for the

keep it simple

GET 22% TAX RELIEF ON A STAKEHOLDER PENSION FOR YOUR CHILD
It might seem premature to start saving for your child's pension, but it could make sense if you have money to spare. You can invest up to £3,600 each year in a stakeholder pension on behalf of each of your children and receive 22% tax relief on your contributions, worth up to £792 a year.
The drawback is that your children can't touch the money until they are at least 55, but because you are investing over such a long period, it could be worth a lot.

child and managing them on their behalf until they turn 18. All income and growth is then taxed as belonging to the child, so they can use their full personal allowance.

Grandparents' gifts Providing they live for seven years afterwards, grandparents can give their grandchildren any amount of money free of inheritance tax.

Coming of age From the age of 16, your child can use their £3,000 cash ISA allowance for low-risk, tax-free savings. From 18, they can use their full £7,000 allowance.

MEETING THE COST OF EDUCATION

With charges going up all the time, it's good to know that there are several ways you can make up for any shortfall in your savings.

Child benefit Don't forget that this continues up to the age of 19 if your child stays on at school. In addition, means-tested education maintenance allowances (EMAs) of up to £1,500 a year are available from September 2004.

Bursaries If your child plans to study an NHS-approved medical or dental course, they may be entitled to bursaries that cover tuition fees in the final years of their course. The NHS Student Grants Unit will supply details. For other courses, there are opportunity bursaries for students from low-income families without a history of higher education. All three Armed Forces also offer bursaries to undergraduates and scholarship schemes to sixth-formers.

Sponsorship Some companies will fund the cost of a university course – especially in engineering, science and technology – based on an agreement that the student will work for the company for a specified period upon completion of their course.

Debt clearance Some employers offer to repay university debts as an attractive part of their salary package. Similarly, if your child goes on to work as a teacher in a subject with a shortage, they could qualify for government help with repaying their loan.

TOP TIPS TRACKING DOWN LOST ASSETS

Nobody likes losing money, but families in Britain are currently letting up to £20 billion slip through their fingers. That's £357 for every man, woman and child in the UK. The money is lying unclaimed in old savings accounts, insurance policies, share certificates, pension schemes and Premium Bonds. Assets can be lost when people move house, lose paperwork or die without telling relatives where their documents are kept. But there are ways of tracking assets down, either free of charge or for a small fee.

■ **Get help tracking down your assets** A number of organisations, such as Funds Reunited and The Unclaimed Assets Register, will help you to locate your unclaimed assets for a small fee (see Resources, left, for details).

■ **Do your own search** You can save money by making a start on a search yourself. Contact the relevant bank, insurer, investment company, National Savings or your former employer. Alternatively, you can contact several organisations that help track down assets held by existing and defunct institutions free of charge (see Resources, left).

BEST WAYS TO BORROW

Borrowing money is easier than ever, with lenders showering us with offers for credit cards and personal loans. Rates range from 0% to more than 30%, which makes a huge difference to your monthly bill, so get the cheapest possible interest rate. What, then, are your credit options?

CREDIT CARDS CAN BE CHEAP – OR DEAR

Spending on plastic is easy and fun, but it can also be pricey. The nation's favourite credit card is also one of the most expensive, so unless you clear your outstanding balance each month, switch to a hungrier, leaner rival.

0% introductory rate Scores of cards now charge an introductory rate of 0% for the first six months or so, to attract new customers. Some offer this only on balance transfers, others on new purchases as well. Visit websites **www.moneyfacts.co.uk** ✉ or **www.moneysupermarket.com** ✉ or check weekend newspapers and financial magazines for the latest best buys.

WATCH POINTS CREDIT CARD DRAWBACKS

Credit card providers now include summary boxes on marketing literature, highlighting details usually hidden in the small print. Always watch out for the following:

■ **APR (Annual Percentage Rate) charged on purchases** This is the most important figure for those who don't clear their balances. Look out for 0% introductory charges, but don't pay a rip-off rate when you revert to the standard APR.

■ **APR on balance transfers** This is interest rate you pay on money transferred from a previous card, and isn't always the same as the rate for purchases. But be warned: a card charging 0% on balance transfers but a high APR on purchases could use your monthly payment to clear the 0% balance first, while your spending attracts hefty interest.

■ **The rate you actually pay** Sometimes companies charge APR according to your credit rating, which means you could pay more than the headline rate.

■ **Interest-free period** Most credit cards don't charge any interest for around 56 days after making a purchase. But a handful charge immediately, which means you still pay interest even if you clear your balance every month.

■ **Annual fee** Some cards don't charge an annual fee, others charge around £20.

■ **Loyalty and cashback schemes** Some credit cards offer rewards such as Air Miles or credit your card account with a percentage of your spending, between 0.1% and 2%.

■ **Penalties** Check on penalties for late payment or exceeding your credit limit.

■ **Minimum payments** Special offers, such as 0% balance transfers, may demand that you spend a minimum monthly sum on your credit card.

---

keep it simple

CUT UP YOUR STORE CARDS AND SAVE POUNDS
There is one simple piece of advice with store cards – give them the chop! Unless you know you will clear the monthly balance regularly, cancel them once you have reaped any benefits they might offer (see *Practical parenting*, page 100). Many charge scandalous rates of interest, exploiting their loyal customers with rates of up to 30%. High street names are often among the worst offenders. Shift your outstanding balance to a 0% introductory offer – if you owe £1,000 on your store cards, you'll save up to £150 over the next six months.

RESOURCES

COMPARE RATES
■ Find out about the potential savings you could make on borrowing by comparing rates of credit cards, loans and mortgages. Check **www.moneysuper market.com** ✉ and **www.moneyfacts.co.uk** ✉.

LOANS BEAT CREDIT CARDS

Personal loans are typically cheaper than credit cards, with the most competitive charge being less than 10%. Unlike credit cards, the repayment term and interest rate are fixed at the outset.

Shop around A bank or building society won't necessarily give you the best deal. For an extensive list of lenders and brokers, visit **www.find.co.uk** ✉ and search for best buys on **www.moneyfacts.co.uk** ✉.

REMORTGAGE TO RAISE CASH

This is the cheapest long-term credit you can get, and many people use it to consolidate more expensive debts such as a credit or store card. This isn't always a good idea, because you may take more than 25 years to pay off your mortgage, which means you end up paying more in the long run.

GOING INTO THE RED? TELL YOUR BANK

If you seem likely to exceed your bank account funds and go overdrawn, always warn your bank. If you don't, you could pay twice as much interest on your overdraft as you would on a personal loan.

CREDIT REFERENCE AGENCIES

Your financial record, including details of all borrowings, arrears and defaults, is kept on file at three credit reference agencies – Experian, Equifax and Call Credit. Banks and building societies tap into their records when deciding whether to lend you money.

A credit rating pays Whereas a bad credit rating can cost you dearly, having no credit rating at all (because you've never borrowed money or had a hire-purchase agreement) can be just as detrimental. You are most likely to be granted a loan if you have a proven record of paying back credit and debt responsibly.

OVERCOME A BAD CREDIT RATING

Millions of people, trapped in costly home loans or paying spiralling loan rates from a loan shark, have a damaged credit rating, and many face problems securing a mortgage or remortgage from the major high street lenders.

Mortgages are available Don't despair, because a growing number of reputable lenders will give you a mortgage, even if you have mortgage arrears, county court judgments (CCJs), discharged bankruptcy, a poor credit rating or no proof of income. You will pay slightly more than the most competitive rates, but it may not be as expensive as you think. Consult an experienced mortgage broker to help you find the best deal.

Restore your standing Sub-prime or non-standard mortgages, as they are known, also allow you to repair your battered credit rating. After a year or two of regular payments, you can remortgage to a lower rate from a different lender.

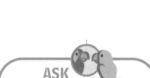

ASK YOURSELF

HOW CAN I MAKE BEST USE OF MY CHILD'S STUDENT LOAN?

Most students will take low-interest loans to help them through their university years. Your income affects the amount of loan your child is entitled to from the Student Loans scheme. Before applying for a loan, consider the following:

■ If you support your child beyond the amount of loan they're entitled to, consider using their full loan entitlement and investing the money. The borrowing will accrue interest at the rate of inflation, which you may well be able to beat.

■ Banks regularly offer student accounts with substantial interest-free overdrafts. If you use your child's student overdraft facility, don't get caught out. Check when the bank expects it to be repaid.

BENEFIT BY JOINING A CREDIT UNION

If you are struggling to get a loan from a mainstream organisation because of previous credit problems, or are tired of your hard-earned cash lining the pockets of banks whose annual profits run into billions, then you should consider joining your local credit union.

What are they? Credit unions are non-profit making organisations owned by their members, which offer basic savings and loan services. There are more than 700 credit unions in the UK, usually serving a local community such as church, trade union or workers in the same industry. The Labour government has encouraged credit unions as a way of getting financial services to those on low incomes who are often ignored by the big banks.

Cheap credit Interest on a loan from a credit union is capped by law at 12.7% a year (at July 2004), although many charge less. At this rate of interest, someone borrowing £1,000 over 12 months would pay £1,067 in total, and there are no penalties for early repayment. The maximum loan available is £10,000.

Savers' rates Profits from loans help pay the interest on savers' deposits. Savings rates are typically 2% or 3%, although some can be as high as 8%. You may also receive a dividend, with any surplus typically shared among members, because there are no shareholders.

Other benefits Savings include free life insurance, giving your main beneficiary double the amount you have saved if you die. Like banks and building societies, credit unions are even regulated by the Financial Services Authority compensation scheme, so in the unlikely event that your union goes bust, your first £2,000 savings will be returned and 90% of the next £30,000.

 **RESOURCES**

DEBT PROBLEMS
If you have debt problems, the following organisations may help:
Business Debtline (for small business owners) Call 0800 197 6026 ✉.
Citizens Advice Bureau Call 020 7833 2181 or visit **www.citizensadvice. org.uk** ✉.
Consumer Credit Counselling Service Call 0800 138 1111 or visit **www.cccs.co.uk** ✉.
Debt Advisers UK Visit **www.debtadvisers.co.uk** ✉.
Insolvency Service (a government information service) Visit **www.insolvency.gov.uk** ✉.
National Debtline Call 0808 808 4000 ✉.
Payplan Call 0845 601 2923 or visit **www.payplan.com** ✉.

DEALING WITH DEBT

If your debts are spiralling out of control, face up to the problem as soon as you can. The quicker you act, the more you will save in the long run. Don't let fines, penalties and high interest charges make a bad situation even worse.

STEP ONE: GET HELP

First of all, accept that you have a problem and take steps to find the help you need to tackle it.

Get free advice and counselling Personal problems often contribute to debt, and even the most conscientious people can run into problems following redundancy or divorce. A variety of organisations give free counselling services to help you to find ways of paying off your debts (see Resources, left). Reputable debt agencies won't make you feel guilty, and they will help you to put things right. Avoid companies that charge a fee for helping people in debt as this will only add to your costs.

Contact your creditors Don't hide from your creditors – they have seen it all before and will view you more positively if you contact them and explain your situation rather than if you just don't pay. They may also be more sympathetic than you fear, particularly utility (gas, electricity water, etc) and financial services companies, who have a social obligation to help you with your problem.

Remember you have rights too Don't be bullied by heavy-handed or threatening creditors and debt collectors. The courts are there to protect your interests as well as help creditors get their money.

Action plan for clearing your debt

The quicker you pay your debts the less they will cost you in the long run.

Make a budget Draw up a personal budget to see how much you are earning and spending each month, and make cutbacks.

Prioritise your debt Pay your mortgage or rent to keep the roof over your head. Then meet utility bills and try to maintain hire purchase agreements, such as a car to get you to work. Finally, look at debts such as credit and store cards.

Draw up a repayment plan If you can't afford to pay all your monthly bills negotiate a debt-management plan with your creditors. This involves paying as much as you can after covering all your essentials. Many companies prefer this to taking you to court, which is expensive and time-consuming.

Pay bills promptly Deal with bills when they arrive – don't let them stack up or the debt spiral will begin again.

Top up your income This might include taking a part-time job, freelancing, or renting out a room in your home. Are you receiving the state benefits available to you?

Maximise your resources Do you have any unwanted but valuable possessions you could turn into cash?

Pay bills by direct debit It's relatively painless as you don't see the money leaving your account.

Consolidate your debts Move expensive borrowings into cheaper forms of debt, such as a 0% introductory credit card rate or a remortgage.

Say no Don't enter into any instant credit agreements you can't afford, no matter how enticing they seem.

CASE STUDY

GETTING TO GRIPS WITH MOUNTING DEBTS

Andy Johnstone, 27, knew he had to take charge of his debts when he found that he owed more than £10,000 on his credit cards. Andy had put off clearing his credit cards for years, simply switching the outstanding balance to new cards with 0% introductory rates. 'I was earning £22,000 a year, which meant the debts were half my annual income. So I really had to take control.'

There are several organisations that help people deal with their debts, and Andy contacted Payplan (see Resources, opposite). 'I was embarrassed to call them at first, but they didn't judge me, and gave me a lot of useful advice.'

They suggested he start by drawing up a list of his regular outgoings, and this helped him identify where he was spending his money – a simple step that might have helped him to avoid debt in the first place. Its advisers also suggested ways of boosting his income, such as taking a part-time job, and Andy now works three nights a week in a local pub, getting paid to serve drinks rather than spending money buying them. Andy has now cut up his credit cards and set up regular standing orders to repay £300 a month, the maximum he could afford.

Once his debts are cleared, he wants to get into the saving habit to put down a deposit on a flat. 'That may be a few years away – and something I couldn't have imagined a few months ago – but at least I'm starting to take control of my finances now.'

SAVVY SOLUTIONS FOR STUDENT DEBT

The interest rate charged on a student loan is very low compared with other loans in the marketplace. Therefore if your child has graduated with other borrowing, such as credit card debt or a bank overdraft, any money earned would be better placed clearing these debts before paying back the student loan.

TOP TIPS ECONOMIES TO HELP YOU SAVE

Here are some financial 'housekeeping tips' to keep your expenses down, allowing you to pay off your debts more quickly.

■ **Prune direct debits** Do you use that gym membership or magazine subscription?

■ **Switch your utility supplier** You can cut the cost of gas and electricity by 25% (see *Household finance*, page 296).

■ **Check overpayments on direct debits** If you have a direct debit for your gas, electricity or telephone, check whether you have overpaid. Your provider could owe you hundreds of pounds and be getting interest on your money.

■ **Shop around for cheaper life insurance** Premiums have fallen 40% over the last six years.

■ **Compare insurance renewal rates** Switching your household and motor insurance companies could cut your premiums by more than 30%.

■ **Find cheaper phone deals** Hunt for a cheaper mobile phone tariff or renounce your phone altogether to save around £60 a month.

■ **Pay promptly** Don't be surcharged or fined by paying off your credit or store cards late.

INVESTING IN THE STOCK MARKET

When you buy stocks, you acquire a share of a company's profits. Although the recent slump in equities demonstrated that stocks and shares can go down as well as up, markets have started to revive.

WHY INVEST?

Long-term returns have beaten every other type of investment, but only invest money you won't need for at least five, preferably ten, years to give you time to bounce back from any shocks.

Little and often Putting a little aside every month is always a good idea, but it is particularly sensible when investing in stocks and shares. If you put a lump sum into the stock market and it crashes the next day, your money could instantly be worth much, much less.

'Pound cost averaging' This jargon means that regular savers actually benefit if the stock market falls from time to time, because their monthly payment buys more shares at the lower price. This is good news, provided the market has bounced back by the time you cash in your investment.

Spread the risks Build a 'balanced portfolio' by starting to invest in major UK blue-chip companies that make up the FTSE 100. Then diversify by putting a smaller amount of money overseas. Spread your money between different fund management companies as well as different types of fund.

DON'T GET GREEDY

Throwing money at the latest fad is a waste. Funds invested in technology, biotechnology, smaller Japanese companies and healthcare have all lost unwary investors a lot of money.

Facts not hype If something looks too good to be true, it probably is. High-income bonds were paying up to 10% at a time when the average savings account was paying 4%, and were sold as a low-risk investment targeted at elderly people

LONG-TERM INVESTMENT PERFORMANCES

This chart shows how £1,000 invested in cash, bonds and equities fared over five and ten year terms.

	5 YEARS	10 YEARS
BUILDING SOCIETY SAVINGS ACCOUNT	£1,099	£1,294
UK ALL-COMPANY EQUITY INDEX	£902	£1,934
UK CORPORATE BOND (AVERAGE)	£1.170	£1,808

Source: Lipper, May 2004

wanting income in retirement. But thousands of investors lost their original capital, which wasn't guaranteed, when stock markets fell. So always read the small print.

AVOID HIGH CHARGES

Most investment funds have two types of charge, an initial charge, paid upfront when you buy the product and taken from your investment, and an annual management fee, taken from your fund each year. Initial charges are typically higher, often more than 5%, meaning that for every £1,000 you invest, the fund management company pockets £50.

Discount brokers To escape those 5% initial charges, purchase your investment funds through a discount broker, such as Chelsea Financial Services, Financial Discounts Direct or Hargreaves Lansdown. These companies will rebate all the initial commission they earn to you, typically slashing initial fund charges from 5.25% to less than 1%, or even as low as 0%. Investing your £7,000 ISA allowance via a discount broker could save more than £350.

No catches Discount brokers can waive initial charges because they don't offer financial advice but sell funds direct to the investor on an execution-only basis, saving on staff, administrative and regulatory costs. They earn their money from a share of the fund's annual charge (you're unlikely to get a worthwhile discount on annual fees).

keep it simple

AGE CONCERN
The older you are, the less you should have in equities and the more in cash and bonds, as you have less time to recoup any losses. If you have only a small nest egg, avoid the stock market altogether.

YOU DECIDE: PROFIT, RISK AND CHARGES		
SAVINGS PLAN	**WHAT IS IT?**	**TYPICAL CHARGES**
Deposit account or cash ISA	Low-risk savings from banks and building societies.	No direct charges. The cost of the account is reflected in the rate of interest.
Unit trust	A pooled stock market fund that invests in a range of different companies to spread the risk of investing in a single stock. Investors buy units in the fund. The basis for most stocks and shares is ISA funds.	Initial charge: 5.25% Annual charge: 1.5%
Investment trust	A pooled stock market fund, similar to a unit trust, but with a more complex structure. Can be slightly higher risk, but has lower charges.	Initial charge: 0%–3% Annual charge: 0.5%–1%
Friendly Society baby bonds	Tax-efficient regular savings plans offered only by friendly societies. You can save up to £25 a month for a minimum of 10 years.	Traditionally high-charging, with initial charges of more than 5%. New bonds are emerging with total fees of just 1% a year.
With-profits bonds	Investment bond sold by insurance companies investing in a range of stocks and shares, bonds, cash and property. Aims to reduce risk and produce smooth returns.	Initial charge: 5%–7% Annual charge: 1.5%

BE YOUR OWN INVESTOR

Investing in individual companies puts you at the sharp end of equity investing. This is where fast money can be made and lost. But direct equities is a slippery game, and you are likely to pick almost as many losers as winners.

ONLINE SHARE DEALING SLASHES COSTS
You can pay less for your share dealing service by using an online or telephone-based broker. There are now dozens of stockbrokers allowing you to trade online in real-time and slashing fees from £50 for each share trade to just £10.
Percentage or flat-rate fees? If you expect to trade relatively small amounts, investing less than £1,000, look for percentage-based fees charged by sites such as The Share Centre, but check minimum charges. Investors trading larger sums might do better paying a flat rate. Ample Share Dealing, for example, charges £10 for all UK trades (see Check Out the Charges, opposite).
Hidden costs When comparing costs, watch out for hidden fees. Some websites charge a quarterly administration fee of around £12 – that works out at an expensive £48 a year – or sting you with inactivity fees unless you make regular trades.
Online brokers As well as offering popular online share dealing services, online stockbrokers give free information, news and analysis on share trading. Visit **www.find.co.uk** for a full list.

MAKE OLD WINDFALLS WORK FOR YOU
Many people will harbour happy memories of the days in the late 1990s when many mutually owned building societies and some life insurers became stock market quoted banks, showering their members with cash windfalls worth thousands of pounds. Some conversions were forced by unscrupulous opportunists (carpetbaggers), who opened dozens of building society accounts in the hope that this would qualify them for a windfall on demutualisation. Most are probably now wasting their time. Many building societies have introduced new rules barring new customers from a windfall during the first three years, although rules vary according to the institution.
Don't sit on your windfall shares Many people simply hold onto their windfall shares, but this can be a big mistake. You won't gain much benefit from the shares if they underperform, so review them regularly. Do you expect the company to perform well or would you be better off investing the money elsewhere?
Diversify your holdings It's too risky to keep a large amount invested in one company. If your windfall shares are the only shares you own, you should move at least some of the money into another share, investment fund or savings account to avoid having all of your eggs in one basket.
Shelter your shares from the taxman You can use your annual ISA allowance to shelter your windfall shares, and any other shares you own, from the Inland Revenue.

Information correct as of July 2004

CHECK OUT THE CHARGES ✉

Interactive Investor £10 for UK deals online and £15 for US trades, regardless of size, with no annual fee.

Comdirect £12.50 for online and telephone deals, plus £25 annual fee.

Fastrade from Charles Stanley & Co £9.99 on share trades below £1,500 and £14.99 above, plus £20 annual fee. Telephone trades cost a minimum £20.

Hargreaves Lansdown Stockbrokers £9.95 per online trade or £15 by telephone, plus £50 a year account management charge.

TD Waterhouse £12.50 per online trade in UK or international stocks, or £11.95 if you trade more than seven times in a quarter (£16.95 on telephone).

The Share Centre 1% on the first £5,000 falling to 0.5% after that, with a minimum commission of £2.50 buying and £7.50 selling.

TAKE UP SHARE OPTIONS

Millions of workers can benefit from having shares in their own company under schemes offering a combination of tax breaks and free or cut-price shares. The two most popular schemes are Sharesave and Share Incentive Plan (SIP). If your company offers such a plan, don't miss out on it.

Sharesave This scheme protects members from any financial losses. By investing between £5 and £250 a month, you get the right to purchase the shares at a set price when the scheme winds up, after three, five or seven years. If the share has fallen, you reclaim your cash, plus tax-free interest on top. If it has performed well, you reap the benefits.

Share Incentive Plan Employees buying shares in a SIP are given free matching shares from their employer. This scheme is slightly riskier, as the stock market will affect share prices.

Minimise tax After cashing in your tax-free company shares, any future profits may become liable to tax. Protect yourself by shifting the shares into your ISA.

CASE STUDY

QUITTING WHILE HE WAS AHEAD

David Allen, 55, thought he could beat the investment professionals and started to trade stocks and shares online. He invested £2,500 – £500 each in a bank, an insurance company, an oil giant, a pharmaceuticals company and a small technology firm. The bank and insurer both grew 20% within weeks, and the technology firm grew a mighty 35%. Within three months, his portfolio had risen 20% to £3,000.

Dazzled by this early success, David became impatient, cashing in slow-moving stock and trading it for new stock without doing his research properly. Then one of his companies tumbled a massive 50%. This movement cost him £250 and, more annoyingly, he had decided against investing in a stock that rose 75%.

David soon realised he was becoming obsessed. He was devoting so much time and energy to his new hobby that his wife was complaining. So he decided that there was more to life than share dealing and decided to call it a day while he was still in profit, banking a £400 gain, closing the account and resuming a normal existence.

Years before you retire you need to find the most efficient way to save for later life. Shrewd savers not only maximise their pension but also make the most of their income once they have finished work.

Planning for retirement

UNDERSTANDING THE BASIC STATE PENSION

We're all living longer these days, so the money we have to save for retirement must stretch further than ever. Don't pin your hopes on the basic state pension – if you want a decent lifestyle in retirement, you should start saving now. Britons need to save an estimated £27 billion to plug the national savings gap, the difference between what we are saving for retirement and what we will actually need.

BASIC STATE PENSION

The basic state pension is barely enough to keep you above the breadline – and that's if you get the full amount. Many people wrongly believe they automatically qualify for this pension. What you get depends on your National Insurance (NI) contributions during your working life.

Who gets the full pension? To get the maximum pension, a man must have contributed for 44 years and a woman for 39 years. By 2020, the retirement age for women will have risen to 65, which means they must also have contributed for 44 years. If you don't make maximum contributions, you will get a reduced pension depending on the number of years you did contribute. You typically need to have contributed for at least 10 years to get anything at all.

Pensions for carers Women taking time off work to look after children, and carers looking after a sick or elderly relative, can also build up benefits under the home responsibilities protection scheme. If you are a carer or disabled person on low wages, or not earning at all, you can also build up entitlement.

Check up on your benefits To find out your current state entitlement, contact the forecasting unit at the DWP (Department of Work & Pensions). The call could be one of the most valuable you ever make. If you have any gaps you may be able to fill them with voluntary contributions, boosting your state retirement income. Call 0845 3000 168 or visit **www.thepensionservice.gov.uk** ✉, and have your NI number ready.

TOP TIPS FIND OUT ABOUT STATE TOP-UPS

If you have requested a pensions forecast, this will set out any additional state pension benefits you might get.
■ **The employed** Those in work may be able to top up their basic state pension with further state-funded benefits, the state earnings-related pension scheme (SERPS) and the state second pension (S2P), which replaced SERPS in April 2002 and targets support towards those on low earnings. The amount you get will depend on your earnings while working and how much you pay in Class 1 National Insurance contributions.
■ **The self-employed** If you are self-employed, you cannot claim any additional state pension. This means you should work harder to build your own savings towards topping up your state pension.

SMART MOVES

Hedging your bets

To ensure you have enough money in retirement, your best bet is to combine a number of different pension savings options:
■ Basic state pension and additional state pension benefits.
■ Final salary or money-purchase occupational pension.
■ Personal pension, including stakeholder.
■ Other investments, including ISAs, stocks and shares, bonds, cash.
■ Property, including your own home.

WORKPLACE PENSIONS

If your company offers an occupational pension scheme, you're one of the lucky ones. Join now, or you'll regret it in the long run. There are two main types of occupational pensions: final salary schemes and money-purchase schemes.

FINAL SALARY PENSIONS

Final salary schemes are the Rolls-Royce of company pension schemes but are increasingly rare – most firms can no longer afford them. Scheme assets may be invested on the stock market, but if equities fall, your company makes up the shortfall, not you.

How it works For every year you work for your employer, final salary schemes pay a proportion of the salary you earned in your final years before retirement. Most schemes offer one sixtieth of your final salary, multiplied by the number of years you worked for the company. For example, if you have worked for your employer for 15 years, you will get 15/60ths (or one-quarter) of your final salary as annual pension.

The benefits You are paid what is called a 'defined benefit' – your retirement income is guaranteed by your employer, so it doesn't depend on stock market performance.

The problems Falling stock markets, rising life expectancy and 'stealth taxes' on pension funds have made final salary schemes too costly for most companies. Many schemes have closed to new members, and some schemes have even collapsed, leaving employees battling for compensation.

New safety net Under new legislation, employers must protect members' benefits in full when winding up a scheme, and further protection is planned. The proposed pension protection fund aims to guarantee that workers will get at least 90% of their pension pot if their company goes bust.

MONEY-PURCHASE PENSIONS

The vast majority of occupational pensions are now money-purchase as they are less risky for employers.

How it works Normally, your boss invests between 3% and 5% of your salary into the scheme, and you contribute a similar amount. This money is invested in the stock market, and elsewhere. At retirement, your pot is used to buy an annuity – an income for life.

The benefits Despite not being as valuable as a final salary pension, it's still a great company benefit. Your employer's contributions effectively double your investments.

The problems Money-purchase schemes are less attractive than final salary pensions because you take the investment risk rather than your employer.

OTHER COMPANY PENSION SCHEMES

Although other types of occupational pension schemes have their drawbacks, consider the options before going it alone.

Group stakeholder pensions All companies with more than five staff have to offer access to a stakeholder pension, unless they already have an approved scheme. Unfortunately,

---

A WORTHWHILE BENEFIT

Your pension is probably your most valuable workplace benefit, so a good scheme is worth several thousand pounds on top of your annual salary. Check benefits carefully when applying for a new job.

Money from your partner's pension

Ensure you will receive benefits from your partner's company pension if your partner dies before retirement. These schemes offer two death benefits:

■ **Death-in-service** This is a lump sum of usually 4 x salary paid to a nominated person, which could be your spouse, partner or anyone you choose.

■ **Spouse pension** This pays a percentage of your pension to your spouse after you die. If you're not married and you want the money to go to your partner, make sure he or she is named on the form.

SMART MOVES

they aren't obliged to contribute, which makes most schemes worthless. If this is all you're offered, start a personal stakeholder pension (see page 346), which you can continue contributing to even after you've moved to a better employer with a worthwhile company scheme.

Group personal pension plan Your company may offer a group personal pension, typically contributing around 3% of salary. Charges have fallen in line with stakeholder plans. As with other money-purchase schemes, your income at retirement will depend on investment growth.

TAX-EFFICIENT TOP-UPS

You can boost your company pension by making additional contributions up to 15% of your salary, and earn generous tax relief into the bargain. There are two main ways of doing this: through additional voluntary contributions (AVCs) and free-standing additional voluntary contributions (FSAVCs).

ADDITIONAL VOLUNTARY CONTRIBUTIONS

As their name suggests, AVCs are additional contributions you can pay into your company's pension scheme.

The benefits They are a low-cost form of saving because your employer pays all the charges for running the scheme, giving you maximum possible benefit from your contribution. You also get tax relief on your contributions, as with personal pension contributions. Higher-rate taxpayers get a handsome 40% worth of relief; basic-rate taxpayers get 22%. At retirement, you can also take 25% of your fund as a tax-free cash lump sum.

Stakeholders vs AVCs Stakeholders also get this tax relief, but you pay the management charges from your pocket. Whether you decide to take out a personal stakeholder pension or opt for AVCs will depend on your individual circumstances, and you should consider taking independent financial advice.

Added years Some final salary schemes allow you to buy something called 'added years' in the scheme. Added years increase the proportion of your final salary you get as a pension and are attractive because they are a defined benefit, underpinned by the scheme. Unfortunately, few private-sector companies offer added years, which means your AVCs buy less attractive money-purchase benefits. Public-sector employees are luckier; not only do they have the option of buying added years, but their schemes are backed by the government, with any shortfall funded by the taxpayer. You can't find a better guarantee.

FREE-STANDING ADDITIONAL VOLUNTARY CONTRIBUTIONS

Unlike AVCs, which go into your employer's scheme, FSAVCs are invested in a separate 'free-standing' scheme run by an insurance company. This means you have to pay the pension company's management charges yourself, which will reduce investment growth. Charges on FSAVCs can also be relatively expensive, so check rates carefully before committing yourself.

ASK YOURSELF

IS A TOP-UP THE BEST OPTION?

■ If your company is making a healthy profit, your final salary scheme is probably safe. But if it's struggling, consider making extra provision by contributing to a stakeholder pension or ISA. As always, don't rely on a single pension savings vehicle.

SAVE MONEY WITH AVCS

Given the choice, you should generally choose AVCs over FSAVCs, because you avoid paying management charges. But there are exceptions:

■ If you don't want your boss to know how much extra you are contributing to your pension; perhaps you fear it could prejudice pay negotiations.

■ If you aren't impressed with the insurance company running your employer's scheme and think another company could do better. Even then, it may be better to use other investments, such as an ISA or a personal stakeholder, rather than FSAVCs.

SAVING WITH A STAKEHOLDER PENSION

If you aren't in a company scheme, either because your company doesn't provide one or because you are self-employed, you'll have to make your own plans. Don't rely on your state pension – supplement it with further savings.

TOP TIPS UNDERSTANDING STAKEHOLDERS

Your first option for your own pension scheme is a stakeholder pension. Before stakeholders were introduced in April 2001, many personal pensions had costly charges and complex, restrictive rules. Stakeholder pensions have swept all that away.

■ **Built-in flexibility** Plans allow you to invest from just £20 a month, and you are free to start, stop, increase or reduce your contributions whenever you wish. This is great news for those who don't want to be tied into a long-term contract, or the self-employed with variable income.

■ **Low charges** Originally, stakeholder pensions were limited to charging an annual 1% management fee. That charge will rise to 1.5% for stakeholders taken out after April 2005 (falling back to 1% if you hold your pension for more than 10 years). This is still a big improvement on old-style personal pensions, when charges were as high as 7%.

■ **A tax gift** You can invest up to £3,600 a year (2004) and earn attractive tax relief on your contributions. This works out as 40% for higher-rate taxpayers and 22% for everyone else, and means a top-rate taxpayer pays £2,160 for £3,600 worth of pension. Everybody else pays just £2,808. This is effectively a gift from the government, so don't ignore it.

STAKEHOLDER TAX TIP

Higher-rate taxpayers earn 40% tax relief on stakeholder contributions. But if their income falls after retirement and they become a basic-rate taxpayer, they will only pay 22% on their pension income. This makes stakeholder pensions even more tax efficient.

CASE STUDY

JULIA'S PRUDENT RETIREMENT PLAN

Julia Armstrong, 25, is already saving a little extra towards her retirement, but she is the only one of her friends who does.

Her first employer didn't have a company pension scheme, so she invested £40 a month into a stakeholder pension from a major insurance company. 'I know it isn't much, but it should stack up over the years. After all, that money has 40 years to grow.' She has since found a new job with an employer who runs a company pension scheme but continues paying into her stakeholder and has index-linked her pension contributions so they rise in line with inflation. 'My friends think I'm mad having two pensions – they'd rather spend the money on going out. But I want a fun old age, and the sooner I start saving the better. The money comes straight out of my bank account each month, so I don't really notice it.'

Stakeholder plans have low charges which means she can stop, start, reduce or increase her contributions. 'This is important in case I stop working to have a family one day.'

SHOP AROUND FOR LOW CHARGES

	TOTAL FUND VALUE	ANNUAL CHARGE
The original maximum annual management fee for stakeholder pensions was 1%, but some pension companies charge less, particularly for those with larger sums to invest. Charging structures differ, but the one shown right is typical and would save somebody with £50,000 in their pension £100 a year. Over 20–30 years, this saving could be worth several thousand pounds.	Less than £10,000	1%
	£10,000-£19,999	0.95%
	£20,000-£49,999	0.9%
	£50,000+	0.8%

■ **Retirement options** You can take 25% of your pension pot as a tax-free lump sum at retirement. The rest must be used to buy an annuity before age 75, and you may pay tax on the income.

■ **Who benefits?** You don't have to be working or even paying tax to claim tax relief. Husbands, for example, can invest on behalf of a wife who has stayed home to look after the children, and claim 22% tax relief.

■ **Death benefits** If you die before drawing your pension, your nominated beneficiary, who can be anybody you like, receives the value of your pension at the time you died, including all tax relief. No charges are deducted. This can be taken as a tax-free cash lump sum.

■ **Choice available** Plans are sold by many insurance and investment companies including big names such as Norwich Union, Prudential and Standard Life, so you have a good choice of plans. Most stakeholder companies offer a range of different funds investing in stock markets in the UK and globally, plus bonds, cash and property funds.

HOW TO DECIDE ON A TRANSFER

After the stakeholder scheme was introduced, many insurance companies switched their expensive old-style pension contracts to the more attractive stakeholder terms. If your contract still applies restrictive rules and hefty charges, you may do better to switch your fund to a stakeholder.

Ask for a projection Ask your current pension company for a projection of your benefits at retirement.

Find out the penalty Confirm how much they will penalise you for withdrawing your money. Subtract this from the projected benefits to determine the 'transfer value'.

Compare the benefits Contact a low-cost stakeholder provider and ask for a projection of your benefits if you invest this transfer value with them. See if the lower charges over the long term offset the penalty incurred by switching.

STAKEHOLDER OR AVCS?

Your decision is complex and will depend on your personal circumstances, and how loyal you feel to your company. If you belong to an occupational pension scheme you can also contribute to a stakeholder, but only if you earn less than £30,000 a year and aren't a director of your company. This rule may change from April 2006.

RESOURCES

STAKEHOLDER PENSIONS
Both the Financial Services Authority and The Pension Service (part of the Department of Work & Pensions) have information on stakeholder pensions on their websites and guides that can be ordered by post:
FSA consumer helpline
0845 606 1234
www.fsa.gov.uk ✉
The Pension Service
0845 731 32 33
www.pensionguide.gov.uk ✉

Who pays the charges? The advantage of AVCs is that your employer takes the money from the payroll and pays all necessary scheme charges. With a stakeholder pension, you must pay the annual management fee yourself.

When is a stakeholder better? Zero charges may give AVCs the edge, but sometimes it is better to opt for a stakeholder, for example if the insurer running your company's pension scheme is a poor performer. Stakeholder pensions are more portable than AVCs, which can be difficult to detach from the company scheme. This gives you greater flexibility if you think you may be going to change jobs regularly.

Tax relief Both schemes offer immediate basic-rate tax relief at 22%. They both offer higher-rate tax relief up to 40%, but with AVCs you get this immediately – with stakeholder you must reclaim it on your self-assessment tax form.

Long-term difference Stakeholder plans allow you to take a tax-free 25% lump sum at retirement, but AVCs don't, under current rules. This may change from April 2006.

TOP TIPS GET STARTED NOW

Whichever method you plan to use for your retirement, start now, because for every year you wait, the more you will have to save each month to catch up.

■ **The price of delay** Saving for retirement has plunged to the bottom of many people's financial priorities, after buying a house, clearing credit card debts or simply having fun. Fewer than half of people under age 30 are in a pension scheme, a lower figure than in the 1950s and 1960s. Most people only start serious pension planning after age 55, and by then it's too late.

■ **How much to save?** The later you leave it, the more you have to save each month. Your basic target for income in retirement should be two-thirds of the average national wage, which means you should be looking to build enough pension to earn an index-linked annuity income worth £15,000 a year at today's prices. Someone aged 55 with no savings would have to put aside a massive £1,200 a month to create this level of annuity income but if they started at 35 the figure would be £270 a month. Starting at 25, their savings would only need to be £105 a month. Early pension contributions are the most important, because they have much longer to grow in value.

GET SAVING

If your current pension arrangements aren't going to yield sufficient funds, decide how best to tackle the shortfall.

■ Consider a stakeholder pension, AVCs, FSAVCs and ISAs. The Inland Revenue offers tax breaks to encourage you to save, so use them.

■ Do you want the discipline of a pension or the flexibility of an ISA? If you are likely to raid your savings, go for a pension.

■ How much can you afford to save each month? If it isn't enough, work out how you can cut back on your spending.

■ Can you afford to do nothing? The answer, sadly, is no.

PENSION ALTERNATIVES

A pension isn't the only tax-efficient way to save for your retirement – millions also invest in an ISA (Individual Savings Account) as well. Others use property to provide pension savings. The safest approach is to build up a combination of pensions, ISAs and property.

ISAS FOR TAX-EFFICIENT SAVING

One in five people use ISAs to save for early retirement. They are more flexible than pensions – you can withdraw money whenever you wish (see table, below) – but this does have its dangers. You could be tempted to dip into your fund, depleting your savings. With pensions, at least you can't touch the cash until retirement age.

PROFIT FROM PROPERTY

Stock markets have struggled in recent years and so stocks and shares have become a more risky investment, but property prices in Britain have risen at mind-boggling speed. Growing numbers of people have been turning to bricks and mortar to boost their pension income in retirement, often giving up on traditional pensions altogether.

Buy-to-let schemes Such schemes are hugely popular, allowing ordinary people to become private landlords. You don't need cash to buy the property outright – you can raise the money through a mortgage and use the rental income to repay the loan. Almost every major lender now offers special buy-to-let loans.

Double blessings Investors benefit from both rental income and capital growth in the value of the property. Many plan to clear the mortgage before retirement and live off the monthly payments from their tenants.

Too good to be true? Think carefully before taking the plunge, because the glory days of buy-to-let may already be over. Interest rates have increased from their recent lows while rents have remained fairly static, reducing returns. Property values are unlikely to rise dramatically in the near future and, if they fall, now could prove a bad time to invest (see Ask Yourself, right).

ASK YOURSELF

IS BUY-TO-LET FOR ME?
- Are you committed for the long term? If investing for 10 years or longer, you should overcome any dips in property values.
- Do you understand the local rental market? Do your research. What type of tenants will you attract, how buoyant is the market and how much can you charge?
- What happens if you can't find tenants for several months? You'll need enough spare cash to pay the mortgage if your property is empty.
- What do you expect to happen to property prices? If you expect them to fall, wait until prices dip to more affordable levels.
- Do you want your pension to depend upon the property market?

PERSONAL PENSIONS VERSUS ISAS	
PERSONAL PENSIONS	**ISAS**
■ Can invest up to £3,600 annually in a stakeholder.	■ Can invest up to £7,000 a year in stocks and pension shares, cash and life insurance (£5,000 from April 2006).
■ Tax relief at 22% or 40% on contributions.	■ No tax relief on contributions.
■ You can take a 25% tax-free lump sum at retirement. Thereafter, all income is subject to income tax.	■ No income tax or CGT (capital gains tax) when you withdraw your money.
■ Cannot touch your money before age 50 (rising to 55 by 2010).	■ Can withdraw your money whenever you wish.
■ Must use your money to buy an annuity before age 75 (rules may change).	■ Can spend your money on whatever you like.

BUYING THE RIGHT ANNUITY

An annuity is a guaranteed income for life that you must buy with your pension fund before age 75 (unless you belong to a final salary pension scheme). This means anybody with a money-purchase occupational pension, stakeholder or other personal pension is faced with this important decision.

YOUR MOST CRUCIAL FINANCIAL DECISION?

Your choice of annuity may be one of the most important financial decisions you ever make. Once you have bought your annuity, you cannot change it and will be living off that income for the rest of your life. Unfortunately, annuities have been hit by both rising life expectancy and falling interest rates. A married couple with £100,000 in the husband's pension fund at age 65 might get a rather unimpressive £6,000 a year, including a widow's pension of £4,000 after he dies. Hardly a great return for a lifetime of saving. The good news is that inflation is low and rising interest rates may improve these disappointing figures in the future.

TREAD CAREFULLY

Before you retire, your pension company will write to tell you how much annual income you can buy with your pot. Many people automatically sign up for the annuity quotation they are given without further thought but this can prove costly, for two reasons.

You are free to shop around Don't assume you must buy your annuity from your pension company. You can go to any company you like (known as taking the open market option) and rival insurers may offer much better rates. You could boost your income by up to 25%: the difference between getting £4,500 a year or £6,000 a year. That's an extra £125 a month for the next 15 or 20 years. You can check your options in three or four minutes by contacting companies such as the Annuity Bureau, Annuity Direct or independent financial advisers Hargreaves Lansdown (see Resources, left).

Don't buy the wrong annuity Your insurer's initial quote will usually be for a 'single life' annuity, which will pay out only as long as the main policyholder, typically the husband, lives. Couples should take out a 'joint life' annuity, which continues to pay a reduced amount, usually half or two-thirds, after the first partner dies. Otherwise, the surviving spouse could be plunged into poverty when her husband dies (see page 354).

PROTECTING YOUR ANNUITY

If you die shortly after buying a single life annuity, your fund will revert to the insurance company – under current rules, you cannot leave it to your dependants. You can prevent this by taking out an income-protected annuity. If you die, say, two years after buying your annuity, the policy will continue to pay for up to five or ten years in total, depending on which option you choose. In return for this protection, you get a slightly lower income. Future governments may allow more flexibility on annuities, such as money-back guarantees up to age 75, but details haven't been finalised.

DON'T RISK YOUR NEST EGG

Some financial advisers like to push more adventurous forms of annuities, such as income drawdown or self-invested annuities. You delay drawing your annuity, and invest your pension pot in the stock market. These are only suitable for wealthy investors who understand stocks and shares and investment risk. Don't do it unless you have at least £250,000, plus other sources of income.

USE YOUR TAX-FREE CASH LUMP SUM

When buying your annuity, you can draw 25% of your pension pot as a tax-free lump sum. This means that you'll get a lower annuity income, but that income is taxable. Although you don't pay tax on the lump sum, you may pay tax on your returns after investing it. Minimise the tax you pay by using tax-free savings, notably your ISA allowance or certain National Savings certificates, where possible.

WATCH POINTS CHOOSING AN ANNUITY

An annuity is the only financial product the government compels you to buy, so make sure you buy the right one.

■ **Taking advice** Members of company schemes should get annuity advice from the trustees, but those with personal pensions won't. You could take independent financial advice, but most advisers won't help unless your pot is worth more than £50,000. Sadly, most people have much less than that. Remember that the right choice isn't always obvious. For information and a comparison of annuity rates based on your personal circumstances, look at the Pension Annuity website **www.pensionannuity.co.uk** ✉ or the Financial Services Authority site **www.fsa.gov.uk** ✉.

■ **A flat rate may backfire** Most people take a level or flat-rate annuity, without inflation proofing, because they get more money immediately. But that could cause problems if high inflation returns because your spending power could rapidly be eroded. Consider the option of an index-linked annuity instead.

■ **Consider life expectancy** If you have health problems, look for an 'impaired life annuity'. These pay higher rates of income to those with certain medical conditions, such as high blood pressure or cholesterol, heart trouble, diabetes and some forms of cancer. Life expectancy is shorter, so the insurance company expects to pay out for a shorter period. It sounds like a brutal calculation but it's one that could work in your favour.

■ **Lifestyle-linked rates** If you are a smoker or drinker or are overweight, you could boost your income with a 'lifestyle annuity'. Again, the insurer pays more because it expects you to die sooner. Almost one in five people over 65 smoke and could get a better-value annuity. A man aged 65 with a 10-a-day habit and £100,000 worth of savings could boost his flat-rate annuity from £6,800 a year to £8,200, worth an extra £115 a month.

ASK YOURSELF

AM I MAKING AN INFORMED DECISION?

■ Have I taken the open market option to find the best annuity rate?

■ Do I need to provide a pension for my partner after I die?

■ Do I want protection against inflation or the highest possible income now?

■ Do I smoke or drink heavily, or have an illness that threatens my life expectancy?

■ Do I understand my annuity choices or do I need independent financial advice?

CASH IN ON YOUR HOME

EQUITY RELEASE
■ Lifetime mortgages are sold by large companies such as Norwich Union ✉ and Northern Rock ✉.
■ Home reversion plans are typically sold by smaller specialist companies such as BPT Bridgewater Equities (Home Reversions) Ltd 01372 742 741, **www.bpt-bridgewater.co.uk** ✉.
■ Contact Safe Home Income Plans (SHIP) at 0870 241 60 60 or **info@ship-ltd.org** ✉. Or log on to their website at **www.ship-ltd.org** where you can find a list of member organisations.

Millions of pensioners are living in poverty despite owning an asset worth tens, or even hundreds, of thousands of pounds – their home. There is an increasingly popular solution, but it won't suit everybody.

EQUITY RELEASE

Retired homeowners are sitting on £693 billion worth of equity, around two-thirds of their total wealth. Equity release schemes, also called home income plans, allow you to turn the capital in your property into ready cash by borrowing money against the value of your home, either as a lump sum or regular income. You don't have to sell or move out of your property, nor will your spouse or partner have to move after you die. The capital raised and interest charged is repaid when the house is finally sold, either after you die or move into long-term nursing care.

Lifetime mortgage The most popular type of equity release scheme is an interest-only mortgage secured on your home. The capital and interest are repaid when the property is sold. As you cannot predict how much you will owe when you die, you could even leave a debt, although most policies won't allow negative equity.

Home reversion plan In this option, you sell a percentage of your property at less than the full market value. You continue to live in your house rent-free, as a tenant rather than owner. When you die or move into care – with relatives or a nursing home – your policy provider will receive a percentage of the proceeds. The rest goes into your estate.

HOW MUCH DO YOU GET?

On a home reversion plan you won't get the full value of your property, because you retain the right to live there for many years. But the older you are, the more you get. If you

PROS AND CONS OF EQUITY RELEASE

ADVANTAGES	DISADVANTAGES
■ Allows you to tap into your most valuable asset to improve your lifestyle.	■ You don't get the full value of your home, but a percentage depending on your age.
■ You can continue living in your home for many years, and can even move house.	■ Trading down to a smaller property is much simpler and less expensive.
■ No negative equity guarantee means never owing more than your house is worth.	■ You won't enjoy the full benefit of any future rises in house price values.
■ Schemes are increasingly offered by reputable household names.	■ Equity release is complex, and you don't know how much you will end up owing.
■ Homeowners without children or who don't want to leave an inheritance can enjoy their money while alive.	■ Much – or all – of your family's inheritance will be depleted.

are 70 years old, you could raise £40,000 on a £100,000 property. Compare quotes from different companies. If choosing a lifetime mortgage, shop around for the lowest interest rate.

WHAT PROTECTION DO YOU HAVE?

Reputable plans offer a 'no negative equity guarantee', which means you can never owe more than the sale value of your home, however long you live. Members of industry body Safe Home Income Plans (SHIP) all offer this guarantee, but check the wording carefully. Equity release schemes are not yet fully regulated by the Financial Services Authority, so be cautious when entering any agreement.

HOW DO YOU CHOOSE THE BEST DEAL?

Equity release is complicated so you must speak to a trusted independent financial adviser and your family solicitor. Discuss your plans with your family and beneficiaries, as you are spending their inheritance. Take time to consider your options and don't be rushed into anything.

ALTERNATIVES TO EQUITY RELEASE

Many people argue against equity release, pointing to the fact that you only get a relatively small proportion of the value of your home, and are selling a share in a valuable asset that may later grow in value. You or your family may prefer to consider alternatives.

Move house A much simpler solution is to sell up, move to a smaller property and invest and live off the difference. Your home may now be too big if you are still in the family home, but your children have moved away. However, moving is stressful and upsetting so think carefully before you decide to leave your home. You won't pay any capital gains tax when you sell your own home, but once you re-invest the money you are liable to pay income tax on the interest. You should therefore you sure tax-free allowances such as ISAs and your personal allowances.

Remortgaging You could raise an ordinary mortgage against your property, taking a relatively small proportion of its value, say £20,000 or £30,000, on what is known as an 'interest-only' basis. This means you repay the interest every month, but not the capital (which can be repaid from your estate when you die). The advantage over equity release is that the debt doesn't grow in value, the disadvantage is that you need enough spare funds to repay the monthly interest.

Get help Your beneficiaries could help you out financially, knowing they will eventually profit from a share in the property. If you decide to follow this route, make sure all your beneficiaries accept the situation and you aren't creating a family dispute. Get a solicitor to draw up a proper agreement.

ASK YOURSELF

IS EQUITY RELEASE RIGHT FOR ME?

- Have I considered alternative ways of raising cash?
- Am I claiming all the state benefits and private pension income owed to me?
- Is my preferred equity release scheme a member of SHIP?
- Does my scheme impose any penalties if I repay the loan early – and how long do they last?
- How much will I pay in arrangement fees?
- Do I want to leave the full or partial value of my home to my loved ones?
- Have I spoken to everybody who will be affected by my decision?
- Can equity release help to avoid my beneficiaries receiving an inheritance tax bill?

WOMEN AND PENSIONS

Women still get a raw deal in retirement – a typical woman's pension is just two-thirds of a typical man's. Most women earn less than men during their working life and are more likely to work part-time and take career breaks to have children. Many still rely on men to save on their behalf, which costs them dearly in the long run.

MARRIED WOMEN'S ENTITLEMENTS

Marriage qualifies you for state pension benefits based on your husband's entitlement, plus a share of any workplace or personal pension benefits. Even if you divorce, you are due up to half your husband's assets, including pension up to the time of divorce. Your share depends on how long you were together, how old you are and whether you have children. You can either transfer a share of his pension into your name or offset assets, taking the house, for example, but leaving his pension fund intact.

WATCH POINTS UNMARRIED PARTNERS

More women choose to cohabit with their partner than ever before, but this could prove financially disastrous as it gives you no protection under family law.

■ **Understand your position** You can live with a man for 30 years and have children together, but if he decides to leave, he doesn't have to give you anything. All you get is a share of any assets held in joint names.

■ **Check pension rights** If your relationship is stable, check what happens to your partner's occupational pension if he dies, either before or after retirement. Is your name down for death-in-service benefits or a percentage of his pension fund?

STATE PENSION BENEFITS

Like men, women don't automatically get the full basic state pension but a sum depending on their NI contributions.

Carers' benefits Since 1975, women taking time off work to look after children, and carers looking after a sick or elderly relative, have also accumulated benefits under the home responsibilities protection scheme, which treats them as if they have been making contributions.

Married and divorced Married women receive up to 60% of their husband's state pension, but only after he retires at age 65. If your husband dies, you get his pension. If you divorce, your entitlement will include your husband's NI contributions during your marriage.

Nothing for partners Unmarried women won't earn any state pension benefits entitlement in their partner's name.

MAKE YOUR OWN PLANS

Build your own pension pot. Even if you don't have any income (perhaps you are at home with children) you can still claim 22% tax relief on stakeholder contributions. If your personal income is low, ask your husband or partner to contribute on your behalf. Clerical Medical ✉, Legal & General ✉ and Norwich Union ✉ offer popular plans.

---

keep it simple

SAVE WITH AN ISA
Instead of a pension, you can save up to £7,000 under your ISA allowance, and take all returns free of most income tax and all capital gains tax. If you have lost faith in the stock market, play it safe by saving up to £3,000 a year in a mini-cash ISA.

Buy a joint life annuity

Even if you and your partner have saved for years, if you buy the wrong annuity at retirement you could face financial disaster. Make sure you and your partner take out a 'joint life' annuity, which pays a reduced amount after the first partner dies, usually half or two-thirds. Take the open market option and seek out the best quote (see page 350).

SMART MOVES

A LATE CAREER CHANGE

The over-50s can enjoy a career change just the same as younger workers. DirectGov **www.direct.gov.uk** ✉ gives professional help through the JobCentre Plus network. Learn Direct **www.learndirect.co.uk** ✉ offers information on more than 700,000 courses to help you get up to speed with computers, office skills and self-development.

JOB HUNTING

Local contacts are often the best when looking for a job later in life, rather than applying for advertised positions. Learn Direct Futures 0800 100 900 or **www.learndirect-futures.co.uk** ✉ can help to match your skills and interests to job opportunities.

'NEW DEAL' CAN HELP

New Deal 50 Plus is a government-funded scheme that offers personal advice and financial support to older job-seekers claiming income-replacement benefits for six months or more. Contact the New Deal helpline on 0845 606 2626 ✉.

WORKING FOR LONGER

Almost one million people continue to work beyond the state retirement age, the fastest growing part of the work force. Many people shudder at the idea, but rising life expectancy will compel many more to do it.

WORKING PART-TIME

Some 654,000 women work beyond age 60 and 336,000 men beyond age 65. Of these, around two-thirds work part-time. Consider working in a local shop or café, which can be both sociable and fun as well as financially sound.

ADVERTISE YOUR SKILLS

www.2young2retire.co.uk is a website that allows over-50s looking for part-time work and consultancy to post their details free of charge so potential employers can contact them by email.

OVER-50S' SUPPORT

Over50 **www.over50.gov.uk** ✉ gives practical information on the advice and support available through government and voluntary organisations.

MAXIMISING YOUR RETIREMENT INCOME

TRACE YOUR PENSION
Don't lose track of your pension entitlement. Contact former employers and insurance companies you have saved with to claim your entitlement. If the company has folded or been taken over, you should still be able to get your hands on the money.

■ The following two organisations may help:
The Pension Schemes Registry 0191 225 6316 **www.opra.gov.uk** ✉, and **The Pensions Advisory Service** 0845 601 2923 **www.opas.org.uk** ✉.

If you're retiring shortly, are already in retirement, or simply don't have the spare cash to build worthwhile savings, you'll need to find innovative ways of getting by. As well as working for longer, there are other options you might consider, depending on your individual circumstances.

DELAY CLAIMING TO BOOST YOUR PENSION

You can still carry on working after reaching state pension age and either claim your pension or delay claiming in return for receiving a higher pension when it is finally paid. This may prove tempting if your salary is enough to live on but your pension benefits are minimal.

What you get now You can put off claiming your state pension for five years. You get an extra 7.5% for each year that you delay. You can claim this as higher weekly pension once you have retired, or a lump sum worth up to £30,000.

Future revisions Under planned pension reforms, which may be introduced by April 2005, you should be able to delay drawing your pension for as long as you like.

Final salary scheme bonus If you are in a company final salary scheme, you could do even better. Delaying retirement by five years could boost your pension by up to 50%.

Other pension types You could also benefit from drawing your money-purchase or personal pension at a later date, but this depends how stock markets perform in the interim. If they take off, you will benefit; if they slump, you could be in an even worse position.

CASE STUDY

FRANK SPICES UP HIS WORKING LIFE
After 30 years working as an insurance agent, Frank Deacon, 62, seized the opportunity to retire three years early. But rather than quietly draw his pension, he decided it was time for a fresh challenge, and launched a handmade pickles business with his wife June.

'I didn't fancy spending the next 25 years watching telly and playing golf, I had too much life in me for that. June has always enjoyed making food, and is a dab hand at jams and pickles, so we decided to turn it into a business.'

Frank used his sales experience to promote June's pickles and relishes to independent food shops and delicatessens. 'I visit food fares and farmers' markets around the country and try to get specialist shops to display our stock. This is harder work than

my desk job, but it's much more rewarding.' The business is now taking off, helped by the growing interest in quality British food – and new premises. 'Our kitchen was small and we were tired of the smell of pickles. It just shows that it's never too late to do something you really enjoy,' Frank says.

WATCH POINTS RETIRING ABROAD

Almost half of us dream of swapping a drizzly Britain for a retirement in the sun, with some 2.3 million people over 50 actively planning to emigrate within the next 10 years.

■ **Will you get your pension?** You can still receive your state pension if you retire overseas in countries within the European Economic Area (EEA), or other countries with social security agreements with Britain, including Barbados, Cyprus, Jamaica, Turkey and America. In these countries, you should get exactly the same as in the UK. But this doesn't apply elsewhere. Some 500,000 pensioners had their state pensions frozen after moving to countries including Australia, New Zealand, Canada and South Africa.

■ **Avoid NI shortfall** Many people who head overseas before the state retirement age unwittingly lose out, because they don't get the NI credit automatically given to British residents after age 60. Consider making voluntary contributions to maintain your 100% entitlement.

■ **Get tax advice** If you have accumulated your personal or company pension fund in Britain it may still be taxed by the Inland Revenue. If you spend 183 days or more in the UK, or your visits average 91 days or more every year over four years, you will pay tax in Britain. Otherwise, you will pay tax in your new country of residence. Rules are complex, so take specialist tax advice.

■ **Exchange-rate problems** If your pension is paid in sterling, you will face a currency risk. Consider switching some of your savings into your new home currency to protect against adverse movement in exchange rates.

■ **Inheritance rules** Laws on inheritance differ overseas, and you may have to write two wills, one for each country.

CASH FOR CLUTTER

Unwanted possessions or hidden family treasures gathering dust in your attic or garage could be converted into ready cash to enjoy today, even if it's only for a special treat such as a meal out or weekend away.

Not just antiques People not only pay good money for antiques and jewellery, but collectables such as kitchenalia and sporting or pop memorabilia.

Know the market Don't sell high value items at a car boot sale – buyers there tend to be a little more thrifty. Stick to electrical goods, clothes, books and bric-a-brac. Price your goods beforehand, enlist a friend, be prepared to haggle and take plenty of change with you.

How to sell valuables You can sell direct to market traders or, for a small deposit, set up your own stall in an antiques market. You can sell valuable items at auction, although the profit is reduced by commission, insurance, handling fees and VAT. Antiques Bulletin (**www.antiquesbulletin.co.uk** ✉) offers advice on buying and selling antiques through auctions, fairs and dealers. For other helpful organisations see Resources, right.

Online auctions The eBay website (**www.ebay.co.uk** ✉) has revolutionised the art of commerce, enabling you to sell almost anything to hundreds of thousands of potential buyers cheaply and easily.

RESOURCES

SELLING ANTIQUES AND COLLECTABLES

For help and advice in selling your prized possessions, refer to:

Buy, Keep or Sell? published by Dorling Kindersley/Reader's Digest, 2004, £29.99 ISBN 1405305959, or contact

Antiques Collectors' Club 01394 389 950 www.antique-acc.com ✉

Antiques Trade Gazette 020 7420 6600 www.atg-online.com ✉

Bonhams 020 7393 3900 www.bonhams.com ✉

Christie's 020 7839 9060 www.christies.co.uk ✉

Sotheby's 020 729 5000 www.sothebys.com ✉.

DIRECTORY OF ADDRESSES ✉

The contact details in this Directory will help you locate the resources given in the book, designated by the symbol ✉. They are arranged chapter by chapter, following a general section of entries that appear in more than one chapter.

Web addresses may change so if any do not work, please use a search engine such as Google, Yahoo or Lycos to find what you are looking for.

This Directory can be used whether or not you have a computer. But if you would like help using the Internet, please turn to pages 8–9 in the front of this book.

GENERAL RESOURCES

A LOT OF ORGANICS
Douglas House, 33 Douglas Road,
Caversham, Reading RG4 5BH
0118 3759375
www.alotoforganics.co.uk

AGE CONCERN
1268 London Road, London SW16 4ER
0800 00 99 66
www.ageconcern.co.uk

ALTON TOWERS
Alton, Staffordshire ST10 4DB
08705 204060
www.altontowers.com

AMAZON
www.amazon.co.uk

ANTIQUES TRADE GAZETTE
Sandy Lane, Old Martlesham,
Woodbridge, Suffolk IP12 4SD
020 7420 6600
www.antiquestradegazette.com
www.atg-online.com

ARGOS
489-499 Avebury Boulevard,
Central Milton Keynes MK9 2NW
0870 600 8784
www.argos.co.uk
www.argossports.co.uk

ASDA
ASDA House, Southbank,
Great Wilson Street, Leeds LS11 5AD
0500 100055
www.asda.co.uk

ASSOCIATION OF BRITISH INSURERS
51 Gresham Street, London EC2V 7HQ
020 7600 3333
www.abi.org.uk

BAA
www.baa.com
www.baa.com/shopping

BENEFITS AGENCY
If you don't have Internet access, find your local office in the *Yellow Pages* under *Social Service & Welfare Organisations or Employment Agencies (Jobcentres)*.
www.dwp.gov.uk

BRITISH TELECOM (BT)
dial 150 from a BT line or 0800 800 150
www.bt.com

CATALINK
Neville House, Station Approach,
Wendens Ambo, Essex CB11 4LB
01799 544655
www.catalink.net

CATALOGCITY
www.catalogcity.com

CIAO!
www.ciao.co.uk

CITIZENS ADVICE BUREAU
If you don't have Internet access, find your local office in the *Yellow Pages* under *Counselling & Advice*.
www.citizensadvice.org.uk
www.adviceguide.org.uk/em

COMET
08705 425 425
www.comet.co.uk
www.clearance-comet.co.uk

CONSUMERS' ASSOCIATION
2 Marylebone Road, London NW1 4DF
01992 822800
www.which.co.uk

CUSTOMS AND EXCISE
0845 010 9000
www.hmce.gov.uk

DEBENHAMS
1 Welbeck Street, London W1G 0AA
08456 055 044
www.debenhams.com

DEFRA (Department for Environmental Health and Rural Affairs)
Ergon House, c/o Nobel House,
17 Smith Square, London SW1P 3JR
08459 3355
www.defra.gov.uk

DEPARTMENT OF WORK AND PENSIONS (DWP)
www.dwp.org.uk

DIXONS
0845 850 0545
www.dixons.co.uk

DOOYOU
www.dooyou.co.uk

EBAY
www.ebay.co.uk

ENGLISH HERITAGE
PO Box 569, Swindon SN2 2YP
0870 333 1182
www.english-heritage.org.uk

EXERCISE ZONE
Unit 12/4c, Anniesland Village
Business Park, Netherton Road,
Glasgow G13 1EU
0141 959 1259
www.exercisezone.co.uk

FINANCIAL SERVICES AUTHORITY
25 The North Colonnade, London E14 5HS
0845 606 1234
www.fsa.gov.uk

FIND
Bucklersbury House, 11 Walbrook,
London EC4N 8EL
020 7329 9901
www.find.co.uk

FOOD STANDARDS AGENCY
Aviation House, 125 Kingsway
London WC2B 6NH
020 7276 8000
www.food.gov.uk

GENERAL INSURANCE STANDARDS COUNCIL (GISC)
110 Cannon Street, London EC4N 6EU
0845 601 2857
www.gisc.co.uk

GLOBAL FLIGHT MANAGEMENT
+49 69-9853-5566 (Germany)
www.globalflight.net

GOOD DEAL DIRECTORY
www.gooddealdirectory.co.uk

GOOGLE
www.google.com

HANDBAG
151 Oxford Street, London W1D 2JG
www.handbag.com

HOMEBASE
Beddington House, Railway Approach,
Wallington SM6 0HB
0845 077 8888
www.homebase.co.uk

HOMESOURCES
Sutton Business Centre, Restmor Way,
Hackbridge Road, Wallington SM6 7AH
www.homesources.co.uk

HSS
25 Willow Lane, Mitcham, Surrey CR4 4TS
0161 749 4400
www.hss.com

IKEA
0845 355 1144
www.ikea.co.uk

INLAND REVENUE
0845 300 3900
www.inlandrevenue.gov.uk

IVILLAGE
01992 632222
www.ivillage.co.uk

KAYS LIFESTYLE
Royal Avenue, Widnes WA88 1TB
0870 333 3725
www.kayslifestyle.co.uk

KELKOO
1 London Bridge, London SE1 9BG
www.kelkoo.co.uk

LAST MINUTE
0871 222 5969
www.lastminute.com

LEGOLAND®
Windsor Park Ltd, Winkfield Road,
Windsor, Berkshire SL4 4AY
08705 04 04 04
www.lego.com/legoland

LONDON ZOO
Regent's Park, London NW1 4RY
020 7722 3333
www.londonzoo.co.uk

LXDIRECT
0845 757 3457
www.lxdirect.com

M AND M SPORT
Clinton Road, Leominster HR6 0SP
01568 616161
www.mandmsports.com

MAJESTIC
Majestic House, Otterspool Way,
Watford WD25 8WW
0845 605 6767
www.majestic.co.uk

MARKS AND SPENCER
Chester Business Park, Wrexham Road,
Chester CH4 9GA
0845 302 1234
www.marksandspencer.com
www6.marksandspencer.com

MATALAN
Gillibrands Road, Skelmersdale,
West Lancashire WN8 9TB
01695 552400
www.matalan.co.uk

MFI
08702 400417
www.mfi.co.uk

MONEYFACTS
66-70 Thorpe Road, Norwich NR1 1BJ
0870 2250 476
www.moneyfacts.co.uk

MONEYSUPERMARKET
Moneysupermarket House, St David's Park,
Ewloe, Nr Chester CH5 3UZ
0845 345 5708
www.moneysupermarket.com

MOTLEY FOOL
2nd Floor, Lasenby House, 32 Kingly Street
London W1B 5QQ
020 7025 5500
www.fool.co.uk

MSN MONEY
www.money.msn.co.uk

**NATIONAL ASSOCIATION OF
FARMERS' MARKETS**
PO Box 575, Southampton SO15 7BZ
0845 230 2150
www.farmersmarkets.net

NATIONAL EXPRESS
Ensign Court, 4 Vicarage Road, Edgbaston,
Birmingham B15 3ES
08705 808080
www.nationalexpress.com

THE NATIONAL TRUST
England and Wales
PO Box 39, Warrington WA5 7WD
0870 458 4000
www.nationaltrust.org.uk
Scotland
0131 243 9300
www.nts.org.uk

NEAL'S YARD REMEDIES
8-10 Ingate Place, London SW8 3NS
020 7627 1949
www.nealsyardremedies.com

NEXT
Desford Road, Enderby, Leicester LE19 4AT
0845 600 7000
www.next.co.uk

NORWICH UNION
PO Box 4, Surrey Street, Norwich NR1 3NG
01603 622200
www.norwichunion.com

NTL
Tel 0800 183 0123
www.ntl.com

**OCCUPATIONAL PENSIONS
REGULATORY AUTHORITY (OPRA)**
Invicta House, Trafalgar Place,
Brighton BN1 4DW
01273 627600
www.opra.gov.uk

OFFICE OF FAIR TRADING
Fleetbank House, 2–6 Salisbury Square,
London EC4Y 8JX
08457 224499
www.oft.gov.uk

ORANGE
150 from your Orange phone or
07973 100 150
www.orange.co.uk

OXFAM
Oxfam House, 274 Banbury Road,
Oxford OX2 7DZ
0870 333 2700
www.oxfam.org.uk
Oxfam Originals, 22 Earlham Street,
London WC2H 9LN
020 7836 9666

THE PENSION SERVICE
PO Box 1005, Newcastle NE98 1WZ
0845 6060265
www.thepensionservice.gov.uk

THE PENSIONS ADVISORY SERVICE
11 Belgrave Road, London SW1V 1RB
0845 601 2923
www.opas.org.uk

PRICERUNNER
78 Margaret Street, London W1W 8SZ
www.pricerunner.co.uk

**ROYAL INSTITUTE OF CHARTERED
SURVEYORS (RICS)**
Surveyor Court, Westwood Way,
Coventry CV4 8JE
0870 333 1600
www.rics.org/public

SAGA
The Saga Building, Middelburg Square,
Folkestone CT20 1AZ
0800 414 525
www.saga.co.uk
For Saga holidays 0800 056 6088
www.sagaholidays.co.uk
For Saga magazine 01303 771525

SAINSBURY
33 Holborn, London EC1N 2HT
0800 63 62 62
www.sainsbury.co.uk

SHOPPING VILLAGES
www.shoppingvillages.com

SPORT-E
www.sport-e.com

SUPERDRUG
Admail 838, Croydon CR9 4WZ
0870 333 5666
www.superdrug.com

TELEWEST
0800 953 5383
www.telewest.co.uk

TESCO
Tesco Clubcard, Freepost, Tesco
SCO 5043, Dundee DD2 9XU
0800 591688
www.tesco.com
www.tesco.com/winestore

THORPE PARK
Staines Road, Chertsey, KT16 8PN
0870 444 4466
www.thorpepark.com

TK MAXX
50 Clarendon Road, Watford WD17 1TX
www.tkmaxx.com

TRADING STANDARDS
0121 248 2000 (Trading Standards
Institute)
www.tradingstandards.gov.uk

USWITCH
PO Box 33208, London SW1E 5WL
0845 601 2856
www.uswitch.com

VIRGIN WINES
St James' Mill, Whitefriars, Norwich
NR3 1TN
0870 164 9593
www.virginwines.com

WHICH?
Castlemead, Gascoyne Way,
Hertford SG14 1LH
0845 307 4000
www.which.net

WICKES
Wickes House, 120–138 Station Road,
Harrow, Middlesex HA1 2QB
0870 6089001
www.wickes.co.uk

ANIMAL MATTERS

THE BLUE CROSS
Shilton Road, Burford, Oxon OX18 4PF
01993 825500
www.bluecross.org.uk

BREEDER DIRECTORY
08700 114115
www.breederdirectory.co.uk

BRITISH VETERINARY ASSOCIATION
7 Mansfield Street, London W1G 9NQ
020 7636 6541
www.bva.co.uk

CAT CHAT
PO Box 358, Ramsgate, Kent CT12 6YP
www.catchat.org

CAT FANCY
3 Burroughs, Irvine, CA 92618, USA
www.catfancy.com

CATS PROTECTION
National Cat Centre, Chelwood Gate,
Haywards Heath, Sussex RH17 7TT
08702 099 099
www.cats.org.uk

THE DOG RESCUE PAGES
www.dogpages.org.uk

DOGS' TRUST
17 Wakley Street, London EC1V 7RQ
020 7837 0006
www.dogstrust.org.uk

K9 DIRECTORY
www.k9directory.com

THE KENNEL CLUB
1 Clarges Street, London W1J 8AB
0870 606 6750
www.the-kennel-club.org.uk
www.doggenetichealth.org

**NATIONAL ASSOCIATION OF
REGISTERED PETSITTERS**
0870 3500 543
www.dogsit.com

OUR CATS
5 James Leigh Street,
Manchester M1 5NF
0870 731 6510
www.ourcats.co.uk

PDSA
Whitechapel Way,
Priorslee, Telford,
Shropshire TF2 9PQ
01952 290999
www.pdsa.org.uk

PET PLANET
10 Lindsay Square,
Deans Industrial Estate,
Livingston
EH54 8RL
0845 345 0723
www.petplanet.co.uk

PET VACCINATION CLINICS
La Fontana, Alcester Rd, Wythall,
Birmingham B47 6AP
01564 823825
www.any-uk-vet.co.uk/pet-
vaccination-wythall

PETS AT HOME
Epsom Avenue, Stanley Green Trading
Estate, Handforth, Cheshire SK9 3RN
0161 486 6688
www.petsathome.com

RSPCA
Wilberforce Way, Southwater, Horsham,
West Sussex RH13 9RS
0870 3335 888
www.rspca.org.uk

UKPETSITTER
01902 417891
www.ukpetsitter.co.uk

Z2CLOTHING
FREEPOST NAT21699,
Wellingborough NN8 5BR
01933 384 844
www.z2clothing.com

BUYING AND RUNNING A CAR

AA
Carr Ellison House, William Armstrong
Drive, Newcastle-upon-Tyne NE4 7YA
0870 600 0371
www.theaa.com
www.aapetrolbusters.com

AUTO EXPRESS
9 Dallington Street, London EC1V 0BQ
020 7907 6000
www.autoexpress.co.uk

AUTOEBID
0870 922 0572
www.autoebid.com

BREAKERLINK
08707 806655
www.breakerlink.com

BSM
0870 010 4322
www.bsm.co.uk

BUY ABROAD
Crostwick Lane, Spixworth,
Norwich NR10 3NG
01692 400 999
www.buy-abroad.com

CAR IMPORTING
www.carimporting.co.uk

CAR PLUS
The Studio, 32 The Calls, Leeds LS2 7EW
www.carclubs.org.uk

CAR SUPERMARKETS
www.car-supermarkets.com

CHEAP CAR INSURANCE UK
2 Compton Way, Witney, Oxon O28 3AB
0800 138 2413
www.cheap-car-insurance.uk.net

COMPETITION
www.europa.eu.int/comm/
competition/car_sector/price_diffs

**DVLA (DRIVER AND VEHICLE
LICENSING AGENCY)**
Sandringham Park, Swansea SA7 0EE
0870 240 0010
www.dvla.gov.uk

THE ENERGY SAVING TRUST
21 Dartmouth Street, London SW1H 9BP
0845 727 7200
www.est.org.uk

FORDS OF WINSFORD
Weaver Valley Road, Wharton Retail Park,
Winsford, Cheshire CW7 3AL
0845 456 3770
www.fow.co.uk

FRIENDS OF THE EARTH
26–28 Underwood Street, London N1 7JQ
0808 800 1111
www.foe.co.uk

GLASS'S GUIDE
1 Princes Road, Weybridge KT13 9TU
www.glass.co.uk

**INSTITUTE OF ADVANCED
MOTORISTS**
510 Chiswick High Road, London W4 5RG
020 8996 9600
www.iam.org.uk

JAMJAR CARS
3 Edridge Road, Croydon, Surrey CR9 1AG
0845 608 1133
www.jamjar.co.uk

MOTORPOINT
Chartwell Drive, West Meadows
Derby DE21 6BZ
0870 12 54321
www.motorpoint.co.uk

PASS PLUS
0115 901 2500
www.passplus.org.uk

RAC
08705 722 722
www.rac.co.uk

**RETAIL MOTOR INDUSTRY
FEDERATION (RMIF)**
0845 758 5350
www.rmif.co.uk

TRANSPORT ENERGY
0845 602 1425
www.transportenergy.org.uk

UK CAR INSURANCE DIRECTORY
The Royal, 25 Bank Plain, Norwich NR2 4SF
01603 283641
www.ukcarinsurance.directory.co.uk

VEHICLE CERTIFICATION AGENCY
0117 952 4235
www.vca.gov.uk

VIRGIN CARS
0870 766 33 11
www.virgincars.com

WATCHDOG GUIDES
www.bbc.co.uk/watchdog_to/
importinganewcar

WHAT CAR?
60 Waldegrave Road, Teddington TW11 8LG
020 8267 5688
www.whatcar.com

BUYING AND SELLING PROPERTY

BIG BROWN BOX
PO Box 2359, Stoke-On-Trent ST3 7WF
0845 890 1153
www.bigbrownbox.co.uk

THE BOXSTORE
www.theboxstore.co.uk

**BRITISH ASSOCIATION OF
REMOVERS**
3 Churchill Court, 58 Station Road,
North Harrow HA2 7SA
020 8861 3331
www.bar.co.uk

CHANNEL 4
www.channel4.com/4money/
mortgages

CHARCOL
0800 358 5885
www.charcolonline.co.uk

EASIER2MOVE
33–34 Clarence Street, Southend-on-Sea
SS1 1BH
07004 327437
www.easier2move.co.uk

ENERGYLINX
The e-Centre, Cooperage Way
Business Village, Alloa FK10 3LP
0845 225 2840
www.energylinx.co.uk

ESSENTIAL INFORMATION GROUP
1A Church Street, Reigate RH2 0AA
0870 112 3040
www.eigroup.co.uk

HOUSE WEB
0845 123 5181
www.houseweb.co.uk

I AM MOVING
www.iammoving.com

L&C MORTGAGES
0800 953 0304
www.lcplc.co.uk

THE LAW SOCIETY
113 Chancery Lane, London WC2A 1PL
020 7242 1222
www.lawsoc.org.uk

**NATIONAL ASSOCIATION OF
ESTATE AGENTS**
21 Jury Street, Warwick CV34 4EH
01926 496800
www.naea.co.uk

OMBUDSMAN FOR ESTATE AGENTS
4 Bridge Street, Salisbury SP1 2LX
01722 333306
www.oea.co.uk

PICKFORDS
Heritage House, 345 Southbury Road,
Enfield EN1 1UP
www.pickfords.co.uk

PRACTICAL CAR & VAN RENTAL
0121 772 8599
www.practical.co.uk

PROPERTY AUCTIONS
01772 621909
www.property-auctions.net

REALLY MOVING
0870 870 4851
www.reallymoving.com

REMOVAL BOXES
01294 313348
www.removalboxes.org

SHELTER
88 Old Street, London EC1V 9HU
020 7505 4699
www.shelter.org.uk

SHOOSMITHS
www.property-conveyancing-
online.co.uk

STUART & COMPANY
Audley House, Berechurch Hall Road,
Colchester CO2 9NW
01206 760600
www.britishlaw.net

UP MY STREET
10th Floor, Portland House, Stag Place,
London SW1E 5BH
020 7802 2992
www.upmystreet.com

USE THE MOUSE
www.use-the-mouse.com

ELECTRONIC EQUIPMENT

3
PO Box 333, Hemel Hempstead HP2 7YW
333 from your 3 mobile or 08707 330 333
www.three.co.uk

118TRACKER
Mostyn Hall, Friargate, Penrith CA11 7XR
01768 866050
www.118tracker.com

ALPHATEL
0845 085 0250
www.alphatelecom.com

BATTERY FORCE
PO Box 363, Tonbridge TN9 1UQ
0870 220 4404
www.batteryforce.co.uk

BUDGET BATTERIES
Unit 13, Drewitt Industrial Estate, 865
Ringwood Road, Bournemouth BH11 8LW
01202 582700
www.budgetbatteries.co.uk

COMPAQ
www.compaq.co.uk

COMPARE PRICES
www.compareprices.co.uk

COMPUTER BUYER
0207 907 6000
www.computerbuyer.co.uk

COMPUTER SHOPPER
020 7907 6000
www.computershopper.co.uk

DELL
0870 907 5818
www.dell.co.uk

DOWNLOAD
www.downloads.com

FREEVIEW
DTV Services Ltd, Broadcast Centre,
(BC3 D5), 201 Wood Lane, London W12 7TP
08708 80 99 80
www.freeview.co.uk

GAMES FRENZY
PO Box 189, South Ockendon RM15 5WR
07956 312227
www.gamesfrenzy.co.uk

IBM
PO Box 41, North Harbour,
Portsmouth PO6 3AU
02392 561000
www.ibm.com/contact/uk

INK FACTORY
9 Newporte Business Park, Bishops Road,
Lincoln LN2 4SY
08707 500 710
www.theinkfactory.com

MDS BATTERY
A12 Hastingwood Trading Estate,
Harbet Road, London N18 3HT
020 8884 4904
www.mdsbattery.co.uk

METROPOLITAN POLICE
020 7230 1212
www.met.police.uk/crimeprevention/
alarms.htm

**NATIONAL SECURITY
INSPECTORATE (NSI)**
Queensgate House, 14 Cookham Road,
Maidenhead SL6 8AJ
0870 205 0000
www.nsi.org.uk

O$_2$
www.o2.co.uk

ONE.TEL
Building 1, Chiswick Park, London W4 5BY
0800 957 0700
www.onetel.co.uk

PC WORLD
PO Box 1687, Sheffield S2 5YA
08702 420444
www.pcworld.co.uk

PLANET TALK
www.planet-talk.co.uk

SHARE WARE
www.shareware.com

SKY
08702 40 40 40
www.sky.com

STAPLES
0800 692 92 92
www.staples.co.uk

SWAPGAME
PO BOX 3795, Coventry CV7 8ZS
01676 549010
www.swapgame.com

TALKTALK
08000 855 900
www.talktalk.co.uk

TELE2
0800 279 51 52
www.tele2.co.uk

TISCALI SMART TALK
PO Box 7206, Milton Keynes MK14 6XG
0800 954 2223
www.tiscali.co.uk/services/smarttalk

T-MOBILE
Hatfield Business Park, Hertfordshire
AL10 9BW
0845 412 2401
www.t-mobile.co.uk

VIKING DIRECT
0800 1971747
www.viking-direct.co.uk

VIRGIN MOBILE
PO Box 2692 Trowbridge BA14 0TQ
789 from a Virgin mobile or 0845 6000 070.
www.virginmobile.com

VODAFONE
191 from your Vodafone mobile or
08700 700 191
www.vodafone.co.uk

FAMILY AFFAIRS

A–Z CARE HOMES GUIDE
PO Box 7677, Hungerford RG17 0FX
01488 684321
www.carehome.co.uk

CARE CHOICES
Valley Court, Royston SG8 0HF
01223 20777
www.carechoices.co.uk

**COMMISSION FOR SOCIAL CARE
INSPECTION (CSCI)**
33 Greycoat Street, London SW1P 2QF
0845 015 0120
www.csci.org.uk

HELP THE AGED
207–221 Pentonville Road,
London N1 9UZ
0800 800 6565
www.helptheaged.org.uk

LATERLIFE
www.laterlife.com

**THE NURSING HOME
FEES AGENCY**
NHFA Freepost (SCE12765),
St Leonard's House,
Mill Street, Oxford
OX29 4BR
01242 253297
www.nhfa.co.uk

**THE NURSING HOMES
DIRECTORY**
Little Grove, Bushey,
Watford, Herts
07092 035131
www.ucarewecare.com

RAIL EUROPE
08705 848848
www.raileurope.co.uk

SENIOR RAILCARD
08457 484950
www.senior-railcard.co.uk

SENIORITY
www.seniority.co.uk

THE SOCIETY OF WILL WRITERS
First Floor Chambers, Roe House, Boundary
South Hykeham, Lincoln LN6 9NQ
01522 68 78 88
www.willwriters.com

TV LICENSING
0870 241 6468
www.tv-l.co.uk

THE WILL SITE
82 Durban Road, Beckenham BR3 4EZ
020 8402 3957
www.thewillsite.co.uk

FOOD AND DRINK

ARBLASTER & CLARKE
Farnham Road, West Liss, Petersfield
01730 893344
www.winetours.co.uk

BBC FOOD
www.bbc.co.uk/food/recipes

BLUE TREE
Parkers House, 48 Regent Street,
Cambridge CB2 1FD
01223 245831
www.thewinetutor.co.uk

CHATEAU ONLINE
0800 169 2736
www.uk.chateauonline.com

CHOCOLATE SOCIETY
01423 322 230
www.chocolate.co.uk

CHOCOLATE TRADING CO
PO Box 114, Alderley Edge SK9 7WG
01625 592808
www.chocolatetradingco.com

COOKS KNIVES
Pots and Pans Ltd,
Geisher Road,
Callander FK17 8LX
01877 33 99 00
www.cooks-knives.co.uk

COSTCO WHOLESALE
0118 920 7105
www.costco.com

CULINAIRE
01293 550 563
www.kitchenknivesdirect.co.uk

DAY TRIPPER
Park House,
239 Stoke Newington Church Street,
London N16 9HP
020 7254 7772
www.day-tripper.net
www.bestferryfares.com

DECANTER
Broadway House,
2–6 Fulham Broadway,
London SW6 1AA
www.decanter.com/learning/
wine_clubs.php

DISCOUNT COFFEE
Dundyvan Estate, Lanarkshire ML5 4AQ
0845 225 5000
www.discountcoffee.co.uk

DONALD RUSSELL
Harlaw Road, Inverurie AB51 4FR
01467 622601
www.donaldrusselldirect.com

FARM SHOPPING
0845 2302150
www.farmshopping.com

THE FISH SOCIETY
Freepost, Haslemere GU27 2BR
0800 279 3474
www.thefishsociety.co.uk

FOOD FIRST
2 Chalk Hill Road, London W6 8DW
www.foodfirst.co.uk

FREEDOM FOOD
Wilberforce Way, Southwater, Horsham,
West Sussex, RH13 9RS
0870 754 0014
www.farmgatedirect.com

FRESHAMPERS
The Old Dairy, Home Farm, Ropley,
Hampshire SO24 0EF
020 7376 3185
www.freshampers.com

FRUGAL LIVING IN THE UK
www.frugal.org.uk

GOURMET COOKWARE CO
Holmleigh House, Manley Road, Frodsham,
Warrington WA6 6HS
01928 740 844
www.gourmetcook.co.uk

GOURMET WORLD
101 Lonsdale Road, London SW13 9DA
020 8748 0125
www.gourmet-world.com

THE GUARDIAN
119 Farringdon Road, London EC1R 3ER
020 7278 2332
www.guardian.co.uk

HOTEL CHOCOLAT
Mint House, Royston SG8 5HL
0870 442 8282
www.hotelchocolat.com

HUGE CHEESE DIRECT
28 Winchcombe Road, Eastbourne
BN22 8DE
01323 641 950
www.hugecheesedirect.co.uk

ICELAND
Second Avenue, Deeside Industrial Park,
Deeside, Flintshire CH5 2NW
01244 842842
www.iceland.co.uk

INDEX
0845 075 2233
www.index.co.uk

KINGS OF HAGLEY
92 Worcester Road, West Hagley Village,
Hagley, Nr Stourbridge, Worcestershire
DY9 0NJ
01562 885 236
www.kingsofhagley.co.uk

LAITHWAITES
0870 444 8282
www.laithwaites.com

LOCAL FOOD WEB
www.localfoodweb.co.uk

MAKRO UK
020 8965 6655
www.makro.co.uk

MARTIN'S SEAFRESH
St Columb Business Centre, Barn Lane
St Columb Major, Cornwall TR9 6BU
0800 027 2066
www.martins-seafresh.co.uk

MERCHANT GOURMET
2 Rollins Street, London SE15 1EW
0800 731 3549
www.merchantgourmet.com

OCADO
PO BOX 659, Hemel Hempstead HP2 7FF
0845 399 1122
www.ocado.com

P&O FERRIES
08705 202020
www.poferries.com

RECIPES4US
www.recipes4us.co.uk

RED MONKEY COFFEE
Unit 8, Berwick Avenue, Shrewsbury,
Shropshire SY1 2NT
0870 207 4831
www.redmonkeycoffee.com

RICK STEIN
The Seafood Restaurant, Riverside,
Padstow, Cornwall PL28 8BY
01841 53270
www.rickstein.com

THE ROSSLYN DELICATESSEN
56 Rosslyn Hill, Hampstead,
London NW3 1ND
020 7794 9210
www.delirosslyn.co.uk

SAINSBURYS TO YOU
1–5 Wilder Street, Bristol BS2 8QY
0845 301 2020
www.sainsburystoyou.com

SCOTCH WHISKY
www.scotchwhisky.net

TRAIDCRAFT
Kingsway, Gateshead NE11 0NE
0870 443 1018
www.traidcraftshop.co.uk

TROLLYDOLLY
www.trollydolly.co.uk

UK WINES GUIDE
www.ukwinesguide.co.uk

THE VEGETARIAN SOCIETY
Parkdale, Dunham Road, Altrincham,
Cheshire WA14 4QG
0161 925 2000
www.vegsoc.org/cordonvert/recipes

WAITROSE
Doncastle Road, Bracknell RG12 8YA
0800 188 884
www.waitrose.com

THE WINE EDUCATION SERVICE
Vanguard Business Park, Alperton Lane,
Western Avenue, Greenford UB6 8AA
020 8991 8212/3
www.wine-education-service.co.uk

WINE & SPIRIT EDUCATION TRUST
1 Queen Street Place, London EC4R 1QS
020 7236 3551
www.wset.co.uk

WINE ON THE WEB
www.wineontheweb.co.uk

WORLD WINES
Unit 5, Westonian Court, Glenavon Park,
Stoke Bishop, Bristol, Avon BS9 1RJ
0870 922 0269
www.worldwines.co.uk

GOOD-VALUE TRAVEL

AIRPORT PARKING SHOP
0870 733 0778
www.airport-parking-shop.co.uk

ANDREW WEIR SHIPPING
2 Royal Mint Court,
London EC3N 4XX
020 7265 0808
www.aws.co.uk

ANYWORK ANYWHERE
www.anyworkanywhere.com

APARTMENTS.CZ
+420 224 990 990 (Czech Republic)
www.apartments.cz

APH (Airport Parking/Hotels)
0870 733 0809
www.parkaph.co.uk

**ASSOCIATION OF NATIONAL
TOURIST OFFICE REPRESENTATIVES**
PO Box 5017, Hove, East Sussex BN23 3ZD
0870 241 9084
www.tourist-offices.org.uk

**ASSOCIATION OF SPECIAL FARES
AGENTS (ASFA)**
www.asfa.net

BANKRATE
www.bankrate.com

BEST AT HOLIDAYS
0870 709 3007
www.bestatholidays.co.uk

BRIDGE THE WORLD
45–47 Chalk Farm Road, London NW1 8AJ
0870 814 4400
www.bridgetheworld.com

**THE CAMPING AND
CARAVANNING CLUB**
Greenfields House,
Westwood Way, Coventry, CV4 8JH
024 7669 4995
www.campingandcaravanningclub.
co.uk

CAMPING AND CARAVANNING UK
www.camping.uk-directory.com

CANVAS HOLIDAYS
01383 629 000
www.canvasholidays.co.uk

CARBISDALE CASTLE
0870 155 3255
www.carbisdale.org

CHALETFINDER
Stalcot, Taberbacle Walk,
Stroud GL5 3UJ
01453 766 094
www.chaletfinder.co.uk

CHEAP HOTELS WORLDWIDE
0871 717 7397
www.cheaphotelsworldwide.co.uk

CHEAP TICKETS
www.cheaptickets.co.uk

CHEEP TRAVEL
www.cheeptravel.co.uk

CONSORT TRAVEL
Wickersley House, Bawtry Road,
Wickersley, Rotherham, S Yorks S66 2BB
0845 345 0300
www.consorttravel.com

CRUISE CONTROL
Stanton Gate, 49 Mawney Road,
Romford RM7 7HL
0870 909 7540
www.cruisecontrolcruises.co.uk

CRUISE DEALS
Mariner Street, Swansea SA1 5BA
0800 107 2323
www.cruisedeals.co.uk

CRUISE DIRECT
85 Oswald Street,
Glasgow G1 1SN
0871 226 0964
www.cruisedirect.co.uk

THE CRUISE PEOPLE LTD
88 York Street, London W1H 1QT
0800 526 313
www.cruisepeople.co.uk

CRUISE PLANNERS
1 Raven Road, London E18 1HD
0870 528 0000
www.cruiseplanners.co.uk

CUNARD
0845 071 0300
www.cunard.co.uk

CURRENCIES4LESS
160 Brompton Road, London SW3 1HW
020 7594 0594
www.currencies4less.com

CYBERCAFES
www.cybercafes.com

DALTONS HOLIDAYS
8th Floor, CI Tower,
St George's Square,
New Malden, Surrey KT3 4JA
020 8329 0195
www.daltonsholidays.com

DISCOVER CRUISES
020 7436 2449
www.discover-cruises.co.uk

EASYJET
EasyJet Airline Company Limited, EasyLand,
London Luton Airport LU2 9LS
0871 7 500 100
www.easyjet.co.uk

EUROCAMP
0870 9019 410
www.eurocamp.co.uk

EXPEDIA
0870 050 0808
www.expedia.co.uk

FAMILYHOLIDAYS.BIZ
0131 446 9753
www.familyholidays.biz

FAMILY TRAVEL
1 Hargrave Road, London N19 5SH
020 7272 7441
www.family-travel.co.uk

FARM STAY UK
024 7669 6909
www.farmstayuk.co.uk

FCO TRAVEL ADVICE UNIT
Consular Directorate, Foreign &
Commonwealth Office, Old Admiralty
Building, London SW1A 2PA
0870 6060290
www.fco.gov.uk/travel

FEDERATION OF TOUR OPERATORS
14-16 Sussex Road, Haywards Heath,
West Sussex RH16 4EA
01444 457900
www.fto.co.uk

FLYBE
Jack Walker House,
Exeter International Airport EX5 2HL
0871 700 0535
www.flybe.com

FOREIGN CURRENCY DIRECT
The Old Malt House, Currencies Court,
Old Amersham, Buckinghamshire HP7 0HL
0800 328 5884
www.currencies.co.uk

FRED OLSEN CRUISE LINES
Fred Olsen House, White House Road,
Ipswich IP1 5LL
01473 742424
www.fredolsencruises.com

GLOBAL FLIGHT
+49 69-9853-5566 (Germany)
www.globalflight.net

HAVEN HOLIDAYS
1 Park Lane, Hemel Hempstead,
Herts HP2 4TU
0870 242 5678
http://online.haven-holidays.co.uk

**HILLSCAPE WALKING HOLIDAYS
IN WALES**
Blaen-y-ddôl, Pontrhydygroes,
Ystrad Meurig SY25 6DS
01974 282640
www.wales-walking.co.uk

HOMELINK INTERNATIONAL
01962 886882
www.homelink.org.uk

IBIS HOTELS
www.ibishotel.com

INFO TRANSPORT
www.infotransport.co.uk

**INTERNATIONAL ASSOCIATION OF
AIR TRAVEL COURIERS**
01291 625656
www.aircourier.co.uk

KINGS COLLEGE
King's College London, London WC2R 2LS
020 7848 1700
www.kcl.ac.uk

LONDON WALKS
PO Box 1708, London NW6 4LW
020 7624 3978
http://london.walks.com

MARK WARNER HOLIDAYS
10 Old Court Place, London W8 4PL
0870 770 4227
www.markwarner.co.uk

MASTERCARD
www.mastercard.com/cobrand/
maestro/atm

NATIONAL RAIL ENQUIRIES
08457 48 49 50
www.nationalrail.co.uk

NETCOVERDIRECT
25 Coolgardie Avenue, Chigwell IG4 5AX
www.netcoverdirect.com

NORWEGIAN CRUISE LINE (NCL)
www.uk.ncl.com

ONE TRAVEL
www.onetravel.co.uk

P&O CRUISES
Richmond House, Terminus Terrace,
Southampton SO14 3PN
0845 3 555 333
www.pocruises.com

PACKAGE TOUR OPERATORS
Cosmos 0870 44 35 285

www.cosmos.co.uk
First Choice 0870 850 3999
www.firstchoice.co.uk
Thomas Cook 0870 750 5711
www.thomascook.co.uk
Virgin holidays 0870 220 2788
www.virgintravel.co.uk

PARK AND SAVE AIRPORT PARKING
0870 733 0542
www.parkandsave.co.uk

**PASSENGER SHIPPING
ASSOCIATION RETAIL
AGENT SCHEME**
020 7436 2449
www.psa-psara.org

QJUMP
0870 0007 245
www.qjump.co.uk

RAMBLERS HOLIDAYS
Box 43, Welwyn Garden City AL8 6PQ
01707 331133
www.ramblersholidays.co.uk

RESPONSIBLE TRAVEL
www.responsibletravel.com

ROOMS TO BOOK
0870 240 7060
www.roomstobook.co.uk

ROYAL CARIBBEAN INTERNATIONAL
0800 398 9819
www.royalcaribbean.com

RYANAIR
www.ryanair.com

SIMPLE TRAVEL INSURANCE
0870 444 3778
www.simpletravelinsurance.co.uk

SKY SCANNER
www.skyscanner.net

SPEED FERRIES
209 East Camber Office Building, Eastern
Docks, Dover CT16 1JA
0871 222 7456
www.speedferries.com

STAY4FREE
www.stay4free.com

TOTAL STAY
98 Great North Road, London N2 0NL
0870 011 2292
www.totalstay.com

TRAVEL INDEPENDENT
www.travelindependent.info

TRAVEL INN
0870 850 3771
www.travelinn.co.uk

TRAVEL-INSURANCE-WEB
www.travel-insurance-web.com

TRAILFINDERS
0845 05 05 891
www.trailfinders.com

TRAVELBAG
0870 814 4441
www.travelbag.co.uk

TRAVELOCITY
0870 111 7061
www.travelocity.co.uk

TRAVELSPHERE
Compass House, Rockingham Road, Market
Harborough, Leicestershire LE16 7QD

0870 240 2426
www.travelsphere.co.uk

UK HOTELS
www.ukhotels-net.com

VILLASTOGO
Maple House, 2, Maple Grove,
Bishops Stortford, Herts CM23 2PS
01279 329 150
www.villastogo.com

VOYANA CRUISE
020 8515 4890
www.voyanacruise.com

WOMEN WELCOME WOMEN WORLDWIDE
88 Easton Street, High Wycombe HP11 1LT
01494 465441
www.womenwelcomewomen.org.uk

THE WORK AND TRAVEL COMPANY
45 High Street, Tunbridge Wells TN1 1XL
01892 516164
www.worktravelcompany.co.uk

WORKING ABROAD
PO Box 454, Flat 1, Brighton BN1 3ZS
www.workingabroad.com

WORLD WALKS
01242 254 353
www.worldwalks.com

WORLDWIDE TRAVEL INSURANCE
01892 833338
www.worldwideinsure.com

THE YOUTH HOSTEL ASSOCIATION OF ENGLAND AND WALES
Trevelyan House, Dimple Road, Matlock,
Derbyshire DE4 3YH
0870 770 8868
www.yha.org.uk

HEALTHY LIVING

ASSOCIATION OF REFLEXOLOGISTS
27 Old Gloucester Street, London WC1N 3XX
0870 5673320
www.aor.org.uk

BEST SHOP SEARCH
www.bestshopsearch.co.uk

BIG BARN LTD
College Farm, Great Barford MK44 3JJ
01234 871 005
www.bigbarn.co.uk

BIOVEA
56 Gloucester Road, Suite 524,
London SW7 4UB
0800 917 4831
www.biovea.co.uk

BOOTS
www.boots.com

THE BRITISH COMPLEMENTARY MEDICINE ASSOCIATION
PO Box 5122, Bournemouth BH8 0WG
0845 345 5977
www.bcma.co.uk

BUMBLEBEE AUCTIONS
www.bumblebeeauctions.co.uk

BUPA
15–19 Bloomsbury Way, London WC1A 2BA
0800 001010
www.bupa.co.uk

PHA GROUP
89 Station Road, Sidcup, Kent DA15 7DN
0870 7700 942
www.cashplan.net

CLINICARE
The Nexus Building, Broadway, Letchworth
Garden City SG6 3TE
01462 688111
www.clinicare.co.uk

DENPLAN
Denplan Court, Victoria Road,
Winchester SO23 7RG
0800 401402
www.denplan.co.uk

THE DEPARTMENT OF HEALTH
Richmond House, 79 Whitehall,
London SW1A 2NL
020 7210 4850
www.dh.gov.uk

ESSENTIAL OILS DIRECT
PO Box 161, Oldham OL2 6FA
0161 633 3952
www.essentialoilsdirect.co.uk

EXPERIENCE MAD
PO Box 7721, Hatfield Peverel,
Chelmsford CM3 2WZ
0870 7607432
www.experiencemad.co.uk

HEALTHY LIVING
0845 278 8878
www.healthyliving.gov.uk

HEALTHSURE GROUP
HealthSure Group Limited,
43-45 Lever Street, Manchester M60 7HP
0800 854 721
www.healthsure.co.uk

HOLLAND AND BARRETT
Samuel Ryder House, Townsend Drive,
Attleborough Fields, Nuneaton CV11 6XW
0870 606 6606
www.hollandandbarrett.com

HSA
Hambleden House, Andover SP10 1LQ
08702 425454
www.hsa.co.uk

INTERNATIONAL FEDERATION OF PROFESSIONAL AROMATHERAPISTS
82 Ashby Road, Hinckley LE10 1SN
01455 637 987
www.ifparoma.org

MASSAGE THERAPY UK
www.massagetherapy.co.uk

MEDICAL TREATMENT CHOICES LTD
17 Seatonville Road, Whitley Bay NE25 9DA
0800 652 2554
www.treatmentchoices.co.uk

NATIONAL INSTITUTE OF MEDICAL HERBALISTS
54 Mary Arches Street, Exeter EX4 3BA
01392 426022
www.nimh.org.uk

NET DOCTOR
85–87 Bayham Street,
London NW1 0AG
020 7424 7850
www.netdoctor.co.uk

NHS DIRECT
0845 4647
www.nhsdirect.nhs.uk
www.nhs.uk/england/dentists

THE PATIENTS' ASSOCIATION
PO Box 935, Harrow,
Middlesex HA1 3YG
0845 608 4455
www.patients-association.com

PHYSIQUE
Jackson Close, Grove Road, Drayton,
Portsmouth PO6 1UP
0870 60 70 381
www.physique.co.uk

POSTOPTICS
FREEPOST, York YO26 6ZZ
0800 038 3333
www.postoptics.co.uk

POWERHOUSE
0800 212729
www.powerhouse-fitness.co.uk

PRACTICE PLAN
Kempthorne House, Park Avenue,
Oswestry, Shropshire SY11 1AY
01681 677954
www.practiceplan.co.uk

PRESCRIPTION PREPAYMENT CERTIFICATE
PO Box 462, Newcastle Upon Tyne
NE99 2DD
0845 850 0030
www.dh.gov.uk/assetRoot/04/05/
02/72/04050272.pdf

PRIVATE HEALTHCARE UK
271 High Street, Berkhamsted HP4 1AA
01442 385019
www.privatehealth.co.uk

PURELY HEALTH DIRECT
PO Box 170, Ashford TN24 0ZX
0800 089 8900
www.purelyhealthdirect.co.uk

REVIEW CENTRE
Premier House, Manchester Road,
Mossley OL5 9AA
01457 833444
www.reviewcentre.com

THE SOCIETY OF HOMEOPATHS
11 Brookfield, Duncan Close, Moulton Park,
Northampton NN3 6WL
0845 450 661
www.homeopathy-soh.com

**THE SOCIETY OF TEACHERS OF
THE ALEXANDER TECHNIQUE**
1st Floor, Linton House,
39–51 Highgate Road,
London NW5 1RS
0845 230 7828
www.stat.org.uk

SOIL ASSOCIATION
40–56 Victoria Street,
Bristol BS1 6BY
0117 314 5000
www.soilassociation.org

SPA SEEKERS
08708 50 55 50
www.healthyvenues.co.uk

THINK NATURAL
FREEPOST NAT15233,
Lutterworth LE17 4BR
0845 601 1948
www.thinknatural.com

TOTALLY FITNESS
020 7467 5925
www.totallyfitness.co.uk

THE TRICHOLOGICAL SOCIETY
19 Balgores Square, Gidea Park
Nr. Romford RM2 6AU
01708 728980
www.hairscientists.org/
hairmineral-analysis.htm

WELEDA
Heanor Road, Ilkeston, Derbyshire DE7 8DR
0115 944 8200
www.weleda.co.uk

WPA
Rivergate house, Blackbrook Park, Taunton,
Somerset TA1 2PE
01823 625000
www.wpa.org.uk

XS HEALTH
0800 2989588
www.xshealth.co.uk

YOUR AROMATHERAPY
FREEPOST NAT21699, Wellingborough
NN8 5BR
01933 384 844
www.youraromatherapy.co.uk

ZIPFIT
0800 028 2875
www.zipvit.com

HOME REPAIRS AND IMPROVEMENTS

1926 TRADING COMPANY
2 Daimler Close, Royal Oak,
Daventry, Northamptonshire NN11 8QJ
0800 587 2027
www.1926trading.co.uk

AMTICO
Solar Park, Southside,
Solihull B90 4SH
0121 745 0800
www.amtico.com

ANDERSEN WINDOWS
Andersen House,
Dallow Street,
Burton-On-Trent DE14 2PQ
01283 511122
www.blackmillwork.co.uk

**THE ARCHITECTURAL
SALVAGE INDEX**
Netley House, Gomshall,
Surrey GU5 9QA
01483 203221
www.handr.co.uk/salvage_home.html

B&Q
0800 444840
www.diy.com

**THE BATHROOM DISCOUNT
CENTRE**
020 7384 4222
www.bathroomdiscount.co.uk

BATHROOM EXPRESS
www.bathroomexpress.co.uk

BATHROOMS
Unit 5, Trading Estate,
Holland Road,
Hurst Green, Oxted RH8 9BZ
01883 732470
www.bathrooms.com

**THE BATHROOM MANUFACTURERS
ASSOCIATION**
Federation House, Station Road,
Stoke on Trent ST4 2RT
01782 747123
www.bathroom-association.org

BEST QUOTE
Hadwyn House, Field Road,
Reading RG1 6AP
0870 165 7280
www.bestquote4conservatories.co.uk

BUILD CENTER
Trowel House, Kettering Parkway,
Venture Park, Kettering NN15 6XR
0800 529 529
www.build-center.co.uk

BUILDBASE
Gemini One, 5520 Oxford Business Park
South, Cowley, Oxford OX4 2LL
0800 107 2255
www.buildbase.co.uk

THE BUILDING CENTRE
26 Store Street, London WC1E 7BT
020 7692 4000
www.buildingcentre.co.uk

THE CARPET FOUNDATION
01562 755568
www.carpetfoundation.com

CLEAR SKIES
Building 17, Garston, Watford WD25 9XX
0870 243 0930
www.clear-skies.org

COLOROLL
Heasandford Industrial Estate,
Widow Hill Road, Burnley BB10 2TJ
01282 727400
www.coloroll.co.uk

CONSERVATORIES
www.conservatories.co.uk

CONSERVATORIES ONLINE
0800 169 2200
conservatoriesonline.co.uk

CONSUMER COMPLAINTS
PO Box 1290, Civic Centre, Glebe Street,
Stoke on Trent ST4 1RX
www.consumercomplaints.org.uk

**COUNCIL FOR REGISTERED GAS
INSTALLERS (CORGI)**
1 Elmwood, Chineham Park,
Crockford Lane, Basingstoke RG24 8WG
0870 401 2300
www.corgi-gas-safety.com

COVENTRY DEMOLITION COMPANY
0247 654 5051

CROWN PAINTS
PO Box 37, Crown House, Hollins Road,
Darwen, Lancashire BB3 0BG
0870 2401127
www.crownpaints.co.uk

CROWN WALLCOVERINGS
Number One @ The Beehive, Shadsworth
Business Park, Lions Drive, Blackburn
BB1 2QS
01254 222800
www.cwvgroup.com

CUPRINOL
Wexham Road, Slough, Berkshire SL2 5DS
01753 550555
www.cuprinol.co.uk

DECORATING DIRECT
Unit G1, Commerce Way, Skippers Lane
Industrial Estate, Middlesbrough TS6 6UR
www.decoratingdirect.co.uk

DIRECT DOORS
5A Fishwives Causeway, Portobello,
Edinburgh EH15 1DF
0131 669 7310
www.directdoors.com

**THE DISCOUNTED CARPET
UNDERLAY COMPANY**
0845 644 0623
www.discounted-carpet-underlay.
co.uk

DIYNOT
www.diynot.com

DIYTOOLS
15–37 Caryl Street, Liverpool L8 5SQ
www.diytools.co.uk

DOORS DIRECT
35 Claro Court Business Centre,
Claro Road, Harrogate HG1 4BA
01423 502040
www.doorsdirect.co.uk

DOORS SELECT
01625 262400
www.doorsselect.co.uk

DRAPER TOOLS
Hursley Road, Chandlers Ford SO53 1YF
023 8026 6355
www.draper.co.uk

DULUX
ICI Paints, Wexham Road, Slough SL2 5DS
01753 550555
www.dulux.co.uk

EHOW
www.eHow.com

**ELECTRICAL CONTRACTORS
ASSOCIATION**
34 Palace Court, London W2 4HY
020 7313 4800
www.eca.co.uk

ENERGY EFFICIENCY
0845 727 7200
www.saveenergy.co.uk

ESTIMATORS ONLINE
12A High Street,
Cheadle SK8 1AL
0161 286 8601
www.estimators-online.com

EXPERT HOME ADVICE
www.experthomeadvice.com

THE FEDERATION OF MASTER BUILDERS
Gordon Fisher House,
14–15 Great James Street,
London WC1N 3DP
020 7242 7583
www.fmb.org.uk

FOCUS DO IT ALL
Gawsworth House, Westmere Drive,
Crewe, Cheshire CW1 6XB
0800 436436
www.focusdoitall.co.uk

THE GLASS AND GLAZING FEDERATION
44–48 Borough High Street,
London SE1 1XB
0870 042 4255
www.ggf.org.uk

HAMMERITE
Prudhoe, Northumberland NE42 6LP
01661 830000
www.hammerite.com

HANDLES DIRECT
Unit 3, Princess Court, Chapeltown, Pellon
Lane, Halifax HX1 5SR
01422 358111
www.handlesdirect.co.uk

HARLEQUIN
Chelsea Harbour Design Centre,
Chelsea, London SW10 0XE
08708 300032
www.harlequin.uk.com

IFLOOR.CO.UK
0800 358 0103
www.ifloor.co.uk

INSTITUTE OF PLUMBING AND HEATING ENGINEERING
64 Station Lane, Hornchurch RM12 6NB
01708 472791
www.plumbers.org.uk

JUST DOORS
Unit 1, Grove Technology Park, Wantage,
Oxon OX12 9FA
0870 200 1010
www.justdoors.co.uk

KERSHAWS DOOR WAREHOUSE
5 Main Street, Woodside Road
Wyke, Bradford BD12 8BN
0845 126 0270
www.door-warehouse.co.uk

THE KITCHEN DOCTOR
Oak House, Sevenoaks Road,
Pratts Bottom, Kent BR6 7SF
0500 855555
www.thekitchendoctor.com

KITCHENS.CO.UK
www.kitchens.co.uk

LIGHTING DIRECT
Unit 39, The Wenta Business Park, Colne
Way, Watford WD24 7ND
01923 333000
www.lighting-direct.co.uk

THE LIGHTING SUPERSTORE
Unit G11, Avonside Enterprise Park,
Melksham, Wiltshire SN12 8BS
01225 704442
www.thelightingsuperstore.co.uk

LIGHTSAVER
10–12 York Road, Erdington,
Birmingham B23 6TE
0121 350 1999
www.lightsaver.co.uk

LOCAL AUTHORITY BUILDING CONTROL
137 Lupus Street, London SW1V 3HE
020 7641 8737
www.labc-services.co.uk

MAGNET
01325 744344
www.magnet.co.uk

MARLBOROUGH TILES FACTORY SHOP
Elcot Lane, Marlborough, Wiltshire SN8 2AY
01672 512422
www.marlboroughtiles.com

NATIONAL BRANDS
Edge Lane, Liverpool L7 2PD
0151 260 8967
www.national-brands.co.uk

NATIONAL FEDERATION OF BUILDERS
55 Tufton Street, London SW1P 3QL
0870 8989 091
www.builders.org.uk

NATIONAL HOME IMPROVEMENT COUNCIL
www.nhic.org.uk

THE ORIGINAL BOX SASH WINDOW COMPANY
29–30 The Arches, Alma Road,
Windsor SL4 1QZ
0800 783 4053
www.boxsash.com

PAINTING AND DECORATING ASSOCIATION
32 Coton Road, Nuneaton CV11 5TW
024 7635 3776
www.paintingdecoratingassociation.
co.uk

PILKINGTON'S
PO Box 4, Rake Lane, Clifton Junction,
Swinton, Manchester M27 8LP
0161 727 1000
www.pilkingtons.com

PLUMB CENTER
08701 622 557
www.plumbcenter.co.uk

PLUMBWORLD
Watts Building, Grosvenor Business Park,
Enterprise Way, Evesham WR11 1GA
www.plumbworld.co.uk

PROTECH
Bermingham House, Whinfield Drive,
Newton Aycliffe Ind Park,
Newton Aycliffe, DL5 6AU
01325 310520
www.thebbgroup.co.uk

THE REPLACEMENT KITCHEN DOOR CO
1 Hollow Cottages, London Road,
Purfleet RM19 1QP
01708 86538
www.replacementkitchendoor.co.uk

ROYAL INSTITUTE OF BRITISH ARCHITECTS
66 Portland Place, London W1B 1AD
020 7580 5533
www.riba.org

ROYAL TOWN PLANNING INSTITUTE
41 Botolph Lane, London EC3R 8DL
020 7929 9494
www.rtpi.org.uk

RUGS UK
93 Highgate, Kendal LA9 4EN
0808 108 9657
www.rugsuk.com

SALVO
01890 820333
www.salvo.co.uk

SCREWFIX DIRECT
FREEPOST, Yeovil BA22 8BF
0800 096 6226
www.screwfix.com

SLATE WORLD
Westmoreland Road, Kingsbury,
London NW9 9RN
020 8204 3444
www.slateworld.com

THE TILE ASSOCIATION
83 Copers Cope Road, Beckenham BR3 1NR
020 8663 0946
www.tiles.org.uk

THE TILE WAREHOUSE
131 Derby Road, Stapleford,
Nottingham NG9 7AS
0115 939 0209
www.thetilewarehouse.com

TOOLBANK
0800 068 6238
www.toolbank.co.uk

TOPPS TILES
Rushworth House, Handforth, Wilmslow,
Cheshire SK9 3HJ
0800 783 6262
www.toppstiles.co.uk

UK CARPETS DIRECT
0191 418 7396
www.ukcarpetsdirect.com

UK KITCHEN BATHROOM BEDROOM SPECIALISTS ASSOCIATION
12 Top Barn Business Centre, Holt Heath,
Worcester WR6 6NH
01905 726066
www.ksa.co.uk

THE WALLPAPER SHOP
www.thewallpapershop.net

WALLPAPER ORDERS UK
Oozewood Road, Royton, Oldham,
Greater Manchester OL2 5SQ,
0161 626 4278
www.wallpaperorders.co.uk

WORLD'S END TILES
Silverthorne Road, London SW8 3HE
020 7819 2110
www.worldsendtiles.co.uk

HOMES AND GARDENS

APPLIANCE DIRECT
Babington Lane, Derby DE1 1SX
01332 547580
www.appliance-direct.co.uk

APPLIANCE WORLD
145 Faringdon Road, Swindon SN1 5DL
0870 757 2424
www.appliance-world.co.uk

BBC GARDENING
www.bbc.co.uk/gardening/design

BEDS DIRECT
25 Chester Street, Chester CH4 8BL
01244 671188
www.bedsdirect.com

BRITISH GAS
0845 600 5090
www.house.co.uk

BUYERS AND SELLERS
120–122 Ladbroke Grove, London W10 5NE
0845 085 5585

CHEAP WASHING MACHINES
www.cheap-washing-machines.co.uk

CHRISTY MILL SHOP
PO Box 19, 19 Newton Street, Hyde
SK14 4NR
0161 368 1961
www.christy-towels.com

THE COTSWOLD COMPANY
1 Apollo Rise, Southwood,
Farnborough GU14 0GT
0870 241 0973
www.cotswoldco.com

THE CURTAIN EXCHANGE
020 7731 8316
www.thecurtainexchange.net

CURTAINS ENCORE
01258 455221
www.curtainsencore.co.uk

DARTINGTON CRYSTAL
Torrington, Devon EX38 7AN
01805 626421
www.dartington.co.uk

DENBY
Denby, Derbyshire DE5 8NX
01773 740899
www.denbypottery.co.uk

DESIGNERS GUILD
3 Latimer Place, London W10 6QT
020 7893 7400
www.designersguild.com

EBID
www.ebid.co.uk

FURNITURE 123
Sandway Business Centre, Shannon Street,
Leeds LS9 8SS
0845 062 2233
www.furniture123.co.uk

FURNITURE BUSTERS
453–457 Lordship Lane, London N22 5DJ
020 8888 7009
www.furniturebusters.com

GONEGARDENING
0845 1 300 100
www.gonegardening.com

HABITAT'S CLEARANCE DEPARTMENT
0161 902 0441

THE HENRY DOUBLEDAY RESEARCH ASSOCIATION (HDRA)
Ryton Organic Gardens, Coventry CV8 3LG
0247 6303517
www.hdra.org.uk

JOHN LEWIS
PO Box 369, Exeter EX1 1DH
08456 049 049
www.johnlewis.com

KNICKERBEAN
0845 130 5900
www.knickerbean.co.uk

LAURA ASHLEY
27 Bagleys Lane, London SW6 2QA
0871 9835 999
www.lauraashley.com

LITTLEWOODS
Sir John Moores Building, 100 Old Hall
Street, Liverpool L70 1AB
0845 707 8810
www.littlewoods-online.com

LOST POTTERY
0870 732 4462
www.lostpottery.co.uk

NATIONAL CARPET CLEANERS ASSOCIATION
0116 271 9550
www.ncca.co.uk

OSBORNE & LITTLE
304 King's Road, London SW3 5UH
020 7352 1456
www.osborneandlittle.com

ROYAL HORTICULTURAL SOCIETY
80 Vincent Square, London SW1P 2PE
020 7834 4333
www.rhs.org.uk

SANDERSON
Sanderson House, Oxford Road,
Denham UB9 4DX
01895 830044
www.sanderson-online.co.uk

THE SHOWHOME WAREHOUSE
11–17 Francis Court, Wellingborough Road,
Rushden NN10 6AY
0870 333 1556
www.showhomewarehouse.co.uk

SISLEY
www.sisley.co.uk

SPODE
Church Street, Stoke-on-Trent ST4 1BX
01782 744011
www.spode.co.uk

TABLEWHERE
020 8361 6111
www.tablewhere.co.uk

TRADING INTERIORS
28 Barwell Business Park,
Leatherhead Road, Chessington KT9 2NY
020 8397 4730
www.roomservicegroup.com

UNBEATABLE
Capital House, Link 10, Napier Way,
Crawley RH10 9RA
01293 543555
www.unbeatable.co.uk

UK APPLIANCES
Castle Mead House, Castle Mead Gardens,
Hertford SG14 1JZ
08707 606600
www.ukappliances.co.uk

VACUUM BAG SHOP
22 Aspen Close, Ipswich IP6 0HQ
07870 697 728
www.vacuumbagsonline.co.uk

VACUUM CLEANERS DIRECT
57 Moreton Street, London SW1V 2NY
0700 424 7247
www.vacuumcleanersdirect.co.uk

WESLEY-BARRELL
Ducklington Mill, Standlake Road,
Ducklington, Witney OX29 7YR
01993 893100
www.wesley-barrell.co.uk

HOUSEHOLD FINANCE

**ANSVAR INSURANCE COMPANY
LIMITED**
Ansvar House, St. Leonards Road,
Eastbourne BN21 3UR
01323 737541
www.ansvar.co.uk

BASIC POWER
Freepost (SCE9229), Chippenham SN15 1UZ
0845 601 2421
www.basicpower.co.uk

DIRECTORY ENQUIRIES
www.118500.co.uk
www.ukphonebook.com
www.192.com

THE ENERGY SHOP
0845 045 0160
www.theenergyshop.co.uk

GREEN ENERGY
9 Church Street, Ware SG12 9EG
0845 456 9550
www.greenenergy.uk.com

MONEYSAVINGEXPERT.COM
www.moneysavingexpert.com

OFGEM
9 Millbank, London SW1P 3GE
020 7901 7000
www.ofgem.co.uk

POWERGEN
PO Box 7750, Nottingham NG1 6WR
0800 015 20 29
www.choosepowergen.co.uk

SAYNOTO0870
www.saynoto0870.com

SCOTTISH POWER
0845 270 6543
www.scottishpower.com

SWALEC
PO Box 7506, Perth PH1 3QR
0800 052 5252
www.swalec.co.uk

SWITCHANDGIVE
Suite 330, 30 Great Guildford Street,
London SE1 0HS
0870 922 0353
www.switchandgive.com

UKPOWER
Barclays Venture Centre, University of
Warwick Science Park, Coventry CV4 7EZ
0800 093 2447
www.ukpower.com

UNRAVELIT
Xelector House, 40 Sandford Road,
Dublin 6
0808 156 3765
www.unravelit.com

VIRGIN HOME ENERGY
Freepost LON14908, Exeter, EX2 7BF
0800 028 8269
www.virginhome.co.uk/virginHome/
homeenergy/home.do

YELLOW PAGES
www.yell.com

LEISURE AND HOBBIES

5 MINUTES AWAY
0905 403 0132
www.5minutesaway.co.uk

5PM
38 Queen Street, Glasgow G1 3DX
www.5pm.co.uk

AA
Carr Ellison House, William Armstrong
Drive, Newcastle-upon-Tyne NE4 7YA
0870 600 0371
www.theaa.com

ABEBOOKS
www.abebooks.co.uk

ACCOR SERVICES
50 Vauxhall Bridge Road, London
SW1V 2RS
0845 3304433
www.luncheonvouchers.co.uk

AMDRAM
PO Box 536, Norwich MLO, NR6 7JZ
www.amdram.co.uk

ASSOCIATION OF CYCLE TRADERS
31a High Street, Tunbridge Wells TN1 1XN
01892 526081
www.act-bicycles.com

BARTER BOOKS
Alnwick Station, Northumberland NE66 2NP
01665 604888
www.barterbooks.co.uk

BBC LEARNING
www.bbc.co.uk/languages
www.bbc.co.uk/learning

BEANS OF BICESTER
86 Sheep Street, Bicester OX26 6LP
01869 246451
www.beansonline.co.uk

BOL
www.uk.bol.com

THE BOOK PEOPLE
Parc Menai, Bangor LL57 4FB
0870 607 7740
www.thebookpeople.co.uk

BRING YOUR OWN BOTTLE
www.wine-pages.com/byoblist.shtml

**CARAVAN AND OUTDOOR
LEISURE SHOW**
Earls Court Exhibition Centre,
Warwick Road, London SW5 9TA
020 7370 8203
www.caravanshows.com/
outdoorleisure/home.php

**CENTRAL COUNCIL OF CHURCH
BELL RINGERS**
www.cccbr.org.uk

CHELSEA FLOWER SHOW
Royal Hospital,
Chelsea, London SW3
020 7649 1885
www.rhs.org.uk/chelsea/2004/
index.asp

**CHESSINGTON WORLD OF
ADVENTURES**
0870 444 7777
www.chessington.com

CONCERT DIARY
www.concertdiary.com

CRAFT DEPOT
Somerton Business Park, Somerton,
Somerset TA11 6SB
01458 27 47 27
www.craftdepot.co.uk

**THE CREATIVE NEEDLE
SEWING CLUB**
PO Box 14, Hinckley,
Leicester LE10 1ZU
01455 615108
www.cross-stitch-club.co.uk

THE DAILY TELEGRAPH
1 Canada Square, Canary Wharf
London E14 1DT
020 7538 5000
www.telegraph.co.uk

DAWKES MUSIC
Reform Road, Maidenhead SL6 8BT
01628 630 800
www.dawkes.co.uk

DAYS OUT UK
PO Box 427, Northampton NN1 3YN
01604 622445
www.daysoutuk.com

DINE ONLINE
www.dine-online.co.uk

DISCOUNT FABRICS & WALLPAPER
08705 239955
www.homeinteriors.co.uk

ENGLAND AND WALES CRICKET BOARD
www.ecb.co.uk

THE ENGLISH NATIONAL OPERA
London Coliseum,
St. Martin's Lane,
Trafalgar Square,
London WC2
020 7632 8300
www.eno.org

ENVIRONMENT AGENCY
08708 506 506
www.environment-agency.gov.uk

EXPLORE BRITAIN
6 George Street, Ferryhill,
Co. Durham DL17 0DT
01740 650 900
www.xplorebritain.com

FEET FIRST
728 Chesterfield Road,
Woodseats, Sheffield S8 0SE
0114 258 9529
www.feetfirst.resoles.co.uk

FLEXIBLE LEARNING
www.distance-learning.co.uk

FLOODLIGHT
www.floodlight.co.uk

FREE!
www.londontourist.org/free.html

FREE SKILLS
www.freeskills.com

FREETODO ENGLAND
www.freetodoeurope.net/
page121.html

FULHAM FC
Fulham Football Club Training Ground,
Motspur Park, New Malden KT3 6PT
0870 442 1222
www.fulhamfc.com

GARDEN VISIT
www.gardenvisit.com

GO-FISHING
www.go-fishing.co.uk

THE GREAT BRITAIN PHILATELIC SOCIETY
Greylands, Melton, Woodbridge IP12 1QE
www.gbps.org.uk

HALFORDS
Redditch,Worcestershire B98 0DE
0870 870 8810
www.halfords.com

HOT COURSES
150–152 King Street,
London W6 0QU
020 8600 5300
www.hotcourses.com

THE INDEPENDENT
Independent House,
191 Marsh Wall,
London E14 9RS
020 7005 2000
www.independent.co.uk

JAGS ONLINE
www.jags-online.co.uk

JESSOPS
Scudamore Road,
Leicester LE3 1TZ
0116 232 6000
www.jessops.com

KAY OPTICAL
020 8648 8822
www.kayoptical.com

LATEST EVENTS
Juniper House, Seager Buildings,
Brookmill Road, London SE8 4JT
0870 787 1787
www.latestevents.com

LEARN DIRECT
0800 101 901
www.learndirect.co.uk

LIFELONG LEARNING
0800 100 900
www.lifelonglearning.co.uk

LINNS STAMP NEWS INTERNATIONAL
PO Box 29, Sidney, OH 45265, USA
www.linns.com

LONDON AQUARIUM
County Hall, Westminster Bridge Road,
London SE1 7PB
020 7967 8000
www.londonaquarium.co.uk

LONDON'S ROYAL ACADEMY OF MUSIC
Marylebone Road, London NW1 5HT
020 7873 7373
www.ram.ac.uk

THE LONDON SYMPHONY ORCHESTRA
Barbican Centre, Silk Street
London EC2Y 8DS
020 7588 1116
www.lso.co.uk
St Lukes 020 7490 3939
www.lso.co.uk/lsostlukes

LONDON THEATRE GUIDE
PO Box 45519, London NW1 0WX
020 7493 4731
www.londontheatre.co.uk

LONDON UNDERGROUND
55 Broadway, London SW1H 0BD
020 7222 5600
www.thetube.com

MANPOWER GLOBAL LEARNING CENTRE
www.manpower.co.uk/jobseekers/
main_global_learning_centre.asp

THE NATIONAL ART COLLECTIONS FUND
Millais House, 7 Cromwell Place,
London SW7 2JN
0870 848 2003
www.artfund.org

NATIONAL ASSOCIATION OF FLOWER ARRANGEMENT (NAFAS)
Osborne House, 12 Devonshire Square,
London EC2M 4TE
020 7247 5567
www.nafas.org.uk

NATIONAL FILM THEATRE
020 7815 1374
www.bfi.org.uk/showing/nft/about/
join.html

THE NATIONAL GARDENS SCHEME
Hatchlands Park, East Clandon,
Guildford GU4 7RT
01483 211535
www.ngs.org.uk

THE NATIONAL PHILATELIC SOCIETY
107 Charterhouse Street,
London EC1M 6PT
020 7490 9610
www.ukphilately.org.uk/nps

NATIONAL SOCIETY OF ALLOTMENT AND LEISURE GARDENERS
01536 266576
www.nsalg.org.uk

THE NATIONAL THEATRE
South Bank, London SE1 9PX
020 7452 3000
www.nt-online.org

NETTO
0845 6000200
www.netto.co.uk

ODEON
www.odeon.co.uk

ONLINE FABRICS
388–394 Foleshill Road,
Coventry, West Midlands
024 7668 7776
www.online-fabrics.co.uk

ONLINE GOLF
0870 20 12345
www.onlinegolf.co.uk

OPERA NORTH
Grand Theatre, Leeds LS1 6NU
0113 243 9999
www.operanorth.co.uk

ORANGE & FILM
150 from your Orange phone or
07973 100 150
www.orange.co.uk/entertainment/
film/cma/overview.html

OUTDOOR MEGASTORE
P.O. Box 36, Bootle L20 4YD
www.outdoormegastore.co.uk

PREPAL
www.prepal.com

PROFESSIONAL ASSOCIATION OF DIVING INSTRUCTORS (PADI)
www.padi.com

RAMBLERS' ASSOCIATION
2nd Floor, Camelford House, 87–90 Albert
Embankment, London SE1 7TW
020 7339 8500
www.ramblers.org.uk

THE RESTAURANT GUIDE
www.restaurant-guide.com

**THE ROYAL HORTICULTURAL
SOCIETY**
80 Vincent Square, London SW1P 2PE
020 7821 3000
www.rhs.org.uk

THE ROYAL OPERA HOUSE
Covent Garden, London WC2E 9DD
020 7304 4000
www.royalopera.org

ROYAL SHAKESPEARE COMPANY
Royal Shakespeare Theatre, Waterside,
Stratford-upon-Avon CV37 6BB
01789 403444
www.rsc.org.uk

**THE ROYAL SOCIETY FOR THE
PROTECTION OF BIRDS (RSPB)**
The Lodge, Sandy SG19 2DL
01767 68055
www.rspb.org.uk

RUGBY FOOTBALL UNION
Rugby House, Rugby Road,
Twickenham TW1 1DS
www.rfu.com

RUNNING CLUBS
www.running-world.net/
clubs-uk.html

THE SCOTTISH OPERA
39 Elmbank Crescent, Glasgow G2 4PT
0141 248 4567
www.scottishopera.org.uk

SCOTTISH RUGBY
www.scottishrugby.org

SCOTTISH SPORT
www.scottishsport.co.uk

SEE
www.seetickets.com

SHAPE
356 Holloway Road, London N7 6PA
020 7619 6160
www.shapearts.org.uk

SIGNET MUSIC
0800 542 1566
www.signetmusic.com

THE SOCIETY OF LONDON THEATRE
32 Rose Street, London WC2E 9ET
020 7557 6700
www.officiallondontheatre.co.uk

SPORT ENGLAND
3rd Floor, Victoria House, Bloomsbury
Square, London WC1B 4SE
08458 508 508
www.sportengland.org

THE SPORTS COUNCIL FOR WALES
Sophia Gardens, Cardiff CF11 9SW
029 2030 0500
www.sports-council-wales-co.uk

STAMP & COIN MART
1st Floor, Edward House, Tindal Bridge,
Edward Street, Birmingham B1 2RA
0121 233 8744
www.stampmart.co.uk

THEATRES ONLINE
www.theatresonline.com

TICKETMASTER
www.ticketmaster.co.uk

THE TIMES
1 Pennington House,
London E1 9XN
020 7782 5000
www.timesonline.co.uk

TOP TABLE
33 Welbeck Street, London W1G 8EX
0870 850 8454
www.toptable.co.uk

TOY TRADER
49 Southfield Close, Dukinfield SK16 5RX
0161 285 0150
www.toytrader.net

UCI CINEMAS
FREEPOST NWW 211 2A,
Manchester M1 9PF
08700 10 20 30
www.uci.co.uk

UGC CINEMAS
Power Road Studios, Power Road,
London W4 5PY
0870 777 2775
www.ugcinemas.co.uk

UK ATHLETICS
Athletics House, Central Boulevard,
Blythe Valley Park, Solihull B90 8AJ
0870 998 6800
www.ukathletics.net

UK DIVE GUIDE
Bleasdale House, 9 Copse Road,
Fleetwood FY5 2AQ
01253 778444
www.ukdiveguide.co.uk

UK SITES GUIDE
136 Hillside Road, Bramcote,
Nottingham, NG9 3BD
0115 9225582
www.uk-sites.com

**THE UNITED KINGDOM
PARLIAMENT**
House of Commons, London, SW1A 0AA
020 7219 3000
www.parliament.uk

VOUCH4ME
64 Clarendon Road, Watford WD17 1DA
www.vouch4me.com

VUE CINEMAS
10 Chiswick Park, 566 Chiswick High Road,
London W4 5XS
020 8396 0100
www.myvue.com

WAY TO LEARN
0870 000 2288
www.waytolearn.co.uk

THE WELSH NATIONAL OPERA
John Street, Cardiff CF10 5SP
029 2046 4666
www.wno.org.uk

WHATSONSTAGE
www.whatsonstage.com

WHIPSNADE ZOO
Dunstable, Bedfordshire LU6 2LF
01582 872171
www.whipsnade.co.uk

WIMBLEDON
The All England Lawn Tennis Club,
Church Road, London SW19 5AE
020 8946 2244
www.wimbledon.org

WISH VALUE
51–52 Causeway Road,
Earlstree Industrial Estate North,
Corby NN17 4DU
www.wishvalue.co.uk

WOBURN SAFARI PARK
Woburn Park, Bedfordshire MK17 9QN
01525 290407
www.woburnsafari.co.uk

WOOL WORKS
www.woolworks.org

WORLD OF CAMPING
Unit 4, Wheal Kitty Workshops,
Wheal Kitty, St Agnes, Cornwall TR5 0RD
01872 552 778
www.worldofcamping.co.uk

WELSH RUGBY UNION
www.wru.co.uk

LOOKING GOOD

ALEXON SALE SHOPS
01743 236319

THE ANERLEY FROCK EXCHANGE
122 Anerley Road,
London SE20
020 8778 2030

AQUASCUTUM FACTORY SHOPS
01964 536759
www.aquascutum.co.uk

ARMSTRONGS
0131 220 5557

ASH SAMTANI CLOTHING
www.samtani.com

ASOS
www.asos.com

AVON
0845 601 4040
www.avon.uk.com

BANG BANG
Goodge Street, London W1
020 7631 4191

BICESTER VILLAGE
50 Pingle Drive, Oxon OX26 6WD
01869 323 200
www.bicestervillage.com

BODY SHOP
Building 4,
Hawthorn Road,
Wick, Littlehampton BN17 7LR
08459 050607
www.uk.thebodyshop.co.uk

BRITISH HEART FOUNDATION
14 Fitzhardinge Street,
London W1H 0DH
08450 70 80 70
www.bhf.org.uk

**THE BRITISH JEWELLER'S
ASSOCIATION**
Federation House, 10 Vyse Street,
Birmingham, B18 6LT
0121 237 1110
www.bja.org.uk

BROWN BAG CLOTHING
PO Box 403, Macclesfield SK10 4WR
01625 859185
www.bbclothing.co.uk

THE BURBERRY FACTORY OUTLET
29–53 Chatham Place, London E9 6LP
020 8985 3344

BUY COSMETICS
FREEPOST 28 ANG20402, London W1E 9HY
0871 871 7207
www.buycosmetics.com

CANCER RESEARCH UK
P.O. Box 123, Lincoln's Inn Fields,
London WC2A 3PX
0207009 8820
www.cancerresearchuk.org

CATWALK QUEEN MAGAZINE
www.catwalk-queen.net

CHOICE FOR YOU
Royal Avenue, Widnes WA88 1TB
08000 686 901
www.choiceforyou.co.uk

CITY COLLEGE
0800 013 0123
www.ccm.ac.uk

CLARK'S FACTORY SHOPS
020 7732 2530

CLARKS VILLAGE
Farm Road, Street, Somerset BA16 0BB
01458 840 064
www.clarksvillage.co.uk

COME-SHOPPING
19 Bridgegate, Retford DN22 6AJ
01777 861600
www.come-shopping.co.uk

THE CONSUMER GATEWAY
www.consumer.gov.uk

CREATIVE BEADCRAFT
20 Beak Street, London W1
020 7629 9964
www.creativebeadcraft.co.uk

CRUSAID
Churton Street, London SW1
020 7233 8736
www.crusaid.org.uk

DEALTIME
www.dealtime.co.uk

DELLA FINCH DESIGNER SALES
020 7233 6385

DESIGNER DISCOUNT
PO Box 7007, Nottingham NG7 5FN
0115 970 3956
www.designerdiscount.co.uk

DESIGNER EXCHANGE
3 Royal Exchange Court, Glasgow
0141 221 6898

DESIGNER SALE UK
01273 470 880
www.designersales.co.uk

DESIGNER SHOWROOM SALE
020 7850 5075

THE DESIGNER WAREHOUSE SALES
020 7704 1064
www.dwslondon.co.uk

DOROTHY PERKINS
www.dorothyperkins.co.uk

ELITE DRESS AGENCY
35 King Street West, Manchester M3 2PW
0161 832 3670
www.elitedressagency.co.uk

ELVI
17 Oxleasow Road, East Moons Moat,
Redditch B98 0RE
01527 506306
www.elvi.co.uk

ESKAYE
PO Box 3192, Sheffield S26 4WZ
0114 254 0941
www.eskaye.co.uk

ESSENTIALLY OILS
8–10 Mount Farm, Junction Road,
Churchill, Chipping Norton, Oxfordshire
OX7 6NP
01608 659544
www.essentiallyoils.com

ESUIT
www.eSuit.com

EVANS
www.evans.ltd.uk

FARA
020 7371 0141

FASHION WORLD
40 Lever Street, Manchester M60 6ES
0870 160 6100
www.fashionworld.co.uk

FREEMANS
PO Box 1761, Sheffield S96 5FS
0870 606 6099
www.freemans.com

**FRENCH CONNECTION/
NICOLE FARHI OUTLET SHOP**
020 7399 7125

THE GALLERIA OUTLET CENTRE
Hatfield
www.factory-outlets.co.uk

GAP
www.gap.com

GET AHEAD HATS
www.getaheadhats.co.uk

H&M
57 Rathbone Place, London W1T IHE
020 7323 2211
www.hm.com

HIRE SOCIETY
16 Imperial Studios, Imperial Road,
London SW6 2AG
0870 780 2003
www.hire-society.com

JAMES & ALDEN
385 Edgeware Road, London NW2 6BA
020 8830 8008

KING OF SHAVES
17–19 Chiltern Court, Asheridge Road,
Chesham HP5 2PX
0800 0838416
www.shave.com

KITBAG
08000 830 010
www.kitbag.co.uk

KNICKERBOX
0845 456 2343
www.knickerbox.co.uk

LANDS END
FREEPOST Mid 15304, Oakham,
Rutland LE15 6ZW
0800 376 7974
www.landsend.co.uk

LA REDOUTE
PO Box 777, Bradford BD99 4WY
0870 050 0455
www.redoute.co.uk

L'HOMME DESIGNER EXCHANGE
50 Blandford Street, London W1
020 7224 3266

THE LOFT
35 Monmouth Street, London WC2
020 7240 3807

LONDON FASHION WEEKEND
0871 222 2314
www.londonfashionweek.co.uk

L'OREAL TECHNICAL CENTRE
020 8762 4292

MCARTHUR GLEN
0207 535 2350
www.mcarthurglen.com

MEN ESSENTIALS
www.menessentials.com

MENKIND STORES LTD
Connect Business Centre, Kingston Road,
Leatherhead, Surrey KT22 7NT
01372 365021
www.menkind.co.uk

MULBERRRY FACTORY SHOP
01749 340583

NEW LOOK
New Look House, Mercery Road,
Weymouth DT3 5HJ
01305 765000
www.newlook.co.uk

OAKVILLE
020 7580 3686

ONE WELLINGTON PLACE
1 Wellington Place, London NW8 7PE
020 7483 0688

OXFAM ORIGINAL
PO Box 1761, Sheffield S96 5FS
0870 606 6099
www.freemans.com

PAUL COSTELLO
0151 357 1681

PEAK VILLAGE FACTORY OUTLET
Chatsworth Road, Rowsley, Derbyshire
01629 735326
www.peakvillage.co.uk

PRIMARK
41 West Street, Reading RG1 1TT
www.primark.co.uk

RAJA FASHIONS
www.raja-fashions.com

REVISIONS
01273 207728

RITA RUSK INTERNATIONAL
498 Great Western Road, Glasgow
0141 357 3333
www.ritarusk.co.uk

SALON LINES
Salon House, 2nd Floor, 47 Allerton Road,
Liverpool L18 2DA
0151 722 4888
www.salonlines.co.uk

SALVATION ARMY CHARITY SHOP
020 7359 9865

SAVE ON MAKE UP
www.saveonmakeup.co.uk

SECONDS OUT
01628 850371

SHOE-SHOP.COM LTD
The Kinloch Building, Northminster
Business Park, Northfield Lane, Upper
Poppleton, York YO26 6QU
08700 117 227
www.shoe-shop.com

SLAPITON BOUTIQUE
25A Castlegate, Newark,
Nottinghamshire NG24 1AZ
01636 611 844
www.slapiton.tv

SOMERSET COSMETIC INGREDIENTS
PO Box 3372, Renton, WA 98056, USA
www.makingcosmetics.com

STITCH UP
45 Parkway, London NW1 7PN
020 7482 4404

SUE RYDER
2nd Floor,
114–118 Southampton Row,
London WC1B 5AA
020 7400 0440
www.suerydercare.org

TAILORED FOR YOU LTD
14 West End, Melksham SN12 6HJ
www.tailored-for-you.com

TIPKING
www.tips.tipking.com

TONI AND GUY
020 7921 9100
www.toniandguy.co.uk

TOP SHOP
www.topshop.co.uk

TRAID
5 Second Way, Wembley HA9 0YJ
020 8733 2580
www.traid.org.uk

TREVOR SORBIE
27 Floral Street, London WC2E 9DP
020 7395 2907
www.trevorsorbie.com

UK HAIRDRESSERS
1–2 The Promenade, Ainsdale,
Southport, Merseyside PR8 2QB
01704 577111
www.ukhairdressers.com

THE UPPINGHAM DRESS AGENCY
2–6 Orange Street, Uppingham, Rutland
01572 823276

VIDAL SASSOON
020 7318 5205
www.vidalsassoon.co.uk

VIRGIN VIE
0845 300 8022
www.virgincosmetics.com

WAHL FASHIONS
020 7499 4000

YVES ROCHER
0870 608 7575
www.yves-rocher.co.uk

PLANNING FOR RETIREMENT

ANNUITY BUREAU
11 York Road, London SE1 7NX
0845 602 6263
www.bureauxltd.com

ANNUITY DIRECT
32 Scrutton Street,
London EC2A 4RQ
0500 506575
www.annuitydirect.co.uk

ANTIQUES BULLETIN
2 Hampton Court Road, Harborne,
Birmingham B17 9AE
0121 681 8000
www.antiquesbulletin.co.uk

ANTIQUES COLLECTORS' CLUB
01394 389 950
www.antique-acc.com

BONHAMS
101 New Bond Street, London W1S 1SR
020 7393 3900
www.bonhams.com

BPT BRIDGEWATER EQUITIES
28 Church Street, Epsom KT17 4QB
01372 742741
www.bpt-bridgewater.co.uk

CHRISTIE'S
8 King Street,
London SW1Y 6QT
020 7839 9060
www.christies.co.uk

CLERICAL MEDICAL
33 Old Broad Street,
London EC2N 1HZ
020 7930 5474
www.clericalmedical.co.uk

DIRECTGOV
www.direct.gov.uk

LEARN DIRECT FUTURES
0800 100 900
www.learndirect-futures.co.uk

LEGAL & GENERAL
www.legalandgeneral.com

NEW DEAL
0845 606 2626
www.newdeal.gov.uk

NORTHERN ROCK
0845 600 0741
www.northernrock.co.uk

OVER 50
www.over50.gov.uk

PENSION ANNUITY
www.pensionannuity.co.uk

THE PENSION SERVICE
Freepost, Bristol BS38 7WA
0845 731 3233
www.pensionguide.gov.uk

PRUDENTIAL
Laurence Pountney Hill, London EC4R 0HH
020 7220 7588
www.prudential.co.uk

SAFE HOME INCOME PLANS (SHIP)
PO Box 516, Preston Central PR2 2XQ
0870 241 6060
www.ship-ltd.org

SOTHEBY'S
020 729 5000
www.sothebys.com

STANDARD LIFE
Standard Life House, 30 Lothian Road,
Edinburgh EH1 2DH
0131 225 2552
www.standardlife.co.uk

TRUSTNET
www.trustnet.com

PRACTICAL PARENTING

BABIESRUS
Freepost NAT 3362, Gateshead NE10 8BR
www.babiesrus.co.uk

BABYCENTRE
www.babycentre.co.uk

BASICS4BABY
20 Mount Gardens, Harrogate HG2 8BS
01423 871093
www.basics4baby.co.uk

CHILD ACCIDENT PREVENTION TRUST (CAPT)
18–20 Farringdon Lane, London EC1R 3HA
020 7608 3828
www.capt.org.uk

CHILDCARELINK
Opportunity Links, Trust Court, Vision Park,
Histon, Cambridge CB4 9PW
0800 096 02 96
www.childcarelink.gov.uk

**CHILDREN'S INFORMATION
SERVICE**
0845 602 1125

DAPPERNIPPERS
14 Glenester Close,
Hoddesdon EN11 9LS
07905 929922
www.dappernippers.com

FOR PARENTS BY PARENTS
c/o 32c Alder Lane, Parbold WN8 7NN
www.forparentsbyparents.com

**GMPTE (Public Transport for
Greater Manchester)**
9 Portland Street, Piccadilly Gardens,
Manchester M60 1HX
www.gmpte.co.uk

HOME SAFETY NETWORK
www.dti.gov.uk/homesafetynetwork

KING'S CAMPS
0870 345 0781
www.kingssportscamps.com

**NATIONAL ASSOCIATION
OF NAPPY SERVICES**
0121 693 4949
www.changeanappy.co.uk

**NATIONAL ASSOCIATION OF TOY
AND LEISURE LIBRARIES**
68 Churchway, London NW1 1LT
020 7255 4600
www.natll.org.uk

THE NATIONAL CHILDBIRTH TRUST
Alexandra House, Oldham Terrace,
London W3 6NH
0870 770 3236
www.nctpregnancyandbabycare.com

**NATIONAL CHILDMINDING
ASSOCIATION (NCMA)**
0800 169 4486
www.ncma.org.uk

NATIONAL FOOTBALL MUSEUM
Sir Tom Finney Way, Deepdale,
Preston PR1 6RU
01772 908 442
www.nationalfootballmuseum.com

NATIONAL HISTORY MUSEUM
Cromwell Road, London SW7 5BD
020 7942 5011
www.nhm.ac.uk

NATIONAL RAILWAY MUSEUM
Leeman Road, York YO26 4XJ
01904 621261
www.nrm.org.uk

**ROSPA (THE ROYAL SOCIETY FOR
THE PREVENTION OF ACCIDENTS)**
Edgbaston Park, 353 Bristol Road,
Edgbaston, Birmingham B5 7ST
0121 248 2000
www.rospa.com

SCIENCE MUSEUM
Exhibition Road, South Kensington
London SW7 2DD
0870 870 4868
www.sciencemuseum.org.uk

SMILECHILD
www.smilechild.co.uk

THE TRAINLINE
www.thetrainline.com

TRICYCLE
269 Kilburn High Road, London NW6 7JR
020 7238 1000
www.tricycle.co.uk

VISIT LONDON
www.visitlondon.com/travel

YMCA
640 Forest Road, London E17 3DZ
www.ymca.org.uk

SAVING, BORROWING AND INVESTING

ADVFN
0870 794 0236
www.advfn.co.uk

BEST INVEST
20 Masons Yard, Duke Street, St James,
London SW1Y 6BU
020 7321 0100
www.bestinvest.com

BLOOMBERG
020 7330 7500
www.bloomberg.com

**THE BRITISH BANKERS
ASSOCIATION**
Pinners Hall,
105–108 Old Broad Street,
London EC2N 1EX
www.bba.org.uk

**THE BUILDING SOCIETIES
ASSOCIATION**
3 Savile Row, London W1S 3PB
020 7437 0655
www.bsa.org.uk

BUSINESS DEBTLINE
0800 197 6026
www.bdl.org.uk

CALL CREDIT
One Park Lane,
Leeds LS3 1EP
0113 244 1555
www.callcredit.plc.uk

CHARLES STANLEY & CO
www.charles-stanley.co.uk

CHILD TRUST FUND
The Children's Mutual,
Abbey Court, St. John's Road,
Tunbridge Wells TN4 9TE
01892 515353
www.thechildrensmutual.co.uk

CITYWIRE
www.citywire.co.uk

COMDIRECT
2 Selsdon Way, London E14 9LA
0870 600 6044
www.comdirect.co.uk

**CONSUMER CREDIT
COUNSELLING SERVICE**
Wade House, Merrion Centre,
Leeds LS2 8NG
0800 138 1111
www.cccs.co.uk

DEBT ADVISERS UK
08000 433287
www.debtadvisers.co.uk

DIGITAL LOOK
8–11 Lime Street, London EC3M 7AA
Tel: 0906 8022 222
www.digitallook.co.uk

EQUIFAX
25 Chapel Street, London NW1 5DS
www.equifax.co.uk

EXPERIAN
PO BOX 7710, Nottingham NG80 7WE
0800 656 900
www.creditexpert.co.uk

FINANCIAL DISCOUNTS DIRECT
PO Box 85, Alton, Hants GI34 1XS
01420 549 090
www.financial-discounts.co.uk

FUNDS REUNITED
PO Box 215, Bletchingley, Redhill RH1 4YA
0870 444 3696
www.fundsreunited.com

THE INSOLVENCY SERVICE
21 Bloomsbury Street, London WC1B 3QW
www.insolvency.gov.uk

INTELLIGENT FINANCE
1 Baird Road, Kirkton Campus,
Livingston EH54 7AZ
0845 609 4343
www.if.com

INTERACTIVE INVESTOR
0845 882 3325
www.iii.co.uk

MONEY EXTRA
Quay House, The Ambury, Bath BA1 1UA
0845 0777 085
www.moneyextra.com

NATIONAL DEBTLINE
The Arch, 48–52 Floodgate Street,
Birmingham B5 5SL
0808 808 4000
www.nationaldebtline.co.uk

NATIONAL SAVINGS
0845 366 6667
www.nsandi.com

PAYPLAN
Kempton House,
Dysart Road,
Grantham NG31 7LE
0800 085 4298
www.payplan.com

SAFEWAY BANK
0800 995 995
www.safeway.co.uk

THE SHARE CENTRE
Oxford House, Oxford Road,
Aylesbury HP21 8SZ
0800 800 008
www.share.co.uk

TD WATERHOUSE
0800 531 6695
www.tdwtrader.co.uk

THIS IS MONEY
2 Derry Street, London W8 5TT
www.thisismoney.com

UKCITYMEDIA
www.ukcitymedia.co.uk

THE UK SHARES GUIDE
www.uksharesguide.co.uk

THE UNCLAIMED ASSETS REGISTER
Leconfield House, Curzon Street,
London W1J 5JA
0870 241 1713
www.uar.co.uk

SPECIAL OCCASIONS

0800-BLOSSOMS
28–30 Jaggard Way, London SW12 8SG
0800 256 776
www.0800-Blossoms.co.uk

BIRSTALL
27–35 Sibson Road, Leicester LE4 4DX
0800 0850005
www.birstall.co.uk

THE BRITISH CARTOON CENTRE
7 Brunswick Centre, Bernard Street,
London WC1N
020 7278 7172

THE BRITISH CHRISTMAS TREE GROWERS' ASSOCIATION
13 Wolrige Road, Edinburgh EH16 6HX
0131 644 110
www.christmastree.org.uk

BUNCHES
Unit 19, Hazelford Way, Newstead Village,
Nottinghamshire NG15 0DQ
01623 750343
www.bunches.co.uk

CADBURY
PO Box 12, Bournville, Birmingham B30 2LU
0121 451 4444
www.cadbury.co.uk

THE CHAMPAGNE CELLAR
PO Box 138, Rochester ME3 7LQ
0800 597 7122
www.champagne-cellar.co.uk

CHRISTMAS DIRECT
07000 962787
www.xmastreesdirect.co.uk

THE CHRISTMAS SHOP
55A Tooley Street, London SE1 2QN
020 7378 1998
www.thechristmasshop.co.uk

CHRISTMASTIME UK
Albion House, Manor Farm, Fillingham,
Gainsborough DN21 5BS
01427 667270
www.christmastimeuk.com

CHRISTMAS TREE LAND
Catchdale Moss Farm, Catchdale Moss
Lane, Eccleston, St. Helens WA10 5QG
0845 230 3663
www.christmastreeland. co.uk

THE COMPLETE CHILDREN'S PARTY SURVIVAL GUIDE
www.kidspartysurvival guide.com

CONFETTI
0870 840 60 60
www.confetti.co.uk

CROCUS
Nursery Court, London Road,
Windlesham, Surrey GU20 6LQ
0870 787 1413
www.crocus.co.uk

DEALTIME
www.dealtime.co.uk

DISCOUNT WINES
www.discountwines.com

DISPOSABLE CAMERA SHOP
Unit 8, Old Great North Road,
Sutton on Trent NG23 6QS
0845 1303 606
www.disposablecamerashop.co.uk

E GREETINGS
www.egreetings.com

INTERFLORA
0870 366 6555
www.interflora.co.uk

IUK WINE
www.iuk-wine.co.uk

JUST CANDLES
1–3 Arterial Road, Laindon, Basildon,
Essex SS15 6DR
01268 546560
www.just-candles.net

LINCOLN'S CHRISTMAS MARKET
City Hall, Beaumont Fee, Lincoln LN1 1DD
01522 881188
www.lincoln.gov.uk

MADAME TUSSAUDS
Marylebone Road, London W1
0870 400 3000
www.madame-tussauds.co.uk

ODDBINS
31–33 Weir Road,
Wimbledon SW19 8UG
0800 328 2323
www.oddbins.com

PRICE'S CANDLES
16 Hudson Road, Elms Farm Industrial
Estate, Bedford MK41 0LZ
01234 264500
www.prices-candles.co.uk

WEB WEDDING
80–81 Tottenham Court Road,
London W1T 4TE
020 7291 7600
www.webwedding.co.uk

WEDDING FLOWERS
www.weddingflowersfreeservers.com

WEDDING GUIDE
PO Box 946, Carr Lane,
Low Moor,
Bradford BD12 0YG
0870 840 6060
www.weddingguide.co.uk

TAX AND BENEFITS

CONNEXIONS DIRECT
080 800 13219
www.connexions.gov.uk

DIGITA
Liverton Business Park,
Exmouth EX8 2NR
01395 270 273
www.digita.com/taxcentral/home/
employment/payslipcalculator
www.taxcentral.co.uk

ENTITLEDTO
www.entitledto.co.u

THE FEDERATION OF SMALL BUSINESSES
Sir Frank Whittle Way, Blackpool Business
Park, Blackpool FY4 2FE
01253 336000
www.fsb.org.uk

INSTITUTE OF CHARTERED ACCOUNTANTS IN ENGLAND
PO Box 433, London EC2P 2BJ
020 7920 8100
www.icaew.co.uk

INSTITUTE OF CHARTERED ACCOUNTANTS IN SCOTLAND
21 Haymarket Yards, Edinburgh EH12 5BH
0131 347 0100
www.icas.org.uk

INTUIT
PO Box 2234, Maidenhead SL6 8WQ
0845 606 2161
www.intuit.co.uk

THE MATERNITY ALLIANCE
Third Floor West, 2–6 Northburgh Street,
London EC1V 0AY
020 7490 7638
www.maternityalliance.org.uk

SOCIAL SECURITY AND JOBCENTRES
If you don't have internet access, find your
local office in the *Yellow Pages* under
*Social Service & Welfare Organisations or
Employment Agencies (Jobcentres).*
www.jobcentreplus.gov.uk/cms.asp?
Page=/Home/AboutUs/OurOffices

SOCIETY OF MOTOR MANUFACTURERS AND TRADERS (SMMT)
Forbes House, Halkin Street,
London SW1X 7DS
020 7235 7000
www.smmt.co.uk

TAX CAFÉ
214 High Street, Kirkcaldy, Fife KY1 1JT
01592 560018
www.taxcafe.co.uk

TAX CREDITS (INLAND REVENUE)
0845 300 3900
www.taxcredits.inlandrevenue.gov.uk

INDEX

This index refers you to the main subjects in the book. See also the detailed tables of contents at the beginning of each chapter, and the Directory of Addresses beginning on page 358 for contact information on the sources and suppliers named in the book.

ACKNOWLEDGMENTS

Cartoons Special thanks to Paul Bommer for supplying all cartoons throughout the book
Front cover illustration
by Bill Ledger c/o Just for Laffs agency

Photographs
10 Digital Vision, **12** Corbis/ John Feingersh, **21** RD ©
27 RD ©/Ken Field, **29** RD © **31** RD ©, **37** Getty
Images/Photodisc, **38** Getty Images/Photodisc, **42-43** Image
Source, **47** Digital Vision, **54** Getty Images/ Photodisc, **58** Digital
Vision,**59** Getty Images/Photodisc, **60-61** Getty Images/Photodisc,
64 Digital Vision, **66** RD ©/ Ulrich Kopp, **77** Stockbyte **91**
Digital Vision, **94** Digital Vision, **99** Digital Vision, **103** Digital
Vision, **107** Digital Vision, **110** Digital Vision, **120** Digital
Vision, **127** Getty Images/Photodisc, **129** Getty Images/
Photodisc,**130** Digital Vision, **135** Digital Vision, **139** RD © **140**
Digital Vision, **145** RD © (GID WSW058_2F), **148** Getty
Images/Photodisc, **152** Getty Images/Photodisc, **161** Digital
Vision, **162** Digital Vision, **164** Digital Vision, **167** Getty Images/
Photodisc, **172** Getty Images/ Photodisc, **175** Digital Vision, **179**
Digital Vision, **186** Digital Vision, **190** Digital Vision, **196** RD
©/Debbie Patterson, **203** RD © (GID HMP127), **207** Getty
Images/Photodisc, **212** Getty Images/Photodisc, **214** RD ©/ Sarah
Cuttle, **216** RD ©/ Debbie Patterson, **220** Getty
Images/Photodisc, **224** Getty Images/Photodisc, **227** Digital
Vision, **232** Digital Vision, **236** RD ©/Colin Bowling & Paul
Forrester, **240** Getty Images/Photodisc, **245** RD ©/ Colin Bowling
& Paul Forrester, **246** Digital Vision, **254** RD ©/Colin Bowling
& Paul Forrester, **257** RD © (GID 051ASK01A), **260** Stockbyte,
274 Digital Vision, **279** Punchstock/Thinkbyte, **280** Digital
Vision, **290** Hemera Technologies Inc., **292** Digital Vision, **295**
Digital Vision, **298** Comstock**301** Digital Vision, **308** Getty
Images/Photodisc, **316** Getty Images/Photodisc, **321** Getty
Images/Photodisc, **324** Getty Images/Photodisc, **329** Getty
Images/Photodisc, **331** Digital Vision, **342** Getty Images/
Photodisc, **348** Digital Vision, **355** Getty Images/Photodisc.

Originated by **Craft Plus Publishing Limited,
53 Crown Street, Brentwood, Essex, CM14 4BD**

Project Manager Sue Joiner
Writers Carol Davis, Kerensa Deane, Jane Egginton, Rachel
Fixsen, Katharine Gurney, Vicky Huntley, Harvey Jones,
David Leck, Barry Plows, Gisela Roberts, Christine Stopp,
Wendy Sweetser
Indexer Diana Lecore
Editors Dawn Bates, Sue Churchill, Judy Fovargue,
Margaret Maino, Patsy North, Gisela Roberts
Sub Editor Bea Agombar
Proofreader Ron Pankhurst
Design Kerrie Blake, Jane McKenna

For **The Reader's Digest Association Limited**
Editor Lisa Thomas
Art Editors Heather Dunleavy, Louise Turpin

Reader's Digest General Books
Editorial Director Cortina Butler
Art Director Nick Clark
Executive Editor Julian Browne
Managing Editor Alastair Holmes
Picture Resource Manager Martin Smith
Pre-press Account Manager Penny Grose

Colour origination Colour Systems, London
Printing and binding Maury Imprimeur SA, Malesherbes,
France

Concept code UK1731/IC
Book code 400-034-01
ISBN 0 276 42947 8
Oracle code 250008866H.00.24